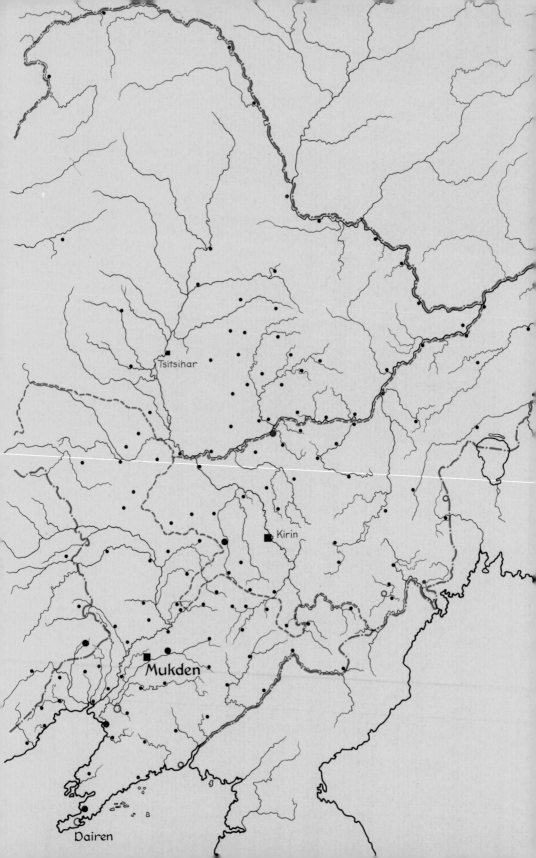

Tsitsihar

Kirin

Mukden

Dairen

THE CHINESE CITY
BETWEEN TWO WORLDS

Contributors

David D. Buck Susan Mann Jones
Mark Elvin Robert A. Kapp
Stephan Feuchtwang Rhoads Murphey
Bernard Gallin Edward J. M. Rhoads
Rita S. Gallin Alden Speare, Jr.
Shirley S. Garrett Irene B. Taeuber
Winston Hsieh

THE CHINESE CITY
BETWEEN TWO WORLDS

Edited by MARK ELVIN *and* G. WILLIAM SKINNER

Stanford University Press, Stanford, California 1974

HT147
C48
d43

Stanford University Press, Stanford, California
© 1974 by the Board of Trustees of the Leland Stanford Junior University
Printed in the United States of America
ISBN 0-8047-0853-3   LC 73-89858

Preface

In 1968–69 the Subcommittee on Research on Chinese Society—financed by the Carnegie Corporation of New York, administered by the Social Science Research Council (New York), and overseen by the Joint Committee on Contemporary China of that Council and the American Academy of Learned Societies—devoted two of its research conferences to the Chinese city. In the wake of these conferences, the Subcommittee planned three volumes, of which this is the second to appear. The first, *The City in Communist China* (edited by John Wilson Lewis), was published in 1971; the third, *The City in Late Imperial China* (edited by myself), is in press. These three volumes in turn form part of a larger series, Studies in Chinese Society, on which particulars are given opposite.

Eight of the papers in this volume were presented in preliminary form at a conference held in St. Croix, Virgin Islands, in December–January 1968–69. (This particular conference was cosponsored by the Subcommittee on Chinese Government and Politics, also under the jurisdiction of the Joint Committee on Contemporary China, in consideration of the many conference papers that treated political aspects of urban life in the People's Republic of China.) In addition to myself and the authors of these eight papers—David D. Buck, Mark Elvin, Stephan Feuchtwang, Bernard Gallin, Shirley S. Garrett, Winston Hsieh, Rhoads Murphey, and the late Irene B. Taeuber—the following China specialists attended the conference and participated in discussions relevant to the volume: Jerome A. Cohen, John Philip Emerson, Edward Friedman, Paul F. Harper, Ying-mao Kau, John Wilson Lewis, Victor H. Li, John C. Pelzel, Janet W. Salaff, Ezra F. Vogel, and Richard W. Wilson. Norton E. Long and Charles Tilly, who attended the conference as discussants, helped us place aspects of China's changing cities in the comparative context of urban development. Sophie Sa Winckler and Edwin A. Winckler, our rapporteurs, produced an incisively organized analytical record of the conference proceedings that greatly facilitated subsequent editorial work. An earlier version of the paper by Rhoads Murphey was published in 1970 (Michigan Papers in Chinese Studies, No. 7). The papers by Susan Mann Jones, Robert A. Kapp, Edward J. M. Rhoads, and Alden Speare, Jr. were later solicited to supplement the eight St. Croix papers.

For the unfortunate delay in the publication of this volume, I offer my heartfelt apologies to its contributors and readers alike. The Chinese Society Bibliography Project, also sponsored by the Subcommittee on Research on Chinese Society, took all the time I had from 1969 until its completion in 1973. That the present volume is ready even now is due largely to my good fortune in obtaining Mark Elvin's invaluable services as coeditor. He has had primary responsibility for the more historical papers and the Introduction, I for the more sociological papers and the maps.

This book is concerned with social process and institutional change in modern Chinese cities. A central concern is the transformation and modernization of traditional urban forms. Because relevant papers on the People's Republic were included in *The City in Communist China*, the historical period covered here extends beyond 1949 only in the case of Taiwan. The Subcommittee originally intended that the analyses of traditional urban institutions and processes in *The City in Late Imperial China* should provide a baseline for the treatment of urban transformation in the present volume, which in turn would provide a starting point for the analyses of mainland cities in *The City in Communist China*. Thus it is particularly unfortunate that publication delays have caused the three books to appear in reverse chronological order. In consequence, continuities as well as discontinuities are underplayed and underanalyzed—a deficiency that I hope to remedy in part in subsequent publications.

The endpaper maps show China's cities as of 1930. The three frames—North China at the front with Manchuria overleaf, and South China at the back—cover virtually all of agrarian China. Within these frames, all capitals of counties and higher-level administrative units are plotted, together with the largest and most important nonadministrative cities. These categories also include all cities with the status in 1930 of municipality or treaty port, the treaty ports being indicated by red symbols. (A key to the symbols will be found overleaf from the back endpaper.)

Standing alone, these maps serve especially to point up the number and distribution of treaty ports in relation to the overall distribution of cities in agrarian China. Changes in the spatial patterning of cities of different types may be traced during a critical four decades of the period treated in this volume by comparing these endpaper maps with those to be published in *The City in Late Imperial China*, which show data for 1894 in comparable frames.

Special thanks are due Bryce Wood for his competent staffwork for the Subcommittee, J. G. Bell for advice on the overall design and general editorial guidance, Autumn J. Stanley for particularly conscientious press editing, T. H. Hollingsworth for advice on certain questions of urban demography, Rhoads Murphey for technical advice concerning the endpaper maps, and Jill Leland for drafting the internal maps as well as completing the endpapers.

The achievements of this symposium volume, modest as they are, have some intellectual significance. The modern transformation of the world's largest premodern urban system is a subject of importance for the comparative study of urbanism as well as for Chinese studies. We see opened in these pages the dialogue between social scientists and historians that is essential to analyzing so momentous a change. The firstfruits of this dialogue are already apparent: a more eclectic and imaginative use of sources, improved methodologies, a more rigorous approach to argumentation, and, above all, an augmented sense of problem.

G.W.S.

April 1974

Contents

Contributors

DAVID D. BUCK received his Ph.D. from Stanford University and is now Assistant Professor of History at the University of Wisconsin at Milwaukee. His research interests center on the history of Chinese cities since 1850. This piece on education in Tsinan is part of a larger study of the city's history covering 1890 to 1949.

MARK ELVIN received his Ph.D. from the University of Cambridge in 1968. He taught at Cambridge and Glasgow before moving to Oxford, where he is now Lecturer in Chinese History and a Fellow of St. Antony's College. He has published translations of Japanese monographs on Sung and Ming economic history in the *Michigan Abstracts* (of which he is the editor), *The Pattern of the Chinese Past* (1973), and articles on land tenure and premodern technology.

STEPHAN FEUCHTWANG is submitting a doctoral thesis on Chinese religion to London University. It is based on observations in Taiwan, 1966–68. He teaches sociology at The City University, London, England. He is the author of *An Anthropological Analysis of Chinese Geomancy* (1974) and of articles on Chinese religion.

BERNARD GALLIN received his Ph.D. from Cornell University in 1961. He is now Professor and Chairman of the Department of Anthropology at Michigan State University. His research over the years has focused on Chinese peasantry, socioeconomic change, and rural-urban migration in Taiwan. He is the author of *Hsin Hsing, Taiwan: A Chinese Village in Change* (1966) and numerous articles.

RITA S. GALLIN received her M.A. in Sociology from Michigan State University in 1973 and is presently a doctoral candidate there. She became interested in China by virtue of her marriage to Bernard Gallin and participated in research during field trips to Taiwan. She has collaborated with her husband on several articles dealing with Chinese society and rural-urban migration in Taiwan.

SHIRLEY S. GARRETT received her Ph.D. from Harvard University. Author of *Social Reformers in Urban China* (1970), she is currently a Fellow at the Radcliffe Institute (Cambridge, Mass.), working on a study of the Chiangs of China and American religious communities.

WINSTON HSIEH, who received his Ph.D. from Harvard University in 1969, is Assistant Professor of History at the University of Missouri at St. Louis. In 1973 he coordinated the Canton Delta Seminar at the University of Hong Kong. He is author of *Chinese Historiography on the Revolution of 1911* (1974) and coeditor of the Chinese-language publications volume of *Modern Chinese Society: An Analytical Bibliography* (1973). An article closely related to his contribution to this volume appears in Jean Chesneaux, ed., *Popular Movements and Secret Societies in China* (1972).

SUSAN MANN JONES received her Ph.D. from Stanford University in 1972. Her research, concerned with economic organization in the Ningpo area and with Chinese politics of the eighteenth century, has paid particular attention to the role of patronage and cliques in late traditional society. She is presently studying political thought in eighteenth-century China at the University of Chicago, on a fellowship from the American Council of Learned Societies.

ROBERT A. KAPP is a member of the Department of History and the Institute for Comparative and Foreign Area Studies at the University of Washington. His doctorate is from Yale and he formerly taught at Rice University. He is the author of *Szechwan and the Chinese Republic: Provincial Militarism and Central Power, 1911–1938* (1973).

RHOADS MURPHEY is Professor of Geography and Associate Director of the Center for Chinese Studies, University of Michigan. He worked in China from 1942 to 1946, mainly in the rural west, and received his Ph.D. from Harvard in 1950. His research interests focus on Asian cities and on nineteenth- and twentieth-century China.

EDWARD J. M. RHOADS received his Ph.D. from Harvard University in 1970 and is presently Associate Professor of History at the University of Texas at Austin. His research has focused mainly on the social and political developments of the late Ch'ing and early Republican period. He is the author of *China's Republican Revolution: 1895–1913*, now at press.

G. WILLIAM SKINNER, Professor of Anthropology, Stanford University, received his Ph.D. from Cornell in 1954. A research interest in Chinese market towns and cities stems from fieldwork in the Chengtu region of Szechwan in 1949–50. He is the author of two books on the Chinese in Bangkok, and the editor of *The City in Late Imperial China* (Stanford, forthcoming). Other publications include *Modern Chinese Society: An Analytical Bibliography*, 3 vols. (Stanford, 1973).

ALDEN SPEARE, JR. spent a year in Taiwan in 1967–68 collecting data for a doctoral dissertation on rural-urban migration. In 1969 he received the Ph.D. in Sociology from the University of Michigan and joined the faculty of the Sociology Department at Brown University, where he is now Associate Professor. He has returned to Taiwan several times as a visiting scholar of the Institute of Economics of Academia Sinica. He has published several papers on urbanization, migration, fertility, and labor force participation in Taiwan.

IRENE B. TAEUBER was Senior Research Demographer, Office of Population Research, Princeton University, when she died in February 1974. She served as president of the Population Association of America and as vice-president of the International Union for the Scientific Study of Population. She is the author of *The Population of Japan* (1958) and numerous articles on the demography of China.

THE CHINESE CITY
BETWEEN TWO WORLDS

Introduction

MARK ELVIN

The city of Peking is a novel sight for a European. . . . He will not weary of admiring the manner in which the nearly three million people gathered within its vast enclosure are ruled by the police as schoolchildren by their masters, and dare even less than these to emancipate themselves. People coming and going fill streets wider than that which faces the Luxembourg Palace in Paris. Some are on foot, some in carts, while others ride on horseback or in sedan chairs. Some carry loads, others cry out the goods they have for sale. The crowd is beyond belief, yet peace reigns everywhere. It is not the business of those on foot to watch where they are going; those on horses or in palanquins must take care not to splatter them with dirt. One of the great will be fearful of jostling a seller of matches. At the slightest cry the soldiers of the nearest guardpost will run up and put an end to all quarreling with a few threats or, if someone fails to obey them instantly, with lashes of the whip.

When night falls, the barriers across the smaller streets are shut, and everyone retires to his own house. There is nothing to be heard but the soldiers sounding the hours of the night; and one meets with no one but the watchmen going on their rounds to care for the public safety. They are so scrupulous in this that there are no reports of thefts or murders. At the least warning of a fire, pumps, soldiers, workmen, mandarins, persons of rank—and even princes—arrive from all directions.

The streets are sprinkled several times each day to lay the dust. In summer there are little booths in every piazza where people may drink iced water. On every hand one can find refreshments, fruits, tea, and eatinghouses. The various kinds of foodstuffs are sold on specific days in specific places. There is entertainment everywhere for the passersby, whether stories being read aloud, short humorous dialogs, or experts displaying tricks and curiosities. In times of natural disaster, the Emperor has rice and clothing distributed to the poor. In times of celebration, all sorts of amusements are permitted to the people. . . .

The police know all that is going on, even inside the palaces of the princes.

They know who has arrived and who departed. They keep exact registers of the inhabitants in every house; and they make sure that all foodstuffs are in abundant supply. They see to it that all the repairs required for convenience, safety, and cleanliness are carried out when needed. Princes and mandarins, citizens and foreigners, soldiers and courtiers, bonzes and lamas, are all subject to their rule; and they keep everyone on the path of order and duty without arrests, and without harsh actions, [seeming] hardly to touch them.

I will say nothing of the grandeur of this capital, of the extent of its suburbs, the beauty of its walls, the width of its ramparts, the variety of its public buildings, the alignment of its thoroughfares, the multitude of its palaces, and so forth. One has to see them to appreciate their effect. Architecture here works on a different plan from ours, its magnificence accords with other ideas, and its taste follows different principles; but European prejudices are powerless before the novelties that one beholds. The palace of the Emperor announces with eloquence his greatness and his power to any with eyes to see.[1]

So wrote Father Amiot of the capital of China in the middle of the eighteenth century. Today his words seem more plausible than they might perhaps have seemed fifty or a hundred years ago. The vision that they evoke of spacious self-confidence, concern for the public welfare, and insinuating control is not altogether unfamiliar to the visitor to the T'ien-an Men in the era of the People's Republic. Between that time and this there lies a century and a half, deceptive in its familiarity, of disruption and transformation set in motion by the inroads of the military and industrial power of Europe and North America. It is this period that concerns the essays in this book: China, and the cities of China, between the two worlds of the old empire at its zenith and the communist government of today.

Why the cities? As I have said, the familiarity of the period is deceptive. China's first encounter with modern industrial civilization took place in the cities; it was in the cities, too, that Chinese efforts at modernization began. Yet we still have had no systematic study of this urban setting. The interrelation of the new trends with the economic and political hierarchies of the central places, the pervasive realignment of lines of movement and points of concentration of men, goods, and ideas, are still almost *terra incognita*. Perhaps we have been bemused by the fact that the Maoist revolution came in from the countryside and seemingly (though only seemingly) bypassed the cities as agents of change.

We have as yet no very clear conception of Chinese cities in late traditional times on the basis of which to evaluate the changes that took place after the middle of the nineteenth century. To some extent this deficiency will be remedied with the publication of the papers from the conference on the city in late Imperial China mentioned in the Preface. Without wishing to anticipate the findings set forth in those papers, I can say that they prompt three conclusions pertinent to our present theme. First, many of the characteristics that caused traditional Chinese cities to play so much less dynamic a role in history than those of western Europe may be traced to the political and economic dominance of transients, migrants, and outsiders. One conspicuous example is the county magistrate, following the rule of avoidance that forbade him to serve in his native province; another is the migrant merchant, member of a guild of fellow-regionals combining to assert their interests against those of the local populace. Second, a process of urbanization had been under way in China at least since the later Ming. In fields as diverse as higher education and the control of water-conservancy projects, almost all the most important institutions and sociopolitical functions were increasingly concentrated in the cities. And third, at least in some regions, what might be termed an "urban involution" was beginning. While the absolute size of the largest cities showed no advance over their Sung dynasty maxima during late traditional times, and their percentage share of the population actually fell, an ever higher proportion of people were gathered together into the lower-level centers, above all the market towns. Thus our evaluation of how thoroughly urbanized China was by the beginning of the present century depends critically on how we define a city. The most dramatically divergent set of figures shows 34 percent of the population living in settlements containing at least 2,500 inhabitants, but only about 6 percent in conurbations of 50,000 or more.[2] The first of these two estimates is unacceptably high—25 percent would find more of a consensus among experts—but it may be quoted here to demonstrate the dimensions of the problem.

As for the processes by which cities grew and functioned, we now know just enough to see how difficult it often is to sort out "modern" phenomena from continuing late traditional ones. Many existing Chinese institutions grew at an accelerated pace until well into the twentieth century. This was true, for example, of guilds, charitable foundations, and small market towns wherever there was the economic vitality to sustain them. Some modern developments, such as the city-based political power of the gentry and merchants that underlay the 1911 revolution, turn out to be trends that were unmistakably present by late premodern times.

As an example of the kind of ambiguity that one often encounters, consider the demographic features of Chia-hsing county in 1928 summarized in Tables 1–3. Are they "modern" or not? The high sex ratios

TABLE 1. THE POPULATION OF CHIA-HSING COUNTY, 1928

Territorial unit	Households	People	Males/ Females	Age 20 or under	21–40	Over 40	Out-migrants from county
Villages and smallest towns	87,007	371,029	204,394 166,635	85,918 65,337	76,940 53,469	41,536 47,829	10,238 1,868
Towns over 1,000 males	7,933	41,822	24,900 16,922	9,594 7,079	9,862 5,378	5,444 4,465	3,127 461
County capital	5,277	36,450	21,898 14,552	8,790 6,207	8,259 4,489	4,849 3,856	4,270 1,286
County	100,217	449,301	251,192 198,109	104,302 78,623	95,061 63,336	51,829 56,150	17,715 3,615

SOURCE: *Chia-hsing hsin chih* (New gazetteer for Chia-hsing county; Chia-hsing, 1929), pp. 108–233.

NOTE: Out-migrants from the county are not included in the other totals. There are some small inconsistencies between the subtotals and totals in the original data, in most cases certainly due to misprints. In general the totals have been followed here.

among the working-age population (relative to rural levels) in the county capital and in other large towns of the county indicates substantial rural-to-urban migration by men (Table 2).* The low survival rates for urban marriage-age females relative to their country sisters suggests some migration by this group out of the capital and larger towns (Table 3).

There are plausible reasons for connecting at least the male migration with modern developments. Twentieth-century Chia-hsing was linked by rail or steam launch with fifteen other urban centers, including Shanghai. Both the county capital and the larger towns had some modern industries, including silk filatures and plants for generating electricity. Although the thrust of male migration toward the larger towns seems to have been almost as strong as toward the county capital (Table 2), the higher proportion of male out-migrants from the county capital (Table 3) shows that male migration *into* the capital was higher relative to the towns than it appears. If we recall that the county's total population in 1928 (449,301) was still less than half what it had been in 1838 (1.12 million), as a result of the deaths caused by the Taiping rebellion, the suspicion grows that we may be dealing here with a largely traditional process of recovery. The aspect most closely linked with modern economic developments was probably the out-migration of the native-

* The purpose of the table is to contrast the relative ratios in the different territorial units, and we shall not enter here into the difficult question of whether or not the absolute level is too high.

TABLE 2. SEX RATIOS AND HOUSEHOLD SIZE IN CHIA-HSING COUNTY, 1928

Territorial unit	Persons per household	Men per 100 women				Out-migrants
		Overall	20 or under	21–40	Over 40	
Villages and smallest towns	4.3	123	131	144	87	548
Towns over 1,000 males	5.3	147	136	183	122	678
County capital	6.9	150	142	184	126	332
County	4.5	127	133	150	92	490

SOURCE: As for Table 1.

born from the county, presumably, in most cases, to Shanghai. As so often, we lack the data that would let us solve the problem. It may be noted here, however, that the chapter by Irene B. Taeuber in this volume shows that city growth in Taiwan under the Japanese, when the island was still an expanding frontier area, probably fell into the traditional category.

We are better off when we turn to qualitative assessments. For a general impression of Chinese cities on the eve of the Western impact, the writings of European travelers such as Fortune and von Richthofen are still unsurpassed. Here we can see, passing before the mind's eye, the uniform height of the houses, broken only by the occasional watchtower or pagoda, the multitudes living in single-room dwellings without special rooms for sleeping, cooking, or eating, the open shopfronts shuttered with heavy boards at night, the painted statues in the temples, looming in the half-darkness thirty or forty feet above the throngs of women worshippers. Here we can glimpse the individual character of the cities: the public bathhouses of Shanghai, packed with bathers and pouring steam from their doors, the icehouses and furniture shops of Ningpo, the silk clothes of the inhabitants of Hangchow and Hu-chou, the golden banners glittering above the bookshops and art shops of Chengtu, splendidly rebuilt after a disastrous fire and renowned as the "Paris of the empire."

More substantially, there are insights to be gleaned into regional differences in patterns of settlement. Here, for example, are von Richthofen's observations on the basin of Szechwan in 1872:

In no other province of China is there such a sharp distinction between Country and City as is the case in [this part of] Szechwan. Chinese like crowding, the tighter the better. They congregate in cities and villages, but dislike to live alone. The difference of villages and cities is generally more in size than in character, and the smallest hamlet has a tinge of the city. In Szechwan, the country is dotted everywhere with farms or small groups of them. There the

MARK ELVIN

TABLE 3. SURVIVAL RATES, OUT-MIGRATION, AND URBANIZATION
IN CHIA-HSING COUNTY, 1928

| Territorial unit | Survival rates | | | | Out-migrants as % of residents, by sex | | Rural-urban population distribution |
| | Group 21–40 as % of group 20 or under | | Group over 40 as % of group 21–40 | | | | |
	M	F	M	F	M	F	
Villages and smallest towns	90%	82%	54%	89%	5%	1%	83%
Towns over 1,000 males	103	76	55	83	13	4	9
County capital	94	72	59	86	19	9	8
County	91	81	55	89	7	2	100%

SOURCE: As for Table 1.

farmer lives, with his numerous family, in the midst of his fields. Those who are given to industrial pursuits or commerce live in market-towns or cities, but the Chinese type of townlike village is little represented. The city is thoroughly city, and the country is thoroughly country. People can live in this state of separation and isolation only where they expect peace; and profound peace is indeed the impression which Szechwan prominently conveys.[3]

The value of this sort of information is that it helps us to put the statistics of urbanization in perspective. According to early-twentieth-century Japanese surveys, Szechwan was the province with the third-highest percentage (9.9) of its inhabitants living in cities.* Kiangsu had about 13.6 percent (including Shanghai), and Hopei 11.2 percent.[4] Assuming that this was so—although the surveys do not inspire great confidence—the reason may have been that the increased prominence of the market towns in the landscape, and the absence of nucleated villages, led the investigators to classify more market towns as important cities.

The subtleties of regional variation in the pattern of late traditional urbanization are yet to be unraveled. Here I can only point to some of the complicating factors. Defense, for example, was at times as important as economics. Alexander Hosie noted in the 1880's that "it is a peculiarity of Kweichow towns that there are no suburbs outside the walls; but when the struggles [against the Miao] that have taken place within the province and the consequent insecurity are considered, their absence is not a matter for surprise."[5] It seems a reasonable guess (but no more than a guess at present) that the high urbanization rates of counties like Huang-yüan in Tsinghai (50.2 percent of the population living in cities and

* Defined by the investigators as conurbations that had over 10,000 inhabitants or, if smaller, were nonetheless "important."

TABLE 4. CHAMBERS OF COMMERCE IN CHINA AROUND 1920

Province	Chambers	Firms per chamber	Inhabitants per chamber firm
Shansi	97	496	306
Fukien (1919)	66	180	936
Kiangsi (1918)	78	160	1,029
Chekiang (1919)	95	200	1,038
Szechwan (1915)	134	343	1,048
Hupeh (1918)	74	269	1,071
Kwangtung (1917)	70	354	1,175
Kiangsu	79	333	1,545
Hopei	121	163	1,608
Hunan (1917)	34	475	1,622
Anhwei	74	174	1,691
Shantung	99	147	2,487
Honan	85	127	2,500
Shensi	37	97	2,671
Kweichow (1916)	17	195	3,114
Kwangsi (1916)	31	155	3,353
Kansu (1917)	43	40	3,981
Yunnan (1914)	5	40	46,500
Total	(1,239)		

SOURCE: Baba Kuwatarō, *Shina keizai chiri shi, seido zempen* (Economic and geographic gazetteer of China, volume on systems; Shanghai: Yuiki gakukai, 1928), pp. 1270–71.

towns) and Jung *hsien* in Kwangsi (59.1 percent in cities and towns) are to be explained as concentration for safety.[6]

A puzzle (or maybe a pseudo-puzzle) of a different sort is provided by the province of Shansi. Consider the figures in Table 4, which show the number of chambers of commerce in each province around 1920, the average number of firms belonging to a chamber, and the average number of inhabitants in each province per firm belonging to a chamber. The figures should not be taken as precise: the total number of chambers and member firms varied sharply between 1912 and 1920, 1915 being the peak year for both. The provincial population figures used in the calculations are also only approximations. At first sight, it looks as if the numbers in the righthand column might provide an index of commercialization (the more inhabitants per firm, the lower the level). Unfortunately, except perhaps as regards the last seven entries, this hope is destroyed by the mutually canceling effects of two opposing trends. Imabori Seiji has pointed out that, at least in the case of Kuei-sui (Huhehot), the coming of modernization and larger enterprises reduced the number of firms belonging to local chambers of commerce. There were 1,800 chamber members in Kuei-sui in 1912, 1,400 in 1925, and only 800 in 1931.[7] Up to a point, no doubt, increased commercialization was reflected in more firms per inhabitant, but after this point this second trend presumably reduced the ratio again.

But the odd position of Shansi, with the highest number of firms per chamber and less than one-fifth the median number of inhabitants per firm (306 as against either 1,608 or 1,622), is intriguing. The number of chambers, though high, is broadly in line with the general tendency for the number of chambers to approach the number of county capitals. A political hypothesis would be that Governor Yen Hsi-shan forced many small firms to join chambers that would not have done so elsewhere. An economic hypothesis would be that the province combined to a unique degree a high level of commercial activity and very expensive transport (due to the difficulty of cutting roads through loess), and that this combination of factors led to a multiplicity of small firms serving rather restricted areas.[8]

Until we have control over the sort of regional variation illustrated in this and the preceding examples, generalizations about China as a whole are hazardous. For this reason all but two of the papers here (those by Rhoads Murphey and Shirley Garrett) are local or regional studies. They are pioneering attempts to pursue detailed analysis at the only level at which it is at present practicable. But before we turn to individual papers, it may be useful to make a few remarks about the probable general development of cities in China. These remarks must in the nature of things be provisional, and the reader should not be surprised if before long they are refined or refuted by further investigations.

First, a caveat. There is no good reason to assume that the overall percentage of the Chinese population living in cities (however defined) grew between 1840 and 1950. There are examples of urban decay in this period as well as of urban expansion. Hsiang-t'an in Hunan, which von Richthofen reckoned as having over a million inhabitants, had less than a third this number by 1917 as the rise of steamer shipping on the Yangtze reoriented trade routes. Chia-ting, and other Szechwanese towns serving the trade in insect wax used for the outer coating of candles, declined with the growing use of imported kerosene. A sample survey of over 200,000 peasants made in 1936 also showed that, at least by this date, the annual city-to-farm migration (1.1%) exceeded the annual farm-to-city migration (0.9%).[9]

What did take place was a restructuring of interprovincial trade and transport, and a corresponding realignment of the urban structure. The opening of the early treaty ports led to the eclipse of the routes running north from Kwangtung via Hunan and Kiangsi. The coastal steamer was responsible for the neglect of the Grand Canal, with the result that the waterway joining Kiangnan and Peking became impassable to through traffic. Some old centers acquired a new character. Until its harbor silted up, Chinkiang was a point of distribution for petroleum. Wuhu exported rice. Kiukiang and Hankow were rival tea-exporting centers. I-ch'ang grew as a port of transshipment at what was for a long time the end of the steamship line up the Yangtze.[10]

The railroads changed the commercial geography of the north as much as the steamships changed that of the south. An example is the building of the Ching-Sui line westward from Peking early in the 1920's. This line transformed Kuei-sui, formerly an entrepôt of the north-south trade and primarily linked with Mongolia, into a center of east-west trade looking to Ningsia and Sinkiang as its hinterland.[11] The economic structure of Shantung was reoriented following the decline of the Grand Canal, and the stimulus given by the German railroad running from Tsingtao into the interior. The construction of the Manchurian lines, and improved harbor facilities, led to a tidal wave of in-migrants, and to massive exports of farm products from what had been an underdeveloped region.[12] The Kwantung Leased Territory and the South Manchurian Railway Zone administered by the Japanese were the scene of an extensive urbanization, in the broad sense of the word; and Manchoukuo saw what was possibly the fastest city growth ever recorded—Mukden's spurt from 0.5 million people in 1935 to 1.4 million people in 1940.[13]

Overshadowing every other aspect of this restructuring process was the concentration of modern communications, capital, and mechanized industry in a handful of coastal cities, foremost among them Shanghai. This concentration, the result of these cities' close contact with the international economy, meant that the quality of life enjoyed by their citizens soon became very different from that experienced elsewhere. One indicator of this is the enormous disparity between the Shanghai-Nanking region and the rest of the country in the volume of mail and parcels per head, and in the numbers of telephones, radio sets, and broadcasting stations. Shanghai, Peking, and Tientsin also dominated the production of newspapers.[14] By 1931 Shanghai had nearly half of the foreign capital invested in China (including Manchuria) and almost two-thirds of the output in China (excluding Manchuria) from factories using power and employing thirty or more people.[15] The growth of production in the modern industrial sector, which meant essentially the major treaty ports and Manchuria, proceeded at a brisk 5.6 percent a year from 1912 to 1949.[16] In short, the contrast between the relatively advanced and the relatively backward areas grew steadily wider.

At the same time the chief cities were linked together more closely than before by rail, steamship, and telegraph. By 1910 there were 560 telegraph offices in China, about 28,000 miles of overhead line, and cable links with Europe and America.[17] The effects of this new political and economic nervous system showed up with particular clarity in the course of the 1911 revolution. Urban center after urban center responded to the Wuchang Uprising, bypassing the intervening countryside almost completely in the process. This geographic pattern of revolution was new in Chinese history, contrasting clearly with that of the traditional rebellion, which spread like a flood over the countryside, engulfing or isolating the cities. The 1911 revolution was also the first large-scale political upheaval in Chinese history that was predominantly urban in origin.[18]

The populations of the expanding modern cities in the first half of the twentieth century were normally dominated by young adult male in-migrants. The only exceptions were places like Wusih, where many women were employed in the silk industry. This process of city formation by sex-selective migration was not inherently "modern." Early in the 1870's, for example, von Richthofen had noted of Kalgan: "Of the resident population, the greater part consider themselves as visitors on a long term, and have their families in some other place or province."[19] It is also not the only way in which cities around the world have grown during their period of modernization. Most British cities in the first half of the nineteenth century, for example, were characterized by female in-migration, and a preponderance of females in the young adult age groups.[20] Conceivably, this too was the continuation of a premodern pattern.[21] What may have been new in early modern China was the combination of a high rate of gross migration (defined as in- plus out-migration divided by total population) and a low efficiency of migration (defined as the percentage that the net migration in or out forms of in- plus out-migration). Table 5 gives the relevant data for Shanghai. One curious feature is that the efficiency of migration in any given year seems to have been remarkably similar for men and women, whereas there were large differences between years and substantial differences between the numbers of men and women migrating in any given year.

Presumably the high turnover was caused by the lack of opportunities for satisfactory permanent employment. In Shanghai during the early 1930's, approximately a third of a million out of a total population of about 3.5 million were recorded as unemployed. In Nanking, Peiping, Tientsin, and Tsingtao the unemployed numbered roughly half of the working-age population.[22] Some of the new urban growth was evidently cancerous.

TABLE 5. MIGRATION IN AND OUT OF SHANGHAI FROM 1930 TO 1936

Migration data	1930	1931	1932	1933	1934	1935	1936
In-migration:							
Males	145,670	178,963	272,733	268,161	248,790	300,765	244,971
Females	108,860	127,749	200,495	190,104	167,287	219,232	169,950
Total	254,530	306,712	473,228	458,265	416,077	519,997	414,921
Out-migration:							
Males	85,562	121,874	117,697	178,830	188,202	299,799	188,393
Females	63,207	86,832	81,345	123,270	128,403	199,182	138,361
Total	148,769	208,706	199,042	302,100	316,605	498,981	326,754
Efficiency of migration:							
Males	26%	19%	40%	20%	14%	2%	13%
Females	26%	19%	42%	21%	13%	5%	10%
Total	26%	19%	40%	20%	14%	2%	12%
Migrants per 1,000 population	131	158	219	228	210	281	198

SOURCE: Yü Hung-chün, ed., *Shang-hai shih nien chien* (Shanghai municipal yearbook; Shanghai: Chung hua shu chü, 1937), section C, pp. 12, 19–21.

NOTE: Efficiency of migration, as noted in the text, is defined as the percentage that net migration in or out forms of in- plus out-migration.

To what degree the conclusions set forth in these chapters are surprising is hard to say for someone like myself, who has grown accustomed to them over several years. Rhoads Murphey's thesis is perhaps the most provocative. Late traditional China, he argues, was strong enough politically to prevent a colonial takeover, but not strong enough to carry out the reforms demanded by twentieth-century conditions. Economically she was even stronger. Her merchants easily resisted all but the most limited Western economic penetration, and so for a long time she failed to appreciate the extent of her need for technical innovation. The result was that confrontation with the West was irritating rather than devastating; it "sharpened the Chinese sense of identity rather than destroying it." He buttresses his argument by showing that the Chinese economy in the middle of the nineteenth century was in better shape than has usually been thought, and suggests that the quality of life in the countryside did not begin to decline seriously until after the 1911 revolution. If it can be sustained, this is an important revision of accepted ideas.

Possibly the most significant new point made by Susan Mann Jones concerns the nature of the transition from late traditional to modern economic institutions in Shanghai. The transition was relatively smooth, she maintains, because the leaders of the old institutions became leaders in the new institutions without relinquishing any of their former positions or ties. Thus personal relationships made and sustained in the premodern matrix guaranteed the functioning of modern banks and chambers of commerce.

Edward J. M. Rhoads's study of Canton focuses on the politicization of the merchants in the closing years of the Ch'ing dynasty. The most interesting of his findings is the way in which the concentration of official and gentry power in Canton, a city high in the political hierarchy, produced different patterns in merchant power from those found in cities like Shanghai (which was a county capital and the residence of a circuit intendant) or Swatow (which was not even a county capital).* Cantonese gentry and merchants competed in causes that elsewhere they combined to promote (setting up, for instance, rival self-government associations); and the social-gravitational pull of the official and gentry world created a split between wealthy merchants who had acquired gentry status and ordinary merchants, the two groups being represented by different organizations.

Winston Hsieh's chapter presents an institution previously known, if at all, only to Kwangtung specialists: the people's army. In a pioneering analysis of the infrastructure of the 1911 revolution in the delta hinterland of Canton, he traces the interlocking of modern means of communication (steamer, railroad, and telegraph) with the traditional lineage organization through which the lowest-level units of these armies were mobilized, to explain the highly selective geographic pattern of the uprisings. He shows how the marketing community, centered on a market town, was the basic spatial component of organization; and then points out that as the revolutionary forces moved up the hierarchy of central places, the unifying factor changed—from the lineage at the lower levels to the secret society at the higher levels.

Robert A. Kapp's paper on Chungking in the 1920's and 1930's shows cities in a different and interestingly ambiguous light. They were key points at which the quasi-feudal warlords tapped the flow of rural and commercial resources, and at the same time the centers of the warlords' drive toward economic modernization. The warlord, then, in the author's vision, was both a predator and an entrepreneur; and the interrelation of the two roles is developed with a nice touch of paradox.

* Attention is called to such distinctions on the endpaper maps, which use distinctive symbols for provincial capitals such as Canton, county capitals such as Shanghai, and cities like Swatow that have no formal administrative role. County seats of exceptional size such as Shanghai may be identified by the larger size of the symbol, in this case a filled circle.

David D. Buck's extensive study of education in and around Tsinan stresses one of the familiar truths about modernization, that the relatively high cost of new skills and new equipment in an underdeveloped environment increases the gap between the haves and the have-nots. Educational advance was gradually confined to fewer and fewer cities as people interested in modernizing education were drawn into Tsinan from all over Shantung, in hopes of getting official financial support for their new schools. The consequences of this concentration are depicted in a way that opens new insights into the sources of social tensions in Republican China. In particular, Buck points out, the modern schools were the main foci of nationalist agitation during the second and third decades of the century; and where modern education was absent, so too, usually, was nationalism.

The section of Shirley S. Garrett's paper on the YMCA demonstrates the urban, Christian, middle-class origins of many of the mass programs now associated with the Communists and the New China. These include effective if localized efforts at mass health, mass education, and even large-scale fly-swatting in the interests of public hygiene. The section on the chambers of commerce takes up on a nationwide scale a theme treated by Rhoads in the context of Canton: the politicization of the merchants. Garrett traces the gradual decline of the chambers from institutions concerned with reformist and national causes to conservative bodies negatively preoccupied with defending the interests of big business. Together the two sections offer a psychological portrait of the new urban middle class in both its idealism and its selfishness.

My own paper on the administration of early-twentieth-century Shanghai depicts the formal transfer of urban power from outsiders to locals. This transition constituted one of the clearest breaks between the early modern Chinese city and its late traditional predecessor, as did the official recognition for the first time of cities as administrative entities in their own right. The main points of interest are two. The "modern" city government that emerged after 1905 was largely a fusion of indigenous institutions that had evolved very late in traditional times, though it was the challenge and example of the West that induced, and to some extent directed, this fusion. The ideal inspiring the new civic leaders was that of a municipal welfare state, pursuing the Confucian goal of the Great Concord, but a little overburdened—at least according to its critics—with "a philosophy of interference" in people's everyday lives.

Stephan Feuchtwang's study of temples in Taipei city during the nineteenth and twentieth centuries combines historical research with anthropological fieldwork. The result is a new typology of urban, popular, religious institutions. In times past, he maintains, they fell into three main groups, albeit with some overlapping. These were (1) temples serving those who had migrated from a common place of origin, (2) those serving a given territory, and (3) those serving a given trade. This leads to the exploration of a new spatial dimension of social structure: the ritual territory. Territorial temples had few or no branch structures, whereas compatriot temples were often articulated into quite extensive structures of many temples. Territorial temples frequently served as the focal points of urban markets, but the areas they served were usually not coterminous with the marketing areas. The ritual territory of a town temple stopped at the edge of the town; it did not embrace the hinterland. Feuchtwang then shows how in recent decades the more modernized parts of the city have seen the appearance of a new type of temple, lacking compatriot, local, or commercial roots, but having a congregation held together by devotion to certain beliefs, more in the manner of a Western church.

Alden Speare and the Gallins analyze migration to the city in two different parts of present-day Taiwan. They also take two different approaches to the data. Speare concentrates on establishing the distinctive characteristics of those who left for the city, whereas the Gallins are interested in what happened to them once they arrived there. Speare shows that migrants to Taichung came disproportionately from the larger farms and the rural nonfarming households. They were better educated than the average, and tended to be later-born sons with numerous brothers but relatively few sisters. They broke away from life in the extended family at a rather earlier age than those who stayed behind. Most of them were also married, which contrasts with the single male migrants who contributed so much to city growth in China Proper and Manchuria between the wars. In the case of the migrants to Taipei examined by the Gallins, there were two distinct streams. Short-distance migrants were better off and better educated; long-distance migrants were poorer and less well educated. The Gallins' most interesting observations are perhaps those that show how the economic characteristics of city life subtly subverted the kin- and village-based relationships from which the migrants had been accustomed to seek support. Bernard Gallin gave an illustration of this during the conference that deserves to be recalled: the reduction of ritual occasions for social contact and solidarity by the urban mortuary funeral.

Irene B. Taeuber's study of demographic data collected by the Japanese government focuses on the relationship between migration patterns and urban growth in the first half of the twentieth century around the periphery of China Proper. Japan is compared and contrasted with Taiwan and Manchuria. In Taiwan, for example, an area of rapidly expanding agricultural production, Taeuber shows that the rates of increase in city populations were inversely related to the size and maturity of the cities, whereas exactly the opposite was true of Japan. But such clearcut contrasts are rare. Her conclusions, based on an analysis of sex ratios, marriage age, educational status, and labor-force participation, reflect a sophisticated agnosticism. Even with data that are markedly superior to any available for China Proper, it is hard to distinguish confidently between the demography of a traditional kind of city growth in a period of economic expansion (Taiwan) and that of an early phase of industrialization (Manchuria).

This brief survey gives some idea of the scope and range of the contributions to this volume. As anyone familiar with modern Chinese history will at once be aware, many important subjects have had to be omitted. There is hardly a word on the industrial working class and the mass movements in which they were involved; there is little on the relationship between the Nationalist government and urban business power; and there is not even a mention of the cities as centers where a new literary sensibility was created, expressed in the regional vernacular novel, the political propaganda play, and other new forms.[23] But if the papers appearing in the following pages can show that a meaningful conceptualization of China's early modernization is impossible without a systematic study of the central places within which that modernization unfolded—or, even better, if they can stimulate further inquiry along these lines—they will have served a useful purpose.

The Treaty Ports and China's Modernization

RHOADS MURPHEY

Prologue

The foreign position in China was consistently seen by its builders as a beachhead. The treaty ports were not necessarily harbingers of a fuller-scale territorial sovereignty, a goal that few even of the most ardent Old China Hand advocates of imperial ambition urged as desirable. But the China coasters did see themselves and the semi-colonial ports whose affairs they dominated as the wave of the future that must sooner of later engulf the whole of the country, as "backward" China came to emulate the "progress" whose banner these Western outposts so confidently flew. Behind these expectations there lay not only the supreme self-confidence of the nineteenth-century West, but the Western colonial experience in most of the rest of Asia. In South Asia and Japan especially (in quite different ways, of course) but to varying degrees also in mainland Southeast Asia, Indonesia, and the Philippines, whatever the administrative status from full colonialism to virtual independence, the leading edge of each society was being transformed by the Western impact, and for the most part along Western lines, through the agency of a few coastal cities, European bases that were analogues of the China treaty ports. Increasing commercialization of the economy under the impetus of foreign investments in production and transport, and the widening of the market in general, was accompanied by the boom growth of these new port cities founded or dominated by foreigners (outside of Japan). They soon became by far the largest in each country, although they had scarcely existed, or were at best small towns, before the seventeenth century. There the full force of the Western impact was concentrated, and this was far more than a commercial or industrial phenomenon. The flow of ideas and of noneconomic institutions was perhaps of greater revolutionary importance in the long run.

These processes are best summarized under the label of "modernization,"[1] a term that should connote not merely economic changes such as were involved in the emergence of a national market and the beginnings of a technological revolution in production and transport, but institutional, organizational, and ideological adjustments to a new order, and the early emergence of Asian nationalism. Although these developments all involved something more than and different from Westernization, they were set in train primarily through the presence and actions of Westerners in Asia, and are appropriately viewed as Asian responses to Western stimuli. The port cities that grew out of a few of the earlier European trade bases[2] constituted a working model of dynamic nineteenth-century Europe. Most of them were under colonial control, and functioned as points of entry into Asia of an alien Western order at a time when the West was in the midst of vigorous economic, technological, and institutional growth and when, as it happened, Asia (except for Japan) was experiencing a relative decline in all of these respects. The European impact was correspondingly devastating, not only in its remaking of the economic landscape in much of Asia but in its action on Asian cultural and national perceptions.

The China treaty ports, whose era may be said to have begun in 1842 and ended with the Japanese invasion in 1937, were a historical and geographical extension of a system established much earlier in South and Southeast Asia. Sixteenth- or seventeenth-century trading factories and forts at scattered points on the coastal fringes of Gujerat, Coromandel, Ceylon, Bengal, Java, Luzon, and elsewhere had by the end of the eighteenth century become urban bases for expanding colonial regimes, centers of a rapidly increasing external trade, foci of new internal transport routes (e.g., the extensive rail networks of India and Java, which in many cases opened new routes to areas previously involved only in limited and local trade), and nuclei of the institutional ferment that was during the nineteenth century to engulf and then to transform most of each country, as ripples spread across a pond from the casting of a single stone. Virtually all of the cities were new, settled on coastal or near-coastal sites that had been neglected when urban functions had been centripetally oriented. The new cities were not particularistically Asian, let alone national in the old sense, nor were they coherent symbols of a homogeneous culture of traditional consensus. They were physically unplanned growths that neatly symbolized the disruption and conflict they had introduced into each Asian order. They belonged more to a "modernizing" and supranational world than to the particular cultures or economies whose oceanic peripheries they occupied.[3]

Promise. The similarities among these cities, including those on the China coast, are striking, extending even to their physical appearance, but the different context in which they functioned in China was primarily responsible for differences in the final pattern of their influence which is the focus of this discussion.* Soon after the opening of the sixteenth century, European traders began their operations at ports from western India through Southeast Asia to Canton and Nagasaki. At all of them the same succession of Westerners, often indeed the same firms and even the same individuals trading in several countries, attempted to promote the same set of goals. India, Southeast Asia, China, and Japan were thus exposed to the same West, and through the same sorts of oceanic vestibules. Why should the Chinese response be different? In India and most of Southeast Asia the foreigners eventually built their own colonial environments in which the port cities could flourish and could act upon the mass. The Japanese provided in effect their own similar environment. Although in China this was never accomplished, it might reasonably be imagined that an expanded foreign trade, through the many-sided agency of the treaty port, would have served as an effective vehicle of modernization.

The contrasting situational patterns provide some clue as to why it did not (see the endpaper maps for this book). With the single and very late exception of Tsingtao,[4] all of the Chinese treaty ports arose beside the walls of existing major Chinese trade centers. Indeed, the Westerners specifically sought such locations, eager (as they put it themselves) to "tap" the China market as close as possible to where the action already was. They destroyed the Cohong and the restrictions of the Canton system, but never seriously attempted to create a new system. In India and Southeast Asia, by contrast, the colonial port cities were genuinely new, not only in character and function but in the sense that they arose independently of existing cities and were founded by Westerners precisely in order to escape from the existing Asian trade centers, and to set up a rival system whose attractions and rewards could overshadow

* The research on which this essay is based was supported by the Guggenheim Foundation, the American Council of Learned Societies, the Social Science Research Council, and the Center for Chinese Studies, University of Michigan. I am grateful to all of them, and to several colleagues at Michigan and elsewhere from whose suggestions and criticism I have benefited while the research was in progress. Discussions and comments at the St. Croix conference in December–January 1968–69 were of course especially helpful. Finally I want to thank Mark Elvin for exceptionally valuable criticism and editorial suggestions.

those of the deteriorating indigenous systems. They sought unoccupied but defensible sites where they could maintain their independence from the local orders, a pattern repeated, in historical sequence, from Goa through Batavia, Madras, Galle, Bombay, Calcutta, Penang, Singapore, and Surabaja. Manila, Rangoon, Colombo, Bangkok, and Saigon had existed as towns and trade centers earlier, but only on a very small scale.

But the foreign bases in China were beachheads of the same alien Western system that was ultimately to overwhelm or to reshape most of the rest of Asia, and by 1842 it was clear that the competitive balance of effectiveness had shifted drastically in China's disfavor. Full colonialism did not follow, but the treaty ports rapidly monopolized a growing external trade and had by the end of the nineteenth century become also virtually the only centers of machine manufacturing, like the colonial port cities in the rest of Asia; and like them, the treaty ports achieved this monopoly despite their strikingly eccentric locations (see the end-papers of this volume). It was also in the treaty ports, following the earlier model in colonial Asia, that Western commercial institutions were planted—banking, finance, insurance—and from them that mechanized transport lines spread, first steamships and then railways. By about the turn of the century or soon thereafter, the largest city in China was the most foreign—Shanghai, the kingpin of the treaty port system—although in 1842 it had been a relatively small center of regional trade whose population was outranked by several cities in the lower Yangtze valley and by perhaps a score or more in the country as a whole. With the single (and significant) exception of Peking, all of the other largest cities by the 1930's—Tientsin, Canton, Wuhan, Nanking, Chungking, Mukden, Dairen, in that order—were coastal or riverine treaty ports dominated (although to different degrees) by their commercial functions as opposed to the administrative character of the largest traditional cities, and dominated by foreigners. Their populations were of course overwhelmingly Chinese, but in part a new kind of Chinese, the treaty port men, who promised to be the indigenous agents for the remaking of China along Western lines in trade, finance, transport, industry, politics, and ideology, following the path of men like Tong King-sing or T. V. Soong and discarding the less appropriate models of Chang Chih-tung or Li Hung-chang and the crippling disabilities of the *kuan-tu shang-pan* system.[*]

[*] Literally, "official supervision, merchant management." In fact, the merchant managers never had a free hand, and their enterprises were stymied or destroyed by official failure to countenance innovation or to provide adequate capital. The official side also used its position to allocate jobs and revenues on a traditional nep-

It would be tempting to assume that the treaty ports, although never in any sense controlling the country at large, had attracted and then transformed enough Chinese would-be agents of modernization to transform China. Many of these recruits, it may be argued, were drawn from traditional merchant groups who could contrast their position under the traditional order with the new entrepreneurial freedom offered in the treaty ports—security of property and accumulation, the protection of nonparticularistic law, a stable civil order, the ready availability of capital at low rates of interest, expanding opportunities for constructive as opposed to parasitic uses of capital—and thus, in traditional parlance, hastened to be transformed. The first Chinese efforts at industrialization were in every case in the treaty port urban areas—the arsenals and other enterprises of the "self-strengtheners," and the first privately owned factories, financed mainly by ex-compradors.

It was also true that the treaty ports acted as havens not only for masses of refugees from mounting internal disorder, but increasingly also for political and ideological dissidents, and in time for open revolutionaries and their political parties. Such activities in the sanctuary of the treaty ports, and openly inspired by their example, helped to throw China into a ferment different from earlier dynastic declines. The revolutionaries were reacting to the model of a different system planted by the West along the seaward face of an undeniably disintegrating Chinese polity, an example of integration, strength, success, wealth, all seen as flowing not only from the superiority of Western technology but from Western institutions as well, especially nationalism. To all Chinese concerned about their country's weakness, the treaty ports offered a powerful goad, and to many it provided an attractive model.

The colonial port cities elsewhere in Asia had played a similar role with great effect. At least with the help of hindsight, it was already clear by the mid-nineteenth century that the Westernized Asian elites emerging in Calcutta, Bombay, Madras, Karachi, and Colombo were to inherit and to shape South Asia's modern development. By the end of the century the same pattern was apparent in each Southeastern Asian country (except for landlocked Laos and bucolic Cambodia), where the new national elites were exclusively concentrated in the colonial ports (Bangkok being of course semicolonial). The treaty port Indian became, without apology, and with all his fundamental Westernization, the dominant modern Indian of independence, the spokesman to and for nearly all

otistic basis, often to the ruin of the undertakings concerned. See A. Feuerwerker, *China's Early Industrialization* (Cambridge, Mass.: Harvard University Press, 1958), *passim*.

politically conscious Indians.[5] The role of the treaty port Ceylonese, Burmese, Thai, Vietnamese, Indonesian, and Filipino was similar. All of these antecedents of Shanghai and Tientsin had indeed worked a revolution. Why should not the apparently very similar pattern in China eventually produce similar results?

The Chinese Context: Political Weakness and Economic Strength

The Chinese context was fundamentally different. To begin with, Chinese sovereignty was never displaced, despite the greater effectiveness of the West, and it tended to preserve many of the incubus aspects of the traditional system. The rigidity of the Ch'ing as a weakening, originally alien, dynasty of conquest meant that there was no effective leadership at the top, Chinese or foreign, toward a new order. Late Ch'ing China was strong (or simply big?) enough to prevent a complete colonial takeover, but not to manage adequately the traditional patterns of its internal affairs, let alone meet the pressures for adjustment to the new circumstances of the nineteenth and twentieth centuries, or to administer "modernization." The change-oriented leaders that were produced—primarily the treaty port Chinese and some of the Western colonialists—held no political power (as the treaty ports themselves had no administrative functions beyond their own boundaries), and were chronically frustrated by government officials in their efforts to promote innovative economic development or institutional change. Neither foreigners nor treaty port Chinese ever had a free field of operation, and certainly nothing to compare with the colonial Westerners and their partners in the rest of Asia functioning in the environment provided by colonialism. The progressive collapse of civil order in China, which no Chinese government after 1850 and until 1949 was able to reverse, may have been another major reason why the treaty port impact was, by comparison with the rest of Asia or with its own apparent promise, blunted. It was not only that the treaty port system failed to build up a respectable volume of new trade, especially in terms of China's scale (a point examined in more detail in a subsequent section), but that it failed to induce a lasting or self-perpetuating variety of modernization. For example, a rail skeleton was built, largely at foreign urging and with foreign capital (and for the most part against the resistance of traditional official/gentry prejudices); but for much of its relatively brief existence, from about 1902 to 1936, many of the lines were blocked, cut, or otherwise hampered in their operation by civil war, troop movements, and commandeering of rolling stock.[6] The contrast with India is particularly clear, and important.

But more than these negative or disabling factors was involved. For all its actual and latent economic and political problems, nineteenth-century China was no such wilderness for the merchant as has sometimes too easily been assumed from the supposed "backwardness" of traditional commercial methods and the heavy hand of the bureaucratic state. The absolute levels of Ming and Ch'ing commerce were extremely large. They are difficult to measure precisely, but the available evidence from local gazetteers[7] and other sources suggests even in per capita terms a level of interprovincial (and perhaps external?) trade equal to or greater than European levels as late as the beginning of the nineteenth century. The absolute total was of course far greater. A large sector of the economy was monetized, and a number of commodities were produced for and distributed over a multiprovincial, national, or external market: raw cotton and woven cloth from several centers in Chihli and Kiangsu, silk from Hangchow and Soochow, rice from the Yangtze provinces, sugar from Kwangtung and Szechwan, porcelain from Ching-te-chen, tea from Fukien, and a long list of lesser goods such as iron tools, paper, dried or preserved foods, and the several commodities distributed as official monopolies, most of which were also traded (and smuggled) privately.

Sample measures. The Japanese consul at Amoy in 1898, Ueno Sen'ichi, reported that in the whole of the Foochow district there had traditionally been no local production of cotton cloth, and that until very recently all cloth consumed had been imported from Kiangsu and Chekiang; his report indicated a similar situation in most of Kiangsi and eastern Kwangtung. Only within the preceding few years had local cloth production begun, almost entirely as a female occupation carried on in households and making use of imported Indian yarn.[8] Much of the cloth supply for these southern areas probably came from Kiangsu. Hatano Yoshihiro in his study of the cotton cloth industry cites data from Ch'ang-shu in Kiangsu in 1901 to the effect that cloth made there had long been sold in large quantities to Fukien, Kwangtung, Kwangsi, and Kiangsi, and as far as Szechwan as well as northward to Shantung, Chihli, and Shansi. These data include estimates of total cloth sales from Ch'ang-shu alone of three million rolls a year, of which only one million were marketed in Kiangsu.[9] Hatano also quotes a memorial of Pien Pao-ti in 1892 from Foochow: "Fukien is barren and the inhabitants have difficulty in making a living. They had no knowledge of how to cultivate cotton or weave cloth, but relied entirely on the merchants from Kiangsu and Chekiang coming to Fukien to sell it." Thus Pien introduces his account of the establishment of a "weaving board" in Foochow in 1891 so that "the poor people (may) have a trade and rely upon it for their livelihood."[10] These are all indications of a high degree of commercialization and a well-developed exchange economy before the onset of any significant foreign influences on production or transport.

Tribute grain shipments, involving as they did a complex transport linkage, provide further indication of regional specialization and exchange. Grain actually transported to the capital averaged over three million *tan* yearly during the Ch'ing, carried in between 7,000 and 8,000 ships from the eight provinces concerned.[11] To this should be added about an equal amount to cover "wastage" in a variety of forms along the route, plus "squeeze" and peculation at the sources.[12] However, the tribute grain shipments became by the nineteenth century a predominantly commercial operation, managed by merchants.[13] The grain ships were officially exempted from customs and transit duties and were authorized to carry a fixed quota of trade goods tax-free, but commonly exceeded this quota and nevertheless paid no tax, in part because customs officials en route feared being accused of delaying the tribute rice.[14] The grain shipment itself was increasingly commercialized by commutting payments into "easy delivery silver," a practice begun as early as Sung but increasingly common in Ch'ing.[15] By 1834, according to the *Veritable Records* for that year, half of the tribute grain was being collected as silver, and in the most densely populated areas of Kiangnan tribute rice money amounted to 20,000 or 30,000 taels yearly.[16]

This was a reflection of a highly monetized economy. Commission fees for commutation, tax farming, sale of tribute grain en route and privately in the capital, and various forms of squeeze associated with each enterprise all helped to nourish a cloud of merchants. It was far from being any longer an official undertaking. Trade goods other than rice appear to have become by far the dominant cargo of the grain ships, especially if illegal and smuggled as well as legal goods are included. By 1799 one scholar asserted that each of the ships carried one to two thousand *tan* of private merchants' goods that successfully escaped inspection and taxation.[17] Grain ships carried a similar stream of commercial goods on the return trip southward, including some of the tribute rice being shipped back on private account.[18] Merchants usually travelled with the boats, buying and selling a wide variety of goods in great volume along the way and acting as virtually the sole managers of the entire affair. The other people on the boats, and even the officials, were in effect the employees of the merchants.[19] One rough measure both of the magnitude of the shipments and of the nature of the late traditional economy is provided in the grain-equivalents used for commutation: one ounce of silver for four piculs of rice, government scrip (*ch'ao*) worth 500 cash for one picul, one piece of cotton cloth for one picul, one *chin* of cleaned raw cotton for 0.2 picul, one ounce of gold for twenty piculs, or one piece of silk for 1.2 piculs.[20] Large numbers of private as well as official merchants were involved in this trade, legal and illegal.[21]

The salt trade was at least equally profitable to many of those engaged in it, and took place on a comparable scale. Indeed, in both Ming and Ch'ing (until the introduction of likin) approximately half of the total national budget revenues in silver was derived from the salt administration, although it was widely acknowledged that the quantity of smuggled salt was at most periods at least as great as the total legally traded, despite the severe penalties for smuggling.[22] Wide variations in salt prices, both temporal and spatial (primarily as a result of fluctuating tax or levy demands, irregular enforcement of regulations, and transport problems, as well as normal economic cycles) encouraged speculation on a massive scale and increased smuggling incentives.[23] There was apparently an even greater "leakage" in the salt trade than in the grain tribute trade. In early-nineteenth-century Liang Huai, for example, the salt tax collection turned over to the government was a little over two million taels, while the actual tax collected was about eight million, and the Liang Huai transport merchants' outlay for that area's share of the salt trade was between twenty and thirty million taels.[24] Merchants and officials invested both in the legal and the illegal salt trade as well as in the rice trade, in pawnshops, etc., using capital derived from speculation and/or smuggling of salt. The wealth of many of them and the size of the trade they manipulated is indicated by the dimensions of the special levies exacted from them at periodic intervals, to meet unusual military expenses or other financial crises: the Liang Huai salt merchants alone "contributed" four million taels toward the expedition against the Gurkhas in 1792, and two million for the Miao campaign of 1795.[25] But our attention should perhaps not be focused too much on the abuses of the system. A study by Professor Thomas Metzger deals with a highly successful, and rational, reform in the system of salt deliveries, quotas, transport, and taxes carried out by T'ao Chu in 1832–34 and designed to reduce smuggling by eliminating the incentives. It worked very well, at least for a few decades. Metzger concludes: "Little could have been accomplished without expert and dedicated officials. . . . The effectiveness of T'ao and his subordinates does not easily tally with the theory that the Ch'ing bureaucracy, except for anomalies, was a mass of corruption, paralyzed by suspicion, and operating on sheer inertia."[26]

As the nineteenth century wore on and population continued to increase faster than production, while disorder mounted, merchants and others with capital sought speculative or predatory activities as the best

means of survival in a deteriorating situation, rather than attempting to
increase or rationalize production or exchange. But this relative decline
was probably fairly slow, at least until 1850, and even after the Taiping
Rebellion did not take place so rapidly or consistently as to destroy the
ability of the traditional commercial sector to continue to manipulate the
market and largely to exclude foreign merchants. Ch'ing official and
actual policy toward merchants and commerce, often characterized as
ruinously oppressive, is probably better seen as reflecting the close mu-
tuality of merchant and bureaucratic interests. The state and its revenues
depended to an important degree on the commercial sector and hence
attempted to ensure that it would thrive. Merchants, for their part, benefited far more from contact with officials (including a share in the management of government monopolies) than they suffered, either from taxation or from periodic special exactions. Commercial success depended
to an important extent on bureaucratic connections, but the embrace was
more nourishing than stifling.[27]

Scale and persistence. Finally there is the sheer bulk of China, geo-
graphically, demographically, and economically, and the huge total of
its production, all of which dwarfed Europe's until very late and helped
both to absorb and to deflect European efforts at penetration or transformation. As John Fairbank has put it: "China was too big a country
[with its] great reservoir of inland provinces" (many on the scale of
separate European states) "to be easily stirred by a marginal sea-frontier
contact with foreign ideas."[28] The level of urbanization in China was
also relatively high; perhaps as much as a tenth or a twelfth of an immense population lived in cities before the planting of the treaty ports
(substantially more in highly commercialized areas such as most of
Kiangnan). The endpaper maps show the generally dense pattern of
urban places, all but a very few of them in existence long before the
treaty ports, including of course those that became treaty ports. Perhaps
half or more of this mass of city dwellers were supported by or in some
way engaged in trade, transport, or manufacturing, or their administration. What more did the European model offer? Even Adam Smith was
impressed enough, at second or third hand, to write:

The great extent of the empire of China, the vast multitude of its inhabitants,
the variety of climate, and consequently of productions in its different provinces, and the easy communication by means of water carriage between the
greater part of them, render the home market of that country of so great extent
as to be alone sufficient to support very great manufactures, and to admit of
very considerable subdivisions of labour. The home market of China is perhaps
in extent not much inferior to the market of all the different countries of
Europe put together.[29]

Smith also remarks elsewhere on China's strong commercial advantage in possessing such a vast network of natural and artificial internal waterways, and on the enormous traffic they carried,[30] matters commented on subsequently by nearly all foreign observers at first hand.

The most important difference between China and the rest of Asia outside Japan in this connection is that in China the traditional indigenous system, at least outside the political sphere, remained very much more effective, right through the nineteenth and into the twentieth century. There was no vacuum the foreigners could fill. The great economic drive of European export to China, in textiles, largely failed to establish any significant share of the market in the face of the superior competitive position of traditional textile production, and, especially after about 1917, of Chinese machine manufacturing. The strong position of Chinese handicraft textiles was apparent quite early, but most foreign merchants continued to dream, despite the accurate assessments of a few. One of the earliest of these was the report originally prepared in 1852 for the Foreign Office by W. H. Mitchell, Assistant Magistrate at Hong Kong, addressed to Sir George Bonham (Governor of Hong Kong, 1848–63), and published with minor emendations as "Report on British Trade with China" in the Blue Book of 1857–59. It reads in part as follows:

Since the British plenipotentiary who signed the Treaty of Nanking in 1842 informed his countrymen that he had opened up to their trade a country so vast "that all the mills of Lancashire could not make stocking stuff enough for one of its provinces" the endeavor to supply China with manufactured cotton has been the most interesting and generally the most perplexing of the enterprises which merchants in this country have been engaged in. The Lancashire and other manufacturers soon found that however correct the plenipotentiary's statement might have been as far as it related to the consuming capacity of China, it was wrong either in ignoring the producing power which the country possessed, or the difficulties in the way of introducing cotton goods into the interior. Amongst the disappointed merchants in China were several who took the latter view, and who thought—even at a time when, as now, the labouring classes of Chinese at Hong Kong, where no duty at all is charged on cotton goods, preferred wearing the more durable fabrics of their own country—that English manufactured cottons were prevented from circulating freely in the interior by the heavy inland duties levied on them, an opinion which led to the emphatic assertion of the transit dues regulation in the treaties of 1858. There were some, however, who saw that it was the producing power in the people which made them independent of foreign supply, and the larger experience of the last few years has made the view of this faction clear enough.

A few years later, the Commissioner of Customs at Tientsin in his Report on Trade for 1866 (pp. 88–90) pointed out that

Cotton is grown extensively in China, and the people weave it into a coarse, strong cloth which is much better suited to the wants of the peasants and working men than the more showy but less substantial product of Foreign machinery. The customers of the British manufacturer in China are not the bulk of the people but only those who can afford to buy a better looking but less useful article.

The Commissioner listed the relative weights and prices of Tientsin- and British-made cloth, indicating that the British article was significantly more expensive per unit of weight, and adding that

the Chinese say that the superiority in strength of the Native article over the Foreign is greater than the difference in weight between them. . . . No transit passes are applied for by Foreigners to protect imported cotton piece goods from undue charges on their way into the interior, and it is to be inferred from this fact that if the inland charges in this part of China exceed the Treaty transit dues [i.e., half of the import duty] the excess is so small that the native merchant does not think it worth his while to try to get his goods passed into the interior under foreign protection.

Note that it was the "native merchant" who remained responsible for the marketing even of imported foreign goods.

As in the case of India, there has long been a too-easy assumption that imports of machine-made cloth ruined a large share of traditional production. Even for India, this is in serious question,[31] but for China virtually all the evidence points the other way, including the chronically disappointing trade figures and the tiny scale of cloth imports even at their peak by comparison with the size of the market. As late as the 1930's in Hopei, Fang Hsien-t'ing estimates that small-scale handloom weavers still accounted for four-fifths of the total cloth production.[32] By that time, machine-spun yarn was in use even by hand weavers (originally imported from India and Japan, later obtained increasingly from Chinese factory production), and foot-treadle and Jacquard looms were common.[33] Virtually all of the cloth was sold commercially, much of it in interprovincial trade, and profitable use was made of mechanized transport, especially the railway lines and motor roads with which eastern Hopei was relatively well supplied.[34]

Hatano's study of the cotton industry cites a Japanese report of 1898 on the areas around Shanghai (of all places!) which suggests among other things that hand-spun yarn continued to be important:

The general characteristics of the producing area are like those of Nara, Ibaraki, or Saitama before the importation of foreign yarn. The people are very primitive, and stress only frugality, diligence, and honesty. . . . The investigators were surprised to find no hired labour from outside either in rich or poor households, all of which were individually operated. They use hand-twisted yarn made by themselves from home-grown cotton for both the warp and the weft. Although some progress has been made in recent years with the importation of foreign yarn, they still stubbornly adhere to their old ways. . . . We have heard that the reason is that they dislike receiving a small price as the result of having to buy the raw materials and not using their home-grown cotton.

In the vicinity of Shasi in Hupeh, the raw materials were either hand-spun yarn alone or a combination of machine-spun warp and hand-spun weft. The cloth was sold in Szechwan, Yunnan, Kweichow, Kwangsi, Hu-nan, and elsewhere, either by local shops directly or through merchant-travelers (*hao-k'o*) sent out from these areas to lay in stock. The system was both economically rational and commercially successful. As late as 1913, according to Hatano, hand-spun yarn continued to be used on a large scale. He refers to the gap between recorded yarn imports in that year (358 million pounds in weight), Chinese-made machine-spun yarn (estimated at between 220 and 250 million pounds), and total yarn con-sumption in China, where power looms used only about 15 million pounds of yarn. Hand-spun yarn used in combination with this machine-spun yarn clearly must have amounted still to a vast quantity.[35]

The persistence of indigenous production so late, and its ability to take advantage of technological innovations, tell us something about the rea-sons for the foreigners' failure either to penetrate the market with their own goods or to see their technology triumph in Chinese hands. Ch'en Shih-chi has provided a broad survey of this and similar areas in Shan-tung and Hunan where hand weaving preserved a strong position into the 1930's.[36] Hand-woven Chinese cloth remained more durable and cheaper by weight than foreign machine-made cloth, and continued to enjoy an enormously greater sale. The traditional cottage-based silk in-dustry saw similar changes after about 1880, when mechanical silk-reel-ing equipment was introduced, although here weaving as well as reeling (the equivalent of cotton spinning) was quickly taken over almost en-tirely by concentrated factory units, leaving the traditional producer only the function of supplying cocoons.[37]

What was true of cloth was, in differing ways, true of almost every other would-be import. Part of the foreign problem was Chinese resis-tance to new commodities, well summarized by S. G. Checkland:

Selling in China of course means discovering within the Chinese consumption pattern hitherto unexplored desires capable of responding to the manufactured novelties and factory processed fabrics of the West. This meant altering the traditional culture of the Empire—the very thing that had rendered the Chinese so hostile to the newcomers. Little was to be hoped for from the attempt to interest the Chinese in a variety of new and untried things.

Checkland's study is based on the private papers of the Rathbone family and on records of the firm of Rathbone, Worthington and Co. at the University of Liverpool. These records graphically illustrate the difficulties all foreign firms experienced in their effort to penetrate the China market. Given the volatile prices, the fluctuating exchange rates, the problems of selling almost anything on commission or on consignment, and the need for multiple Chinese agents, business "expenses in China were heavy beyond all Indian experience." The firm ultimately made most of its profits in speculation on the great variety of money exchanges, currency, and credit. As early as 1851, one of the partners accurately foresaw this: "Profits will be made as much in the management of the funds and the exchanges as in any other way."[38]

But a great deal of the Chinese reluctance to buy foreign goods or to adopt foreign business methods or technology was entirely rational and not culture-bound: traditional Chinese goods and methods were equal or superior, especially in cost terms. The only significant exceptions were cotton yarn (though its success was far from complete, as pointed out above), kerosene, and cigarettes, the last two being items not present at all in the traditional economy and, at least in the case of kerosene, demonstrably superior to domestic alternatives without being substantially more expensive. However, cigarettes, like machine-made yarn, matches, and a number of other lesser goods of originally foreign manufacture, came increasingly after about 1915 from Chinese producers using Chinese raw materials.

As the Chinese producer successfully moved into the production of goods that had been foreign monopolies (and as the consumer accepted clearly preferable new alternatives like kerosene), so the Chinese entrepreneur took advantage of changing conditions to invade new fields of trade and investment. He had never been replaced as the commercial manager of the domestic market either for imports or for exports, despite foreign efforts. After about 1860, and especially after 1920, he took advantage as an investor of the new opportunities for profit offered by foreign innovation in steamships, mining, banking, and factory production in the treaty ports. One estimate gives a total of 400 million taels of Chinese capital invested in foreign enterprise in the late 1890's, by which time Chinese owned about 40 percent of the stock of Western firms in shipping, cotton spinning, and banking, and held shares in roughly 60 percent of all foreign firms in China.[39]

Steamship enterprises attracted the earliest major Chinese investment outside of trade itself. Chinese merchants subscribed about a third of the original capital of the first three foreign steamship companies founded at Shanghai between 1862 and 1868, and nearly 80 percent of the initial capital of the China Merchants Steam Navigation Co., the first such enterprise owned and operated by Chinese, in 1873–74.[40] Large amounts of Chinese capital were later invested in new mining and manufacturing enterprises, especially cotton textiles and tobacco.[41] By 1894 Chinese investors, and managers, were represented in about three-fifths of the foreign firms in China.[42] Profits obtainable from landholding (especially as land prices rose in response primarily to continued population increase) and from the traditional government monopolies such as salt were static or declining, and Chinese investors were fully able to perceive and to act on changed circumstances which made foreign-managed innovative enterprises an attractive outlet, followed in time by Chinese-managed enterprises.[43] Foreign undertakings were more attractive to Chinese investors than the officially sponsored *kuan-tu shang-pan* efforts, which were chronically plagued by capital shortages.[44]

Identity

To return to the contrast between China and colonial Asia, but in sociocultural rather than economic terms: colonial rule may be said to have created nationalism and national consciousness almost *de novo* in most of South and Southeast Asia, whereas in China a vigorously self-conscious cultural nationalism, national identity, and a tradition of an integrated national state and culture had existed for some two thousand years before the Westerners arrived. The treaty port system in China merely refocused and sharpened the traditional Chinese insistence on a self-sufficient and self-satisfied identity, and the traditional resistance to foreign models. One may say that the ports were a new negative in Chinese society, which in the end called forth a new negative in response. By contrast, most politically conscious Indians, lacking a national tradition and seeing crippling deficiencies in their regional traditions, valued Western models and indeed welcomed British rule as the obvious path to progress, a Western concept which they enthusiastically adopted.[45]

India, like Ceylon, like all of Southeast Asia, like Japan, experienced a long identity crisis. In each country, to differing degrees, indigenous attitudes, cultural styles, techniques, patterns of thought, notions of po-

litical organization—the whole stuff of traditional society—were found
wanting and to varying extents rejected, directly or indirectly, in favor
either of outright Western models or of the colonial hybrid that in the
end prevailed: the Calcutta-Bengali model and its unambiguously urban-based parallels created by the new Westernized national elites in
Bombay, Colombo, Rangoon, Bangkok, Singapore, Saigon, Batavia, Manila, Tokyo, and so on. This has of course brought its agony to the intellectuals and other nationalists involved, and in most cases a painful process of readjustment has followed independence, a re-sorting that has
been referred to as "second-wave nationalism."[46]

Although in the end she may have accepted a partly alien modernization as the price of self-respect, China never had an identity problem;
perhaps it would have been better if she had. The Western challenge
merely reinforced existing Sinocentric pride. All foreigners had always
been barbarians, to whom China had been willing to condescend. After
1840, foreigners revealed themselves also as bandits, clever, effective in
certain ways, but alien and frequently evil. There was more than a grain
of truth in this assessment. By comparison with China before the nineteenth century, all foreigners could with some reason be dismissed as
barbarians; their nineteenth-century role in China can with equal reason
be seen as banditry. The Chinese perception in these respects, still
strongly evident today, is really not warped. But despite the blows to
which China was subjected and the apparent sharp contrast between
Western effectiveness and Chinese ineffectiveness at least in political
terms, the strong sense of cultural continuity and identity prevented any
surrender. There was certainly a deeper and a wider awareness of their
own national cultural tradition on the part of most Chinese than existed
among most Indians or Southeast Asians, and a firmer commitment to it.
And the confrontation with the West heightened the Chinese sense of
identity rather than destroying it, in part because the treaty ports had
so little cultural impact. *Shen-pao* and other, more radical, treaty-port-
based journals circulated quite widely, especially after 1911, but their
influence strengthened the Chinese sense of crisis, not the cosmopolitan-
ization of China. The Japanese situation was different because of the
vastly greater size of China and its contrasting experience over two mil-
lennia with cultural borrowing. To China, *foreign* had come to mean
inferior, whereas to Japan it could still mean *possibly better*, in a country
which in any case was too small and too accessible to ignore foreign
pressures. A German physician who visited Japan in the middle 1870's,
a few years after the Meiji Restoration, received a startling but revealing
reply from a Japanese friend whom he questioned about Japanese his-

tory: "We have no history; our history begins today."[47] Such an attitude at any period, including the present, is utterly inconceivable in China.

It may be argued that the May Fourth Movement and its aftermath (an urban affair, after all, and largely a treaty port one) had some of the elements of an identity crisis, and that in any case Chinese intellectuals suffered deeply from a growing awareness of the deficiencies of their own tradition as early as 1842 and with increasing sharpness up to 1949. But despite the second thoughts about Confucianism or the prescription of large doses of Science and Democracy, there was no real loss of identity. Criticism of certain traditional values did not, in anyone's mind, mean abandonment of cultural membership. As Levenson has stressed (see note 49), there is an important difference between "culturalism" and nationalism; both may, however, be symbols or bases of identity. In the Chinese case, as some traditional values came to be questioned by the relatively small numbers affected by *Kulturschmerz*, Chinese identity was newly buttressed by the beginnings of nationalist feelings and loyalties. It was, as Levenson describes it, a shift from cosmopolitanism to provincialism, but it left identity intact. There was keen interest on the part of some in learning English, in adopting certain clearly Western ideas or institutions, and in rejecting large blocks of the Chinese past (although it is important that many, perhaps most, of these critics and seekers were outside the treaty port milieu). But no one in China wondered, in all this turmoil, who he was, as nearly all other Asian intellectuals caught up by Westernization did wonder while they groped for solutions. China was in danger, but not Chineseness. Even among expatriates and emigrants this was true. Which China to embrace or to try to build was sometimes a problem, but "a sense of where you are"[48]— what game, what team, what league—was never lost. The Japanese agony may have been briefer, perhaps even confined to the first decade or so of the Meiji; but Western pressures involved a real threat to national identity. China suffered infinitely more, at least in part because she never even briefly flirted with the idea of not being Chinese. This was perhaps a losing game after 1850, but to play any other was nevertheless unthinkable.[49]

Time and Dichotomies

Economically, China was in no sense undeveloped, nor was she disastrously deteriorating until perhaps the second or third decade of the twentieth century. Our perceptions in this respect have been warped by projecting into the nineteenth century the economic conditions prevailing between 1920 and 1949, the period which is now best known. This was, however, a seriously unrepresentative time. What evidence we have demonstrates not only a drastic deterioration beginning in the early 1920's (the famine-flood-warlord years), and (less concretely but nevertheless convincingly) a general level of economic vigor in the traditional system throughout most of the nineteenth century and into the first two decades of the twentieth that makes most comparisons with the post-1920 period inappropriate. The Taiping Rebellion marks a watershed in the course of China's economy in the nineteenth century as it does in so many other respects, and there seems little question that it was followed by a steepening of a downward trend that may have begun more slowly in the latter part of the eighteenth century as mounting population pressure joined with declining governmental effectiveness. But even by 1911 it is doubtful that the economy had degenerated enough to make it closely comparable with conditions in the 1920's or 1940's.

One important source of ambiguity is the commonly overlooked distinction between the more or less measurable aspects of the economy (primarily in its "modern" sector) and the readily observable deterioration of the political and institutional order on the one hand, and on the other hand the ability of the traditional commercial system to continue functioning with reasonable success and little change, not merely despite the failures and problems in railway-building or industrialization, and the disintegration of the national administrative order, but almost wholly apart from such developments and the quite different sphere in which they were taking place. The two systems touched one another very little, their interaction was minimized by the concentration of the modernizing sector in the few scattered islands of the treaty ports, and of political struggles in Peking and Nanking. In what seems, especially through foreign eyes, to have been a catastrophically disintegrating China, the vast, predominantly rural bulk of the country, including its "little tradition" sector of livelihood and commerce, was only marginally affected. By the twentieth century, it too was in mounting economic trouble, but not to any important extent because of failures in the modernizing sector. Its problems were the long-familiar Malthusian ones, aggravated by the progressive breakdown of civil order after 1911; but even by the 1920's or 1940's it was not yet so weakened that it could not continue to operate more or less as it had always done, and to show occasional signs of regeneration or adaptability to changed conditions. There was of course some common ground: many of the same goods, capital, and in some cases (see below) even merchants operated in both systems. But in terms of technology and more generally of the structure and character of the two systems, they were separate and only incidentally tangential.

For the purposes of our argument here, the persistence of the traditional commercial system may best be seen in the ability of traditional merchants to invade the treaty ports themselves, as well as to maintain their control over the internal marketing even of foreign goods, including those that were genuinely new to China such as kerosene, cigarettes, and machine-spun yarns, despite determined Western efforts to force their way in. It was not, as the foreigners perennially complained, the resistance of Ch'ing officials, the foot-dragging of the gentry, the "backwardness" or xenophobia of the Chinese consumer (although this had some relevance, in the sense that traditional wants persisted), the inadequacy of the railways, the continuation of likin, or the lack of support from their home governments that aborted their dreams, but the fact that they were attempting to invade a traditional Chinese system fully able to meet and beat them at their own game of commerce, on its home ground.

Outside the relatively few big cities and those served by railways, steamships, or motor roads—in other words in most of the country—changes related to the modernizing sector were minimal even up to 1948. G. W. Skinner's three-part study of the rural marketing system[50] estimates that by that year only about 10 percent of the traditional standard markets in the country as a whole had yielded to "modern" trading systems; in Szechwan, where most of his primary data were gathered in 1949–50, he found none that had so altered. Over most of China, the long-established nested pattern of marketing systems survived basically unchanged until the advent of the Communists, covering the economic and social landscape with its intricate and efficiently operating honeycomb of commercial and social interaction and remaining without much question the predominant channel of internal trade. It was vigorous and flexible enough to adjust as necessary to changes in population, regional political conditions, local disorder, and new commodities, but was seldom seriously disrupted, and then only briefly. It was a much less fragile and uncertain sector than the many times smaller one in which modernization was being attempted. Its relative success in riding out essentially undamaged the mounting storm of disaster that, from a Western point of view, overtook China after 1850 or after 1900 is ample testimony to its effectiveness, and suggests among other things that our attention may have been focused to a misleading extent on the failures of modernization and national integration, causing us to jump to the erroneous conclusion that China and the Chinese economy were degenerating or no longer viable.

Skinner's study is a useful corrective to this view, and in effect shows us a larger China where the old currents of trade and social integration continued largely unruffled by the winds tearing at the more obvious official edifices of the traditional system. This was the network that managed much, perhaps most, of the ultimate marketing even of goods imported by the foreigners. It was of course not proof against innovation, and indeed had no reason for being so, or for drawing invidious distinctions between goods on the basis of their origin. Western cloth or kerosene, factory-made matches or cigarettes, and even (by the 1940's) American fountain pens, were sold in the standard markets along with traditional Chinese goods. But there was no need and no room for foreign traders to establish a "modern" marketing system along Western lines or with the participation of "modern" merchants. The existing system was fully capable of managing the country's commerce, and the foreign or "modern" role, by comparison of little significance, was confined to the few small dots of the treaty ports and a share in the manipulation of external trade.

In the political-administrative sphere, as the center weakened and finally rotted, regional and local continuity in administration kept most of the functionally beneficial aspects of the system going. Indeed, it may be argued that the decline of the center had a net positive effect on actual welfare, at least until 1911, by removing the exploitative burden of the official bureaucracy and allowing the assertion not merely of local self-interest through the gentry management of local affairs but even of some innovation in local administration. The self-regulating society that ideally was part of the traditional system at the local level was freed from the dead hand of reaction and corruption, the major contributions of a decaying center, and was thus better able effectively to confront local problems. Western attention has been concentrated on political events at the national level, where the picture was indeed one of progressive disintegration, or has viewed the post-1850 rise of regionalism as both a symptom and a cause of general deterioration. Such a perspective may well be misleading. Unfortunately, we have very little evidence from the local sphere, especially before it in turn succumbed (at least in some respects) to mounting chaos with the outbreak of chronic civil war and banditry after 1911. But it is surely unsafe to generalize from political happenings at the center about actual welfare at the local level, where the bulk of the population lived, and regarding which neither the direct nor the indirect socioeconomic data summarized above in any way suggests a parallel disintegration, at least not for fifty or sixty years after 1850.[51]

Exclusive attention to the recorded political events at earlier periods in Chinese history may be similarly misleading. The Japanese monk Ennin, who made detailed observations in late T'ang within a few years of the final collapse of the dynasty,[52] records no political chaos but depicts relative order and prosperity as well as cultural sophistication; presumably there were ample indications of decay at the center, but these drew no comment from Ennin and the implication is that they did not importantly affect the basic fabric of Chinese civilization with which he was concerned. One may reach similar conclusions from a reading of accounts of late Sung, as for example Jacques Gernet's absorbing descriptions focused on Hangchow.[53] Even in the Sung capital within a few years of its ultimate downfall, one is shown an effective, successful system in operation in which individuals and communities appear to have been very little affected by the weakening of the central bureaucracy. In late Ming, too, by Ricci's account,[54] the undeniable ossification, corruption, and mounting ineffectiveness of the national administration were not reflected in any important way in what was happening at the local level. Ricci shows us a prosperous, well-ordered, commercially vigorous, and highly civilized China that, like Skinner's picture of the 1940's, may be a useful antidote to generalizations based on the knowledge of imperial political decline.

Because we know a good deal more about the last few decades of the Ch'ing we may be correspondingly reluctant to find a similar pattern there, in the sense that the catastrophic weakening of the center with which we are so familiar seems hard to reconcile with continued order and economic effectiveness in the bulk of the country. We may be mesmerized by our data showing exclusively the sickness of the center. After 1911 this sickness unquestionably did spread to engulf large parts of China in chronic disorder. Such disorder had by no means been absent before, especially after 1850, but it certainly attained a new order of magnitude after 1911. There may be reason to think that in the preceding decades the traditional system managed to continue functioning with much less impairment, little enough at least to enable it to hold the field against foreign encroachments and to buttress its own sense of self-sufficiency. Its principal problem may have been the slower-acting one of mounting overpopulation, rather than the more dramatic collapse attributed to it by extrapolation from what was happening on the official plane.

One informant's recollections of village life in Kwangtung from about 1880 to 1950 offer some support for such assertions.[55] The quality of life and even the character of the landscape in his village and its area, some hundred miles southwest of Canton, changed radically after 1911. During the last two decades of the nineteenth century, the village was orderly, reasonably prosperous, largely free of banditry, and surrounded on all hillsides by extensive forest. After 1911 it was increasingly overtaken by troop movements, massive banditry, interruptions in its normal communications, and wholesale removal of the trees, both by troops and by villagers. Emigration of young adult males became common especially after about 1900, and by the 1920's the area fit the stereotypes of twentieth-century Kwangtung. The point here is that this condition was reached relatively recently, not in the nineteenth century. In Szechwan, more remote from the forces operating in Kwangtung, and thus probably more typical of most of China, both Skinner's data and my own observations from the early and middle 1940's suggest that even on the eve of the Communist conquest the quality and conditions of rural life had not yet drastically changed. The people were suffering the kind of slow decline one might expect from growing overpopulation, and were beginning to be more seriously troubled by civil disorder (mainly in the form of banditry, whose causes were probably more economic than political), but they had certainly not fallen into chaos in the way that many Western generalizations about China, lumping together the whole of the period after 1850, and based on a reading of major political events, would have us believe.

The foreigners' activities probably strengthened China's economy far more than they weakened it. Some of the capital generated in the treaty ports was, it is true, drained off as profits or for investment in the metropolitan countries, but this was more than balanced by investment in China. More important, foreign efforts to widen external markets were certainly accompanied by increased Chinese production of foreign trade goods, even if this was not a large proportional increase over traditional levels of production. The availability of certain imported goods, such as machine-spun yarn, also benefited indigenous production and improved its ability to compete. Taking the increased level of commercial activity in general also into consideration, there seems no question that Chinese incomes gained rather than suffered as a result of the foreign presence. Moreover, new industrial employment was created in the treaty ports after 1895. The treaty ports themselves provided invaluable training grounds for an emerging industrial labor force, as well as for technicians.[56]

The importance of the example set by foreign commercial, transport, and industrial techniques, especially for wealthy treaty port Chinese, and the imitative efforts inspired thereby should be stressed. Foreign innovation in the treaty ports, and foreign technological and institutional effectiveness also made an important ideological impact on many Chinese intellectuals. The question remains how deep or widespread these influences were; or perhaps more pointedly, what form they took. "Modernization" ultimately came to China, but hardly in the form the treaty ports represented or strove for, except as altered through Maoist glasses. There can be no doubt, however, that the treaty port chapter in modern Chinese history was critically important to this Maoist version of modernization, of which more in the final section of this paper. Perhaps the imitative behavior of treaty port Chinese and "Western-style" Chinese entrepreneurs or industrialists was in effect a poison helping to corrode the traditional system, a poison injected, wittingly or otherwise, by the imperialists. Marion Levy's work may suggest some such analysis.[57]

But whether the foreign system strengthened or weakened the Chinese economy, its contributions were in any case too marginal to be seen as aspects of transformation. The treaty ports were like a fly on an elephant; the fly could ultimately irritate its host enough to provoke a violent counterreaction, but not enough to change the elephant's basic nature.

Trade and Technology: Coals to Newcastle?

China's relative economic success, if only in keeping foreign competition minimal, helped to mask crucial respects in which China was technologically backward by comparison with the modern West, and also to buttress resistance to technological change. China was to some extent caught in what has been referred to as a low-level (perhaps better a *high*-level) equilibrium trap. Its traditional system produced high agricultural yields per acre, adequate manufacture of most essential goods (especially textiles), an efficient exchange linkage by low-cost water transport in the areas of greatest population and production, and altogether a respectable level of per capita income which probably surpassed that of most of the rest of the world (including Europe) until some time in the nineteenth century (see below). Although it became technologically backward by comparison with the post-eighteenth-century West, its degree of pragmatic success and self-sufficiency made it difficult to change. Western technology was resisted because it was not easily seen as advantageous, not simply because it was foreign. The most obvious exception, the speed and eagerness with which Chinese merchants took advantage of steamship transport, can be seen as a logical extension of the traditional system, which had also been for many centuries evolving its own increasing commercialization, growing long-distance trade, and urban concentration. However, that it was principally foreigners—colonialists—who were pushing for change, and that the technology involved was exclusively Western, fed understandable Chinese resistance and resentment, not to say xenophobia. The foreigners complained about the low level of Chinese technology and about the obstructionism they encountered in their efforts to open coal mines or build railways. But their own accounts of the economic condition of the country, especially before about 1900, do not suggest a decaying system of livelihood and commerce, or one where they could expect easily to make a place for themselves as "developers" with something attractive to offer. My most direct evidence for asserting the absence of the kind of disaster in the traditional economy that many foreigners have assumed took place long before 1920, or even before 1900, is foreign accounts of the country outside the treaty ports. These are very numerous and range through the period with which we are concerned.[58] It would be tedious and I trust unnecessary to reproduce more than a fraction of these accounts here. They are quite consistent, both before and after the Taiping Rebellion, in giving a picture of general prosperity, enormous productivity, thriving commerce, tranquility, and a well-ordered system of control, transport, and management.

A few examples must suffice here. As a one-sentence summary of what he found from the late 1830's into the mid-1850's in a wide area in Kiangsu, Chekiang, Anhwei, Chihli, Hunan, Kwangsi, Kwangtung, Kiangsi, and Fukien—the economic and commercial heartland of the country—Robert Fortune includes a startling remark: "In no country in the world is there less real misery and want than in China."[59]

H. H. Lindsay made one of the few foreign efforts to guess at the volume of Chinese trade on the eve of the treaty port system.[60] His report enumerates 400 junks, averaging between 100 and 400 tons, entering the port of Shanghai weekly during July of 1832. If this was broadly typical of the year as a whole,[61] Shanghai was already one of the leading ports of the world, with a volume of shipping equal to or greater than London's.[62]

The Elgin expedition up the Yangtze reached Hankow in December 1858, barely two years after the restoration of local order in the wake of the Taipings, but already trade and shops there were "upon a much grander scale than at Canton or any of the open ports. . . . We could scarcely credit that only two years and four months ago this bustling city had been levelled to the ground. . . . No stronger proof could be afforded of the vitality of trade at this point. . . ."[63] This impression is confirmed in equally grand terms by Bickmore's account of the same area, including trade on Tung-t'ing Lake as well as at Hankow, in 1866.[64]

Fortune's several accounts are full of surprises, and yet his manner gives the reader confidence in his honesty, accuracy, astute observation, and detailed personal knowledge of what he writes about. His spoken

Chinese and his costume, queue, and tinted skin were good enough to deceive nearly everyone whom he met on his extensive travels (except of course for his own Chinese servants) into believing his explanation that he came from a distant province, and he appears to have lost few opportunities to quiz the local people wherever he went. His books were the first important and comprehensive efforts to describe and analyze China from an objective point of view (as opposed to missionary tracts or reflections) after the revised edition of Sir John Francis Davis's *The Chinese*,[65] and the first to be based on wide and repeated personal observation of extensive areas outside Canton or the five ports by a private individual not representing a government or a religious mission. Fortune had no cause, but wished solely to inform Western readers about this huge and newly "opened" country whose civilization he clearly, but in no sense uncritically, admired.

He describes it as tranquil, prosperous, and enormously productive. His account of a trip in 1848 through the important silk district south and west of Shanghai includes the following information:

The merchant and silk manufacturer will form a good idea of the quantity of silk consumed in China when told that, after the war, [i.e. 1840–42] on the port of Shanghae being opened, the exports of raw silk increased in two or three years from 3000 to 20,000 bales. This fact shows, I think, the enormous quantity which must have been in the Chinese market before the extra demand could have been so easily supplied. But as it is with tea, so it is with silk—the quantity exported bears but a small proportion to that consumed by the Chinese themselves. The 17,000 extra bales sent yearly out of the country have not in the least degree affected the price of raw silk or of silk manufactures. This fact speaks for itself.[66]

Fortune points out that China and the Chinese should not be judged by the foreign experience in the five ports, or in Kwangtung, which he, in company with virtually every other European observer at every period, gives a very low character, saying that it is full of petty thieves, bandits, surly and xenophobic peasantry, "insolent troublemakers," and scheming or otherwise unpleasant townspeople. Shanghai, Ningpo, Amoy, and Foochow he found only a little better, and bearing little comparison with the towns, countryside, and people he observed in the course of his several long trips inland. He gives a lengthy description of Hangchow[67] as a thriving and bustling place, full of evident prosperity, and, like other cities and towns in the China he saw, with its walls, streets, temples, and public buildings in excellent repair. Hangchow was "a place of wealth and luxury," where "all except the lowest labourers and coolies strutted about in dresses composed of silk, satin, and crepe." His Chinese servants, who came from elsewhere, "said there were many rich men in their country, but they all dressed modestly and plainly, while the natives of Hangchow, both rich and poor, were never contented unless gaily dressed in silks and satins."[68] Apparently neither sumptuary laws nor fear of the public display of wealth had any force in the city of Hangchow.

Fortune's attention was also drawn to the prosperous appearance of the agricultural countryside, with its well-tended fields, heavy crops, and high productivity. Like other observers both earlier and later, he was impressed by the immense traffic on the waterways and the profusion of boats, as well as by the numerous water mills using the current to power their machinery, and the system of transferring even the largest boats from one water level to another in both streams and canals by the use of a windlass and an inclined plane. Most of his journeys he made by water, which also carried of course the great bulk of the trade of Central and South China, but in the few places where he did use the roads, he comments on the excellent state of their stone paving and the dense traffic they carried. Apparently the description of the imperial road system as "Good for ten years and bad for ten thousand" was not then so apt a witticism as it seemed to be in the twentieth century. And like so many other Western travelers, he several times remarks on the strong commercial propensities and skills of the Chinese in general, not only the Cantonese, whose merchants he found widely scattered throughout central China, but the people of all areas he visited.

Davis's earlier work (see note 65), though less thoroughly based on direct observation, gives a similar if more generalized picture. In a way, Davis's positive assessments are the more convincing when one remembers the nature of his experience: the frustrations of East India Company operations under the Canton system, the humiliation and provocation of the Amherst Mission, the chronic tension and irritation of his dealings as interpreter with the Cohong and the Kwangtung administrations, and his maddening and long-drawn-out controversy with Ch'i Ying and others over the infamous Canton "city question" from 1844 to 1848, which last he took back with him to England as his parting memory of China. Yet Davis was profoundly impressed by the smoothness and effectiveness of China's self-regulating society (the phrase is mine, not his), based on the central virtue of filiality and its ramifications in the five relationships. He saw the system's tranquility as an important basis of the prosperity he also recognized: "the machine works well."[69] He makes the by now familiar comments on "the cheerful industry" of the

Chinese, and adds, "It is certain that the bulk of the native population enjoys the results of its industry with a very fair degree of security, or it would not be so industrious."[70]

Despite his own experiences, Davis clearly cannot help liking the Chinese, whom he regards as immensely good-humored and yet substantial (an impression most foreigners in China were still receiving in the 1940's), as well as admiring their civilization and economic success. Indeed he pays them the supreme compliment of comparing them with the English: "There is in short a business-like character about the Chinese which assimilates them in a striking manner to the most intelligent nations of the west. . . . It does not seem too much to say that in everything which enters into the composition of actively industrious and well-organized communities, there is vastly less difference between them and the English, French, and Americans than between these and the inhabitants of Spain and Portugal."[71] In fact, "The Chinese are very much our superiors in *true* civilization—in that which frees the majority of men from the brutality and ignorance which, among many European nations, place the lowest classes of society on a level with the most savage beasts. . . ."[72] Economically also, he anticipates in a more general sense Robert Fortune's remark about misery and want quoted above. In addition to Davis's already-cited statements on the level of prosperity, one can cite his observation that as of the 1840's potatoes were still not widely grown even in Kwangtung, though they were "common" in Macau,[73] and had of course been introduced to China, via the Spanish base in the Philippines, in the sixteenth century. Like the delayed spread of kaoliang in the north after its original introduction from central Asia in the late sixteenth century, this may suggest that overpopulation and economic distress were still not pinching hard enough in these areas to make "inferior" or culturally devalued food crops acceptable. Another straw in the wind is Davis's observation that "the middling and poorer classes are amply accommodated with taverns and eating houses, where for a very small sum a hot breakfast or dinner can be obtained in a moment."[74] He joins the chorus of wonder over China's multitudinous inland water routes, its great volume of water traffic, and its stone-lined Grand Canal, and points out that in many of the lesser towns "by far the most considerable buildings were the commercial halls belonging to the associated merchants and dealers."[75] Finally, *mirabile dictu*, "Europeans resident in China have generally found that their property has been as secure from violent invasion as it would be in any other country of the world. . . . The efficiency of the police has proved . . . that the government was not

only willing but able to do . . . summary justice."[76] Did Davis have access
to a time machine and arrange to transport himself into the era of the
People's Republic?

The Abbé Huc's widely read travel account[77] of a journey from Tibet
down the Yangtze and over the Meiling Pass to Canton in 1850–51
contains the first important foreign description of Wuhan, some ten years
before it became a treaty port:

> We took more than an hour to traverse the long streets of Hanyang. . . . [Wu-
> chang is also] an immense town, a vast city, with multitudes of enormous
> junks and a prodigious mass of shipping in the anchorage, one of the chief
> commercial places in the Empire. . . . [There is finally] another immense
> town called Han-keou . . . at a confluence of a river that throws itself into the
> Yang-tse-kiang almost under the walls of the capital. These three towns, stand-
> ing in a triangle in sight of one another, and only separated by the river, form
> a kind of heart from which the prodigious commercial activity of China circu-
> lates to all parts of the Empire. They are calculated together to contain nearly
> eight millions[78] of inhabitants, and they are so closely connected by the per-
> petual coming and going of a multitude of vessels that they may almost be said
> to form one.

This picture suggests no obvious place for the kind of innovation the
foreigners attempted to introduce. Huc writes of Chinese trade with the
West as follows:

> This commerce is doubtless of considerable importance to England and the
> United States, but its influence is very little felt in this vast Chinese Empire
> and this immense population of traders. The trade with foreigners might
> cease suddenly and completely without causing any sensation in the interior
> provinces. The great Chinese merchants in the ports open to Europeans would
> doubtless feel it; but it is probable that the Chinese nation would not experi-
> ence the least inconvenience.

He goes on to say:

> European productions will never have a very extensive market in China. . . .
> As foreign commerce cannot offer them any article of primary necessity [i.e.,
> which they do not already produce themselves] nor even of any real utility,
> they will interest themselves very little in its extension, and they would see it
> stopped altogether not only without uneasiness but with a certain feeling of
> satisfaction. . . . China is a country so vast, so rich, so varied that its internal
> trade alone would suffice abundantly to occupy that part of the nation which
> can be devoted to mercantile operations. There are in all the great towns im-
> portant commercial establishments into which, as reservoirs, the merchandise
> of all the provinces discharges. There is a constant bustle going on about them,

a feverish activity that would scarcely be seen in the most important cities of Europe.

The immense population of China, the richness of its soil, the variety of its product, the vast extent of its territory, and the facility of communication by land and water, the activity of its inhabitants, all unite to render this nation the most commercial in the world. . . . The stranger is struck by the prodigious bustle and movement going on everywhere under the stimulus of the thirst of gain. . . . From north to south, from east to west, the whole country is like a perfect fair. . . . And yet when one has not penetrated to the centre of the Empire and seen the great towns Han-yang, Ou-tchang-fou, and Han-keou, facing one another, it is impossible to form an adequate idea of the amount of internal trade.

What did the introduction of the treaty port system add to this? Huc's concluding remarks, about Hankow, make one wonder:

Han-keou especially, the Mouth of Commercial Marts, must be visited, for it is one great shop. . . . In all parts of the city you meet with a concourse of passengers, often pressed so compactly together that you have the greatest difficulty to make your way through them. . . . The shops are crowded with buyers and sellers. The factories also contain a considerable number of work-men and artisans. . . . The great port of Han-keou is literally a forest of masts, and it is quite astonishing to see vessels of such a size and in such numbers in the very middle of China. . . . Han-keou is in some measure the general mart for the eighteen provinces. . . . Perhaps the world could not show a town more favorably situated and possessing a greater number of natural advantages.

The perspective of these observers was of course not ours. Theirs was the Europe of Charles Dickens and his Coketown, the Chartists, the Great Hunger in Ireland, David Ricardo, and the early Marx. But many of their statements are simple factual observations, and the China they show us, unrecognizable though it may be, was real enough. If they were right, matters are most unlikely to have changed enough even by the end of the century to put the Chinese economy for the whole of the post-1850 period in the category to which we have uncritically relegated it through familiarity with conditions in the 1930's and later. It is not easy to be more specific with dates or with precise measures of the rate and scale of economic decline. The economy probably never recovered, especially not in per capita terms, from the Taiping disaster; and there are varied indications (partial and imprecise) that after about 1870 the decline became more rapid. The rate of decline was probably uneven, however, and there may have been brief periods of partial recovery, especially between 1917 and 1921. Even if it were possible to pin this argument down (and I am not convinced by the few existing attempts, including Perkins's analysis of agricultural development already cited, that it is possible), this is not the place to do it. My point here is that the decline is unlikely to have produced before the 1920's, or perhaps even the 1930's, an economic situation totally different from that pictured by foreign observers up to 1850, or an economy unable to cope (as it clearly did) with foreign competition.

Into this immense, still relatively prosperous, well-ordered, and commercially thriving country a small group of Westerners attempted to introduce an alien trade under their own management, to alter production and divert trade flows toward external markets, and to invade the domestic market with foreign goods. It is not surprising that Western accomplishments fell far short of these goals. China remained without much question the world's most productive area of even approximately comparable size until perhaps as late as 1850, both in terms of absolute totals and of yields per acre in China Proper. One is tempted to guess that even in per capita terms, China in the first half of the nineteenth century compared favorably with Europe. Precisely how important the commercial sector was as a proportion of total production or population is difficult to say, but the partial and impressionistic evidence on which one is largely obliged to base judgments of the volume of shipping, the scale of trade flows, the size and number of towns in which trade was an important function, and the extensive networks of merchants and trade guilds, does not suggest that this was in any way a commercially backward system.

One important aspect of any economic comparison between Europe and China at this and perhaps at any period is the very much more even income distribution in China. There were almost certainly fewer wretchedly poor and fewer very rich Chinese than Europeans. It is misleading to imply the possibility of precision, but there is little question that Chinese society was composed overwhelmingly of small peasant proprietors, tenants, landless laborers, and small artisans, a number of petty but only a few large merchants, and a very small and fluid body of officials. China offered little basis or opportunity for the kind of skewed income distribution characteristic of Europe. Miserable poverty there doubtless was at every period, as in virtually all societies then and now; but until the latter part of the nineteenth century, the number and the proportion of the total Chinese population living in economic deprivation were probably quite low by comparison with Europe, both in the scale and in the degree of misery. Indeed, through most of the first two-thirds or three-quarters of the nineteenth century, median economic welfare in

Europe probably declined as a concomitant of the early stages of the industrial revolution. Foreign observers in China before about 1870 rarely mention poverty except in connection with military devastation. The first large famine to attract European attention came in the 1870's. What happened from then on was not so much a steepening of the distribution curve as a progressive drop in absolute levels of income across the board. After 1911 especially, the total and relative numbers of wretchedly poor people grew at a rising rate, and by the end of the 1920's China as a whole more nearly fit the stereotypes of rock-bottom poverty that have inappropriately been applied to the preceding century or two. Dwight Perkins nevertheless goes so far as to suggest that throughout the nineteenth century and up to 1957 Chinese per capita grain production and consumption remained high by world standards.[79] According to this argument, the economy as a whole retained a significant margin even at its nadir.

Equally important was China's economic self-sufficiency, both real and imagined, material and psychic. Little or no need was seen for technological or institutional change, or for increased foreign trade. Benefit and individual profit were to be sought in the manipulation of the extensive existing trade. In spatial terms, the Canton delta, the Yangtze delta, the Wuhan area, the string of natural harbors along the southeast coast, the seaward face of the North China plain—in fact all of the sites of the major treaty ports—were, long before 1842, the chief foci of traditional Chinese commerce, and would have remained so even if the treaty ports had never existed. The treaty port system fell far short of making the kind of impact on the Chinese economy many Westerners felt it should, and therefore must, have done.

Statistics vs. Reality. One important reason for this sort of misinterpretation may have been an incomplete understanding of the statistical pitfalls even in so generally careful a series as the figures of the Maritime Customs, one of the few oases in the statistical desert of the Chinese economy. These figures show a steady and substantial, if not breathtaking, increase in trade through the treaty ports from 1864 (when the series begins on a basis more or less comparable with later years) until the 1930's. It is not only that the dimensions involved look a good deal less impressive when compared with the mass of the Chinese economy, or with European trade with a great number of smaller and less productive countries. A closer look at the figures, in the light of some study of the Customs *Reports on Trade* and other contemporary accounts, suggests that to an unmeasurable but significant extent the foreigners merely absorbed into their system and their statistics existing Chinese trade, and deflected some (though by no means all) of it into export channels. Some—perhaps a great deal—of the increase in the Customs figures represents only a change from junk transport (whose cargoes were not recorded) first to foreign steamships and then to Chinese steamships as well. Much of the remainder can be accounted for by steady improvements in the completeness of the Customs statistics. The last point especially is often overlooked. What happened in effect was a spread of the Customs' statistical net from the original five ports to cover by the 1920's most of the country, through a total of 69 treaty ports, 47 of them with Customs offices (see the endpapers of this volume). Their returns continued to swell the total of recorded trade, but the extent to which this growth represented actual trade increases is difficult to establish. The real increases that took place were heavily concentrated in foreign trade, but even there the peak of growth was unimpressive on any per capita or international scale.

The total recorded value of the "whole" trade (i.e. domestic as well as foreign) of all the treaty ports (including Chinese goods imported from one treaty port to another, most of which went unrecorded in earlier years) rose relatively slowly until about 1890, and then more steeply to a peak in 1929–30, which it never subsequently regained, owing to Chinese boycotts, the world depression, civil war, and the Japanese invasion. The total in 1870 was just over a hundred million Haikuan taels. In 1890 it was 241 million, by 1910 just over one billion, and by 1930 just over three billion, an overall increase since 1870 of some thirty times. During the same period foreign trade alone increased approximately twenty times in Haikuan tael values. It should be noted that these totals included Manchuria, which by the 1920's represented *nearly a third* of the total of Chinese foreign trade, but was in effect a separate economic system under Japanese management after 1905.[80]

For China Proper, how much of the increase in the Customs figures represented a real rise in trade and how much a shift from Chinese to foreign carriage, and from unrecorded to recorded, is impossible to say; but the amount that should be deducted from the figures on such grounds seems unlikely to be less than half and may be closer to two-thirds.[81] To give one specific example whose scale can at least roughly be measured, the tribute grain shipments, traditionally moved by junk from central to northern China by the Grand Canal and by sea, began after 1872 to move by steamer (both Chinese- and foreign-owned) whose cargoes were recorded. During the same period the value of the Haikuan tael fell more or less continuously, dropping altogether by about two-thirds (from the equivalent of US $1.60 in 1870 to US $0.46 in 1930), as recorded in the yearly sterling and dollar equivalents published in the Maritime Customs Annual Returns of Trade and Trade Reports. We may thus be left with a real increase of the trade of *China Proper* (mainly in foreign trade, although some of this may in turn have been deflected from previously domestic channels) of three or four times at most.

But even without attempting to adjust the Customs trade figures to take account of all of the points noted above, the total dollar-equivalent value of the foreign trade of China (less Manchuria) by the end of the 1920's put it in the same approximate foreign trade class as Mexico, Chile, New Zealand, Brazil, and the Union of South Africa, and far behind Argentina, Australia, Canada, Denmark, the Federation of Malaya, India, Indonesia, or of course any of the industrialized countries of the West, or Japan.[82] China's foreign trade never exceeded 1.5 percent of the total value of world trade, and exceeded 1 percent only briefly. In per capita terms, it remained negligible, and even at its peak probably smaller than that of any country in the world, including Tibet.

It is not perhaps surprising, when even in trade the foreign impact was unremarkable, that that impact was so small in the broader sphere of modernization. Almost as if it were in traditional Chinese terms, the treaty port men—foreign, traditional Chinese, or re-molded Chinese— took their opportunity to manipulate the system they found rather than transforming it, as the colonialists and their Asian partners did elsewhere. As pointed out above, trade alone was not, and should not really be expected to be, a sufficient agent of transformation. It did not produce innovation or the equivalent of modernization in the great premodern centers of trade in the West, such as Portugal, despite Portuguese domination of overseas trade, especially with the East, for over a century after da Gama. The foreign and treaty port role in China may in fact with some appropriateness be compared to the Portuguese century in Asia, and Portugal's extremely limited impact on the areas whose trade she appeared, like the foreigners in China, so completely to control. Like the China treaty port merchants, the Portuguese never eliminated the Asian merchant groups, and, perhaps more important, did not significantly alter the nature of existing trade, let alone affect the conditions or commodities of production. They were merely one more in a long succession of briefly successful entrepreneurs who left the Asian economy little changed from what it was when they found it and as it had been manipulated by others before them, including the Chinese. As George Masselman puts it:

Nor did the Portuguese succeed in eradicating the Moslem traders. On the contrary, the old established trade flourished as never before.... We may conclude that the volume of Portuguese trade was exceeded many times over by the trade carried on by the peoples of Asia.... Thus the Portuguese, notwithstanding their strongholds, never succeeded in establishing even a rudimentary type of colonial administration in the sense of a European power gaining significant control over large areas. The long established pattern of Asiatic trade remained the same.[83]

Even as the only significant change brought about by the Portuguese was the introduction of Christianity (although often through forced conversions), one may reasonably argue that, despite the discouraging total of converts, the post-1842 missionary effort in China was a more effective direct and indirect vehicle of change, and of ultimate modernization (primarily through the mission-founded schools), than the seemingly more impressive but evanescent commercial activities in the isolated islands of the treaty ports. Like the Portuguese, the treaty port foreigners and their Chinese imitators had a dominantly speculative attitude. They were neither free to try nor for the most part interested in trying through investment and management to improve the means of production, or to "develop" the Chinese economy. Like traditional Chinese merchants, they were more often content to compete for slices of the cake rather than trying to make the cake bigger. Sir Frederick Bruce, the British Minister, writing from Peking in January 1864, put it more pretentiously in arguing against Western efforts to force modernization on China: "Our office is that of the schoolmaster who educates, not of the tyrant who imposes."[84] But an alien schoolmaster was in a poor position to make a significant dent in a country as vast, effective, and self-satisfied as China, at least in the absence of the climate that full colonialism, its sanctions and its organizational structures, could create. The Indian and Southeast Asian experiences underline this point, and help to explain why Western schoolmasters in China failed. A tyrant in some form was indispensable. In the end, the Chinese supplied the solution themselves, which is certainly the most important reason why it has been so successful.

The Manchurian Case. The great exception to these generalizations, and one that may be taken to support their validity, is Manchuria. After 1905, Manchuria was increasingly a piece of colonial property, probably even more effectively so than India or Java, seeing that Manchuria was almost unoccupied before about 1900, had no inherited economic, social, or political system whose vigor or inertia could resist change, and was therefore the more easily shaped by planned Japanese investment and

Japanese development policy in general. Without any of the built-in drags against change that characterized China Proper—its immense size and population, the sanctity and relative effectiveness of its existing system, and simple national or xenophobic resistance to foreign-inspired change—Manchuria was the kind of place where a developmental blueprint could most easily and quickly be translated into reality by a determined manager with technology, organization, and capital to invest. The degree both of development and of transformation accomplished by the Japanese in less than forty years in Manchuria is extremely impressive. It tends to suggest not merely that trade alone changes little, but that for effective impact on any established Asian system, complete colonial control or territorial sovereignty was necessary. The cases of Java, Luzon, Ceylon, Malaya, lower Burma, Vietnam, and India confirm these suggestions. The course of colonialism, though brief, and the level of foreign impact in Manchuria were much closer to the experience of the Asian nations just listed than to that of China.

Accomplishments

What then was the treaty port impact? How much of what can be ascribed to it was genuinely new? One can be reasonably certain that the treaty port system produced at the very least a substantial net increase, both relative and absolute, in foreign trade, and consequently some increased stimulus of commercial production for export. This was true even in long-established export industries such as tea and silk, which the foreigners merely tapped but for which they did create a greatly expanded overseas market, as well as in commodities like tung oil, eggs, bristles, wool, hides, peanuts, and straw braid. Production of such goods undoubtedly rose as a result of the wider external markets made available through the treaty ports, although the rise was small in terms of the Chinese economy as a whole.

There were in more general terms certainly the beginnings of a more efficient and particularly a more concentrated commercial structure. A few dominant nuclei began to emerge as transport improved and long-distance marketing became increasingly important. This process was similar to the one that took place under similar conditions in Europe and America with the growing dominance of one or a few metropolitan commercial and port centers in each country, especially for external trade, and the progressive relative decline of lesser centers (Bristol, Hull, Charleston, Bordeaux). In China one can clearly discern three levels emerging. Shanghai and Hong Kong were central places and quasi-monopolistic ports for foreign trade for the country as a whole (like London,

New York, Buenos Aires, Calcutta, and Bombay). At the second level, Tientsin, Hankow, and Canton played the same kind of role for North, Central, and South China respectively. (Dairen's position in Manchuria was similar, but as stressed above, the Manchurian economy as a whole was unlike that of China.) The third level, of smaller regional or provincial service centers, was represented by places like Changsha, Chungking, Foochow, or Wu-chou, all of them also part of the treaty port hierarchy. It was of course an overlapping hierarchy in which Shanghai and Hong Kong (like New York or London) included aspects of the whole country in their commercial hinterlands, just as Hankow, for example, included much of Central China. But the growth of commercial nodes at these three levels was a symptom of increasing commercialization and exchange beyond traditional levels, and one that in many cases bypassed or superseded traditional centers and lower-order systems.

Study of the yearly Customs *Returns of Trade* throughout the period 1864–1936 shows something of the nature of this hierarchy, at least for recorded flows. Shanghai, Hong Kong, Tientsin, Canton, and Hankow increasingly exchanged primarily with one another, in the commodities destined for export and in the distribution of foreign imports (Canton dealing in both respects largely with Hong Kong). For each of the four ports on the mainland, the other three were consistently the main trade partners by a large margin. Shanghai supplied Tientsin and Hankow with the great bulk of their goods of foreign origin, as Hong Kong supplied Canton. However, recorded re-exports from each port accounted in every year for only a very small fraction of the value of the whole trade of the port. This suggests that much, perhaps most, of the actual re-exports were not recorded (principally because they were moved by Chinese carriers), that their total amount was probably not very great, and that each port was the dominant consumer of its own imports. The treaty port system was to a large extent an enclave economy.

The four chief ports plus Hong Kong dominated the urban hierarchy in other respects as well, each serving as the cultural as well as the industrial and foreign-trade node for its quarter or so of the country, in terms at least of the "modern" sector. This is apparent in the concentration there of both Chinese and English-language newspapers, and in the role of these cities as intellectual and (periodically after 1900) revolutionary centers. Canton spoke for "modern" South China (aided in this case no doubt by the remoteness of Peking), Shanghai for the Yangtze valley, and so on. The even more marked concentration in these four ports of traditional and "modern" schools, technical colleges, and universities makes the same point. Outside of Manchuria, these four were also the first to develop a structure of both light and heavy industry, beginning with arsenals and shipyards, but going on into textiles, milling, and other consumer goods. Skinner's study referred to above shows the early effects of rising commercialization and concentration on those rural marketing systems for which he has data and which were near enough to major centers of trade to be acted on by the growing centripetal developments.[85]

Expanded credit facilities for external trade, lower interest rates in the treaty ports where capital was relatively secure, the development of collection networks for export goods over much of the country by foreigners and their Chinese agents, and the emergence for the first time of a system of shipment of goods under single ownership from interior provinces through the hierarchy of treaty ports to Shanghai or Hong Kong for export, all encouraged economic growth and helped to account for the process of concentration referred to above. This contrasted especially with the traditional series of middlemen and other agents who had earlier passed goods along from one part of the country to another, as the proliferation of *hui-kuan* contrasted with the much larger-scale operations of a few dominant firms now dealing on a national basis. All of this brought obvious economies, and was accompanied by an increased volume of business.

By the end of the nineteenth century a few foreign banks largely controlled trade credit for the internal movement of most goods destined for export, or at least for those readily discernible through the files of the Customs Service and the records of foreign companies. Notes issued by foreign banks in the treaty ports circulated all over China and were freely accepted at face value; they constituted an important element in the system of currency and had largely displaced the traditional notes of credit and transfer previously associated with this trade. By the end of the nineteenth century, the famous Shansi banks, for example, had largely lost their role in the financing even of internal trade to both foreign and Chinese banks, although other Chinese "native" banks, engaged to a greater extent in local commercial financing, survived and remained vigorous. Foreign banks appear to have shared the financing of trade with them in an increasingly nationwide and interlocking system of credit that extended from Hong Kong and Shanghai through Chinese "native" banks in the interior to local dealers and collectors. Periodic financial crises in the treaty ports, for example, can clearly be seen to have involved or to have been contributed to by the failure of "native" banks in the provinces.

Other evidence suggests that in fact the great bulk of commerce, including much if not most of the increase attributable to foreign enterprise in widening the market, remained in the hands of Chinese merchants. Customs *Reports on Trade* at the treaty ports, the series of British, American, and French consular trade reports, and comments by a great variety of individual foreign observers all voice this complaint repeatedly from the beginnings of the treaty port system in the 1840's, again after the Treaties of Tientsin when the new terms failed to produce the hoped-for results, through the aftermath of the Treaty of Shimonoseki in 1895, and into the 1920's and 1930's. One is struck by the persistence of both traditional-style guilds and new Chinese commercial organizations in the treaty ports themselves, and indeed the continued increase in the numbers of both, at least up to 1911 and, one may safely assume, for some time thereafter. Far from being eliminated by foreign competition or Western models, the guilds maintained their effective control over much of even the newly developed trade.

Traditional-style guilds did not of course have it all their own way,[86] but it was still Chinese jostling Chinese for control of the growing commercial sector. The precise means whereby the control was exercised is hard to observe, secrecy and discretion being part of the guild system, but the results are clear. One is here in the position of the astronomer who deduces the existence of a planet from its effects on the behavior of other bodies—in this case the continued foreign complaints about the Chinese "stranglehold" on trade. A revealing yet tantalizing illustration is provided by the Swatow Opium Guild case in 1879–80, tried before the Mixed Court in Shanghai and reported in some detail in the *North-China Herald*,[87] in which two foreigners attempted to sue the guild, charging "a conspiracy against foreign trade." The charges were ultimately dismissed, after the hearing of large amounts of evidence which at least circumstantially supported the plaintiffs, who remarked, "Not a single one of us can trade independently and the treaty is no good at all so long as this underground system exists."

The "particularism" and "functional diffusiveness" of the traditional merchant, in Parsonian terms,[88] obstacles to "modern business," were strong assets in his successful efforts to exclude foreign competition. In this society where long-established family and personal connections counted for everything, no outsider (a status that carried far greater handicaps in China than anywhere else in the world) could hope to win a viable place beyond the artificial realm of the treaty ports. Many observers have seen the absence in traditional China of qualities associated with commercial and industrial success in the West—"universalism" and "functional specificity" (the labels and circumlocutions vary)—as crippling disadvantages for economic development. Perhaps this was so, although it is arguable even beyond definitions of "economic development." But there can be little argument that as China was constituted even up to 1949, the traditional system was almost ideally designed to resist outside manipulation and to protect the Chinese merchant. The familial web enhanced rather than stultified his enterprises, and at the same time ensured that he would not be seriously challenged in his commercial control of this vast and self-contained economy.

The Chinese merchant was also slow to make "modern" use of capital or to contribute to the building of an economic infrastructure. Without doubt this was a major roadblock to economic development however defined. But it rested on an individual rationality that was economically sound in the conditions prevailing in China, especially after 1850. Speculation, moneylending, and other parasitic or predatory uses of capital were both safer and more profitable, as well as faster. Where innovation offered reliable and immediate rewards, the Chinese merchant was quick to adopt it. The best illustration here is probably the almost instant response to the introduction of steamships. Merchants began by traveling on and shipping their goods by these safer and faster ships and not long thereafter ended by owning and managing the largest single shipping fleet in East Asia, the China Merchants' Steam Navigation Company.[89] But most industrial or long-term commercial investment could not begin to match the rate of return, security, and anonymity of traditional speculative and usurious ventures. The sharply varying prices of many commodities from one time and place to another offered strong attractions for speculation to those who possessed even small amounts of capital, and had the further important advantage of permitting the quick and not easily detected movement of funds from one venture to another. This minimized the risks both of normal commercial loss and of attracting unwelcome attention to the possession of money. To be a registered shareholder or involved in any "modern" enterprise, including those launched by officials after 1860, dangerously exposed one's wealth and was to be avoided.[90]

It would appear that after 1911 this reluctance began to break down, and perhaps for other reasons as well industrial investment became more popular among Chinese merchants. Yen Chung-p'ing's study of the cotton industry lists nineteen cotton mills established in Shanghai, Tientsin, and Hankow between 1897 and 1910, of which twelve were founded by officials, three by compradors, and only two by traditional merchants or gentry (the remaining two involved families or individuals whose status is unclear).[91] However, of thirty-two cotton mills established in the same cities between 1916 and 1922, eighteen were founded by merchants (the term is not defined), only six by officials, three by "industrialists," and two by gentry. Two were owned publicly, and one was owned jointly by an official and two warlords.[92] The principal difficulty about these data is that none of the different status groups is defined. In both periods concerned, there was in fact often a good deal of blurring of distinctions between "merchant," "gentry," "comprador," and "official." If we take the data entirely at face value, they would suggest that the Chinese merchant-capitalist-investor was becoming more willing to risk his money in "modern" enterprises because many of the earlier objections to such investment were losing their force: profitability and security were attaching proportionately less to traditional uses for capital (land, usury, speculation) and proportionately more to industrial investment.

But again it was Chinese investors moving in on a previously foreign-dominated field, as much because industrial investment was in their own economic interest as because it was patriotic or "modern," let alone Western-inspired. Indeed it may be argued not only that this might have happened without the presence of the treaty ports at all (as it did in the Japanese case), but that the semi-colonial position of the foreigners and the aggressive role they attempted to play from their urban bases of special privilege may in fact have retarded rather than hastened the Chinese shift toward modernization. Modernization was clearly and exclusively of foreign origin; the special position and imperialist behavior of the foreigners made them resented rather than admired; and the innovations the foreigners brought and attempted to push onto China were accordingly resisted. In pre-Meiji Japan too, foreigners were often resented. Many were even murdered by patriotic samurai. It was not only the new leadership after 1869 that changed Japanese attitudes, but the end of the "unequal treaties," the concessions, the imposed tariff, and the special position for foreigners. Even in Japan, the enthusiasm for Western-style innovation so characteristic of the late nineteenth and early twentieth centuries would be hard to imagine if the foreigners there had kept to the treaty port world as they did in China.

When the Chinese entrepreneurs (as opposed to officials) did make up their minds to enter factory-based industry, they seem to have made a very creditable job of it. It was to an important extent their success, not merely Japanese- and Western-owned factories in China, that was by the 1930's impinging on the previously dominant position of the hand weavers in the cotton textile industry, and this in the face of Western and Japanese competition already in the field and with larger and cheaper sources of capital.[93] At first, in a pattern familiar in India and elsewhere, Chinese mills concentrated on the production of coarse cloth, but by 1930 "it is only a question of time until they crowd their competitors of today out of the market in most of the finer counts also."[94] This trend continued up to the outbreak of the war in 1937.[95] By 1934 imports of cotton yarn had also been largely displaced by domestic factory production.[96] The Chinese businessman may have been, for a variety of reasons, slower than his Japanese counterpart to jump into the industrial revolution, but despite the obstacles he still faced in the 1920's and 1930's— domestic disorder, high interest rates, strong foreign competition, and many surviving traditional business practices—he apparently proved able to adjust successfully and to begin squeezing out the foreign devils even in this, their own field.[97]

Two Worlds

But the two systems, Western and Chinese, though competing in the same market at least within the treaty ports and their immediate environs, remained for the most part separate. The commercial, technological, and institutional innovations that were, from a Western point of view, so strong and attractive a part of the Western system did not spill over into the traditional Chinese system, which saw no need for them. One may draw the obvious analogy with the noneconomic aspects of the confrontation between China and the West, where the same considerations apply in the realm of ideas and institutions as in technology. But, as suggested above, the relative success of the Chinese commercial sector in competing with the foreigners helped to blur the appropriateness of technological innovation, which was also stymied because of its foreign origin and impetus. To some extent, this was also an urban-rural split. The treaty ports represented a new and exclusively urban phenomenon following Western models, whereas the rest of China remained not only predominantly rural but characterized by cities of a fundamentally different sort, bearing a close symbiotic relationship with their rural hinterland. The sharpness of the legal lines around the treaty ports was paralleled in almost every other respect.

In addition, none of the treaty ports ever had any administrative or political role outside their own concession areas, even in the legally separate but functionally integrated conurbation at each port outside the concession lines. This further distinguished them from the colonial ports in the rest of Asia as well as from traditional Chinese cities. It helps to explain their separateness from the Chinese system as a whole, and accounts in part for the failure of their model to spread. This is not to say that there was no spillover at all. For example, the commercial sale of agricultural goods and the tenancy rate were both significantly greater within a twenty- or thirty-mile radius of each treaty port than elsewhere in the country, and in some cases such as the Yangtze delta hinterland of Shanghai there was a degree of satellite urban development with an in-

creased commercial and light-industrial base (Wusih, Soochow, Hu-
chou) related to Shanghai's proximity. But such developments were a
result more of simple urbanization than of the particular model of urban
growth represented by the treaty ports, and indeed were direct continua-
tions of trends already apparent in traditional urban and demographic
growth long before the founding of the treaty ports.

Industrial development in the immediate hinterlands of some of the
treaty ports, such as silk reeling and silk and cotton spinning in Wusih or
Soochow, and coal mining and associated metal industries in Tangshan,
were perhaps more specifically connected with the new kinds of economic growth centered in Shanghai and Tientsin respectively; but extensions of this sort were largely lacking in the hinterlands of Canton,
Wuhan, and the lesser treaty ports. Part of the explanation is presumably
that most of the capital earned in treaty port trade, both foreign and
Chinese, sought investment outlets in commercial speculation or land-
owning rather than in industrial development. In any case, capital for
industrial investment selected locations that offered maximum advantage, predominantly within the treaty ports themselves. Only in special
cases, such as the Kaiping mines or the silk and cotton areas around Lake
T'ai, did maximum advantage appear obtainable in the hinterlands of
the treaty ports.

The separateness of the two systems, traditional Chinese and "modernizing," was also reflected in the development of banking. Here most
of the data refer to the treaty ports, where one might perhaps expect the
modern sector to be dominant. In fact it seems reasonably clear that even
in the treaty ports "native" Chinese banks of the traditional type did
at least as much financing of domestic trade as was done by both foreign
and "modern" Chinese banks, and possibly more.[98] Chinese merchants,
who as stressed above continued to dominate the marketing even of imported goods, preferred to do business with the "native" banks, which
were more liberal with unsecured loans and in general part of the same
traditional system to which the bulk of the Chinese merchants belonged.
There the interlocking network of personal and group associations was
more important than Western notions of contract and liability. The "native" banks were also active, however, in speculative buying and selling
of exchange on Hong Kong. Like the traditional merchant firms, they
were quick to take advantage of new commercial opportunities created
by foreigners and successfully manipulated the changed conditions to
their own advantage. The native and the modern-style banks did, it is
true, draw capital from some of the same sources, and there was some
interlocking financing between them that involved the foreign banks as

well. But such connections provided a necessary link between the treaty port sector of largely foreign trade and the far larger and mainly separate system of domestic production and exchange.

On the other hand, the "modern" Chinese banks which grew up, especially after 1911, and were overwhelmingly concentrated in the treaty ports—an apparently promising Chinese response to Western pressures and models for modernization—never became involved to any important degree with the financing of either trade or manufacturing. Private individuals and public institutions, not commercial or industrial firms, were their leading depositors, and they concentrated on government financing through loans and bond issues. These carried a high rate of interest and had the further attraction of greater security than commercial loans. Partly because of the relatively high interest rate paid to depositors, rates charged to borrowers were higher than most commercial enterprises found attractive.[99] The foreign banks continued to dominate the financing of foreign trade, while Chinese "native" banks, with their wide geographical dispersal and network of connections throughout the traditional system, remained dominant in domestic commerce.[100] In brief, modernization and innovation in the treaty ports was mainly confined there, in banking as in other respects, while the traditional system, largely inviolate, continued its vigorous survival and indeed invaded even the treaty ports with notable success.

The backwash and multiplier effects of simple economic growth, let alone innovation, in the treaty ports were also limited by the separateness of the two systems. The pattern of innovation waves elsewhere in the world suggests that even in relatively small and highly developed countries such as Sweden the chain of innovation that links urban areas may have little or no connection with the temporally, spatially, and substantively different diffusion of innovation between rural areas.[101] In semi-colonial China there was similarly little connection between the urban centers and channels of Western-directed innovation and the mainly rural mass of the Middle Kingdom; the two might almost have been on different continents.

Even if one acknowledges that the emergence of a more clearly national market for capital as well as for goods, the relative security of capital, the lower interest rates, and the substitution for the earlier fragmented commercial systems of the more efficiently concentrated one represented by the treaty port hierarchy were all to some degree innovations and directly traceable to the foreign presence, how much did any of this touch, let alone transform, the bulk of the Chinese economy? Admittedly, one may pose the same question even for India, but one suspects that the qualitative as well as quantitative differences between the Indian and the Chinese context become clearer merely in the raising of the question.

Trade Figures and the Chinese Scene

In comparing the Chinese Maritime Customs figures on trade with general knowledge, or detailed accounts, of what was going on in the area theoretically being influenced or served by each treaty port, one is immediately struck by the inverse correlations between flourishing treaty port trade (at least in recorded statistics) and catastrophic economic disaster in the supposed commercial hinterland. Customs returns at Tientsin, for example, show unbroken increases in the port's trade throughout the dreadful famine years in Hopei in the 1870's, and again in the 1890's and 1920's. In fact, boom years for trade coincide with or immediately follow the years of worst famine, flood, and (in several cases) rampant civil disorder. The 1870's were a grim decade for most of the inhabitants of North China.[102] From 1875 through 1879, with successive total crop failures beginning in 1876, there were severe famine conditions "of unparalleled extent and destructiveness over the greater portion of North China commercially connected with Tientsin"; but this "has exercised only a comparatively small influence on the figures representing the trade of Tientsin."[103] The influence is hard to find, since the trade figures continue their unbroken increase, although the same Customs Report estimates that by 1879 60 percent of the population of Shansi alone had died or fled and that conditions were only moderately better in Hopei and Shantung.[104]

The floods of 1890, judged the worst in the thirty-year history of the foreign settlement at Tientsin, laid waste extensive parts of North China. Chinese officials estimated that 20,000 people had been drowned in Hopei alone, but as so often has happened in North China the excessive rainfall came too late to do more than wash away what few crops had survived the preceding drought of spring and early summer, so that 1890 and 1891 were famine years also. The trade of the port, however, continued to flourish, and indeed both 1890 and 1891 were record years of outstanding magnitude.[105] In 1899, "the dry summer and consequent meagre crops have caused much distress; nevertheless, trade has flourished."[106] The beginnings of the great North China famine of the 1920's were apparent in 1919–20, when it was already being described as "the worst that has ever visited China" and as covering all of Hopei and large parts of Shantung, Honan, Shansi, and Shensi.[107] But the trade of Tientsin for 1920 was the second best on record and the slight drop from 1919 was attributed entirely to exchange problems. Toward the end of this tragic decade and its "atmosphere of civil war which has hung over North China with very little intermission . . . civil war, bad harvest, depletion of the rural population, and constant interruptions of the means of communication have all combined to hamper trade [in 1928], and yet the total volume of imports and exports constitutes a fresh record in the history of the port."[108]

With the cumulative effect of successive years of crop failure, Shensi is estimated by 1928 to have lost 40 percent of its population by combined death and migration.[109] The Decennial Customs Report for 1922–31 repeats the paradoxical juxtaposition of unprecedented catastrophe in the hinterland ("internecine wars with attendant dislocation of transport facilities, successive years of dearth caused by droughts and floods, brigandage waxing rife in the interior, the silting of the Hai-Ho above Tangku") and unprecedented prosperity in the treaty port: "disturbed as it was by drought, flood, and civil war, trade continued to show advances in value . . . despite continual military interference with railway transport."[110] "Disorder and banditry were rampant everywhere"[111] and secret societies mushroomed; the report estimates that the Red Spear Society had 100,000 followers in Hopei and 600,000 in Honan by the end of the decade.[112] This was of course in addition to the chronic fighting on a large scale between the Fengtien, Chihli, and other cliques in the immediate hinterland of Tientsin until 1927, which repeatedly cut the major rail lines for long periods; the attacks on the Kuo-min-chün by Chang Tso-lin, Wu P'ei-fu, and Chang Tsung-ch'ang during 1926; and the fighting that accompanied the final push of the Northern Expedition. All of this meant not merely dislocation of the economy and widespread destruction but an almost complete break in rail and other long-distance overland shipments; the Decennial Report states that "most of the rolling stock was carried away by the retreating forces; that available for trade fell off to only 5 percent of normal."[113] It goes on to remark that "the deplorable state of the Hai-Ho continued to cause anxiety" (i.e., internal trade movements by this channel were also sharply curtailed) and that there were successive poor harvests in which "crops suffered partly from being laid waste by military operations and partly from drought, followed by excessive rains" (a cruelly familiar pattern in North China). "It is a pleasant surprise to note, however, that notwithstanding the obstacles described above, the total value of trade exceeded the record of any previous year."[114]

The paradox is completed by what happened after 1929 (1927, 1928, and 1929 each in turn saw the value of trade rise to a new height): there was "an exceptionally good harvest in this province"[115] in 1930, an absence of flooding, and a temporary end to significant civil disorder in the Tientsin hinterland; rail lines and waterways functioned more or less normally and traffic moved well on the Hai Ho. There was a marked *decline* in the total value of the trade of Tientsin for 1930. The year 1931 continued the same pattern: an excellent harvest, relatively peaceful conditions, and a decline in the trade of the port. (The drop in world trade as a whole beginning in 1930 was of course another reason for this trend.) One might have surmised that a part of this paradox is accounted for by imports of grain and flour in famine years; but in fact such imports remained a small proportion of total imports during those years, and were in any case totally inadequate to make any impression on the gross food shortages. The continued increases in Tientsin's trade 1919–29 (with the single exception of 1926) likewise cannot be explained by postponed consumption in the city's hinterland in the early years of the decade. Grain and flour imports largely disappeared in 1930 and 1931, but the Customs reports apparently do not regard this as an important factor in the overall trade decline. With the recovery to something like normal conditions in North China, "cheaper foreign cotton piece goods were largely supplanted by native ones, which not only compared favorably with foreign products but were sold at such low prices as to defeat most competition."[116]

Two conclusions seem inescapable: (1) Tientsin's trade, for all its importance among the treaty ports, was a drop in the bucket of the economy of North China; and (2) Tientsin was not serving to any significant extent as the commercial center even of Hopei, either for the collection of goods for export or for the distribution of imported goods. Although Tientsin is an especially clear case, the same paradoxical pattern is discernible at Hankow, and to some extent at Canton, as well as in a more general sense at Shanghai and for the treaty port system as a whole, which continued to show vigorously rising levels of trade while the Chinese economy deteriorated, and declining levels whenever there was a brief recovery. The most likely explanation is probably the swelling of treaty port populations by refugees or temporary migrants during periods of distress or disorder in the surrounding areas, including perhaps especially wealthy Chinese.[117] Both the normal and the "emergency" Chinese populations in the treaty ports probably included a larger proportion of relatively wealthy people than was characteristic of the dominantly rural hinterlands, and both they and the less prosperous elements developed consumption patterns that included growing amounts of Western-style goods. Some, perhaps most, of the remaining inflow of consumer goods may have been destined for higher income and/or semi-Westernized groups in the satellite towns within easy radius of the major treaty ports. Industrial growth, almost entirely concentrated in the treaty ports and a few satellite towns, came after 1895 to be responsible for increasingly major shares of import totals, including many raw materials (such as wheat for flour milling) available domestically but deliverable at lower cost by sea transport from external sources. Such sources became additionally important whenever the domestic hinterland was disturbed.

Internally, domestic producers were doubtless hurt by famine, flood, and disorder, and their output presumably fell during such periods. Their access to market, as well as the actual cost of transport, was also affected adversely, and the combined effect of all the above created an enhanced opportunity for foreign imports in the treaty ports at the expense of the usual domestic suppliers. Consumers in the hinterland may also have turned to foreign sources of supply in troubled periods for the same reasons. Even in normal times foreign cloth was cheaper, and economic distress had the effect of reducing consumption of the slightly higher-priced but more durable Chinese cloth. But all of such changes were temporary, as the Customs trade figures suggest, and it seems in any case unlikely that they were on a very great scale, especially since the foreign accounts do not mention any significant enhancement of the market for foreign goods outside the treaty ports that could be attributed to such causes.

Predictably, the detailed trade figures show a highly mixed pattern, as different commodities succeeded one another (for widely varying reasons) in both the import and the export trade. Careful analysis and plotting of the mass of figures at Tientsin for the three periods mentioned above shows no gross and few significant exceptions to the general statement that the trade of the port increased when its supposed hinterland was in economic distress and decreased when that distress was relieved. Among foreign imports this was true even for opium (1876–81 and 1890–93), as it was for cotton and woolen cloth and piece goods in aggregate, and for "sundries." The major exception, in the period 1919–31, was the combined category of metals and machinery, which showed a more or less continuous increase through 1931—and this was not an item likely to reflect economic developments outside the city itself, except for railway expansion and the growth of the Kailan mines. The overall picture is not altered, and is indeed mirrored for the most part, by an analysis of so-called native imports. The figures for exports are less conclusive. Although in perhaps half of the dominant commodities there were unbroken or only slightly interrupted increases, usually relatively modest in any one of the three periods, most of the remaining export items showed substantial (though often erratic) rises during the supposed bad years, followed by declines like those in imports, once economic distress in North China was eased. Disaggregation of the trade confirms the general pattern and provides few clues, at least to me, that could either challenge or extend the conclusions stated above. The only suggestion is the obvious one—that in bad times producers in the hinterland became proportionately more dependent on selling whatever goods they could to consumers in Tientsin, other treaty ports, or abroad, who in such times were the only ones able to buy.

But none of this constitutes a substantial interrelation between what was happening in the treaty ports and the mass of the Chinese economy. It may be possible to explain why treaty port trade figures rose and fell at certain periods, but not (except negatively) by reference to what was going on in the country beyond their limits—the area they were supposedly transforming. The market served by the treaty ports consisted of themselves and their local satellites. Their sharp political and cultural isolation from the rest of China was mirrored economically. Something must be wrong with our assumptions about the key role of the treaty ports in the redevelopment of China.

The Failure of Modernization

The technological element in the treaty port impact was critical, and of obviously greater significance than was trade itself as an agent of transformation. But technological innovation acquired even a modest momentum late in the day, mainly after 1919, and its progress was hampered if not hamstrung by developments outside the treaty ports. A standard survey estimates that, as of 1933, the total output of all of the "modern" industrial sector (i.e., eliminating handicrafts) was 3.4 percent of net domestic product. By including estimates for the output of construction, modern trade and finance, and modern transport and communications, the same source shows the modern sector accounting for 13 percent of net product in the same year, while total employment in factory industry, "modern" mining, and utilities is estimated at about two million, or not more than 4 percent of the then current nonagricultural labor force.[118] What one may call a railway system, as distinct from a few separate lines, did not begin to emerge until after 1900, only a few years before the civil order began to collapse. All that the presence of railways theoretically should have been able to do to accelerate economic growth was vitiated; most of the time, the railways could offer neither security of goods in transit, nor speed, nor lesser cost by comparison with traditional carriers, which continued to account for the bulk of transport.[119] It is hardly surprising that rail lines made so little impact on the economy of the areas through which they ran: that the Shanghai economy, for example, was so little dependent on them;[120] that Hopei and Shantung differed so little, in ways attributable to the presence of railroads, from Szechwan, which had not a single rail line.

In political or ideological terms, the treaty ports did not help to integrate China, as the port cities helped to integrate South and Southeast Asia, in many cases for the first time. Instead, the treaty port system created, or perhaps accentuated, a deep dualism. There was no blending of China and the West, but only a sharpening of the confrontation. No *national* group emerged from the treaty port context to speak or to act for China. The ports multiplied the divisions among the traditional or reactionary gentry and official elite outside the concessions, the treaty port Chinese, and the new revolutionaries: the Chinese Communist Party and its student allies. The perspective of Communist China has revealed the treaty ports as tiny and isolated islands—as the endpaper maps also suggest—in an alien Chinese sea that all along resisted and finally rejected them. In contrast with the foreign ports in the rest of colonial Asia, they remained foreign in everyone's eyes, clearly distinct from the country as a whole—external, fragile, superficial grafts. When even the foreigners distinguished "China" from "treaty port land," it is hardly surprising that the Chinese did the same, and could in the end more easily reject the ports as having nothing to do with their contemporary national experience. Traditional resistance to innovation as representing disharmony and chaos was succeeded by the CCP's bitter denunciation of the entire treaty port model.

Many Asian nationalists, including the Chinese (Ch'ing, KMT, and CCP alike), blamed colonialism for Asia's unsatisfactory economic and political progress, even for its moral and social problems. In South and Southeast Asia, the evidence seems on balance to argue the contrary, whereas in China the semi-colonial system was never as effective as the nationalist argument implied. Even the treaty port Chinese remained a resented and feeble minority, divorced from the traditional order and never able to dominate or successfully rival it. The KMT was controlled at least as much by unregenerate gentry types as by treaty port men, as exemplified by Chiang Kai-shek himself, who was both, but dominated by the former. And the Nanking Government represented the apogee of power for the treaty port Chinese—a not very impressive achievement. The treaty ports also produced very few intellectuals or political dissidents who exercised any influence on the course of events from outside positions of political power. (The reformers of 1898 were certainly treaty-port-tainted, but hardly treaty port men.) Significantly, this sort of role was played instead by students, whose spiritual and material base was primarily Peking and whose first political activities took the form of protests and boycotts *against* the treaty ports and all they represented, i.e., "national humiliation." Students and other protesters and potential revolutionaries were of course both sheltered in and stimulated by the treaty port world, the principal arena of national humiliation and the point of maximum contact with the foreigners who were exploiting China, and at the same time an example of strength through nationalism. But the student and other leaders—especially the leaders of boycotts— used the treaty ports as their *target*, never as their even indirect model. It was, as perhaps it had to be, a new group, divorced from both the traditional order and the treaty ports, that inherited modern China.

Epilogue

In spite of all that has been said here, contemporary China is inconceivable without the treaty port experience. The very vigor with which it was rejected demonstrates its profound impact on the Chinese mind. Materially, it made little impact. The lifestyle of the great majority of Chinese was unaffected, directly or indirectly. Over most of the landscape, as in the production process or in the urban centers outside the foreign concessions, there was almost no sign that external forces were attempting to reshape the country. The volume of *new* trade was unimpressive. But there was a big traffic in ideas, and a psychological shock of deep significance. Perhaps more than anything else, it was this that galvanized China's national life, provoking political action and the emergence of a new ideology. In their role as beachheads of an alien system, the treaty ports highlighted the ineffectiveness of the national political order. That order was unable to prevent their incursive nibblings at Chinese sovereignty or to shield individual Chinese from bitter humiliation. Arrogance, highhandedness, and gunboat diplomacy also accompanied the missionary effort. The foreigners may have been largely frustrated in their trade and "modernization" dreams, but they sorely wounded the Chinese psyche. Their technology, too, though it failed for the most part to spread, let alone to transform, the country, was ideologically important in its revelation of China's backwardness; it hurt China psychologically more than it helped her economically, at least up to 1949.

The center was politically, technologically, and ideologically powerless. "China" was humbled, and one result was the rise of a regionalism or provincialism which (whatever its real meaning or worth) was ultimately read, and resented by Chinese nationalists, as a sign of weakness and national disintegration. For much of this, nationalists could argue, the treaty ports were to blame. It was they, and the system they represented, that had assaulted and emasculated the center, had helped to prevent its overthrow by the Taipings and the regeneration that might have followed. It was they who had in effect kept the Ch'ing in office as a client regime, profiting from its growing weakness, bleeding it through unequal treaties, imposed tariff levels, Customs revenues, and indemnities, while they manipulated it to yield more and more concessions. In such a context, those Chinese who collaborated with foreigners, who lived in and made a good thing out of the treaty ports—perhaps especially those who adopted foreign techniques and attitudes (i.e., the pre-1949 "modernizers," the apostles of "progress" from a Western point of view)—were by definition traitors, as the treaty ports themselves were cancers on the Chinese body. In the perspective of 1970, it is possible that the Chinese response to the West may appear more rather than less effective than the Indian or Southeast Asian, precisely because single-mindedness, ideological fervor, and xenophobia—the major legacies of the treaty ports—unite, organize, and invigorate more effectively than compromise or cosmopolitanism.

The foreign presence was almost exclusively urban,[121] as was the kind of modernization the foreigners tried to promote. Contemporary China is consequently anti-urban. Anti-urbanism is directed primarily against the former treaty ports (which with the single exception of Peking include all of the largest cities), but it involves by association *all* cities. Those least affected by this dogma are those farthest removed from the treaty port legacy: cities newly created or having experienced their greatest growth since 1949, cities located in remote and previously underdeveloped parts of the country—Urumchi, Ta-ch'ing, Paotow, Lanchow. Anti-urbanism is a central part of the Chinese Communist view of the world. It provides a developmental model for the new China and a microcosm of the party's revolutionary struggle for power. It also influences CCP perceptions of the political and ideological struggle in the rest of the world. Lin Piao's now-famous dictum about city and countryside in the battle against contemporary imperialism[122] echoes Mao's earlier formulae and experiences, but is clearly understandable only in light of the psychological impact of the treaty port experience and all that it came to symbolize in the minds of Chinese nationalists.

Admittedly, CCP anti-urbanism has not always been entirely consistent, and its basic contradiction with the equally strong commitment to pro-industrialism makes it partially inconsistent even now. But the

CCP strategy of the 1920's was aimed at the cities, in the expectation that the oppression they created would breed revolution. It took the failure of uprisings and attacks at Canton, Changsha, and Wuhan and the Kuomintang coup of 1927 in Shanghai to persuade the Communists that the cities were not ripe for their purposes, and to convince them decisively of the rottenness, moral corruption, and politically counterrevolutionary character of the cities. Such a characterization arises equally understandably, however, from the treaty port image, an image attached to virtually all large cities in China, making them and their inhabitants evil.

The theme of paradox or contradiction is of course basic to Chinese Communist ideology, and is in practice often revealing. Exclusiveness vs. universality in international affairs, elitism vs. mass participation in domestic affairs, expertness vs. redness, national economic growth vs. regional development—"walking on two legs" in a great variety of contexts in a way that at least partially blends contradictions to create or release new energy—these things are seen as the very stuff of revolution, and the implicit conflicts are glorified. But there is a residue of hard reality in many of these conflicts that can only retard progress toward one or the other of the conflicting goals. Anti-urbanism/pro-industrialism may be the most important of these. It is difficult to question that industrialization is most cheaply and efficiently based in cities, or that cities tend to be the biggest and the fastest-growing points in nearly all economies. It is equally clear that the former treaty ports represent most of the optimum locations for manufacturing within China as a whole, if the goal is rapid industrialization at least cost. China has chosen to pursue other goals as well, goals which may certainly be more important. The eventual result may be a marked improvement over Western models for economic development. But Chinese decisions involve a willingness to subordinate some strictly economic goals to other considerations, in a way that reflects, among other things, a response to the treaty port experience.

The colonial and running dog entrepreneurs may have pursued their own profit rather than the national good of the Chinese economy in siting their factories and planning railways, but they were necessarily sensitive to cost factors; it was economics far more than politics that shaped the pattern of industrial location before 1949. Shanghai, Tientsin, Wuhan, Dairen, and the other major treaty ports that were also manufacturing centers offered and still offer unbeatable cost advantages, mainly as a result of their low-cost transport connections (by river, rail, and sea) and nearness to markets. The absence of nearby raw materials, except for agricultural products, has never been a significant cost disadvantage for

Shanghai, which completely dominated the pre-1949 industrial map of China Proper, whereas Wuhan and the treaty port urban centers in Shantung, Hopei, and southern Manchuria are close to major sources of coal, iron ore, and other raw materials. The skilled labor pool, Chinese managerial and technical skills, special services, satellite industries, and capital market that accumulated in each of the industrialized treaty ports were further important reasons why their near-monopoly of manufacturing developed and why it might logically continue.

Since 1949, however, the great bulk of new industrial investment has been located elsewhere. Manufacturing in the former treaty ports has not been cut back for the most part, but it is maintained almost apologetically while the excitement as well as the funds and commitment have been shifted to new industrial centers in previously backward and often remote parts of the country.[123] The former treaty ports still dominate manufacturing as a whole, as they dominate the urban hierarchy, but one would not guess it from most of the Chinese press. The big news stories are reserved for the rapid transformation into industrial centers of places like Changchun, Loyang, Kunming, Chungking, or Chengchow, or the creation out of the wilderness of manufacturing towns such as Paotow or Ta-ch'ing. Noneconomic goals are being pursued in investment decisions about the location of new industry in a way which at least in net terms is detrimental to national economic growth. Every *yüan* invested in Lanchow or Kunming is one fewer *yüan* available for investment in locations closer to market and thus not only less costly but sooner in operation. The opportunity costs of pursuing regional development for its own sake (as the Soviets have also done, and seemingly also as an article of faith) or of basing industrial decisions on ideological considerations are high, though they may well be worth paying.

As if they were still controlled or manipulated by the imperialists, all cities are seen as corrupt and corrupting, potential centers of counterrevolutionary revisionism or worse, artificial hothouses where even workers can be dragged down into the moral rottenness of "economism"—Mao's version of "creeping capitalism"—in which people are seduced into elevating personal material gain above the needs of society. This and the other cardinal sins of "bureaucratism" and "status quoism" are perhaps understandable products of urbanism, but without urbanism the industrialization which Chinese Communism so determinedly wants is literally unattainable. Chinese improvements on Western models—for which there is certainly plenty of room—should come from reforming cities. These qualities of urbanism are not peculiar to former treaty ports, and indeed that is, from Mao's point of view, their devilish harm. But it is questionable whether so pointed an anti-urban attitude is intelligible without the treaty port experience.

The *hsia-fang* movement puts this attitude into sharp perspective; no one, it seems, can hope to remain ideologically or behavioristically pure in the foul environment of a city, and must periodically be sent to the countryside for self-redeeming, purging labor in order to recoup his socialist vision. It is, to say the least, curious that a society bent on technological modernization should regard cities as evil and the still largely undeveloped countryside as the wellspring of wisdom and truth, the model for the behavior of Chinese Communist man. This is not comparable with the American tradition of Populism, or its earlier European semi-parallels. These were rural, know-nothing reactions to an urban-based power that was seen as oppressing the farmer, attitudes that were a mixture of resentment and envy. Nor is the Chinese Communist posture a latter-day version of a Jeffersonian, let alone a Gandhian, image. It is a piece of dogma unrelated to present circumstances, indeed in direct conflict with them as well as with other current goals, and imposed from the top. Emphasis on the wickedness of the city is related not to backwoods or underprivileged scorn/covetousness, still less to a Virgilian or Jeffersonian eulogy of a society based on the yeoman or gentleman farmer, but to a revolutionary vision of a socialist world where selfishness, oppression, and luxury must give way to selfless austerity in the service of society as a whole.

Austerity is a familiar theme in revolutions, and China is here consistent with earlier revolutionary experiences in Russia, France, and Cromwellian England. But by historical circumstance, cities became the targets of the Chinese revolution rather than its breeding grounds or power bases, and the association of cities with colonialism in the Chinese context has further sharpened ideological anti-urbanism. The colonial capitalists were rich, ostentatious, and urban; the proper nationalistic Chinese Communist must therefore be poor, austere, and at least ostensibly anti-urban (he can hardly be non-urban if he is to man the drive for the industrialization and technological modernization that have proved to be more important goals than anti-urbanism). Such an ideologically structured contradiction may have its political value but must sooner or later be resolved in favor of the city, as technological and industrial growth proceed. Even the new cities, or those whose major growth has come since 1949, must breed the kind of revisionism, economism, or bureaucratism that Mao execrates. The Maoist vision of a true socialist society is inspiring, but one of its principal goals, industrialization, can be won only at the cost of seeing urbanism triumph, with the risk that urbanism's anti-Maoist tendencies may persist. The root meaning of the word "bourgeoisie" is no accident.

Communist China takes pride in having freed itself from colonialism. "Self-reliance" is the watchword, revealing an attitude that may be seen as an overreaction to the alien and resented models of the treaty ports. But though it was never conquered by colonialism in the first place, China is haunted by its semi-colonial past to a degree not found elsewhere in Asia, even where the foreigners had it all their own way. Perhaps it was because the treaty ports did fail to make a significant material impact, and hence to produce the kind of blending that took place in the rest of Asia, that the Chinese could continue to regard them as alien and hence can still resent and attempt to reject them, and with them all of modern urbanism. Whereas India is ruled, with no sense of its being inappropriate, from the Edwardian monument of Luytens' and Baker's Viceregal Secretariat, China can be ruled only from untaintedly Chinese Peking, the only major city that was never a treaty port, where the T'ien-an Men remains the chief monumental symbol of the state, as it was before the Westerners arrived. The much greater strength of national cultural awareness in China than in India or the rest of Asia outside Japan, especially during the period of Western dominance, undoubtedly has something to do with this, as does the greater effectiveness of the traditional Chinese system as a whole in its ability to maintain itself even into the twentieth century despite the crumbling of its central political power. But although China remained unconquered economically, culturally, or politically, the semi-colonial interlude may, perhaps because of its very ineffectiveness, have made a sharper and deeper impression on Chinese intellectuals, Communist and non-Communist, and in the long run helped to put greater forces into train than all the imperial achievements of Westerners in the rest of the world east of Suez.

The Ningpo Pang and Financial Power at Shanghai

SUSAN MANN JONES

From about 1800 to the 1920's, control of the organization of Shanghai finance lay primarily in the hands of a group known as the "Chekiang financial clique."[1] Who these people were, and how they perpetuated their power, can be explained in part by exploring the careers and organizational ties of some of the leading members of the clique. Such an investigation raises questions about the nature of economic and social organization in China's modernizing urban centers, and in particular about the ways in which traditional rural relationships carried over into the new urban context.

There is a widely accepted notion that "modernization or urbanization weakens kinship ties, and creates a new type of social organization on entirely different bases."[2] The rise of nationalism has likewise been widely viewed as a process tending to replace local and regional loyalties with a broader allegiance to the new political order.[3]

One aim of this study is to examine the validity of these arguments as they relate to a specific group at a specific time: the Ningpo community at Shanghai during the late nineteenth and early twentieth centuries. As a locally based and supported native-place association with a long history of domination by certain major lineages, the group of Ningpo residents at Shanghai shows in its recent history how traditional locality and kinship ties were adapted to meet the needs of modernization. It also demonstrates the role played by new forms of commercial and social organization in providing alternatives to traditional forms.

The Origins of the Chekiang Financial Clique: Ningpo Entrepreneurship and the Native Banks

The city of Ningpo was an entrepôt in the foreign and coastal trade of China as early as the tenth century. In T'ang times, in fact, Ningpo served as the major port of entry for China's trade with Japan, and has been referred to as one of the oldest seaports in China.[4] Although the city played a respectable role in the cultural hierarchy of central places in China (as a producer of degree-holders and a repository of literary collections), it was best known for its entrepreneurs—who were in turn best known for their fierce loyalty to their native place. As traveling men in the nineteenth century, Ningpo merchants created a vast network of native-place associations along internal trade routes, particularly in the lower Yangtze valley and in the north around Tientsin. They took with them the guarantee of sound financial backing provided by lineage estates at home in Ningpo. And they created among themselves an informal system of credit that eventually became institutionalized as the transfer-tael (*kuo-chang*) system.

Commercial acumen was an acknowledged gift of the Ningpo trader. But he faced a formidable array of competitors, particularly to the south, where Canton and Foochow challenged Ningpo's hegemony in foreign trade during the late Ming and early Ch'ing periods.[5] During the late eighteenth century Ningpo traders sought new markets to the north in the coastal trade[6] and eventually began to leave Ningpo for good, abandoning some of their interests to the Foochow guild there. It was part of this search that sent Ningpo merchants in ever-increasing numbers to the growing port city of Shanghai toward the last years of the eighteenth century.

Shanghai was no fishing village when it was opened to foreign trade in 1842. The city had begun to emerge as a commercial center in Yüan times, when it played an increasingly important role in coastal trade, as a port for the northern goods, especially beans, that were exchanged for rice.[7] By the time Shanghai was formally opened as a treaty port in 1842, it was "a rich commercial city with a population of about 270,000."[8] By 1850 the volume of foreign trade there had surpassed that of Canton.[9]

However, Shanghai's extraordinary potential as a port of trade escaped the attention of most Western merchants who were seeking a way out of the Canton system.* And so, for an interesting period between about 1757 and 1842, we find Western merchants using all their wiles to break into the trade at Ningpo, while Ningpo merchants were seeking with equal ingenuity a way to break out of it. As we shall see, hindsight rapidly confirmed the soundness of the Chinese strategy.

---

* After 1757, foreign trade with China was confined by imperial decree to the port of Canton. Foreign merchants were required to conduct their transactions through members of the Cohong, a group of some dozen Chinese merchant families to whom the government had granted a monopoly over commercial transactions with foreigners.

Representatives of the British East India Company in the 1830's expressed great enthusiasm for opening trade at Ningpo or possibly one of the outlying Chusan (Chou-shan) islands. But they were not the first foreigners to take an interest in the port. The Portuguese had come to Ningpo in 1522, and in two decades built up a large permanent foreign community including inns for traveling merchants, a courthouse, two churches, and two hospitals. However, a violent clash between the Portuguese and Chinese residents in 1549, during which 800 foreigners were killed, temporarily ended Portuguese influence in China outside Macau.[10] At the beginning of the eighteenth century, the British government established a "factory" in Chusan, but it functioned less than a year before closing in the face of the high tariffs imposed by the Chinese government.[11] In 1753, after a second overture had been rebuffed, the East India Company declared it "essential" that trade be opened at Ningpo. Successful negotiations to that effect with the local authorities were concluded in 1755, but the agreement was overturned in Peking.[12] At that time Ningpo was the scene of a flourishing coastal trade, with 600 to 700 junks from Shantung province and Manchuria alone passing through her harbors each year.[13] Further assaults on the Ningpo trade were launched by the British in 1756 and 1757, but these proved equally fruitless, and precipitated the formal imposition of the Canton system by the Chinese government.[14]

Ningpo remained a tantalizing source of profit in the mind's eye of British traders. An emissary of the East India Company wrote in his journal in 1832:

In extent, it may vie with Fuchau, and in population it is not inferior to many of the large trading towns of Europe. It surpasses anything Chinese which we have yet seen, in the regularity and magnificence of the buildings, and is behind none in mercantile fame. The Portuguese traded to this place as early as the sixteenth century. They found here a ready market for European products, and they exported hence to Japan a great amount of silk.[15]

But a century later, the report of the Internal Maritime Customs morosely summed up Ningpo's history as a treaty port as follows:

Ningpo was officially opened in December, 1843. Great hopes were held of the development of trade here in view of its past history as a Portuguese factory and a port visited by early British traders, but they were ill-founded and doomed to failure. In 1844, the first year, foreign trade amounted to $500,000, but five years later it was less than one-tenth of that amount. With the development of Shanghai, Ningpo was left to all intents and purposes without a "hinterland" for either the sale of commodities or their purchase. In the second half of our present period [1843–58] foreign shipping began to partici-

pate in the carrying trade, first by means of small fast-sailing vessels and lor-
chas, and later by steamers of the American river type. This trade, though
under foreign flags, was merely a coastal carrying trade with Shanghai, and
the direct foreign trade of Ningpo was then, as it is now, practically nonexistent.[16]

The decline of Ningpo as a port of trade was clearly a function of the
rise of Shanghai. But there are many indications that the rise of Shanghai
predated the opening of the treaty ports by nearly a century, and that
this process was both anticipated and facilitated by the activities of
South China's merchants—primarily the Cantonese and those from Foochow, but ultimately the Ningpo traders themselves.[17] The most important index of this trend is the record of the founding of native-place and
occupational guilds (hui-kuan) and associations (kung-so) in Shanghai,
allegedly dating back to the Sung period. However, the first proliferation
of guild activity occurred in the Ch'ien-lung period (1736–95) and was
followed by a period of steady and then phenomenal growth in the
course of the nineteenth century.

Merchants seek new markets primarily as a source of profit. But in
traditional China, the search for new markets embodied another concern:
to contain the profits of trade within the circle of a group of merchants
from the same native place, thereby ensuring that some of this money
would be fed back into the local system from which the group was drawn.
At home this money would serve further to enhance the standing of
those trading and traveling abroad, and to replenish the coffers of family
and friends who stood by with financial aid in times of crisis—a necessity
in a market where risks were high, communications slow, and particularistic ties of trust and confidence the underpinnings of interregional
trade. Ningpo merchants in time also contributed substantially to the
modernization of their native place as a whole by investing in schools,
hospitals, and transportation systems there. In a sense, then, the Ningpo
merchants seeking new markets left their own local system and abandoned their stake in its prosperity as a port of foreign trade, precisely in
order to preserve that prosperity (albeit in a different form, with Ningpo
as a port of transshipping and domestic trade).[18] They pinned their future as members of a common local system on the success of another
local system, and thereby built on the profits of two central places instead
of one.[19]

Whatever drew them there, we know that by 1797 Ningpo people had
gathered in Shanghai in sufficient numbers to finance the construction
of a meeting hall for an organization known as the Ningpo Guild (Ssu-

ming kung-so).* Little is known of the earliest founders except their names.[20] But soon after its founding, the leadership of the organization fell into the hands of a lineage that remained prominent in the Ningpo community at Shanghai and in Shanghai finance as a whole for a century thereafter: the Fangs of Chen-hai.[21]

The original hall of the Ningpo Guild was built on a site later incorporated into the French Concession. Additions to the building, prior to the opening of Shanghai as a treaty port, were made in 1798, 1803, 1819, and 1836.[22] The last phase of expansion, 1834–36, was financed primarily by funds supplied by two brothers from the Fang lineage, Fang Hsiang-ning and Fang Hsiang-hung, who spent an estimated 16,000 *yüan* in Republican currency. The massive investment on the part of the Fangs was reflected in their control during the 1830's and 1840's of the Guild's board of directors, which numbered only five or six men. This control was maintained by the lineage for several generations.

The Fang lineage had a considerable stake in Shanghai trade ventures. By the 1830's two generations of Fangs from Chen-hai had been doing business there, primarily in sugar and silk. Fang Hsing-chai, who inherited both silk and sugar companies from his older brothers, was the first Fang to enter native banking in Shanghai. His initial venture, founded around 1830, was a diversified business that combined retailing in cloth and sundries with the functions of a traditional bank. The business was named the Lü-ho Native Bank (*Lü-ho ch'ien-chuang*), and was located in the south market. Even after its reorganization a decade later as the An-k'ang Native Bank, the company had a capital of only 60,000 to 70,000 taels.

A similar but more modest groundwork in Shanghai was laid by another Chen-hai lineage, the Li. Li Yeh-t'ing worked his way up into managerial positions from the menial job he had had as a teenager employed to carry wine to junk crews. He eventually became a crewman himself. Then with the money he made on the goods he was allowed to trade privately, he founded his own junk company, and later acquired property to build his own wharf. Although Yeh-t'ing came to Shanghai in 1822, his rise as an entrepreneur coincides with the opening of foreign trade at Shanghai, and thus belongs to a new stage in the growth of the Ningpo financial clique.

---

* Ssu-ming was the name of the mountain range west of the city of Ningpo; it was associated with the seven counties that traditionally comprised Ningpo prefecture: Yin *hsien*, Tz'u-ch'i, Chen-hai, Feng-hua, Ting-hai, Hsiang-shan, and Nan-t'ien.

The precise origins of native banks in Shanghai, or elsewhere for that matter, are unclear. True banking functions appear to have been an outgrowth of large-scale commercial enterprises like those of the Fang lineage, wherein accumulated capital was lent out at interest to other traders. Even after native banks became specialized economic institutions, the relationship between borrower/depositor and lender/banker tended to be highly particularistic: native banks, even into the modern period, assumed unlimited liability for their clients. There are strong suggestions that the institutionalization of native banks proceeded with the increasing use of the so-called transfer-tael system of credit associated with Ningpo.[23] The occupational association representing the native bankers in Shanghai, the Shanghai Money Trade Guild (*Shang-hai ch'ien-yeh kung-so*), may be of very early origin,[24] but the earliest unquestionable record of it dates from the Ch'ien-lung reign, when a guild hall was constructed in the inner courtyard of the temple of the city god in Shanghai.[25] It is impossible to tell whether at that time the organization represented owners of actual native banking institutions, or simply private financiers. The first specific references to native banks and to the transfer-tael system do not appear until the early nineteenth century, although clearly they were both institutionalized by 1842.

The earliest Ningpo entrepreneurs in Shanghai played formative roles in both of these infant institutions, the native-place association and the occupational association founded to regulate, protect, and promote the banking business there. The significance of this combined organizational strength was not fully realized for some decades. But there were good reasons why such dual control enabled Ningpo traders not only to create an important monopoly in Shanghai commerce, but to exercise a powerful influence in the financial structure of all China.

Traditional Chinese traders in an alien setting tended to cluster into two kinds of groups or cliques (*pang*), on the basis of common place of birth or ancestral home (native place) and on the basis of common occupation.* Formally these groups were organized into guilds (*hui-kuan* or *kung-so*).[26] The guilds were legitimate, self-regulating, voluntary as-

* There was a third type of *pang* in traditional Chinese cities that functioned primarily as the urban analog of the rural secret society. The best-known of these *pang* were the Green Gang and the Red Gang of Shanghai. Their members were largely lower-class workers. They were therefore a relatively new phenomenon, originating with the appearance of an urban-industrial working class in the late nineteenth century. However such gangs were not, strictly speaking, occupational groupings. Their leadership, like that of the secret societies, was in the hands of a segment of the local elite, and their influence reached at least the fringes of the *déclassé* elements in the city—beggars, prostitutes, and vagrants.

sociations. In the absence of a governmental administrative apparatus for urban centers in traditional China, they assumed considerable political power in the judicial, economic, and military spheres. They adjudicated disputes between members, they regulated commerce and trade, they provided flood and famine relief, and they maintained private militias against enemy or bandit incursions.

Much of the power in the traditional Chinese city rested with these organizations or, more precisely, with the influential cliques within them. The structure of power in Shanghai is therefore best explored through a study of the composition of these groups, and of their changing relationships with each other and with rival power groups, notably the foreign community and the representatives of the central government. The organization of Ningpo traders in Shanghai illustrates the manner in which a hold on power could be perpetuated through the channels of the Chinese *pang*.[27]

The Introduction of New Elements: Foreign Capital and Modern Banking

Shanghai was a focal point of trade not only for the north-south coastal trade, but also for trade up and down the Yangtze, and vast quantities of money and trade goods were already funneling through the city by the 1830's. Shanghai was potentially the central port of trade for all China, but neither the Chinese government nor the foreign trader had created channels for tapping the profits and regulating the flow of this trade. These conditions placed Ningpo traders in an advantageous position. They had a strong native-place organization, and they were backed in their undertakings by large financial reserves at home.

By the middle of the nineteenth century, Ningpo traders possessed diversified business interests throughout the lower Yangtze valley. But the greatest concentration of their resources was in native banking. There were strong reasons why the traditional Chinese entrepreneur with capital to invest looked to money and banking rather than other forms of investment. Transactions in money—money-changing, speculation on exchange rates, and loans at high rates of interest—were some of the most lucrative forms of commercial investment in traditional China. Profits hinged on the inherent instability of the Chinese monetary system, which was a function of (a) the absence of effective central government control over the coinage and distribution of currency and the issue of credit or bank notes, and (b) the presence of a foreign currency supply in the form of the silver dollar.

A capricious monetary valuation not only invited speculation; it also

demanded that those engaged in trade create a means of regulating or
at least setting bounds to the fluctuation, and a method of standardizing
currency and exchange rates within and between various trade centers.
The organization that could do both of these things would in some measure control both currency and prices. Such regulation of currency exchange and interest rates was a function assumed by Chinese native
banks until the first national bank in China was founded in 1897.

Native banks were divided into two large informal groups (*pang*):
a northern group (the Shansi banks) and a southern group (the native
banks proper, or *ch'ien-chuang*).* The informal leadership of the southern group of native banks was in the hands of a so-called Chekiang
financial clique (*Che-chiang pang*), and the core of the Chekiang financial clique was the Greater Ningpo clique (*Ta Ning-po pang*), a group
so influential in the Chekiang clique that the names were often used interchangeably.

The Ningpo traders were known as the fathers of the native banks.
Fang Ch'i (Fang the Seventh) was their legendary first founder. But
all that is known of the early association between membership in the
Ningpo Guild and membership in the Money Trade Guild is that the two
organizations coexisted for several decades prior to the opening of the
treaty ports. By the 1860's, however, a reference to the Ningpo *pang*
implied not only a common native-place group, but a common occupational bond as well: native banking.

At what point did Ningpo people come to dominate or control the
organization of native banking? Kagawa Shun'ichirō argues that cliques
sharing both native-place and occupational ties were formed during
periods of political and social crisis, to provide members with a system
of mutual legal and economic aid because none existed in the larger
sociopolitical context.[28] Two crises immediately suggest themselves as
likely stimulants to the marked solidarity of the Ningpo merchant banking community at Shanghai. The first was the opening of Shanghai as a
treaty port in 1842, and the ensuing influx of foreign traders, missionaries,
and other new residents. The second was the series of rebellions in the
1850's that disrupted trade routes and cut off the copper supply from
Yunnan, creating a shortage of copper cash. In addition, during the Taiping Rebellion most of Shanghai, along with Ningpo and other cities
in the Yangtze valley, was occupied.

---

* In this paper the term "native bank" is used to distinguish banks of the southern
group (*ch'ien-chuang*) from the Shansi banks. Both were obviously "native" as opposed to modern Western-style banking institutions; this translation is selected for
convenience only.

Assuming that such crises fostered and strengthened *pang* groupings, what happened to the native-place/occupational alliance when the crises subsided?

One authority contends that in a stable and expanding market like that of Shanghai in the 1870's and 1880's, concerns for profit and increased efficiency within an occupational group would have tended to weaken particularistic ties such as those based on common native place. In their stead, so this argument goes, would have arisen business practices based on "universalistic" criteria.[29] Kagawa postulates in a similar vein that when order was restored and, even more important, when a legal system was created by the government to subsume functions originally performed by the *pang*, the influence of groups based partly on native-place ties—and consequently the influence of those ties themselves in commerce and business—would have begun to wane. In addition to the loss of their para-governmental functions, such groups would face unbeatable competition from independent firms whose business practices tended to be less particularistic.[30]

Whereas modern organizations appeared in Shanghai to take over the functions of native-place and occupational organizations—the chambers of commerce and the modern banks, for example—there is evidence that the notion of native-place ties and the ascription of a native-place *pang* affiliation to all powerful individuals nevertheless retained much of their traditional significance. This might not have been so, had the Ningpo bankers not retained control of the one resource indispensable to the contenders for power after 1911: money.*

Kagawa calls control of this sort "feudal," meaning that the money was retained within regional, territorially based groups, and was not subject to collection and redistribution by the central government. This "feudal" control was institutionalized through groups (*pang*) of native banks owned by people who shared a common native-place tie; it was reinforced by the decentralization of taxes and levies during the Taiping Rebellion.[31]

As the expansion of trade at Shanghai after 1842 cast deeper shadows over the prospects for trade at Ningpo, the Ningpo traders redoubled their effort to secure control of the instruments of the Shanghai trade. In this effort they enjoyed a number of advantages. The proximity of Ningpo to Shanghai made possible speedy communication in business crises. There was an already-established network of Ningpo business

---

* To what extent the conclusions drawn here can be extended beyond the field of native banking is an open question and one that I have not attempted to explore.

along the Yangtze and in northeastern Chekiang. The Ningpo traders were experienced in the transfer-tael system of credit, which had given Ningpo a reputation for reliability and sound financial backing. Finally, there was a close-knit and carefully controlled system for recruiting Ningpo youths into trade in Shanghai.

This system was institutionalized in a number of ways. At the outset, recruitment was based primarily on kin relationships. The few case studies available indicate that successful entrepreneurs tended to recruit nephews rather than sons to assist in and eventually inherit the family business.* Young men from Ningpo who had no relatives in Shanghai were recruited or gained access to employment through the Ningpo Guild. Thus for some time the Guild served as the main channel through which Ningpo people entered trade in Shanghai.

As the Ningpo Guild expanded, occupational cliques emerged as specialized groups within the larger native-place organization. These cliques in turn sought to control various occupational guilds in the city, enabling people from Ningpo to be recruited directly into an occupational guild through the good offices of a Ningpo clique within the guild. The power of the Ningpo community at Shanghai thus infiltrated several organizations, and Ningpo entrepreneurs began to build their own small networks of patronage and loyalty outside the Ningpo Guild.

This trend away from the concentration of recruitment functions in the Ningpo Guild was extended when modern industry and foreign-style native enterprises were founded in Shanghai at the end of the nineteenth century. Then Ningpo men were able to use their appointive powers as officers or administrators of companies to create staffs composed entirely of people from Ningpo and its environs. Prominent businessmen from Ningpo eventually established themselves as "guarantors" who would contract with an apprentice from Ningpo seeking employment in any trade, and serve as bondsmen responsible for financial losses in his behalf. Where this kind of bonding (*pao*) was deemed unnecessary, a simple introduction (*chien*) was readily provided. Losses on the part of guarantors increased as this system became less particularistic, and finally a "mutual guarantee system" (*lien-pao fa*) was devised, whereby a candidate had to share equally in all losses he incurred.[32]

One more way in which the Ningpo native-place tie was used as a basis for recruitment was in the selection of compradors for foreign firms

---

* Whether sons were sent through the civil service system instead is not clear. Probably the primary consideration underlying this tendency was the perpetuation of corporate family landholdings. The family estate was often the key to remaining solvent during crises in the business world; landholdings must have constituted the mainstay of such estates.

in Shanghai. Foreign firms sought compradors with two main qualifications: sound financial backing (personal wealth or access to wealth through kinship or native-place ties) and experience in the peculiarities of the Chinese financial system. As Nishizato puts it, the Ningpo merchants in Shanghai formed a veritable "standing army" with precisely these qualifications.[33]

The Ningpo *pang* was thus the mechanism whereby Ningpo traders were able to retain control or powerful influence in three critical areas: Shanghai finance, trade relations with the foreign community at Shanghai, and the trade and native banking in the lower Yangtze valley and northeastern Chekiang that served as the foundation of all their activities. In each of these areas, their role was that of the broker. In Shanghai, native bankers mediated between foreign banks and native banks; between governmental and native banking interests; between borrowers and lenders of different social classes; between native banks in Shanghai's economic hinterland and foreign traders and bankers.[34]

During the last half of the nineteenth century, modernization and urban change subjected the role of the Ningpo broker to increasing strain. Native banks became increasingly dependent on loans from foreign banks to ensure their solvency. Foreigners became increasingly bold in their efforts to expand territorial and financial control over the Shanghai market. To Shanghai were drawn increasing numbers of Ningpo people who were not businessmen or investors or would-be apprentices, but rather menial laborers and vagrant elements seeking unskilled jobs.

The creation of modern Chinese banks (*yin-hang*) after 1897 and the rise of Western-style urban organizations in Shanghai further challenged the traditional modes of financial and guild organization. But none of these strains destroyed the Ningpo *pang*. Rather they served to demonstrate the kinds of choices that were presented to the traditional elite in urban China during this period, and the facility with which many of these choices were made and carried out, in the context of the traditional *pang*.

In what follows several case studies are presented showing the ways in which Ningpo brokers solved their conflicts of interest and preserved their identity as a native-place group in Shanghai. These cases demonstrate a clear trend in the *pang* away from kin-centered leadership based on ascribed characteristics and toward leadership based on achievement. They also indicate, as Ōya's study suggests, a clear movement away from the guild hall (*kung-so* or *hui-kuan*) as the center of economic and political activities. The economic and political functions of the guilds were gradually assumed by modern organizations such as chambers of commerce and unions or cooperatives; guilds retained significance as centers for religious and philanthropic activities.[35] In the course of these developments, the original autonomy of the native banking system was gradually compromised: first by its dependence on foreign capital in the form of the chop loan,* then by the steady extension of central government control over the size of reserves and the issuance of bank notes.

Throughout this process of change, however, ran a thread of human as well as institutional continuity. Ningpo people moved from positions of leadership in traditional organizations into prominent roles in modern institutions; and the success of the Ningpo traditional banks, as merchant banks, continued into the 1930's.

The Fang clan. The most powerful and most prominent kinship group in the Ningpo *pang* at Shanghai from the early nineteenth century into the 1930's was the Fang lineage.[36] As late as 1936, an edition of *Who's Who in China* contains a photograph and biography of Fang Chi-fan, the grandson of Fang the Seventh. According to this biography, Chi-fan was vice-president of the Shanghai Chamber of Commerce, a former member of the Board of Directors of the Shanghai Mint, and manager of both the Tung-lu Bank of Shanghai and the Nantao Branch of the Commercial Bank of China. He was also a former director of the Ningpo-Shaohsing Steam Navigation Company, the Chinese Merchants' Stock Exchange, the Hung-an Steamship Company, and the Chinese General Insurance Company of Shanghai.[37] Not until the 1870's did other Ningpo lineages begin to challenge the Fang hegemony in Shanghai trade.[38]

The Fang lineage reinforced ties of kinship through the maintenance of two large residential compounds in Chen-hai, where members of the lineage lived and maintained ancestral temples, and through the corporate ownership of various business enterprises, including some native banks.[39] The family's primary field of investment was native banking, but Fang native banks did not exist as separate specialized institutions until after the opening of the treaty ports. Prior to that time, all native banking capital was diverted from profits in other branches of business. By the 1860's, however, the Fang lineage had established a comprador relationship with a foreign firm called the Li-pai-li Company,[40] for whom a Fang company (Fang-chen-chi) acted as wholesale purchaser. Fang-chen-chi traded Hu-chou silk and Shao-hsing green tea for foreign cloth, which it sold in Hankow. At various times between 1866 and 1950 members of the Fang lineage owned seventeen native banks in Shanghai, five in Ningpo, one in Hankow, and one in Hangchow.[41]

* Chop loans (*ch'e-p'iao*) were funds deposited with native banks by foreign banks, through their compradors, on a short-term basis (usually from two to seven days).

Several of these native banks in Shanghai endured through the Revolution of 1911; three survived until 1950.[42] Each of them tended to develop a specialized clientele and a well-defined sphere of operations. For example, the An-k'ang Native Bank, founded in 1870, conducted exchange transactions between Shanghai and Ningpo, Hangchow, Chia-hsing, Hu-chou, Chinkiang, Yangchow, T'ung-chou, and Nanking, its main clientele being drawn from the cotton industry. The An-yü Native Bank, founded in 1879, catered primarily to silk merchants. The Ch'eng-yü, founded in 1892, had a diversified clientele drawn from the silk and tea trades and the trade in metals and imported goods, and conducted exchange transactions between Shanghai and Ningpo, Soochow, Hangchow, Hu-chou, Nan-hsün, and Hankow.[43]

Another branch of the Fang lineage was also active in native banking in Shanghai, but none of its native banks survived the Revolution of 1911. Some possible causes for this are discussed later.

Fang hegemony within the Ningpo *pang* and the Shanghai Money Trade Guild (where the most powerful member banks were the three Fang native banks just mentioned) remained unchallenged until the Kuang-hsü reign (1875–1908). In the 1870's other kin groups rose to prominence within the Ningpo *pang* at Shanghai, most prominent among them the Li and Yeh (also of Chen-hai) and the Tung of Tz'u-ch'i.[44] Of these two, only the Li lineage was able to continue native banking after the Revolution of 1911, however, and then only after an eight-year period of recuperation following the general collapse of the family's business enterprises in the Rubber Crash of 1910 and the upheaval surrounding the revolution.[45]

The decline of kin-based leadership. Why did leadership within the Ningpo *pang* begin to slip out of the hands of these powerful families? Part of the reason was that after 1870 there were simply more Ningpo families engaged in Shanghai native banking and trade. Although these families were neither so large nor so wealthy as the Fang lineage, they challenged its control of the Ningpo *pang* by the sheer weight of their numbers. Another part of the reason was that processes of political and economic modernization in the late nineteenth century diminished the influence of kinship relations within the *pang*. The rise of nationalism appealed to loyalties transcending the local level. The founding of modern-style banks and commercial associations afforded new options for employment. The presence of foreign capital and foreign business in Shanghai enabled compradors to attain positions rivaling those of members of prominent lineages.

Members of powerful Ningpo families did not formally accept positions as compradors, although they might perform the same brokerage

function through a company like Fang-chen-chi. Lineage resources made
it unnecessary for them to subserviate themselves in that manner. However, Ningpo traders who had no access to lineage support found the
role of the comprador attractive. The best-known Ningpo comprador
was Yü Hsia-ch'ing, who came from Lung-shan in Chen-hai. Born in
1863,[46] he was apprenticed at the age of fifteen to a Shanghai cosmetics
firm through an introduction by a relative. Yü received two shares of
stock in the business, and in time was able to invest an additional 200
taels of his own, thereby making himself one of the major stockholders.[47]
But Yü was looking to better things. He attended night school to learn
English and by the age of 27 (in 1893) had abandoned cosmetics to
serve as a comprador to Western firms. By the end of his career, during
which he had worked for two large Western banks, Yü had served a
term as president of the Shanghai General Chamber of Commerce, and
been for fifteen years a member of the Chamber's executive committee.
At his home near Ningpo Yü also founded the Ningpo Bank (Ssu-ming
yin-hang), the Ning-Shao Shipping Company, and the San-pei Shipping
Company. He was the chief financier of the modern road that linked
the city of Ningpo with Chen-hai to the east and Tz'u-ch'i to the west.
At the age of sixty, he was regarded in Shanghai as "one of the most
prominent merchants and public-spirited citizens of the city."[48]

Although he was a native of Chen-hai, Yü lacked the connections with
"better families" that could have made him influential in the Ningpo
Guild.[49] He remained therefore a relatively unknown figure in the Ningpo pang at Shanghai until 1898, when he became a celebrity overnight
as a result of his role in a clash between the authorities of the French
Concession and the Ningpo Guild. The crisis, which had been brewing
for a long time,[50] is worth recounting here, for it exemplifies the many
conflicts between Western and Chinese interests that were developing
in Shanghai during this period. It also shows how these conflicts acted
to uncover the latent differences within the increasingly diversified
Ningpo community at Shanghai.

The mourning hall and the cemetery for indigent members of the
Ningpo Guild occupied over seven acres of land that had been incorporated into the French Concession in 1849. During the 1860's the French
authorities sought to lease the area occupied by the cemetery, proposing
first to construct a school and a hospital there, and then, in 1873, to
build a road through the property. These overtures were rebuffed and
the Guild lodged a formal protest with consular and settlement authorities. Finally in 1874 the French sent troops to forcibly occupy the land.
The resulting skirmish left seven Chinese dead, and touched off a riot

in which shops and homes in the French settlement were looted or destroyed. The case came to a hearing before the Tsungli Yamen and representatives of the French Concession in 1878. The terms of the settlement reaffirmed the permanent land rights of the Guild, forbade further efforts at foreign construction thereon, and ordered the Chinese government to pay 37,000 taels as indemnity for the losses incurred by French merchants. The Chinese received 1,000 taels for each Chinese life lost.

It was with this precedent before him that the president of the Ningpo Guild received a communiqué from the office of the French consul on May 13, 1898, stating that Lots 186–91 of the French Concession (the lands occupied by the cemetery), long in the hands of the Ningpo Guild, were now to be "returned" to the French to permit the construction of a public school, a hospital, and a slaughterhouse. Five days later, with the Guild leadership still debating an appropriate course of action, French troops arrived to tear down the cemetery wall.

The entire Ningpo community was thrown into an uproar. Ningpo merchants closed their shops; Ningpo people employed by the French walked off their jobs. A boycott on goods and services was then extended to the entire Western community in Shanghai, and pressure on the French forced them to withdraw. The boycott lasted six months, and is now viewed as the first political strike against a foreign power in the history of modern China, forerunner to the massive anti-Japanese boycotts of the 1930's.

The strike and its success had a significant effect on the internal organization of the Ningpo community in Shanghai. It discredited the then leaders of the Ningpo Guild because they failed to take prompt, decisive action against the French. Further, it brought to the forefront of the community two new leaders, representing new elements in the Ningpo power structure: Yü Hsia-ch'ing and an obscure figure named Shen Hung-lai. Yü, as a comprador, was able to invoke personal ties with Western merchants and businessmen in explaining the grievances of the Guild. At the same time, because of his own background as a poor youth, he could appeal to the workers for cooperation and support. He thus successfully negotiated a settlement that recognized and upheld the legitimate property rights of the Guild.

The actual mobilization of the vast number of Ningpo laborers in the city fell to Shen Hung-lai. Shen was a native of the Ningpo region who had come to Shanghai following a stay in Japan, where he had been caught up in the emerging Chinese nationalist movement. Convinced that part of China's weakness lay in her lack of effective organization at all levels, he had formed a group at Shanghai called the Long Life Society (*Ch'ang-sheng hui*). Membership was drawn primarily from Ning-po people in the service of foreigners, and from petty traders and artisans. Shen used the Long Life Society as the focal point for organizing the strike of Ningpo laborers in the city.

The alliance of necessity which this incident forged between the leisured elite and the laboring masses from Ningpo at Shanghai proved to be short-lived. While it lasted, however, it precipitated some dramatic changes. After the strike the Long Life Society affiliated with the Ningpo Guild, and by 1901 had won a measure of control within it, Shen Hung-lai being elected business manager.[51] Yü Hsia-ch'ing likewise improved his position in the wake of the strike—not only in the eyes of the Ningpo *pang*, but in those of the foreign community as well. In 1902 he accepted a position with the Banque Russo-Asiatique, transferring a year later to the Bank Nederlandsche Handel-Maatschappij.

The introduction of modern institutions. In the first years of the twentieth century, then, we can observe within the Ningpo *pang* at Shanghai a new balance of power that was to shift further with the weight of political and social change in the decades that followed. The twentieth century, however, introduced a new factor into the contest: the rise of modern or Western-style organizations and other private interest groups that could have acted to destroy or permanently weaken the hierarchical order worked out, until that time, within the confines of the Ningpo Guild. But as these new organizations appeared, they served rather to underline the persistence and adaptibility of a power structure organized on native-place principles.

As the account that follows will demonstrate, the new organizations presented a wider range of social and political options to the Ningpo merchants in Shanghai. For a brief period many of these options were explored, indicating perhaps some tentative alterations in the traditional alliance between commercial wealth and political power. But in the end the Ningpo merchants reverted to the preservation of the status quo rather than staking their future on its reform. This tendency was characteristic of the nouveaux riches—the most immediate beneficiaries of the changes of the time—as well as of the established Ningpo merchant elite.

It will be recalled that prior to 1902, when the first chambers of commerce were formed, the power of the Ningpo merchants in Shanghai was concentrated in two organizations: a native-place association, the Ningpo Guild, and an occupational association, the Money Trade Guild, whose leadership they controlled. In the early 1900's the Ningpo Guild had been forced to expand its membership to include Ningpo workers and petty traders; it had also been forced to permit (albeit briefly) one of their spokesmen to hold office in the organization. At the same time that the organization was accommodating these new elements, institutional challenges to Ningpo commercial hegemony in Shanghai as a whole were arising from another quarter in the form of modern banking institutions and the new Shanghai Chamber of Commerce. To appreciate the nature of this challenge, however, it is necessary to understand the continuity of personal control that persisted through the rise of new institutional forms.

At the end of the nineteenth century and in the early twentieth century, the most prominent leaders in the Ningpo Guild included Yeh Ch'eng-chung, Shen Tun-ho, Yen Hsin-hou, Fang Shih-ju (of *the* Fangs), and Chou Hsiang-yün. These men made up the "traditional" conservative elite in the organization: they were wealthy, independent businessmen, not compradors. Two compradors had also distinguished themselves sufficiently to win places in the leadership of the organization: Yü Hsia-ch'ing and Chu Pao-san.[52] In the first decade of the new century an effort was made to "democratize" the Ningpo Guild: the group was reorganized so that meetings were conducted as a general assembly, with an open forum for speakers; a representative from every occupational group within the Guild was appointed to serve as a trustee and to participate in the monthly audit of funds; and a post was created for an officer to be elected by the general assembly at large. When the lower ranks of the membership lost their spokesman with Shen Hung-lai's death, power within the Guild reverted to the original board of directors; but the general assembly was by then too well entrenched to be denied access to the decision-making process, and thus continued to play a role in the formulation of policy.[53]

Doubtless one way in which the traditional board of directors kept its control over the organization was through its control of other sources of wealth and power in Shanghai: the modern banks and the new chambers of commerce. As Kagawa observed in 1948, "the large native banks in Shanghai are bound up inextricably with the capital of the modern banks held by the Chekiang financial clique. Nevertheless the relationship between them is based on personal ties, and clearly where this relationship has become a formal connection, it has been based on mutual agreement between the members of the clique themselves, maintained and expanded by their own design."[54] The first modern-style bank in China was the Imperial Bank of China (*Chung-kuo t'ung-shang yin-hang*), founded in 1897 by Sheng Hsüan-huai as a *kuan-tu shang-pan** enterprise, and converted in 1905 to private status as the Commercial Bank of China.[55] It was followed in 1904 by the first national bank of China, the Hu-pu Bank, also known as the Ta Ch'ing Bank and later as the Bank of China (*Chung-kuo yin-hang*).[56] In 1907 the Bank of Communications (*Chiao-t'ung yin-hang*) was founded to serve with the Ta Ch'ing Bank as a repository for official funds.[57]

The president of the Imperial Bank, Yen Hsin-hou, was prominent in the Ningpo community at Shanghai, as were two of the most prominent investors, Yeh Ch'eng-chung and Chu Pao-san.[58] The managerial staffs of these new Western-style banks at Shanghai included several bankers from Shao-hsing, the prefecture west of Ningpo, and a part of Ningpo's economic hinterland. When the Hu-pu Bank at Shanghai was reorganized as the Ta Ch'ing, the assistant manager was Hu Shan-teng of Yü-yao. In 1900 Sung Han-chang, also of Yü-yao, was made an assistant to the manager of the Imperial Bank of China, and in 1906 he was placed in charge of the Peking Savings Bank, which had been established to handle the savings accounts of the Ta Ch'ing Bank, then in liquidation. By 1912 Sung was manager of the Bank of China.[59]

Ningpo bankers at Shanghai became dissatisfied with their dealings with these new banks, "combining as they did the taints of 'officialdom' and 'foreigners.' "[60] Accordingly, one of China's two earliest[61] private merchant banks, the Ningpo Bank (*Ssu-ming yin-hang*), was organized in 1908 by ten prominent Ningpo merchant bankers, including the compradors Chu Pao-san and Yü Hsia-ch'ing. The Ningpo Bank was underwritten by Li Yün-shu and other wealthy Ningpo financiers, and was the first modern bank in China organized as a limited stock company.[62]

Accompanying the rise of modern banking institutions at Shanghai during the first decade of the twentieth century was the creation and growth of modern chambers of commerce, designed to articulate and protect the interests of the Chinese community against Western competition in every sphere. From the time of the founding of the Shanghai General Chamber of Commerce, the influence of the Ningpo *pang* was asserted in a familiar pattern. The proposal that resulted in the formation of this Chamber was addressed by Sheng Hsüan-huai to Yen Hsin-hou in 1901. In 1902 Yen rented a building for a meeting of a group which he called the Shanghai Merchants' Assembly Guild (*Shang-hai shang-*

---

* *Kuan-tu shang-pan* means "official [governmental] supervision, merchant [private] management." See Albert Feuerwerker, *China's Early Industrialization: Sheng Hsuan-huai (1844–1916) and Mandarin Enterprise* (Cambridge: Harvard University Press, 1958).

yeh hui-i kung-so), composed of the presidents of every native-place and occupational organization in the city, and also of the leaders of the larger new clubs and associations.[63] In 1904 the name of the organization was changed to Shanghai General Chamber of Commerce (*Shanghai shang-wu tsung-hui*) at the request of the government, which was seeking to curtail and control guild influence in urban areas.[64] This group

in effect became the organization of the Shanghai bourgeoisie. . . . Clearly it embodied all the formal characteristics of traditional guild organization. At the same time, it represented an alliance between the Ch'ing governmental apparatus and the merchant organizations of Shanghai; it represented the emergence of a more modern type of organization.[65]

From the start the leadership of the Chamber was composed of Ningpo merchants and "other famous merchants from the Chekiang and Kiangsu *pang.*" As of 1911 this leadership included Chu Pao-san (president), Shen Tun-ho (president of the general assembly), and Yü Hsia-ch'ing.[66]

*Revolution and the New Order: The Established Elite
Seeks Its Role*

As leaders of a representative organization of the urban elite in Shanghai, the officers of the new Chamber of Commerce represented an important body of support that might be thrown behind any of the rival political forces emerging from the Revolution of 1911. The immediate impulse of these leaders, as will be seen below, was one of enthusiastic support for the revolution. But this enthusiasm and the flood of funds that accompanied it were soon cut short in favor of a more calculated effort to ensure that investments would be repaid. Merchants became increasingly aware that their interests lay in the maintenance of peace and order, and accordingly supported whichever political movement offered the best promise of achieving this goal.[67] Mark Elvin has noted, for example, that the T'ung-meng Hui received generous contributions from the Shanghai merchant community directly following the rubber crash of 1910, in which the imperial administration had been sharply criticized for corruption and mismanagement.[68]

One critical observer of the Shanghai financial elite in this period insists that much of the early support for the revolution from that quarter was motivated by a true sense of nationalism.[69] However, the record seems to bear out Negishi's conclusion that the wealthy Ningpo merchants in Shanghai "reflect the traditional commitments of China's gentry elite. . . . Although they maintained an official posture of aloofness from politics, . . . they were likely to be heavily involved not only in philanthropy, but also in the maintenance of political order."[70] In 1905, for example, Yü Hsia-ch'ing had founded the China Merchants' Drill Team (*Hua-shang t'i-ts'ao hui*) as a counterpart to the militia maintained by the Concession authorities. In the fighting at Shanghai in 1911, Chinese merchant militia in various contingents throughout the city became the main strength of the revolutionary forces.[71] Yü Hsia-ch'ing was personally responsible for the conversion of the governor of Kiangsu, Cheng Te-ch'üan, to the revolutionary cause by providing him with a million taels with which to pay his troops. The province of Kiangsu was thereby enabled to declare its independence (and to ensure the security of revolutionary movements in Shanghai). The president of the Chamber of Commerce personally pledged 50,000 taels to the revolution in early November, and most of the nearly seven million dollars needed to carry the revolution in Shanghai in 1911 was supplied by businessmen there.[72] During this period the primary arm of political action for the Ningpo *pang* in Shanghai remained the Chamber of Commerce, which became "in reality a political body controlled by the Chekiang financial clique."[73]

In the period between 1911 and 1927, a clear transition took place characterized by three major changes: the diminishing power of workers, petty merchants and artisans, and other non-elite elements in the Ningpo community at Shanghai; the growing tendency for the merchant elite, which retained and increased its power, to reflect conservative gentry interests and to play traditional roles in the urban context;[74] and, toward the end, the marked convergence of the Shanghai merchants' interest in preserving order and unity with the right-wing Kuomintang's interest in achieving these goals.

The failure of the workers and other non-elite strata to win a permanent and meaningful voice in the Ningpo community at Shanghai became apparent in March 1911, when they felt compelled to form a new organization in order to escape what was termed the "elitist domination" in the Ningpo Guild. Known as the Association of Ningpo Residents at Shanghai (*Ning-po lü-Hu t'ung-hsiang hui*), it was open to all traders, artisans, workers, and students from the seven counties in Ningpo prefecture.[75]

Ironically, effective leadership in the fledgling Association was promptly assumed by Shen Tun-ho, Chu Pao-san, Yü Hsia-ch'ing, and others who, although not of the "old guard" in the Ningpo Guild leadership, were nonetheless by that time clearly identifiable as members of the elite.[76] In this context is worth noting that native-place ties, like traditional caste ties in India,[77] had served as effective instruments of vertical mobilization (cutting across class lines) in the cause of nationalism and party politics in China, as they did in the strike of 1898. The character of this new interclass alliance is ambiguous, however.[78]

In the period immediately following the Revolution of 1911, the composition of the Ningpo merchant elite itself underwent considerable transformation. Between 1911 and 1919 the entire financial structure of the nation was in a state of upheaval, and banks were subject to periodic runs reflecting the political crises of the moment. This chronic instability hit both native and modern banking institutions with equal force, although the former had also been weakened by the effects of the stock market crash of 1910.[79] Only about 30 percent of the native banks survived the revolution at all.[80] Accordingly an effort was made to ensure that the new powers emerging in Chinese politics would be interested in maintaining and protecting the status of the commercial elite at Shanghai. Both Yü Hsia-ch'ing and Chu Pao-san, in addition to providing financial support for the revolution, also accepted offices in the provisional government created at Shanghai on November 4, 1911.[81]

The key to maintaining one's position as a banker in this precarious time appears to have been diversification of interests and organizational ties, so that regardless of which institutions or fortunes fell prey to the vicissitudes of politics, one could still fall back on a sizable financial base. Of the five most prominent Ningpo native banking families at Shanghai, two closed their banks for good in 1911 (Tung and Yeh), two survived on a considerably diminished scale (Li and Fang), and one continued to prosper after 1911, primarily as a result of investments in Shanghai real estate (Ch'in).[82] The Li family incurred severe losses in the revolution and did not reenter the field of native banking until the 1920's or the 1930's. Most of the family's resources were invested in real estate. Nishizato suggests that one of the major weaknesses of the Fang native banks was simply the inverse side of their greatest strength: corporate resources. Money from Fang native banks was pooled for investment in lineage enterprises, and when many of these failed in 1911 and 1912, the lineage had no way of reimbursing its clients. The Fangs were still operating three native banks in Shanghai in 1950, but all native banks there owned by the oldest branch of the lineage closed after 1912, and by 1925 the only Fang still active in Shanghai banking was Chi-fan (C. P. Fong).[83]

After 1913, as the demands of warlords began to impinge upon the prerogatives of the merchant community at Shanghai, the commercial elite there increasingly turned to local sources of control to protect their investments against both the West and the whims of the new powers in government. Until the establishment of the Nanking regime in 1928, merchants at Shanghai enjoyed an extraordinary range of initiative in the management of urban affairs.[84] Their influence in provincial politics was further increased by the Republic's regulation on voter qualifications, which gave the urban merchant elite a voice in the provincial assemblies.[85] Throughout this period a critical locus of decision-making rested in the hands of the Ningpo *pang*: in the Shanghai Chamber of Commerce, and in the native banks and bankers' guilds that controlled all Shanghai banking. Like the Money Trade Association (*Ch'ien-yeh kung-hui*), the modern Bankers' Association (*Yin-hang kung-hui*) was "heavily influenced by traditional forms,"[86] being divided into four regionally based cliques, and controlled by the Ningpo sector of the Chekiang clique. The Bankers' Association was founded in 1915 by a group of bankers led by Chang Chia-ao (Chang Kia-ngau) and Sung Han-chang, the latter from Yü-yao. [87]

Both the Money Trade Association and the Bankers' Association paid nominal respect to government regulations in the formal organization of their membership.[88] But the manner in which they exercised their power through the Shanghai Chamber of Commerce resulted in a persistent effort on the part of the government to curtail and control their activities. As Ms. Garrett indicates elsewhere in this volume, however, this effort did not bear fruit until after 1927. That most of this power was vested in the hands of a few individuals can be seen in the following few examples. Ch'in Jun-ch'ing of Tz'u-ch'i, the "founding father" of modern Shanghai finance, was noted for the introduction of modern banking practices and administrative techniques in the organizations where he held office.[89] For many years he served concurrently as manager of two large native banks, as the executive director of the Money Trade Association, and as president and general manager of the China Development Bank (*Chung-kuo k'en-yeh yin-hang*). After 1927 he became auditor for the Central Bank of China. Others from the Ningpo clique who served concurrently as stockholders or investors in native banks and as high officials (manager or president) in modern banks were Sun Heng-fu, Hsieh Kuang-fu, and Yü Tso-t'ing.[90]

Within the guilds and the Chamber of Commerce likewise, the organizational leadership testified to the economic and political power of the Ningpo clique. The founder and first president of the Chamber of Commerce, Yen Hsin-hou, was a native of Tz'u-ch'i who first acquired contacts in Shanghai while serving as a member of Li Hung-chang's personal staff.[91] An early industrialist (in 1895 he was co-founder, with Chou Chin-piao, of the T'ung-chiu-yüan Cotton Mill at Ningpo), Yen served

as the first director of the Commercial Bank of China and was a founder
of the Ningpo Commercial Bank.[92] Yen was made president of the
Shanghai office of the Commercial Bank when it was merged with the
Hui-t'ung Customs Bank, of which he was manager.[93] Following his
appointment as president of the Chamber of Commerce, Yen appointed
Chou Chin-piao vice-president.[94] Within the Chamber of Commerce as
a whole, controlling interests were represented by the Bankers' Association and the Money Trade Association, which of course controlled the
money, credit, and exchange rates that were the foundation of Shanghai
finance and commerce. However, the representatives of these associations
made up only 10 percent of the Chamber's total membership, and thus
they controlled the Chamber not with their own votes but through their
control of the Ningpo *pang*, whose members did dominate the Chamber
in actual numbers.[95]

Until 1927 the Shanghai Chamber of Commerce and the interests
represented within it enjoyed much the same kind of autonomy in urban
affairs that had traditionally been accorded the gentry in the rural
sphere. Prominent members of the Ningpo elite (most notably Yü
Hsia-ch'ing) organized welfare and relief projects,[96] saw to the keeping
of peace and order, and used their personal offices to guarantee the financial security of their clients and fellow members of the Ningpo *pang*.
During this period (1911–27), the interests of the Shanghai financial
elite became increasingly aligned with the political interests of the Nationalists under Chiang Kai-shek, who offered political reunification and
an end to the warlord rivalries that struck at the heart of their financial
interests.[97]

Like the rural gentry, however, the urban bankers soon found their
prerogatives under pressure from the central govenment. In December
1926, the Chamber of Commerce at Shanghai (along with others
throughout China) was ordered to reorganize as a Merchant-People's
Cooperative (*Shang-min hsieh-hui*). The new organization was to be
open to "middle and petty" merchants as well as to the elite. The Chamber of Commerce not only refused to obey the order (when the new
cooperative was formed, the Chamber retained its identity as a separate
organization), but its Ningpo leadership infiltrated the new Cooperative
just as it had the Ningpo Residents' Association in 1911.[98] Yü Hsia-ch'ing,
for example, became chairman of the finance committee.[99]

The events of 1927 in Shanghai and the nature of the banking interests
that supported Chiang Kai-shek in his break with the Chinese Communists have been described elsewhere in vivid detail.[100] The more
obscure linkage between Chiang and the Ningpo financial clique in

particular can be traced to Chiang's birthplace in Feng-hua county of Ningpo prefecture. Chiang's thirteen years as a broker in Shanghai, during which he was undoubtedly affiliated with the Ningpo *pang* there, remain an unexplored facet of this political and interpersonal alliance based on native-place ties.[101] The nature of the continuity of control within the Ningpo *pang* at Shanghai, and the political ties of the leadership of the *pang*, raise a number of interesting questions for the period after 1927. What, for example, was the role of native-place associations in determining political alliances within the labor movement at Shanghai in the period between the spring of 1925 and the spring of 1927—when it appears that the Chinese Communist Party won significant influence among urban workers? To what extent were the political ties between the Ningpo elite and the Kuomintang able to rechannel the allegiance of urban workers toward the Kuomintang after the White Terror? What became of native-place ties, in short, during the rise of class consciousness and mass political movements in Shanghai in the 1920's?

The economic policies of the Kuomintang in the 1930's, particularly the nationalization of private modern banks and the wartime inflation, made the relationship between financial elites and the government ambiguous at best. For example, native-place ties with Chiang Kai-shek did not keep the Ningpo Bank from being nationalized in 1935.[102] Whether the events of the 1930's and the 1940's seriously undermined the strength of the resilient *pang* affiliations in Shanghai is a problem that remains to be explored.

The record of the Ningpo community at Shanghai offers substantial evidence that, prior to the 1930's, native-place ties provided the primary channels through which family, class, and business interests were articulated in Chinese cities.

Merchant Associations in Canton, 1895–1911

EDWARD J. M. RHOADS

Chinese merchants and the Chinese city, like practically every other social group and institution in China, underwent a profound change in the last fifteen years of the Ch'ing dynasty. In the traditional city the demands of bureaucratic administration generally took precedence over commercial development. Consequently the merchants, although economically vital, were socially isolated and politically weak. They congregated naturally in cities but kept to themselves and avoided involvement in political matters, which they recognized as the prerogative of the gentry-officials.[1] This traditional pattern was on the whole dominant down to the last decade of the nineteenth century, when, as a result of China's humiliation in the war with Japan in 1894–95, it began to weaken. During the next decade and a half the merchants emerged from their shadowy position in society and became deeply involved in the contemporary political scene. In short, they became politicized. This process, which is a characteristic feature of modernization, was reflected in the development of new forms of merchant associations. I propose to examine here the politicization of merchants and merchant associations in Canton between 1895 and 1911.[2]

The City and Its Gentry and Merchants

Canton is an ancient city whose history goes back at least to the Han period.[3] For most of the ensuing two thousand years it has been the metropolis of South China. Its population in 1965 is estimated as slightly over three million. However, much of this growth has been recent. In 1921 the population was only 788,000. It is therefore reasonable to assume that at the beginning of the century it was about 600,000.[4] Like most traditional Chinese cities, Canton was a walled city, though not a

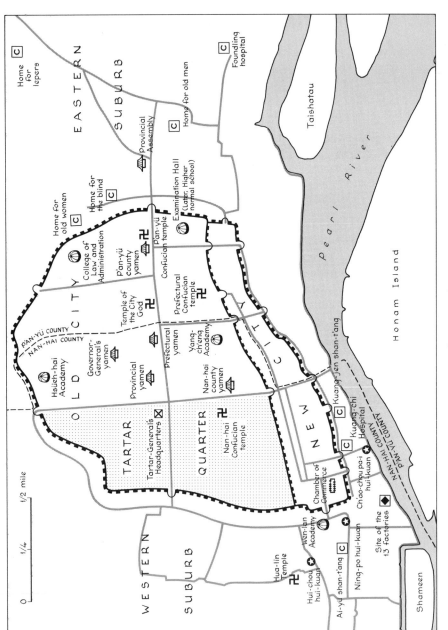

MAP 1. CANTON, 1895–1911

regular one. It lacked the rectangular city walls and the grid of avenues oriented to the compass points that were characteristic of many other cities, particularly in North China.[5] The walled city comprised the Old City, whose walls in their final form dated from the 1380's, and the New City to the south, enclosed in the 1560's (see map). Twenty-five feet high and six miles around, the walls encompassed an area of scarcely two square miles.[6] The city within the walls was thus extremely congested. According to an early nineteenth-century account, "there are several long streets, but most of them are short and crooked; they vary in width from two to sixteen feet, but generally they are about six or eight feet wide."[7] A later account describes Canton as "a labyrinth of some 600 evil-smelling, dimly lighted stone-flagged streets, packed with a seething mass of humanity."[8] The population necessarily spilled over into the suburbs, particularly to the west and south (even across the river to Honam island) and to a lesser extent to the east. The hilly area to the north, however, was relatively sparsely populated. There was also an immense boat population living aboard sampans and junks on the river.

Canton functioned as a center of political administration and as a central market for much of Ling-nan, the region "south of the ranges." Politically, it was both the nerve center of an administrative system that encompassed two provinces and the center of the several layers of administration within its own neighborhood. During the Ch'ing period, it was the seat of the governor-general who ruled over both Kwangtung and Kwangsi and of the governor of Kwangtung, until the two posts were amalgamated in 1905. (Earlier, in the Ming period, the provincial capital had been located at Chao-ch'ing, fifty miles upriver from Canton. It was moved to Canton in 1630, reportedly so that the provincial officials would be better situated to keep an eye on the foreign traders.[9]) Canton was also the seat of Kuang-chou prefecture, which took in the surrounding fourteen counties, and within the prefecture, of the two counties of Nan-hai and P'an-yü. In addition, it was the seat of the Tartar-general, whose garrison of 47,000 Manchu and Chinese bannermen, descendants of the army that had conquered China for the Ch'ing in the seventeenth century, lived in the so-called Tartar Quarter of the city.[10] The official presence, in short, was pervasive. As a mid-nineteenth-century observer pointed out, "a glance at the map of Canton will shew how vast a proportion of its area is taken up by their yamuns."[11]

Canton was equally important as a commercial city, as the irregularity of its physical layout would suggest. Located in the middle of the densely populated Pearl river delta at the confluence of the West, North, and East rivers, Canton had long been the hub of a marketing network that covered most of Kwangtung and Kwangsi. It was also an entrepôt for South China's foreign trade with Southeast Asia and beyond. It enjoyed its greatest prosperity in the days of the "Canton system," the late eighteenth century and early nineteenth century, when all the goods of China flowed south to Canton for export to the West. With the opening of other ports to foreign trade in and after the mid-nineteenth century, Canton quickly lost its preeminence to Shanghai and Hong Kong—and soon lost much of its prosperity as well. Nevertheless, down to the present it has retained its commercial importance within its own region.[12]

Since Canton was both a political and a commercial center, both gentry and merchants congregated there. The gentry were the local political elite, the holders of examination degrees that qualified them for government service. However, for many of them, officeholding, which by the rule of avoidance had always to be away from home, was infrequent and brief.[13] When not holding office, they lived at home and often acted as intermediaries between the local populace and the officials appointed by the central government.[14] Unlike their English namesakes, the Chinese gentry were an urban elite, though they probably derived much of their income from landholdings in the country. They were drawn to the city in large part because that was where the officials, whom they were privileged to advise, lived and worked.[15] Thus Canton, with its four levels of administrative officials, attracted large numbers from the various strata of the Kwangtung gentry. Members of the higher, or provincial, gentry, such as those holding the degrees of *chin-shih* (metropolitan graduate) and *chü-jen* (provincial graduate), were on hand to advise the governor-general and the governor. For example, the *chin-shih* Liu Hsüeh-hsün was the agent for Governor-General Li Hung-chang in his curious dealings with Sun Yat-sen's revolutionary group in the summer of 1900,[16] whereas the *chin-shih* Chiang K'ung-yin did much the same for Governor-General Chang Ming-ch'i in 1911.[17] Members of the lower, or local, gentry, such as holders of the *kung-sheng* (senior licentiate) degree, were similarly on hand to advise the prefect of Kuang-chou and the magistrates of Nan-hai and P'an-yü.

The merchants were drawn to the city, of course, because of its central marketing facilities. Canton was predominantly a commercial rather than an industrial, or even industrializing, city. In the first decade of the twentieth century, it had little more in the way of modern industry than an electric light company, a waterworks, a cement factory, and a railway company.[18] The principal reason for Canton's failure to industrialize, which stood in sharp contrast to Shanghai's rapid development in the late nineteenth and early twentieth centuries, was the proximity of British Hong Kong, which offered greater security and stability not only to foreign but also to Chinese entrepreneurs. In 1905, for example, when Chien Chao-nan and his brother Yü-chieh founded the Kwangtung Nanyang Tobacco Company, they located it in Hong Kong and not Canton.[19] The merchants of Canton were thus mostly shopkeepers, traders, and craftsmen rather than industrialists.[20]

The distinction between gentry and merchants was not, of course, always clearcut. On the one hand, with the growth of modern commerce and industry in the late nineteenth century, some members of the gentry, most notably Chang Chien of Kiangsu,[21] chose a career in business rather than in government service. On the other, some merchants, especially the wealthier ones, were able to buy some of the lower degrees and titles and so obtained gentry status. Thus, many of the compradors, like Cheng Kuan-ying, held the title of expectant taotai (circuit intendant) by right of purchase.[22] Despite this undeniable overlap, however, gentry and merchants remained self-consciously distinct. This was the case, at least, in Canton.

In Canton, the division between merchants and gentry could virtually be drawn on a city map. Most of the commerce and handicrafts, and most of the merchants, were concentrated in the western half of the city, especially the Western Suburb. According to J. G. Kerr, a missionary doctor and longtime resident, "the Western suburbs contain a large part of the business, wealth, and manufacturing industry of the city."[23] For example, Canton's famous silk weavers were all located here, particularly in the area centering on Ch'ou-ch'un-tung street, outside the West Gate of the Old City. Similarly, most of the Chinese banks, including the Canton branch of the new Imperial Bank of China, were established on T'ai-p'ing Street, near the T'ai-p'ing Gate leading into the New City.[24] (As in the T'ang period, over a thousand years earlier, each trade or craft still tended to congregate together in one street or on one side of a street. John Henry Gray, another missionary and longtime resident of Canton, pointed out: "The shops of the various tradesmen are not, as is the case in many English towns, scattered indiscriminately, as it were, throughout the city. . . . For each branch of trade has its distinct and separate locality, and to which, as a rule, it is restricted."[25]) The Western Suburb was also where the Anglo-French settlement of Shameen (Sha-mien) was located, and where the thirteen foreign factories had been located in the days of the Canton system. Finally, it was where many of the leading Chinese merchants lived.

Thus, wealthy descendants of the former Cohong merchants had their town mansions on Shih-pa p'u (in the Eighteenth Ward), which, according to Kerr, was "the street of Canton millionaires."[26]

The eastern half of the city, on the other hand, was the stronghold of the gentry. The old examination hall, the prefectural Confucian temple, and many of the new provincial schools decreed by the post-Boxer reforms, such as the College of Law and Administration (*Fa-cheng hsüeh-t'ang*) and the Higher Normal School (*Yu-chi shih-fan hsüeh-t'ang*), were located here. Many of the old-style academies (*shu-yüan*) were also located in or near the eastern half of the city. Most of the book-sellers, too, were found in this same general area, on Shuang-men-ti (Double Gateway Street), close to the schools. The street was, again according to Kerr, "a resort of the literati."[27]

Moreover, relations between the two groups were often strained and suspicious. The gentry looked on the merchants as vulgar economic parasites, whereas the merchants, as one of their group put it in 1906, "dread the gentry as they do tigers."[28] The merchants resented the gentry's hauteur and, more immediately, envied them their social and political prerogatives. For, in the traditional society, Canton's importance as a center of political administration generally overshadowed its commercial importance. Nothing expressed this subordination of trade to bureaucracy and of the merchants to the gentry-officials so well as the division of Canton into two separate administrative districts. The city was split almost down the middle, between P'an-yü on the east and Nan-hai on the west, in complete disregard of its organic unity. Canton simply did not exist as an administrative entity. Nor was Canton unique in this respect. Many of the other provincial capitals were divided in a similar fashion, as Hangchow had been during the Southern Sung period.[29]

Of course, neither the gentry nor the merchants of Canton had any formal say in the government of their city. Its officials, from the two county magistrates to the governor-general, were all appointed from outside the province and were responsible to the central government. There was no home rule for either the province or the city. But the gentry were at least often consulted by the officials, and their consequently easy access to the officials made them influential in the affairs of the city. The merchants, by contrast, who probably had a greater personal stake in the city than the gentry with their extensive land-holdings in the country, had practically no access to the officials. Only the gentry-merchants among them could participate to any extent in the government of their city.

Traditional Merchant Associations

The Ch'ing dynasty generally frowned on private voluntary associations lest they threaten its monopoly of power. Thus, late in the nineteenth century the gentry were still barred from forming even study associations (*hsüeh-hui*).[30] The merchants, on the other hand, perhaps because of their very weakness, were free to organize their own associations, notably guilds and *hui-kuan* (Landsmannschaften or clubs of fellow provincials).[31] At the turn of the century there were over a hundred different guilds (*hang*) in Canton,[32] virtually all of them located in the western half of the city. They were usually organized on the basis of specific services, crafts, or products, such as the North River Porters' Guild, the Boots and Shoes Guild, and the Native Silk Guild, respectively. At least three, however, all called *pang-hang*, seem to have been created on a geographical basis: the Tientsin Public Alliance and the Shanghai and Szechwan Alliances. Most of the guilds were probably fairly old, but some, the Electrical Equipment Guild for example, were obviously of recent origin. With the possible exception of the three *pang-hang*, they were probably all local organizations, with little or no connection to similar guilds in other cities. The guilds probably included most of the merchants who were Canton natives.[33]

Merchants who were not native to the city were organized in *hui-kuan*. These were associations formed on the basis of common geographical origin. They were open to gentry-officials as well as to merchants, but outside Peking they existed mainly to serve interregional trade.[34] The *hui-kuan* were thus primarily, if not totally, associations of merchants. In Canton at this time there were about twenty-five *hui-kuan*, representing many provinces and several prefectures.[35] The most substantial were the "Swatow Guild" (*Ch'ao-chou pa-i hui-kuan*), which actually represented the entire prefecture of Ch'ao-chou in eastern Kwangtung, the "Guildhall of the Green Tea Merchants" (*Hui-chou hui-kuan*), representing a prefecture in Anhwei, and the Ningpo Guild (*Ning-po hui-kuan*).[36] All of these, and the *hui-kuan* for Shensi and Hunan as well, were also located in the western half of the city. However, in contrast to the guilds, the *hui-kuan* were relatively unimportant in the life of Canton, perhaps simply because their members were all, strictly speaking, outsiders. It is clear, in any case, that the twenty-odd *hui-kuan* in Canton did not have the power or influence that the combination of six *hui-kuan* known as the Wan-nien feng had in Swatow, or that the Five Guilds, really a combination of five *hui-kuan*, had in Ch'iung-chou on Hainan island, or that the Cantonese Guild (*Kuang-Chao kung-so*), composed of natives of Kuang-chou and Chao-ch'ing prefectures, had in Shanghai.[37]

The guilds reflected the economic vitality and political weakness of their merchant members. The functions of traditional Chinese guilds were almost exclusively economic. Each guild concentrated on protecting its de facto monopoly from interlopers and regulating conditions of work. Each guild policed its own members and tried to settle disputes in its own court. The guilds thus exercised considerable authority over commercial affairs.[38] But the authority that they exercised was not formally delegated to them by the officials. Although they were encouraged by the officials to regulate their own affairs, they had no independent authority, and existed at the sufferance of the officials.[39] Moreover, the guilds were further weakened because they were divided. Each guild kept to itself, and there was little or no cooperation among guilds, even for economic purposes.

The only sphere in which the guilds and the merchants overcame their parochialism and developed some degree of city-wide cooperation was philanthropy. The merchants were the principal backers of the several charitable institutions (*shan-t'ang*) of Canton. These institutions should be distinguished from the older, government-supported charities located in the Eastern Suburb, like the Foundling Hospital (*Yü-ying t'ang*, founded in 1698) and the homes for old women (*P'u-chi yüan*, 1722) and for the blind (*Ku-mu yüan*, 1747).[40] The oldest of the later, private institutions was the Ai-yü Shan-t'ang, founded in 1871 and said to have been modeled after a similar institution in Shanghai, the P'u-yü T'ang. Called the Chinese Dispensary by Westerners, the Ai-yü Shan-t'ang provided free outpatient care to the indigent sick, financial support for destitute widows, and free coffins for the poor; it also supported several free primary schools for the children of the poor. Other charitable institutions, performing similar services, included the Kuang-jen Shan-t'ang founded in 1890 and the Kuang-chi Hospital founded in 1893. These later banded together to form the Nine Charitable Institutions (*Chiu shan-t'ang*), from which, incidentally, the older charities were excluded.[41]

Although the gentry and officials gave assistance, it was the merchants who principally financed and directed the charitable institutions. It is no surprise, then, to find that the charitable institutions were located in the Western and Southern suburbs. (The Ai-yü Shan-t'ang was built on the site of a mansion in the Eighteenth Ward that had belonged to a descendant of the Cohong merchant Puan Khequa.) The directors of the various institutions presumably constituted the merchant elite of the city. Certainly this was the case for two similar institutions in Hong Kong, the Tung Wah Hospital (*Tung-hua i-yüan*), founded in 1870, and the Po Leung Kuk (*Pao-liang chü*), a refuge for women, founded in 1880.[42] Similarly, in Macau the board of directors of the "Chinese Hospital" consisted of "the most influential and highly respected members of the Chinese Community."[43]

In short, the merchants of Canton on the eve of the Sino-Japanese war were organized but divided, despite some cooperation in the work of the charitable institutions. Moreover they lacked independence. They were far from challenging the gentry-officials' monopoly on political power.

New Forms of Merchant Association

The reform movement of the late 1890's, together with the subsequent post-Boxer reforms, initiated great changes in Chinese thought and society, including a reevaluation of the role of the merchant in the society. The main precipitant of change was the widespread anxiety among both government officials and private individuals for China's future as a sovereign nation. One component of this concern was economic: China, as the Cantonese comprador-reformer Cheng Kuan-ying and others like him saw it, was engaged not only in a military but also in a commercial struggle with the imperialist powers. How was she to meet their economic competition? How was she to recover the many economic rights and privileges already lost to them in the "Scramble for Concessions"?[44] One answer was greater cooperation among the traditionally divided merchants in order to strengthen China's commercial and industrial power. The result was the formation of newer, more complex forms of merchant association.

The short-lived reform government of 1898 took the first step. It ordered each province to establish a Bureau for Commercial Affairs (*Shang-wu chü*) to promote the development of commerce. But the bureau was an official body, headed by a government-appointed official; in Canton the head was apparently the provincial treasurer. For this reason, despite its merchant representation, the bureau was never very popular with the merchants. They would have preferred a body that was more nearly representative of their own rather than the government's interests.[45]

In Canton, by coincidence, circumstances led the merchants to meet this need themselves. In 1899 the Manchu Grand Secretary Kang-i came to Canton to raise funds for the Imperial Treasury. Kang-i reorganized the collection of the likin or internal transit tax, then made the merchants

guarantee to increase its annual yield from 2.8 to 4 million taels. It was
an extreme case of the government's habitual practice of putting the
squeeze on the merchants. To take charge of their new responsibility
the heads of 72 guilds, led by the silk, tea, timber, and banking guilds,
combined to form the Merchant-Guaranteed Likin Bureau (*Shang-pao
li chü*). They found it impossible, however, to collect as much likin as
Kang-i had demanded and gave up the attempt within five months. They
presumably made up the difference to him and returned the function to
the old Likin Board. But they did not cease to consult with one another.
Their association became formalized as the Seventy-two Guilds (*Ch'i-
shih-erh hang*).[46] It was probably no more than a coordinating board that
exercised a small degree of supervision over all the guilds of the city.
Like the guilds themselves, it had grown up spontaneously and without
formal authorization from the government. It was an organization of,
by, and for the merchants. And like the guilds again, it was tolerated by
the officials but had no formal standing with them. In Shanghai, too,
the merchants expressed dissatisfaction with the official character of the
Bureau for Commercial Affairs. In 1902 they formed their own Shanghai
Commercial Association (*Shang-yeh hui-i kung-ssu*), though, unlike the
Cantonese merchants, they did so with the prior approval of local officials.[47]

Clearly responding to these unauthorized activities, the Court finally
in January 1904 called for the creation of chambers of commerce in the
provinces and cities.[48] The Kwangtung General Chamber of Commerce
(*Shang-wu tsung-hui*) was accordingly founded in Canton in July 1905,
after months of discussion among the officials and the merchants. Unlike
the bureaus for commercial affairs, which had been official bodies for
the promotion of trade, the chambers of commerce were, like the Seventy-two Guilds in Canton, merchants' organizations. The Kwangtung
Chamber was financed by the merchants, with each guild and shop in
Canton contributing to the expense of the Chamber in varying amounts
according to the size of its business or capital. It was composed exclusively of merchants. It was led by merchants who, furthermore, were
selected by the members from among themselves; they were not appointed by the officials.[49]

However, unlike the Seventy-two Guilds, the Chamber of Commerce
was an officially authorized merchant association. It was decreed by the
Court and was regulated by the Ministry of Agriculture, Industry, and
Commerce, from which it received its seal and its authority. Thus, one
of its main functions was to represent the merchants officially. It served
as an intermediary between the guilds, which still had no formal stand-

ing, and the officials. For example, when the Taxpayers' Guild of Canton, which handled the payment of taxes and duties for its clients, complained in 1912 about a new arrangement that the Commissioner of Customs had instituted for examining cargoes, the Chamber acted as the mediator between the guild on the one hand and the Governor and the Customs Commissioner on the other. The guild, incidentally, was able, through the Chamber, to convince the Commissioner to revert to the former system of examining goods.[50]

Another of the functions of the chambers of commerce was to provide the institutional framework for greater cooperation among the merchants. The Canton Chamber, as a "general chamber," was responsible for coordinating the activities of all the merchants across the province. It thus stimulated merchants in other cities and market towns to form local branch chambers. By early 1908, the Canton Chamber was overseeing a network of at least fourteen branches that extended to all but the Swatow region of Kwangtung.[51] (Swatow, by virtue of its economic independence of Canton, had its own General Chamber.) Within Canton itself the Chamber broke down the barriers between guilds, and created a city-wide merchant organization. It served as an arbitrator in disputes between guilds and promoted harmony among the city merchants. The Chamber thus overcame the parochialism that had been so characteristic of traditional merchant associations. It provided a formal and officially recognized channel for linking the guilds and merchants not only in Canton but across most of the province. The chambers of commerce were the most inclusive merchant associations yet founded.

A third function of the chambers of commerce was to promote China's commercial and industrial development, particularly to improve her competitive position in the "commercial war" with the foreign powers. The regulations of the Canton Chamber suggested some of the ways it might do this: encourage cooperation among the merchants, publicize modern business practices, discourage traditional obstacles to commercial development (like belief in *feng-shui* or geomancy), investigate and make known local business conditions, open a products exhibition hall, and publish a commercial newspaper.[52] The *Chamber of Commerce News* (*Tsung shang-hui pao*) began publication in Canton shortly afterward, in 1905.[53]

If the new chambers of commerce had been expected to supersede unauthorized associations like the Seventy-two Guilds, then the Canton Chamber did not meet expectations. Despite an apparent duplication of effort, the Seventy-two Guilds flourished as an independent—indeed a rival—organization. For example, in 1907 it began to publish, in competition with the *Chamber of Commerce News*, its own newspaper, the *Seventy-two Guilds Commercial News* (*Ch'i-shih-erh hang shang-pao*), which quickly became one of the most influential dailies in the city.[54] How is this situation to be explained?

For most merchants of Canton the Chamber was probably too cosmopolitan, too remote. It was concerned not only with Canton but with the whole province. Moreover, it had quasi-official duties that made it in part dependent upon the officials. Finally, and perhaps most importantly, it was dominated by gentry-merchants. The first chairman of the Canton Chamber, Tso Tsung-fan, held a regular *chü-jen* degree, while the first vice-chairman was the ex-comprador Cheng Kuan-ying, who held the title of expectant taotai. Tso's successor as chairman was Chang Pi-shih, a wealthy overseas-Chinese entrepreneur who held various high official posts, while one of Cheng's successors as vice-chairman was the *chü-jen* Ou Tsan-sen.[55] These men were all closely identified with the world of the gentry officials. The leaders of the Seventy-two Guilds, by contrast, were generally inconspicuous, in part because their association had no official standing, but probably also because they were not men of high reputation, as we shall see in our later discussion of the Self-Government Society. In short, the Chamber of Commerce was evidently a creature of the wealthy gentry-merchants, whereas the Seventy-two Guilds was more nearly representative of the ordinary merchants.

The Merchants and Nationalism

As the merchants became more highly organized, they also became politicized. This had not been the official intent. The regulations of the Canton Chamber of Commerce specifically restricted its sphere of activity to commercial development. It was expected to avoid politics as the traditional guilds had. But the merchants, encouraged by the formal recognition granted them by the officials, quickly took the lead in the urban mass nationalist movement that emerged in the post-Boxer decade.[56] Later, as the Court began to take steps leading toward eventual constitutional government, they participated in that movement too. Finally, in 1911 they helped to arrange the transition to republican rule.

In Canton, the first involvement of the merchants in political agitation was the anti-American boycott. The Shanghai Chamber of Commerce initiated the boycott, a traditional weapon of the merchants, in May 1905 as a protest against the exclusion of Chinese laborers from the United States in the Sino-American treaty of 1894 and, more generally, against the discriminatory treatment of Chinese immigrants there.[57] Merchants and merchant associations in other cities responded promptly.

In Canton, the merchants of the Seventy-two Guilds, the Nine Charitable Institutions, and the just-founded Chamber of Commerce set up the Society to Oppose the Treaty (*Chü-yüeh hui*) in July to direct and coordinate the boycott locally. The main leader of the boycott society was Cheng Kuan-ying, who was then vice-chairman of the Chamber of Commerce. Another leader was Wu Chieh-ming, one of the Chamber's several resident managers and director of the Kuang chi Hospital, which served as the headquarters of the society. The success of the boycott was ensured by the guilds, who threatened to discipline any of their members who broke ranks and sold or bought American goods. As a result of the cooperation of the various merchant organizations, the boycott in the Canton area was surprisingly effective and lasted from August 1905 to February 1906.

An ad hoc group of merchant leaders had directed the anti-American agitation. Two years later, in November 1907, a more lasting organization of politically minded merchants was formed, the Self-Government Society (*Tzu- chih hui*).[58] It quickly assumed local leadership of the mass nationalist movement from the Chamber of Commerce, which thereafter tended to concentrate on strictly commercial affairs. The merchants' Self-Government Society was only one of several similar groups formed in Canton at this time. The gentry, for example, founded the Kwangtung Association for the Study of Self-Government (*Tzu-chih yen-chiu she*),[59] while some students organized the National Rights Recovery Society (*Kuo-ch'üan wan-chiu hui*).[60] The inspiration for all of these organizations was the Court's several decrees in September and October 1907 promising that a constitutional regime would eventually be created and calling for the immediate formation of associations for the study of self-government.[61] The Court of course had the gentry in mind when it issued these edicts. The other groups, however, were able to use these decrees to justify creating their own associations. Shortly afterward, a protest movement against Britain for sending its navy to police the West River gave them the opportunity to do precisely that.

Whereas the gentry's Association for the Study of Self-Government had been founded in accordance with imperial instructions, the merchants' Self-Government Society, like the students' National Rights Recovery Society, was entirely without official standing. Ever suspicious of such unofficial activities, the Court issued an edict on December 24 denouncing "those who on the pretext of constitutionalism have interfered in recent years in all domestic and external governmental affairs."[62] The reply of the Self-Government Society, in an open letter to its "brethren at home and beyond the seas," was immediate and emotional:

The calamity of partition confronts us. Yet our government does nothing. It does not even strive to devise a solution. On the contrary, because the Self-Government Society has sent it some blunt telegrams, it has ordered the Society disbanded. Why do we wait meekly for our race to be annihilated, our nation destroyed, our families killed? Why not, while we are still alive, strive for cooperation and organization? Perhaps then we may yet survive![63]

However, the society had the tacit approval of Governor-General Chang Jen-chün and survived despite imperial disapproval. Other unofficial groups such as the National Rights Recovery Society were not so fortunate; they had all wilted by 1908.

Membership in the society was open to anyone who paid its annual dues of one dollar. There seems to have been no bar on gentry membership, and at least one prominent gentry member, Chiang K'ung-yin, was active in the society. But the society was predominantly a merchant organization, as its full name, the Canton Merchants Self-Government Society (*Yüeh-shang tzu-chih hui*), made very clear. The gentry in general resented the merchants' presumption. One group of unidentified "orthodox gentry" was moved to complain indignantly to the central government early in 1908 about the "uncivilized" behavior of the merchants and to question the respectability of their leaders.[64]

The Self-Government Society seems to have functioned almost as the political action arm of the Seventy-two Guilds. The chairman of the society, Ch'en Hui-p'u, regularly signed his telegrams of protest to the Foreign Ministry in the name of the "merchants of the Seventy-two Guilds."[65] Moreover, one of his principal associates in the society, Lo Shao-ao, was editor of the *Seventy-two Guilds Commercial News*— which, coincidentally perhaps, began publication only shortly before the formation of the society itself. The Chamber of Commerce, by contrast, had practically no connection with the society. With the exception of Huang Ching-t'ang, a gentry-merchant who presided over its inaugural meetings, none of the officers of the Chamber was notably active in the society. The leaders of the Self-Government Society clearly lacked the high social standing of the leaders of the Chamber. Ch'en Hui-p'u, said his gentry detractors, was nothing but a "bankrupt banker."[66]

According to a statement of purpose made at one of the first meetings in November 1907, the "sole object" of the Self-Government Society was "to safeguard the sovereign rights and privileges of the Nation."[67] As we shall see, this was not its only purpose. But its principal activity was indeed to promote nationalism, specifically resistance to foreign encroachments and the recovery of lost concessions. The society thus initiated and led a series of nationalist demonstrations in Canton and Kwangtung between the end of 1907 and the beginning of 1910, which involved it in successive controversies with Britain, Japan, and Portugal.[68] The protest against the British West River patrol, which was, as noted above, the occasion for the formation of the society, lasted from November 1907 to January 1908. When the Japanese government took a hard line on the capture of the arms-smuggling vessel *Tatsu Maru* off the coast of Macau, the society instituted an anti-Japanese boycott that lasted from March to December 1908. Finally in November 1908, when a Chinese passenger aboard the British river steamer *Fatshan* was allegedly murdered by the Portuguese night watchman, intense feeling was aroused both against Britain and against Portugal. The British operators of the *Fatshan*, the firm of Butterfield and Swire, were boycotted from December 1908 to August 1909. The society also supported the Chinese Foreign Ministry's coincident attempt to redefine the boundary of Macau and to restrict the Portuguese to the original Ming-dynasty leasehold.

During such controversies, the Self-Government Society was capable of attracting thousands of people to attend weekly meetings at its Hua lin temple headquarters in the Western Suburb. It enjoyed the support of the local officials as well. It was a highly effective instrument for mobilizing popular support for the local nationalist movement. It also organized Cantonese participation in nationalist efforts originating elsewhere, such as the movement initiated in 1909 by the Tientsin Chamber of Commerce to form National Debt Societies to raise funds from among the people to help pay off China's various foreign loans.[69]

The Self-Government Society furthermore promoted nationalism by encouraging and helping merchants to compete more effectively with foreign goods and services. During the agitation against the British West River patrol, the society joined with the merchants of Wu-chou, Kwangsi, to establish a steamship company that would undercut British shipping on the river.[70] The society may also have encouraged some of the match factories that were founded in Canton and its vicinity during the anti-Japanese *Tatsu Maru* boycott. These factories helped to reduce Canton's dependence on wooden matches imported from Japan.[71] The society regularly suggested specific ways to improve China's trading position. For example, at its meeting on September 8, 1908, it advised trunk makers and bamboo weavers to produce "foreign-styled luggage cases" rather than the "old-fashioned trunks." It encouraged one company to go into the business of making "portable bottles for the use of the army" so that China would not have to purchase them from abroad. It finally recommended the improvement of Kwangtung's fishing and salt indus-tries.[72] The activities of the Self-Government Society in this area were identical to those specified by the Court for the chambers of commerce.

Merchants and Constitutionalism

The merchants, through their Self-Government Society, also partici-pated in the Court's constitutional program. In January 1908, shortly after the Court had declared its commitment to the principle of constitu-tional government, the society distributed copies of basic readings in civics in order to popularize the program and prepare the citizens of Canton for their future responsibilities.[73] It moreover joined like-minded groups in other cities to press the Court to be more specific about its plans. Representatives of the society met in Shanghai in March and April 1908 with delegates from the rest of China to map out an unprece-dented nationwide campaign to petition for the early establishment of constitutional government.[74] In Kwangtung the petition gathered at least 150,000 signatures.[75] Responding to the campaign, the Court issued de-tailed instructions in July regarding the organization of the provincial assemblies; in August, it set up a definite schedule for the realization of constitutional government within nine years.[76] When the provincial as-semblies were being organized the following spring, the society helped to publicize the elections.[77] It also set up at the Hua lin temple a self-government instruction office (*Tzu-chih yen-chiu so*), which gave an eight-month course on local self-government.[78]

The Court's constitutional program, however, hardly benefited the merchants. The qualifications for voters in the provincial assembly elec-tions clearly discriminated against them and favored the gentry:[79] three years devoted to teaching or some other form of public service in the province; or graduation from middle school or its equivalent; or posses-sion of the *kung-sheng* degree; or service in the government at or above the seventh rank for civil posts or the fifth rank for military posts; or ownership of a business or property valued at $5,000. Only the last of these was directed at merchants, and then only at great and wealthy merchants. Predictably, the Kwangtung Assembly was overwhelmingly composed of gentry members. Twenty-three, or over half, of a limited sample of 42 assemblymen held at least a regular *kung-sheng* degree and thus qualified as members of the regular gentry.[80] On the other hand, out of the total membership of 94 assemblymen only five are known to have been merchants, three of whom were leaders of the chambers of com-merce at Canton, Swatow, and Chia-ying-chou.[81] None of them was asso-ciated with the Canton Self-Government Society. In short, the Kwangtung Assembly represented the gentry first and foremost. It was probably no coincidence that the assembly hall was located outside the East Gate, in the gentry-dominated eastern half of the city.

Finally, the actions of the Kwangtung Assembly during its three years of operation generally reflected the concerns of the gentry, particularly their efforts to formalize and expand their role in local government at the expense of the officials.[82] The Assembly tried, for example, to extend the gentry's authority over local schools at the expense of the magistrate's authority. It rarely dealt with matters that concerned merchants. It gave but slight encouragement to the development of commerce and industry. It did urge the government to sanction the formation of a merchant militia (*shang-t'uan*) similar to the Shanghai Chinese Merchants' Volunteer Corps, something the Canton merchants had repeatedly asked for to supplement the incompetent city police. (The merchants were probably also anxious to duplicate and counterbalance the gentry's rural militias.)[83] But the Assembly included the merchants' militia in a general request for permission for all types of popular militias (*min-t'uan*), which the government in any case evidently rejected.

There were, however, other aspects of the Court's constitutional program from which merchants might have benefited. In January 1909, the Court approved a set of regulations for the formation of self-government bodies at the sub-county level—in cities, towns, and rural areas. The regulations defined a city (*ch'eng*) as a county seat, together with its suburbs. The rest of the county was then divided, according to population, into townships (*chen*) and rural areas (*hsiang*). By 1913 each city, town, and rural area was to have both a deliberative and an executive council, with the deliberative council to be elected by the people and the executive council to be appointed by the deliberative council from among the electorate. The franchise for the local deliberative council elections was considerably broader than that for the provincial assembly elections. The only qualification for voting was financial, based either on a man's tax payments or on his charitable contributions. Furthermore, the financial qualification was made less demanding. For example, ownership of a business worth $5,000 had been necessary to qualify for voting in the provincial assembly elections, but annual payment of $2 in direct taxes sufficed for the local deliberative council elections.[84] Thus merchants clearly had a much greater opportunity to participate in self-government at the city and town level than they had had at the provincial level. The 22-member Swatow deliberative council (*I-shih hui*), elected in August 1910, demonstrated the possibilities. It was controlled by local merchants in the same way the gentry controlled the Provincial

Assembly. The vice-chairman of the Swatow Chamber of Commerce headed the council, and issues of interest to merchants dominated its proceedings in March and April 1911. Merchants similarly controlled the Chinese municipal council in Shanghai.[85]

The merchants of Canton were less successful in taking advantage of these local government opportunities. Swatow and Shanghai were both more commercial and less political than Canton; Shanghai was only a county seat, whereas Swatow was not even that. Consequently, their merchants were not so thoroughly overshadowed by the local gentry-officials as those of Canton were. Moreover, Swatow and Shanghai were not divided cities as Canton was. Since both Nan-hai and P'an-yü had their county offices there, Canton qualified under the local self-government regulations as two separate cities. The regulations, however, also provided that such a divided city could unite under a single municipal council. Both the Chamber of Commerce and the Self-Government Society, along with the local officials, favored the union of Nan-hai and P'an-yü. So did the Association for the Study of Self-Government, the representative of the provincial gentry. Nevertheless, in May 1910 the local gentry of P'an-yü refused to go along. As they advised their county magistrate, "Although the people of Nan-hai and P'an-yü live together in one common city, their manners and habits are foreign to one another." Perhaps a more compelling reason for their opposition was their fear that union would give the merchants, concentrated in the more populous Nan-hai, a dominant voice in the municipal council.[86] In the end, nothing was done in either half of the city toward the formation of separate city councils, probably because negotiations continued to explore, without success, the possibility of a single municipal council.

In a related bid to modernize the city, the provincial gentry of Canton petitioned the officials in 1909 and 1910 to tear down the city walls and replace them with spacious carriage roads in order to relieve the terrible congestion in the city. They took as their model the bund that had just been built along the south shore of the city on mud-flats reclaimed from the Pearl river. However, in the wake of the New Army mutiny in February 1910, when the walls were thought to have kept the mutinous troops from attacking the city, the officials understandably rejected the petition.[87] Thus, on the eve of the Revolution, Canton still retained much of its traditional character. Its walls were intact. The city was administratively divided. There was no local self-government. The merchants were subordinate to both the gentry and officials. Only the gentry, through the Provincial Assembly, had managed slightly to enlarge their role in local government at the expense of the central government officials.

Merchants and the Revolution

By 1911, largely as a result of the post-Boxer reforms, the merchants had been organized and politicized. As they became politicized, they became more and more resentful that the Ch'ing reform program, particularly the self-government program, discriminated against them and was aimed instead at the gentry. Their efforts to make the regime more responsive to their demands were repeatedly frustrated either by the central government or by the gentry. As a result, they felt no personal stake in the future of the Ch'ing dynasty, or of a regime in which power was monopolized by the gentry-officials. Although merchants did little to bring on the revolution, they did just as little to avert it, and many in time sympathized with the revolutionary cause. When the revolution came, few rushed to defend either the dynasty or the regime.

In Canton, it was the officials and gentry who responded first to the revolutionary crisis initiated by the Wu-ch'ang Uprising on October 10, 1911. On October 25 leading members of the provincial gentry, with the consent and encouragement of Governor-General Chang Ming-ch'i, met at the Wen-lan Academy to work out a response to the crisis. They decided that provincial autonomy within a loosely organized federal Ch'ing empire would be the most expedient solution. It would, they hoped, break enough of Kwangtung's ties to Peking to satisfy the republicans and avert an attack, while preserving enough of these ties to avoid reprisals in case the dynasty should rally and defeat the republicans. Moreover, it would assure a continuity of rule, only slightly modified, by the centrally appointed officials and the local gentry. The governor-general would still administer the province, but would be subject to greater control by the gentry-dominated Provincial Assembly. As a concession to groups outside the gentry, like merchants and students, the meeting called for the creation of a second popular assembly, larger and more representative than the Provincial Assembly, that would "supervise" the operations of the provincial administration and "back up" the Assembly. It was a minor concession that would scarcely have disturbed the gentry-officials' monopoly on power.[88]

The merchants found no satisfaction in the solution proposed by the gentry. First of all, practically none of them had been involved in formulating it. The Wen-lan Academy meeting had been dominated by the gentry. It is perhaps significant that the meeting took place at an academy, a traditional stronghold of the gentry, even though the Wen-lan Academy itself was located outside the T'ai-p'ing Gate in the Western Suburb. With the exception of Lo Shao-ao, editor of the *Seventy-two Guilds Commercial News*, no merchant leader had been active in its proceedings. Second, the merchants resented the gentry's self-aggrandizement. Third, and most important, they questioned whether the gentry's measures were adequate to cope with the crisis. They doubted that the republicans, already gathering in Hong Kong, would be satisfied with such equivocation. They were particularly worried about rumors of an imminent attack on Canton by Lu Lan-ch'ing's "people's army" on behalf of the republicans. If there was to be any fighting in the streets of Canton, the merchants of course would be the main losers. Consequently, some of the merchants, led by Ch'en Hui-p'u of the Self-Government Society, met at the Ai-yü Shan-t'ang on the morning of October 29. (The choice of the meeting place, a charitable institution, is once again suggestive.) They agreed among themselves that the seriousness of the revolutionary threat warranted a clear-cut decision in favor of the republicans. They voted to declare Canton independent of the Ch'ing. They also voted to form the merchants' militia that had so long been denied them.[89]

On October 29, however, the success of the revolution was still far from assured, so Governor-General Chang Ming-ch'i repudiated the merchants' action. He preferred the original formula he had worked out with the gentry: autonomy within a federal Ch'ing empire rather than outright independence. The officials and the gentry, assisted by the compliant Chamber of Commerce, sought to reassure the merchants, especially those who had been involved in the abortive declaration of independence. They promised that "the officials will not go deeply into the incident" and that "all merchants can therefore relax."[90]

But how could the merchants relax when, in the first week of November, the republicans and their people's armies began to advance on Canton from Hong Kong and Macau? On November 5, as the revolutionaries captured Shih-ch'i,[*] their first county capital in Kwangtung, the guilds and charitable institutions in Canton received a letter from the republican headquarters in Hong Kong warning them that Governor-General Chang's actions had made a bloodless takeover impossible.[91] The merchants promptly went to Chang once more to impress upon him their anxiety for the safety of the city.[92] Realizing the futility of further resistance and fearful of foreign intervention, the Governor-General finally bowed to the wishes of the merchants. On November 8 he sent his sec-

---

[*] See the account by Winston Hsieh in this volume.

retary to meet with the merchants and arrange for the transition to re-publican rule.[93] That afternoon, Chang issued a public proclamation ending the equivocation and declaring that "in this national crisis a majority of the people favor independence."[94] The next day, after Chang had secretly escaped to Hong Kong, a much-enlarged provincial assembly met formally to declare Kwangtung independent and to welcome the revolutionaries to Canton.[95] The day after that, Hu Han-min arrived from Hong Kong to take charge for the republicans.[96] Despite the attempts of the gentry and officials to turn the occasion to their own advantage, the merchants were thus the ones who steered Canton through the revolutionary crisis.

No one should conclude from this that the republican revolution in Canton was by any means a bourgeois revolution. The merchants, newly emergent and still weak as a political force, did not dominate the new regime. The system of home rule for the province, which replaced the traditional system of rule by officials from outside of the province, bene-fited the gentry at least as much as, and probably more than, the merchants. The first republican governors of Kwangtung, Hu Han-min and Ch'en Chiung-ming, both came from the old gentry class.

Nevertheless, the revolution had broken the gentry-officials' traditional grip on political power. The new regime was far more responsive to the interests and needs of the merchants than the previous regime had ever been. The Canton merchants, for example, received permission at once to form the volunteer corps that they had requested unavailingly for so long. The Provincial Assembly was greatly enlarged to provide for merchant and other non-gentry representation. Moreover, the new regime was much more inclined than its predecessor to consider the special needs of Canton. One of its first acts was to begin tearing down the city walls. Also, in the elections for the provisional Provincial Assembly that replaced the old gentry-dominated Assembly in December 1911, it designated Canton and Honam island as a single electoral unit separate from the rest of Nan-hai and P'an-yü counties, entitled to twenty representatives of its own.[97] The administrative division of the city, however, continued down to 1918.

In summary, for all of their weaknesses, the merchants were the ones who determined the fate of the revolution in Canton. The revolution succeeded in 1911 because of their support, including heavy financial support in the first days of the new regime. It was to fail in 1913 because of the withdrawal of their support.[98]

Peasant Insurrection and the Marketing Hierarchy in the Canton Delta, 1911

WINSTON HSIEH

In the wake of the Wuchang Uprising of October 10, 1911, many thousands of peasant bands in the Canton delta region rose at their local market towns and marched toward the cities. In a few weeks some of these poorly equipped but enthusiastic "people's armies" (*min-chün*) had reached the regional capital of Canton, while others had taken over county capitals throughout the delta. It would be an exaggeration to say that the armies conquered Canton; they simply swarmed over it unresisted. For several weeks they dominated the Canton scene. Carried away by iconoclastic fervor, some of them stunned the public by attempting to destroy the Temple of the City God and by other acts of violence. From surrounding towns came the more alarming news that the rebels controlled many county governments, that some were forcing travelers to cut off their pigtails, and that others had gone so far as to attack the houses of the privileged gentry.

The spontaneity and destructive power of the people's armies astonished many contemporary Western observers, but in local and historical context they seem less extraordinary. Peasant disturbances and mass uprisings are a familiar element of local politics in the Canton delta. Gazetteers and other Chinese sources record numerous instances of collective violence during the century preceding 1911, including intervillage and interlineage feuds, mass attacks on tax collectors, luddite destruction of silk-reeling machines, fighting between local militia and government troops, and secret-society rebellions. Information is far richer and more specific on the people's armies of 1911 than on dissident forces in earlier years, thanks to the special attention given the Revolution of 1911 in Chinese historiography.[1] Thus, the case of the people's armies is a strategic one for illuminating collective violence and the wide distribution of paramilitary forces in the delta region. The study of people's armies in 1911 also provides historical perspective on the armed peasant forces that were to play such a prominent role during the Republican period in the revolts against Yüan Shih-k'ai and various warlord regimes, in the conflicts between communist-directed peasant associations and traditional militia organizations on the eve of the Northern Expedition, and in the anti-Japanese guerrilla activity along the Pearl river tributaries during World War II. Specifically, what we learn about the geographic origins, composition, main sources of support, and basic motivations of the dissident peasant forces of 1911 is often applicable to the dissident peasant forces of later decades as well.*

Since information on given local uprisings during 1911–12 is usually incomplete and superficial, I have fleshed it out with socioeconomic data from local gazetteers and geographic data from large-scale local maps both contemporary and of more recent vintage. Such supplementary data not only help correct for the errors inevitable in such sources as the reminiscences of participants, but also shed light on many otherwise isolated or seemingly insignificant events. Most important, however, tracing the movements of insurrectionary armies on the map of local marketing systems helps to reveal the channels through which these bands were drawn to the centers of conflict and the patterns of mobilization at various levels of the marketing hierarchy.

These historical and methodological considerations underlay my selection of the two case studies presented below: the Shih-ch'i uprising in Hsiang-shan (now Chung-shan) county and the Kuan-lan uprising in Hsin-an (now Pao-an) county. With the help of five consecutive editions of Hsiang-shan gazetteers, spanning 250 years of the county's history, I have been able to reconstruct the trend of urbanization in the city of Shih-ch'i, where a major uprising was staged in 1911. The second case involves a movement encompassing several towns near the border of the Hong Kong New Territories. Using a recently unearthed daily chronicle on the uprising in conjunction with large-scale local maps, I have been able to demonstrate the central role of market towns in local uprisings and to delineate the pattern of revolutionary mobilization.

The Shih-ch'i Uprising

On the eve of the uprising, the secret organization of the revolutionary party, the T'ung-meng Hui, had infiltrated much of the county of Hsiang-

* This chapter is part of an ongoing research project on the Canton delta region. For substantive comments and advice, my thanks go to the two editors of this volume and to those participating in the Canton Delta Seminar at the University of Hong Kong in 1973.

shan, which bordered on the Portuguese colony of Macau and was cut through by many waterways connecting delta cities with Hong Kong (see Map 1). More specifically, Hsiang-shan students and émigrés in Hong Kong, Macau, and Honolulu had used their family and personal connections to build a secret network in Lung-tu, an area west of and commercially dependent on the central market of Shih-ch'i, the county capital of Hsiang-shan. Naval officers assisted the revolutionaries by smuggling weapons into the walled city, and revolutionary fervor was so intense that the commander of the militia and the chief of the county magistrate's bodyguards had both joined the T'ung-meng Hui. An enterprising Shih-ch'i merchant, certain that a local uprising would follow the Wuchang Uprising within days, made up a batch of several hundred republican flags for sale.

The T'ung-meng Hui's clandestine activities were not limited to the Shih-ch'i area. Contacts were maintained with pirates in the town of Hsiao-lan to the northwest. Efforts were also made to infiltrate the New Army at Ch'ien-shan, a military stronghold overlooking the Macau border. Following the T'ung-meng Hui's decision to appeal to the local armed bands for revolutionary action, a headquarters was set up at Macau to coordinate and finance the various activities across the Hsiang-shan border. On November 2, the pirates made the first move, taking over Hsiao-lan; the next day, a band of militia sent by the magistrate to suppress the pirates joined them instead. Two days later, the major uprising took place at Shih-ch'i.[2]

Mobilization of the insurrectionary troops. The peasant bands from the Lung-tu area first gathered at their local centers and then marched to Shih-ch'i. When the bands met in front of the Temple of the Dragon Emperor at the Shih-ch'i market, they were organized into two brigades, one marching into the walled city by the West Gate, the other by the South Gate. Because the militia officers at the West Gate and the garrison forces at the county magistrate's yamen cooperated with them, they took over the city without difficulty. The *hsün-fang-ying* patrol forces attempted to resist at the South Gate, but they were easily routed and their commander was slain on the spot.[3] By this time the uprising had developed into a spectacle, with thousands of people watching along the riverside. The county magistrate, who had studied in Japan and was sympathetic to the ideas of revolution and change, made a public pledge to support the republican cause and to remain in his post for the transition period. Gentry and merchant leaders with lineage ties to the rebels offered to raise funds. For the office of the new government, the ancestral hall of the Kao lineage was preferred to the county yamen, symbol of the old regime.

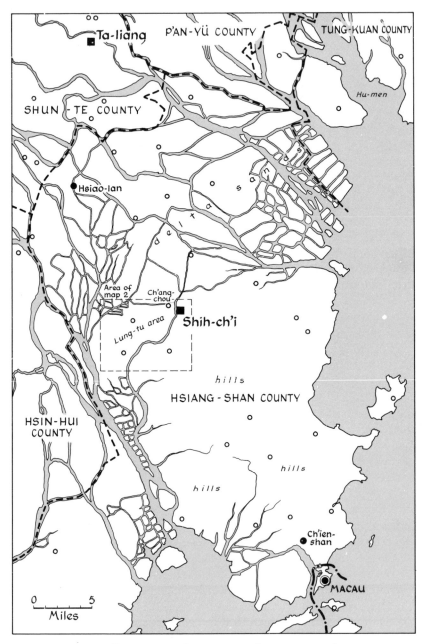

MAP 1. HSIANG-SHAN COUNTY AND SURROUNDING AREA

The fall of Shih-ch'i alarmed the provincial authorities in Canton, who dispatched a gunboat to suppress the uprising. But the people's armies had both banks of the river near the Shih-ch'i market under heavy guard, and when New Army forces under revolutionary command arrived from Ch'ien-shan the gunboat left. Most Chinese accounts of the uprising shift their focus at this point, leaving Shih-ch'i itself and going on to relate how the New Army troops were reorganized into the Hsiang-shan Army (*Hsiang-chün*), how the Army acted in Canton, and how it was incorporated into the expeditionary force sent to fight the Ch'ing army at Nanking. Our concern, however, is with what the process of mobilizing a people's army was actually like, and for this we must piece together data on the local uprising and analyze them in the light of background material provided by local gazetteers.

The reminiscences of Cheng Pi-an, a T'ung-meng Hui leader, provide crucial information: the names of the commanders of the ten major bands participating in the uprising, the names of the communities where the bands originated, and the surnames of the majority of the soldiers in each band (see Table 1). The correspondence of followers' and leaders' surnames suggests that the bands were organized along lineage lines; and indeed Cheng remarks that the band from An-t'ang consisted of the young men from the Lin lineage, the Hsi-chiao band of those from the Liu lineage, and so on. In each case the lineage cited by Cheng for which documentary sources are available is shown to be the principal lineage of the community in question.[4]

The impressive number of volunteers from each of these lineages suggests that each band was supported by the whole lineage. Cheng estimates the total number of volunteers involved in the uprising at between 2,000 and 3,000 men. Since it is unlikely that a smaller number could have halted the gunboat from Canton, Cheng's estimate seems reasonable. Thus the average lineage would have provided some 200 to 300 volunteers, which should cover almost all the young males in a local lineage who were capable of fighting. In earlier times such a massive turnout would have occurred only in a major lineage feud.

Cheng's account also suggests that the leaders whose names he gives, though belonging to the lineages involved, may have been titular rather than actual commanders of the bands, since many of them no longer resided in their native towns. Indeed, they were, in a sense, outside agitators. As Cheng recalls, some were activists from overseas Chinese communities who had hurried home to participate in the revolution. Some had been studying in Hong Kong. Probably all of them were T'ung-meng Hui members, for otherwise Cheng would not have been so likely to remember all their names.

TABLE 1. MAJOR BANDS PARTICIPATING IN THE
SHIH-CH'I UPRISING, 1911

Local community	Dominant lineage	Band commanders
An-t'ang	Lin	Lin Hsiu Lin Shao-yü Lin Yao-nan
Hsi-chiao	Liu	Liu Cho-t'ang Liu Wei-ch'ih Liu Jih-san
Nan-wen	Hsiao	Hsiao — - —
Lung-chü-huan	Liu	Liu Han-hua
Hsiang-chiao	P'eng	P'eng Hsiung-chia
Hao-t'u	Kao	Kao Sheng-hu
Shen-ming-t'ing	Yang	Yang Tsao-yün
K'an-hsia	Liang	Liang Shou
Kang-t'ou	Hu	Hu K'ung-ch'u
Ch'ang-chou	Huang	Huang Yao-han Huang P'u-ming

SOURCE: *Hsin hai ko ming hui i lu*, 2: 338–42.

Thus the mobilization can be reconstructed as follows. T'ung-meng
Hui agitators were sent to local communities where they had family
ties to win over the leaders who controlled the lineages' fighting bands,
to spread revolutionary propaganda, and to prepare for the uprising.
When the call finally came, they marched with the local bands, armed
with guns acquired for use in the local feuds, to the Temple of the
Dragon Emperor in Shih-ch'i. (Thus, two prominent T'ung-meng Hui
members, Lin Chin-hun, the top leader of the uprising, and his cousin
Lin Chün-fu, were both natives of An-t'ang; and the Lins from An-t'ang
formed the largest band that fought at Shih-ch'i, numbering over 500.)
The success of the uprising was undoubtedly furthered by money from
Hong Kong and Macau and by the persuasive power of republican
agitators, but there would have been no uprising without personal access
to the existing "war machine" for lineage-based feuds.

It should be pointed out that this pattern of mobilization has its limitations. In the immediate neighborhood of the villages that produced
revolutionary forces, many other communities played no part in the uprising (Map 2). While the revolutionaries' lack of access to the lineage-
sponsored armies in these communities provides a major explanation,
certain questions remain. Why, for instance, did such powerful communities as Hsi-chiao and Shen-ming-t'ing fail to sway their neighbors and,

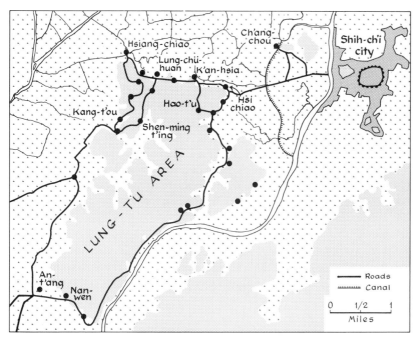

MAP 2. PLACES OF ORIGIN OF THE MAJOR BANDS PARTICIPATING IN THE SHIH-CH'I UPRISING, 1911. Areas over 20 feet in elevation are shaded. Settlements from which few or no participants originated are not labeled.

in particular, how does one account for the inactivity of the intervillage militia bureau, which had come into existence in the mid-nineteenth century specifically to coordinate local forces? The events of 1911 seem to indicate that control of such forces had shifted from the general militia office to individual villages. Could this shift, then, be taken as an index to the general decline of the traditional, intervillage dependence of the area under the modern impacts from the Shih-ch'i market? What looms large in the background of the revolutionary mobilization seems to be a situation close to what Skinner found in his rural marketing study: As individual villages were increasingly pulled to the modern urban trading system, "much of their communal significance devolves on component villages, and a gradual change in emphasis places the self-interest of each little community above intervillage cooperation."[5] To grasp the nature and scope of such changes, we must investigate the urbanization process in the Shih-ch'i marketing system during the decades preceding 1911.

Differential urbanization. As a comparison of Table 1 and Map 2 will show, nine of the ten lineage-sponsored bands involved in the Shih-ch'i rising came from an area traditionally known as Lung-yen-tu, or simply Lung-tu, and the tenth from an area between Lung-tu and Shih-ch'i called Ch'ang-chou. Although the Lung-tu and Ch'ang-chou areas were separated from the market by the Shih-ch'i "sea," a major branch of the Pearl river system in the delta region, all evidence suggests that both areas had belonged for centuries to a local marketing system dependent on Shih-ch'i.* For instance, the 1911 map of Shih-ch'i shows five major wharves along the Shih-ch'i sea: three of these were apparently for the long-distance steamer and junk lines connecting Shih-ch'i with Shun-te, Macau, and Hong Kong; but two were for local ferries to Ch'ang-chou and Lung-tu. A map in the 1759 gazetteer shows a canal used by Lung-tu ferryboats to reach Shih-ch'i, which indicates that such ties across the Shih-ch'i "sea" had developed long before the arrival of steamers.

On the other hand, there is no record of major bands coming to join the uprising from any place outside the Shih-ch'i marketing area. The pirates who had taken over Hsiao-lan a few days earlier showed no interest in joining the Shih-ch'i insurrection, nor was there any response from the area known as "Sixteen Delta Sands of the Eastern Sea" (*Tung-hai shih-liu-sha*), an area of alluvial land to the northeast of Shih-ch'i, where the local self-defense organization had probably the best fighting capacity in the county. Since it is hard to imagine the T'ung-meng Hui overlooking this potential source of support, we must look elsewhere for an explanation. One is provided by the local gazetteers of Hsiang-shan and Shun-te counties, which reveal that although the Sixteen Delta Sands area was officially under the jurisdiction of Hsiang-shan county, the local militia organizations had actually been under the control of gentry leaders in neighboring Shun-te county for decades, if not centuries. Hsiang-shan magistrates had repeatedly attempted to wrest

---

* In its narrowest sense "Shih-ch'i" designated the market district that centered on the Grand Temple of Shih-ch'i and extended from the waterfront of the Shih-ch'i sea to the West Gate of the walled city. This is the district loosely described in gazetteers and in Tables 2 and 3 as "Outside the West Gate." However, the Shih-ch'i market directly served a major sectoral marketing system within the city trading system, whose precise boundaries are difficult to determine but which clearly extended westward from the West Gate, across the river, and through Ch'ang-chou to the Lung-tu villages. I call this system the "Shih-ch'i marketing system."

The Shih-ch'i market also provided services, as a higher-level market, to the less developed sectoral marketing communities outside the walled city's other three gates, thus gaining such dominant status that its name was commonly extended to the city as a whole. In formal administrative terms, the city was sometimes referred to as Hsiang-shan because it was the county capital; but in local references and among Hsiang-shan emigrants I interviewed in Hong Kong and elsewhere the city is called Shih-ch'i.

TABLE 2. HOUSEHOLD DISTRIBUTION IN SHIH-CH'I

| District | Kind of household | | Total | District percentage of total urban population |
	Regular	Irregular		
Walled city	803	239	1,042	8%
Outside the West Gate	4,341	683	5,024	36
Outside the South Gate	2,486	484	2,970	21
Outside the North Gate	1,778	690	2,468	18
Outside the East Gate	1,294	366	1,660	12
Hou-hsing Street (northwest of the city)	659	69	728	5
Total	11,361	2,531	13,892	100%

SOURCE: The 1910 census survey, cited in HSHCHP, 1924 ed., ch. 2, pp. 1b–2a.
NOTE: "Irregular" households are those HSHCHP designated *fu-hu*, which seems to mean either recent settlers or temporary residents whose officially recognized native places were elsewhere. The disproportionate number of such households in the northern district is probably to be accounted for by the location in that district of the *hsün-fang-ying* provincial patrol forces, for families of the soldiers could have been counted as *fu-hu*.

control of this richly productive area from Shun-te leaders, but to no avail.[6] Thus the local bands of the Sixteen Delta Sands were indifferent to the Shih-ch'i uprising because they were controlled by Shun-te gentry leaders.

Seemingly, then, the Shih-ch'i uprising was confined to a single marketing community, namely the Shih-ch'i sectoral marketing system, and there was no spontaneous response from other sectoral marketing communities even within the large trading system centered on Shih-ch'i. This case fits the general proposition that revolutionary energy, the explosive potential underlying the uprisings during the autumn of 1911, was concentrated in certain marketing communities rather than evenly permeating the peasantry of the Canton delta.

Why should the Shih-ch'i marketing community have been more readily mobilized for revolution than adjacent communities? To answer this question, it is necessary to investigate the development of Shih-ch'i during the decades preceding the revolution, during which the city grew to some 14,000 households, with a population of around 70,000. Table 2 shows an enormous degree of urban expansion by 1910: over 90 percent of the population lived outside the walled city.

Map 3 shows Shih-ch'i in 1911. The district lying outside the West Gate, in which the Shih-ch'i market was located, was the most heavily settled part of the city, with a total of over 5,000 households, almost five times more than within the walled city. Here also were the thickest concentration of streets and the city's more modern institutions, e.g. the post office, telegraph station, and Western hospital. The data in Table 3,

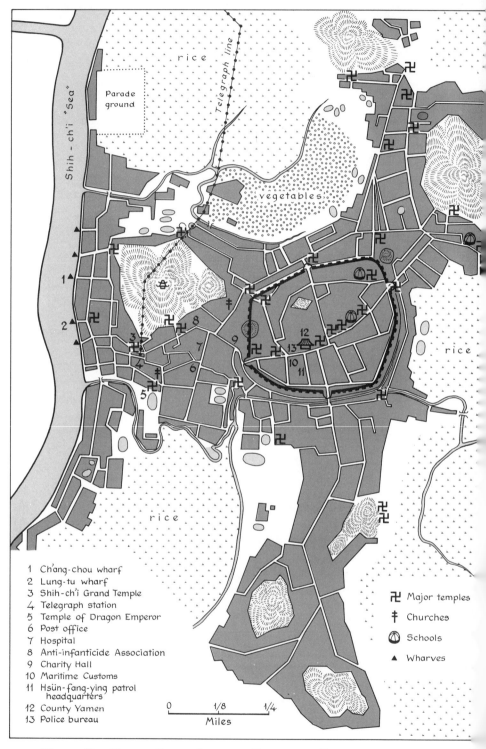

1 Ch'ang-chou wharf
2 Lung-tu wharf
3 Shih-ch'i Grand Temple
4 Telegraph station
5 Temple of Dragon Emperor
6 Post office
7 Hospital
8 Anti-infanticide Association
9 Charity Hall
10 Maritime Customs
11 Hsün-fang-ying patrol
   headquarters
12 County Yamen
13 Police bureau

꒯ Major temples

✝ Churches

⊛ Schools

▲ Wharves

0   1/8   1/4
Miles

MAP 3. THE CITY OF SHIH-CH'I ON THE EVE OF THE REVOLUTION

TABLE 3. GROWTH OF DISTRICTS OUTSIDE THE WALLS OF SHIH-CH'I
(*Number of li*)

District	1673	1750	1827	1873	1911
Outside the West Gate	1	10	15	15	30
Outside the North Gate	2	5	13	15	8
Outside the East Gate	4	9	10	11	6
Outside the South Gate	12	14	14	21	21
Total	19	38	52	62	65

SOURCES: HSHCHP, 1673, 1750, 1827, 1873 and 1924, sponsored by Shen Liang-han, Pao Yü, Chu Huai, T'ien Ming-yao, and Li Shih-chin, respectively. Although the latest edition (by *Li*) was published in 1924, most of its data precede 1911.

NOTE: *Li* refers to a territorial unit whose basic function in the late Ch'ing period was probably the allocation of tax quotas.

taken from five successive editions of the county gazetteer, point up the rapid growth of the western district in the decades immediately preceding 1911. In fact, whereas all four suburbs expanded during the two centuries preceding 1873, growth after that year was limited to the western district.

The spectacular growth of the western district and the simultaneous attrition of the other districts were perhaps opposite aspects of the same development. It often happens that when the introduction of more efficient transportation favors trade at a particular location, commercial facilities in nearby centers relocate; thus the western district seems to have absorbed many of the marketing functions of the northern and eastern districts. With marketing activities now increasingly shifted to the western district, the center of gravity of the city also shifted there. This helps explain the rebels' easy takeover of the other districts of the city following the conquest of the Shih-ch'i market.

The impact of commercialization. A major factor in the rapid growth of the Shih-ch'i market was the introduction of steamboats. By virtue of its location, the western district monopolized steamshipping, and between 1873 and 1911 the city's major wharves increased from three to five. The map in the 1873 gazetteer shows a cluster of market streets surrounding the Grand Temple, with shops spreading along the roads connecting the temple with the wharves and with the West Gate; to the south of these streets there were still many vacant areas marked with the character *t'ang* (ponds). On the 1911 map, not only has the market expanded enormously, but all the areas previously marked *t'ang* are filled with streets and residential lanes. Nothing like the same growth occurred in the other districts.*

---

* The tremendous impact of steamboats on transportation and marketing in China was due not merely to their shipping capacity and speed, but also to their low cost

Even prior to the introduction of modern transportation, Hsiang-shan county exported agricultural products to the urban centers of Shun-te and other delta counties. The introduction of steamboats on the Shih-ch'i "sea" encouraged farmers near the city to grow rice primarily as a commercial crop. By 1911 the seasonal export of rice from Hsiang-shan reached such high levels—an annual value of over five million taels, or almost three-quarters of the county's total exports—that some 300,000 taels' worth of cheaper Siamese rice had to be imported annually for local consumption.[7] Shih-ch'i had thus developed into a leading transit port for rice on the delta, and Lung-tu merchants had become prominent in the rice trade, as they are in Hong Kong to this day. In addition to its high-quality rice, the Lung-tu area was noted for the production of raw silk and silk cocoons and of fruits and vegetables, and exports of these products also initially increased with the growth of steam transport. Commercialization was particularly marked in the Lung-tu area, not only because of its intimate ties to the Shih-ch'i market but also because of the favorable ecological setting of the village communities in question. Almost all of those involved in the Shih-ch'i uprising were situated on the outer rim of a hilly area—note the twenty-foot contour on Map 2—between the level fields where rice and mulberry trees were cultivated and the hills where fruits and vegetables were grown.

Precisely because Lung-tu villages had responded vigorously to the initial steady expansion of commercial opportunities, they were particularly vulnerable to subsequent fluctuations in the export markets. Indeed, Lung-tu was hard hit in the first decade of the twentieth century not only by instability in the fruit and vegetable trade but by a secular decline in silk exports. A major blow came with the opening of the Canton-Kowloon railroad in 1906, which made it possible to ship Siamese rice to various delta cities directly from Hong Kong and greatly reduced demand for the higher-priced rice from Hsiang-shan county.

Resentment against the Ch'ing government. Considering the impressive and long-sustained urban growth of the Shih-ch'i marketing community, one may well question whether the economic setbacks immedi-

---

per ton-mile—a factor hardly noticed until J. Lossing Buck's study of China's rural economy supplied the relevant data. Although one may question whether Buck's 1929–33 data are applicable to the late Ch'ing period, steamboat shipping clearly cost far less than the two common forms of transportation on the Canton delta: flat-bottomed junks and human runners carrying loads balanced at both ends of a pole. Using Buck's data (*Land Utilization in China, Statistics* [Nanking, 1937], pp. 346–47, Tables 3 and 4), G. William Skinner calculates the following comparative costs in silver dollars per ton-mile for medium distance transportation in early twentieth-century China: pole-carrying runner, 1.39; junk, 0.21; railroad, 0.09; steamboat, 0.08.

ately preceding 1911 warranted so extreme a response as an uprising. But the absolute measurement of such setbacks is far less important than their perceived effect, exacerbated in this case by the dashing of expectations nurtured by a prolonged period of prosperity. T'ung-meng Hui agitators in the county made every effort to blame its economic troubles on the evil rule of the Manchu dynasty, and to transform the widespread dissatisfaction into revolutionary action. Meanwhile, the representative of that dynasty in Kwangtung, as if playing into the revolutionaries' hands, pushed through a series of reformist programs to strengthen political control, build up new armies, and increase revenues. To cite one especially unpopular instance, a province-wide police system, an unprecedented innovation, was established in 1910. In Hsiang-shan county this meant a corps of 515 men in eleven bureaus— seven in Shih-ch'i and four more in the local market towns, including one in Lung-tu and one in Ch'ang-chou.[8]

All these reforms, of course, cost money. Indeed, the form of governmental oppression most acutely felt by Hsiang-shan people during the late Ch'ing period was the seemingly endless tax increases.* Tax riots were frequent in the Canton delta, as elsewhere, in the years before 1911, and on occasion census surveyors, mistaken for tax collectors, were beaten up.[9] An episode in June 1910 attests the widespread resentment concerning taxes in the Shih-ch'i area.[10] When a bureau was established in the city to collect the newly imposed "levies on witches, priests, monks, and nuns," a group of priests and monks came together on June 7 to organize resistance; envoys were dispatched to surrounding towns and villages. On June 12, a mob—many from Lung-tu—formed in front of the bureau and began demolishing the building. About 9 P.M., when the *hsün-fang-ying* patrol forces moved in to back up the local police, the mob stoned the battalion commander, knocked his sedan chair to pieces, and beat up the chief of police. The new tax bureau was completely destroyed by 10 P.M., when the mob, now swollen to several thousands, moved on to assault the house of Ch'en Shan-yü, collector of the taxes for coastal defense and the excise tax on pottery. At midnight, when Ch'en's house was demolished, the mob turned to the salt-monopoly

* For a dramatic illustration of the Ch'ing government's aggressive and persistent efforts to tighten administrative control in Kwangtung during the years leading up to 1911, see my "Triads, Salt Smugglers, and Local Uprisings: Observations on the Social and Economic Background of the Waichow Revolution of 1911," in Jean Chesneaux, ed., *Popular Movements and Secret Societies in China, 1840–1950* (Stanford, Calif.: Stanford University Press, 1972), pp. 145–64. The drastic increase in salt taxes in the Waichow region in 1909–11, which cut deeply into the well-established and secret-society-based salt trade, looms unmistakably in the background of the Waichow uprising.

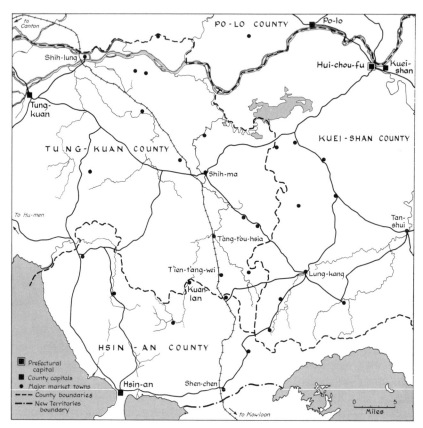

MAP 4. SETTING OF THE KUAN-LAN UPRISING

bureau, which was looted and burned. This riot dramatizes the widespread resentment against the Ch'ing government, a feeling that must
have contributed to the T'ung-meng Hui's rapid success in raising
people's armies throughout the Canton delta.

The Kuan-lan Uprising

The background of the second uprising we shall examine had much in
common with that of the first. Bordering on the British colony of Hong
Kong—in fact, with a large portion of its land recently carved off as part
of the Kowloon New Territories—Hsin-an county had been as directly
exposed to Western influences as Hsiang-shan. The impact of urbanization and commercialization was also felt strongly here, if only because of
the demand for servicing metropolitan Hong Kong. And finally, the newly

built Canton-Kowloon railroad had brought economic reverses to certain districts of both counties. In particular, the Kuan-lan market, where the forces of the uprising were first rallied, had recently felt the competition of a booming new market in nearby T'ien-t'ang-wei, the railroad station; and many other market towns involved in the Kuan-lan uprising, as we shall see, were also located on or near the railroad.

Possibly, then, our explanation of the Shih-ch'i uprising may be applicable to Kuan-lan: namely, that insurrectionary forces tended to appear in those marketing systems in which expectations raised during a sustained period of urbanization and commercialization were dashed by a sudden sharp reversal of economic fortunes. Although there is abundant documentation for a detailed study of urbanization in Hsin-an county in the decades preceding 1911, I would prefer to use my space here to explore some other facets of the Kuan-lan uprisings. In particular, thanks to the recent publication of a daily chronicle kept by the commander of the revolutionary troops and annotated by a fellow participant, both members of the T'ung-meng Hui, we have a rare opportunity to observe in detail the actual development of an uprising and the metamorphosis of a people's army. The next four paragraphs offer a résumé of this chronicle, and much of what follows is based on it.[11]

The initial uprising was staged in Kuan-lan on October 30; the major battle was won in a neighboring town, Lung-kang, on November 3. On their way back to Kuan-lan from this battle on November 4 the revolutionaries were ambushed by a band from the town of Tan-shui, which attempted to take custody of the captured government troops. A patrol officer from the *hsün-fang-ying* troops stationed in Hsin-an city defected to the rebels at Kuan-lan on November 5, bringing 80 soldiers with him.

On November 6 news arrived that the county authorities at Hsin-an city were prepared to surrender, but before Kuan-lan forces reached the county capital peasant bands from other towns had already poured into the walled city. The revolutionary forces, after reestablishing order, left only a few garrison forces there; the main force departed on November 7 for the prosperous town of Shen-chen, some 60 *li* to the east. In exchange for generous donations from Shen-chen merchants, the revolutionary leaders assigned a band of 40 men to police the local market.

Two days later the revolutionary troops started north toward Canton along the Canton-Kowloon railroad. Their first major target was Shih-ma (now Chang-mu-t'ou), a flourishing market town at the junction of the principal roads connecting the Waichow region with the railroad. Before they reached Shih-ma, however, they heard rumors that routed Manchu battalions were approaching from Waichow. The revolutionaries accordingly stopped and concentrated their forces at T'ang-t'ou-hsia (or T'ang-hsia), a big market town on the rail line.

The next morning (November 10), when they found the rumors were false, the bands poured into Shih-ma. On November 11 they occupied the larger market town of Shih-lung, located at the junction of the East River and the railroad to Canton. That same day they received the news that the provincial capital had been taken by other revolutionary forces. The chronicle ends with a very brief account of the Kuan-lan troops' march to Canton, where they joined forces with other revolutionary troops.

The role of market towns. The strategic importance of market towns and their central role in such local uprisings can be seen even in this very sketchy account of events. The two revolutionary chroniclers obviously took the towns rather than the villages as their points of reference. As far as they could recall, it was in the *towns* that various kinds of support were secured; from one *town* to another that the military moves were directed; and over the security or control of *towns* that battles were fought. The chronicle mentions eight towns, not including the county capital of Hsin-an, but not a single village.

Indeed, individual villages seem to have no identity of their own. The term *hsiang-min*, meaning the people of a community, invariably appears after the name of a market town, not a village: thus "Kuan-lan hsiang min" for participants from the area around the town of Kuan-lan, "Lung-kang hsiang min" for those from around the town of Lung-kang. This suggests that what mattered to our chroniclers was the marketing community, the town and its dependent villages as a unit. Serving as the node of a marketing system in peaceful times, the market town also played the central role in revolutionary operations within that system. Further, as we shall see, the subsequent development of the mobilization process reflected the hierarchy of marketing centers, which was of course not identical with the formal hierarchy of administrative centers. Let us begin with the operations at the market town of Kuan-lan.

The revolutionaries who came from Hong Kong to organize the uprising brought with them only revolutionary ideals, enthusiasm, and a handful of Hong Kong paper currency. Presumably they also had some preliminary contacts with local elements. But they needed men, weapons, and funds, which had to be raised in the Kuan-lan area in the few days following the uprising. A local theatrical troupe made the first donation, and many merchant households in Kuan-lan also contributed. The headquarters of the revolutionary bands was a large store at the market, borrowed from someone who was presumably a clansman of the band commander. Volunteers were recruited from neighboring villages, and a loan of one hundred Mauser rifles was secured.

As the movement developed, Kuan-lan changed from a launching pad for the uprising to a center for revolutionary operations. As soon as a sizable band had been organized, a mass rally was held in the town and brigades were dispatched to occupy strategic points, to attack other towns, and to ambush government troops. News of other uprisings was received and pondered; negotiations with envoys from the county magistrate were conducted there. After the main forces had marched to Lung-kang, Kuan-lan was still retained as a logistical center. As soon as they had won the battle at Lung-kang, the bands returned to Kuan-lan, along with hundreds of captured government soldiers.

Kuan-lan's importance was to diminish after the county capital was taken, however, and especially after the revolutionary troops had moved on to the big and prosperous town of Shen-chen. By then the movement had shifted from the local level to higher levels of the marketing hierarchy. While the revolutionary leaders were busily engaged in planning the march to Canton, many local bands left Shen-chen for home.

To judge from the presence of at least one store large enough to serve as a revolutionary headquarters, from the ability of local merchants to contribute handsomely to the revolutionary coffers, and from the existence of a theatrical troupe in the town, Kuan-lan was evidently a local economic center of some importance. That it was also a natural political center is clear from the revolutionaries' "instant" acquisition of men and weapons from surrounding villages and perhaps especially the loan of a hundred rifles overnight at a time when guns were considered more precious than a villager's life. Whatever form of personal credit may have been involved, it worked effectively: on the eve of the revolutionaries' entering of Canton, the rifles were duly returned.

The Kuan-lan community. As we have seen with the "Sixteen Delta Sands," the alignment of a natural area like the one dependent on Kuan-lan has no necessary relation to the boundaries of formal administrative units. The movement of local bands in the Kuan-lan area during the thirteen-day crisis clearly points to a case of cross-cutting alignments.

Kuan-lan in 1911 was located very near, and possibly right on, the border between Hsin-an and Tung-kuan counties, and was within walking distance of the border of Kuei-shan county (later known as Hui-yang).* At the next level up, Kuan-lan can also be seen to lie near the

---

* An 1892 provincial atlas places Kuan-lan in Tung-kuan county (see Liao T'ing-cheng et al., eds., *Kuang-tung yü ti t'u shuo* [Explanatory notes for the

border of two prefectures, namely Kuang-chou prefecture, which included Hsin-an and Tung-kuan counties, and Hui-chou prefecture, which included Kuei-shan county. The local marketing community dependent on Kuan-lan naturally fell within the administrative domain of these three counties and two prefectures. As our chronicle clearly indicates, the administrative authorities took Kuan-lan as part of Hsin-an county; but trade and commerce in Kuan-lan were traditionally oriented toward T'ang-t'ou-hsia, a big market town downstream, and, more recently, toward T'ien-t'ang-wei, the nearest railroad station, where a new market was flourishing. Both T'ang-t'ou-hsia and T'ien-t'ang-wei were on the Tung-kuan side of the county border. It is obvious that Kuan-lan's marketing activities could not have been confined to a single county. Both Hsin-an and Tung-kuan counties (and probably even Kuei-shan county as well) shared the territory and revenues of this prosperous marketing community.

The battle at Lung-kang and its aftermath further demonstrate to us, if further evidence is needed, that the local marketing community around Kuan-lan and Lung-kang functioned as a natural political unit regardless of administrative boundaries. Government forces had been drawn to the area initially by the disturbing news that massive people's armies were gathering at Tan-shui in preparation for a siege of Waichow. In order to attack the Tan-shui bands from the rear, a battalion of the *hsün-fang-ying* patrol forces set out from the Bogue, passing by Kuan-lan en route.

To the T'ung-meng Hui leaders from Hong Kong, the prospective siege of Waichow by the Tan-shui forces was exciting news; but to their local followers at Kuan-lan, both Tan-shui and Waichow seemed too remote to be of any immediate concern. The rumor of approaching troops, however, was another matter. The Kuan-lan leaders' first reaction was to dispatch a band of one hundred men to intercept the troops. When they were told that this band was far outnumbered by the invading forces, they followed up by mobilizing all the fighting bands available from Kuan-lan.

Despite their superior arms, the government troops fought only halfheartedly. After an initial skirmish lasting about half an hour, the troops pulled away and raced toward their assigned destination at Tan-shui.

Kwangtung atlas], 1892, ch. 1, p. 20b), as does the Tung-kuan county gazetteer of 1919. However, an earlier Hsin-an county gazetteer places Kuan-lan in Hsin-an county, and a provincial survey conducted in 1934 indicates that jurisdiction over the town was then still disputed between these two counties (see local maps in Min cheng t'ing, ed., *Kuang-tung ch'üan sheng ti fang chi yao* [A province-wide survey of local conditions in Kwangtung], 1934).

This move suggested weakness and invited attack from a local mob in the Lung-kang area. Before nightfall the government troops were encircled on a small hill south of the market of Lung-kang. The local people generously aided the fighters from Kuan-lan, providing them with food and bedding, lighting the hillside with an ocean of torches, and finally cutting off the water supply to the hillside where the government troops were encamped. The troops surrendered the next day.

The enthusiastic support given the Kuan-lan revolutionaries by the people of Lung-kang contrasts strongly with their cool and distant attitude toward Tan-shui, even though Lung-kang was in the same county and prefecture as Tan-shui. In spite of the strategic importance of the battle at Waichow, the Kuan-lan and Lung-kang bands made no move to join forces with the Tan-shui bands. Their first concern was with the security of their own community. They were also attracted by the soldiers' weapons, and when the Kuan-lan leaders marched into the government encampment following the surrender, they found that rifles and ammunition had been looted by the Lung-kang mob.

My informants from the area tell me that the Lung-kang dialect is closely similar to that of Kuan-lan, but different from that of Tan-shui; that old feuds have left lingering hostility between the inhabitants of Lung-kang and Tan-shui; and that the county line was redrawn in the 1950's so as to include the town of Lung-kang in Pao-an (previously Hsin-an) county. The hostility between the two communities may be seen in the above-mentioned incident following the victory at Lung-kang, when a band from Tan-shui attacked the Kuan-lan bands on their way home and tried to take away their government prisoners. The fighting was called off only after the revolutionary leaders from the two sides reached a compromise: those soldiers who were familiar with the Bogue fortress should stay with the Kuan-lan bands to assist in future attacks on the fortress, and the rest might go with the Tan-shui band. The Tan-shui revolutionary leaders could not dissuade their followers from attacking until it was clear that the prisoners no longer had their rifles.

The metamorphosis of the revolutionary forces. The Kuan-lan uprising may be divided into two phases. In the initial phase, i.e. during the nine days before the occupation of Shen-chen, it was strictly a local uprising. The insurgents were mainly concerned about establishing control over the local market towns; their ultimate goals extended little beyond taking over the county capital. After the rebel troops moved into Shen-chen, however, the operation shifted to the higher-level urban centers, and the insurgents began to think of occupying the remote provincial capital, Canton. Although the same revolutionary leaders were in command throughout the movement, the major participating forces differed greatly in character during the two stages.

One is struck in the accounts of the first nine days by the predominance of local bands and the mobs with which they were so closely associated. The revolutionary chroniclers understandably praise the idealism and discipline of the revolutionary forces, but the facts they present suggest that the tiny revolutionary contingent under the T'ung-meng Hui leaders' direct command was dwarfed by the local mob. The latter's support had its attractions: the victory at Lung-kang, for instance, would have been impossible without them. But they also posed problems of public order, notably in Hsin-an city and Shen-chen.

In effect, the "revolutionary army" probably differed less from the mob than some chroniclers would have us believe. For instance, certain revolutionary troops from towns other than Kuan-lan who had agreed to confine their operations to Tung-kuan county, leaving Hsin-an county to the Kuan-lan forces, rushed toward Hsin-an city when they heard that the county authorities were ready to hand over the city. The Kuan-lan forces themselves were little better. Three of their leaders and over a hundred troops left Shen-chen for home as soon as they learned that the town was already controlled by an armed police corps. They had no enthusiasm for a "northern expedition" to Canton.

As more and more peasant bands melted away during the expedition to Canton, their place was taken by other elements, among them the newly surrendered regular soldiers, recruits from among the railroad workers, and forces sponsored by the secret societies. Before the troops had reached Shih-lung, for instance, a Triad force of over a hundred men, calling itself the Fourth Army, had taken control of traffic on the East River; after intercepting a navy gunboat carrying rice to the government troops at Waichow, they shared their loot with the revolutionaries. To be sure, some local bands that had personal ties with the revolutionary leaders followed the troops to Canton, but the difference in the character of the main forces at the two stages is clear.

Conclusions

Although any conclusions derived from these two episodes in the Canton delta must of necessity be tentative, certain interesting common themes emerge. First, the two dissident forces—and indeed such forces in all the local uprisings reported throughout the delta during the revolutionary months of 1911—came exclusively from marketing communities that had enjoyed prosperity for a significant period but had recently encountered sharp economic reversals.

Of the many examples of other uprisings that might be adduced here, two must suffice. The decline of the silk trade was no less devastating in the town of Le-ts'ung, south of Fo-shan, than it was in the Lung-tu area. Founded in the early eighteenth century as a center for processing and marketing silk cocoons, Le-ts'ung became a major silk center in the nineteenth century after the introduction of semi-modern machine-reeling techniques. In the years around 1911, after a large number of Le-ts'ung's silk workshops had been closed down, several disturbances and uprisings occurred in the town.

Similarly, the Kowloon-Canton railroad affected not only Shih-ch'i and Kuan-lan but many other cities and market towns. Shih-lung, for instance, which had for centuries been a key transit port for flat-bottomed junks plying their trade along the East River between the Canton delta and the Waichow region, lost much of its trade to Shih-ma with the opening of the railroad. Although both towns were close to the new railroad, Shih-ma was advantageously situated at the junction of the railroad and the principal highways leading directly to the Waichow region. In 1911 the Triads staged an uprising at Shih-lung.

Second, the local uprisings of 1911 clearly reflected the importance of natural marketing systems, and their independence of formal administrative boundaries. Thus although Shih-ch'i, for instance, was the administrative seat of the whole of Hsiang-shan county, the Shih-ch'i uprising attracted no forces from outside the city's western sectoral marketing community. Conversely, the cooperation of Kuan-lan and Lung-kang against government troops suggests a natural political community persisting in the face of an administrative division. Of the towns mentioned above, Shih-lung, T'ien-t'ang-wei, and Shen-chen were all situated close to county or prefectural borders, and the marketing communities dependent on them crossed those borders.

Third, as the prairie fire of revolution spread, the movements of the people's armies closely reflected the hierarchical structure of the marketing systems. We see this pattern not only in the Kuan-lan uprising, but in the way young peasants from the Lung-tu area congregated at the Shih-ch'i market, the way secret-society forces gathered at market towns like Tan-shui and Shih-lung and then jointly laid siege to Waichow, and the way the revolutionary armies that had assembled at Fo-shan, Shih-ch'i, and other cities in or near the Canton delta were ultimately brought by T'ung-meng Hui leaders to metropolitan Canton.

There are obvious reasons why any successful revolutionary movement had to climb this hierarchy. For one thing, the local centers could provide neither the influence nor the resources that such a movement would eventually need; these could come only from higher-level centers, the nodes of larger, higher-order marketing systems. For another, the goal of political revolution is after all to conquer the central places in the formal administrative hierarchy—the county, prefectural, and provincial capitals—and through them to control the territories they administer; and in practice control of the major economic central places in an area facilitates seizure of its administrative nerve center. In these terms the aims of revolutionary activity have long been clear. What the marketing-hierarchy approach adds is a deeper understanding of the mechanisms by which these aims are achieved or frustrated.

Fourth and last, careful attention to the marketing hierarchy facilitates the researcher's task of distinguishing among various kinds of people's armies. Militia forces, "clan-feud" bands, delta defense corps, and the like usually operated at the lowest levels of the hierarchy: villages and small, low-order market towns. As "people's armies," they rose in 1911 to resist, ambush, and rout the government troops that invaded their territorial communities. These peasant bands would attack higher-level urban centers only after they had been aroused. As soon as the revolutionary tide ebbed, they would return to their ordinary life at the lower reaches of the hierarchy.

In order to mobilize such troops for activity extending beyond their local areas, a broader network of communication, organization, and coordination was necessary. It was here that secret societies became prominent.* Although lineage ties were not the sole bond of the local forces and secret-society ties were not the only ties operating at higher levels, there is no disputing this general pattern. It reflects a decline in organizational effectiveness as one moves from localized lineages to higher-order lineages and on to clans, and the increasing heterogeneity of kin groups as one moves from villages to standard marketing communities and on to higher-level, more extensive marketing systems. At these higher levels the secret societies, with their own kinds of ties, their far more extensive organizational network, and their own financial bases, seem increasingly to have replaced the lineages as channels of mobilization.

It seems safe to conclude, then, that the stage on which the drama of peasant insurrection unfolded in 1911 was not an undifferentiated platform on which the peasant actors moved at random, but rather a hierarchical structure of nested local economic systems in which urban centers occupied strategic positions. Indeed, perhaps no movement of dissi-

---

* For a more detailed discussion of the role of secret societies in local uprisings during the revolution, see the article cited at p. 131n.

dent peasant forces in Chinese history can be fully understood apart from this hierarchical system of marketing centers. At a still higher level of generalization, our findings raise questions about the differential political effects of urbanization in rural China. Why, for example, was revolutionary energy in the Canton delta region heavily concentrated in less urbanized marketing systems that had recently suffered severe economic reversals after sustained periods of commercial and urban growth? Why did the larger and more prosperous urban centers of the region—Canton, Fo-shan, and Waichow—play so minor and passive a role in the agitations of 1911?

Chungking as a Center of Warlord Power, 1926–1937

ROBERT A. KAPP

In 1905 Archibald Little, the Englishman who introduced steam navigation to the Upper Yangtze region, wrote glowingly of the prospects for Chungking. French visitors, he said, predicted that Chungking would become "the Lyons of China"; Americans saw the Chungking of the future as "another St. Louis."[1] Whatever specific points these observers might have had in mind, there is no doubt that Chungking's actual importance to the economy of Szechwan province and its potential significance to the economy of twentieth-century China were very great.

Located at the confluence of the Yangtze and one of its major tributaries, the Chia-ling, Chungking was the focal point of a vast trading system. The city's hinterland included virtually all of Szechwan, as well as portions of neighboring provinces to the south, west, and north. Roads, which in Szechwan prior to the 1930's meant stone-slab paths used by human and animal carriers, connected Chungking with Chengtu on the northwest and with the productive region which lay between the two great Szechwanese cities. Other land routes followed the Yangtze upriver to I-pin and downriver to the major port of Wan-hsien.[2] Beyond the Szechwan basin, land routes from Chungking led to Kweiyang in Kweichow province, to I-ch'ang in Hupeh, and through the southeastern arm of Szechwan into Hunan. See Map 1.

It was water transport, however, that made Chungking so important commercially. In addition to the Chia-ling, which connected Szechwan with Shensi and Kansu and was navigable nearly to the Shensi border, other major tributaries conveyed the products of Szechwan and adjoining provinces into the Yangtze above Chungking. The T'o river emerged from the rich Chengtu plain, ran southeast through the Szechwan basin, and met the Yangtze at Lu-hsien, where goods from southern Szechwan

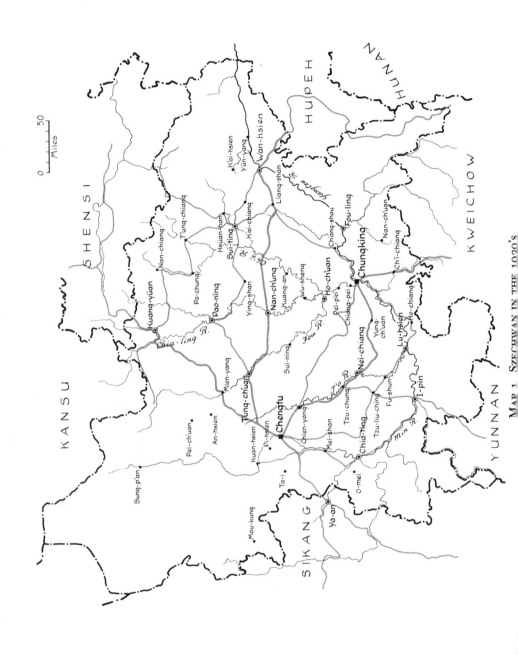

MAP 1 SZECHWAN IN THE 1920'S

and adjacent areas of Kweichow also collected. The Min river dropped south from the Chengtu plain, passing through important silk- and salt-producing areas before reaching the Yangtze at I-pin in southwestern Szechwan. I-pin was also the principal Yangtze outlet for opium and other exports from northern Yunnan. Two other major water arteries, the Fou and the Ch'ü rivers, fed into the Chia-ling at Ho-ch'uan, above Chungking. The Fou extended northwest through central Szechwan; navigable to a point just east of the Chengtu plain, it carried more commerce than any other Yangtze tributary in the province. The Ch'ü, unique in that it ran generally northeast-southwest, brought the products of northeastern Szechwan down to the Chia-ling at Ho-ch'uan and thence to Chungking.[3]

Chungking's position rested on the fact that a very large proportion of Szechwan's exports, plus products from neighboring provinces, passed through the city or its customs houses on the way to Central and East China. Conversely, Chungking's location made it the principal trading center for imports to Szechwan from the rest of China and from abroad. It goes without saying that the Yangtze was by far the most important connecting link between the Szechwan basin and the political and economic centers of China downriver.[4] The main components of Szechwan's (and thus Chungking's) export trade during the early twentieth century were raw materials and, except during the brief period when it was effectively suppressed, opium. Among the province's exports were silk, tung oil, hog bristles, medicinal products, and animal hides.[5] By the 1930's, Szechwan's chief imports were cotton yarn and piece goods, dyes, metals and industrial metal products, kerosene, and luxury goods.[6]

In 1891 Chungking was opened as a treaty port, the westernmost on the Yangtze. Szechwan's distance from the coast and its geographic isolation from the rest of the country served to weaken the foreign impact on the province, but Szechwan was not completely neglected. After Chungking was opened, it became the center of foreign commercial and naval activity in Szechwan. Lured by the vision of an untapped market of fifty million Chinese, foreign firms that included Standard Oil, Asiatic Petroleum, and British-American Tobacco established operations in Chungking. Although the port of Wan-hsien east of Chungking on the Yangtze was opened to foreign commerce in 1902, Chungking remained the principal foreign-trade and gunboat port in Szechwan through the last years of the Ch'ing and into the Republican period.

The political-military history of Chungking from the Revolution of 1911 through the end of 1926 was as disordered as were conditions in Szechwan as a whole. The city was one of Szechwan's two revolutionary centers in 1911, the other being the provincial capital of Chengtu. An independent military government was established in the city late in 1911, only to merge a few months later with the revolutionary-militarist regime that had taken power in Chengtu.[7] Thereafter, the city changed hands frequently, sometimes falling under the control of non-Szechwanese armed forces. In the wake of the unsuccessful "Second Revolution" against Yüan Shih-k'ai in 1913, for example, Kweichow forces helped to drive the revolutionaries from Chungking and to occupy the city. For most of 1914 and 1915 and for part of 1916, Chungking was occupied by military forces specially sent by Yüan Shih-k'ai, including a division under Ts'ao K'un in 1916. For Chungking, as for other parts of Szechwan, Yüan's defeat brought still another invasion of "guest armies" from Yunnan and Kweichow. Only at the end of 1920 did Yunnanese and Kweichow forces retire from the city.[8]

Even after this, Szechwan was invaded by forces from other areas from time to time until 1926, as Szechwanese militarists sought outside aid in support of their own struggles within the province. In addition to brief forays into Chungking by elements of Wu P'ei-fu's armies from Hupeh, the Kweichow militarist Yüan Tsu-ming arrived in Chungking in 1923 and remained there, sharing the occupation of the city with a succession of Szechwanese commanders, until his final expulsion in the spring of 1926. When there were no outside forces in Chungking (and sometimes when there were), a variety of Szechwanese armies held the city and Pa *hsien*, of which Chungking was the capital. It is indicative of the instability of military politics in eastern Szechwan during the early years of the Republic that Pa *hsien* had twenty-eight magistrates between 1912 and 1926.[9]

The Garrison Area System

The first fifteen years of the Republic in Szechwan saw the rise of a large number of independent native militarists, many of whom professed transitory allegiance to one or another of the rival claimants to national power in Canton and Peking. The frequency with which the province was invaded by outside troops testifies to Szechwan's immersion in external conflicts, even though no extraprovincial political power proved capable of controlling the entire province after the death of Yüan Shih-k'ai. By late 1926, however, a degree of stability had come to Szechwan's internal politics. The ejection of Yüan Tsu-ming opened for Szechwan a decade free from noncommunist external military interference.[10] Moreover, by 1926 the field of significant provincial military commanders had narrowed, as older figures were driven from power by their younger subordinates and weaker militarists were overcome or absorbed by their stronger colleagues. By the end of 1926, when the remaining Szechwanese militarists went through the motions of proclaiming their allegiance to the victorious Kuomintang regime at Wuhan, the number of provincial militarists holding the highest rank had dwindled to seven, two of whom had been deprived of all real military power.[11]

Each of the seven militarists known after 1927 as Army Commanders (*chün-chang*) used his military forces to occupy a number of contiguous districts which together formed a "garrison area" (*fang-ch'ü*). As generally used, the term "garrison area" denoted a parcel of territory within which the occupying Army Commander enjoyed de facto independence from outside authority (see Map 2, 1928). Each garrison area, in this sense, functioned like a separate province; in terms of size, some garrison areas were comparable to provinces, containing as many as sixty or more of Szechwan's 140-odd counties.

The leading Szechwan militarists, all of whom were personally well acquainted with one another, plotted continually to add territory and revenue to their existing assets at their rivals' expense, but by comparison with the first fifteen years of the Republican period, political conditions in Szechwan during the late 1920's and early 1930's were relatively quiet. A rough balance of power prevailed among the provincial commanders until 1933 (see Map 2, 1932), when the two most powerful men, Liu Hsiang and Liu Wen-hui, went to war and Liu Wen-hui was driven to remote Sikang. Even after the "Two-Liu War," the "garrison area system," as it was called, persisted in modified form for several years, until the advent of central government military power in Szechwan changed the dimensions of provincial political life.

Chungking Under Liu Hsiang

From 1926 to 1935, the city of Chungking was the site of the military and administrative headquarters of Liu Hsiang, the provincial militarist who rose gradually to predominance among the Szechwanese Army Commanders. The city itself at the start of Liu's tenure was not substantially different from what it had been in the late Ch'ing. After the establishment of the treaty port in 1891, a few foreign-style buildings had been erected near the waterfront, but the foreign community remained small, never exceeding a few hundred people.[12] Built on a hilly promontory, the city was surrounded by a wall with seventeen gates. Of the nine gates that actually opened, all but one faced the Chia-ling or the Yangtze. From the riverbanks to the higher levels of the city, long

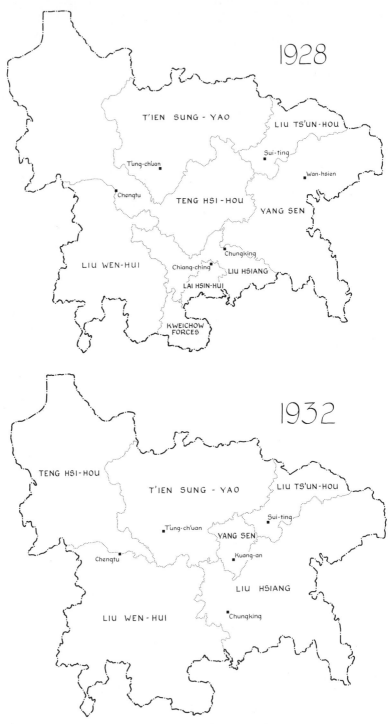

MAP 2. SZECHWAN GARRISON AREAS
Top, 1928; bottom, 1932

stairways served as streets, while narrow stone-slab streets ran in more horizontal fashion at every level. Prior to 1927 no wheeled vehicles, not even wheelbarrows, could be used on the tortuous streets and stairways of the city.[13] The only all-land route into Chungking was the Great East Road from Chengtu, which ran down the peninsula on which Chungking was situated to the T'ung-yüan Gate. For the rest, traffic heading for Chungking from the south had to cross the Yangtze by ferry, and traffic from the northeast had to cross the Chia-ling from suburban Chiang-pei.[14]

Chungking first became a separate administrative entity in 1921, when Liu Hsiang during his first sojourn there established the Office of the Chungking Treaty Port Director (*Ch'ung-ch'ing shang-pu tu-pan*). The name of the governing authority changed with successive changes in military occupation. Late in 1927, Liu Hsiang's subordinate in charge of Chungking had the city's name changed from a treaty port (*shang pu*) to a municipality (*shih*), and the name Ch'ung-ch'ing *shih* was formally adopted in 1929.[15] The boundaries of the municipality were adjusted from time to time as the result of discussions between the city government and the county governments of Pa *hsien* and Chiang-pei; at all times, however, the municipality extended beyond the city walls to include adjacent communities on the peninsula and nearby settlements on the Yangtze's south bank and the Chia-ling's north bank.[16]

Modern public works and industry were scarce when Liu Hsiang took sole possession of Chungking in 1926. All water for the city was drawn from the Yangtze and carried in buckets up the slimy staircases by thousands of water-bearers.[17] An electric power company was first organized in Chungking in 1903, but its output was tiny and its customers few.[18] Telephone service was also very poor—so poor, in fact, that clients often preferred to use runners to carry their messages rather than bother with the phone at all.[19] Industry in Chungking was largely confined to handicraft operations such as silk-reeling, hog bristle treatment and dyeing, and other processes related to Szechwan's exports of raw materials. A mint, located on the south bank of the Yangtze about three miles from the heart of Chungking, added to the city's economic and strategic importance.

In the decade after 1926, during which Liu Hsiang rose to the height of his power in Szechwan, Chungking underwent some conspicuous changes. Liu and his powerful military subordinates were deeply involved in most of these developments.

In the first place, the expansion of the main city beyond the city wall and the construction of modern streets and roads got under way in 1927.

A new business area (*hsin shih-ch'ang*) was planned outside the T'ung-yüan Gate, in the midst of the huge cemetery area lying just beyond the wall. The delicate problem of excavating and moving the remains of the dead was handled by a committee of prominent gentry figures, in cooperation with city authorities.[20] Funds for construction of the new business area were secured from the Chungking Chamber of Commerce, which parceled out the financial burdens among the banks, guilds, and merchants of the city.[21] The city, or, to be more precise, the leading figures in the city administration, bought up or expropriated land along the projected routes connecting the main city with the new area.[22] After the connecting route, which was the first modern road-building project in Chungking, was finished in 1927, city authorities ordered merchants and businesses located just inside the city wall to move to the new business area, ostensibly to facilitate the construction of modern streets and roads inside the wall, but also so that speculators might realize profits from the sale of land in the new area.[23]

In subsequent years, especially after 1932, wider streets with pedestrian sidewalks appeared in the main city.[24] Street-widening was often a ruthless business that necessitated pulling down the front parts of buildings bordering the old narrow lanes. Generally, the front rooms of existing structures were lopped off, and new façades put up in front of what had been the inner rooms of the buildings.[25]

Some industrial development in the city and its environs also took place after 1927, although road construction and the introduction of wheeled traffic to Chungking were the most visible alterations during the late twenties and early thirties. Chungking's industrial growth was noteworthy more because Chungking started with so little than because so much was accomplished. In the late 1920's and early 1930's, two industrialization programs began, each directed by a private corporation with the support (and, in many respects, under the orders) of the Chungking military authorities. One program was carried out by the Min-sheng Company, and the other by the West China Development Corporation.

The Min-sheng Company (*Min-sheng shih-yeh kung-ssu*) operation was above all the creation of Lu Tso-fu, a native of Ho-ch'uan county north of Chungking. In 1925, Lu joined with several wealthy figures from Chungking to establish a small steamship line serving Chungking and Ho-ch'uan, which lay at the junction of the Fou, Ch'ü, and Chia-ling rivers.[26] In 1927, Lu became the director of a militia committee established by the four Chia-ling river counties between Chungking and Ho-ch'uan in an effort to eliminate the rampant banditry disturbing the area.

Under his direction, the region was pacified and commerce was restored between Chungking and Ho-ch'uan.[27]

In 1929, seeking to regain for Chinese shipping the dominant role in the Upper Yangtze trade, Liu Hsiang made Lu Tso-fu the chief of his new Navigation Bureau at Chungking. The Bureau, which levied taxes on all shipping passing through the port, gave special tax relief to the Min-sheng Line, and Liu Hsiang backed Lu's successful efforts to acquire the ships of numerous small and unprofitable Chinese lines operating in Szechwan.[28] Adherence to regular schedules, elimination of corruption and inefficiency in shipboard operations, and provision of equal treatment for Chinese and foreign passengers enabled the Min-sheng Line rapidly to expand its fleet and its routes over the Upper Yangtze. Eventually, Min-sheng ships worked the Yangtze all the way to Shanghai.[29]

As Min-sheng shipping operations grew, the company expanded into industrial development in its base area along the Chia-ling north of Chungking. Small coal mines that had shut down for lack of profits were revived and combined into a single coal company, with the financial backing of Min-sheng shareholders.[30] Szechwan's first railway, a short narrow-gauge line connecting the mountain coal mines with the Chia-ling river, was constructed in 1931.[31] At the Chungking suburb of Pei-p'ei, a dyeing plant and a refrigerating plant were built, along with a model industrial community later called "the most outstanding instance of city planning in China."[32] The Min-sheng Company further developed machine shops and shipyards on the Chia-ling at Chiang-pei, thus eliminating the need to send ships to Shanghai for repairs.[33] In 1935, Min-sheng capital helped finance a cement works, only the second in Szechwan, on the south bank of the Yangtze.

The Min-sheng Company's conspicuous success rested first of all on the Yangtze river trade. By buying out the smaller Chinese shipping companies and even buying ships from foreign lines, the Min-sheng Company reestablished Chinese predominance in Upper Yangtze steamship navigation. This would not have been possible without the support of the Chungking military authorities; more than anything else, tax relief at Chungking permitted Min-sheng to compete successfully against the foreign carriers.[34] Through financial arrangements and personal associations, the Min-sheng Company, though remaining a private enterprise, was dependent on and helpful to the militarists and politicians of Liu Hsiang's Twenty-first Army.

Whereas the Min-sheng Company's original purpose was to recapture the Upper Yangtze trade for native shipowners, the West China

Development Corporation (*Hua-hsi hsing-yeh kung-ssu*) was established in response to Liu Hsiang's growing interest in the development of the modern sector of his garrison area's economy, particularly at Chungking. The first serious planning for industrial growth in Liu's territory commenced in 1931. The West China Development Corporation was formed the same year, specifically to develop industries and businesses requested by Liu Hsiang's own Office of the Szechwan Rehabilitation Director.[35] Most of the initial capital for the Corporation was raised among wealthy Szechwanese acquaintances of Liu Hsiang's chief financial advisor and emissary to the Chungking business community, Liu Hang-shen. Later on, several Chungking banks invested in the Corporation.

The first project of the West China Development Corporation was an electric power plant for Chungking, for which investments were attracted by the authorities' guarantees of tax exemption.[36] The electric plant was producing power for Chungking by mid-1934, and was further expanded in 1936.

The second West China Development Corporation project was a machine-building factory, which used machinery discarded from a Shanghai plant. Designed to make boilers and simple machinery for such Chungking industries as silk-weaving, the machine factory later turned to the manufacture of arms for Liu Hsiang's forces.[37] Other enterprises developed by the West China Development Corporation prior to 1935 were a cement works, which broke Szechwan's dependence on cement imported from downriver ports,[38] and a small steel plant set up in 1934. The principal investor in the cement works was the Bank of Chungking, which in turn drew most of its capital from the military establishment in the city.[39] Capital investment for the steel plant came primarily from Liu Hsiang himself and from Liu's financial advisor Liu Hang-shen.[40]

Prior to the advent of central government power in Szechwan in 1935 and especially to the transfer of much of China's portable industrial plant to Szechwan during the Sino-Japanese War, that was the extent of modern industrial development in Chungking. By comparison with Hankow or Shanghai, Chungking remained an underdeveloped, even primitive place. It was notoriously dirty, overcrowded, and opium-ridden; public health remained deplorable, unemployment high.[41] A popular expression held that the "three plenties" (*san to*) of Chungking were prostitutes, singing beggars, and ordinary beggars.[42] But given the low level from which the city started in 1927, it was true that the face of Chungking had changed significantly by the middle 1930's. See Map 3.

Liu Hsiang's control of Chungking and his special position in Szechwanese military politics were more than coincidentally related. In considering the role of Chungking in militarist Szechwan during the late 1920's and the early 1930's, there are two key questions: first, how did Chungking affect the course of military and political affairs throughout Szechwan; and second, what was Chungking's function within the garrison area of Liu Hsiang's armies?

The Function of Chungking in Provincial Military Politics

As the high turnover rate among military and civilian authorities in Chungking and Pa *hsien* indicated, Liu Hsiang was not the first military leader to realize the importance of Chungking to military success in Szechwan. Nor, when Liu came to Chungking in late 1923 along with Yüan Tsu-ming and other militarists, was it the first time that troops under his command had been stationed in the city. Liu had entered Chungking first in late 1920 on the heels of the retreating Yunnanese, and had occupied the city with the title of Commander in Chief of Szechwan Armies until provincial rivals forced him to "retire" to his native Ta-i county during 1922.[43]

However, after Liu Hsiang managed with the help of other Szechwanese commanders to drive Yüan Tsu-ming back to Kweichow in mid-1926, he emerged as the dominant military figure in Chungking. In 1927 and 1928, the city was the headquarters of a garrison area that stretched from Tzu-chung county to the west through the rich sugar-producing region around Nei-chiang, eastward to Nan-ch'uan near the Kweichow border. At this time, Liu Hsiang's portion of the Yangtze reached from Chungking upriver as far as Lu-hsien. Below Chungking, the Yangtze belonged to Liu's rival Yang Sen, who had formerly been Liu's subordinate and ally.

The garrison area of Liu's Twenty-first National Revolutionary Army expanded to the east in 1929. Defeated in a war with Liu, Yang Sen was forced out of his Yangtze territories, withdrawing to his native Kuang-an county. Yang maintained a small army and garrison area in the vicinity of Kuang-an for a number of years. Liu Hsiang took over most of Yang's former territory, so that he claimed eastern Szechwan all the way to the Hupeh border, as well as the southeastern corner of the province adjoining Hunan and Kweichow. Although Liu Hsiang lost several counties on the west side of his garrison area to his uncle Liu Wen-hui in the next few years, his victory over Yang Sen in 1929 gave him several valuable Yangtze prizes: Fou-ling, Szechwan's biggest opium port, which lay at the junction of the Yangtze and the principal water artery

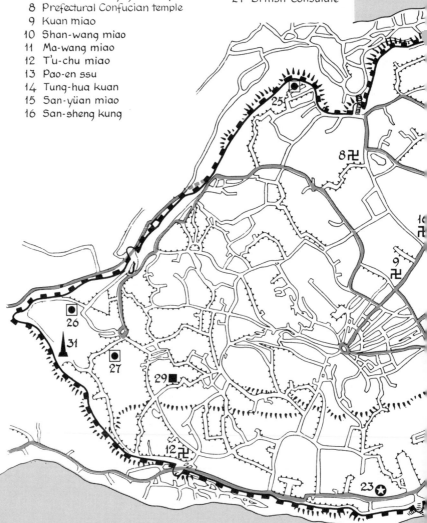

⛩ Civil Offices
1 Pa hsien government offices
2 Chungking municipal govern-
    ment offices (after 1928)
3 Head Post Office (as of 1933)
4 Maritime Customs (as of 1933)
5 Central Telephone Office (est.
    1930) (location approximate)

☒ Military Offices
6 HQ, 21st Army and Szechwan
    Rehabilitation Director
    (Liu Hsiang) (after 1926)

卍 Religious Institutions
7 Prefectural City-god temple
8 Prefectural Confucian temple
9 Kuan miao
10 Shan-wang miao
11 Ma-wang miao
12 T'u-chu miao
13 Pao-en ssu
14 Tung-hua kuan
15 San-yüan miao
16 San-sheng kung

✪ Guild and Native Place
    Associations
17 Che-chiang hui-kuan (Chekiang)
18 Shan-hsi kuan (Shansi)
19 Hu-kuang hui-kuan (Hupeh & Hunan)
20 Chiang-nan hui-kuan (Kiangsu & Anhwei)
21 Kuang-tung hui-kuan (Kwangtung)
22 Shen-hsi hui-kuan (Shensi)
23 Yün-Kuei kung-so (Yunnan & Kweichow)
24 Fu-chien hui-kuan (Fukien) (Loc.appro)

◉ Consulates
25 German Consulate
26 French Consulate
27 British Consulate

MAP 3. CHUNGKING, 1935

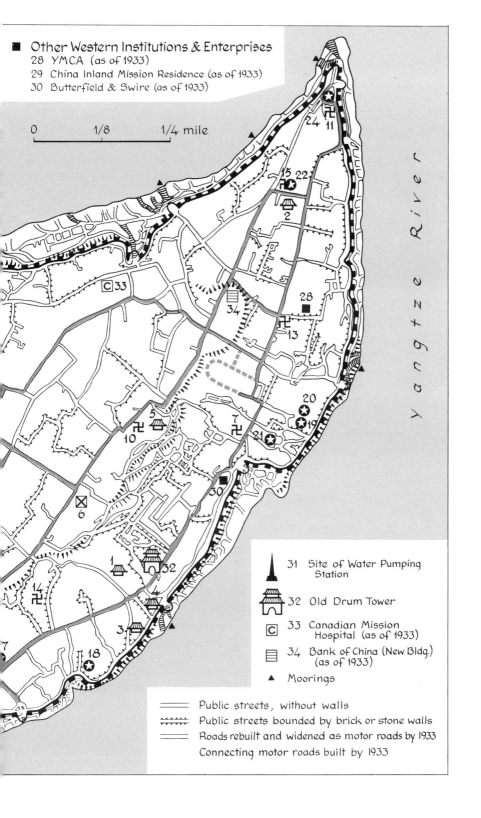

Other Western Institutions & Enterprises
28 YMCA (as of 1933)
29 China Inland Mission Residence (as of 1933)
30 Butterfield & Swire (as of 1933)

0   1/8   1/4 mile

Yangtze River

31 Site of Water Pumping
    Station

32 Old Drum Tower

33 Canadian Mission
    Hospital (as of 1933)

34 Bank of China (New Bldg.)
    (as of 1933)

▲ Moorings

══════ Public streets, without walls
┼┼┼┼┼┼ Public streets bounded by brick or stone walls
══════ Roads rebuilt and widened as motor roads by 1933
        Connecting motor roads built by 1933

to Kweichow; the treaty port of Wan-hsien, center of Szechwan's vital tung oil trade; and Yün-yang, near which lay the trading center of Yün-an Market (Yün-an-ch'ang).[44] Beginning with his victory over Yang Sen in 1929, Liu Hsiang clearly became Szechwan's most powerful militarist. What role did Chungking play in this process?

Chungking's primary value to Liu lay in the revenues it produced for him. The city supplied enormous amounts of money to Liu's armies, which by 1932 numbered nearly 100,000 men.[45] Most of this money came from taxation. But by virtue of its economic and political position in Szechwan, Chungking also enabled Liu and his associates to profit from personal investments and commercial enterprises that could not have been undertaken elsewhere in the province.

Taxation throughout Szechwan during the garrison area period was heavy, and it grew heavier as the years passed. By the late 1920's, land taxes were being collected in advance, and by the middle 1930's many districts had reportedly paid their land taxes into the 1970's and 1980's.[46] The roads and rivers of Szechwan bristled with hundreds of customs stations, where transit taxes were levied on goods without regard to the larger effects of taxation on Szechwan's internal commerce. Chungking, however, offered something special in taxation opportunities. A welter of individual levies applied to all merchandise coming into Chungking or neighboring Chiang-pei. In the early years of Liu Hsiang's tenure in Chungking, each tax was controlled by a separate agency; the time and effort required to obtain chops from each of the numerous tax authorities was a source of severe frustration for foreign businessmen in Chungking.[47] Beginning in 1929, many of these individual commerce taxes were incorporated under a general taxation agency called the Bureau of Taxes and Levies (*Shui-chüan chü*), headed by Liu Hsiang himself, but although the collection process was simplified, few of the many varieties of taxes collected in Chungking were actually eliminated.[48]

In addition to taxes on the great river commerce of Chungking, Liu Hsiang procured revenue from taxes on Chungking's other economic activities. Levies on meat, wine and tobacco, tea and other daily necessities, taxes on various kinds of businesses, and a stamp tax on sales also added to Liu's revenues. Two other taxes in particular deserve mention. One was the "local surtax" (*ti-fang fu-chia*), levied on imports and exports at a fixed percentage of the Maritime Customs assessment. Liu Hsiang's surtax agency set up operations immediately next to the Customs office, and goods coming out of the Customs were shunted into the surtax building for inspection and additional taxation. The surtax was significant because it was tied to the central government's Maritime Customs and because it became a source of controversy both between

Liu Hsiang and Nanking and between Nanking and foreign shippers.[49]

The second tax of special interest applied to "illegal" shipments of opium. The center of Szechwanese opium production actually lay in the Yangtze districts below Chungking; the city of Fou-ling was the principal export center for native opium bound downriver.[50] However, considerable quantities of Kweichow opium came overland to Chungking; heavily guarded opium caravans half a mile long were a common sight on the Kweichow Road. In addition, Yunnanese opium poured down the Yangtze from I-pin on its way to central and eastern China. In Chungking itself, the opium business flourished. There as elsewhere in Szechwan, opium addiction was widespread; a foreign diplomat estimated in 1926 that the population of Chungking spent as much money on opium as it did on rice.[51] Thus "opium-suppression" taxes levied in Chungking added to the occupying militarists' revenue supplies.

Other forms of revenue available to Chungking military authorities were forced loans and contributions from the mercantile community. Powerful merchant guilds, banks and money shops, even foreign-owned firms operating in the city were liable to occasional lump-sum assessments.[52] The avowed purpose of the loan might be road construction or military defense or some other project; but increasingly in the early thirties, when forced loans became more important to Liu Hsiang as a source of revenue, the loans were devoted to paying off the interest on and some of the principal of previous loans. Though foreign firms often successfully resisted attempts by the Twenty-first Army to wring money from them, there seems to have been little serious resistance by the Chungking Chamber of Commerce, individual merchant guilds, or banks in the city.

There were, to be sure, cases of merchant opposition to Liu Hsiang's fiscal measures during the late 1920's and early 1930's. For example, the customs surtax referred to above led to a paralyzing merchant strike when Liu first introduced it in 1929.[53] In general, though, Liu Hsiang managed to live comfortably with Chungking's mercantile community despite his repeated demands for special contributions. He was able to do this partly because of the way he treated the merchants and partly because the merchants themselves were well disposed toward him.

Liu Hsiang was careful whenever possible to avoid alienating the Chungking trading and financial community. To this end, he maintained contact with the community, and his advisers consulted leading merchants on important political as well as economic issues.[54] For example, in 1927, an Office for the Receipt and Disbursement of City Operating Funds (*Shih-cheng ching-fei shou-chih so*) was set up by P'an Wen-hua, Liu Hsiang's subordinate in charge of the government of Chungking. The head of this office, chosen by the powerful associations (*fa-t'uan*) of the city, was invariably a merchant.[55] Unlike the revolutionary student-labor movement, which Liu Hsiang ruthlessly attacked in 1927 and throttled thereafter,[56] the businessmen of Chungking enjoyed a relationship with Liu that followed familiar and recognized rules. Settlements of disputes such as the surtax matter might be long in coming, but they were reached through a process of negotiation, pressure, and compromise.

At the same time, the merchants and bankers of Chungking had an interest in cooperating with Liu Hsiang, not because they were particularly attached to him personally, but because support of the incumbent Chungking militarist generally worked to their advantage. Inconsequential as the frequent changes in military control in Szechwan might appear from the outside, such military upheavals could spell disaster for the merchants of the affected region. In the first place, each garrison area, including Liu Hsiang's, circulated its own currency, and the fall of a militarist in Chungking meant heavy losses for the unfortunate bank or trading house caught with stocks of the defeated commander's money.

Similarly, no matter how hollow a ruling militarist's promises to repay forced loans might be, they were less hollow than a defeated militarist's promises. From 1927 to 1937, even after he had become the strongest of the provincial militarists, Liu Hsiang lived in fear of a hostile coalition of rival commanders. The possibility of his being forced out of Chungking paradoxically served him well in his relations with the Chungking commercial community, linking his survival and the merchants' economic interest in a symbiotic relationship.

This symbiosis between Liu Hsiang's military organization and the businessmen of Chungking produced some strange results. By earmarking his customs surtax for repayment of his obligations to the merchants, for example, Liu Hsiang made it worth the merchants' while to support his continuation of the surtax even though the National Government demanded that it be abolished. The independently levied surtax had definite political implications; it was one symbol of Liu Hsiang's financial and political independence from Nanking. Despite the advantages that the Chungking trading community might logically have expected from greater economic integration into Nanking's sphere of influence, the immediate factor of Liu Hsiang's short-term obligations to them was enough to ensure merchant support of Liu's provincial separatism on the surtax issue.[57]

Besides providing revenue from taxation and loans to Liu Hsiang's military establishment, Chungking offered its militarists excellent opportunities for private economic ventures. More than the commanders of any other region in Szechwan during the garrison area period, Liu Hsiang and his powerful subordinates in southeastern Szechwan indulged in profitable enterprises, most of them oriented to Chungking or its nearby suburbs. The list of such enterprises is long; a few examples will suffice. In 1925, Liu Hsiang, in conjunction with a lesser militarist then in Chungking, invested in a river steamer in order to ship opium to I-ch'ang under a military flag and thus avoid inspection by the Maritime Customs at Chungking or Wan-hsien.[58] The former bandit leader Fan Shao-tseng, now a division commander in Liu Hsiang's army, operated a morphia factory in the vicinity of Chungking.[59] Lan Wen-pin, another subordinate whose base was in the city of Chungking itself, profited heavily from his opium transactions as well as from a chain of theaters which he owned and policed with his own troops.[60] One of Division Commander Wang Ling-chi's operations was a tung oil export firm.[61]

Real estate was another good source of funds; a small clique of militarists and bureaucrats accumulated large holdings in Chungking and profited from rents and sales.[62] Another investment sphere, banking, showed most clearly the extent to which Liu Hsiang and his ranking subordinates were tied to the city of Chungking and its commercial activities. At a time when trade and production in eastern Szechwan staggered along under the burdens of intermittent war and ever-increasing taxation, the banking business flourished in Chungking. Of the nine Chungking-based banks operating at the beginning of 1935, before the advent of central government power in Szechwan, seven were established after 1927; the only non-Szechwanese bank, the Chungking branch of the Bank of China, dated from 1915.[63] Militarists invested heavily in Chungking banking, usually in concert with local mercantile investors. Whether or not high-ranking militarists became the executive officers of Chungking banks, as Division Commander T'ang Shih-tsun did in one case, the banks served as treasuries for military funds. By lending money and by actually trading in important commodities like tung oil and opium, the Chungking banks helped make the fortunes of their military backers.[64]

In addition to offering Liu Hsiang and his powerful lieutenants a fine field for personal investment, Chungking in its role as the economic and administrative center of Liu's garrison area enabled Liu to allot lucrative official posts to his advisers and subordinates. The large and cumbersome Twenty-first Army Headquarters bureaucracy was filled with loyal if generally powerless civil officials. Posts that were more important to the maintenance of Liu's position, such as Mayor of Chungking,

Director of the Highways Bureau, or Commissioner of Salt Transport, could be granted to Division Commanders like P'an Wen-hua, T'ang Shih-tsun, or Wang Tsuan-hsü, all Liu's longtime supporters. Chungking's role as control center of the garrison area, which in turn derived from its economic position in Szechwan, was thus indirectly but supremely important to the preservation of Liu's predominance within the world of provincial military politics. In a province and an era when disloyalty and defection at the highest military levels were routine, the unusual stability of Liu Hsiang's corps of ranking subordinates was a major factor in his military and political success. In his relations with these men Liu undoubtedly invoked old military school ties and career associations.[65] But without the reinforcement of lucrative appointments in Chungking it is highly doubtful that these sentimental attachments would have kept Liu's generals loyal to him for such a long time.

The Role of Chungking in the Garrison Area

Though Chungking provided Liu Hsiang with special resources that other Szechwanese commanders did not enjoy, Liu would not have been able to thrive in the province if he had not had a sizable and productive garrison area of his own. The garrison area provided Liu with revenue from land taxes and other exactions; it also provided manpower, both for the army itself and for the labor force that served the army. The resources of some of Liu's districts—tung oil, opium, and coal, for example—provided him with necessary commodities for use within the garrison area and with valuable exports.

What was the connection between Liu's occupation of Chungking in the late 1920's and the 1930's and his possession of a large and expanding independent garrison area? Recognizing that Chungking was crucial to the maintenance of Liu's army and his relative strength in provincial military affairs, can we assume that control of Chungking was also the key to control of the dozens of counties and the millions of people in Liu's garrison area? To answer these questions it is necessary to ask how control was channeled within the Twenty-first Army itself, how control was extended from the Army structure to the nonmilitary sector, and what "local control" meant in Liu Hsiang's area. Reliable data on these issues are scarce; in the discussion below, information about places belonging to other Szechwanese militarists has occasionally been combined with data about Liu Hsiang's own area, on the assumption that conditions in the different regions were sufficiently similar to justify such pooling of information.

Taking data on one garrison area and projecting their meaning onto another implies, of course, that the dimensions and shapes of the Sze-chwan garrison areas were not clearly and rigidly determined by the economic geography of the province. This was indeed the case. Certain features of the garrison areas remained constant; for example, the counties comprising a garrison were always contiguous, no county ever being surrounded by the territory of another militarist. However, the frequency with which the major garrison areas changed size and shape, as counties were traded or conquered, suggests that there was nothing "natural" about the exact distribution of militarist territorial holdings at any given moment. Chungking's dependence on rice supplies from the Chengtu Plain and other regions outside of Liu Hsiang's control suggests, moreover, that economic self-sufficiency was not indispensable for a garrison area's survival.[66]

Besides the definition suggested earlier, a garrison area could be defined as the territory occupied by military forces whose high officers in turn professed allegiance to a common highest commander. The distribution of authority and the degree of independence enjoyed at various levels of the military hierarchy varied from area to area, commander to commander, and year to year.

Within the Twenty-first Army hierarchy, subordinate officers at different levels seem to have enjoyed considerable autonomy. The phenomenon of "garrison areas within garrison areas" was a feature of Sze-chwanese military politics in the 1920's and 1930's.[67] P'an Wen-hua, one of Liu Hsiang's chief subordinates and Mayor of Chungking from 1927 to 1935, described the situation in eastern Szechwan to an American naval officer in 1924, early in Liu Hsiang's occupation of Chungking:

General P'an illustrated the conditions of affairs by placing several water-melon seed[s] on the table, in a row, and pointing them out as Chungking, Changshow, [Fou-ling], etc., down the river, to the Hupeh border. Pointing to one seed, Chungking we will say, he said a certain military official is appointed to that town and the surrounding country with definite limits. He is given absolutely no financial support, but must levy his own taxes, pay his own soldiers, and support his own force from anything he can raise in that particular district. He is an absolute sovereign in that particular district, he knows nothing of Peking and cares less. Although at the present time General Liu Hsiang is supposed to control this stretch of river, it is in name only; actually he has no control. General P'an admitted he was in charge from Wan-hsien to [Fou-ling], but actually exercised little or no control over the officers stationed in the various districts under him.[68]

Direct references to this sort of independence among subordinates are scarce, but it can be assumed that P'an Wen-hua's description of

the relationship of powerful subordinate officers to Liu Hsiang's headquarters at Chungking remained valid after 1927, just as similar situations existed in other garrison areas.[69]

In the Twenty-first Army, upward loyalty to Liu Hsiang was not only
compatible with a high degree of downward autonomy; it was dependent on it. Even if, as was not the case everywhere in Szechwan, the
land tax revenue collected locally was forwarded to Army Headquarters
for further distribution, other forms of locally raised taxes such as meat
taxes or "commerce-protection fees" levied along the land routes of a
given area were retained by lower-level commanders. At Wan-hsien,
for instance, the revenue from "Navigation Taxes" in 1929 was kept by
the local commander for the upkeep of his troops, not sent to Liu Hsiang
in Chungking.[70]

Thus, within the garrison area, officers at successively lower levels
enjoyed considerable freedom of action. Loyalty to Liu Hsiang lay in
not rebelling against him, acting in concert with Liu's other forces in
provincial campaigns, and submitting certain revenues to Army Headquarters in return for ammunition, weapons, and other military supplies. But such loyalty did not preclude the significant autonomy that
Liu Hsiang's most trusted military supporters did in fact enjoy.

Liu Hsiang's ability to establish such a *modus vivendi* with his divisional commanders and back it up with lucrative posts in the central
administrative structure at Chungking did not, however, solve the problem of local control. In the final analysis, the internal dynamics of Liu's
army were one thing; the exercise of army power over the people of the
garrison area was another. Occasionally, army troops themselves were
used to secure civilian and especially peasant compliance in such matters as tax payment and labor conscription.[71] Far more often, the Twenty-first Army relied on intermediaries to bring about the desired local
responses to its demands.

Securing local compliance with Chungking's directives was the essence of local control in Liu Hsiang's garrison area. It was not enormously complicated. Popular mobilization, in the sense of active political commitment or mass participation in economic development projects, was not at issue in the days when Liu Hsiang held Chungking.
The primary elements in local control were the effective collection of
revenue, the raising of manpower for the army and for army-connected
services such as the transport of supplies, and the maintenance of sufficient local tranquillity to permit the first two tasks to be carried out.
Having replaced the Ch'ing bureaucracy as the governors of Szechwan
after 1912, the provincial militarists introduced no radical changes in

local administrative practice. The burst of reformist energy that had in many cases accompanied the creation of local "self-government" institutions in the last years of the Ch'ing was not sustained in Republican Szechwan.[72] Even though by 1932 the province supported as many troops as the Ch'ing had maintained in all of China in 1911, Szechwanese local institutions generally followed the pattern laid out in the late Ch'ing, at least superficially.[73] Of course, during the garrison area period the tax burden on the Szechwanese population increased enormously over late Ch'ing levels; labor and military conscriptions were carried out ruthlessly and constantly; social disorder and banditry erupted sporadically, especially in the mid-1920's and mid-1930's. Nonetheless, the functions of local administration under the Twenty-first Army after 1927 differed little from the functions of local administration before the Revolution.

The techniques of garrison area administration rested on the basic fact that although subprovincial armies like Liu Hsiang's might have looked like "local" forces when viewed from Nanking or from a foreign embassy, from the standpoint of the localities they occupied these armies were often outsiders imposing their presence on the local communities. The provincial armies remained somehow separate, despite their great numbers, from the life of the areas they held. In this sense, though the armies differed from the Ch'ing bureaucracy both in their numbers and in the very fact that they were military forces, their position in the society approximated that of the Ch'ing administrators. Installed in a region of which few of them (and especially their officers) were natives, the military forces employed familiar methods to bridge the gap between the world of provincial military and local nonmilitary life.

There were essentially two ways of bridging this gap. One was the appointment from Chungking of civilian administrators for each county in the garrison area. The other was reliance on local leading elements, some more orthodox than others, to carry out the military's commands among the civilian population.

One of Liu Hsiang's prerogatives as Army Commander and chief militarist was personal approval and appointment of all county magistrates in his garrison area. This power of appointment ensured for Liu a degree of local control independent of the subordinate military commander on the scene in a particular county, although Army Headquarters in Chungking often approved magistrates' nominations submitted by local brigade or division commanders. Similarly, Army Headquarters, in effect Liu Hsiang himself, retained the power to appoint the heads of certain county government bureaus (*chü*), including the Revenue Collection

Bureau (*cheng-shou chü*). The Revenue Collection Bureau was the most important, though certainly not the only, tax-gathering agency in most counties.[74]

Actually, appointment of magistrates and revenue bureau chiefs from Chungking performed a dual function. In addition to providing Liu Hsiang with a semi-independent lever in local administration, the power of appointment enabled Liu to reward faithful civil servants and bureaucrats, or special friends, with administrative positions in which they could make their fortunes in a short time. In other words, Liu's power to appoint these local administrators helped him to maintain and consolidate in the Twenty-first Army organization a body of loyal nonmilitary personnel, for whom the vision of riches accumulated in a county job was often compelling.[75] Not all county officials appointed by Army Headquarters did belong to the Twenty-first Army bureaucracy; some were themselves military officers, others were educated civilians but not hangers-on of the Army. However, the most common background for high county government officials was either long service in the Army bureaucracy (frequently the so-called Secretariat) or else personal connection with Liu or one of his close associates.[76]

Even the injection of Liu Hsiang's appointees into county government in the garrison area did not solve the problem of local control. As was true before the Revolution, county government remained remote from the daily lives of much of the population. The other means on which the Army relied to achieve local control was the use of native intermediaries. The Army's reliance on these local people, and the resulting difficulties that sometimes arose, showed most clearly how the occupying military forces remained alien to the territories that they garrisoned.

The collection of the land tax may be taken as an illustration. Methods of collection differed from area to area. Occasionally, army units themselves demanded and collected the grain tax from landlords and peasant families.[77] In other counties, the Revenue Collection Bureau was responsible for gathering the revenue. Sometimes branch countinghouses (*fen-kuei*) were set up in several *hsiang* within a county, and taxpayers were required to bring their taxes to the countinghouses. When the army itself was not actually raising the revenue, the job often fell either to special local tax collectors (*liang-ting*), who knew the financial details of every family within their area just as their predecessors had during the Ch'ing, or to local militia (*t'uan*) under the command of "militia lords" (*t'uan-fa*), who extorted the taxes from the landlords and peasants and then were supposed to turn the revenues over to the county governments for remission to Army Headquarters.[78]

The rapid expansion of militia forces in Szechwan had begun after the collapse of Yüan Shih-k'ai's power in the province. In the wake of Yüan's overthrow and the subsequent invasion of Yunnanese and Kweichow troops, banditry flourished, and the disorganized "regular" armies in Szechwan were unable to stem the rising tide of brigandage. Militia forces under the command of local gentry were organized to protect market towns. Arms were purchased and taxes collected to pay for the provisions of the new militia and the salaries of their officers. Official pronouncements to the contrary, the expanding militia forces were organized and controlled within each *chen* (township) and *hsiang* (rural administrative area), the economically determined territorial units of which each county was composed. As early as 1923, the militarist Liu Che'ng-hsün, then holding the titles of Provincial Governor and Commander-in-Chief of Szechwan Armies, ordered an end to independent militia management and collection of militia funds by the thousands of *chen* and *hsiang* of Szechwan, but the order was ineffectual. In December of the same year, the magistrate of Pa *hsien* explicitly directed each *ch'ang*, or market town, to handle its own militia affairs, in contradiction to Liu Ch'eng-hsün's command. A specific prohibition against separate collection of militia funds by individual *hsiang*, included in the Twenty-first Army's Three-Year Militia Funding Plan in 1933, indicates that the organizational base of local militia remained the market-oriented communities within the county.[79] By the early 1930's, the size of Szechwan's militia forces was estimated at several thousand per county, or five to six hundred thousand for the entire province.[80]

The extent to which local militia forces held the key to local control was acknowledged both by Liu Hsiang and by the frustrated organizers of the revolutionary peasant movement in Szechwan in 1927. Liu complained bitterly that "bad gentry" had usurped control over local militia forces, turning popular military units into "villains' tools," setting up independent subgovernments, taking over the power of taxation, and even exercising the power of life and death over local residents.[81] The organizers of the abortive peasant movement, dispersed by Liu Hsiang and the other provincial militarists in the spring of 1927, maintained that local "militia lords" had conspired with the generals to destroy their movement, but their assessment of the militia forces' local strength coincided with Liu's. Because the militia forces were natives of the area in which they operated, they knew every move of the local people; they set up their own customs barriers on the roads, forced peasants to plant opium, and executed victims without consulting any other authority. County magistrates, said the defeated peasant organizers, had thus in effect lost the power to govern.[82]

The independence of local militia forces was acceptable to provincial army leaders as long as it did not interfere with the vital functions of local control, namely tax collection, manpower provision, and the maintenance of social order. When the fragile partnership of army and militia was functioning smoothly, there seemed to be enough resources for both.[83] Nonetheless, Liu Hsiang's military organization constantly sought ways to lessen militia autonomy and increase Twenty-first Army power over local armed forces.

From time to time the latent tension between army and militia developed into hostile confrontation. Specific references to army-militia conflicts in Liu Hsiang's area during the late 1920's and in the 1930's are less numerous than one would expect. Much of the available data on militia resistance to provincial armies in Szechwan concern northern, western, and southwestern areas that were not part of Liu Hsiang's garrison area. In Mei *hsien* in the southwest, for example, hostilities broke out between army and independent militia forces when the militia set up their own transit-tax stations on the county roads.[84] In 1932 three overlapping groups—the Ko-lao Hui secret society, the militia, and impoverished peasants—joined in forming a "tax-resistance army" that operated in several counties belonging to Liu Wen-hui.[85] In Ch'i-chiang, south of Chungking, a letter to the *North-China Herald* reported in 1929, "the people's bands are up in arms against the excessive taxation that has been imposed upon them. . . . The commander of the train bands sends groups of propagandists daily into the countryside who distribute printed handbills to the people explaining why they have taken up arms."[86] Another report in 1934, which mentioned no specific locality, described an additional source of friction between militia and army:

Another source of terror to the people of Szechwan, besides the Reds and troops, is the Militia Corps, which has developed throughout the province. Though nominally these militiamen are volunteers and formed under the auspices of the local gentry for the protection of the localities, they are all under the influence of the local partisans and used as a tool to oppress the innocent people. They have been able to expand their forces by intercepting small bodies of stragglers of the army. For this reason they have attracted the enmity of the militarists and brought untold suffering to the localities. In many instances whole villages have been razed to the ground by the troops who return with large forces to avenge their comrades.[87]

Within Liu Hsiang's area, a British diplomat noted in 1929 the existence of a Szechwan Provisional People's Army Military Committee (*Ssu-ch'uan min-chün lin-shih chün-shih wei-yüan-hui*), whose purpose was to combine with local militia elements to oppose military overtaxation.[88] Conflict between Liu Hsiang's Twenty-first Army and local militia extended even into Pa *hsien* itself: in June 1929, the magistrate of the county joined with Jao Kuo-hua, a deputy brigade commander in the area, to disperse by force of arms the militia in two adjoining areas of the county. As the county gazetteer cryptically remarked, "At this time the power of the militia people and their arrogance went beyond the limit, often intruding into administrative and legal matters."[89]

In the period after 1927, when Liu Hsiang was firmly ensconced in Chungking, the Twenty-first Army Headquarters attempted to reorganize local militia affairs in such a way as to ensure army control over militia finances and activities. In 1932, Headquarters ordered the abolition of the local countinghouses, situated in several market towns in each county, leaving only the central countinghouse (*tsung liang-kuei*) in the county capital. This made it harder for peasants to bring their tax payments to the collectors, but on the other hand it left less room for unsupervised militia abuses in the collection of the land tax.[90] In the same year, Headquarters issued a plan for the regulation of militia operating funds and activities. The plan called for closer scrutiny of county budgets to prevent misallocation of funds to militia units, and it prohibited individual *hsiang* from privately collecting militia funds, as indicated above. A phased three-year program aimed at consolidation and coordination of militia forces was issued, with provisions for censuses, registration of weapons, and the training of militiamen and unit leaders.[91]

The Twenty-first Army also attempted to resolve the problem of militia independence by making county magistrates appointed from Chungking concurrently chiefs of the county Militia Affairs Committees, and giving these Committees control over lower-level militia units. Headquarters proclaimed its ultimate purpose with regard to militia affairs in the garrison area with the slogan, "All the people militia, all the people soldiers."[92]

Despite these efforts to remove the vital militia forces from the control of "bad gentry" and to eliminate militia autonomy, the Twenty-first Army seems not to have fully conquered the problem by 1935, when central government troops and political advisers moved into Szechwan in large numbers. One of the first orders of business in 1935 was militia reform, although to be sure the reforms of 1935 were directed at the entire province and may have been addressed to conditions in other areas besides Liu Hsiang's. In a new multi-phased program proposed in 1935, the first step in militia reorganization was still the consolidation of control at the county level.[93] Liu Hsiang's principal financial adviser warned in May 1935 that local finances had to be thoroughly rearranged if local control was to be wrested from the hands of bad elements and the *chen* and *hsiang* were not to become tiny garrison areas in their own right.[94]

The era of Liu Hsiang's solitary control of Chungking ended early in 1935. The previous year, Liu had faced a triple crisis: in northern Szechwan, provincial militarists had failed to confine the communist threat presented by Hsü Hsiang-ch'ien and Chang Kuo-t'ao; the economy of the garrison area had declined severely under the burdens of vastly increased taxation and collapsing external markets; and the beginning of the Long March had made Szechwan a likely target for Chu Te and Mao Tse-tung. Late in 1934, therefore, Liu Hsiang had made the first journey of his life outside Szechwan, to seek help in Nanking. As a result of his conferences with central government leaders, Nationalist penetration of Szechwan began in earnest. A Staff Corps from Chiang Kai-shek's headquarters arrived in Chungking in January 1935 to advise Liu Hsiang on ways to fight the communists and reorganize Szechwan's armies. Civilian advisers affiliated with Yang Yung-t'ai, the architect of Nanking's local administrative reform schemes, accompanied the Staff Corps to Szechwan.

As the communist menace to southern Szechwan receded in the summer of 1935, the Provincial Government established in February moved from Chungking, the seat of Liu Hsiang's power, to the traditional administrative center at Chengtu. Meanwhile, despite initial understandings that central government forces would not move into Szechwan, National armies came up the Yangtze from Hupeh while others entered western Szechwan after pursuing the communists north from Yunnan. After first concentrating heavy forces along the Szechwan-Kweichow border to forestall a communist advance into the province at Ho-chiang, Liu Hsiang transferred troops to western Szechwan, along with other provincial militarists, to keep Chu Te and Mao Tse-tung away from the Chengtu plain. Foreign observers noted at this time that provincial troops were being sent to remote fronts while central government forces were occupying key economic and strategic centers in the Szechwan basin.[95]

Although the Provincial Government, of which Liu Hsiang was Chairman, was relocated in Chengtu, Liu Hsiang maintained his military presence in Chungking. Not until June 1937, after several weeks of extreme tension and ostentatious war preparations by the Twenty-first Army and central government forces around Chungking, did Liu relinquish control of the city and move his headquarters westward to Yung-ch'uan.[96] Liu's withdrawal from Chungking a month before the outbreak of full-scale war between China and Japan turned out to be a major step in making Chungking the seat of the national government less than a year later. When hostilities erupted in East China, Liu Hsiang was made Commander of the Seventh War Area, but he died—some said he was killed—in a Hankow hospital in January 1938.

The notion that occupying a given territory militarily is not the same thing as ruling it is nothing new; it is expressed in the adage that one can conquer on horseback but one cannot govern on horseback. Over and over in Imperial China, dynasts realized that their tenure depended as much on the fulfillment of accepted social and ethical norms as it did on the imposition of military force. In the early Republican period, despite the elimination of the Imperial institution and effective central authority, despite the disappearance of formally standardized and centralized bureaucratic procedures and structures, the distinction between military occupation and local control remained. Liu Hsiang and his division commanders, operating out of Chungking and other cities in the garrison area, did not have to worry so much about the legitimacy of their authority; in the absence of recognized higher authority the formal administrative structures that had embodied prestige and legitimacy were theirs to manipulate. Nonetheless, while Liu was able to make the formal bureaucratic apparatus his instrument, he was still constrained by durable local social forces outside his Twenty-first Army structure.

That these forces were more often "bad gentry," "militia lords," or "local bullies" than "old landlords" or "upright gentry" was a highly significant reflection of early-twentieth-century social changes that require much deeper study. The phenomenon might be seen as the continuation —or rather the result—of a metamorphosis of the traditional local subofficial elite that had commenced long before 1911.[97] It probably also reflected provincial military commanders' ill-treatment of wealthy and respected gentry families, especially the imposition of ruinous taxes that forced old families to abandon their lands and permitted less honorable individuals to acquire land. Changes in the pattern of landholding in Szechwan were clearly visible to investigators in 1935.[98]

From still another standpoint, the autonomous power of "militia lords" and "bad gentry" in the Szechwanese countryside during the garrison area period reflected a longer-term evolution of the late Ch'ing gentry-led militia itself.[99]

The point is, however, that while the cast of characters had changed by the early Republican period—militarists and puppet bureaucrats replaced governors-general and centrally appointed magistrates; bullies and "militia lords" replaced "upright gentry"—the relationship of higher-level authority to local control remained substantially unchanged. In the case of Liu Hsiang and the other militarists of Szechwan, at least, the familiar chasm between official rulers and populace remained un-bridged.[100] The traditional functions of local control—taxation, labor requisition, and maintenance of order—also persisted. The urban-based regime of Liu Hsiang depended, as had its bureaucratic predecessors in the Ch'ing, on knowledgeable local natives to carry out essential con-trol functions in the garrison area. The waves of political modernization, such as they were, that crested in Szechwan in 1911 had receded after the Revolution, and long-established forms of local administration and control endured into the 1930's.

During the garrison area period from 1927 to 1935, when Liu Hsiang was in sole possession of Chungking, the city was vital to his military position in Szechwan but only indirectly important to his control over the garrison area. Liu's army and his regime were based on the city; revenues from Chungking (as well as Wan-hsien and other trading cen-ters) enabled Liu to equip enormous forces and keep the loyalty of his ambitious subordinates. Without the armed forces that possession of Chungking enabled him to raise, Liu Hsiang would not have been able to hold the territory of his garrison area against coalitions of hostile rivals.

If Liu had not held his counties, someone else would have, in which case the revenue and manpower of those counties would not have been Liu's to use. In that sense, too, Chungking's importance to Liu's military strength was basic. Once the fact is accepted that Chungking enabled Liu to occupy as many counties as he did, however, it should be noted that the essential ingredients of local control were not dependent on the city at all. The urban base that permitted Liu to rise to military pre-eminence in Szechwan had little to do with Liu's relationship to local militia and other elements whose intermediary functions were indispens-able to local control.

Educational Modernization in Tsinan, 1899–1937

DAVID D. BUCK

"How are educational systems shaped by and how do they in turn affect the structures of society that allocate resources, exercise power and provide social order?"[1] Thus Burton R. Clark phrases the question asked in what might be called the political approach to the study of education, the approach I will be using here. This approach permits me to investigate who controlled the schools and how these people sought to modernize education. It also fits the available records. Materials on the organization and control, the numbers and functions, and the prescribed curricula of schools in Shantung province are reasonably complete. Histories of individual schools and biographies of individual educators and students can be found. Several incidents in provincial history during the decades dealt with in this volume centered around the schools or around student activities. Thus an account can be given of how Shantung society shaped the early modern school system and how the schools in turn shaped the society.

An attempt will also be made here to consider the educational modernization of Tsinan in relation to the central-place hierarchy as analyzed by G. William Skinner.[2] In this attempt, frequent reference will be made to the operation of the provincial educational administration located in Tsinan as well as to the schools in other parts of the province. In this fashion I hope to show the difference between education in Tsinan, the topmost city in the central place hierarchy in Shantung, and other parts of the province.

Traditional and modern educational systems have a number of things in common, the most basic of which is that both preserve and transmit cultural values and resources. Both train the ruling elite. In another perspective, both train those who would become the elite; both must be seen, in short, as important determinants of upward social mobility.

The two kinds of systems differ in important ways, however. In modern educational systems schooling ceases to be an experience for the privileged alone and becomes a general, often compulsory, experience of youth. Closely related to the mass character of modern educational systems is state control over education. Although such control is not logically necessary for the functioning of a mass education system, in practice the modern state usually intervenes as the agent that sustains schools. In traditional societies, religious or local secular institutions supported the schools. In China, guilds, lineage organizations, and village groups were the secular organizations that most often operated schools.

Another major difference between modern and traditional educational systems is the professionalization of the teacher in the modern system. In the traditional system the teacher is one who possesses a general education—or merely more education than the average for the area—and is appointed, often self-appointed, to teach children. In modern systems teachers receive special training in addition to their regular education, and then are certified by the state or professional society before being allowed to teach. Typically in modern systems there arise strong professional groups, usually acting in cooperation with the state, to improve education and protect the teachers' interests.

Modern education has a number of other characteristics that follow from its state-controlled, mass, professionalized nature. One rather obvious example is that "education becomes more differentiated, more internally complex and more elaborately connected with other features of society."[3] From this it follows that modern education becomes a major determinant of every individual's economically usable skills. Thus, education comes to play a larger part in determining social roles and status. Modern education also contributes an important part of the homogenization of political, economic, and social norms required in the modern nation-state.

In traditional China the state did not control schools directly. Instead it dominated education by means of the examination system. The schools faithfully prepared their students for these examinations, thereby providing all educated men with a common intellectual background. Primary schooling in late traditional times was conducted in a wide variety of schools. Some were operated by families, some by clans, some by villages and some by voluntary associations such as guilds. An important variety of these traditional primary schools was the endowed school (i-hsüeh) operated from contributions of benefactors. The quality of primary education varied widely. Because of financial difficulties or other considerations the primary schools would have only a short life. The compiler of the educational portion of a Shantung gazetteer from the 1890's suffixed his listing of primary schools in his county with the remark, "The difficulty with community schools (*she-hsüeh*) is not in establishing them, but in sustaining their operation."[4]

The real work of preparation for examinations took place in the academies. Every county seat ordinarily had an academy.[5] The level of instruction in individual academies corresponded to the type of examinations given in that city. In an ordinary county capital the academy would prepare students for the county examination (*hsien-k'ao*), whereas academies in the prefectural capitals specialized in preparing students for the various prefectural examinations (*yüan-k'ao, sui-k'ao,* and *k'o-k'ao*). The provincial capital usually boasted several academies. One or more would have special courses to prepare students for the triennial *chü-jen* examinations (*hsiang-k'ao*).

I have subdivided the history of educational modernization in Shantung into four periods. The first starts with Yüan Shih-k'ai's governorship of Shantung in 1899 and extends until the new Board of Education (*Hsüeh-pu*) began to create a national educational system for China. This first period is marked by official dominance and control. The second period, during which the gentry increased their control over education, begins with the new national educational system and extends until 1914–15 when Yüan Shih-k'ai acted decisively against gentry power in parliament and in the provincial assemblies. The third period begins after Yüan's death in 1916 and extends to the last stages of divided political control in China before the success of the Northern Expedition in 1927–28. This third period I have characterized as a time of liberal, professional reform. It includes both the May Fourth Movement and the golden age of Chinese capitalism (1917–23).[6] The fourth period, marked by Kuomintang control, begins in 1928 and ends when the Japanese invasion of North China reached Shantung in the last months of 1937.

Official Programs for a National School System, 1899-1905

Education was one of the first subjects on which the Empress Dowager entertained reform proposals after the Boxer debacle. Yüan Shih-k'ai, who had been governor of Shantung during the height of the Boxer crisis, joined other prominent officials in presenting memorials to the throne on the subject of education.[7] Yüan's ideas for a national school system were drawn from Chang Chih-tung's *Ch'üan-hsüeh p'ien* (Exhortation to Study) published in 1898.

Yüan's memorial proposed that each province establish a three-tiered

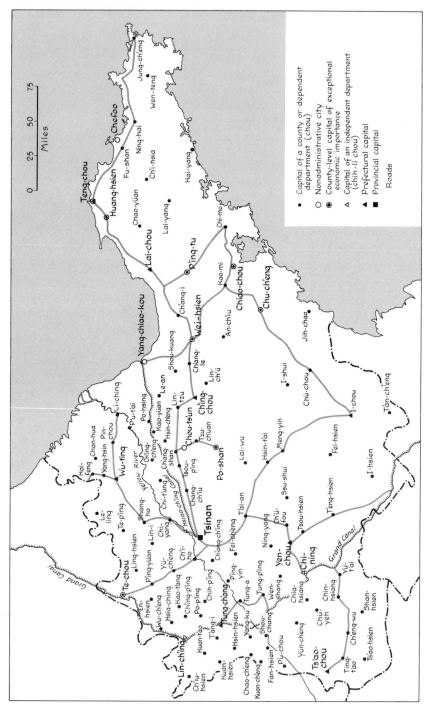

MAP 1. SHANTUNG IN THE 1890's

Legend:

- Capital of a county or dependent department (chou)
- ○ Nonadministrative city
- ◉ County-level capital of exceptional economic importance
- ▲ Capital of an independent department (chih-li chou)
- ▲ Prefectural capital
- ■ Provincial capital
- — Roads

Miles
0 25 50 75

Place names (as labeled on map):

Jung-ch'eng, Wen-teng, Chefoo, Ning-hai, Fu-shan, Chi-hsia, Huang-hsien, Chao-yüan, Teng-chou, Lai-yang, Hai-yang, Lai-chou, P'ing-tu, Ch'ang-i, Kao-mi, Chi-mo, Yang-chiao-kou, Wei-hsien, Chiao-chou, Chu-ch'eng, Shou-kuang, An-ch'iu, Chang-le, Li-ching, Po-hsing, Lo-an, Lin-tzu, Lin-ch'ü, Jih-chao, P'u-t'ai, Kao-yüan, Hsin-ch'eng, Chou-ts'un, Ching-chou, Chan-hua, Ching-ch'eng, Chang-ch'iu, Tzu-ch'uan, I-shui, Chü-chou, T'an-ch'eng, Wu-ting, Yang-hsin, Pin-chou, Tsou-p'ing, Po-shan, Lai-wu, I-chou, Hai-feng, Le-ling, Shang-ho, Chi-yang, Chi-tung, Hsiao-ch'ing Canal, Chang-ch'iu, Tsinan, Li-ching, Meng-yin, Fei-hsien, I-hsien, Te-p'ing, Chi-ho, Ch'ang-ch'ing, Fei-ch'eng, T'ai-an, Hsin-t'ai, Ssu-shui, Teng-hsien, Te-chou, Ling-hsien, P'ing-yüan, Lin-i, Ch'i-ho, Ch'ang-ch'ing, Ning-yang, Chü-fou, Tsou-hsien, Wu-ch'eng, Hsia-ching, Kao-t'ang, Ching-ping, Po-p'ing, Ping-yin, Tung-a, Wen-shang, Chia-hsiang, Chin-hsiang, Kuan-t'ao, T'ang-i, Hsin-hsien, Yang-ku, Shou-chang, P'u-chou, Yün-ch'eng, Chü-yeh, Cheng-wu, Shan-hsien, Tung-ch'ang, Tsao-hsien, Chiu-hsien, Kuan-hsien, Chao-ch'eng, Fan-hsien, P'u-chou, Tsao-chou, Ting-t'ao, Grand Canal, Yellow River school system with the most important school (*ta-hsüeh*) at the provincial capital, the second-level school (*chung-hsüeh*) at the prefectural level, and the third-level school (*hsiao-hsüeh*) in each county seat. The terminology adopted for these schools was the same as that later used for university, secondary, and primary schools, but clearly neither Chang nor Yüan intended the three levels to work in quite that way. Both Chang and Yüan intended separate lower primary schools (*meng-yang hsüeh-t'ang*) to provide primary education. These schools, which would instruct children ages six through thirteen in the classics, simplified astronomy, geography, and mathematics, could be located in any town or village without reference to the administrative hierarchy.

Both also suggested that the existing academies be transformed into the three-tiered school system. Completing the course of study in these schools would become the equivalent of passing the examinations held at the county, prefectural, and provincial levels. Initially both Chang and Yüan had thought the schools could be combined with preparation for the examinations. However, later they suggested the examinations should be abolished because preparing for traditional degrees continued to be more attractive to students than the modern schools.[8]

In his 1901 memorial Yüan also adopted Chang Chih-tung's *t'i* and *yung* distinction whereby Chinese classical studies were the core of an education and Western political and scientific studies were added. Yüan went on to explain the connection between education and the power of the state: "The strength or weakness of a country is seen in its human talent. The abundance or scarcity of human talent is the source of the state. Schools are the means by which human talent is developed. Today the world has changed greatly and the times are extremely difficult. To obtain men to govern, we must increase learning and thereby we will assemble talent."[9] Yüan was typical of late traditional bureaucratic leadership in that he equated national strength with the worth of a nation's officials and not with the worth of its general populace.

Yüan's proposal was accepted by the throne and in September the academies were ordered transformed into three tiers of official schools. In Shantung, the higher-level school (*ta-hsüeh*) was already established at Tsinan during Yüan's tenure. This school became known as the provincial college.[10] After Yüan had been transferred to Chihli his successors carried out the establishment of the second and third tiers of schools in the prefectures and counties.[11] This marks the beginning of the modern school system in Shantung.

In Tsinan, Yüan transformed the Le-yüan Academy, the best in the city, into the new provincial college. American missionaries from a school near Chefoo were hired to teach there. The missionaries resigned after a controversy over regulations requiring all students to participate in Confucian ceremonies.[12] Japanese educators were hired as replacements.

In addition to his college program, Yüan also was responsible for other modern educational projects in Tsinan. The Shantung Military Preparatory School (*Shan-tung wu-pei hsüeh-t'ang*) was established in 1902 as part of the system of military schools Yüan created to provide officers for his modern armies. Yüan also created an orphanage (*Chiao-yang ch'u*), meant to train youngsters from poor families in handicraft skills such as carpentry, shoemaking, weaving, rope making, and straw braiding. Another project Yüan supported was the establishment of handicraft bureaus (*kung-i chü*) to promote local handicrafts in various areas of Shantung.[13] All were first begun in Tsinan. The Tsinan schools were intended to serve both as models and as resource centers to provide the personnel and expertise for establishing similar operations at lower levels in the administrative hierarchy.

Many of Yüan's proposals were actually carried out by his successors in the governorship. Chou Fu, a former secretary to Li Hung-chang, was governor of Shantung from 1902 to 1904. Yang Shih-hsiang, a close political ally who was also related to Yüan by marriage, was governor from 1905 through 1907. Both did much to put Yüan's plans into effect and even to elaborate on them.

In January 1904 Chang Po-hsi, Chang Chih-tung, and Jung-ch'ing submitted to the throne a new national education program.[14] As with many reform ideas in China after 1895, this plan was modeled on the Japanese system. In part, it also was a further elaboration and rationalization of the 1901 program. The provincial-level school retained its status as a college; the prefectural school became more recognizably a middle school; the county school became a higher primary school.[15]

The higher primary school in the county seat is a key to understanding the whole system. In the 1904 plan these higher primary schools were the bottom rung of the official schools. Below that level, education remained the responsibility of the local community. Locally supported schools, called lower primary schools, provided the first years of education. The higher primary school, with official financial support, duplicated the schooling available in the lower primary schools but also provided the two or three years of instruction required for entrance into middle school. Thus, entrance into a higher primary school was decisive in a student's chances for a middle-school education. In spite of several changes in the name and the duration of the higher primary school, its character as the chief selection point for higher education was retained.

Other important features of the 1904 plan were the establishment of special normal schools for the training of teachers and vocational schools to teach commerce, industrial and handicraft skills, farming, and the skills necessary to become a clerk in the bureaucracy. At Tsinan the first teacher training school had been established as part of the provincial college in 1902. The handicraft bureaus helped provide the beginnings for the vocational schools.

The official attitude toward education after 1901 also encouraged local gentry to establish unofficial modern schools both at the primary level and above. In Tsinan in 1903–5 about half a dozen such schools at the secondary level were started by groups of individuals.[16]

This early period of educational modernization is distinguished from the later ones discussed in this paper not so much by the form of the school system as by the purposes for which education was intended. Unlike the programs developed after 1906, these early programs were not intended to train young Chinese for the responsibilities of citizenship. In the minds of reformers such as Chang Chih-tung and Yüan Shih-k'ai, educational reform was meant to produce more and better-educated officials. The concept of education as training for citizens had to wait for the acceptance of the idea of constitutionalism by the dynasty.

The Development of the Concept of Popular Education

Just as the ideas of Yüan Shih-k'ai and Chang Chih-tung about the purposes of education fit closely with traditional Chinese concepts of the polity, so the ideas of the reformers and revolutionaries matched their conceptions of a modernized polity. Many of these new leaders were in exile in Japan, where a growing community of Chinese students was gathering in hopes of learning Japan's secret. Liang Ch'i-ch'ao was the leading intellectual spokesman for Chinese reformism in those days. His arguments about the connection between education and national strength went far beyond the ideas of Chang Chih-tung. Liang came to stress the popular, mass character of education as well as the changes in curriculum that would be needed to make education contribute to a strong, modern China. In 1902 he wrote,

During the nineteenth century [European] statesmen of great vision clearly recognized that the aim of education lay in the rearing of citizens (*kuo-min*). . . . Today, China cannot simply desire to promote learning. If we desire to promote learning, the government must use its interventionist powers to start a primary education system.

Since the goal is to create citizens, then the system must educate the sons of the whole country.[17]

Liang's explanation of the aim of education betrays a strong constitutionalist bent that separated him from men who continued to serve the Manchu empire.

Liang made no effort, however, to solve the problem of China's military weakness. This humiliating deficiency was of great concern to many politically aware Chinese. The desire for a militarily strong China was one of the few common concerns shared by many young Chinese students in Tokyo and reform-minded officials with the imperial administration.

Some young men had no difficulty combining a concern for constitutionalism with plans for a strong military in China. In 1902 Chiang Fang-chen contributed an article entitled "Education for Militaristic Citizenship" to Liang Ch'i-ch'ao's magazine *Hsin-min tsung-pao* (New People's Journal).[18] In it Chiang introduced a new concept of citizenship called "militaristic citizenship" (*chün kuo-min*). He defined it as patriotism, public morality, honor, character, and patience. Chiang argued that good citizens and good soldiers should have the same personal qualities, and therefore some direct connection should be made between the schools and the army. He suggested that students be organized into military formations. Chiang Fang-chen and others who elaborated on this concept admitted that their prescriptions for militaristic citizenship were largely based on the Japanese example.

As students returned from Japan, their concern with constitutionalism and a strong China was conveyed directly and indirectly to others in their home areas. Many of these students, both the military and the civilians, had been sent to Japan specifically to prepare to become teachers. These teachers included members of the T'ung-meng Hui and many who did not join that organization. Most seem to have imbibed the principle that China's strength could be increased by educating people about their relationship to the state in terms of the Western concept of citizenship.

Reform Under the New Board of Education, 1906–11

Before the Board of Education (*Hsüeh-pu*) was established and the old examination system abolished in late 1905, some of the proposals of the 1904 official reform plan had already been put into operation in Shantung and other provinces. The real start of the new education system in China was delayed until the spring of 1906, when the Board of Education began to issue directives to set up a national school system.[19] Schools were divided into primary, secondary, and higher levels. Primary education was split into steps. The first took the young student from age six through age eleven. The higher step took the student up to age fifteen. Graduates of higher primary schools would be eligible to enter middle or vocational schools.

The new Board was divided into general and vocational sections. The general section dealt with teacher training, middle school, and primary school. The vocational section was responsible for the wide variety of commercial, administrative, and agricultural schools to be established at the secondary level. In addition to the ordinary bureaucratic trappings the Board had an office of educational inspectors and an office that approved textbooks for use in the schools. There was also a special section responsible for Peking University (see Figure 1).

The goals of education under the new Board were to teach loyalty to the throne, reverence for Confucius, respect for military and public service, and moreover to provide an education that had practical application.[20] The most radical shift, however, was in the open declaration that the new education was to have a mass, popular character. In the new statement of educational goals, the Board argued: "In promoting education today, China properly emphasizes general education and has decreed that none of the people of the state should be without some schooling."[21] The same document explained respect for public service as closely related to patriotism and adopted the term "militaristic citizenship" in explaining the usefulness of respect for military service. In these aspects the new Board was carrying out a program deeply indebted to the dynasty's critics.

In the provinces a new commissioner of education (*t'i-hsüeh shih*) replaced the old commissioner (*hsüeh-cheng*), whose chief responsibility had been administering the triennial examinations. The new commissioner was nominated by the central Board, but served under the control of the provincial governor. The office of the commissioner was organized along the same lines as the central Board. In addition to the general and vocational educational sections there was a set of educational inspectors and a special group of gentry advisers (*shen i*) (see Figure 2).

At the county level an educational promotion office (*ch'üan-hsüeh so*) was established. This new office was to "coordinate all educational work within the borders of the county."[22] The county magistrate selected the general administrator (*tsung-tung*) of the new office. The general manager in turn selected several local men to serve as educational promotion officers for the school districts (*hsüeh-ch'ü*) of the counties. The local promotion officers were to be selected from "among those interested in education who possess the upright moral character of gentry."[23]

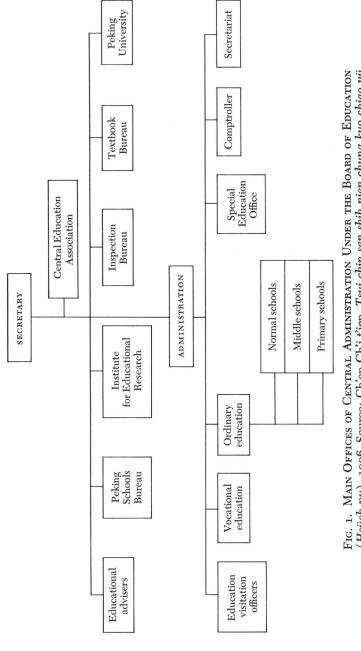

FIG. 1. MAIN OFFICES OF CENTRAL ADMINISTRATION UNDER THE BOARD OF EDUCATION (*Hsüeh-pu*), 1906. Source: Ch'en Ch'i-t'ien, *Tsui chin san shih nien chung kuo chiao yü shih*, 1930, chart between pp. 75 and 76.

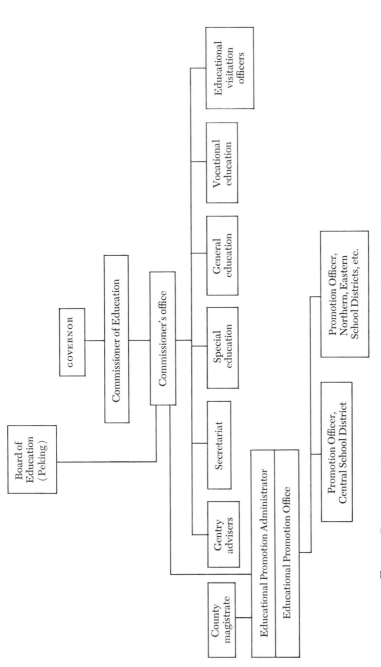

FIG. 2. PROVINCIAL EDUCATIONAL ADMINISTRATION UNDER THE BOARD OF EDUCATION. Source: Same as for Figure 1.

These regulations gave the local gentry control over education within the county and its educational subdistricts. The logic of such a policy was obvious: the school districts depended upon local resources to underwrite both the lower primary schools and most expenses of the county-level higher primary school.

The first task of educational promotion officers was to convert community property such as academies, temples, and endowed schools (*i-hsüeh*) into property of the state school system. In Shantung the first example of this kind of change, which became common after 1906, is found in the transformation of the Le-yüan Academy into a provincial college. Official records in Tsinan report but do not describe the transfers. For a description of the actual process, we must go to the Shanghai gazetteer. The board of directors of a Shanghai academy met and voted that under a new educational system they would turn the school over to official control. The directors made certain restrictions, and a one-year trial period was established during which the agreement was apparently revocable.[24] In addition to the buildings and grounds, these community institutions owned land and had investments, ordinarily in the form of money placed with pawnshops for lending.[25]

Between 1906 and 1911 many schools and large properties suitable for use as schools became state property. This conversion program is a major turning point in the educational modernization of China. It marks the decision by the gentry to let the state take over responsibility for sustaining local schools.

The concept of the educational promotion office is closely related to the new interest in constitutionalism that swept through the Ch'ing imperial system in 1905. The Empress Dowager gave her consent in that year for moves toward the creation of a constitutional monarchy in China. The Manchus felt that by creating some representative institutions they could continue to reign and to rule over China. The most conspicuous evidence of the Court's new attitude was the dispatch of a mission under the Manchu noble Tsai-tse to investigate constitutional arrangements in other countries.

Even before Tsai-tse's mission returned to write a favorable report, the Ch'ing authorities began to press for more local influence in administration through widening local control in the national education system. Thus historically there was an important connection between the establishment of educational promotion offices at the county level and the growth of local representative institutions prior to the 1911 revolution.

The character of the educational promotion office drew heavily on the tradition of official reading of the Sacred Edicts, or imperial instructions. During the Ch'ing dynasty the County Director of Studies (*chiao yü*) and his assistants were responsible for seeing that the Sacred Edicts were read at the appropriate occasions in the Confucian temples in the city, at public ceremonies, and at gatherings in the markets and villages. By the nineteenth century this tradition had fallen into general disuse, although there were attempts to restore it in the post-Taiping period of reconstruction and again around the turn of the century.[26] The 1906 regulations for educational promotion offices revealed the Manchu reformers' intent to have the new officers continuing to conduct the traditional ceremonies:

> Conduct of public lectures: Every locality will establish a lecture place and, following the former regulations for proclaiming the Sacred Edicts, will invite special officers to proclaim [the edicts] at appropriate times. For the towns and villages, a lecturer should be sent on market days to lecture. The responsibility for managing this lies with the educational promotion office as overseen by the local magistrate.[27]

The new promotion officers also carried the joint designation of Director of Studies until 1910.[28]

The material authorized for use in the lectures included the Sacred Edicts, the 1906 statement of educational aims, the imperial edict announcing the preparation for a constitutional regime, and a wide range of other materials including tracts on ethical education (*hsiu-shen*), history lessons, and Chang Chih-tung's *Exhortation to Study*.[29] The new regulations specifically enjoined the lecturers from making use of their post to give partisan political speeches.

The financial aspect of the new education program set the general pattern of educational finance in Republican China. Central government funds sustained the Board of Education and its operations. The provincial treasury provided for schools designated as provincial (*sheng-li*) schools. Schools at the county level, however, did not receive official funds and had to depend on local resources for both capital and operating budgets. The program's designers probably intended the same gentry who served as educational promotion officers to support the schools through donations. This intent, however, did not prevail. A series of local surtaxes, collected, for instance, on the ordinary land tax, and other special local levies became the chief source of local school revenues. Thus, local schools were supported by general local taxes.[30]

The position of educational promotion officer and the men who filled it were critical to the financial viability of the new national education program. First, the establishment of schools depended upon their endeavors; then, the schools' survival came to depend upon their willingness to impose local surtaxes.

The local gazetteer of Wei *hsien* contains information on the background of the educational promotion administrators.[31] Of the three men who occupied that post before 1912, two were *sheng-yüan* and one was a *chü-jen* degree holder. All were prominent men who went on to have extensive careers in public office. The most active was Chang Yü-ying, who had been a member of a local Society for the Study of Mass Education (*Chih-ch'ün hsüeh-she*) established in Wei-hsien in 1903. Chang started his own primary school at Wei-hsien in 1906. In 1908 he became head of an institute for retraining older teachers in the aims and techniques of the new education. Chang served as head of the Education Promotion Office in Wei-hsien from 1909 through 1912. While in that post he also held the presidency of the Wei-hsien Chamber of Commerce. He made a large donation to Wei-hsien primary school.[32]

Chang Yü-ying did not support the forces that operated against Yüan Shih-k'ai in eastern Shantung during 1915 and 1916. He became secretary for the Shantung provincial assembly in 1918. From 1923 to 1928 he served as head of the Wei *hsien* tax office. Chang Yü-ying typifies the gentrymen who dominated the school system after the 1906 reforms were enacted. He came from a wealthy family and was interested in educational modernization. His interests led to increased personal power, which took shape in his home district and then was transferred to the provincial capital.

Like the progressive gentry, the members of the T'ung-meng Hui were deeply involved in educational modernization. Mary Backus Rankin has noted in her study of the pre-1911 revolutionary movement in Chekiang that the revolutionary elements were able to obtain the support of progressive merchants and gentry to establish schools.[33] Once in existence these schools became centers of revolutionary ideas and actions. This pattern is also evident in Shantung.

The Society for the Study of Mass Education mentioned above exemplifies how this cooperation worked. In Wei *hsien* the members of that society included, in addition to Chang Yü-ying, the head of the local academy (who became the principal of the Wei-hsien middle school), the future chief compiler of the local gazetteer and a local gentry leader who served as county magistrate in 1928. In 1906 these men, along with a retired county magistrate who was then serving as an educational adviser to the Shantung governor, all contributed funds to a school founded by a member of the T'ung-meng Hui. This school, the Shantung Inland Public School (*Shan-tso kung-hsüeh*), was a center of revolutionary propaganda and activity until forced to close by provincial authorities in 1907.[34]

Unlike the Lower and Middle Yangtze valley branches of the T'ung-meng Hui, the Shantung branch confined itself primarily to educational work until the Wu-ch'ang Uprising. The Shantungese in Japan who were early members of the T'ung-meng Hui were P'eng Chang-yüan, Hsieh Hung-t'ao, and Ting Wei-fen. Lin Kuan-san, the founder of the Shantung Inland Public School, was the leading member within the province. Except for Ting Wei-fen, who remained in Japan, the other three leaders all became involved in creating schools in Shantung. P'eng Chang-yüan helped create a middle school at the prefectural seat for Ts'ao-chou (Ho-tse) in southwestern Shantung. Hsieh Hung-t'ao started a comparable school at Yen-t'ai, adjacent to his home district.[35]

It appears that the T'ung-meng Hui in Shantung was working on a general plan to establish revolutionary schools in the prefectural seats in Shantung. The Ch'ing officials were able to shut down T'ung-meng Hui schools, but they could not make a concerted drive against all of its members connected with education. Many supporters remained on the teaching staffs of the secondary schools, where they had relative freedom in spreading revolutionary ideas. In some places the military drills, sanctioned by the national educational program's use of the concept of militaristic citizenship, were used to prepare students to overthrow the dynasty. Even in Tsinan it was possible for teachers to teach the ideas of the T'ung-meng Hui openly in the schools.[36]

Nevertheless, the real control over education continued to lie with the Ch'ing officials. Typical of these men was Fang Yen-nien, a *chin-shih* from Anhwei who first came to Shantung when his fellow provincial Chou Fu was serving as Governor. Fang was appointed head of the first teacher-training classes in Yüan Shih-k'ai's provincial college. He remained involved in teacher training for several years. For a brief time in 1907 Fang served as Educational Commissioner for Shantung. While in that post he closed down Liu Kuan-san's Shantung Inland Public School because of its revolutionary character.[37] Officials such as Fang had great power to influence the new education through their access to provincial funds. Fang could arrange for subsidies from the provincial treasury to help in establishing schools that would follow the modern scheme of education.

In addition to the provincial (*sheng-li*) schools, there were two other kinds of schools found in Tsinan before 1911. One was a private (*ssu-li*) school; the other a public (*kung-li*) school. Both were supposedly independent of the provincial treasury. Official subsidies, however, became common. In Shantung the schools that received the subsidies usually were located in Tsinan. This meant that aspiring educational modernizers from all over the province were drawn into Tsinan in hopes of obtaining official monies to support their new schools. The period between 1905 and 1911 saw private and public schools in Tsinan increase at a rate much faster than the official schools. This fact, together with the practice of granting subsidies, increased the importance of the Tsinan schools in the Shantung school system.[38]

Education and the Early Republic, 1912–16

Under the new Republic the national education office assumed a new name, Ministry of Education (*Chiao-yü pu*) and a new set of educational goals. The Ministry announced that in the new Republican order there would be "an emphasis on moral education, supplemented by vocational and militaristic citizenship training, rounded out by aesthetic education."[39] Moral education remained the foremost consideration, but meant instilling a spirit of loyalty and service to the Republic rather than to the Ch'ing throne.

The first official acts of the new Ministry sought to abolish the emphasis on memorization and on the Confucian classics, to introduce coeducation into primary schools, and to add handicraft and military drill to the primary school curriculum. Although these bold pronouncements established a general direction for educational reform, the Ministry's directives were not followed by most educational authorities.

The new orientation obviously necessitated new textbooks. The Ministry established an office to approve texts. The new books departed from the old classical primers in trying to relate the process of learning to read more closely to the child's actual experience. During the early Republican period Chinese educators became convinced that the new materials could promote nationalism as well as, if not better than, the traditional materials.[40]

As part of the new Republican program, teacher-training institutes were established to retrain experienced teachers. At these schools teachers received short-term courses of instruction both in the new aims of education and in the use of education to support the Republic. One such institute was established in Tsinan in the fall of 1911 just prior to the October revolution. The institute closed because of the Wuchang Uprising, but resumed operation in 1912. In 1913 the institute came under the management of the Shantung Provincial Education Association. It passed out of existence sometime in 1915 or 1916.[41]

Classes of about 150 teachers studied in a course of unknown duration, probably two or three months, at the end of which they were expected to return to their home districts to conduct similar institutes for teachers in their own areas. Records from Wei *hsien* show that such an institute operated there from 1913 through 1915.[42] Martin Yang's account of his boyhood education in eastern Shantung notes that the teacher in his village school, a Mr. P'an who was head of a wealthy clan, went to the district seat at Chiao-chou to attend such an institute.[43]

The investigations of Huang Yen-p'ei, the Kiangsu educational modernizer and promoter of vocational education, reveal that the resistance of teachers was the main impediment to the success of the program. Huang Yen-p'ei visited Shantung in 1914 to inspect the province's schools. In Po-shan the district magistrate told him that older teachers had refused to change their teaching methods or their materials to fit the standards taught in the institute.[44] This was a serious setback for the educational modernizers, who had hoped to reform education at the provincial capital and then to use teacher-training programs to spread reform quickly into the lower reaches of the central-place hierarchy.

The new national program, the new textbooks, and even the new educational philosophy did not produce a major shift in the locus of power in education. As in the years since 1905, the real power in education lay with local gentry leadership. There was a shift to younger men with more modern educations, but in a more important sense the republican period did nothing to stop the increasing power of the gentry. Many of the men elected to the first provincial assemblies in 1909 and to the provincial legislatures in 1912 had been prominent in the development of modern education. For example, the head of the Tsinan teacher-training institute was elected to the provincial and then the national legislature in 1912.[45] This is only one of several dozen cases showing that involvement in education prior to 1911 was a main avenue for the development of nonmilitary provincial leadership in the early Republic.

The career of Wang Hung-i illustrates the close connection between politics and education in the early Republic.[46] Wang was the first Commissioner of Education for Shantung under the Republic. He was a returned student from Japan, who had, as already noted, joined with others to create a middle school at the prefectural seat of Ts'ao-chou (Ho-tse). Wang was then a member of the Revolutionary Alliance. After the Republic was established, he broke away from the leadership of Sun Yat-sen and the parliamentary Kuomintang to follow some of the smaller, more conservative anti-Japanese political groups.*

Under Wang's direction and with the support of the provincial legislature, a plan to establish sixteen provincially financed middle schools

---

* In Shantung a split over the proper attitude to take toward Japan developed along geographical lines. Individual political and commercial leaders from the Wei-hsien trading system were somewhat more tolerant toward the Japanese than were the inland leaders.

and ten normal schools, all at the secondary level, was adopted in 1913. Three of the middle schools were in Tsinan; twelve of the remaining thirteen were located at the site of the ten prefectures and two independent departments that were the next level of administration below the province under the old Ch'ing system.[47] The thirteenth was a middle school to be located at Ch'ü-fu, the home of Confucius. Important commercial places such as Chou-ts'un and Wei-hsien were given no provincially financed schools. By contrast, less commercially prominent administrative places such as Ho-tse, Hui-min, or Lin-i received schools.

The background of the three provincially sponsored middle schools in Tsinan is revealing. One had always been an official middle school. The other two, however, began as early nonofficial middle schools. The principals of the two schools were both prominent men with close connections in the provincial legislature. One of these men, Chao T'ung-yüan, became a member of the provincial legislature in 1918 while he was still principal of Tsinan's largest middle school.[48] The new provincial legislature continued to provide large subsidies to the nonofficial schools in Tsinan.[49]

In Tsinan no record survives of public objection to such favoritism. Reports from rural areas in southern Chihli and northern Shantung, however, show that in 1913 irate rural residents rioted over alleged misappropriation of school funds resulting from collusion between the provincial legislature and the county-level bureaucracy.[50]

The heyday of the educational modernizers and the provincial legislatures proved to be short. Yüan Shih-k'ai directed a dramatic reversal in national policy from Peking in the latter half of 1913. At the beginning of that year, after the election of the new national parliament, Yüan felt he was faced with two major, related internal problems. One was the power of the parliament itself. The other was the continuing crisis in the central government's finances. By the beginning of 1913 it was obvious that the Peking government must rely upon foreign loans unless the provinces resumed remittances of tax revenues.[51] This financial crisis had a deep impact on the course of the young Republic. On the one hand it forced Yüan to entertain almost any foreign loan proposal. On the other it gave his distaste for representative government a very practical basis. When the provinces persisted in their refusal to turn over revenues, and the national parliament spent as liberally as if the revenues had come in, Yüan dissolved both parliament and the provincial legislatures in his retrenchment program.

Shantung, unlike the Central Yangtze provinces, was under Yüan's firm control even before the Second Revolution of 1913. The Governor was

Chou Tzu-ch'i, a trusted subordinate of Yüan. The province was garrisoned by the Fifth Division, one of the units in Yüan's Pei-yang Army. The commander was Chin Yün-p'eng, a Shantungese who was educated in the Pei-yang military school system.[52] When the Second Revolution broke out in the summer of 1913, some men such as Wang Hung-i resigned their bureaucratic posts. There also were some small uprisings in eastern Shantung led by supporters of Sun Yat-sen, and manned by teachers and students. These flare-ups were put down ruthlessly by Chin Yün-p'eng.

Chin was promoted to Governor of Shantung in late 1913. In early 1914 Yüan disbanded both the national parliament and the provincial legislatures. The financial crisis, however, remained unsolved. Chin proceeded with a rapid program of financial reform in Shantung. County magistrates who were behind in their tax remittances were removed from office, a new system of provincial control over county tax revenues was put into operation and several new taxes were imposed. Chin resumed remittances to Peking.[53]

The financial retrenchment program caused a 25 percent reduction in educational expenditures in Shantung.[54] The sixteen middle schools called for in 1913 were reduced to ten, all in former prefectural seats; the ten normal schools were reduced to four, one for each of the four circuits (*tao*) that had replaced the prefecture as the next major level of administration below the province.[55] Subsidies were withdrawn from the nonofficial schools in Tsinan, and several closed as a result.

Although among the cities of Shantung Tsinan was the most seriously hit by the cutbacks, it remained the center of education in the province. Tsinan still had four provincially supported schools at the secondary level. Provincial funds also went for two model primary schools, a military preparatory school and a girls' middle school as well as a girls' normal school.[56] Two good nonofficial middle schools continued operation, as did the Catholic mission schools. The surviving schools were larger, better equipped, better financed and better staffed than those at the prefectural seats.

Prior to retrenchment Tsinan had boasted 24 primary schools supported by provincial monies. The total number of provincially supported primary schools in Shantung had been only 36, and no other city had had more than one. This inequitable use of provincial taxes for the benefit of Tsinan residents was reduced somewhat in 1915 and 1916, when financial responsibility for some primary schools was turned over to the administration of Li-ch'eng county (Tsinan was the seat of this county).[57]

The opposite situation prevailed in Wei-hsien. As of 1914 a total of

TABLE 1. DISTRIBUTION OF COUNTY-SUPPORTED MIDDLE SCHOOLS IN SHANTUNG, 1912–30

| Date school established | County name and location within province | | | |
	Eastern Circuit	Southern Circuit	North Central Circuit	Northwestern Circuit
1912	Huang *hsien*			
1913	Wei *hsien*		Ch'ang-shan	
1914	Kao-mi			
1919			Lai-wu	
1920	Lai-yang			
1924	Chu-ch'eng Jih-chao Shou-kuang Lin-chü Chao-yüan Ch'i-hsia	I-shui	Po-hsing	
1925	Wen-teng Lin-tse An-ch'iu	Chü *hsien*		Kao-t'ang
1926			P'ing-yüan Lo-ling	
1927	Fu-shan			
1930	Kuang-jao	Chang-ch'iu		
Total:	15 of 28 counties or 54%	3 of 33 counties or 9%	5 of 29 counties or 17%	1 of 17 counties or 6%
	Overall total: 24 of 107 counties or 22%			

SOURCE: *Ti i tz'u Chung-kuo chiao yü nien chien*, 3: 270–72.

four counties in the entire province of Shantung supported their own middle schools (see Table 1 above). All four were located within the Wei-hsien trading system.*

In 1915, after the fiscal retrenchment policy was well established, Yüan Shih-k'ai promulgated a new set of educational aims to correct the liberal excesses of the early Republic.[58] Yüan stressed a return to the classics both for principles of conduct and for teaching materials. The aims were never realized, because many of the politicians and officials driven out of the legislatures and government administration in 1913 and 1914 returned to their home districts to become educators. Wang Hung-i, to cite an example already mentioned, was the principal of the middle school at Ho-tse during these years. Other men, former legislators and administrators, especially those from eastern Shantung,

* Ch'ang-shan was part of the city trading system centered on Wei-hsien even though it lay outside the Eastern Circuit.

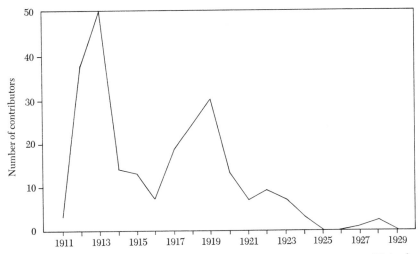

FIG. 3. CONTRIBUTORS TO SCHOOLS IN SHANTUNG, 1911–30. Source: *Ti i tz'u Chung-kuo chiao yü nien chien* (1934), 5: 358–59.

returned to their home districts to teach and to work for Yüan Shih-k'ai's overthrow.[59] These men came to dominate local education authorities and the local education associations (*chiao-yü hui*). From there they blocked implementation of Yüan's conservative education program.

While political leaders in Shantung were withdrawing from politics into education, gentry contributions to official schools dropped dramat- ically (see Figure 3). The sharp rise in such contributions in 1912 and 1913 is good evidence of the gentry's support of the new Republic. Wealthy men were willing to see this new form of government, which they largely controlled, take over the formal responsibility for maintain- ing the schools they had once managed as nonofficial public institutions. As Yüan withdrew power from the national and provincial legislatures, however, the gentry lost interest in donating their own money to the state's schools. Although gentry contributions rose again temporarily after Yüan's passing, the spirit never fully revived.

In summation, the early Republic saw the modern school system ex- pand rapidly along lines most favorable to the gentry leaders who domi- nated the provincial legislatures. Yüan Shih-k'ai halted this expansion, but was not able to destroy the power of the gentry over education even after the representative bodies were disbanded. His attempt to reintro- duce more traditional materials and principles into education failed be- cause of the resistance of his opponents who occupied important posi- tions in the school system.

The question remains whether the schools called provincial middle schools and county primary schools were really modern. Missionary educators were quick to claim that schools were modern in name only.[60] The reports from Huang Yen-p'ei, a leading Chinese authority on educational modernization, are mixed, but mildly encouraging. In Tsinan, Huang found that the best provincial primary schools had good facilities, plenty of modern equipment, and adequate teachers. He found the teachers reluctant to use all the teaching aids available, but found the standard textbooks in use. On the other hand, Huang also found a primary school, Li-ch'eng County Primary School 11, that was exactly like traditional primary schools (*ssu-shu*). The school was dark, windowless, and had only a single teacher. Few books, let alone any other supplies, were available. In his travels to other parts of the province, Huang found the same variation. Most provincial or county-supported schools were real centers of modernization, but the general school system was still composed largely of small schools that were modern only in name.[61]

Education and the Pei-yang Warlords, 1916–28

Yüan Shih-k'ai's scheme to become emperor destroyed the hope that China could be ruled as a republic. Yüan's death in June 1916 left the central administration in the hands of the North China military and bureaucratic cliques who had been his chief supporters. The rapid succession of warlord cabinets at Peking failed to produce any plans for the development of China. In these circumstances it is little wonder that the central bureaucracy lacked a coordinated purpose, that policies shifted rapidly to fit short-term political alignments, and that the lower echelons sometimes ignored directives from above.

Professionalization of education. Surprisingly, in spite of all this, the Ministry of Education developed a reasonably well-coordinated policy. The key to this success was the Ministry's use of professional associations of educators as policy advisors. The Ministry would incorporate certain of the professional associations' suggestions into its policies and give them its official sanction. Putting the policies into effect, of course, depended on the inclinations of the administrators and teachers in the provinces. But the very fact that educational policy was being made in this way—on the basis, for example, of recommendations from the annual national conventions of Provincial Educational Associations (*Ch'üan-kuo chiao-yü hui lien-ho hui*) or the prestigious China Educational Improvement Association (*Chung-hua chiao-yü kai-chin hui*)— made it easier to obtain the support of local educators. Publications such as *Chiao-yü tsa-chih* (Education magazine), *Hsin chiao-yü* (New education), and *Chung-hua chiao-yü* (Chinese education) were devoted to promoting educational reform. These magazines helped inform and convince the teachers about new Ministry policies.

Cyrus Peake, in his perceptive account of education in the early Republican period, dates the important change in the character of professional education groups to 1915, about a year after Yüan Shih-k'ai had made his dominance over the Republic clear and complete. According to Peake, "From 1915 on we note a new spirit among educators. They commenced to grasp their problems more realistically and to adopt toward them a more professional attitude."[62] This turn toward professionalism within the ranks of Chinese educators is an important sign of modernization.

The first regulations for official educational associations had been promulgated in 1906 along with the rest of the modern education program developed by the new Board of Education.[63] Prior to that time there had been organizations such as the Society for the Study of Mass Education in Wei-hsien, and Ts'ai Yüan-p'ei's China Education Society (*Chung-kuo chiao-yü hui*) in Chekiang. Ts'ai's group was deeply involved both in revolution and educational modernization. The group at Wei-hsien was not revolutionary, but was nevertheless quite political.

Until the provincial assemblies were formed in 1909, the local educational associations probably were local political forums. After 1909 this function devolved on the new representative bodies. When Yüan Shih-k'ai had undertaken his drive against the legislatures and political parties, we have seen how many men who had been combining careers in education and politics began to emphasize education. After Yüan Shih-k'ai's death, when it was clear that no one group in China could hold national leadership, education must have seemed an attractive alternative to the uncertainties of a political career.

While the early warlord struggles disrupted orderly government, the educational associations began to claim China could build herself into a power through education. This direction of effort produced the intellectual spirit of the May Fourth Movement. The emphasis on nonpolitical but progressive professional reform showed the influence of Chinese students educated in the United States. American educators such as John Dewey and Paul Monroe from Columbia acted as critics and advisors to Chinese educational circles.[64] At the same time the professional identity and independence of education was growing, the ranks of teachers were filling with more and more young people who had received specialized teacher training. For them teaching was a profession, a modern and progressive profession that could help transform China.

A review of the resolutions passed at the annual national conventions of the Provincial Education Associations between 1911 and 1925 reveals that the Associations' enduring interests were 1) promoting nationalism in the schools, 2) standardizing the Chinese language, both written and spoken, 3) developing physical education, usually along the lines of military drill, and 4) increasing the control of professional educators over schools and school finances.[65]

After the May Fourth incident of 1919, China produced even bolder improvement programs. At the instigation of professional educators, the Ministry promulgated a plan to spread compulsory four-year education from the provincial capitals and treaty ports in 1920 to the smallest village by 1928.[66] The program, which was modeled on a Shansi province project, proved totally unworkable because of shortages of teachers, schools, and financial support. Nevertheless, it is of interest here in that it clearly shows the key role of provincial capitals such as Tsinan. The provincial capital or treaty port was to be the center from which reform would spread to the lower reaches of the central-place hierarchy. A 1922 survey undertaken by teachers in Tsinan to determine how compulsory education was working revealed that only 60 percent of the students entering primary schools in Tsinan finished four full years. The survey could not produce any figures about the percentage of eligible children who actually attended.[67]

Another product of the May Fourth Movement was the new national education program announced in November 1923. The aims of this new program, which drew heavily on the theories of American educators, were to promote social reform, to spread education among the masses, to contribute to China's economic development, and to train individuals in economically usable skills.[68]

Educational circles in Shantung quickly responded to these developments. In 1922 the national convention of the Provincial Educational Associations was held in Tsinan. Afterward there was an obvious increase in professional interest in the province. The *Shan-tung chiao-yü yüeh-k'an* (Shantung education monthly) became the official voice of professional education for the province. Published monthly in Tsinan for three years, the magazine contained articles on local, national, and foreign developments in education.[69] In January 1923 a Research Society for Implementing the New Educational Program (*Shih-hsing hsin hsüeh-chih yen-chiu hui*) was founded in Tsinan.[70]

In line with the professional interests of educators, the reforms called for an increased voice for teachers in the administration of schools. In 1921 the annual Education Association convention said the name of the educational promotion office no longer accurately reflected the work of the office and recommended the name be changed to education bureau (*chiao-yü chü*). This was done in 1923.[71] The change reflected a change in the character of local education administration. The Educational Promotion Office had ceased to be the preserve of the local gentry and had come to be dominated by professional teachers. These changes had not occurred suddenly in 1921, but had been developing for almost a decade. When the regulations for the Educational Promotion Office were rewritten in 1915 and 1916, the qualifications for promotion officer were changed from gentry status plus an interest in education to teaching or administrative experience in a modern school and a modern education.[72]

Tsinan's schools. In Tsinan these 1915 and 1916 regulations gave the Li-ch'eng county education office some independence from the provincial authorities for the first time. Still the provincial capital's schools continued to be supported primarily by provincial and not county monies. The records indicate that only after 1923 did Li-ch'eng county bear anything like its proper share of the financial burden for the many schools located in Tsinan. Tsinan continued to have an advantage, for a 1927 survey of education showed that all Tsinan schools at the secondary level were supported by provincial funds and the county merely financed the primary schools.[73]

The 1927 survey came just before serious external problems temporarily closed many schools in Tsinan, at the height of the improvements that had been possible under the liberal reforming attitudes of the May Fourth Movement. At that time Tsinan was just beginning to develop a provincially sponsored university. This was the first attempt at an officially sponsored university-level institution in Tsinan since Yüan Shih-k'ai's college. The new university was to combine a number of advanced classes from the city's middle, normal, and vocational schools. There was also at this time a thriving and well-endowed Protestant school, Cheloo University, located in Tsinan. Cheloo had moved from Wei-hsien to Tsinan in 1917. The missionary university had a medical school and a hospital as part of its facilities.[74]

There were nine secondary schools supported by provincial funds in Tsinan.[75] These included a boys' and a girls' middle school, a boys' and a girls' normal school, and five vocational schools. Provincial funds also supported four higher primary schools.

The Li-ch'eng county Education Bureau was subdivided into eleven school districts. The first school district, located in Tsinan city, had seven higher primary schools. The second, located at Le-k'ou, Tsinan's port, had five higher primary schools. The other nine school districts were rural and had only four higher primary schools among them. In addition there were 325 four-year lower primary schools, and 194 old-style primary schools (*ssu-shu*) in operation in Li-ch'eng county. The locations of these schools were not specified. A list of recommendations accompanying this survey called for the rapid spread of primary schools into the neglected rural districts and the creation of teacher-training institutes to prepare teachers for these rural posts. Education in the rural areas of Li-ch'eng county clearly lagged behind those in Tsinan city.

In 1927 an American, H. F. Smith, investigated rural schools in eastern Shantung. He used a Tsinan private primary school for comparison with the official rural schools.[76] Although Smith did not rate the Tsinan school highly, all its four teachers had graduated from modern normal schools, whereas the rural teachers were typically older men with traditional educations. The building and the curriculum in the Tsinan school were much more modern than in the rural schools. The rural schools lacked lavatories, playgrounds, adequate lighting, and regular school hours. The rural curriculum continued to use the Chinese classical texts, and the rural teachers used the traditional rote-recitation teaching methods. Huang Yen-p'ei had found similar conditions in some Tsinan schools in 1914. By 1927 such conditions had disappeared in Tsinan but persisted in rural areas.

Educational improvement was concentrated in but not limited to Tsinan during this period. Education also improved in the provincially financed secondary schools in other cities. In addition, the number of county-supported secondary schools increased significantly (see Table 1). In 1924 eight additional county-supported middle schools opened; the following year another five started operation. An interesting geographical split emerges in the pattern of new county-supported middle schools. Of the thirteen cases cited above ten were in the eastern half of Shantung. Thus, while education was improving in the Tsinan area and to the east through the Wei-hsien trading system, the inland areas to the west of Tsinan and the mountain areas to the south of the capital lagged behind.

Educational finance underwent no basic changes during the warlord era. The provincial government continued to confine its support to those schools designated as provincial schools. And since Yüan's retrenchment program had not solved the fundamental problems of provincial finance, even this support became shaky. Normally the teachers' pay was several months in arrears because of warlord exactions from the provincial treasury. On at least one occasion in 1921 the provincial schools in Tsinan were forced to close because of a financial crisis.[77]

Budgets during these years were a special kind of bureaucratic fiction.

TABLE 2. SHANTUNG PROVINCIAL BUDGET (YÜAN), 1922

Receipts			Expenditures	
Land		1,542,000		
Taxes	1,267,000		Education	741,000
Rent	28,000		Administration	263,000
Reclamation	199,000		Finance	230,000
Miscellaneous	48,000		Industry	89,000
Consumer taxes and			Total	1,323,000
license fees		291,000		
Other taxes		45,000		
Extraordinary income		13,000		
Total		1,891,000		

SOURCE: FO 228/3277 Tsinan Intelligence Reports, 1st Quarter 1918 and 3d Quarter 1921.
NOTE: This budget does not include military expenditures, the largest item in the total provincial budget, estimated at 5,600,000 yüan for 1917. The source of military funds is not clear. All figures are given to the nearest thousand yüan.

Allocated funds were often unavailable; military expenditures usually exceeded the entire civilian budget. The 1922 Shantung budget gives an indication of the priority education received in provincial affairs during these years.

Finally, a question arises about the influence on education of the prosperity of Chinese capitalism and commerce between 1917 and 1923. The Chinese bourgeoisie wanted two kinds of education. The first, and most important, was a general education for their own sons and daughters. That education, controlled by the educational modernizers, was strongly nationalistic, stressing patriotism and development of China's strength. The Chinese bourgeoisie accepted these qualities as virtues. However, the bourgeoisie, like the rural population, continued to look to modern education as the door to the official career that was still considered the height of success in Chinese society.[78]

At the same time the bourgeoisie wanted to develop a well-trained corps of workers and craftsmen to operate the factories and the railroads. Vocational schools served this purpose. Vocational schools at the secondary level specialized in agriculture, commerce, and industry. In Shantung there were also vocational schools for educating government clerks and mining engineers.[79]

In a society that had always attached greatest value to general education, people from the middle schools and secondary normal schools looked down on the vocational schools, whereas the vocational school administrators tried to imitate the tone and curricula of the middle schools. This division surfaced in Tsinan as early as 1922 when a fight broke out between the vocational educators and the generalists over control of the Shantung Provincial Education Association. The vocational interests temporarily won, but the Ministry of Education intervened to give control back to the generalists.[80] This incident tells little about the bourgeoisie's impact on education, but shows quite clearly that there were struggles among the modernizers. Interestingly, the traditionalists had retired from educational policy matters in Tsinan.

In summary, then, the warlord period was marked by the rise of professionalism and liberal ideas in education. The goals of education remained strongly nationalistic. Support for education was especially strong in the cities; professional educators tended to teach and to operate from the cities. Their plans for educational modernization, like those of their predecessors, saw the city as the point from which modern education would be broadcast into the countryside. In spite of the vagaries of warlord politics, there was some success with this program in Shantung. Tsinan's schools, however, improved at a much faster rate than those of the countryside. As a result Tsinan developed quite a modern educational program, especially at the secondary and higher levels.

Education and the Rise of Nationalism

The outstanding characteristic of modern education in China has been its championship of Chinese nationalism. Cyrus Peake pointed this out over forty years ago, and his judgment accurately captures the tone of modern education from 1906 through the 1930's. The May Fourth demonstrations show how well the students learned their lessons in modern nationalism. Tsinan, as the leading center of education in Shantung, was the center of May Fourth activity in the province.

In Tsinan the tension over the Versailles negotiations had been building during March and April of 1919.[81] Public meetings protested the continuing Japanese control of Tsingtao, the Shantung railroad, and the adjacent mines. There also was considerable feeling against Japanese merchants. Men like Chin Yün-p'eng, former governor of Shantung and future head of the Peking government, the leading industrialist P'an Fu, and Wang Hung-i encouraged these growing anti-Japanese sentiments.[82]

Prior to May 4 there had been some mass meetings in Tsinan, but the nationalist movement was weak and divided along the lines of earlier political struggles in the province. After students in Peking and Tientsin transformed the anti-Japanese feeling into a national student movement, anti-Japanese political groups in Shantung worked to broaden the base of the movement in Tsinan. Merchants began to show their support.

The governor, Chang Shu-yüan, remained loyal to the position of Tuan Ch'i-jui's Peking government, but for a few weeks general popular support made the boycott against Japanese goods effective. Japanese residents of Tsinan and the Japanese consulate took precautionary meas-ures including increasing the military garrison and evacuating some Japanese nationals, but Tsinan's Japanese were never attacked. In accounts of the May Fourth incident produced on the mainland during the late 1950's, it was argued that merchants abandoned the stu-dents and caused the nationalist movement to collapse in Tsinan.[83] The reports of the British Consul in Tsinan, John Pratt, fully corroborate this allegation. Pratt reported that merchants found themselves without any stocks after the boycott had been running several weeks. At the same time, Governor Chang Shu-yüan was "embarking on trading ventures with the Japanese and reaping handsome profits." As a result merchants dropped their support of the boycott and the students.[84]

The students continued the boycott. The next few months produced a riot at a newspaper that supported Tuan Ch'i-jui, mass arrests of stu-dents, and some student deaths. Finally, Chang Shu-yüan was forced out of office and replaced by a new general, T'ien Chung-yü, who had ties with the anti-Japanese party in Shantung. T'ien Chung-yü, under great pressure from the Japanese, proved to be no great friend of the students. Educators, prominent among them the missionary educators at Cheloo, felt the student movement had gone too far and encouraged students to return to their studies.[85]

Outside Tsinan at cities with secondary schools, there were reflections of the May Fourth demonstrations. Students led boycotts of Japanese goods in T'ai-an, Liao-ch'eng, Wei-hsien, and Chefoo. A few students even began to take their nationalistic message from the cities into the villages, although they apparently did not receive much of a hearing there.[86]

Anti-Japanese sentiments remained strong in Shantung cities, how-ever. When the Washington Conference started to take up the question of Shantung in 1922, tension mounted in Tsinan. In the complicated ne-gotiations to restore the former German concessions to Chinese control, local and national interest were combined for the Shantungese. Those active during the negotiations in 1922 and 1923 were students, business-men, and local politicians.[87]

At the time of the next great nationalistic outburst following the May Twenty-fifth incident in Shanghai, Tsinan and Shantung were under the control of Chang Tsung-ch'ang. That warlord would not tolerate dem-onstrations. The only indication of opposition in Tsinan were some pru-dently mild demonstrations by the protected students at Cheloo Uni-versity.[88]

These events help to define the character and geographical distribution of nationalism in Shantung. At the center in Tsinan the main support for nationalism came from the teachers and the students. Size estimates of the crowds participating in the demonstrations never exceed several hundred, and the demonstrations were confined to Tsinan and to the other cities in Shantung that supported secondary schools. The presence of a secondary school was obviously related to measurable support for nationalistic causes in Shantung during the 1920's. The great majority of these schools were located in former prefectural cities or in cities within the developing Tsinan–Wei-hsien corridor. Throughout the province at the level of the central market town and below there was little or no interest in nationalistic causes. Even when nationalistic causes were tied to provincial interests as in the case of Japanese control of Tsingtao, rural areas gave little support.

The Impact of Banditry, Warlordism, and Civil War, 1923–32

While education, commerce, and industry advanced at Tsinan and other Shantung cities during the early 1920's, a serious problem developed in rural life. The evils of landlordism were part of this problem, but even more visible was the rapid decline of local administration.[89] Yüan Shih-k'ai had broken the beginnings of county self-government in his drive against political parties and financial insolvency. The warlords who inherited Yüan's system were more interested in extracting revenues than in providing decent administration for the people under their control. The variety of local taxes, special levies, and contributions required by the warlords to maintain their armies was a serious drain on both merchants and farmers. Yet the warlord armies could not effectively maintain order outside the cities where they were garrisoned, and in the early 1920's the problems of banditry began to increase. In Shantung the worst area was I *hsien* in the southern part of the province.

In response to the rise of banditry, local self-protection groups with secret-society overtones flourished in southern and southwestern Shantung in the mid-1920's. Some were known as the Red Spears (*Hung-ch'iang hui*) and others were branches of familiar secret societies such as the Big Sword Society (*Ta-tao hui*). In mid-1923 the British consul at Tsinan reported thirteen different self-protection groups operating in thirteen different counties.[90] Many of the groups had special arrangements with the bandits of their local areas. The provincial military units showed little interest in either the secret-society protection groups or the bandits as long as their operations were confined to small areas and no large groupings developed. By the mid-1920's, banditry and the resulting self-protection groups were common in the northwest portion of the province and were beginning to appear in the Tsinan–Wei-hsien corridor.[91]

The self-protection associations, because they were strongly identified with particular localities, probably had no detrimental effect on education. In fact, evidence from the 1930's indicates that such groups may have encouraged schools in rural villages. These schools, however, were traditional schools, one-room affairs taught in the traditional manner and based on the traditional Confucian primers. The existence of local self-protection groups indicates that the people rejected government's exclusive claims to the means of social control, and that rural areas were breaking away from the regular administration. The state could not establish or sustain schools in those areas.[92]

The situation in Shantung took a serious turn for the worse in 1925 when Chang Tsung-ch'ang became governor of the province. Illiterate and ill-tempered, Chang Tsung-ch'ang has become the archetype of the evil warlord. He had been born on the Shantung peninsula but had emigrated to Manchuria, along with thousands of other Shantungese, to seek his fortune. He had been both a bandit and a soldier. After the 1911 revolution he served in military posts in North and Central China before joining Chang Tso-lin, the warlord of Manchuria, in 1921. In 1925 with the backing of Chang Tso-lin and some Japanese interests, Chang Tsung-ch'ang returned to Shantung as governor.

Fighting for control of Shantung. Most of the warlords who ruled Shantung before Chang Tsung-ch'ang had managed to stay clear of serious military involvements. Chang Tsung-ch'ang, however, kept his armies in the field during most of his three-year tenure. First he fought against Feng Yü-hsiang's Nationalist Army (Kuo-min-chün). Then, in 1926, he prepared to face the Northern Expedition. More taxes were levied and more contributions demanded. The official Shantung bank began printing large amounts of worthless paper money.[93]

Chang Tsung-ch'ang's activities had a disastrous impact on education in Shantung. All the official schools in Tsinan closed in October 1926 for lack of money. The schools remained closed until Chang declared them open after the lunar new year of 1927. Even then, few of the students and teachers in the government schools returned to their studies. At the best private school in Tsinan only 400 of the 1,300 students resumed classes.[94] For the first time, the school system in Tsinan had been seriously damaged by a warlord's policies.

In the spring of 1927 ordinary business stopped as Chang prepared for the expected onslaught of Kuomintang forces. The Japanese cabinet, fearful for the safety of its nationals, dispatched a division of troops to garrison the Shantung railroad line and Tsinan. The anticipated Kuomintang offensive into North China did not occur in 1927.

In the 1928 campaign Chang Tsung-ch'ang was driven out of Shantung. The first Kuomintang armies to reach Tsinan found themselves facing a Japanese division sent to protect Japanese nationals. The two armies clashed in the streets of Tsinan. Subsequently the Japanese shelled the city, and the Chinese suffered several hundred military and civilian casualties. The Kuomintang armies withdrew from Tsinan and the representatives of the Nanking government established a skeleton administration at T'ai-an, the former prefectural city south of Tsinan. The schools in Tsinan were closed all during 1928. The Shantung schools and educational administration did not function that year.

The political situation in Shantung remained unsettled during 1929. Various Chinese and Japanese forces garrisoned some parts of the province. In other areas gangs of ex-soldiers and bandits roamed about. There was no real central educational authority in Shantung in 1929. The Kuomintang administration at T'ai-an announced plans for the new educational system, but it was only a paper plan. The Kuomintang was in no position to put any such plans into operation.[95]

Chiang Kai-shek did not want Feng Yü-hsiang to control the province. He bought off Feng's subordinate commanders Han Fu-chü and Shih Yu-san. As a reward for his support for Nanking, Han Fu-chü received the chairmanship of the Shantung provincial government in late 1931.

This digression into the military operations in Shantung illustrates how widespread and serious the disruption of ordinary life had been in Shantung during the 1920's and early 1930's. Business, industry, schools, water conservation, and many other aspects of life in Shantung were affected. Disruption in cities such as Tsinan, Wei-hsien and Chi-ning had been preceded by growing disorder in the countryside, and the rural disorders persisted during the worst years in the cities.

The situation in education in Wei *hsien* illustrates the general conditions.[96] In the early 1920's there were three middle schools in Wei *hsien*. One was the county middle school; another, a missionary school. In 1925 the third, a private middle school, was established in the market town of Han-t'ing east of Wei-hsien. In addition three new teacher-training institutes were established between 1923 and 1925, two in Wei-hsien and the third in a school district south of the city. In 1925 there were 22,000 students enrolled in all the various primary schools of the county. These statistics indicate that Wei-hsien was experiencing the steady expansion in modern education that would be expected for a city of its size and importance. This growth was taking place without any major assistance from the provincial educational administration.

In 1928 when Chang Tsung-ch'ang was driven out of Shantung, Wei-hsien was garrisoned by Japanese troops. Both urban and rural schools were closed. In Wei-hsien the local gentry temporarily took over administration of the city and control of the schools. By 1929 the schools in Wei-hsien were back in operation, but the number of primary-school students dropped by more than a third, to 15,000. The middle school in Han-t'ing never reopened. The teacher-training institute outside Wei-hsien also remained closed. The two secondary-level schools inside the city, however, managed to reopen.

This situation at Wei-hsien was duplicated throughout the province of Shantung. All the schools had been closed by the general disorders. But once peace returned to Shantung, the city schools found it easier to resume operations than the schools in market towns and villages.

Education Under the Control of the Nanking Government, 1929–37

In 1928 a national conference on education met in Nanking to formulate a new set of educational goals. The first goal was to promote nationalism in order to "instill in the minds of the people the national spirit [and] to keep alive the old cultural traditions."[97] The second aim was to use education to help the Chinese attain democracy. The third was to use education to increase economic well-being. In other words the Ministry adopted a program that committed the Chinese school system to Sun Yat-sen's Three People's Principles: Nationalism, Democracy, and People's Livelihood.

Not only did education help attain these goals, but it became the primary medium for spreading Sun's ideas among the Chinese. Shanghai publishers quickly produced a new set of textbooks fitted to this task. The Kuomintang openly proclaimed it would use the schools to indoctrinate Chinese youth in its political philosophy as part of its program of nation building.[98]

In 1931 the League of Nations sent a team of experts to China to review the existing educational system. The investigators did not visit Shantung or Tsinan, but their observations fit what we know about the Shantung school system. The report begins by noting that Chinese schools ignored the nation's social needs.

The result of all these conditions [political instability, financial uncertainty, educational experimentation] is the creation and development in China of schools and educational institutions not conducted on a strict system and not suitable to the needs and conditions of the country. The result is a favouring of schools of higher standard, especially rising far above the condition of the impoverished country whilst the primary and vocation instruction most indispensable for the people is neglected.[99]

TABLE 3. EDUCATION EXPENSES PER STUDENT IN CHINA, ABOUT 1930
(MEXICAN DOLLARS)

Type of school	Cost per student	Ratio to lower-primary cost
Lower primary school	$4.0	—
Higher primary school	17.0	4.25:1
Secondary school	60.0	15:1
Vocational school (secondary level)	120.0	30:1
University	600–800	150–200:1

NOTE: Ratios are calculated using the per-student cost in lower primary schools ($4) as 1.
SOURCE: C. H. Becker, et al., *The Reorganization of Education in China* (Paris: League of Nations, Institute of Intellectual Co-operation, 1932), p. 51.

In administration the report noted, "Each school possesses an administrative personnel whose numbers are out of all proportion to practical requirements."[100] That situation is reflected quite clearly at Shantung Normal School in Tsinan where the ratio of administrators to students declined from 1:50 in 1916 to 1:25 in 1929.[101]

Educational finance. The League of Nations team's findings on finance constitute an excellent criticism of the situation that existed in Tsinan. The report described three tiers of financial responsibility: national, provincial, and local. Each level supported a different level of education; that is, university, secondary, and primary. Calculating the cost per student at various levels in the national education system, the League's investigators found that university-level education might cost up to 200 times as much as lower primary education (see Table 3). The report went on to note that such ratios were unheard of in Europe where the ordinary cost ratio between primary and university students was on the order of 1:8 or 1:10. A similar but somewhat less inequitable situation existed in the pay scales of teachers in the various levels of schools.

Ronald Yu Soong Cheng compiled additional data on the finances of Chinese schools during the early 1930's. Mr. Cheng provides information on the percentage of total educational costs borne by each level of government. His figures reveal a clear division in educational expenditure according to level of administration (see Table 4). The League's investigators had commented on this situation, "All governments, however, have found where a department does not contribute in the matter of financial resources it can exert no influence. Considering the tremendous importance of primary education for the nation, it is essential that the Central Ministry should have an interest therein, and consequently that it should bear a share of the cost."[102] These recommendations were never put into effect. The Central Ministry only specified

TABLE 4. EDUCATIONAL COSTS BY ADMINISTRATIVE LEVEL IN CHINA, 1930–31

Administrative level	Primary	Secondary	Higher
National	0%	3%	62%
Provincial	8	63	38
County	92	34	0

SOURCE: Ronald Yu Soong Cheng, *The Financing of Public Education in China* (Shanghai: Commercial Press, 1935), pp. 39–41.

curricula. The Kuomintang apparatus atttempted to have Sun Yat-sen's ideas taught in the schools. In Shantung such attempts at ideological education were only moderately successful because the governor, Han Fu-chü, actively disliked Sun Yat-sen's theories, and the Kuomintang was weak.

Ronald Cheng's work also provides information about sources of school funds in Shantung province. Provincial educational expenses depended totally upon annual allocations contained in the provincial budget. County school systems derived an average of 15 percent of their annual expenses from endowments. Unlike provincial educational funds, the county educational funds in Shantung came from special educational surcharges on the land tax. In some places this tax was collected and spent by a separate educational tax office. In other places the educational finances were handled as part of the general county administration.[103]

In 1933 Nanking decreed a nationwide reorganization of county-level educational administration. The Education Bureau became the fifth section of the county administration. This change in no way altered the functions of county educational bureaucracy, but it did mark a decline in the independence of education from county administration. Educators had felt that such independence was not merely desirable but necessary during the 1920's, when the warlords were tapping every possible source of revenue. In the 1930's they were more inclined to accept administrative reorganization done in the name of the Nanking regime. The policies of the Nanking administration, and those of Han Fu-chü's administration in Shantung, however, would inevitably decrease the financial independence of the schools.

The education program in Shantung. Education in Shantung during the 1930's complied in general with the Nanking government's directives. The Kuomintang interpretations of Sun Yat-sen's ideas did not receive the emphasis devoted to efforts to revive traditional Chinese cultural values. Consequently, the schools took on a style and tone somewhat independent of Nanking. The four men who created this difference were Han Fu-chü, the governor; Ho Ssu-yüan, the educational commissioner;

Liang Shu-ming, the philosopher and rural reconstruction leader; and Wang Hung-i, the progressive gentry leader and politician.

Han Fu-chü began his seven-year tenure as Chairman of the Shantung provincial administration in late 1930. Never a Kuomintang stalwart, this former subordinate of General Feng Yü-hsiang used his wiles to remain largely independent of Nanking. Han Fu-chü's interest in education apparently stems from his wife's family. His father-in-law had become a prominent leader in adult education in Peking during the early Republic.[104] Prior to coming to Shantung, Han had served as Governor of Honan where he sponsored Liang Shu-ming's rural work. In Shantung, Han continued to be a good friend of educational causes and especially those of Liang Shu-ming.

Ho Ssu-yüan was a Kuomintang man appointed to head the Shantung educational bureaucracy in 1928.[105] Ho came from Ho-tse in southwest Shantung. He had returned to China in 1926 after receiving both a B.A. and a M.A. in American universities. During the Northern Expedition Ho served as the assistant chief of a political education unit attached to the expedition's headquarters. He remained in charge of educational affairs in Shantung until the Japanese invasion.

Ho Ssu-yüan was quite open in his favoritism for men who had an American education or who came from his home area in Ho-tse. A 1929 list of Shantung educational bureaucrats shows eight with degrees from American schools.[106] Of the 55 positions in this list, men from Shantung filled 27. Nine of the twenty-seven hailed from Ho-tse. It is difficult to know in what order Ho Ssu-yüan ranked his commitments to the Kuomintang, modernization, and his native place. It is clear, however, that Ho reconciled party loyalty with other more traditional commitments.

Liang Shu-ming was a philosopher and educator who wanted to rebuild China's strength through developing her rural majority.[107] Liang believed reconstruction must be based on China's unique social characteristics rather than on the false picture of Chinese society given in Marxian analysis. Liang's greatest difference with the communists concerned class conflict in rural China. Liang believed the basic forces in Chinese rural life were Confucian principles such as harmony, benevolence, and community responsibility. Liang sought to harness these forces to rebuild China. He believed the Kuomintang concerned itself too much with urban and military problems and largely ignored the rural problem.

Liang Shu-ming first worked out the philosophical basis for China's revival while lecturing at Peking University after the May Fourth incident. At that time Wang Hung-i had become his devoted follower.[108]

Wang helped Liang Shu-ming with his first practical experiments in rural areas at Ho-tse, Wang's political base in Shantung. This first attempt did not succeed and Liang undertook a number of different experiments in other parts of China before returning to Shantung in 1930. This time Liang's program was centered in Tsou-p'ing county in eastern Shantung. At first Liang's Institute of Rural Reconstruction worked under the regular county administration. Later the Institute took over the administration of all affairs in the county. In 1933 the Institute received authority to work in Ho-tse county in southern Shantung.[109]

Wang Hung-i, whose career in Shantung education and politics began around 1906, died shortly after the rural reconstruction program made its start in early 1931. This progressive gentry leader had a dual influence on the direction of education. First, Wang from his earliest experiments before the 1911 revolution was interested in strengthening the economy of rural areas and providing education for rural children. Second, in the best tradition of assisting his home area, Wang had promoted all kinds of educational and handicraft industry projects in Ho-tse. One mark of his influence can be seen in the large role of Ho-tse men, led by Ho Ssu-yüan, in educational affairs after his death.

Liang Shu-ming received excellent support for his work from both Han Fu-chü and Ho Ssu-yüan. In Tsou-p'ing Liang tried to develop schools and other community organizations such as marketing cooperatives. In education the main techniques employed were the establishment of peasant schools (*hsiang-nung hsüeh-hsiao*), an adult school that specialized in teaching literacy and modern farming techniques, and touring teams who used demonstrations and lectures to teach literacy, hygiene, and new techniques of farming.[110]

Liang concentrated his efforts within a single county, but planned to place specialists in rural education in all of Shantung's 108 counties. The touring lecturers ranged far and wide in Shantung visiting the county seats and prominent market towns in their tours. Liang explained the techniques he had perfected in Tsou-p'ing: "My method, in all sizes of rural communities (the most typical are villages from 200 to 500 households) is to establish a peasant school. At the beginning you must establish a board of directors for the peasant school. If you want to promote these [schools] in the countryside, there is no way to be successful without first obtaining the consent and agreement of the rural leaders."[111]

Liang's program, with its emphasis on public lectures, on using local gentry leadership, and on developing schools as a key to community organization, bears a striking similarity to the program outlined in the 1906 regulations for the Educational Promotion Office described earlier.

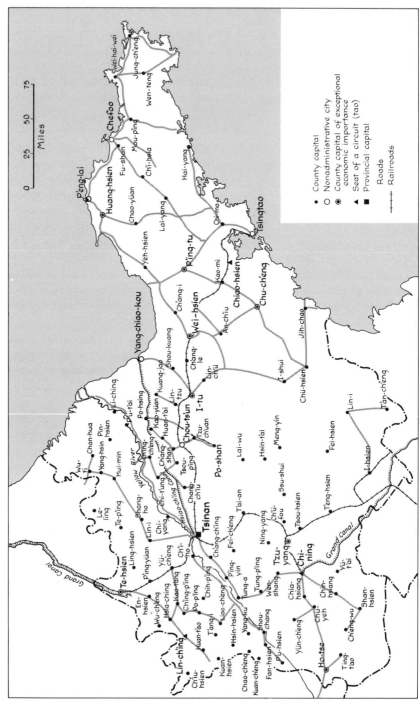

MAP 2. SHANTUNG IN THE 1930'S

Education in Tsinan. Administrative reorganization in Tsinan under the Nationalists produced a city school system with an increasingly urban character. In fact, this reorganization cut Tsinan from many of its previous rural ties. Tsinan received a special status as an urban area under direct control of the Shantung provincial administration. This paralleled the national city status accorded to Tsingtao and several other large coastal cities.

Approximately one-tenth of the area of Li-ch'eng county became part of Tsinan city. The Li-ch'eng administration moved to the village of Hung-chia-lou.[112] Under the new arrangement Tsinan city consisted of the old walled area, the new settlement district, the Huan-t'ai port terminus for the Hsiao-ch'ing canal, the Yellow river port of Le-k'ou and some adjoining suburban and rural land.

Chang Hung-chien, from Ho-tse county, became head of the Tsinan city education office. This was the best-paid such post in the province. The Tsinan school system did not include control over provincial schools in the city, but consisted of thirty-two higher primary schools and a large assortment of adult- and special-education institutes.[113]

The educational attainments of the teachers in Tsinan's primary schools reflect the continued superiority of the city's schools. A 1931 survey showed that 83 percent of Tsinan primary teachers had received special teacher training or a modern education as a professional teacher. Figures from Wei-hsien show only 25 percent of primary teachers with such qualifications.[114] Since Wei-hsien was a progressive city in educational matters, its schools were much better than those of most county capitals in Shantung. These figures reflect the continuing concentration of talent in Tsinan and the widening gap between Tsinan and other places.

On the matter of Kuomintang influence, it seems likely that party influence in Tsinan was greater than in schools elsewhere in the province. In one group of 36 primary teachers in Tsinan, four were Kuomintang party members.[115] A 1:9 ratio of party to nonparty teachers gave the Kuomintang a strong voice in education in Tsinan and ensured that party standards would be met. Figures on party affiliation are not available for teachers outside Tsinan, but the percentages of Kuomintang members certainly were much lower than in Tsinan.

Tsinan's secondary schools, both provincially controlled and private, remained the best in the province. The Protestant-supported Cheloo University flourished in the 1930's after the school's administration came to terms with Kuomintang demands for some control over curricula.[116]

The best Chinese institution of higher education was a new national university established in Tsingtao.

Education in Wen-shang county. The educational work of Liang Shu-ming in Tsou-p'ing was the model for rural education in Shantung and therefore not a proper comparison with urban education. The research conducted in 1935 and 1936 by Liao T'ai-ch'u in Wen-shang county, however, reveals the great differences that had developed in the course of educational modernization between the provincial capital and an ordinary county.[117]

Wen-shang is located near the Grand Canal, about fifteen kilometers north of Chi-ning and sixty kilometers southwest of Tsinan. The county supported no major handicrafts and depended upon wheat, kaoliang, cotton, and peanut cultivation. Wen-shang lies in the ancient state of Lü, the home of Confucius. That area took pride in its reputation as the heartland of traditional Confucian values.

Liao T'ai-ch'u found the government schools in Wen-shang county closed for lack of students. Traditional schools, however, flourished in almost every village. Because of government prohibitions against such traditional schools, these schools operated clandestinely with secret-society overtones to their finances, management, and recruitment of students. Liao asked a sample of parents why they sent their children to these schools rather than government schools. The replies cited four principal reasons. First, the people feared the government schools as an arm of government that would give access to their earnings for taxes and their sons for soldiers. Second, the people disliked what they saw as the foreign orientation of government schools. Third, the teachers in the new schools were thought to be inferior to those in traditional schools, especially in their ability to teach proper discipline. Finally, the people felt the government schools were inflexible to local needs.[118] The antimodern and culturally conservative views reflected in these replies were the very sentiments Liang Shu-ming was attempting to overcome.

The evidence indicates that Wen-shang rejected official government schools in the middle and late 1920's. In 1900 Wen-shang had two traditional academies, both of which were converted into primary schools by 1912. In 1917 Wen-shang supported lower primary schools and a higher primary school. These schools may have been largely traditional, but at least the people in Wen-shang were willing to work within the government system to operate schools. In the early 1920's Wen-shang reached the height of its modernizing tendencies when the county attempted to operate an agricultural middle school. Sometime between 1925 and 1930 this middle school and the other government schools went

out of existence because of endemic political instability, financial shortages, and administrative disorder. Reconstruction programs undertaken
during Han Fu-chü's governorship did not reach into Wen-shang.[119]

The contrast between Wen-shang's schools and those of Tsinan in the
1930's was startling. Tsinan's schools were typically multi-teacher schools
housed in specially constructed buildings that had well-lighted rooms
and regular school grounds. The teachers were usually young men in
their thirties and forties with modern educations. Supervision and control by the regular educational bureaucracy was an ordinary part of
operations. Party influence over the content of education was considerable. The curricula included Sun Yat-sen's Three People's Principles,
the Kuomintang interpretation of China's history and cultural heritage,
the national language, mathematics, and science.[120]

In Wen-shang, Liao found the schools conducted in one-room buildings donated for school use. Conversion to a school ordinarily meant
simply adding benches and a blackboard. The teachers were older men,
usually in their fifties and sixties. The hours were longer and the discipline more harsh than in the city schools. The curriculum was built
around the Confucian classics. The school was ranked by the local people
on the teacher's ability to impart traditional moral virtues to the children. Science had no place in the curriculum.[121]

In summary, education in Shantung under the Nanking regime showed
a widening gap between rural and urban standards, in spite of the efforts
of Liang Shu-ming. In Tsinan and other cities such as Wei-hsien and
Tsingtao, educational modernization made considerable strides. The lower reaches of the central-place hierarchy, however, experienced no sustained general improvement during the 1930's.

The pattern of educational modernization in Tsinan and Shantung
bears out the theory of Ichiko Chūzō about the power of the gentry in
late-ninteeenth- and early-twentieth-century China.[122] Ichiko has argued that the gentry proved able to adapt to the challenges of the late
Ch'ing and early Republic by assuming whatever political coloration
was needed to maintain power. He believes the gentry changed from
opponents of reform in 1898 to proponents of reform after 1905. Reformism became Republicanism after 1911; and he argues that the gentry
maintained power against all challenges until 1949.

My research stops in 1937, but up to that date the data confirm much
of Ichiko's theory. The 1906 plan for educational promotion offices gave
the gentry an access to both political power and educational power that
they quickly used. Throughout the last years of the Ch'ing the gentry
expanded their control in education. Gentry power in politics and educa-

tion in Shantung received a considerable setback as a result of Yüan Shih-k'ai's assault. As a result, the gentry turned away from the more obvious forms of political control to local dominance through a professionalized approach to modern education. Professional educators were strongly nationalistic, willing to cooperate with the state, and convinced of the value of new approaches to education. The evidence from Shantung shows that these men dominated education in Tsinan after 1915 and were responsible for a sustained effort to spread modern schools into the lower reaches of the central-place hierarchy.

Professionalization was an excellent defense against the vagaries of warlord politics until Chang Tsung-ch'ang arrived in the mid-1920's. Then the whole system of modern education in Tsinan and throughout the province was disrupted by internal disorder, civil war, and foreign intervention. The central administration was dismembered and most schools were closed for long periods.

During the period of Kuomintang control the continuing professionalization of educators produced some bad effects. Professional educators found it easy to reopen modern schools in cities such as Tsinan or Tsingtao where the urban attitudes, urban occupations, and political interests of the Kuomintang were centered. Outside the cities, however, the professionalization of educators was a drawback. Young professional teachers, frequently the sons of older gentry leaders, found they lacked both the ability and the desire to teach in China's villages and market towns. Modern education had made beginnings in many of these places during the first years of the Republic, but these beginnings could not be revived in the 1930's.

The Chambers of Commerce and the YMCA

SHIRLEY S. GARRETT

Chinese city life in the era between the sedan chair and the collective farm had both its bright and its dark sides. In the years after the Boxer uprising some aspects of city life improved visibly, as city walls went down, streets were widened, and electricity, telephones, and trolley cars appeared. New schools, hospitals, movie houses, and—sign of a modernizing economy—factories went up. To long-time observers, Canton and Shanghai seemed marvelously transformed in the 1930's. "Wide streets take the place of narrow, ill-smelling crooked alleys," declared an American. "All the mechanical gadgets of our civilization have been taken over and put to work . . . the Chinese are able successfully to function as a modern corporate society."[1] At the same time the modern age exacted its toll. In the silk mills of central China eight-year-old girls stood twelve hours a day, stirring silk cocoons in steaming water. In the cotton industry women and children worked between twelve and twenty hours a day, seven days a week, while babies crawled between the machines. As peasants crowded into city slums to escape famine and rural disorder, epidemics became more and more frequent. The Industrial Hospital in Shanghai was kept busy trying to repair the mangled hands of industrial workers. More than twenty percent of the children admitted as patients had tuberculosis, and one-third had intestinal parasites.[2] The new schools and universities teemed with the children of merchants and professionals, while their fathers' apprentices remained prisoners of illiteracy. The price of modernization was high.

Yet Chinese cities did not altogether ignore the problems that attended urban growth. Some progress was made, and even greater progress envisioned. In spite of the lack of money and the constant political uproar, streets were widened and water supplies provided in some cities. There were public-health measures, popular-education campaigns, relief for the poor, hospitals, fights for labor safeguards. One is struck by the new vision of the city expressed in various reform movements: drives to stop the importation of opium, to provide pure water, to end the trade in girls, to kill flies. These movements were not altogether façades. They represented the beginnings of a struggle to reform urban Chinese society, and they reinforce the truism that in the life of a city there is rarely total progress or total decay.

A functioning urban dynamic had existed in traditional China, but it had lost momentum in the early twentieth century. It was not that the Chinese were growing callous, but that they had arrived at a sad time in their history. Only a century before, there had been many visible official and private organizations concerned with general urban functions as well as with famine relief, charity, and the care of children. Many such organizations survived into the twentieth century, but the demand for their services now far outran the supply. In part this situation reflected the urban bloat caused by the immigration of peasants from the country-side and the poverty and disease caused by overcrowding—a phenome-non visible today in the swollen and terrible suburbs of Calcutta or Rio de Janeiro. Existing resources simply could not fill even traditionally accepted needs. In addition, new questions were being raised about urban needs. Is illiteracy a community responsibility? Should everyone care about hookworm? Which ills are mere blemishes on society's skin and which are cancers? Each society answers these questions in a dif-ferent way. In transitional China there was a remarkable change in the concept of social responsibility, due in part to new circumstances, in part to missionary influence, and in part to exposure to innovations in the treaty ports.

Granted a growing awareness of social ills and a desire to ameliorate them, someone still had to get things done. Who? In the past, a compli-cated web of official, semi-official, and unofficial institutions had helped to make both cities and countryside function. The missionary S. Wells Williams observed in 1803 that "the people crystallize into associations in the town and in the country," and added "these habits of combining themselves quicken the vitality of the mass."[3] Thus gentry, clans, pro-vincial clubs, mutual loan associations, guilds, and secret societies per-formed a variety of functions including self-government, social welfare, and economic regulation. Without these institutions traditional urban society could not have functioned.

Neither the traditional institutional arrangements nor the existing ad-ministrative structure nor the available financial resources were adequate to meet twentieth-century urban needs, however. The combination of public and private institutions that had supported such social services as existed in the nineteenth century could not provide the police, roads, teachers, health services, fire protection, crime prevention and economic investment that Chinese cities needed. Government alone was unable to meet these needs. Part of the problem was that cities generally did not govern themselves, but continued to be governed, as in the imperial era, as mere sections of provinces. Officials concerned with local municipal problems were unable to adopt long-range policies, since the continuing succession of warlords made planning for the future seem futile. Money too was a constant problem, as revenue sources were limited and unreliable. A major source of public income in Canton in 1913 was a tax on brothels, which had been closed in the name of social reform and promptly reopened in the interest of municipal solvency.[4] Peking once found itself unable to pay its police for ten months.[5] Trying to meet the pressing needs of the growing cities and to expand social services meant certain frustration for local government.

This did not mean, however, that urban areas were devoid of resources. These were available throughout the city—some skills, some manpower, some organizational talent—distributed among individuals and also among the organizational subgroups on whom the government had always depended in part. Any one of these subgroups could hire fire-coolies, build a school, or undertake other relatively small projects. Yet small-scale, uncoordinated projects could barely make a dent in modern urban problems. Coordinated and mobilized into mass action, however, they could do a great deal more. As S. Wells Williams had noted, the Chinese had an unsurpassed ability to organize for practical ends. One result was that the physical and social changes in transitional China were effected not only by the bureaucracy but also—I am tempted to say primarily—by scores of quasi-official or completely private institutions that kept functioning despite the political chaos.

These "voluntary" associations played a leading role in the early years of the Republic, particularly until the advent of the Nanking regime in 1927. A city-wide health campaign in Foochow in 1919 numbered among its sponsors the Chamber of Commerce, several guilds, and the YMCA. A school in Hangchow was run by the Silk Guild, mirroring similar efforts by guilds in other cities. Local temporary "self-governing" councils in Chekiang in 1921 included representatives of the Educational Association, the Agricultural Association, the Industrial Association, and the Chamber of Commerce. Strike arbitration in Canton in 1919 was handled by the Chamber of Commerce and the Kwangtung Educational Association. The mass education movement of the 1920's was originated and organized by the YMCA. Famine relief in 1919 was administered by the Chinese Red Cross and staff from the YMCA. An effort in 1925 to get a child-labor law passed in Shanghai was made by the YWCA and the women's clubs of Shanghai. There was a dawning awareness that the new era demanded new organizational ingenuity.

The organizations in the truncated list given above are strikingly diverse. Some of the institutions were deeply rooted in Chinese traditions, some were new; some were secular, some religious; some Western, some indigenous. The contexts in which they appear are sometimes startling, for they often improvised far beyond their early goals in order to meet new challenges. Their names also hint at a growing phenomenon in China, that of city-wide, regional, even national voluntary associations.

For the Western reader, the organizational titles can be deceptive. Organizations with Western origins or names, for example, cannot be understood simply in terms of their Western counterparts, for the Chinese institutions developed their own identities. Another peculiarity is the degree to which these organizations tended to be interrelated, drawing membership and support from the same members of the middle class. And although the list alone cannot show the influence and effects of the organizations, their work sometimes produced profound results. YMCA fly-swatting campaigns have their echo today in the present regime's passion for public health, including fly-swatting. Popular education movements swelled into the great achievement of national literacy for the young during the communist era. Even the failures had their effect. The YWCA movement to improve labor conditions for women in Shanghai did not succeed, but it helped to radicalize women workers. Social service by students and staff in the YMCA did not transform urban poverty, but it revolutionized many young participants.

The moving spirit behind most of the organizations I have listed was the urban middle class, the shifting mixture of merchant and gentry that has become the official scapegoat for the era's massive failures. It becomes increasingly clear that this group played an energetic and probably indispensable role in urban affairs during the first half of the twentieth century. The middle class had a new urban vision and the wealth and organizing talent to translate that vision into action. They provided the dynamic for much public action in transitional China.

Time and further research may reveal the influence of many institutions that are barely mentioned here. The provincial educational associations, for example, were certainly important as consolidated expressions of the opinions and power of the intelligentsia. The role of the shopkeepers' street unions in Shanghai deserves further study, for they have been called the most influential organization in Shanghai during the 1920's.* The women's groups, especially the YWCA, worked steadily to improve the lot of working-class Chinese women. A thorough history of middle-class urban action should include the work of and interrelationships among all these organizations. Here I shall deal with the two I believe were the most prominent of all.

There is little doubt that the key organization in the urban life of Republican China, central to the running of many cities, was the chamber of commerce, or more accurately, the chambers of commerce. Vastly more powerful than their Western counterparts, they exerted political as well as economic influence, and even served for short periods as the governments of a number of Chinese cities. Without their backing many of the urban functions in transitional China could not have been carried out. Furthermore, the chambers were related in varying degrees to many other middle-class organizations, both political and philanthropic. One such organization was the Chinese YMCA, which for more than half a century pioneered in urban social reforms and was the most important social welfare group in China. The separate yet interwoven destinies of these two organizations, briefly described in the following pages, illustrate the vigorous and sometimes constructive activities of the urban business class in the transitional years while China groped its way through chaos to revolution.

The Chambers of Commerce

There is guesswork involved in writing even briefly about the Chinese chambers of commerce. They are described by several observers as the most powerful local centers of influence throughout the early Republic, yet the record is more suggestive than definitive. It is nevertheless worth presenting, as much for the lines of inquiry it opens up as for the evidence it presents. The chambers, or *shang hui*, were officially ushered into being in 1902 by the Ch'ing government. The industrialist-official Sheng Hsüan-huai had been impressed by the power that Western merchants in China had achieved through their ability to cooperate under the auspices of the joint foreign Chamber of Commerce. Under his prodding the government decreed the establishment of an organization that would bring together for cooperative economic action the merchant guilds of each city. Newly appointed commercial taotais were instructed to establish such organizations in all cities of commercial importance, although at that time the government provided no official regulations. Member-

---

* Chow Tse-tsung makes this claim on p. 255 of his *The May Fourth Movement.*

ship was not mandatory and merchants were suspicious that it was merely a scheme to extort money from them, but after a slow start the chambers began to flourish. In 1908 there were chambers in 31 major and 135 smaller cities, and after the successful participation of the merchants in the Revolution of 1911, growth accelerated. In 1915 one set of statistics showed 1,242 chambers with a quarter of a million members.[6] In 1929[7] there were allegedly 1,447 chambers in existence. *

This does not mean that a Western economic prototype was grafted onto China by decree, for actually the new chambers had deep roots in Chinese tradition. To oversimplify a complicated picture, the chambers were a kind of super-guild that added to traditional guild powers the imposing force of city-wide federation. Their twentieth-century history flowed from guild tradition rather than from the example of Western commercial organization.

The general contours of guild power in China are well known. Since the imperial government expected business to regulate itself, guilds fulfilled many functions. They adjudicated disputes among members, regulated prices and production, and collected taxes. They performed philanthropic services for members and their families, and sometimes acted with other guilds for city-wide philanthropic service. Their power over members, symbolized by worship of a guild's patron god and institutionalized in a guild court, was strengthened by the accepted right to boycott guild members who did not cooperate. Thus they had a wide array of powers that could be translated to a larger area if the opportunity should arise. The guilds' power over their members is a central factor in the story of the chambers of commerce.

These powers affected others besides the business community. By the waning years of the Ch'ing dynasty, merchants in some cities were acting cooperatively as de facto urban administrators. In Newchwang, Manchuria, for example, there was in the 1890's a "Local Guild" made up of the principal native merchants of the city, which combined in itself a large number of administrative and economic functions. The guild, it was reported,

maintains order in the streets, takes care of the roads, drains, and reservoirs; controls public lands, administers poor relief, subsidizes charitable institutions, controls banks, regulates exchanges of trade, marts, and transportation. It finances its activities by taxation upon transactions between merchants not natives of the city but residing and doing business therein, by collecting bridge-dues upon carts transporting goods, and shop dues; for all of which the guild has the authorization of the local civil officials.[8]

---

* There was reportedly a drop around 1919–20, but the figures may be incomplete. Compare also those given in the Introduction, Table 4, p. 7.

Thus Newchwang had an unofficial merchant administration working under or with the formal government appointees. If that formal framework should disintegrate, coordinated merchant action could keep the city functioning. Mark Elvin's studies show an impressive set of guild functions in Shanghai, Chungking, and Kuei-sui, and similar patterns of guild administration were reported in Swatow, Shasi, and Chia-ting.[9]

Here, then, was a ready-made cast of administrators waiting in the wings for a star role, not unlike the young samurai in the last days of the Tokugawa regime. They were a trained managerial class, well-to-do and increasingly sure of themselves. As the imperial regime crumbled and the traditional gentry class became more and more demoralized, the guilds became the most powerful traditional institutions still functioning. Distrust of chamber membership evaporated as merchants recognized the additional power to be derived from city-wide consolidation, and chambers became the main channel for merchant opinion and action. It was the Shanghai General Chamber that in 1905 announced the boycott to protest American legislation aimed at excluding Chinese. At the same time, chamber leaders in Shanghai and elsewhere began to spearhead the drive for a constitutional national regime in which merchant power could be represented. In Shanghai the chamber head, Tseng Shao-ch'ing, led the constitutional movement and in Chengtu the chamber agitated for a provincial assembly.[10] A number of writers have emphasized the importance of the merchants' role in nourishing sentiment for political reform.

When the Ch'ing government reluctantly sanctioned local deliberative councils and provincial assemblies, chamber members were prominently represented. The government had so limited the franchise to the well-to-do and educated that in Szechwan, for example, a man had to own five thousand *yüan* in capital or real estate to hold legislative office, the same qualifications set for membership in the chambers.[11] The lists of those eligible for the councils were short. In Swatow, with a population of perhaps 300,000, there were only 1,600 qualified voters in 1910.[12] Thus the prosperous merchant loomed conspicuously among those enfranchised and the chambers of commerce sometimes controlled the deliberative councils. In Swatow the vice-president of the Chamber was also president of the Council.[13] In both Swatow and Newchang the close affinity of chamber and council is suggested by the fact that chamber headquarters served also as the meeting place for the council.[14]

As other authority failed, the chambers moved easily into the vacuum and in places assumed local governing power. Declaring itself early in 1911 to be "the final authority on local concerns," the Swatow Council/Chamber collected taxes, looked after sanitation and traffic control, handled the financing of the police, and acted as trustee of public property.[15] In An-tung the chamber collected funds to build an electric lighting system.[16] As revolution spread, chambers set up volunteer corps, as in Hang-chow, or took over the administration outright, as in Ying-Y'ou.[17] Thus by 1911 the chambers were often already serving as temporary governments run by merchants. When official local governments reemerged, the chambers were on hand to advise and assist.

In the wake of the revolution the prestige of the chambers grew, along with their power and functions. In several cities they were given requisitioned temples to use as offices or grants of land on which to build headquarters.[18] The new government expressly granted chambers the right to address provincial governors as equals, as well as the right to petition the national government.[19] Yüan Shih-k'ai specifically requested that regional merchant bodies support him in his abortive attempt to become emperor.[20] These incidents demonstrated the burgeoning power and prestige of the merchant class and encouraged the growth of new chambers of commerce. By 1912 there were almost 800 chambers scattered about the country; four years later there were more than a thousand.[21]

The growing power of these institutions presented a dilemma to Yüan Shih-k'ai and his successors. The chambers could not be allowed to grow unchecked, for they were beginning to assert local power independent of central authority. They nevertheless represented a helpful administrative device for the new republic. Furthermore, they were too strong simply to obliterate. What Yüan tried to do, therefore, was to clip the chambers' political wings and restrict them to an economic function. He dissolved the local self-governing bodies that had crystallized merchant political power, and issued a national code for the chambers which, if honored, would have turned them into purely economic bodies. The code is worth a brief look both for what it says and for what it does not say.

Promulgated in 1914, the national code legitimized the chambers of commerce but at the same time subordinated them to the national government by attempting to place them under the control of a newly formed Ministry of Agriculture and Commerce. Upon petition of thirty qualified persons in any town or city the Ministry could authorize the establishment of an ordinary chamber. In provincial capitals and major commercial ports, general chambers could be established on the petition of fifty persons. There was also provision for a National Chamber. Membership in the chambers was open to company officers, guild directors, and agents for industrial or commercial enterprises. Each chamber elected a number of directors,* four-fifths of whom had to be members

---

* General chambers had 30 to 40 directors, regular chambers 15 to 30.

of guilds. With Ministry approval, a president and vice-president were elected, each limited to two terms of two years each.

The chambers' duties were almost entirely economic. The chambers were "to consult about industrial and commercial reform," to be responsible "for maintaining order . . . when there is a money panic," and were "to settle industrial and commercial disputes at the request of a party concerned" in chamber courts. The chambers were also charged with investigating industrial conditions and running commercial schools. The only hint of other functions came in a vague sentence that called on chambers "to cooperate . . . in the matters assigned by the highest executive officials of the Central Government or the local executive officials."[22]

Obviously the code was an attempt to limit the chambers' powers by rotating their leaders and restricting them to economic activities. A supplement to the code, dealing with the settling of disputes through chamber of commerce courts, further underscored these attempted restrictions by forbidding the courts to accept civil or criminal cases.[23] The code, however, reflected aspiration as much as it did actuality, for many of its spoken and unspoken prohibitions were ignored as chambers continued to play a larger role wherever they could. Rules about the selection and regulation of leadership, for example, were sometimes ignored. In Chefoo and Tientsin it was evidently difficult to dislodge the natural leadership. It was reported from Chefoo in 1920 that one "T'an T'ai" had been president of the chamber almost uninterruptedly since its inception.[24] That the Ministry was sometimes unable in practice to control the most powerful chambers was demonstrated when the government tried unsuccessfully in 1919 to unseat Pien Yüeh-ting, the head of the Tientsin Chamber, for leading the boycott movement against Japanese goods.[25] In Shanghai, on the other hand, the presidency kept changing hands, probably reflecting the active rivalry for leadership among a number of powerful guild heads and bankers, although not until 1927 is there evidence that the government was able to force a change in leadership.

It also proved difficult for the government to restrict chamber activities. In the fifteen years after the fall of the Ch'ing the chambers emerged as important local power holders, with diverse but unmistakable influence in local administration, in urban modernization, in monetary regulation, in social welfare programs, and in the great national boycotts. Never a major national influence, and jostled for local control by other contenders, the chambers nevertheless appear to have been the most influential nuclei of local power well into the 1920's. The journalist Upton Close wrote in 1920, "It is safe to say that in the cities and county seats this 'Merchant Society' . . . is regarded by the populace as the most important local institution, and is more in the public eye than the officials."[26] In Hankow in 1917 the government was reported to have found cooperation with the Chamber necessary in order to govern the city. The Chamber was carrying out political and judicial as well as economic functions, with the latter described as the least important of the three.[27] In Changsha in 1916 there was "a close connection" between the government and the Chamber.[28] The Peking Chamber was officially given charge of mediating labor disputes[29] and in Ningpo in 1917 the Chamber served as the arbitrator of a strike.[30]

Chambers were prominent in the local self-government movement that sprang up during this period. In many provinces they were purportedly active in initiating provincial legislation and well represented in the provincial assemblies.[31] As late as 1924 the An-tung Chamber still described itself as the municipal government.[32]

These examples suggest that, wherever possible, chambers served as overarching, multipurpose institutions, with profound influence in many areas of urban life. The most familiar and dramatic example of such influence was the chamber role in the great boycotts. National in effect, the boycotts were organized locally, and the chambers were the indispensable element, able to make or break the boycott in their own cities. In Tientsin in 1918 the Chamber's most powerful guild, the Tientsin Yarn, Piece Goods, and Silk Guild, held up delivery of four million dollars' worth of Japanese goods, and the Chamber forced other guild members to cooperate in the boycott.[33] In Peking in 1919 the Chamber successfully objected when the government tried to remove the chief of police, suspected of sympathy toward students.[34] In Canton, however, the Chamber failed to support the boycott of 1919 enthusiastically, since many merchants were dependent on Japanese goods such as coal, chemicals, drugs, and cotton yarn. Japanese goods continued to be exhibited openly in front of the big stores and the boycott was never really successful in that city.[35] This uneven success of the boycotts demonstrated the chambers' power to defy the Japanese and the central government when they wished, and to manipulate the economy of a city.

Immense power was also reflected in the chambers' responsibility for monetary and fiscal order, which had been specifically mentioned in the 1914 code. Decisions concerning the kinds of currency that would be accepted locally, as well as the power to set exchange rates among the various currencies, lay with the chamber of commerce. Thus chambers, acting together with individual members who were bankers, were in a position to determine local money movements. Since they guaranteed local currency, especially that of small banks and business concerns, the chambers could regulate the money market and determine the worth of paper currency. Some time before 1917 in Hankow and two other nearby localities, the chambers temporarily issued their own currency. Chambers were often said to refuse to accept or purchase the government bonds issued by national or provincial commissions of finance. They or their powerful banking members could often also simply open or close local banks at will.[36]

How often did chambers use these formidable economic powers constructively for the welfare of the cities? Chambers did divert some of their energies and funds to urban modernization, particularly waterworks, harbor-control projects, and city lighting. Individual guild members might be induced to invest in public projects, as in An-tung where the electric lighting plan of 1912 was financed by shares sold by the chamber to its member guilds.[37] With surpluses accumulated from fines, fees, and contributions, chambers invested in local businesses or in public projects. Thus in Nanking in 1914 the Chambers were working on plans for a waterworks. In 1919 they helped the municipal government of Nanking to dredge the harbor and the municipal government of Nanning to dredge the river shoals.[38] In Hanyang in the same year the Chamber worked on plans to supply electric lighting.[39] Upton Close reports that the chambers exercised a decisive influence in port development in Chihli, in river and canal conservation, in mining development, and in railroad construction. Their control of banking in Hankow made chamber support vital for the success of any public loan.[40] Even assuming that in each case the hope of profit as well as public spirit dictated support of worthwhile projects, chamber backing seems often to have made the difference between success and failure. In 1921 at Hsü-chou in Kiangsu, for example, a waterworks plan fell through because of difficulties between the promoter and the local Chamber of Commerce.

Furthermore, chambers and their member guilds often provided the crucial support for social welfare activities. Chinese businessmen were of course as happy as Americans to lend their names to philanthropic causes. As I shall show, however, chambers and their member guilds gave more concrete aid to social welfare projects as well.

Although some of these varied responsibilities were officially assigned to the chambers in the national code, they could not have been met without the cooperation of member guilds. In the final analysis the key to the chambers' influence, economic and otherwise, lay in their ability to evoke guild solidarity. A good deal of this power was regulatory and potentially coercive. Chambers had the virtual power of life and death over any local business. The regulations enumerated in the code only hinted at the organizations' wide prerogatives. It was allegedly "practically impossible" for a new business to start in any city without obtaining the sponsorship of the chamber of commerce. Chambers guaranteed the credit soundness of new firms.[41] In Foochow all new businesses had to register with the Chamber and pay a fee.[42] Chambers collected business taxes and import taxes. In Amoy, for example, the Chamber inspected and levied taxes on imported yarn.[43] Chambers could investigate the books and stocks of any business firm in town, whether a chamber member or not. A business that refused to pay its debts could be liquidated by the local chamber.[44] Any protests or petitions to official sources had to be made through the chamber. It was thus little wonder that even a major guild would hesitate to challenge chamber actions.

Chamber influence over its members, however, was more than coercive, for there were unmistakable advantages in having the support of a city-wide organization with wealth and political power. Chambers attempted to protect their members from being double-taxed and from law suits in government courts. In 1924, for example, when the municipal government of Canton levied a merchant tax to pay for rebuilding city streets, the Chamber called a trade strike and organized a militia to oppose the tax. Chambers also protected individual members, as in the previously cited support given Tientsin Chamber chairman Pien Yüehting in 1919. Protection did not extend only to the mighty; in Hankow the Chamber sometimes acted as surety for a merchant or even assumed his debts.[45] Chambers occasionally disseminated information on trade conditions, ran industrial exhibitions, and exchanged information with chambers in other cities. In 1919, for example, the Taiyuan Chamber requested information about Hupeh cotton mills from the Hankow Chamber.[46] The advantages of being a chamber member were such that no business of any consequence, or so it was said, could afford to stay out.[47] Thus coercion and reward linked guilds to the local chamber. Major guilds sometimes bypassed the chamber as a channel in such matters as paying taxes, but practically speaking it was more advisable to be a chamber member and try to exert influence from within than to stay aloof. Since in some instances chamber votes were determined by the size and wealth of each guild,[48] there was an added incentive for the largest and richest organizations to support chamber activities.

It seems clear that chambers of commerce were at the peak of their prestige and aspirations in the early 1920's. Expensive chamber headquarters and office buildings went up in Hankow, Shanghai, Tsinan, Chefoo. In Shanghai, membership was restricted to the more important merchants and companies,[49] and such was the Chamber's social prestige that honorary memberships were awarded as a recognition of public service.⁵⁰ The Shanghai General Chamber began in 1921 to publish a monthly journal. Biographies of Chinese bankers and industrialists made prominent mention of their chamber membership. As foreign business-men became aware of chamber power, the first Western-Chinese club, the Union Club, was established for big businessmen and diplomats, with membership arranged through foreign and Chinese chambers of commerce. "One can hardly peruse vernacular or English newspapers from China without finding some reference to the Chinese Chamber of Commerce," wrote Upton Close.⁵¹

It was indeed a period of relative optimism for the urban middle class, even in the midst of the problems that beset the country. The Fed-eralist movement was gaining momentum, the cultural renaissance was under way, social reform movements in health and education were making headway, and the success of the boycotts seemed to indicate that merchants could guide China's destinies. The Shanghai Chamber intensi-fied its long fight for Chinese representation on the municipal council of the International Settlement, jockeying to monopolize such represen-tation for its own leaders. Businessmen began to express ambitious plans to run not only cities but provinces and even the entire country. In Tientsin in 1920 the silk merchant Chao Chun-ching told the Chamber of Commerce that the commercial public should accept responsibility for the welfare of the country.⁵² At the end of 1921 the National Cham-ber heard a speech stating "We know the conditions of our country and we know her needs and we can bring to her our experience and knowl-edge . . . ; only the merchants, educationists, industrialists and bankers can have leisure and experience and can command the respect of the people."⁵³

But it was already becoming evident that these ambitions would not go unchallenged. The merchant power concentrated in the chambers of commerce was threatened from many directions. One occasional source of harassment was the government itself. Understandably enough, the Peking government had been displeased by chamber support of the stu-dent movement in 1919. As a result, at the end of 1919, the Ministry of Agriculture and Commerce ordered its Hupeh branch to see that no unfit persons were admitted to membership in the chambers of com-merce, and that the list of all those elected was sent to the Ministry for approval.⁵⁴ In 1920, police dissolved the Tientsin Yarn and Piece Goods Guild, and regulations began to pour from government agencies. From local governments the challenge was often more pointed. There was much overt hostility over taxes between the Chamber and the radical Canton government in 1924. The issue was settled summarily when the municipal government called in the Whampoa military to disarm the merchant militia. In 1923 the Chamber head in Kiaochow Bay (Tsingtao) personally asked the American consul, Walter Adams, to secure foreign representation in local government as a check on the Municipal Bureau of Finance.[55] These incidents suggest that local chamber power was by no means unlimited during the era.

Another major source of annoyance came from the armies that tramped across the countryside, living off the land. In 1916, local chambers were forced to raise funds to maintain troops in Changsha, Ch'ang-te, and Yüeh-chou.[56] During the fighting around Peking in the summer of 1920, military officials asked the Chamber for contributions of $3,000,000. They received only about $100,000.[57] Sometimes the chambers and the military were able to find ways to live together. Commanders could and occasionally did divert fighting from the business district; in some Shantung cities, armies closed the gates to all persons not guaranteed by chamber officers.[58] Yet it was the military that held ultimate power, as the Canton Chamber had found in 1917 when Kwangsi militarists kept Chamber candidate Wu T'ing-fang from becoming governor of Kwangtung despite vocal protests by local businessmen. In November 1922 a national conference of chambers of commerce advanced a plan for the demilitarization of China, and in 1924 a Hupeh chamber, probably Hankow's, announced its intention to resist warlordism.[59] Nevertheless, power clearly remained with armed force, and chambers had to accommodate themselves to this fact.

A threat that appeared harder to come to terms with now began to emerge from militant labor. During the period of violent strikes in the early 1920's, chambers began for the first time to feel the impact of a self-conscious proletariat organized by communists. Now and then business response to labor demands was constructive. In Chefoo, for example, the Chamber arranged Sundays off for workers.[60] Usually, however, management reaction was hostile. During the May Thirtieth boycott movement, chamber enthusiasm was muted because of the accompanying labor agitation. The Shanghai General Chamber omitted from the petition it transmitted to Peking the demands for trade union organization and the right to strike that the Federation of Workers, Merchants and Students had inserted. The Wuhan and Changsha chambers both tried to curb local boycott committees. As strikes became more widespread and violent, the chambers' primary goals of survival and retention of economic privilege reasserted themselves over abstract declarations about public welfare. In 1927 the Canton Chamber declared that "no power on earth can ever make the workers into a privileged class."[61]

In Shanghai, the Chamber might have added, "and no power on earth can make the lower middle class into the upper middle class," for in that city the Chamber was becoming a tool of big business. Many merchants were not even permitted to join, and directorships were reportedly allocated according to the wealth of the participating guilds and companies. When small businessmen began to organize block by block into street unions in 1920 and to challenge the Chamber for power they were called radical by Chamber leadership. The Shanghai Chamber worked hand in hand with foreign interests in the Settlement against the street unions.[62]

Events of the mid-1920's, then, impelled many chambers to define themselves as agents of the upper middle class, inimical to new urban movements and institutions that might threaten that class. The depredations of the militarists, the rise of militant labor and of the left wing of the KMT, and the subsequent redefinition of chamber interests, prompted them to seek a champion who would save them as well as China. In the spring of 1927 they threw their support to Chiang Kai-shek. In March of that year, Chiang held a meeting in Shanghai with a group of prominent men headed by Yü Hsia-ch'ing, head of the Chamber. On March 29, according to Harold Isaacs, a confederation of more than fifty leading banks and commercial associations made available to Chiang between three and seven million Shanghai dollars in loans in return for his pledge to rid the city of communists, strikes, and insurrections.[63] Thus they hoped to reach an accommodation with a militarist who was sympathetic to their aims.

Chiang took care of the businessmen's enemies with great efficiency in a series of brutal purges. This did not mean, however, that he was willing to tolerate any political rivalry or independence on the part of the chambers themselves. Within weeks he ousted the leaders of the Shanghai Chamber and forced its reorganization. Then ensued a tug of war. A resolution to abolish all the chambers of commerce was introduced at the third party congress of the Kuomintang in 1929 but failed to pass. Accordingly Chiang announced a plan to "reorganize" the chambers to make them more influential in their work. Regulations for this reorganization were issued in August 1929.* A year later it was announced that the reorganization of the local chambers of commerce had not yet been completed, and that the National Association of the Chambers was to be dissolved by order of the Executive Yüan.[64] Six months after that, however, in the middle of 1931, the National Association

---

* I have not seen these regulations, which were reportedly calculated to dislodge incumbent leaders.

sponsored a party for Yü Hsia-ch'ing, the long-time chairman of the Shanghai Chamber, and both T. V. Soong and H. H. Kung of the Chiang family and the government were there. There is some question, therefore, how much power the Chambers had retained. An anonymous letter to the *North-China Herald*, printed in July 1929, charged that the general chambers had "ceased to function," and that leaders were now figureheads, officials, or economists.[65] Yet at the end of 1929 a Chinese delegate to an International Chamber of Commerce meeting proclaimed that businessmen were now in an unparalleled position of influence in China.[66] The distinction may be that Chambers continued to serve urban business interests but that as institutions they were being shut out of the new government.

In the 1930's, chambers of commerce continued to perform a number of economic functions. In 1933 the local chamber in Peking[67] was still represented on a committee handling bond redemption, and until 1935 chambers were still a repository for reserve notes.[68] The Shanghai Chamber's journal was issued as late as 1946. But the name of the institution itself appeared less and less in discussions of public affairs. The chambers apparently do not figure in political and economic accounts of the late Nanking era.

The foregoing discussion raises far more questions than it answers, owing largely to the general and scattered nature of the data used in this account. There was, naturally, no typical city and no typical chamber. In Shanghai, the Chamber leaders were big bankers and industrialists; in Peking and Hankow all directors were guild members. What difference did this make in their goals and in their insights about the needs of the modern city? The Canton Chamber confronted a radical government, but what of cities where government and chamber were identical or close in their aims? What was the difference between the general chambers and the hundreds of ordinary branch chambers scattered throughout the country? Such questions can be approached only by studies of individual chambers.

Another problem concerns the behavior of chambers over time. Did they in fact wield continuing influence until Chiang's accession to power, or were they only occasionally active? I think the former is true, but the evidence so far is admittedly scanty. Furthermore, the lack of general publicity about the chambers in the 1930's is not a conclusive indication that their power had disappeared. That era too needs further study.

The whole question of an "establishment" deserves more attention. In Shanghai, as I have indicated, the Chinese Ratepayers' Association that arose during the Rights Recovery Movement of the 1920's was organized and virtually controlled by the Chamber. Since these two organizations and the street unions were the three bodies that elected representatives to the Shanghai Municipal Council, the Chamber in fact controlled the election through its double vote. How often did this kind of interlocking leadership occur elsewhere, and what effect did it have on local affairs?

Finally, we need a judgment of the chambers' overall contributions during this transitional era, which would amount to a general assessment of the middle class's contribution. This larger judgment must be left to future scholars. In the remainder of this paper I shall attempt to evaluate it in only one area, that of the urban businessman's involvement with Chinese social welfare.

The YMCA and the Middle Class

The private sector was of major importance in carrying out urban reforms during the early Republican era. Many wealthy and influential people founded schools, sponsored hospitals, and donated large sums to charity. Guilds continued their charitable work, joined by chambers of commerce, which, for example, ran children's refuges in Peking and elsewhere. Christian organizations and branches of American universities continued to found hospitals and colleges. A number of new voluntary associations also played an important role. By 1919, for example, the Chinese Red Cross had 117 branches carrying on public service work in nineteen provinces, and a multitude of educational associations worked to expand the school system and to develop popular and vocational education.

Chief among these service organizations for many years was the Chinese YMCA, which was officially established in Tientsin in 1895 and survived into the communist era. As the first modern community association working in the field of urban services it pioneered in many areas, notably education, recreation, and social welfare. These programs were not only worthwhile in their own right but, perhaps more important, they provided prototypes for other private and public organizations. They included part-time schools offering English, college preparatory courses, and commercial subjects; reading rooms stocked with modern periodicals; employment agencies and passport services; modern athletic programs, paving the way for successful Chinese participation in the Olympic Games; recreational services for both members and non-members, including dormitories, meeting rooms, swimming pools, and public playgrounds; block-by-block "little teacher" movements begun in Shanghai long before the famous movement of the nineteen-twenties;

social-service work using students as teachers and public lecturers on health and citizenship; city-wide campaigns for public health and for mass education in which not only student YMCA members but also other members of the community participated.

Although it would take an urban philosopher to decide whether a swimming pool, an English course, a playground, or a public health association did more to modernize a city, one achievement of the YMCA is particularly important. Although the Association acknowledged the need for strong government action, it also believed in community self-help and cooperation under vigorous middle-class leadership. It further believed that certain large community problems could be solved only through such widespread community cooperation. Moreover, it had the managerial ability to pinpoint areas where community cooperation would work and the energy to get a movement started. Its great talent was the ability to get the middle class into motion. Strong local roots, well-organized leadership, and a capacity to bring together disparate groups made it an organization unique in its ability to coordinate private groups for action. It had no great wealth and of course no coercive power either over its own members or over nonmembers. It could not expect to achieve the results that an active government might have achieved, but it did have one invaluable asset: grass roots appeal among the middle class it served. This gave it a solid base from which to work.

Middle-class support was indispensable to the organization. This support had been won the hard way, for the Association had no indigenous roots, no built-in constituency, no massive financial power. Why should China support an association run by foreign Christians and demanding local financing when it had no idea what such an association meant, did not trust Christians or foreigners, and had other things to spend its money on? An analysis of the organization's success provides insight not only into its institutional vigor but also into the imperatives of urban community action in the Republican era.[69]

The YMCA was an alien growth in China but not in itself a new organization. Associations had existed in America since the middle of the nineteenth century to serve young, male, urban, Protestant businessmen, for whom they provided recreation, athletics, lectures, courses in commercial skills, and religious programs. In addition the Associations had developed a tradition of social service. They received the hearty moral support of the Protestant churches, for whom they represented a supradenominational integrating institution, and the financial support of the business community, which saw in them a source of trained personnel and a transmitter of the values of self-improvement, thrift, and social concern. In addition to the city Associations, student Associations oriented toward religious observance and social service existed in hundreds of colleges.

When the YMCA came to China with the avowed purpose of serving students and subsequently young businessmen, its timing was good, for urban Chinese were ready for an innovative institution. The young in particular were eager to learn new skills, read new periodicals, and take on new styles in behavior. The YMCA, as the first organization in China to concentrate on work with middle-class urban youth, swiftly attracted a progressive, intelligent membership—the best young men in Shanghai, one staff member in that city reported in 1901. By 1911 the Association was operating popular programs for the young in seven major cities on the mainland, was organizing in five others, and had a thriving program for Chinese students in Tokyo, where its tacit acceptance of the student revolutionary movement made it especially popular. For several years thereafter the YMCA was widely acknowledged to be the most important youth association in the country.

However, it was soon evident that the organization's appeal and usefulness were not confined to the young, but extended to their elders. The YMCA brought to China a value system comfortably adaptable both to Confucian tradition and to modern middle-class aspirations. The same historical developments that had produced a political vacuum in China had also seen the breakdown of the Confucian order. Traditional Confucian values were not meeting modern needs, yet nothing else had replaced them. Perhaps Chinese youth had no need for a connection with the past but the adult middle class yearned for one. Progressive adults wanted an ethic that embodied some notion of progress but that also left room for the familiar Confucian values of individual morality and social stability.

The YMCA was able to speak to both needs. Despite its firm Christian roots it was far less concerned with dogma than with a general view of man and society that coincided remarkably well with Confucian tenets. The YMCA moral man, bent on improving himself and doing good in society, was a counterpart of the Confucian *chün-tzu*. This insistence on moral virtue was accepted and applauded by a middle class viewing with alarm the more volatile declarations of the younger generation.

Moreover, the YMCA extolled the values dear to the middle class. It placed its basic faith in education, self-help, thrift—all prominent in the Chinese lexicon of virtues. Such values, it believed, would eventually redeem Chinese society. If large numbers of people could learn to read, if laborers would stop gambling and brush their teeth, if beggars could be trained to useful occupations, if people as a whole could hear lectures on the importance of health and good citizenship, China might yet pull itself up by its bootstraps.

Another major source of the YMCA's appeal to the Chinese middle class was its conservatism in contrast with competing radical prescriptions for reform. There was no call for revolution to frighten a conservative middle class, but there was a promise of progress. The burgeoning middle class of merchants, educators, and officials had no desire to become the victims of radical change. The YMCA assured them that a reasonably stable order could produce the necessary innovations.

The organization was also fortunate in having efficient leadership to put its version of modernized Confucianism into practice. Chinese urban problems needed not only intelligent social prescriptions but also managerial talent to translate prescriptions into actualities. The Association leaders were well qualified for the task. They were paid professionals known as secretaries, the best of whom were dedicated to their tasks and highly organized. Their most notable quality was an ability to get things done. They spent little time formulating abstract justifications of what they were doing. Most of their energies went into the practical tasks of raising funds, starting schools, teaching, arranging lectures, and running dormitories. If they were not always businessmen, they were at least business-like, a quality found admirable by their supporters.

A further reason for the growing Chinese acceptance of the Y was its policy of recruiting native leaders. The Association appointed its first Chinese secretary in 1900, and by 1912 the staff included more Chinese than Westerners. C. T. Wang served briefly as general secretary after 1911 before he entered the government. Soon thereafter the Association was headed by David Yui, a former journalist, who began to develop close ties with the business community. This predominance of Chinese in the leadership, never achieved by Christian church organizations in China, further cemented the confidence of nationalistic Chinese and encouraged them to feel that the YMCA was more Chinese than alien.

Such acceptance was necessary, for the YMCA did not expect to be wholly supported from the United States. Except for the salaries of Western secretaries, all running expenses had to be locally financed. American millionaires might donate money for buildings, but the land had to be donated by local citizens or bought with locally raised funds. In the United States the business community was the main source of YMCA support. This tradition—and necessity—dictated that the Y court the business community in China.

Thus staff members paid many calls on Chinese businessmen, addressed them flatteringly as leaders of society, and devoted many programs to business needs. In Shanghai, the YMCA started classes for clerks in business establishments who wanted to learn English and commercial skills such as bookkeeping. As one secretary commented, "Everybody knows that a Y education means a raise."[70] Commercial and English courses became an important part of the Association program in most cities. To business management the courses meant that people with modern commercial skills were available in growing numbers. These practical courses boosted membership and generated substantial financial support from merchants.

Another practical consideration for businessmen was the Association's network of powerful business friends and sponsors in the United States. John Rockefeller gave millions to the work of the International Committee under whose auspices the Chinese Associations were established. William Howard Taft dedicated the new Shanghai YMCA building when he was Secretary of War, and later, when he was President, presided over a fund-raising meeting for the YMCA in the White House. To the Chinese this indicated a close and potentially useful nexus between the Chinese YMCA and influential Americans inside and outside the government.

To the cold considerations of profit and power, however, other dimensions should be added. One was pleasure, as Associations began to provide a variety of acceptable recreational programs ranging from major athletic exhibitions to film shows, available to adults as well as younger people. One photograph shows a clearly gleeful man of some seventy years with a beard falling below his waist, dressed in a YMCA gym suit and clutching a basketball. National pride was fostered by such events as the victory of YMCA-trained athletes in the 1915 Far Eastern Olympics. Good human relations were a further attraction; Association staff members were pleasant young people and the Chinese liked them. All of these factors opened pocketbooks during yearly financial campaigns. Furthermore, it seems justifiable to attribute some degree of social concern to the urban middle class. Staff members reported that businessmen seemed to have no trouble understanding their responsibility for improving society, realizing, for one thing, that someone must take up the role of stewardship once played by the gentry class. Even for those whose main interest was in keeping the revolutionary young at bay, the visible expression of that interest was money that could be translated into services.

Thus as early as 1903 one secretary had reported that "the subscription books of the Association in every city include the names of leading officials and merchants, and the public receptions and other gatherings have been graced by the presence of men of national reputation."[71] At a fund-raising luncheon in Shanghai in 1905, an honored guest was Chu Pao-san, several times head of the Chamber of Commerce. Another early friend and contributor was Tseng Shao-ch'ing, also a chamber head.

With the advent of the Republican era the Association's popularity became even more marked, and one finds the names of officials, educators, Buddhist priests, police chiefs, and warlords among its supporters. Yüan Shih-k'ai and Sun Yat-sen both hailed the Association as a constructive influence for youth; heads of colleges and ministers of education attended its public functions. But most prominent are the names of businessmen, many of whom may be identified as chamber of commerce and guild members. In Chengtu in 1914, among the local luminaries who became "team captains" pledged to fill financial campaign quotas were the president of the Chengtu Chamber of Commerce, as well as the vice-president of the provincial assembly and the local chief of police. Support by guilds and guild members was common. Some of those mentioned in the archives as supporters are the president of the Hangchow Silk Guild, and, in Foochow, members of the Timber Guild, the Canton Guild, the Bankers' Guild, and the Tea Guild.

Some prominent Christian businessmen served as members of YMCA local and national boards of directors. Charles Soong was an early member of the Shanghai board. On the national committee of the Association's journal *Chin-pu* (Progress) were K. S. Wong, manager of the Hanyehping Iron and Coal Company, and C. C. Nieh, owner of the Heng Feng Cotton Mill. S. C. Lin of the Peking branch of the Bank of China was a YMCA member and N. L. Han, president of the China Express Company, was a member of the Association's national executive committee. Some YMCA directors were also prominent in the Chinese chambers of commerce. C. C. Nieh was one such man. Elected to the Municipal Council of the Shanghai International Settlement, S. U. Zau was not only a former chairman of the YMCA but a member of the central executive committee of the Shanghai Chamber of Commerce as well. Many Christian businessmen gave time and effort to the Association, but most financial contributions came from the larger non-Christian business constituency, although no non-Christian was eligible to serve on the board.

The YMCA, in turn, was sensitive to business interests. David Yui, head of the national YMCA, closely supported the concerns of the business community. On at least one trip to the United States he represented Chinese commercial interests. With C. C. Nieh he headed the chamber of commerce demilitarization movement of the 1920's. He also worked hard for the Rights Recovery Movement in Shanghai and was a leading spirit in the movement for self-government in the 1920's. Furthermore, during the labor agitation of the same period Yui expressed sympathy for industrialists.

Many members and supporters, of course, gave the Association only tacit approval, the prestige of their names, or a small financial contribution. The cumulative weight of their support, however, created a climate in which the YMCA could ask for and receive cooperation in many of its efforts. Early in the Republican era, YMCA leaders began to branch out from their original purpose of serving their own middle-class members to the wider one of serving the community. Their network of allies made this feasible.

One form of serving the community was merely to involve YMCA student members in social-service work, an extremely important pioneer effort. Other efforts required the cooperation of other organizations. In Nanchang the Association was able to persuade several guilds to release their apprentices for part-time study and recreation, and several guilds offered rooms for classes. More impressive was the YMCA's ability to gather organizations of many kinds together for a concerted action. Between 1915 and 1921, the Association sponsored and organized city-wide health campaigns in six cities, backed by a variety of community groups. These campaigns sometimes led to the establishment of hospitals and city health leagues.

The most dramatic example of such collaboration occurred in 1920 when the YMCA was asked to mobilize the city of Foochow against a threatened cholera epidemic. The head of the campaign, Dr. W. W. Peter, enlisted the cooperation of city officials, educators, churches, newspapermen, the Chamber of Commerce, and the Canton Guild. These organizations, through their networks of adherents and acquaintances, succeeded in rounding up household servants, owners and employees of restaurants, ricksha coolies, and boatmen to listen to lectures on sanitation. Guilds and schools opened their doors for health lectures. Students, boy scouts, and the military governor's band marched in a parade of floats showing the dangers of unsanitary handling and preparation of food. In Foochow the Association also introduced a massive fly-swatting campaign that was imitated years later by the communist government.

The mass education movement, patterned on the movement begun by James Yen in France under YMCA auspices, was one of the most successful examples of the Y's talent for community-wide cooperation. The mainland movement began in Changsha in 1922 with the organization of leading citizens, including businessmen, college presidents, editors, public officials, guild leaders, clergymen, teachers and students. Guilds representing the manual trades sent shopmasters to meetings on the importance of education and gave apprentices time for study. More than sixty buildings were secured throughout the city for use as school halls, including existing schools, churches, guild halls, temples, club houses, private residences and police stations. Student volunteers recruited teachers from government, mission, and private schools, and later from among gentry and businessmen. This coordination of agencies was a remarkable achievement for a private organization and the first of its kind that I know of in modern China.

Such activities brought the YMCA to the peak of its reputation early in the 1920's. By 1922 there were city Associations in thirty-six cities with over 50,000 paid memberships, as well as more than two hundred student Associations. Some 450 staff members with considerable local autonomy administered the city programs, which were generally supervised from Shanghai by the national staff headed by David Yui. Annual receipts and contributions of more than one million dollars further solidified the organization's belief that it was securely rooted in a Chinese society where middle-class programs might shape the future.

Before long, however, the impact of new social movements began to erode Chinese confidence in the YMCA. As the anti-Christian agitation that started in 1922 began to produce recurring attacks against religious institutions, the Y found its buildings papered with hostile posters, and its members avoiding religious programs. When investigations by Westerners began to publicize the horrors of working conditions throughout urban China, students pressed the YMCA to denounce capitalism and shift its entire resources to industrial work, which it had largely ignored. In the pervasive nationalist reaction to the May Thirtieth incident, Chinese staff members began to protest against any controls by Americans within the organization. To its dismay the YMCA now found itself accused of being a foreign religious institution and a tool of the upper classes and the imperialist powers. In 1925 and 1926 well-organized local attacks by student unions and the left KMT managed to wreck several financial campaigns, terrorize members, and bring several Associations to the brink of dissolution. Though deeply disturbed by such attacks and anxious to develop relevance to new movements, the YMCA found itself locked into its own identity. It was unthinkable to abandon Christian ties, unfeasible to free itself completely from American ties and support, and most impolitic to bite the hand that fed it. As Yui knew and as his staff reminded him, the students made the noise but the business community brought in the money. There seemed little room for maneuver. As students deserted the organization and younger staff members pressed the YMCA to politicize itself, the national leadership awaited the future with trepidation.

With the ascendance of Chiang Kai-shek, urgent problems of survival disappeared, for the connection between the YMCA and the new regime was close and mutually useful. David Yui had presided at the marriage of the General and Madame Chiang. Madame's brother-in-law, H. H. Kung, was a former YMCA secretary, and Madame herself had long been interested in YMCA and YWCA work. Former YMCA General Secretary C. T. Wang was a member of Chiang's cabinet, and by 1930 one hundred and forty-eight former YMCA secretaries were said to be in government service.[72] When Chiang started his New Life Movement to restore Chinese moral tone, a YMCA secretary from Mukden was its first head and David Yui's son-in-law its second. As Yui observed, the YMCA was considered to be close to Nanking, indeed, "too close."[73] But this intimacy had certain benefits as receipts and membership figures began to rise once again, and businessmen and political figures appeared once more as Association boosters. In 1930 the head of the YMCA National Committee was S. C. Chu, general manager of the national Bank of Industry. By 1936 Kung, T. V. Soong, C. T. Wang, and Sun Yat-sen's son Sun Fo were all listed as honorary officers of the Nanking YMCA.

Yet even a nonpolitical organization with no ambitions beyond general service had to pay a price for survival in an increasing repressive atmosphere. It would be unfair to assert that the YMCA did no constructive work during the 1930's. A few secretaries had already begun to carry their services into the countryside. Staff members conducted citizenship training programs, a literacy campaign, and a mass singing program that proved immensely popular as a morale booster during the early war years. Yet by 1930 vitality was clearly ebbing from the organization. Part of this was due to the routinization that was inevitable as more and more work was performed by the paid professional staff rather than by community volunteers. Suitable Chinese staff members became increasingly difficult to recruit as they found alternate and often better-paid employment in government offices or in mission schools and universities. Remaining secretaries often appeared apathetic, but how, asked national leaders, did you revitalize someone who didn't want to be revitalized?[74] This enervation appeared to reflect a split within the staff over the YMCA's proper constituency and goals. One group, largely the younger Americans and Chinese, wanted to recapture student enthusiasm by becoming an agency for social revolution. The other and more powerful group viewed such aspirations as organizational suicide, and it was this view that prevailed. When economic depression in the United States forced a cutback in the number of Western secretaries in 1933, the institutional men were retained rather than those interested in developing large movements.[75] Those who remained had a modest vision of the organization's possibilities in an era of revolution and polarization. As one of its staff members observed in 1934 after thirty years of service in China, "The 'Reconstruction of a New Social Order' is not anything the Y can do. It will only come out of tremendous struggle and turmoil and differences of viewpoint. The Y may develop some of the men who will help to do it."[76]

Although the organization engaged in constant discussions about the way to revive student interest, the city YMCA's now spent their time running barber shops, restaurants, billiard rooms, public baths, and film performances.[77] Educational work dwindled and religious work was practically nonexistent. In 1936 a veteran secretary wrote, "We are now primarily a series of institutions for the social service of middle class professional men and merchants."[78]

During the war, American and Chinese staff members kept debating what part the organization might play in creating a better postwar society. Victory of the Communist forces rendered this question irrelevant as the day of the private welfare agency ended in China. Like the middle class, whose energies and limitations it had embodied, the YMCA had no role left to play.

By no means, however, could the half-century's work be accounted a failure. Transitional China owed the YMCA a great debt. It not only carried on many activities that were, to use an unfashionable term, good works, but it also harnessed the energies of the only group in China at the time with the ability to carry on social welfare in the cities. During the few years in which the urban business class grasped power in China, the YMCA was the primary institution attempting to channel some of that power into social reform.

The Administration of Shanghai, 1905–1914

MARK ELVIN

On the surface at least, city government in China was transformed in the first ten years of this century. In 1909, after three years of local experimentation with municipal self-rule, the central government issued the *Regulations for the Local Self-Government of Cities, Towns and Rural Communities*. Here, for the first time, cities were recognized as administrative units in their own right. Much substantive power was removed from the imperially appointed county magistrates and placed in the hands of elected bodies of representatives. New tasks were undertaken by the official bureaucracy and the city councils, notably the creation of police forces and the operation of primary schools with partially modernized curricula. It was accepted at the time that there had been a break with the past, and more than half a century later there is no good reason to quarrel with this judgment.

The causes behind the break are not so clear. The first Chinese city administrations that were indisputably modern appeared in two of the three most Westernized Chinese cities, Shanghai and Tientsin, in 1905 and 1907 respectively. In immediate origins these administrations were demonstrably a response to the Western presence, and they were created by Chinese who had a knowledge of Western (and Japanese) urban institutions. But this did not mean that they were intrinsically Western, any more than their modernity meant that they were in some sense the opposite of their "premodern" predecessors. By and large, in fact, the contrary was true. Early modern urban government in China sprang directly from a fusion of previously existing institutions: the assembly of county gentry gathered to advise the magistrate, the gentry-run charitable foundation, the late traditional merchants' guild, and the local government board with a specialized administrative function.

Moreover, municipal governments independent of the imperial bureaucracy, and in the hands of local gentry and merchants, had already appeared by the middle of the nineteenth century in at least four cities: Kuei-sui on the edge of Inner Mongolia, Chungking in Szechwan, Hung-chiang in Hunan, and Chia-ting in the Yangtze delta.[1] Further research will almost certainly turn up others. Since the four traditional institutions just mentioned did not become widespread until the eighteenth century or later, it is probable that there was an evolutionary trend at work that would have transformed the sociopolitical structure of China even in the absence of Western influence.

For this reason the analytical separation of indigenous and Western elements is difficult. The main object of this paper is to show how it may be done in the case of the earliest modern Chinese city council, that of Shanghai. Other cases, notably that of the city government of Canton discussed by Professor Rhoads elsewhere in this volume, reveal patterns broadly comparable in outline but significantly different in detail.

Urban Administration in Shanghai
Before the Twentieth Century

The institutions that were to serve as the basis of modern municipal government in Shanghai came into existence in the eighteenth and nineteenth centuries. The first public charitable institution to be managed by members of the gentry, the Hall of Infant Care (*Yü-ying t'ang*), was founded in 1710.[2] The first of the late traditional guilds, the Merchants' Shipping Guild (*Shang-ch'uan hui-kuan*), appeared in 1715.[3] The earliest local board with a specialized administrative function was the Shanghai Board for the Sea Transport of Kiangsu Tribute Grain (*Chiang-su hai-yün Hu-chü*), founded in 1825 and partly run by "gentry directors."[4] The first county-wide assemblies of gentry known to me in Shanghai are those that advised magistrates on water conservancy in 1864, 1870, 1880, and 1895,[5] but there is reason to suspect that they are older than this. Thus K'ang Yu-wei, writing in 1902, observed: "There are at present, as a matter of course, in our various provinces, prefectures, departments, and counties, public boards where the gentry and scholars meet for discussions. If there are important matters [to be discussed], the Hall of Human Relationships in the Confucian Temple is opened for a public debate, and the authorities usually send a deputy to attend it."[6]

These institutions were relatively new; and what was new about them was related to long-term trends in the evolution of Chinese society, as will be briefly indicated in the discussion that follows. Since their origins may, for the most part, be traced to the period preceding the decline of central government power in the last part of the Ch'ing dynasty, it would be wrong to regard them as being simply the characteristic products of a time of dynastic decay. It is likely, however, that the weakening of imperial effectiveness did give them greater scope for development than they would otherwise have had.

Private gentry charities, designed to benefit the members of the founder's clan, had appeared during the Sung dynasty.[7] Charities located in the county capitals and administered by the county government were at least as old.[8] At Shanghai, an official Hall of Provision and Relief (*Yang-chi yüan*) had been founded in 1374. Perhaps significantly, it was not rebuilt after it burned down in 1812.[9] What was distinctive about the new gentry-run charities, of which there were five in the city by 1850, was that they represented a modest form of institutionalized gentry power in the domain of public affairs. They were endowed with considerable grants of land, and often received official subventions.[10] They observed quite elaborate rules and procedures, and sometimes published their accounts for public scrutiny.[11]

Many of their functions are well known. They gave food, money, and cotton clothing to the poor, provided free medicines and the services of doctors and midwives, and took care of abandoned children and vagrants. They buried corpses left in the roads or streams, sold coffins on credit or gave them away free, ran homes for old people and widows, and maintained a number of free schools. They bought birds, fishes, and animals in the market place and released them in special sanctuaries, thus acquiring merit, according to Buddhist belief. They also collected and ritually disposed of unwanted paper with written characters on it, put up memorials to chaste wives and filial sons, repaired tombs and temples, and burned obscene books.[12]

Some of their other functions were of a kind that one would not normally have expected of a charity. The Hall of Effective Care (*Kuo-yü t'ang*) maintained a fifty-man fire brigade.[13] The Hall of Impartial Altruism and Support for the Fundamental (*T'ung-jen fu-yüan t'ang*) dredged waterways and, toward the end of the nineteenth century, collected a vehicle tax and a shop tax to pay both for a small police force maintained by the official Roadworks Board, and for the cleaning and lighting of the city streets.[14] According to the *Continuation of the Shanghai County Gazetteer* (SHHHC), edited by Yao Wen-nan, a former director of this Hall:

It undertook every charitable work, and was relied upon to promote the cleaning of the roads, the lighting of the streets, the building of bridges and thoroughfares, the repair of temples, and the management of militia defense. It was, in fact, the starting point of local self-government.[15]

The appearance of institutionalized gentry power in the charities was part of a wider movement in the eighteenth century toward a partially independent local gentry administration. The Shang-hai gazetteer for the T'ung-chih reign tells us of the county capital's waterways in 1775, "This year for the first time the levying of funds and the dredging were done by the gentry and scholars. Hereafter, all the work done on the county capital's commercial waterways followed the proposals [now] first made." A similar system was instituted in the countryside, in the hope that, with members of the gentry in charge, "the network of personal obligations will work in its accustomed manner, and neither public nor private interests will be thrown into confusion."[16] What was new was not, of course, the control of water conservancy in certain instances by members of the gentry. It was their emergence, following the disappearance of the manorial order in the countryside and the increasing urbanization of the elite, as more or less professional directors, rather than as landowners directly interested in the results of their managerial labors.

By the latter part of the nineteenth century, and possibly much earlier, it seems to have been accepted that major matters of local policy, such as supplementary taxation, required the approval of a gentry assembly. In 1907, for example, the Shanghai City Council thought that for "the imposing of a levy on the whole county" to finance a water-conservancy project, it was necessary to "call a meeting of the gentry of the various charitable halls and the directors of the [gentry] boards in the various rural communities in order to deliberate upon this matter." In 1906, twenty-four of the Shanghai gentry complained to the authorities that the City Council was planning to pull down the walls of the county capital, but had "not invited together the scholars and gentry of the entire county for a public discussion"; and their protest led to the convocation of an assembly in 1908.[17]

Guilds of the late traditional type (hui-kuan, kung-so) developed in Shanghai at the same time as in most of the rest of the country, becoming numerous by the end of the eighteenth century, and enjoying their most rapid period of growth in the nineteenth.[18] There were eleven in the city in 1800, 23 in 1850 and 52 in 1900.[19] These guilds had a corporate character, with members worshipping together and affording each other mutual help. They should be distinguished from the medieval guilds (hang) of T'ang and Sung times, although some of their functions were of course comparable. These earlier guilds seem to have developed from an officially sanctioned quarter consisting of merchants engaged in the same trade, and were linked with the system of officially regulated markets, resembling the Roman *collegia* rather than the more autonomous guilds of medieval Western Europe. After the regulated market system collapsed in the ninth and tenth centuries, guilds seem to have played little part in economic life except as mechanisms of official control, such as the tea guild connected with the Sung tea monopoly, and as corporations for the provision under guarantee of specialized labor such as domestic servants and porters.[20]

Trade guilds of some sort existed in Ming times, although astonishingly little is known about them.[21] The institutional prototype of the late traditional guild was the association of fellow-regionals engaged in regular long-distance trade in some specific place away from home. Interregional trade in basic commodities had existed in Sung times, but on an ad hoc basis, serving mainly to remedy temporary local deficits. The permanence of the late traditional guilds of fellow regionals indicates that trading patterns in late Ming and Ch'ing times were probably more stable than before. The members of these institutions were well-to-do and powerful, and their status was reflected in the ornate and splendid guild-houses they built. In Shanghai at least, membership was not simply open to anyone who came from the appropriate locality, as was the case with the later regional associations (*t'ung-hsiang hui*).[22]

The institutional form assumed by important guilds of local merchants was assimilated to that created by the guilds of fellow regionals. It is sometimes thought that a distinction between the two may be traced in the differential usage of the terms *kung-so* and *hui-kuan*, the former being used for guilds of local people with a common trade and the latter for guilds of outsiders with a common place of origin. The SHHHC correctly points out that such an assumption is untenable for Shanghai.[23] Furthermore, the two organizing principles of shared trade and shared origin were often used in conjunction. Many guilds consisted of merchants from a given area who also specialized in a given trade. The Chin-hua Ham Guild and the Hankow Grain Guild are examples.[24] A regional guild might be subdivided by trades as well as by localities. This was the case with the Ningpo Guild and the Huai-Yang Guild.[25]

The late traditional guilds provided the founders of early modern urban government with models of large corporations managing their affairs through a system that, at its most developed, was characterized by publicly selected directors,* the discussion of problems at public meetings,

---

* The commonest Chinese term for "public selection," *kung-chü*, is notoriously hard to interpret. See Hsiao Kung-ch'üan, *Rural China, Imperial Control in the Nineteenth Century* (Seattle: University of Washington, 1960), 271–75, for a statement of the general problem. Contemporary Westerners called it "election" (e.g. *North-China Herald*, Dec. 16, 1905, p. 671; Nov. 29, 1907, p. 516).

and the principle that policy had to be accepted by a majority. The rules of the Money Trade Guild of the South City of Shanghai laid it down that:

When there are public matters that need to be debated, the directors shall notify the monthly controllers, and, calling the members together, they shall hold a joint discussion. The directors shall investigate with particular care the circumstances on both sides of any quarrel and deliver a fair judgment.[26]

The 1906 regulations of the guild for natives of Kuang-chou and Ch'ao-chou prefectures were even more explicit:

It is generally to be hoped that when the guild gathers to discuss public matters everyone will speak in turn, regardless of how many people there are. There should be no hubbub of many voices speaking at once, as this leads to unsystematic confusion. If someone at the meeting puts forward a view that meets with general approval, appropriate action shall be taken at once. If the views put forward do not meet with general approval, the matter shall be repeatedly discussed until agreement is reached. In the main, a question shall be settled when six or seven out of ten agree.[27]

This limited democratization of the cities seems to have followed that taking place in the post-manorial countryside; and Imabori Seiji is probably right when he speaks of the practice of collective consultation as having been "transferred from the villages to the guilds."[28]

The Shanghai guilds taxed their members and settled disputes between them; ran primary schools, infirmaries, and fire brigades; and provided members with loans, support in old age, and coffins and land for burial. They did not, in the nineteenth century, constitute a municipal government. For this a confederation of guilds would have been needed, such as did exist in certain other Chinese cities at this time.

Historically, such an institution emerged in one of two ways. Sometimes a "great guild" (ta-hang) formed by in-migrants would become differentiated, as numbers grew, into constituent guilds for various trades and localities. This was the case at Kuei-sui.[29] Alternatively, independent guilds of fellow-regional merchants would combine into an overarching association. This was the origin of the Ten Guilds of Hung-chiang and the Eight Guilds of Chungking, both of which bodies assumed governmental functions in the course of the 1850's during the crisis brought on by the Taiping Rebellion. Their duties included welfare work, education, the management of police and militia, collection of certain taxes, famine relief, standardization of weights and measures, resolving disputes between members, and advising the authorities. Nor were they simply merchant institutions. Thus a text of 1888 refers to the "gentry and merchants of the Ten Guilds" in Hung-chiang, and almost all the leading Chungking merchants had official titles or degrees. Furthermore, with the passage of time, the differences between in-migrants from different regions tended to disappear (except in the important matter of which gods they worshipped at their guilds); and the functions of the guilds expanded from serving their members to serving society.

In Chungking, at least, the gentry and merchant power concentrated in the confederation of guilds was fragmented by the new local political institutions of the early twentieth century. The Eight Guilds organization lost its control over trade to the General Chamber of Commerce, its charitable work to the municipal welfare committee, its police power to the Police Board, and most of its other functions to a new municipal government. Its decline opened the way for the takeover of the city by militarists not long after the 1911 revolution; and the office of the Eight Guilds was closed in 1916 or 1917.[30] In Shanghai, as we shall see, a lesser but somewhat similar loss of powers weakened the City Council after the 1911 revolution.

Not having a confederation of guilds, Shanghai was spared the duplication of city-wide merchant organizations that appeared in Chungking and, as Professor Rhoads points out elsewhere in this volume, in Canton. In 1902–4, however, Yen Hsin-hou and other presidents of the principal guilds founded a Chinese General Chamber of Commerce.[31] In 1905, a Consulting Committee of the Chinese Merchants of the Shanghai Settlement was designed, though without success, to serve as a Chinese counterweight to the Municipal Council of the International Settlement, which was under foreign administration.[32] Various corps of merchant militia also came into being about this time.[33] The leadership of these bodies overlapped, and they worked effectively together. Most important of all, directors of guilds and members of the new Chamber of Commerce accounted for fourteen out of the 38 members of the original Chinese City Council of 1905, while another six were or had been engaged in commerce.[34]

The last of the late traditional institutions that contributed to the establishment of early modern city government was the specialized board attached to the county or some higher administrative unit. By 1862 there were at least eleven of these boards in Shanghai. They included a Board for the Boat Levy and the Catching of Pirates, originally run by merchants, a Joint Defense Board, a Board for Security and for the Wards and Tithings (*pao-chia*), and a Free Ferry Board. Many more were created in the following forty years. They were mostly charged with such tasks as collecting taxes on wood, opium, alcohol, sugar, and cotton cloth, manufacturing and storing weapons and munitions, and operating telegraphs, telephones, and postal services. They were usually managed by expectant officials serving as "deputies" (*wei-yüan*). Service of this sort was one way for apprentice bureaucrats to become familiar with the intricacies of local administration. A few boards, whose work bore directly on some branch of commerce, were managed by a deputy together with the directors of the guild of the trade concerned. This was the case with the Board for the Inspection of Raw Cotton for Evidence of Watering. Other boards, like the Free Ferry Board for a time, were run by gentry directors.[35]

The immediate precursor of the City Council was the South City Roadworks Board (*Nan-shih ma-lu kung-ch'eng chü*), founded in 1895 to build a main road along that part of the bank of the Huang-p'u river lying south of the boundary of the French Settlement. Shortly afterwards, this board, to quote its own words, "imitated the settlements" by establishing a police force containing more than sixty men, and setting up a police court.[36] From the point of view of the services it performed, the new City Council can be seen as an expanded version of the Roadworks Board. Its original name, "The General Works Board" (*Tsung-kung chü*), implies as much. In 1907, the executive committee of the Council described its own ancestry as follows: "Our Board's regulations for taxation, and for the imposition of fines, are basically those of the former Roadworks Board, which was under official management; and the Roadworks Board was in fact modeled on the Municipal Council of the International Settlement."[37] In other words, there was conscious institutional plagiarism. The development of the indigenous tradition is therefore not in itself adequate to explain the rise of modern urban administration. We have also to consider the stimulus provided by European models and ideas.

Western Influences in the Creation of the Shanghai City Council

The history of the municipal institutions of the International Settlement and the French Settlement is a familiar one and need not be recapitulated here.[38] The question is to what degree these institutions influenced the Chinese. By the 1880's, the growth of the Chinese city had led to increasing difficulty in meeting such problems as fire hazards, rubbish disposal, traffic circulation on waterways and streets, public order, and the supply of drinking water. Editorials in the newspaper *Shen-pao* indicate that the canals were silting up and choked with filth;

there was little water for washing in, or for fighting the fires that frequently swept through the closely packed houses; the garbage-removal
service run by the charities was breaking down; drinking water cost
several hundred copper cash a load; traffic was being obstructed—indeed nearly halted—by stalls and protruding shopfronts; and crime was
spreading.[39] Seen against this background, the achievements of the foreign Municipal Council in the nearby International Settlement were
impressive. We may quote the words of a leading article in the *Shen-pao*
in 1883:

When strangers first come to Shanghai, wander about the Settlement, and see
how clean and broad the streets are, and how thorough the patrol maintained
by the police, how regular the marching of the militia when drilling, how close
the houses are, like the prongs on a comb or the scales on a fish, and how
revenue from taxes is going up, they cannot help asking in delight: "Who has
had the power to do this?" We tell them: "The Westerners have established
a Municipal Council, which has directors and holds a general meeting every
year for discussions. All permanent regulations are debated and resolved upon
before being put into effect. The Council sees to the patrolling of the streets
by the police, the drilling of the militia, and the cleaning and paving of the
roadways; and it levies a tax from the residents to meet the costs. A superintendent is in charge of the police force, in which both Chinese and Westerners are employed. The police are also responsible for collecting taxes. The
funds are spent on [useful] matters, and not wasted. This is why those who
come to Shanghai all think it a fortunate place, and are unwilling to depart.
There are some petty thieves, brigands, and vagrants who try in a small way
to practice their tricks, but the police arrest them as soon as they see them,
and take them before the Mixed Court, where Chinese and Western officials
together examine their guilt. Once a decision has been reached, they are punished. . . . Thus the inhabitants can sleep without worry.

None of this could have been achieved but for the Municipal Council. . . .
Ever since Shanghai has had its Municipal Council the narrow and uneven
streets have been transformed and improved. A miserable rustic area has become a market to which men of all nations hasten like rivers to the sea, and
to which merchants come with no regard for distance. The streets are sprinkled
and swept every day. Crooked streets are straightened; bumpy streets are
leveled. If there is a fire, the police ring a bell to alert the fire brigade. These
days there is also piped water, which makes it possible to pour water onto a
fire from a source nearby. It is very effective and convenient. . . . The Council
does some things of which public opinion does not approve, but this does not
happen often. Its other actions have greatly benefited the locality. . . . If the
Chinese area is compared to the Settlement, the difference is no less than that
between the sky above and the sea below.[40]

The leader writer did not openly advocate the creation of a comparable council in the Chinese city, but such a thought must have been at the back of his mind. The *Shen-pao* was in favor of provincial parliaments and greater gentry power in local affairs.[41]

By the 1880's, an admiration for Western technology was becoming common in Shanghai. In 1884, Li Chung-chüeh, who was later to become General Director of the City Council, almost succeeded in the double venture of setting up a Chinese waterworks and piping purified water into the Chinese city from the Settlement. In 1887, he wrote *A Record of the Customs of Singapore* in which he praised the municipal administration of the British authorities there.[42] Like many members of the Shanghai gentry, he seems to have conceived of macadamized roads, primary schools, hospitals, piped water, and tramways as natural extensions of the services which it had been the honor and to some extent the profession of the late traditional local elite to provide.

Li is interesting as an embodiment of the combination of Chinese values and Western technology often advocated by Chinese statesmen in the later nineteenth century. He belonged to a generation that could assimilate the externals of European civilization without anguish, because they understood too little of its true nature to feel seriously threatened. His creed was the practical and severely moral Neo-Confucianism that flourished in Shanghai during the 1860's and 1870's, especially at the Lung-men Academy where he studied for ten years. He was a gifted practitioner of traditional medicine, with an interest in combining Chinese and Western therapeutic techniques. As an entrepreneur he won high praise from foreigners for the quality of the modern waterworks he built at Cha-pei. He was a director of banks, shipping firms, and insurance companies, and one of the first Chinese to appreciate the automobile and the telephone. He was also a resolute patriot, and while serving as county magistrate at Sui-ch'i in 1899 he levied forces and led them against the French annexation of Kuang-chou-wan. Li Hung-chang, then Governor-general at Canton, hurriedly removed him from his post, while remarking privately that, with a few more county magistrates of the caliber of Chung-chüeh, China would have no further worries with foreigners. Yet he enjoyed many friendly relationships with Westerners in Shanghai, and in his youth had written leading articles for the Chinese edition of the *North-China Herald*.[43]

Li's gentry colleagues on the City Council were equally preoccupied with the challenge of the West, while remaining firmly convinced of the value of their own heritage. Ts'ao Hsiang, who was a pioneer in Chinese-English lexicography and the author of a primer on the English language, spent much of his life restoring his clan's ancestral temple, publishing its records, and composing pietistic Confucian literature.[44] Yao Wen-nan wished to "synthesize the system of *The Rituals of the Chou* with the methods of education and personal cultivation used by the Westerners."[45]

Of the merchants on the Council we know less. It seems clear from their activities, though, that they were well acquainted with everyday Western civilization. Su Pen-yen, who came from a gentry family, was an expert on commercial law, the founder of the Chinese Cigarette Company, and a cofounder of the Commercial Press.[46] Chu Pao-san was a self-made millionaire with interests in banking, shipping, piped water, coal mining, flour milling, textiles, and newspapers. He was the founder of the Silk Thread Manufacturing Company and of the China United Assurance Company, for which he hired a Western manager.[47] Shen Man-yün was a banker, and the promoter of the Hsin-ch'ang Rice Hulling Company and the Industrial Bank. His initial political sympathies were constitutionalist, but he became a republican early in 1911 and did much to finance the revolution in Shanghai.[48] Yü Huai-chih had studied at the foreign language school set up in Shanghai by Li Hung-chang, and was a pioneer in the use of improved strains of cotton seed from the United States.[49] Wang I-t'ing, who is still remembered as a painter, was the comprador of the Japanese Nisshin Steamship Company. He was active in both the first and the second revolutions.[50] Yao Po-hsin was the founder of the New Theater, and the editor of the *Hsin-wen pao,* "the one profitable newspaper in Shanghai."[51] The experience of successful innovation in a partially Westernized business world must have fostered the self-confidence such men needed when they were faced with the challenge of creating a new political institution.

Direct Western provocations provided a final stimulus. In particular, the councils of the French and the International Settlements built and policed roads in Chinese areas, giving as a pretext the improvement of the amenities. It was these encroachments, according to the *Shanghai Self-Government Gazetteer,* that made the gentry "apprehensive at the growth of foreign power and the loss of sovereignty," and caused them to establish the City Council.[52] Even afterwards, fear remained a spur. In 1907, Intendant Jui-ch'eng remarked to the Executive Committee: "It will be very difficult to find the money to set up our own electric tram company in the Chinese area, but I am apprehensive that if we do not do it ourselves, things will end with the foreigners interfering." Five years later a Chinese tram company was successfully floated, in order, it was said, "to resist the covetousness of the foreigners," and the *North-*

China Herald complimented the promoters on "the excellence of the work done."[53] Chinese pride was also hurt by derisive foreign comments on the filthy state of the Chinese city.[54] Modernization became the price of self-respect.

The Structure of the Shanghai City Council

The new Council was set up late in 1905 on the initiative of Li Chung-chüeh, then Deputy Director of the Kiangnan Arsenal just south of the city, and Yüan Shu-hsün, the Shanghai intendant. Yüan authorized "directors publicly selected by the local gentry and merchants" to manage "all matters connected with main roads, electric lighting, and police in the city and its suburbs."[55] Permission was also granted for the Council to collect special taxes and to run its own police court: and in the following year a number of merchant militia forces were organized under Council leaders.[56]

There followed four years of vigorous growth. The Council enjoyed the general approval of the higher authorities (though they sometimes thought it too powerful),[57] without having any well-defined place in the Chinese polity. This experimental phase formally ended in 1909. The Council, and a number of other embryonic municipal institutions in various parts of China,[58] became subject to the new *Regulations for the Local Self-Government of Cities, Towns and Rural Communities*. Apart from a widening of the franchise, these regulations had no immediate practical effect on the city of Shanghai. They did give rise to new self-government bodies in the surrounding townships and country areas.

With the introduction of provincial assemblies in the same year, the Shanghai Council became part of a short-lived national system of gentry democracy, the creation of the partially modernized late traditional urban elite. In alliance with other forces, it was strong enough in 1911 to undermine the Ch'ing government in central and southern China, but it proved too weak to replace the old imperial bureaucracy. As the alliance of gentry, merchants, and revolutionaries that had sustained the revolution subsequently fell apart, it was succeeded by the increasingly militarized presidential rule of Yüan Shih-k'ai, a former imperial official with no commitment to democracy. Among Yüan's first victims were the erstwhile victors of 1911; and the Shanghai City Council was disbanded early in 1914.[59]

These events had little direct bearing on the internal organization of the Council, which remained fairly constant throughout its lifetime. The only changes worth mentioning are those that affected its sphere of operations after the revolution. It lost its court and its police force at this time; but acquired responsibility for primary education and for the supervision of the newly formed Association of Charities. In no other respect is there a need to make distinctions between subperiods, and the following analysis therefore ignores the numerous changes in the names of officeholders and departments that were unaccompanied by any changes in function.

The Shanghai City Council may well have been the first Chinese institution of any kind in which the making of policy was formally separated from its execution. Policy was made by a Consultative Assembly (*I-shih hui*) of 33 consulting directors (*i-tung*), and carried out by an executive committee (*ts'an-shih hui* or *tung-shih hui*), the core of which consisted of five managing general directors (*pan-shih tsung-tung*), or simply directors (*tung-shih*).[60] The relationship between the two was summed up in the Council's regulations. First, "The affairs the Council has to undertake shall be discussed and resolved upon by the consulting directors, and then carried out by the managing general directors." Second, "The Executive Committee ought carefully to observe the limits of its powers in matters not resolved upon by the Consultative Assembly. It does not have the power to initiate on its own and without authorization."[61] More particularly, the Assembly had the power to determine the annual budget, and require the Executive Committee to answer its questions. It could also review the judgments of the Council's court.[62]

There were two exceptions to the general rule that the Consultative Assembly was the supreme authority regarding matters delegated to it by the national government. The Executive Committee did not need the Assembly's approval to carry out minor tasks assigned by regular officials, though in practice they clearly preferred to have it. They might also delay the implementation of any Assembly resolution that seemed impracticable or beyond their legal powers. This was done by referring such a resolution to the Assembly for further discussion; and in the case of a matter thought to exceed their authority, the Committee might also appeal to higher-level assemblies.[63] In fact, however, since the Assembly elected the directors, there were few serious differences of opinion between the two bodies.[64]

Proposals for debate in the Assembly might be put forward by the Executive Committee, by members of the Assembly, or by members of the public who had the sponsorship of at least two members of the Assembly.[65] After 1909, the discussions were open to limited segments of the public.[66] Argument seems to have been vigorous, at least if the reports in the press may be taken as a guide.[67] Each item was given three "readings," and decided upon by majority vote.[68]

Resolutions that had been approved, and the annual budget, were passed on to the Executive Committee. The composition of this latter body fluctuated considerably; at the period of its fullest development it consisted of four salaried directors and twelve honorary directors (*ming-yü tung-shih*) elected by the Assembly. The divisional directors (*ch'ü-chang, ch'ü-tung*) of the South, West and Central divisions of the city, or their deputies, were entitled to attend the monthly meetings, but might vote only on matters that exclusively concerned their own divisions.[69] In general terms, the system may be described as a form of collective leadership under the chairmanship of the leading director.* The Committee resolved questions put before it by majority vote. Once decisions had been made, a member who opposed them anywhere except at Committee meetings could be punished. Minutes were kept of all proceedings, and members were regarded as having equal responsibility for any course of action adopted, regardless of whether or not they had been present in person at the time.[70]

Beneath the Executive Committee, and subject to its orders, was a bureaucratic apparatus. By 1912 it comprised ten departments (*k'o*) charged with the following responsibilities: the documents of the Executive Committee, the documents of the Assembly, the Council's accounts, the collection of its taxes, the provision of general services, the organization of public works, the care of public health (including the cleaning of the streets), primary education, "household registration" (or, more accurately, electoral surveys), and the registration of the boat population that lived and worked on the city's waterways. These departments were staffed by executive officers (*pan-shih yüan*); and each of them, except the last, was headed by a person commonly referred to as the department administrator (*k'o-chang*). He had a varying number of managerial assistants (*chu-li yüan*) as his subordinates. Before 1909, appointments to the senior posts were made by the Executive Committee, subject to the approval of the Assembly. Thereafter, they were in the gift of the general director. Department administrators may possibly have selected their own assistants.[71]

The bureaucracy also included three branch administrative bureaus (*fen-pan ch'u*), in the South, West, and Central divisions, under the three divisional directors. There was no separate divisional administration for the East division, since the main Council buildings were located there. Before 1912, there was a judicial office (*Ts'ai-p'an so*), or court, presided over by two judicial officials (*ts'ai-p'an kuan*), and a police force for the Chinese suburbs outside the old walled city, under a police

---

* Usually styled the General Director (*tsung-tung*).

administrator (*ching-wu chang*). All of these officials were elected by the Consultative Assembly.[72]

The divisional administrations handled the collection of local taxes, the cleaning and lighting of the streets, and the maintenance of order, subject to the general supervision of the central authorities. In particular, their rota officers (*tang-chih yüan*), or police case officers (*ching-fa li-shih yüan*), carried out the preliminary examination of suspects brought in by the police. If they thought a charge unjustified they might dismiss the accused; if they thought it justified, but of no great importance, they might impose a small fine. Serious cases were passed on to the court, which also maintained its own rota officers for the same service in the East division.[73]

The divisions also disposed of the services of a number of assistant officers (*tsan-chu yüan*). These were distinguished local residents who served without pay on a semipermanent basis. In theory they were meant to have a dual status, being assigned both to a particular executive department in which their special skills would be most useful, and to the division in which they lived. They were supposed to attend regular meetings of two types: one with their departmental colleagues, and one with their divisional colleagues. This does not seem to have been strictly adhered to in practice; the divisional tie seems on the whole to have been stronger than the departmental. The post was an important one: many of the leading gentry and businessmen who held it were later elected to the Assembly. The assistant officers' most important function was probably, as the regulations stated, "to establish a rapport between the locality and the various sectors of the Council" by keeping the latter in touch with public opinion.[74]

At the bottom of the municipal administration were the tax collectors, police, road sweepers and lamplighters, and also a number of agents and workmen hired and controlled by contractors (*ch'eng-pan jen*) and foremen (*fu-t'ou*). Generally speaking, contracting was used for inter-mittent work like road-building,* for matters concerning the intractable boat population, and for services, such as night-soil collection, where the profits to be made enabled the Council to charge the contractor a monthly fee in return for guaranteeing him a monopoly. There was an additional advantage: if a contractor made himself unpopular, the odium did not fall directly on the Council, which could, and often did, replace him.[75]

---

* A limited number of long-term workers (*ch'ang-kung*) and short-term workers (*tuan-kung*) were directly hired by the Council for the repair of roads, drains and buildings.

It was at this lowest level, as with most large Chinese organizations,[76] that the problem of systematic control was most difficult. It was tackled in a variety of ways: The actions of the taxation assistants (*chüan-wu pan-li yüan*), who assessed and collected the locality tax and vehicle tax, were checked on through a system of forms and registers. These effectively prevented them from defrauding the Council, though offering only a limited protection against unauthorized additional charges on the public.[77] To their credit, though, they were never accused of such malpractices. This is in marked contrast to the almost continual complaints raised against the collectors (*shou-chüan jen*) employed by the merchants who had contracted for the boat tax and related levies. Extortion was made almost inevitable by the manner in which the Council auctioned to the highest bidder the right to collect these taxes,* and its reluctance to become involved in any disputes between contractors' agents and aggrieved boatmen.[78]

The road cleaners (*ch'ing-tao fu*) and lamplighters (*teng fu*) were directly employed by the Council, and control over them was exercised in the first instance by foremen; but the city authorities were at pains to avoid giving these intermediaries the degree of independence they enjoyed in most Chinese industries at this time.[79] Wages were paid directly to the workmen; and their efforts were inspected by divisional officials, who recorded appropriate comments in a diligence register (*k'o-ch'in pu*), inflicted fines upon the dilatory, and rewarded those who consistently did well.[80]

When workmen were not directly employed by the Council, there were often abuses. In 1910, for example, the Council felt obliged to issue the following proclamation to the foremen with whom it contracted for the removal of the city's rubbish by boat to a dumping ground some way up the Huang-p'u river:

The Council's rubbish boats were previously told to deposit their loads . . . at Lung-hua point. . . . They have long since become careless, and often . . . dump them in the middle of the Huang-p'u river, or on the banks of the creeks; or else leave them in the P'u-tung area on the pretext of "manuring the fields." People who have seen this have laid plaints against them on several occasions. . . . The foremen who are in charge of rubbish disposal all scheme to profit themselves by cutting wages, and so hire workmen of this lazy and thievish character, making no attempt whatever to discipline them. . . . If they have the audacity to continue to act in the old corrupt way, . . . we shall confiscate the boats concerned in order to provide a warning to others.[81]

---

* The object of this procedure was "to prevent the privileges being solicited on behalf of friends of the directors."

This use of a proclamation by the Council to control those who were, at one remove, its servants shows the extent of the gulf created by contracting.

The police force presented a special problem. This was partly the consequence of a tainted past history; the constables inherited by the Council from the Roadworks Board had a notoriously bad record, and the Water Patrol (*Shui-hsün*) was in the hands of the boss of the city's underworld. The Council struggled hard to introduce satisfactory standards of honesty and efficiency. They disbanded the Water Patrol altogether between 1905 and 1910; they set up a Police Academy (*Ching-wu hsüeh-t'ang*); they insisted that every new recruit be personally guaranteed by a member of the gentry or by a merchant; and they attempted to ensure good performance by means of a schedule of rewards and fines. Even so, corruption proved hard to eradicate; and in the early years substantial numbers of policemen had to be dismissed.[82]

The Council were fortunate in being able to call on a merchant militia as a reserve force. The members of this municipal army were young employees in local businesses. They were so obviously respectable that the imperial authorities allowed them to carry firearms. The initial nucleus was the 350-man Association of Merchant Militia (*Shang-t'uan kung-hui*) founded in 1906 by Li Chung-chüeh and Tseng Chu, one of Li's colleagues on the Executive Committee and president of the Chinese General Chamber of Commerce. Their immediate objective was to suppress the disorders threatened upon closure of the city's opium dens. The Association consisted of five bodies of militia created earlier the same year, all of them under the command of one or more members of the Council. Besides meeting the opium-den crisis successfully, it preserved order in Shanghai on a number of occasions when the county government found its powers inadequate, most notably during the rent agitation in the winter of 1910 and the rice riots of September 1911.[83] In the months before the revolution, the mounting national political crisis led to the rapid expansion of the Association under the leadership of members of the Council such as Wang I-t'ing and Shen Man-yün, both of whom had strong republican sympathies and personal contacts with the chief revolutionaries in the city. In November the merchant militia played the crucial role in the fall of the local imperial administration.[84]

The internal structure of the various merchant militia forces is obscure. Their regulations show them, formally at least, to have been democratic. They elected their leaders and officers, and decided policy at mass meetings of members.[85] The Council occasionally made use of them to carry out functions not directly related to their work as militia. Once, for example, it had them organize a public meeting to pronounce on a local problem.[86]

The City Council did not supersede the older existing system of local control by wardens (*ti-pao*), warders (*ti-chia*),* district directors (*t'u-tung*), and sector directors (*tuan-tung*), all of whom were answerable to the county magistrate. Rather, it assumed joint control over the system with the magistrate. Warders and district directors often reported both to the county magistrate and to the Council; and the Council issued orders to them either on its own account or on the instructions of the county magistrate.[87]

The late traditional system thus incorporated into the Council was based on a combination of two sharply contrasting classes of person: directors from the gentry class and agents of a relatively lowly social status. In this it resembled the rural compact boards (*hsiang-yüeh chü*) of nearby Wu-hsi and Chin-hua—bodies with many of the powers of local government, in which rural compact leaders (*hsang-yüeh chang*) were subordinated to directors of rounds (*shan-tung*).[88] The Shanghai district and sector directors seem to have controlled the wardens and warders less closely, but they certainly worked with them and supervised them. After 1909, they had to stand as guarantors for the probity of new appointees. It was customary for directors and agents to hold joint meetings from time to time.[89]

The reason for the low status of the wardens and warders was that, unlike the police constables, they were held personally responsible for the good order of the districts to which they were assigned. They could be severely beaten or otherwise punished if they failed in this respect. The attraction of the post, which had to be bought for a substantial sum of money, was the opportunity it gave to become rich through a variety of illegal means, especially by collusion with dishonest real estate agents. Even after a modern police force had been created, the wardens and warders were indispensable. No one else could certify the ownership of land being bought and sold, guarantee the truth of statements made to the authorities by residents and businessmen, and supply other such kinds of information that needed a lifetime's familiarity with an area and the city's dialect to acquire. The Council therefore retained them after the revolution under the more dignified title of Household Registration Police (*hu-chi ching-ch'a*).[90]

The district and sector directors were notables whose accepted func-

---

* Wardens operated in rural areas, warders in urban ones. There was no difference in functions. See SHSTCC, Docs section C, pp. 71b, 83a.

tion it was to speak for public opinion, to help organize public works such as dredging and the repair of temples, and to urge citizens to pay their taxes promptly. The sector directors appear to have begun as the staff of the Militia Defense Board (*T'uan-fang chü*) set up in 1862. They were eminent people, appointed by the authorities, but not necessarily holders of titles or degrees. The branch boards in the walled city and its suburbs were disbanded in 1905 and 1906; but the incumbent directors retained their titles and at least some of their duties in the years that followed.[91]

This description of the complex structure of the City Council needs to be completed by a brief account of two partially autonomous bodies with which it was closely connected: the Amalgamated Firefighting Association (*Chiu-huo lien-ho hui*) and the Association of Charities (*Tz'u-shan t'uan*). The Firefighting Association was formed by Li Chung-chüeh in 1907 out of the thirty-odd existing fire brigades; it was largely financed by Mao Tzu-chien, who later became the director of the Council's Central division.[92] Other members of the Council also belonged to the Firefighting Association, and the Association's building housed the Central division offices. The Association of Charities was founded in 1912. It was a federation of existing institutions and two new foundations under the control of a manager (*ching-li*), and other officers, appointed by the Council's Executive Committee. Its budget had to be submitted to the Assembly. Otherwise it enjoyed freedom of action within the compass of rules laid down by the Assembly. There were six departments, which dealt respectively with (1) the issuing of relief to a restricted number of widows, old people, and orphans, (2) the burial of abandoned corpses, and the distribution of free coffins, (3) the care of infants, (4) the lodging of orphans and old people unable to care for themselves, (5) training the unemployed for a trade, and (6) the operation of a workhouse for widows.[93]

Such was the provision made for the needs of an urban population of nearly a quarter of a million people.

The Impact of the City Council on Life in Shanghai

There were precedents in earlier times for most of the policies of the new municipal administration, but taken together they marked a perceptible advance upon the past. A determined attempt was made to provide for welfare and primary education. There was a vigorous program, characterized by an extensive use of regulatory law, to improve the physical environment, to modernize customs and ways of thought, and to create a society that was healthier, safer, more efficient, and more humane. For some of its spiritual resources this campaign drew on the centuries-old mission of the Confucian scholar to eradicate evil ways among the common people, and on the traditional assumption that in a time of disaster it was the government's duty to provide relief. From the West it took the content of many specific undertakings, and also the general ideal of economic and social progress. One by-product of this was a spate of new local laws. The Shanghai public disliked the Council's police for what the Council described as their "philosophy of interference" (*kan-she chu-i*).[94] The phrase might not inaptly be extended to the Council's work as a whole.

The Council's Highway Code, the first in China, is a good illustration of its attack on the easygoing ways of the past. It laid down that vehicles were to keep to the lefthand side of the road, to slow down at bridges and crossroads, and to turn left or right only after having given the prescribed hand signals. Heavily loaded carts had to travel at a walking pace. Those who left their vehicles unattended or blocking a roadway and those who indulged in racing were liable to a fine. Cars, horse-drawn vehicles, rickshas, carts, and barrows had to meet defined standards of roadworthiness, and be equipped with lights for travel after dark. Bicycles had to have bells and lights, and the rider might be fined or have his machine confiscated if he hurt people or did damage to property. For the morning rush hour there was a rudimentary system of one-way streets. Pigs might not be driven along the roads except at certain times of day; nor might cows or horses be left unattended. Further regulations covered the siting of shop counters and railings, the placing of shop signs and roadside stalls, and limited the amount of merchandise that might be piled up in the streets.[95]

Public health laws forbade food shops to sell rotten meat or meat from animals or poultry that had died of disease. Establishments selling smoked meats, breads, warmed wine, or snacks were not permitted to offer wares prepared on the previous day; and comestibles had to be covered with gauze as a protection against insects. Selling watermelon by the slice was discouraged but, if this was "unavoidable," each slice had to be wrapped in paper. Ice creams, iced lemonade and flavored ices were banned, not only because cold things are injurious to the (Chinese) stomach, but also because these products were made with unboiled, and therefore probably unhealthy, water. Other suspect foods were examined by the Council's Public Health Food Analysis Office (*Shih-wu wei-sheng hua-yen so*). Uncovered kerosene lamps were not allowed in food stores or food stalls lest the lampblack enter customers' throats or digestive systems. Coffins, dead animals, bricks, tiles, or other rubbish might not be left in waterways or on public roads. Urinating or defecating in the streets was forbidden. Ordure carriers had to fit their tubs with lids; and the clothes of those who had died might not be burned on the pavements.[96]

It was illegal to carry a gun, a knife, or any other lethal weapon. Kerosene warehouses were restricted to the P'u-tung area across the Huang-p'u river. In order to prevent the repetition of a disastrous fire that had started in a kerosene store, retailers were not allowed to have more than fifteen containers of the fuel on their premises at any one time. People were not permitted to light fires in densely populated areas; shop signs could not be put up near uninsulated electric wires, because of the fire hazard; and the traditional wooden drainage boards were supposed to be removed from all roofs and replaced by lead guttering and drain-pipes, in order to retard the spread of fire. Kite-flying was forbidden because the strings might catch in overhead wires. Municipal engineers were meant to inspect factory boilers to make sure that they were safe.[97]

Builders had to obtain a permit for any major construction work. This was to make sure that they complied with the lines laid down by the Council for the fronts of buildings in such a way that the streets would gradually be widened as houses and shops were replaced. Advertisements, plays, films, and musical recitals were subjected to censorship. Proclamations forbade gambling, worshipping traditional Taoist and Buddhist deities, sailing "dragon-boats," acting as a spirit-medium, or playing children's games in which there was an element of gambling. Men and women might not sit together in teahouses, cinemas, or theaters. Transvestism was banned, and sometimes punished by strangling. It was illegal to operate "nightflower gardens," sell dirty books or dirty pictures, sing obscene songs, flirt with women in public, or make noise late at night.[98]

"Nothing but paper regulations" (*chü wen*) might be the unimpressed Chinese reaction to the foregoing. The 1,700 cases a year handled by the Council's court, and the steady flow of rota bureau fines, would suggest that this was not altogether so.[99] The effective suppression of the opium dens in 1907 also shows that the police, if supported, were capable of accomplishing reforms in the face of considerable popular resistance.[100]

The goal was a municipal welfare state. Since the Council believed that education was of "the first importance" for the development of society, they charged no fees at all at five of their twenty-three primary schools, and fees far below cost at the others. They ran night schools and literacy classes for adults.[101] They started, though they could not long maintain, a hospital in which patients paid only for their board and lodging or, if really poor, were admitted free.[102] In 1912, when they founded a new institution for crippled beggars and other unfortunates, they observed: "In the age of the Great Concord (*ta-t'ung chih shih*) it is certain that the old will complete their allotted span of years, and that the mature will have the means to grow to their full strength. The widowers, the widows, the lame, and the ailing will all be cared for by someone. In its own modest way, the establishment of the Hall of Wide-spread Care pursues this ideal."[103] When the price of rice in the city rose as the result of a genuine scarcity, they imported rice from other parts of China, or from abroad, for sale at a reduced price (*p'ing-t'iao*). When the price rose because the local merchants were hoarding supplies, they used the technique of price stabilization (*p'ing-chia*) invented by Tseng Chu: selling imported grain at a price that was continually lowered so as to undercut the market price by a given margin until the latter could be made to fall no further.[104]

Between late 1905 and early 1914 the Council spent more than half a million *yüan*, or the equivalent of £60,000 at 1906 rates of exchange, on roads, bridges, sewers, and staithing.[105] Their most spectacular achievement was demolishing the city walls, which had choked the economic life of the central area by constricting the circulation of traffic, and building a magnificent circular boulevard, equipped with a tramway, in their place. They subsidized the formation of an electric light company under the direction of a member of the Assembly; they rescued and expanded the failing Shanghai Inland Mains Water Company; and they promoted a successful tram company, which was also managed by a member of the Council.[106] By 1914 they had earned the grudging tribute from the *North-China Herald* that "progress has been made to some extent in roads and, more notably, in the formation of companies for light and waterworks, [and] tramways."[107]

The influence of the modern West was apparent in almost every aspect of the Council's work, from the bridges built of steel frames and concrete to the enthusiasm for physical education, gardening, commercial studies and limited student self-government in the schools.[108] Perhaps the most important effect of all was in the court, where the "weight of the evidence" was adopted as the basis for verdicts. This was a change of pivotal significance. Confession was no longer essential for a verdict of guilty, and so it became possible to do away with torture and to conduct trials in a manner consonant with human dignity.[109] There was a strong current of opinion in Shanghai favoring legal reform, and the first jury trial in China was conducted on the Council's premises early in 1912.

It was not enough of a success to be repeated, but it shows the temper of the times.[110]

In 1912 and 1913 the prospects of social progress in Shanghai gradually darkened. The increase in crime that followed the 1911 revolution, the rise to power of underworld leaders connected with that revolution, the destruction of much of southern Shanghai in the fighting of 1913 with the consequent loss of about a third of the municipal revenue, the reign of terror and demoralization that followed the victory of Yüan Shih-k'ai and the influx of his agents into the city, the forcible disbanding of the Merchant Militia, and then of the Council itself, brought to an end eight and a half years' effort to realize what the Council's leaders had called "the way of humanitarianism."[111]

Conclusions

The Shanghai City Council was an impressive attempt by a still cohesive and self-confident traditional Chinese social order to adapt itself to modern Western ideals of democracy and of organizational and technological efficiency. There were no particular technological problems— any more than for Chinese industries in the city—presumably because of the existence of a pool of skilled labor trained in local Western factories and in repair shops handling Western machinery. Democracy, at least of the limited type whose franchise included, at its broadest, only about one adult male in four, and no women, seems to have come with equal ease. Clearly it had solid roots in Chinese tradition. Most surprising, perhaps, is the absence of corruption. Even its worst enemies never accused the Shanghai City Council of being corrupt. Possibly this was because affairs were transacted in committee, the Assembly could call for documents and question members of the executive, and Assembly proceedings were open to the press. Yet this must have been true of most other self-government bodies, and many of them were denounced as corrupt.[112] It should be noted that some of these denunciations are doubtful. Yamen clerks of the old variety hated self-government, and rural bullies sometimes tried to exploit popular resentment of such typical self-government policies as the conversion of temples to primary schools.[113] Shanghai's unusually good record, however, still awaits explanation.

Reflection on the foregoing material leads us to question many commonly accepted notions about Chinese history in the early years of this century. Change was necessary and inevitable; but if the late traditional elite was generally capable of the creative energy it showed in Shanghai, then the revolution, which led to the rapid breakdown of the framework for peaceful change, was a disaster. It is not unreasonable to speculate that, if the Imperial Court in 1910 and 1911 had possessed one or two politicians with either the intelligence or the flexibility to have conciliated the constitutional movement, not only might there have been no overt revolution, but a new political order, of which the municipal council studied in this paper may stand as an exemplar, might have had the time to establish foundations that could not have been so easily swept away.

City Temples in Taipei Under Three Regimes

STEPHAN FEUCHTWANG

Some of the most prominent institutions of Chinese cities are their temples* and festivals. This essay describes the major temples of popular religion in Taipei, taking as its main theme the relationship between these institutions and the successive governments that have ruled Taiwan since the nineteenth century.

My principal findings may be summarized briefly as follows. During the Ch'ing period, temples in Taiwan—Taipei's among them—functioned both as a proto-government and as rallying points in the communal divisions of society. During the later decades of the nineteenth century, under conditions of greater political stability, Taipei's nonofficial temples could be subdivided into three overlapping types: the compatriot, the territorially based, and the commercially based. In all of these the closed and oligarchic character of the management of the temple property contrasted with the relatively open and popular character of the management of temple festivals. The tighter control exercised over temple organization by the Japanese (1895–1945) and the Republicans (since 1945) has sharpened this contrast. The earlier distinctions between types of temples lost much of their relevance during these two periods, and new distinctions emerged, notably between Buddhist-aligned temples once associated with guilds but now associated with central government, and Taoist-aligned temples retaining a rather more compatriot or territorial form of organization. In the richer and more recently developed parts of the city, meanwhile, new temples were

---

* For the reader's convenience in distinguishing at once between the temples and the deities for whom the temples are named, the following system will be used throughout the text, "the Ch'ing-shan-wang miao" (temple); "Ch'ing Shan Wang" (god).

founded, characterized by syncretistic beliefs, followers organized into congregations, a strong governmental orientation, and a lack in most cases of any specific affiliations with a locality.

My evidence comes primarily from personal observations and investigations of the most flourishing of Taipei's temples during 1967–68.[1] I have drawn on secondary historical materials for the background to the broad pattern of change that I hope to establish.

Taipei Before 1895

Taipei lies on the east bank of the Tan-shui river between the mouths of two of its tributaries, the Hsin-tien and the Chi-lung. These rivers drain a fertile and humid basin surrounded by mountains on all sides but the northwest, where the Tan-shui flows into the Taiwan Straits facing the mainland. It was here, near the harbors of the Tan-shui estuary, site of the present-day town of Tan-shui, that the first Chinese settlements in northern Taiwan were established during the first half of the seventeenth century, and perhaps earlier as pirate bases. The Chinese encroachment into the Taipei basin proceeded up the Tan-shui and then eastward until the middle of the nineteenth century, after which no new settlements were established.[2]

As the best land was appropriated, leaving only hill land for further expansion, boundary disputes probably became frequent. Whatever the cause, there was large-scale rioting or rebellion in the area during almost every decade from 1760 to 1870, with the disputants recruiting aid from people who spoke the same language or dialect and came from the same native place. One effect of all this was to strengthen these speech-group and native-place ties and to sort the Taipei basin into settlements that reflected them, settlements peopled predominantly by descendants of immigrants from one prefecture, one county (*hsien*), or even one district (*hsiang*) of Fukien province, for example. It is to this principle of organization and identification that I refer by the word "compatriotism."

Another effect was that the military side of government predominated. Meng-chia, now part of Taipei (see Map 1), had already been established as a military garrison, and drew to it in 1809 the civilian administration of an assistant county magistrate only ten years after a yamen for him had been started in Hsin-chuang. Meng-chia had also become a port for trade with Ch'üan-chou and Foochow, whereas Hsin-chuang, although an older settlement, was farther upriver and had not grown so quickly, or become a center of trade with the mainland. But despite the presence of central government in Meng-chia (a public granary in 1831 and an academy (*shu-yüan*) in 1841), and the institution of *pao-*

chia registration for the control of the population, riots continued, culminating in the battles of the early 1850's.

At this time Meng-chia was approaching its heyday as Taiwan's most important commercial center, leaving T'ai-nan and Lu-kang behind. It was populated by immigrants from five counties of Ch'üan-chou prefecture in Fukien, and links with the mainland were sustained as part of Meng-chia's function as a port. Two merchant guilds (*chiao*) were the chief organizations of this trade with the mainland. The Ch'üan *chiao* had the monopoly of trade with Ch'üan-chou city, the capital both of the prefecture and of Chin-chiang county.

The Hsia *chiao* (Amoy Guild) had the trade with Amoy, which was also associated with T'ung-an county. The guilds were thus not only commercial but place-of-origin organizations, and as such were at the center of the communal riots. Indeed, the riots were known as the Ting-Hsia riots, "Ting" referring to the Ch'üan *chiao* and two other guilds with which it had formed an alliance, namely the Ting *chiao*, which had the monopoly of trade with ports north of Shanghai on the coast of China, and the Pei *chiao* (Northern Guild), which had the monopoly of trade with Shanghai itself. The Ting alliance was also an organization of compatriots of Chin-chiang county and its two neighboring counties, Hui-an and Nan-an, which were collectively known as the "San I," the Three Counties. The two groups were territorially as well as commercially defined, T'ung-an people living in a settlement called Pa-chia-chuang that adjoined Meng-chia.

The fifth Ch'üan-chou county represented in Meng-chia was An-ch'i. As an inland county, it had no port guild, or apparently any other commercial organization at this time, although An-ch'i people were later to be strongly associated with the tea trade. In the struggle between T'ung-an and the San I in Meng-chia, An-ch'i men tried to remain neutral. At one point they did side with the San I, but still managed, both then and later in the development of Taipei, to settle in large numbers in the urban territories of both the San I and T'ung-an people.

The communal battles ended when the T'ung-an people were defeated and left the vicinity of Meng-chia, taking the Amoy Guild with them. Some of them moved only a couple of kilometers downriver and built another trading center called Ta-tao-ch'eng; others moved farther downriver toward another T'ung-an settlement called Ta-lung-t'ung.

The 1860's saw an end to the rioting in the Taipei basin. Meng-chia became a full-fledged county capital in 1866, and a local pro-government militia was organized. Tan-shui had been opened to foreigners by treaty in 1860; and in 1862 the treaty was extended to include Meng-chia,

TABLE 1. THE ORGANIZATION IN TAIPEI OF IMMIGRANTS FROM CH'ÜAN-CHOU
PREFECTURE AROUND 1850

County of origin		Area of residence	Guild affiliation		Trading region
Chin-chiang		Meng-chia	Ch'üan	Ting	Ch'üan-chou
Hui-an	San I	Meng-chia	Ting	alli-	North of Shanghai
Nan-an		Meng-chia	Pei	ance	Shanghai
T'ung-an		Pa-chia-chuang (later, Ta-tao-ch'eng) and Ta-lung-t'ung	Hsia		Amoy
An-ch'i		Nonspecific	(Tea trade)		—

SOURCE: This and all other tables in the chapter are based on Li T'ien-ch'un, "T'ai-pei ti ch'ü chih k'ai shih yü ssu miao" (Temples and development of the Taipei area), *T'ai-pei wen hsien*, 1 (1962): 67–77.

the foreigners having found that most of the trade was done there, and not in the estuary. During the next thirty years Meng-chia's and Ta-tao-ch'eng's exports to the mainland and overseas rose well above those of all the other ports in Taiwan put together, the main commodity being tea. In 1866 John Dodd of Dodd and Company had brought slips of tea plant from An-ch'i to Taiwan and encouraged their cultivation in the hills around the edge of the Taipei basin. It was the export of this tea, mainly to America, that formed the bulk of the expanding trade. Probably because Amoy was the market for more than half of Taiwan's tea exports, Ta-tao-ch'eng rather than Meng-chia became the center of the tea trade and the site of the major foreign warehouses and processing works. By the 1880's Ta-tao-ch'eng (see Map 1) had surpassed Meng-chia in commercial importance, tea accounting for over 80 percent of Taiwan's total exports between 1880 and 1892.[3]

The increasing commercial importance of Meng-chia and Ta-tao-ch'eng and the presence of foreigners there would seem to have attracted a stronger Chinese central government interest. In 1875 northern Taiwan was made a prefecture and a new walled city (T'ai-pei-fu; see Map 1) was built for its administration just inland of Meng-chia. It was the military headquarters of the future governor Liu Ming-ch'uan in the war against the French in 1884–85; and in 1894, when Taiwan was raised to the status of a province, Taipei was made its capital. The next year, following China's defeat in the Sino-Japanese War, Taiwan was ceded to Japan.

At the time of cession to Japan, then, Taipei was made up of four sub-cities: Meng-chia, developed during the century of riot and rebellion 1760–1860, and populated by people of San I and An-ch'i origin; Ta-tao-

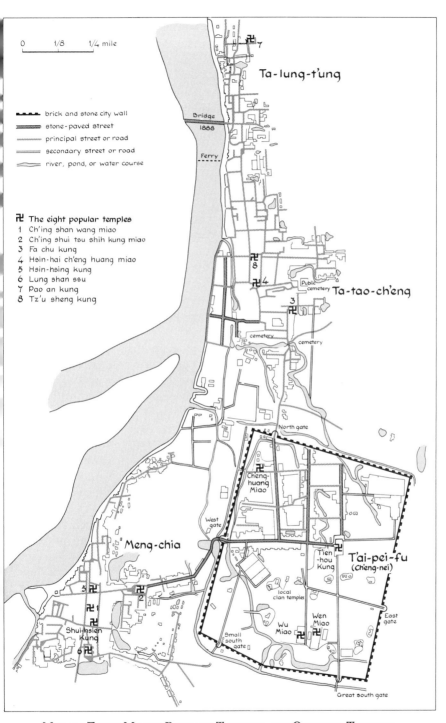

MAP 1. EIGHT MAJOR POPULAR TEMPLES AND OFFICIAL TEMPLES
IN TAIPEI, 1895

ch'eng, developed after 1860 during the years of increasing Western and central government presence; the new walled city, containing the central government itself as well as its own markets and commerce; and, much the smallest, Ta-lung-t'ung, the center of T'ung-an culture and scholarship, famous for the number of degree-holders it had produced.

Temples as Centers of Communal Solidarity

The administrative hierarchy that radiated down from the national capital to its smallest units, the counties, left great areas of social life unadministered. Religion was one of the chief means by which a low-level social system was articulated. Like the marketing structure, and unlike Catholic Christianity, the structure of popular religious institutions was built from the bottom up. Within popular religion there were no congregations.* There were families of professional religious practitioners who passed down religious texts and traditions, and there were cults, with their own histories. The two were separate; the cults of gods developed and continued, and temples were built for them, without clergy and according to their popular repute and manifestations of efficacy (ling).

A local cult might start as a sect, the worship of its god being exclusive to a defined membership. Were it to grow, it would become a center of pilgrimage; and if situated in a town or village it would become inclusive, its temple and festivals open to all those living within its locality. Many villages and almost every marketing system—in short, every local social system—had such a local temple, with a ritual tax on every head within the area to pay for its regular festivals. In many cases the temple was in the central place of the marketing system, with a periodic market or row of permanent shops in front of it. Any of the major Ch'ing dynasty temples of Meng-chia, Ta-tao-ch'eng and Ta-lung-t'ung can serve as an example of this.

It was common for an old temple to have several branch temples. Center and branch temples (and also temples and surrounding domestic shrines) were ritually linked by division of incense (fen-hsiang) or of efficacy (fen-ling). This ritual consisted simply of taking incense dust from the incense burner of the original shrine and placing it in the burner of the branch shrine. Subsequent pilgrimages with the incense burner back to the root shrine, as it was called, renewed the link. The major Ch'ing dynasty temples of Taipei had themselves been set up by mi-

---

* By a congregation I mean people who regularly assemble because they consider themselves to be joined in a faith or cult and bound by the rules of devotion.

grants from Fukien who brought incense dust from shrines of their local temples on the mainland, often as protection on the voyage across the straits. Later they and their descendants made pilgrimages to these root shrines, reenacting history and ritual genealogy. In this way the branches of mainland cults became centers for communities of compatriots in Taiwan.

Taiwan was a frontier region until late in Ch'ing times, and far removed from central administration. Temples were built in its central places long before government officials appeared. As old men in the City God temple of Hsin-chu, just south of the Taipei basin, told Michael Saso, when there was no official government "the gods were our officials."[4] In Fukien and Kwangtung, local-level organization was frequently based on patrilineal kinship. But, unlike the larger solidarity based on common locality of origin, kinship solidarity was neither so easily transferred to Taiwan nor so quick to develop there, in part because of official Ch'ing restrictions, lifted only in 1875, on men's taking their families with them when migrating to Taiwan. Early gazetteers remark on the Taiwanese settlers' having many neighbors but few kin. For defense and mutual aid these neighbors cooperated closely. People from the same home town were as dear as blood relatives, helping each other in illness and at burial, and joining together in contributing toward the welfare of the poor.[5] Temples, or rather the more essential organization around an incense burner, would have been one of the chief means of articulating this organization of neighbors. As Lin Heng-tao has summarized it, popular temples were a form of self-government in the immigrant settlements.[6] Even when Taiwan was fully settled and was more closely scrutinized by the central Chinese government, temples were still important in local-level organization. And the first Japanese governor of Taiwan in 1896 saved the temples from destruction on the grounds that they were the foundation of order and security.[7]

Each of the native-place communities in Taipei had a temple as its focus. The Ting alliance of guilds and San I people had as a headquarters and shrine for their guilds' patron deities the Lung-shan ssu in Meng-chia. The T'ung-an people had the Pao-an kung in Ta-lung-t'ung as a headquarters during the riots, and as a cultural center thereafter. The T'ung-an guild's patron deity was housed in the Tz'u-sheng kung in Ta-tao-ch'eng, originally a shrine in Pa-chia-chuang.* Another temple, the Hsia-hai ch'eng-huang miao, was also first organized by

---

* For the sake of convenience I will use the original place names even for the present period, when they are no longer used.

TABLE 2. COMPATRIOT TEMPLES IN TAIPEI AROUND 1895

Temple	Location	Area of origin	Guild affiliation
Lung-shan ssu	Meng-chia	San I	Ting Alliance
Tz'u-sheng kung	Ta-tao ch'eng (originally in Pa-chia-chuang)	T'ung-an	Hsia
Pao-an kung	Ta-lung-t'ung	T'ung-an	——
Fa-chu-kung kung	Ta-tao-ch'eng	An-ch'i	(Tea trade)
Ch'ing-shui tsu-shih-kung miao	Meng-chia	An-ch'i	——
Compatriot before 1885			
Hsia-hai ch'eng-huang miao	Ta-tao-ch'eng (originally in Pa-chia-chuang)	T'ung-an	——
Compatriot before 1868			
Ch'ing-shan-wang miao	Meng-chia	Hui-an	——

T'ung-an people in Pa-chia-chuang. When its shrine was set on fire by San I and An-ch'i people during the riots, the image of its main god was rescued and a temple built for it in Ta-tao-ch'eng, where it became the local territorial temple. The An-ch'i community had as its focal symbol the Ch'ing-shui tsu-shih-kung miao in Meng-chia. Burnt down during the riots, this temple was subsequently rebuilt on the same site. Later, when the tea trade prospered, tea merchants built the Fa-chu-kung kung in Ta-tao-ch'eng, dedicated to a cult that had started there for people from An-ch'i.[8]

All of these Taipei temples, and several others built before Taiwan was taken into the Japanese Empire in 1895, are still flourishing. Just over one-third of all temples within the areas of the city that had been developed prior to 1895 date from the Ch'ing dynasty, the highest concentration and proportion of them in Meng-chia.[9] Indeed, all the temples that have more than one annual festival date from the Ch'ing.[10] In short, the majority of the most popular and the most communal temples of Taipei have existed throughout the entire modern period of fast urban growth and have survived two major changes of government with much of their original character intact.

Local Temples in Late Ch'ing Times

My sources indicate that 29 of the present-day temples in Taipei date back to Ch'ing times,[11] 18 of them in Meng-chia and 11 in the T'ung-an sub-cities Ta-tao-ch'eng and Ta-lung-t'ung. Eight of these 29 stand out as popular local temples (see Map 1). They will be considered here.*

Probably the most public, and certainly the most demonstrative, of all temple rituals is the festive procession. A procession is a display of the sponsors of the festival and their cult. Its route defines the territorial extent of a community. One of the ways in which the eight temples stood out was in the area covered by their processions.[12] In the case of the six of them that still have processions today, the routes of each pass through all the streets of at least one modern Taipei borough.

Nothing is spared to enhance the repute of sponsors and cult. Personal and formal associations with other cults, as well as the lay associations of the sponsors in the field of recreation—bands, lion dancers, orchestras and military gymnasts—are called upon to add contingents to the procession and increase its panache. The procession is a clear expression both of the collective local power of the association the cult represents, and the individual wealth and prestige of that year's sponsors. Repute and panache are the social translation of a god's efficacy or responsiveness and of a place's or a building's topographic power (*feng-shui*). Just as a domestic shrine is the focal point of a house, oriented if possible to take the best advantage of the power available in its site, so the altar of a local temple is situated within a territory at the point where its forces, most commonly represented in the image of a dragon, can best be concentrated. The procession, the theater, and the feasting, both communal and within every household in the territory, are the external aspects of a festival; the worship and rites, both at the temple's incense burner and at the incense burners of the domestic shrines linked to it, are the internal aspects.

The ritual that most of all enhances the local and all-inclusive char-

---

* Most of the remaining 21 are devoted to plague spirits, to the earth or local-place tutelary gods, or to the unworshipped dead and their guardians. All of these are, in the popular religion, very closely attached to a place and very low in the religious hierarchy. It would be unusual for the worship of any of them to develop into the central cult of a local temple of a place as central as Meng-chia or Ta-tao-ch'eng. On the contrary, their shrines mark subdivisions of the territories of the main town temples. Of the rest, two are temples of retreat (both of them Buddhist vegetarian houses), two were established by and for the literate and those with aspirations to scholarship, and two housed cults of the same character as those of the large local temples. These last two were built very shortly before the Japanese came and, probably because they did not differ sufficiently in character from the big ones to be attractive as alternatives, they failed to grow significantly. There may be a functional limit to the number of communal, local temples that can be supported at any one level of the central-place hierarchy. Certainly only one temple can represent a locality taken strictly as a territorial unit, though there may be other unifying or dominating factors within the same territorial compass, such as native-place or occupational ties.

acter of a temple is that of consecration and periodic renewal—the *chiao* (*tsiao*). It is a Taoist ritual in which a territory is marked out with symbols of the four quarters, guard-posts of the god's spiritual forces, with the temple at its strategic center, its altar and incense burner at the dragon's head. In the course of the *chiao* the territory is purified. The temple is closed to all but the representatives of the community. Within the temple the Taoists erect their own altar from which all but they are excluded. They then put the territory's metaphysical forces into harmony by meditation and by interceding with higher deities or cosmic beings on behalf of the representatives and their community's gods; they feed and calm and exorcise wandering ghosts and pestilential influences, and they secure the force of the territory's dragon in a secret rite. This renewal, including a rite in which all the fires and lights are extinguished and then relit from the sacred area, involves all those inhabiting the marked territory. They are all expected to observe the preliminary abstinence from meat, and every household is canvassed for a subscription to provide for the *chiao*. Posting the names of all subscribers' households outside the temple proclaims the completion of the *chiao*. Local leaders (and, in modern times, candidates for elective offices in local government) make large contributions and are listed prominently, thus converting their wealth into prestige and possibly power.

The anniversary of a local temple's main god is a lesser form of *chiao*. The god's procession past every household in the territory is a sweeping away and warding off of malicious spirits, and is followed by local people carrying incense either in penitence and in order to redeem their fortunes or in gratitude for an improvement in fortune. What I have been calling a local temple is the nearest temple a person knows. It is the temple of the territory in which he resides. He subscribes to the temple and can make use of it for worship or divination or social gathering. The smallest division of territory to have a temple as its focus is that of the earth god—T'u Ti Kung. It is a subdivision of the territory of a village or town ward local temple. The latter has in addition to its central god its own earth god, as does every temple. The village or ward temple is itself part of the territory of the local temple in the next higher level of the central-place hierarchy. But the festival of the local temple of that central place, a town, marks only the territorial extent of the town itself, not the whole system of which it is center. Moreover, selection and stratification affect participation in the festivals of local temples at higher levels, as I shall show.

Now, by no means all popular temples are in the strictest sense local, that is territorial, temples. It is because there is in practice no strict categorization of local and nonlocal temples that I outline the rituals of territoriality so that their occurrence may be noted as an index of the local character of a temple. All eight of the temples being discussed here had large processions that indicated their public character. But the big processions of two of them, the Lung-shan ssu and the Ch'ing-shui tsu-shih-kung miao, were not tours of an area. Rather, they carried lanterns to the river where they were set afloat bearing invitations to orphan souls (wandering ghosts) to partake of the seventh-month feast. This is a festival that had and retains strong Buddhist overtones and a Sanskrit name (Yü-lan-p'en in Chinese, from *ullambhana* or alternatively *avalambana*).[13] These and a third lantern procession from the Pao-an kung were the three biggest of all the many seventh-month processions organized by wards and streets of the Taipei cities. As the three were the ritual headquarters of people from San I, An-ch'i, and T'ung-an respectively, their processions were on separate days and in competition with each other for length, splendor, and the height of the frames upon which the lanterns were hooked.

The central gods of the other temples and of the Pao-an kung had and still have processions on the gods' anniversaries. The Pao-an kung god tours Ta-lung-t'ung. Perhaps because Ta-lung-t'ung was such a small settlement, the Pao-an kung combines in itself the functions of territorial guardian and native-place association.

Two temples have large processions around Ta-tao-ch'eng, as they had in the Ch'ing dynasty. They are the Hsia-hai ch'eng-huang miao and the Tz'u-sheng kung. But only the Hsia-hai ch'eng-huang miao has the figures of generals Fan and Hsieh installed in it.* The procession of a local temple's god deliberately around a bounded territory had as a secular model the tour of his kingdom by a monarch and of its subdivisions by his official administrators. The local temple that most closely followed this model was that of the City God (Ch'eng Huang Yeh) of an administrative capital. The City God's procession was above all judicial and regulative. His post was the purgatorial equivalent of the local magistrate's, and his procession always featured two figures, one tall and white, the other short and black. These were the god's spiritual detectives, generals Fan and Hsieh, who captured any spirit about to

---

* Large city processions almost always include figures of generals Fan and Hsieh even when they do not come from the temple whose god's anniversary is being celebrated, because other temples in the area contribute side figures of their gods in palanquins accompanied by their own procession retinues and bands. One of these gods will be the territorial guardian god, and its band will take out the figures of the two generals. Some bands, indeed, have their own figures of the two, unattached to any temple.

die in order that it should receive its just reward or punishment. In central places below the county level and in centers of the "natural" or marketing system, the local temple's god and his procession had a more military character. But figures of generals Fan and Hsieh, or instruments of torture, or the military retinue and attributes of the god himself were the marks of a procession from a local territorial temple anywhere. As its name implies, the Hsia-hai ch'eng-huang miao is the temple of a City God, although here it is not an official City God, since Ta-tao-ch'eng was never an administrative capital. The name Hsia-hai refers to a region of T'ung-an county. The god represents a compatriots' religious association that developed with Ta-tao-ch'eng and became its territorial guardian temple.

The Tz'u-sheng kung was the headquarters of the Amoy Guild. The temple's deity and the guild's—and that of a great many other guilds—was Ma Tsu, the protectress of seafarers and a favorite deity of merchant associations linked with Fukien, her mortal birthplace. A guild in Taiwan was, like so many other kinds of groups, organized around an incense burner, a form of organization shortly to be described. It was usual for a guild to have for its annual general meeting a festival with a procession and theatrical performances on the patron god's anniversary. It was also usual for the annual public occasion of a guild to be the seventh-month festival, which is a time for charity to the poor as well as to the orphan dead. Although both the Hsia-hai ch'eng-huang miao and the Tz'u-sheng kung were associated with the T'ung-an origin of most of Ta-tao-ch'eng's inhabitants, one can distinguish them functionally as local temples at least before the demise of the Amoy Guild during the period of Japanese rule. Hsia-hai Ch'eng Huang Yeh was responsible for the welfare of the sub-city's inhabitants in his capacity as guardian of the territory, whereas Ma Tsu watched over its commercial interests in her capacity as guardian of the dominant organization of its trade.

A similar distinction can be made between the two temples whose major annual processions tour Meng-chia. The territorial guardian of Meng-chia is Ch'ing Shan Wang. Installed in his temple are the figures of generals Fan and Hsieh, brought out in the procession by the bands attached to the temple. It is headed by two groups of Eight Generals, the god's immediate retinue, impersonated by penitents and the young sons of penitents. Their faces vividly painted, they clear the way with a ritual march of threatening steps, shaking instruments of torture to dispatch wrongdoers, demons, and the ritually unclean. The procession still makes a point of touring every street of Meng-chia, taking three days and dividing itself up to do so. The new borough boundaries, which exclude some of the old parts of Meng-chia, are ignored.

The other temple is the oldest Ma Tsu temple in Meng-chia—the Hsin-hsing kung, as it was called in Ch'ing times. But generals Fan and Hsieh are not kept in the temple for its annual procession. And even the latest rebuilding of this temple, which took place in 1957, was more heavily sponsored by trading associations (such as the Fish Marketing Association and the West Gate Market Merchants Friendly Society) than was the Ch'ing-shan-wang miao's (1938). The Hsin-hsing kung's function as a ritual focus for commerce was much more distinct in Ch'ing times, when it was built and maintained by the guilds of Meng-chia and had in front of it one of Meng-chia's biggest markets, at a ferry terminus. The temple was from the start (in 1747) a guild merchants' association, never one of compatriots. The Ch'ing-shan-wang miao, on the other hand, began (in 1846) as an association of traders from Hui-an county (one of the San I), and was a branch temple of the god's cult in that county before becoming more generally known and taking on the characteristics of a territorial guardian. Its territorial function may have been sealed in 1868, when the subprefect of Tanshui prayed to the god for rain to relieve a drought in northern Taiwan and three days later it rained.[14]

I have included the Fa-chu-kung kung, which has already been mentioned as the An-ch'i and tea merchants' temple in Ta-tao-ch'eng, as one of the leading eight on the grounds that its procession (as I saw it in 1967) ranked for natives of Taipei as one of the six biggest. This procession included the temple's own generals Fan and Hsieh. But it and the whole festival are now part of a development (characteristic of the Republican period) that I shall describe in a later section. The procession may have been initiated just before the Japanese took over, since a proper temple was built for the god in 1895 after he had gained repute for saving people in his neighborhood from an epidemic sickness. In any case, the Fa-chu-kung kung is in striking contrast with the main An-ch'i temple, the Ch'ing-shui tsu-shih-kung miao, which was neither commercial nor territorial and has never had a tour procession.

Taipei's local temples may thus be loosely differentiated into three kinds of association—compatriot, territorial, and commercial (see Table 3). Plainly these are not precise and categorical distinctions. They are at most emphases on particular aspects within institutions that embodied all three, evolving as they did in historically distinctive territories dominated by compatriots from specific parts of Ch'üan-chou prefecture and mainly commercial in their occupational structure. All eight temples

TABLE 3. EIGHT MAJOR LOCAL TEMPLES IN TAIPEI, 1895

Type and name of temple	Deity	Religious orientation	Procession		Seventh-month festival	Branch temple(s) or linked festival(s)
			Tour with own figures of generals	Tour without own figures of generals		
Compatriot only						
Ch'ing-shui tsu-shih-kung miao	Tsu Shih Kung	Buddhist	—	—	Yes	Yes
Compatriot and Commercial						
Lung-shan ssu	Kuan Yin	Buddhist	—	—	Yes	Yes
Tz'u-sheng kung	Ma Tsu	Buddhist and Taoist	—	Yes	—	—
Commercial only						
Hsin-hsing kung	Ma Tsu	Buddhist and Taoist	—	Yes	—	—
Compatriot, Commercial, and Territorial						
Fa-chu-kung kung	Fa Chu Kung	Buddhist and Taoist	Yes	—	—	Yes
Compatriot and Territorial						
Pao-an kung	Ta Tao Kung	Taoist	—	Yes	Yes	Yes
Hsia-hai ch'eng-huang miao	City God from T'ung-an	Taoist	Yes	—	—	Yes
Ch'ing-shan-wang miao	Ch'ing Shan Wang	Taoist	Yes	—	—	—

share some characteristics of the others, and all of them are and were locally popular.

At this point perhaps the clearest contrast is between territorial and compatriot temples. As one of the executive committee of the Ch'ing-shan-wang miao said in 1967, his temple's kind of procession is called unifying (*t'ung-i*) and it is Taoist. The Lung-shan ssu and the Ch'ing-shui tsu-shih-kung miao are Buddhist and so do not have this kind of procession, he said. The Lung-shan ssu's main god is the bodhisattva Kuan Yin; and Tsu Shih Kung of An-ch'i was a hermit who attained

Buddhahood on a mountain in that county. Not all the temples of compatriot associations are Buddhist, however. The Pao-an kung's main god was a famous eleventh-century doctor named Wu. He was from T'ung-an; hence his patronage of T'ung-an people. He has no Buddhist connotations yet is so fiercely associated with T'ung-an that, according to an old man in the temple, when the T'ung-an people in Hsin-chuang put on theater for another god, several houses were suddenly discovered to be on fire. Divination revealed that the T'ung-an god was angry because he had not been invited to share the spectacle. It is, however, appropriate that, in towns that were, like Meng-chia, big enough to produce more than one local temple, a culturally sectional association such as one of compatriots should be related to Buddhism, which in China has lacked Taoism's tradition of local bases and mass participation.

There is a last organizational distinction between territorial and compatriot temples. The former have few or no branch temples, whereas the latter have several branch temples or linked festivals in the relevant communities of compatriots in the Taipei basin. The Lung-shan ssu too, without any San I communities outside the city to speak of, nevertheless had and still has several branch temples in the Taipei basin.

Temple Management and Festival Management

We now leave aside the differences between the local temples and concentrate on the form common to them all, the incense-burner association. We shall see that a distinction appears between the festivals of the association and the association itself considered as a corporation. We may compare the relationships between territorial temples and less territorial temples, between local temples generally and temples of retreat, and between a Taoist orientation and a Buddhist orientation to the relationship that exists between the organization of festivals and the management of the corporate temple associations. Festival organization is relatively open and democratic. Association organization is relatively corporate and exclusive.

An incense-burner association[15] starts as a periodic feast for all its members. At this feast the host for the next feast is chosen either according to a rota or by divination, and in any case after the approval of the patron deity has been ascertained by divination. The new host takes with him the incense burner and, if the association possesses one, the figure of the god. The usual title for the host is "master of the incense burner" or "host of the incense burner" (*lu-chu*), and he cannot hold the office again until all the others in the association have held it. He leads in whatever worship the association has decided upon.

The members may have decided to invite a figure of their deity from

a temple already established for him. They may be prosperous or numerous enough to hire a theatrical troupe to perform for the god's and
their own entertainment. The master of the incense burner is responsible for hiring the troupe, choosing the play, and collecting money from
the members to pay for the whole performance. If the association becomes well established, the passage of the incense burner from the
house of the old to the house of the new master, or the arrival of an
invited figure of the god, may be elaborated into a procession. If so, it
is the master's responsibility to organize the procession. By this time the
god's local following may have grown so large that the periodic feast
occurs not only in the master's home but in every follower's and member's home as well, with accompanying worship at domestic altars. However, the master's altar with the association's incense burner remains
central, the place where the association's offerings are made and the
next master is chosen. The foregoing is characteristic of the development of an association that started with a small number of pioneer settlers
and grew with their natural increase and with the coming of more settlers. Eventually the members' feast becomes a festival, its cost greatly
increases; and assistants, called t'ou-chia, have to be selected at the
same time as the master to take on the increased responsibilities.

The corporate property of the association—and its costs—also increase beyond the initial incense burner. First, a figure of the god must
be carved and consecrated. Then, even in quite small associations, land
may be bought, the rent from it regularly covering the expenses of the
feast. Finally, the membership may decide it can afford to build a permanent residence for its incense burner and god. Temple and estate
together provide capital to be used in the interest of the association, and
also in the private interest of its managers. The greater the corporate
property, the more likely it is that the master no longer manages both
it and the festival, and that a separate, more exclusive, longer-term management is created to look after the property.

The ideology of the incense burner and of the feast is egalitarian.
"The happy ties of the brethren are with incense fire solemnized: / After
burning the incense can there still be barriers between you and me?"
is a couplet from the Triad society's initiation ceremony.[16] As one of the
feasters said at the Meng-chia festival of Ch'ing Shan Wang in 1967:
"You may be an official tomorrow and I just a common person, but at
table we are all equal." Even when a temple has been established and
has become the temple of the local territorial guardian, if the locality is
small and relatively poor and the expenses of the festival not too great
or its organization too complicated, then master and assistants will be
chosen from a list of all household heads in the territory.

But where, as in the case of the large city temples, the festival is expensive, a principle of selectivity intervenes in addition to the traditional exclusion of women and those who are not the heads of their households. In modern Taipei, for the festivals of the territorial guardians of Meng-chia and Ta-tao-ch'eng, the list presented to the god for the selection of the master is made up only of those who have volunteered to be put on it. In these cases a festival organizer stands to spend a great deal of money, on the hiring of a band and of one day's theater at the very least, as well as on the feast at his home. He does so in the name of the god, and therefore of the community. His reward is to have his name publicized in this act of patronage. In Meng-chia, for instance, a young son of his will be carried as his representative in the procession before the god. The ritual reason given for volunteering is gratitude to the god for granting prosperity.

There is also a formal principle for the selection of managers of temple property. In Taiwan these managers are often called *lao-ta*, and Schipper[17] has pointed out the derivation of this designation from *ch'i-lao* or *san-lao*, the terms for the virtuous elders of a locality and for the heads of politico-religious local community houses in the second-century Taoist movements.[18] Practically speaking, in both festival management and temple management, a secular principle is also at work, namely qualification by wealth. Indeed, to be seen to sponsor a festival or to contribute to the building of a temple is a way of legitimating wealth and power. But even when both kinds of management are governed by these selective principles, the management of temple property is more exclusive and festival management more open to all classes in the temple's community. The temple managers are in long-term and inconspicuous positions; the festival organizers change from year to year and are well publicized. Apart from the main god's festival there may be other festivals in the year, based on the same temple but for other gods and their incense-burner associations. Once a temple is established, it is treated as a vessel or lodging for the gods of local associations. Any one festival, moreover, may include days of theater and contingents in its procession that are sponsored separately by any number of associations. Such is the case, anyway, with the festivals of the eight large Taipei local temples. Their management, however, remains constant and distinct from the management of all of these festival groups.

The distinction was there very early in the development of at least six of the eight; and it was made by the original owners of the incense burner, perpetuating their own positions as an inner core of the growing following of their cult. (I have not been able to find detailed enough accounts of the original founders of the Lung-shan ssu and the Pao-an kung.) In these six, the incense burner and figure of the god around which an association was formed were already the domestic incense burner and god of one of the members. That member's house became the center of the association. It is known that the benefactors who endowed the original temples for Ch'ing Shui Tsu Shih Kung, for Ch'ing Shan Wang, and for Hsia-hai Ch'eng Huang Yeh were the heads of the households containing the original domestic shrines to these gods. The Hsia-hai ch'eng-huang miao is even now run by descendants of the store-owner whose domestic altar it originally was. But each proposal to build, rebuild, or make major repairs to a temple creates an opportunity for someone to donate enough to become a main sponsor and thus become important in the management of the general subscription fund for building or repair, or for the ensuing consecration *chiao*, and thenceforward in the management of the temple and its property.

Each renewal and its subscription appeal also formalize the temple's following, and the consecration *chiao* defines it territorially. Thus the original construction of the Lung-shan ssu was organized in 1738 by a merchant who collected 20,000 *yüan* not only from the Chin-chiang county people who had started it, but from people of all three counties of the San I. Some years later the temple was extended with a new shrine, and so given a new constituency and character, for the shrine was to house the Ch'üan Guild's figure of Ma Tsu. Shortly after that, the Northern Guild attached itself to the same shrine. The temple's repute and local standing were further enhanced in 1814 when its fund to repair earthquake damage was managed by, among others, a local notable who had been honored with a yellow robe by the central government. Yet each enlargement of the temple's constituency and standing must have been at the same time a removal of its management from the popular constituency consolidated in the drama of the accompanying *chiao* and subsequent festivals.

Official and Literati Temples

No account of Taipei temples in Ch'ing times would be complete without some consideration of the official cult and its relationship with popular religion. Of all the temples built by the central government, from its funds and the wealth of the local gentry, the temple of the City God and the School Temple (Wen miao) for the cult of Confucius were the most basic.[19]

The state religion was centralized, hierarchical, and exclusive; it also functioned as a form of ideological control over popular religion. The City God temple was the chief point of contact between the two kinds of religion.[20] Local temples developed as adaptations of the official City God temple, and sometimes popular cults and temples were adopted into the state rites. The worship of Ma Tsu, which started as a local cult in Hsing-hua prefecture of Fukien, was one such, being adopted into the official rites in 1720, with the goddess receiving the title of Empress or Consort of Heaven (T'ien Hou or T'ien Fei). An official temple was built for her in the walled administrative city of Taipei, apart from the many temples for her in the adjacent natural cities (see Map 1).

Even without being formally adopted into the official rites, a popular temple could be attended by officials and local gentry. They might choose to enhance the deity's reputation by writing a eulogy in praise of his or her powers to be inscribed in stone or on wooden boards and displayed in the temple. They might even recommend the deity to the central Board of Rites and achieve for the temple, and its management and the community, the honor of a eulogy with the emperor's seal. All the main local temples of Taipei display such eulogy boards—the institution continues with the officials of the Republican Government—and a few have emperors' seals of approval as special attractions. The Tan-shui subprefect's prayer for rain to Ch'ing Shan Wang is recorded with a eulogy in his temple. The Lung-shan ssu, the Ch'ing-shui tsu-shih-kung miao, and the Hsia-hai ch'eng-huang miao all received imperial eulogies for their gods' efficacy in repelling the French in 1884–85, the Lung-shan ssu in particular because guild merchants and local gentry had used it as headquarters for mustering militia in support of Liu Ming-ch'uan, thus dissuading him from moving his administration south.

Even before an administrative capital was attached to a natural city, the city's gentry and merchants frequently set up on their own the more exclusive religious institutions of literati ruling-class culture—temples to Confucius and to Wen Ch'ang, the patron of scholars, with a school or academy attached. A Wen Ch'ang temple in Ta-tao-ch'eng was one such. All in all, by the end of the Ch'ing period, the Taipei basin and its central place were no longer very remote from central government. In fact they had evolved to a close approximation of what was typical for mainland regions. Ta-lung-t'ung had become the resort of scholars, secluded from the commercial bustle of prospering Ta-tao-ch'eng. Despite its much shorter history it had produced twice as many (six) *chü-jen* degree-holders as had Meng-chia, owing, it was said, to its favorable geomantic setting. Two local descent groups of the Ch'en surname in Ta-lung-t'ung and in Ta-tao-ch'eng were prominent among degree-holders, and their members were severally responsible for the building of the Wen Ch'ang temple and a school in Ta-tao-ch'eng, for the Ch'en surname hall in the new walled city next to the Wen miao, and for the couplets inscribed on the gates of the Pao-an kung. An eminent Meng-chia degree-holder wrote the couplets inscribed on a gate of the Lung-shan ssu.

By the time of the Japanese, the Lung-shan ssu had become a strongly Buddhist institution under the sponsorship of the Ch'üan Guild, which in 1845 had rebuilt an older Buddhist temple of retreat near Taipei, its head priest becoming at that time joint head priest of both temples. This suggests a removal of at least the managers of the guild and temple from the compatriotism and parochialism of the earlier years of the Lung-shan ssu. This is not to say that the Lung-shan ssu (or the Pao-an kung) ceased to be local temples, losing their parochial and territorial appeal altogether. Even when the local merchants and gentry were able to move on a national or provincial level, they would also have maintained a local base; and the Lung-shan ssu and the Pao-an kung were evolving into respectable instruments for mediation between state and local levels.

Ch'ing Local Temples Under Colonial and Republican Regimes

The Japanese destroyed all the temples in the official walled city, but few temples outside it. The effect of this upon the local gentry and merchants was to remove the orthodox exemplars of their religious and cultural institutions, leaving their own institutions intact and releasing them from the ideological control of officials. The Japanese did build Shinto and Buddhist shrines and pursue a policy of slow conversion to Japanese culture, but theirs was an alien and colonial regime that, in the fifty years it lasted, never acquired the cultural legitimacy of the former Chinese rulers.

The Japanese resorted far more than the Ch'ing to direct, legal, and supervisory means of controlling temples. They were interested more in the organization than in the culture of the temples, though the latter was of course indirectly affected. The Republican regime also lacked, at least initially, the ideological controls of the former Chinese imperial government, and also resorted to legal and direct controls. In this respect the two post-Ch'ing regimes can be considered together. In general, the controls imposed on temples are part of the extension, originally undertaken by the Japanese but continued under the Republicans, of central-government power in Taiwan below the county level, reducing the local political autonomy of gentry and merchants. Two other long-term effects of Japanese policies should be noted for their impact on local temples. One was the halting of migration and trade with the mainland; the other was the replacement of guilds with secular trade associations defined on a commodity basis. Their effect was to undermine the compatriot parochialism that had so strongly marked the settlement of the Taipei basin and the organization of its overseas trade. Taiwan's economy was "rationalized" to make the island produce as much surplus as possible for the Japanese homeland. As a result of these policies, compatriot temples, and especially guild temples, lost their former social significance.

Only the Amoy Guild continued, being revived at the time of a rebuilding of the Tz'u-sheng kung in 1908. But this exception was itself an example of Japanese methods of controlling temples. We have seen that a temple's renewal could occasion a change in the leadership of its management. The Japanese and Nationalist governments caused almost all the main Taipei local temples to need renewal, simply by billeting troops in them. The Pao-an kung and Lung-shan ssu housed troops just after the Japanese take-over. When Taiwan was returned to China, they and the Ch'ing-shui tsu-shih-kung miao, the Ch'ing-shan-wang miao, and the Tz'u-sheng kung were used first to house troops and then, for many years, to house retired soldiers. A Japanese city-planning and road-widening scheme had necessitated the demolition and rebuilding at another site of the Tz'u-sheng kung in 1908. The local government of Taipei contributed funds for the rebuilding and at the same time revived the incense-burner association of the Amoy Guild as a model religious organization for the island of Taiwan. This body, the Shen-ming Hui, had a separate building in the forecourt of the temple, but all twelve members of the temple's management committee belonged to it.[21] In the temple forecourt were also the offices of a branch of the quasi-governmental Buddhist Youth Association, and a school for the study of Confucian scriptures. From none of these did the temple receive rent.

The newly rebuilt Tz'u-sheng kung was popular among Japanese living in Taipei. At its consecration *chiao*, as is customary, enormous multi-storied outdoor altars were built at the four quarters and center of the temple's new territory and the most precious treasures of its inhabitants were exhibited to show off their locality's prestige and prosperity. One of these altars was filled on this occasion with objects from Japanese museums, and guarded by Japanese police. All subsequent festivals of the temple were also closely surveyed by the police, according to the present temple-keeper, whose father held that position before him in Japanese times.

Two of the most powerful members of the revived Amoy Guild were Ch'en T'ien-lai, the executive secretary of the Taipei Tea Traders' Association, and another man who, according to the temple-keeper again, held a virtual monopoly of Taipei's rice and salt trades. It is doubtful whether the guild in its revived form ever functioned to any great extent as a merchants' association. Whatever such functions it did have, they did not survive the Pacific War. In contrast, the Taipei Tea Traders' Association, itself successor to a tea traders' organization started in 1889 at the instigation of Governor Liu Ming-ch'uan, has its own successor today in the Taiwan Tea Exporters' Association. Neither the tea traders' organizations nor the present rice traders' association has religious functions.

Ch'en T'ien-lai was also an assemblyman of Taihoku shū, the district of which Taipei was the capital.[22] Under the Japanese, Taiwanese served in government only by appointment and in a consultative capacity. Nevertheless to have such a connection with the government was virtually a necessity for a temple, even though the government used the connection for supervision or intelligence. In order to collect funds or to begin construction or extension of a building, permission had first to be sought. This is also required under the present regime. Similarly, assemblies and processions, such as occur at festivals, need police permission. Permits are much more easily obtainable if someone in local government is a member of the temple's management committee.

Possibly as a result of this necessity for having a connection with the government, a number of temples have committee members in common. Perhaps this was so in the Ch'ing period, too, but it is certainly remarkable in the two twentieth-century periods, and of course it works in the interests of greater control when those with multiple membership are the government connections themselves. The model Shen-ming Hui at the Tz'u-sheng kung also worshipped at the Hsia-hai ch'eng-huang miao and at the Pao-an kung. Ch'en T'ien-lai was a member of the managing committees of the Lung-shan ssu, the Fa-chu-kung kung, and the Tz'u-sheng kung. An equally well-connected man was Ku Hsien-yung, who had grown wealthy in the tea trade. He was given the highest position of any Taiwanese under the Japanese, in the governor-general's consultative committee. When the Ch'ing-shan-wang miao was to be rebuilt in 1938, it was to him that its management appealed for permission to collect funds and to start reconstruction. He himself contributed 20,000 yüan. By that time he was already on the management committee of the Lung-shan ssu and an honorary manager of the Pao-an kung.[23] An instance from the Republican period is Wu Yung-nien.

Apart from being head of the Sixth Trust Cooperative Society and of the borough that covers most of what was Meng-chia, Wu was on the management committee of the Ch'ing-shan-wang miao and, allegedly, of the Lung-shan ssu as well. Three of his brothers were on the Lung-shan ssu's committee, one of them a representative to the Taipei municipal assembly.

This method of control, by infiltration of management committees, was and is made possible by the requirement that a temple (or any other association) must be registered with the competent local authority. This means having a formally constituted management committee which is responsible to the government for taxes, where previously there had been an informally defined and unfixed management. Membership in the registered committee was held permanently, there usually being no provisions for elections, and was inherited, a practice that has continued even into the present period. The brothers Wu mentioned above, for instance, are the sons of Wu Ch'ang-ts'ai, manager of the Lung-shan ssu's repair fund in 1913, and himself the son of the general manager of a consecration *chiao* for the Lung-shan ssu that was held in 1892. Ku Hsien-yung's son was a manager of the Lung-shan ssu in 1965.

Under the present regime, elections for the replacement of retiring members should be supervised by a representative of the government. In fact when a membership has lapsed or been resigned (for instance, when none of the sons of a member want to take their father's place), in many cases it has been phased out, no replacement being elected. Official records, such as those of the Taiwan Historical Commission, give numbers of "the followers" (*hsin-t'u*) of the temple, as if they constituted a congregation. In fact there is always a number of worshippers who attend the temple more regularly than others, and when elections have been held it is they, according to the temple keepers and managers interviewed, who are the electors.

One effect of this government interference in temple organization has been to consolidate any existing tendency toward exclusiveness in the management committees. Another effect has been that temples once open to a local community, with a very vague religious definition created by the repute of the god, have tended to become more like membership organizations, no longer focused on the community at large, but specifically as religious institutions. We shall see these effects much further advanced in the temples discussed in the next section.

Some temples have changed their registration from "association" (*hui*) to "nonprofit corporation" (*tsai-t'uan fa-jen*). The advantages of taking this step are, as one of the managers of the Ch'ing-shan-wang miao said, that tax need no longer be paid and official sanction for the temple's activities is more easily obtained. However, nonprofit status means that the authorities not only supervise elections, but also inspect the temple's books. The Ch'ing-shan-wang miao has not yet taken this step. Those temples that have (see Table 4) seem to conform to a certain standard organization, one of the features of which is running a charity. Some temples that have not formally become charitable organizations have also nevertheless started small charities. These involve the annual collection and redistribution of money, rice, and clothing to those in the temple's locality who are listed in government records as being below a certain socioeconomic standard. The local Kuomintang party branch or the local government office supervises or even takes over the distribution side of the charity—indeed the Kuomintang has its own winter charity. But collection is best left to the temple, since temples are acknowledged to have a more powerful moral pull than party or government.

Two other measures taken by the Republican regime may be thought to have had an effect on temples: land reform and local elections. Land reform has reduced the amount of land that can be held by an association or corporation. Regrettably, I could find out very little about Taipei temples' landholdings, knowing only that they had their forecourts and some real estate in their immediate neighborhood as sources of rent. Where the reform has in fact succeeded in reducing temple landholdings, and there are numerous ways of circumventing it, the effect must have been to turn the interest of management committees toward maintaining their temples' large daily offerings of cash and meeting the expenses of their annual festivals.

Elections for local government office make the local politician's position, between a partly alien and dictatorial central government and his local constituency, ambivalent. The temple, in its capacity as the focus for a local community, is used as an instrument to legitimate local power and as a proper medium for the publicization of a name. In other cities of Taiwan, T'ai-nan and Lu-kang for instance, local temples are used as symbols for competing local factions, but to my knowledge no politician has ever been able to use a temple or network of temples as a power base in the way that Farmers' Associations have been used.[24] Nevertheless, appearing, at least in name, on the management of its temple, charity, or festival is a virtual necessity for winning support in a locality. The brothers Wu of the Ch'ing-shan-wang miao and the Lung-shan ssu achieved their local government offices by election. All of the managers of the Ch'ing-shan-wang miao and of the Pao-an kung are heads of wards (*li-chang*; also elected offices).

Even so traditional a form as sworn brotherhood still plays an important part in the weaving of a local network. One kind of local power is wielded through the groups of young men called *liu-mang*, their loyalty often sealed by sworn brotherhood, who run a kind of righteous protection racket. They are, of course, secret; but local groups of young men in general manifest themselves publicly in festival processions, in bands of musicians, as lion dancers, or in military arts troupes. Groups of men who act as volunteer fire brigades also frequently join festival processions as lion- or dragon-dancing contingents. During a festival, lion contingents compete with each other for prowess, measured by the number of times they are asked to perform privately for individual households or firms. Above all, they are sponsored by the festival managers. In short, a festival procession is one occasion on which the holders of local informal power show themselves.[25]

The translation of informal power into official authority, or its association with official authority, is difficult. The Kuomintang's former reliance on the power of secret societies notwithstanding, such societies and the sworn brotherhoods that form their nuclei are generally if not rigidly proscribed. The Ch'ing government also occasionally prohibited sworn brotherhoods. The Japanese government's thorough efforts to register every religious organization in police records was part of a more successful campaign against them. On this firm basis, with an even larger police force, the present government maintains a keen watch against religious organizations that might become fronts for political activity. At the same time, local police and government officials are expected to reduce the number of festivals in their areas, ostensibly, as in the Ch'ing period, because of the economic waste, the extravagance of the feasting, the frivolity of the theatrical performances—in short, because of the unproductive spending of time and money.[26] As has already been remarked, however, it is precisely the feasting, the processions, and the theater that express and reaffirm local solidarity.

Sworn brotherhood and feasting have not been stopped; indeed they are still important means of sealing alliances and forming networks. Yet they are officially deplored and have to some extent been curtailed. How is a local politician to use them and at the same time remain a member in good standing of the Kuomintang or its government? The resolution of this problem in the context of temple organization has implied, and also in effect been made possible by, the contrast between festival and corporate management. The festival manager and his assistants continue to be selected anew at every festival, whereas the management of the temple itself has, as we have seen, become a long-term and exclusive group. The festival is an open and demonstrative local community occasion, whereas the kind of management molded by the government turns the temple into a self-contained institution. Festivals are not intrinsically—or, in the initial development of an incense-burner association, in practice—attached to a temple. The two look easily separable. But as long as festivals are still sponsored by temples, the two forms of management, that of the festivals and that of the temple, provide separate but linked loci for the legitimation of the two kinds of power, unofficial and official, related to the same local base.

Certainly, managers toe the official line. They express scorn for extravagance and for people who pray and are grateful to the gods for wealth and health, believing in their practical efficacy. Worship, in the opinion of these managers, is not for practical effect but for moral protection, for meditation upon that which is virtuous for the sake of consolation and in order to clear the mind of wrong thoughts and attitudes. This they say to a stranger working as a collaborator of a foreign anthropologist, possibly a Christian and possibly attached to an institution of their government. Nevertheless, the feasts and theatrical performances are offerings asking the gods or thanking them for wealth and health. And despite official intentions and exhortations, all the temples so far considered are attended by a mass of local people and people from the Taipei basin hinterland because they believe in the practical efficacy of their gods.

The managers' official line is reinforced by the rationality of secondary-school education (mass secondary education for Taiwanese was introduced under the present regime) and by its emphasis on national culture and Confucian ethics. This education absorbs almost all the time and attention of young people at an important period in their lives, and then sends them out into executive, professional, and administrative jobs, divorced from the superstitions (*mi-hsin*) of popular religion. The philosophy underlying this education rejects mass participation and the exaltation of local community. It stresses charity to the masses and acts of individual devotion. It appeals to Confucian and Buddhist abstemiousness. An example of the philosophy in practice is the printed notice sent to all the main local temples in Taipei in 1967 over the signature of the mayor of Taipei, a notably skilled manipulator of the ambivalent relation between official and unofficial power. The notice begins by stating that the seventh-month festival is in memory of Mu Lien who showed extraordinary filial piety to his mother. To have feasts and to worship Heaven as the ancestors' equal is to act against original principles and against the Ming patriot Koxinga, in the memory of whose son's early death the festival had been established in Taiwan. The Ch'ing Manchus and the Japanese were guilty of perpetrating the fallacy of feasts, which are like nausea and madness and seriously affect health, strength, domestic economy, and social order. True Buddhism rejects the slaughter of animals and the drinking of wine. There should be only domestic offerings, and these only of fruit and flowers, out of that filial piety and gratitude to our ancestors which constitute our national cultural essence. Finally, as I have paraphrased it, the notice declares that feasts are against the spirit of the New Life Movement and especially wasteful at a time when the country is at war.

Possibly as a result of the government's ideological influence, there has been an increased orientation toward lay Buddhist practices in all but one (the Fa-chu-kung kung) of the eight local temples discussed above. The period of increasing prosperity from the mid-fifties onward, when there has been more surplus to spend on ritual activities, has seen either the introduction of Buddhist liturgy chanters or an increase in their numbers. These are groups, mainly of women, led by or having been instructed by a Buddhist priest or monk, who chant sutras and abstain from meat on certain days in the month. Even the Hsia-hai ch'eng-huang miao, which does not house any god with a Buddhist name or legend, has a small group of devout women who chant sutras in the temple nine times a month and run a small charity. The exchange of resident groups to chant in each others' temples, and of congratulatory wreaths of flowers and baskets of fruit at festival time, are the ways in which the temple managements express their links with each other. The same period has seen in Taipei, but nowhere outside the city, a decrease in the number of *chiao*. In fact, apart from one in a suburb in 1963, there has been only one *chiao* in Taipei since the war. Presumably this reflects the greater effectiveness of government influence in its capital.

The exception is the Fa-chu-kung kung, which during the Japanese period was frequented by Buddhist priests but has since abandoned them, whereas Taoist practitioners still perform rites in the temple for the improvement of individual luck. The temple was center of a *chiao* held immediately after the war, covering the whole area of the city, to celebrate liberation from the Japanese. The *chiao* has been followed by an annual procession, which tours the locality within which the temple stands, on a fixed lunar date near Retrocession Day, October 25. Possibly the size of the *chiao* and the absence of Buddhist priests are related to the temple's association with anti-Japanese feeling. Certainly the temple had been put forward as a symbol of tacit resistance to the Japanese. When the Japanese were redesigning the city they wanted to tear the temple down because it blocked the path of a road. It is said that just before demolition a Taiwanese came to take the god out of the temple, but as he made to do so his nose started to bleed. He would proceed no further. When a Japanese then decided to do it, his nose started to bleed too, and he left the god in place. Then Japanese policemen came to tear the temple down. But as soon as they climbed up ladders to start work, they fell off. In the end, the temple was left standing. Only its back hall was removed to make way for the road.

This, it will be noted, contrasted strongly with the fate at that time of the Tz'u-sheng kung, which, it will be remembered, was completely removed. The two temples are still in contrast, the Tz'u-sheng kung's present management taking a pro-Buddhist and anti-Taoist line. As a nonprofit corporation, furthermore, it remains under close government supervision.

During the war the Japanese wanted to remove the Fa-chu-kung kung and clear the area to make fire fighting and evacuation easier during air-raids. But again the temple stood, while the houses around were destroyed. This time its fate was in strong contrast with the Hsin-hsing kung, which the Japanese did destroy at the time, for the reasons given. Its main figure, of Ma Tsu, was installed in Lung-shan ssu until being given temporary accommodation after the war in a Japanese shrine controlled by three government appointees. In 1957 the present temple was built and a Ma Tsu Association formed to run it. The management is pro-Buddhist, issues invitations to Buddhist priests, and finances one of Taipei's largest charities and an associated sutra-chanting group.

The removal of a temple, even by a few streets, dislocates its constituency. It separates real devotees—who go with it—from casual users of its divination and other facilities. The Hsin-hsing kung and the Tz'u-sheng kung are no longer in the now comparatively less prosperous centers of their respective sub-cities Meng-chia and Ta-tao-ch'eng, where the territorial temples (respectively the Ch'ing-shan-wang miao and the Hsia-hai ch'eng-huang miao) remain. They are on the more recently developed fringes, both of them on broad new streets containing the more expensive stores.

A correlation between close government control and a Buddhist orientation is indicated, carrying over from the Japanese period (see Table 4). The Lung-shan ssu provides an example of the phenomenon. Since Ch'ing times it has housed a number of Buddhist monks and indeed

TABLE 4. STATUS OF EIGHT MAJOR LOCAL TEMPLES IN TAIPEI DURING THE REPUBLICAN PERIOD

Name and organization of temple	Religious orientation		Procession maintained		Former guild links	New location	Official tourist and recreation center
	Taoism maintained	Buddhism now/still dominant	With own figures of generals	Without own figures of generals			
Nonprofit corporation							
Lung-shan ssu	—	Yes	—	—	Yes	—	Yes
Tz'u-sheng kung	—	Yes	—	Yes	Yes	Yes	—
Hsin-hsing kung	—	Yes	—	Yes	Yes	Yes	—
Private associations							
Ch'ing-shui tsu-shih-kung miao	—	Yes	—	—	—	—	Yes
Pao-an kung	Yes	—	—	Yes	—	—	Yes
Fa-chu-kung kung	Yes	—	Yes	—	—	—	—
Hsia-hai ch'eng-huang miao	Yes	—	Yes	—	—	—	—
Ch'ing-shan-wang miao	Yes	—	Yes	—	—	—	—

between 1919 and 1938 was managed by, among others, its Buddhist head priest, or abbot. Ku Hsien-yung, Ch'en T'ien-lai, and Wu Ch'ang-ts'ai (father of the brothers Wu) were also managers of the Lung-shan ssu during this period. They bought a large piece of land in front of the temple and cleared it to be an open space for the enjoyment of the people of Meng-chia. A recreation association was formed to manage the funds for this and other such projects. The postwar managers of the revived recreation association were also managers of the Lung-shan ssu, which had become a nonprofit corporation. They organized in 1967 the building of the covered market on the far side of the open space from the temple, after the temple had been designated a tourist attraction. The open space is still traversed by all processions that pass through Meng-chia, but none of them is now based on the Lung-shan ssu, whose last *chiao*, to consecrate repairs, was held in 1927.[27]

The Fa-chu-kung kung, the Ch'ing-shan-wang miao, and the Hsia-hai ch'eng-huang miao, by contrast, are still run by private associations. All three tolerate Taoist practitioners. In the case of the Hsia-hai ch'eng-huang miao, two families of Taoists hold a concession to maintain a practice within the temple that dates back over two generations. All three also house figures of generals Fan and Hsieh, are the centers of Taipei's biggest festival processions and have not been designated tourist attractions. In short, they are still territorial, local temples.

It appears that of the eight main Ch'ing temples of Taipei, those most

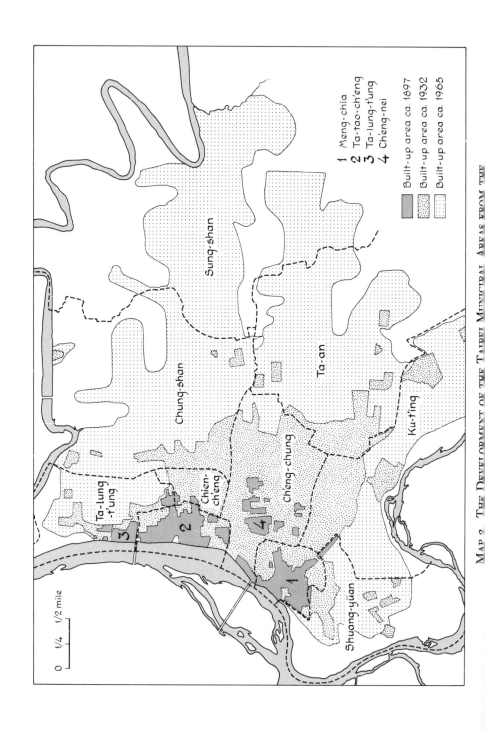

MAP 2. THE DEVELOPMENT OF THE TAIPEI MUNICIPAL AREAS FROM THE

0   1/4   1/2 mile

Ta-lung-t'ung

Chien-chéng

Chung-shan

Sung-shan

Ta-an

Chéng-chung

Ku-t'ing

Shuang-yüan

1 Meng-chia
2 Ta-tao-ch'eng
3 Ta-lung-t'ung
4 Chéng-nei

Built-up area ca. 1897

Built-up area ca. 1932

Built-up area ca. 1965

closely identified with guild merchants—the Lung-shan ssu, the Hsin-hsing kung, and the Tz'u-sheng kung—have become, at least partly by the policy of their managements, more closely identified with the two post-Ch'ing governments than have the most local, territorial temples. Furthermore this governmental identification has been accompanied by an increased inclination toward Buddhism and away from Taoism, and toward self-contained as opposed to open temples.

Like the Lung-shan ssu, and unlike the other temples, the two temples still organized on the basis of native-place ties—the Ch'ing-shui tsu-shih-kung miao and the Pao-an kung—have cooperated with the government's Cultural Renaissance movement in recent years. Their contribution, linked to the government's other recreational and touristic schemes, is jointly to hold a lantern-making competition and an exhibition of lanterns for the fifteenth of the first lunar month, the last day of the New Year season. But otherwise they are less closely identified with the government than are the three former guild temples. Both are still run by private associations. The Ch'ing-shui tsu-shih-kung miao was already pro-Buddhist in inclination, but the Pao-an kung is the territorial temple of Ta-lung-t'ung, and maintains a Taoist practitioners' concession.

Seventh-month processions are no longer competitive in Taipei since their dates have been amalgamated. This is the result partly of the colonial and Republican governments' programs to reduce the number of festivals and partly, for the compatriot temples, of the reduced function of native-place ties in a city whose people are immigrants from other parts of Taiwan, as well as from a great variety of mainland places besides the native places of the groups that originally established the temples.

Five Temples Founded in the Twentieth Century

The modern boroughs that cover Meng-chia, Ta-tao-ch'eng, Ta-lung-t'ung, and Chien-ch'eng (the Japanese-period expansion of Ta-tao-ch'eng) are the most densely populated areas of Taipei and the only parts of the city in which more than half the population has been born in Taiwan (see Map 2). Meng-chia and Ta-tao-ch'eng contain a higher proportion of poor households than other parts of Taipei, and they stand out for the high percentage of their inhabitants who are wage-laborers or small self-employed operators in transport and commerce. All three of the old sub-cities now also have a substantial proportion of their populations working in local factories: metalworking in southern Meng-chia and in Ta-lung-t'ung, food processing and textile production in Ta-tao-ch'eng. The walled city, where most of the government offices are still to be found, and the borough of Chung-shan, built up since the Pacific War, are notable for the high number of financial institutions located in them and for the high proportion of their populations in the professions, hotel and catering services, and private and civil-service industries.[28]

One of the five twentieth-century temples that I will now turn to is in the walled city and one is in Chung-shan borough; two of the other three are in the borough that includes Ta-lung-t'ung, which continued to serve as a resort for the sub-official culture of local gentry and merchants. The fifth is in a suburb. They are by far the best known and most prosperous of Taipei's twentieth-century temples. They are physically removed from all eight of the Ch'ing local temples discussed above except the Pao-an kung. This removal is related in the first place to class and in the second place to a separation of government from the governed that was reinforced during the Japanese period by an ethnic separation and even now reflects a subethnic distinction between Taiwanese and mainland Chinese. But it should be remembered that all the temples I am describing, including these five new ones, are Taiwanese. Both their managers and the mass of their sponsors and users are Taiwanese, though the closer interest shown in the new temples by government officials, with mainland Chinese among them, is, as I shall maintain, an attempt to encourage a religious symbolism and ideology that conceals social divisions. These divisions are within the Taiwanese population, and are both expressed and obscured by temple organization.

Twenty-one years after the official Wen miao was destroyed in 1896, an Association for the Veneration of the Sage was started. Its Japanese chairman and its two Taiwanese vice-chairmen organized the performance of spring and autumn rites of veneration in temporary quarters, which included the Lung-shan ssu and the Pao-an kung, until in 1925 a Confucian temple, the K'ung-tzu miao, was built in Ta-lung-t'ung under the management of three Taiwanese. The head of Taihoku *shū* and the head of its education department attended the Confucian ceremonies.[29]

One of the vice-chairmen of the original association was Li Ching-sheng, who served in the government of Taihoku *shū* under the Japanese and started the Hsin-kao Bank. He was the eldest son of Li Ch'un-sheng, a tea merchants' comprador who became one of the richest men in Taipei after branching out into his own tea-exporting business. The elder Li owned a great deal of real estate in the Ch'ing administrative city—for whose walls and temples his money had helped pay—and in Ta-tao-ch'eng. Apart from official temples he had also contributed to the building of churches in Ta-tao-ch'eng, for he was a professed Christian. He once expressed his religious syncretism as follows: "Confucius' teaching is for governing the nation, Jesus' teaching is for the salvation of the world; the two are complementary, not contradictory."[30] Apparently his son followed his example with regard to Confucius. The K'ung-tzu miao is part of a syncretic religious movement. The movement does not include Jesus, though it propagates a universal ethic that embraces Christian morality; and if Sakyamuni replaced Jesus in Li Ch'un-sheng's statement, it would conform to sentiments very often expressed by Taiwanese bourgeois.[31]

One of the executive managers of the K'ung-tzu miao when it was built in 1925 was the ubiquitous Ku Hsien-yung, and among the members of its committee were Ch'en T'ien-lai and Wu Ch'ang-ts'ai, who have also been introduced already, in the context of the Lung-shan ssu and the managerial network of certain of the local temples in the Japanese period. Two other executive managers of the K'ung-tzu miao were Huang Tsan-chün and Ch'en P'ei-ken. Huang was one of the main ideologues of the new religious syncretism and took a special interest in education, founding a college and adding a Wen Ch'ang shrine to the K'ung-tzu miao complex. He also managed the Pao-an kung for five years and wrote a history of it and of the cultural attainments of Ta-lung-t'ung.[32] Ch'en P'ei-ken was, to judge by their given names, the brother of Ch'en P'ei-liang, one of the founders of the spirit-writing group that was the beginning of the Chüeh-hsiu kung, an important center for the propagation of the new religious style. The three temples, the K'ung-tzu miao, the Pao-an kung, and the Chüeh-hsiu kung, are close to each other in Ta-lung-t'ung.

The Association for the Veneration of the Sage and its temple, the K'ung-tzu miao, were revived by the Republican government after the war, under the official management of the mayor of Taipei. The assistant managers included the head of Taipei's education department and the son of Ku Hsien-yung. Its autumn rites, a replica of those performed in the Wen miao in all Ch'ing dynasty administrative cities, are a much-vaunted tourist attraction, and the chief worshipper at them is always the mayor or an equally exalted official. The K'ung-tzu miao includes in its complex of shrines one to Kuan Ti, the god of war and trade, called the Wu miao after the Ch'ing dynasty state temples of which he was patron deity. But recently another temple for Kuan Ti, the Hsing-t'ien kung, has been sponsored by high city and national government officials whereas formerly only the K'ung-tzu miao was so openly government-sponsored. Judging by the number of worshippers that come to it every day, the Hsing-t'ien kung is also the most popular temple in

Taipei. In 1958 the annual accumulation of daily contributions from worshippers was around 350,000 new Taiwanese dollars, so much that enough could be put aside to build a vast new branch temple outside Taipei, prettily situated in the hills toward Tan-shui, a temple that soon became a center of pilgrimage and a tourist attraction. In addition, the religious style of the Hsing-t'ien kung attracted enough sponsorship from the wealthy men of Taiwan (the wealthiest of whom gave 50,000 new Taiwanese dollars) to allow it to build on a different site a new temple for itself, the largest in the city. The chief worshipper at its opening ceremony in 1968 (which was not a *chiao*) was the Minister of the Department of the Interior in the national government; other prominent worshippers were the mayor of Taipei and lesser dignitaries of the municipal government. At least one newspaper at the time began to call the temple the Wu miao.

Kuan Ti is popularly referred to in and around Taipei (and with reference to the Hsing t'ien kung) as En Chu Kung. This is in fact the title given to each of the five gods, Kuan Ti included, worshipped together in this temple. Temples dedicated to sets of three or five En Chu Kung proliferated through Taiwan during the colonial and Republican periods. In Taipei two of the first were the Chüeh-hsiu kung, founded in 1908, in which the main god of the set is Lü Tung-pin (canonized as Fu Yu Ti Chün), and the Chih-nan kung, founded as a monastery late in the Ch'ing period but converted to a temple for popular worship, again mainly for Fu Yu Ti Chün, around the same time as the Chüeh-hsiu kung was founded. The Chih-nan kung, built on a mountain above the satellite town of Mu-cha and overlooking Taipei, has been promoted by Taiwan's main tourist agencies and has long been one of Taiwan's centers of pilgrimage.

The sets of En Chu Kung nearly always include Kuan Ti, Fu Yu Ti Chün, and Ssu Ming Chen Chün (the god of the stove). What is most notable is that they are all national gods, lacking any particular local significance in Taiwan or in the mainland provinces from which most of its inhabitants originally came. Very often, in fact—and this is certainly the case in the Hsing-t'ien kung, the Chüeh-hsiu kung, and the Chih-nan kung—figures representing Buddhism, Taoism, and Confucianism, namely Sakyamuni, Lao Tzu, and Confucius, are added in side shrines to make the cult interdenominational as well as national in scope. This syncretism is on the one hand similar to that of the temples dedicated jointly to Kuan Ti and Confucius that were founded by local merchants and gentry in several central places as versions of the Ch'ing state religion. On the other hand, and especially in the origins of some of its temples as semi-secret spirit-writing and vegetarian cults—it is similar to that of the syncretic cults proscribed by the Ch'ing state.[33] In the absence of the religious authority of the old imperial government, there is no central control of religion. Moreover, the universalism or pan-Chinese stance of both the state cults and the syncretic sects fits the new conditions that have destroyed the parochialism of native-place associations, and serves well the interests of those who move at economic and political levels beyond and above the local.

The title En Chu Kung is significant. "En" means beneficence, and for those who follow and practice the cult in the Hsing-t'ien kung and the Chüeh-hsiu kung it implies "public spirit" and "charity." The gods are exemplars of civic virtue which their followers learn from them and try to practice. This involves reciting moral texts in the temple, equivalent to the chanting of sutras by vegetarian women's groups in the local temples, and operating charities, which in the local temples are usually also run by the Buddhist women. The Hsing-t'ien kung did, in fact, start in the main market street of Ta-tao-ch'eng in 1937 as a vegetarian hall for the cultivation of virtue and the breaking down of superstition.[34] In 1949 it moved out of this traditional Taiwanese area and into Chung-shan borough. Its latest move has left it still within Chung-shan but on the most newly developed side of the borough.

The moral texts are received from spirit-writing that has taken place either in the past on the mainland or else in sessions held in the earlier stages of the temples' own development. Yet I have heard them and the ceremonial accompanying them called Confucianism and the Confucian Way (or Confucian Taoism, *ju-tao-chiao*) by their practitioners in the Hsing-t'ien kung and in the Chüeh-hsiu kung, showing some inclination toward the religious culture of the literati and the former ruling class. One person who referred to this new religion as *ju tao chiao* said it was island-wide and was intended to encourage the eight virtues. It was of this world and so did not lay stress on the Buddhist Nirvana. My informant was at the time a guide for the chief worshipper at a ceremony in a new (i.e. Republican) City God temple, the Sheng ch'eng-huang miao, built near the site of the razed official City God temple in the walled city. This man and two other guides at this ceremony were also guides for chief worshippers at the K'ung-tzu miao, and my informant was in addition a manager of the Chüeh-hsiu kung. When I asked him which temples belong to the *ju-tao-chiao* he told me that the Hsing-t'ien kung, the Chih-nan kung, the Sheng ch'eng-huang miao, and the Chüeh-hsiu kung all did. Although these temples are linked in many ways—such as by exchanging readers for their moral texts and ritual

TABLE 5. FIVE TWENTIETH-CENTURY TEMPLES IN TAIPEI

Temple	Location	Principal deity and religous orentation	Procession	Branch temple(s)
K'ung-tzu miao	Ta-lung-t'ung	Confucius/syncretic Confucian	—	—
Hsing-t'ien kung	Ta-tao-ch'eng, then Chung-shan	Kuan Ti/syncretic	—	Yes
Chüeh-hsiu kung	Ta-lung-t'ung	Fu Yu Ti Chün / syncretic Taoist	—	—
Chih-nan kung	Mu-cha (suburb)	Fu Yu Ti Chün/ syncretic Buddhist	—	—
Sheng ch'eng-huang miao	Ch'eng-chung	City God/syncretic	Yes	—

NOTE: All of these are government-sponsored temples or nonprofit corporations or both.

experts as guides for their ceremonies—they are not, as he said, in any coordinated or centralized organization.

If there is anything like a center it would be the Chüeh-hsiu kung, because it was there that the new religious style first developed. This temple supplied ritual experts to the Hsing-t'ien kung before the Hsing-t'ien kung started training its own practitioners, and still supplies them to the Sheng ch'eng-huang miao. The Chüeh-hsiu kung began in the 1910's (as the Hsing-t'ien kung began later) as a spirit-writing and re-formist association. But it was also a curing cult and a center of Han medicine.[35] The Chüeh-hsiu kung has continued to promote proper ceremonial, training practitioners of a new religious style that shuns the ritualistic and magical arts of Taoists yet professes Taoism, and bases itself largely on the civil ceremonial of the state cults. The curing side of its activities seems to have lapsed, but spirit-writing sessions are still held wherein personal problems can be put before the gods as well as new texts composed for its litany. Since the Republican period began, the Chüeh-hsiu kung has become a nonprofit corporation organized into three departments, one for instruction, one for charity, and one for publishing. Several of its texts have been printed and distributed free, particularly through the modern temples discussed in this section. It is considered to be an act of merit to sponsor the publication of morally edifying books. The chairman of the Taipei municipal assembly has sponsored many of them and is honorary publisher of the Chüeh-hsiu kung's monthly journal Cheng-yen (Correct words). He is also on the managing committee of the Pao-an kung. Officials who are in the national government, and thus of even higher standing, have contributed congratulatory calligraphy and articles for the journal.

Another link between these temples may be found in the person of Huang Tsan-chün, who seems to have waged a one-man campaign for Chinese cultural renaissance until his death in 1952. Not only did he manage the Pao-an kung and contribute to the establishment of the K'ung-tzu miao, he also contributed to the building of the Chih-nan kung and published a number of magazines on culture and ethics. Later, he participated in the activities of a number of cultural and good-works organizations that had moved to Taiwan from the mainland. One of these was the Universal Ethical Society (*Wan-kuo tao-te hui*), which at one time established branches in the Tz'u-sheng kung and the Sheng ch'eng-huang miao.[36]

Receiving texts and guidance can and does turn into receiving advice on personal and practical affairs of the same kind as that for which Taoist practitioners are consulted in the Hsia-hai ch'eng-huang miao and the Pao-an kung, a development that dissolves all sense of moral reform and rearmament against "superstition." In fact it is for benefi-cence in this practical sense, in the hope that a god will respond with practical benefits, that the mass of worshippers attends the Hsing-t'ien kung and the Chih-nan kung. In these temples they are saved the costs of traditional religious practitioners and of expensive offerings. The ex-ponents of the new religious style receive no fees. They are trained for self-cultivation and the propagation of propriety in the five relationships (*wu-lun*). They must be clean, and in the temple ceremonies wear long blue gowns that entirely cover their worldly Western-style clothing. The emphasis is on simple and direct communication between individual and deity, without the mediation of priests, elaborate offerings, or spirit money—just incense, flowers, and fruit. Self-manipulated divination by lot is the most mediation allowed in the Hsing-t'ien kung. People who come for solutions to personal and practical problems take the texts thus selected (they are in classical, poetic form)[37] to post-office-like kiosks for interpretation by the blue-gowned helpers. Their monetary contributions to the temple are collected, now that the new buildings have been completed, for charitable work. Loudspeakers harangue them with moral teaching from the roof beams.

But apart from this mass of worshippers, the trained practitioners and regular attenders of the Hsing-t'ien kung and the Chüeh-hsiu kung are much closer to a congregation than are the regular attenders of the local temples. The Chüeh-hsiu kung has an association of followers (*hsin-t'u hui*), membership in which cost (in 1968) ten new Taiwanese dollars a month. The "congregation" of the Hsing-t'ien kung must be much larger. In addition, both have something more like a Christian church's weekly assembly, held in a congregation hall with pictures of the President at one end and of the National Father Sun Yat-sen at the other, like all civic halls in Taiwan, and starting (as do all civic meetings) with the national anthem and bows to these two pictures. Unlike the local temples, these two temples and the Chih-nan kung and K'ung-tzu miao have no processions, no theater, no bands, and no professional ritual practitioners. The K'ung-tzu miao and the Sheng ch'eng-huang miao have a territorially defined community, within Taiwan, by virtue of their much closer identification with the old Ch'ing state religion. Otherwise they are autonomous institutions to which the mass of worshippers has no diffuse bonds of loyalty, just specific ritual needs. People come to the Hsing-t'ien kung and the Chih-nan kung from all over the island, without distinction of place.

Among the twentieth-century temples here considered, the Sheng ch'eng-huang miao is the only exception in this regard. It is local, has theater and a procession containing generals Fan and Hsieh that tours its borough on Retrocession Day which (in contrast to the practice of the Fa-chu-kung kung) is reckoned by the solar calendar and so always falls on October 25. But its locality is that of all the central government offices and some of its residences, and of the offices of Taiwan's main financial and commercial enterprises. The management of its procession is taken in turns by the heads of the administrative wards (*li*) of the borough. It was built after Retrocession at the instigation of the head of the borough, in order, so one of its present managers said, to restore patriotism. Thus it is not surprising, given its location and its origins, that it is linked to the networks of the more eminent and universalistic Chüeh-hsiu kung, Hsing-t'ien kung, and K'ung-tzu miao.

Conclusion

It looks as if these twentieth-century temples are developing a Republican version of the imperial state religion. Certainly their religious style is sufficiently distinct from that of the local temples so that quite eminent government officials can openly associate themselves with it. Among the local temples, the old guild temples (as specified in Table 4) and maybe the Pao an kung have been sufficiently transformed in the direction of the new religious style of the five to be on the verge of adoption into it. The degree of government control over the management of the old guild temples has to some extent forced this development.

The new religious style departs most radically from the imperial state religion in having a mass following of worshippers. Only the K'ung-tzu miao is not open every day to all worshippers who wish to make offerings and seek guidance and response, although in all of them regular active participation in their ceremonial is reserved for a defined and trained group of members.

Taipei has become a large city in a very short time (see Map 2),[38] submerging or dissolving the former local communities by means of cheap modern transport. The texts of the new temples appeal to a mass readership. Transportation across the whole island having become faster and cheaper, Taipei's industry has attracted a great number of immigrants from elsewhere in the island, as well as from the mainland. The gods of the new temples have no local significance, nor are they branches of older local cults. They stand for power on a national scale. The morality preached in their name, and the stress of their religious style, is on the individual as a universal atom, receptacle of and responsible to "society" and "Chinese culture," and duty-bound to perform good works.

This amounts to what many social scientists would call the natural process of "modernization" or, more significantly, Westernization. But perhaps the sponsorship of temples that can attract a mass following, and whose deities and ceremonials at the same time transcend local loyalties, was and is a matter of conscious political decisions made by a government of Nationalist mainland exiles on Taiwan for the sake of enhancing its own legitimacy.

It is perhaps surprising that local, territorial temples continue to flourish at all. But when one looks at all the temples considered in this paper, one sees a sharp division between the festivals of the territorial temples in the poorer and older parts of Taipei and the autonomy of the universalistic temples in the newer and wealthier parts of the city, their ceremonials closely identified with the central government.

Migration and Family Change in Central Taiwan

ALDEN SPEARE, JR.

One of the many social changes accompanying urbanization and industrialization is a change in family and kinship relations.* The movement of people from rural areas to cities and from agriculture to industry has typically been viewed as disruptive to the traditional extended family where married brothers, their families, and their parents all lived together under one roof.[1] The change from agriculture to nonagricultural employment undermines one of the primary functions of the extended family—the provision of food and employment for the family members. It is further argued that dealing with the new stresses accompanying industrial work requires stronger relations between husband and wife than are found in traditional extended families. Finally, since industrialization and urbanization usually require geographical mobility and small family units can move more easily than large ones, migration naturally results in an increase in the number of conjugal units and a decrease in the number of extended units.

The general pattern of family change is clear, but the extent of the change and the role of the extended family in facilitating or retarding urbanization and industrialization is not at all clear. Several writers have criticized the view that most people in traditional societies lived in extended families.[2] They argue that mortality and economic hardship severely limited the opportunity for all but the wealthy to live in large ex-

* This research is an outgrowth of the fieldwork conducted for the author's doctoral dissertation. The research was supported by a grant from the National Science Foundation and a fellowship from the Population Studies Center of the University of Michigan. Tunghai University in Taichung provided local sponsorship and student interviewers for the study. The author is indebted to Ronald Freedman, David Goldberg, and Mark Thelin for their advice and to Hui-sheng Lin and Rong Rong Lo for their assistance in the field work.

tended families. On the other hand, Litwak and others have argued that the extended family is not necessarily inconsistent with a modern industrial society and that extended-family relations can be maintained even when all family members do not live in the same household.[3]

In this chapter we shall take up several aspects of the relationship between urbanization and family change in central Taiwan. Our analysis will be based on survey data collected from a sample of male migrants to the city of Taichung and a sample of men living in the rural and semirural areas from which the migrants moved.

Taiwan provides an opportunity to study the processes of urbanization and industrialization while they are occurring. Industrialization, which began during the Japanese occupation in the 1930's, has been particularly rapid during the postwar period. Between 1952 and 1967 industrial production increased more than fourfold, and the Gross National Product grew at an average rate of 7 percent per year in constant dollars.[4]

Urbanization in Taiwan has accompanied and kept pace with economic growth. Between 1950 and 1966, the percentage of the population living in the ten largest cities increased from 23 percent to 29 percent, as a result of rural-to-urban migration. Not all of this migration involved changes from agricultural to industrial employment. The majority of the migrants had worked at nonagricultural jobs in rural areas before moving, and many found employment in sales or service occupations in the city.[5] However, most migrants found jobs in the city within a short time after their arrival, and the general availability of urban employment that enabled them to do this can be attributed to increases in industrialization and trade in the cities.

The pattern of recent urban migration in Taiwan stands in contrast to that found in many other Asian nations where despite slower industrialization there is greater rural-to-urban migration and greater urban unemployment.[6] One of the factors acting to keep rural-to-urban migration in line with economic growth in Taiwan has been the steady improvement of agriculture throughout the twentieth century. Progressive increases in agricultural yield, the more uniform distribution of land that resulted from the 1953 Land to the Tiller Act and the rural reconstruction program have increased the attractiveness of farming for small farmers. Thus although land was scarce, most farm families could make a living during the 1952–67 period.

Furthermore, some of Taiwan's industrial growth has occurred outside the largest cities. According to household-registration statistics, 44 percent of all men employed in manufacturing resided outside the ten largest cities.[7] These men either worked in factories in smaller urban centers or rural areas or commuted to work in one of the large cities. This means that men were not forced to migrate to one of the large cities if the family landholdings were insufficient to support them, but could choose to move to a nearby urban center or even remain in their traditional home and commute to work. Thus for most men the decision to move to the city was based more on the comparison of job opportunities in the city with those in the rural area than on an absolute need to find employment.[8]

With this background in mind, several questions will be raised concerning the role of urbanization and industrialization in family change. First, we shall inquire into the extent to which various forms of the extended family are valued and desired and whether or not migrants differ from nonmigrants in the extent to which they profess adherence to the traditional family norms of South China.

Although the extended family may still be an ideal, it has been argued that few people in traditional China had the opportunity to live in one. Parents and one or more sons might die before any son married, or economic pressures might force all or all but one of the sons to leave a household. Thus, our second question will be what proportion of men could, if they wished, live in various kinds of extended families.

Third, we shall examine the actual extended-family experience of those men who have the opportunity for it. What proportion have ever lived in extended families? What proportion are still living in such families? Were migrants (before they moved) as likely as nonmigrants to have lived in extended families? What proportion of moves resulted in a change from an extended family to a conjugal family?

Fourth, we shall look at the effect of farm background on family structure. Since the extended family has most commonly been identified with subsistence agriculture,[9] one would expect to find more extended families among farm households than among nonfarm households. However, among farm households the size of the farm places a limit on the number of persons who can derive their sustenance from it. Thus, in testing these expectations, we shall investigate large farms, small farms, and nonfarm households separately. In addition we can look at the relation between migration and farm background. Even if an extended family breaks up, the departing members need not leave the village. Thus, although farm size may be related to the presence of extended families, it need not show the same relationship to migration to the city.

Fifth, we shall investigate the relationship between number and sex of siblings and migration. If migration is in part a response to family tensions or economic pressures, or both, we would expect to find more migration from families where there were many brothers than from those where there were few. We shall also be interested in the effects of birth order and number of sisters on migration.

Finally, we shall examine the interaction patterns within extended families divided by migration. To what extent does migration to a nearby city curtail interaction? Do migrants keep up extended-family relations after migration? Are they able to return for major festivals, weddings, funerals, and other large family gatherings?

Description of Data

The Taichung Migration Study was originally designed to provide a detailed study of the determinants of migration for male migrants moving to one of the larger cities in Taiwan. The research design provided for a controlled comparison between recent migrants to a major city and residents of the counties from which the migrants had come. The research was conducted in 1967. Taichung city* with its surrounding area was chosen as the site of the study because of the availability of support from Tunghai University and the Taiwan Population Studies Center, both located in Taichung, and because, of Taiwan's five major cities, it was the one most widely separated from the others. Taichung is the fourth largest city in Taiwan, with a population of about 392,000 in 1967. It ranked third in rate of growth between 1959 and 1967. The surrounding counties are primarily rural, with rice and sweet potatoes the major crops. However, these counties contain one small city and several urban centers where some industry is located.

Because of the difficulties of sending interviewers out to rural villages, the nonmigrant sample area was limited to the four counties immediately surrounding Taichung city: Miao-li, Chang-hua, T'ai-chung, and Nan-t'ou (see Map 1). Within these four counties, 46 villages and subsections of urban towns were selected by random sampling. Within each of these areas, households were systematically selected from the household registers, and males for the nonmigrant sample were obtained from these households.† Using the in-migration records of Taichung city for 1966

---

* I follow here official usage in Taiwan, which renders as "city" the term (*shih*) that might better be translated "municipality" since it refers to a bounded territorial unit rather than to the central place per se.
† The nonmigrant sample is composed of men who had not moved to a major city

and 1967, we drew our migrant sample from among men who had moved from one of these same four counties. These counties furnished 71 percent of all migrants from rural and semirural areas to Taichung city for the years studied.

Several controls were introduced into the sample design through the use of individual characteristics available on both the migration and household records. First, we restricted the sample to men aged 23 to 42. The lower age limit was chosen because most men in Taiwan would have completed the two years of required military service by that age. The upper limit was chosen to provide a twenty-year age range and exclude most men who were likely to have married sons. We thus have a sample of men who would comprise the middle generation of a three-generation family—the generation primarily responsible for the continuance or termination of large extended families.

Second, mainland Chinese were excluded from the sample because they differ from native Taiwanese in their propensity to move and in many other characteristics. Aborigines were likewise excluded.

Third, because several studies have shown that migration rates decline with distance from the destination, we built into the sample design a control for distance. The nonmigrant sample was divided into two rings centered on Taichung city and the selection probability in each ring was made proportional to the migration rate from that ring. This means that our nonmigrant sample overrepresents those living close to Taichung city and thus is not necessarily representative of the overall population of the four counties. However, on none of the variables discussed in this paper were there any significant differences between the distributions shown and the distributions obtained after weighting to make the sample representative.

Finally, the migrant sample was restricted to men who had actually moved to Taichung city and who had stayed there at least three months. We excluded men who had merely transferred their legal residence to Taichung to conduct business without actually moving and men who

---

during the two years prior to interview. They were nonmigrants only in this limited sense. Approximately half of the men had moved at some time in their past. The majority of these moves were either short-distance moves within the sample area or short-duration moves with a return to the place of origin. At the time of interview 80 percent were living in the same township where they were born, and 90 percent were living in the same county. The effect of prior migration on the ability to live with relatives can be considered to be minimal. However, some of the prior moves were to large cities and even though these were typically of short duration, they may have had an effect on the respondents' attitudes toward the extended family.

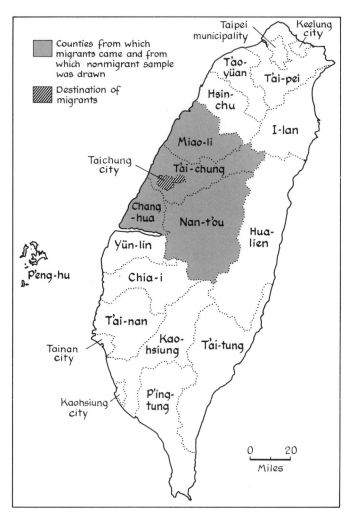

MAP 1. TAIWAN, 1968, SHOWING STUDY AREA

were transients or seasonal migrants who left the city after less than three months.

We attempted to interview everyone in the selected households or on the selected migration records who fit the characteristics listed above for our two sample groups. Thus our ultimate sample was a probability sample of persons and not households. This fact is of some consequence for our determination of the proportions living in different types of extended families, for the calculation of number of siblings, and other measures of family relations. Using the person as the base for these calculations, we arrive at larger proportions living in extended families than if we had used the household as a base. An extreme example will help to illustrate this point. Consider a small village that contains 72 people in ten households: one large household with 36 members and nine small households with an average of four members each. Using the household as the base, one would observe that 90 percent of the households were small. However, using the person as the base, one would conclude that half of the people in the village lived in large households. We feel that we can obtain a more accurate picture of extended-family life by using the person as the base.

Our sample contained 370 interviews with nonmigrants and 480 with migrants. These figures represent 90 percent of the nonmigrants and 70 percent of the migrants who were selected from the records and defined as eligible to be interviewed. The lower response rate for the migrant sample was due to the fact that many migrants could not be located because they were no longer living at the address listed on the registration record. In addition, many of the interviews with migrants had to be excluded from the analysis because the interviewees had actually moved at a much earlier date than that shown on the migration record,* or had not actually lived in the sample area prior to moving. These exclusions reduced the total number of usable migrant interviews to 321.

The relatively low response rate for the migrant sample raises some question about the representativeness of the sample. An extensive analysis of this question was done from data available on the registration records for those who were sampled but not interviewed.[10] This analysis yielded the tentative conclusion that registered migration is representative of actual migration, and that the migrants included in the analysis are similar with respect to age, education, occupation, and other observed characteristics to all registered migrants. With one exception, all the differences observed between migrants eligible to be interviewed and migrants actually interviewed and included in the analysis were smaller than the probable sampling error. This exception was a statistically significant difference in the percentage moving alone, which was 25 percent for those included in the analysis and 31 percent for all those eligible to be interviewed. The migration record does not indicate marital status at the time of the move, but this difference may indicate a some-

---

* An arbitrary decision was made to exclude all migrants who moved before 1965, more than one year before our sample period.

what greater proportion of single movers in the overall sample than in the respondent group, and, in turn, a slight bias in favor of married men among our migrant respondents. This seems plausible, since single migrants would presumably be more likely than married migrants to have moved again since coming to the city, or to have living arrangements that made them difficult to locate, or both.

Almost all of our interviews were conducted in Taiwanese by students from Tunghai University.* The average interview lasted about an hour and fifteen minutes and covered about 200 questions from a printed schedule about the economic and family situation of the migrants both before and after the move to the city. Comparable questions were asked of nonmigrants about their situation at the time of interview. Because the migrant respondents had moved so recently, they had little trouble recalling their situation prior to the move, and accurate comparisons with the situation of nonmigrants were thus possible.

Our study is based entirely on information obtained from male respondents and may not provide a complete picture of the family situation. Since most of our analysis deals with married men and almost all of these were living with their wives, however, there is little bias in the sample selection. The probability of selecting a given family for our sample would have changed very little had we selected married women rather than married men as respondents. However, the responses to some of the attitudinal questions would very likely have been different had females been the respondents. It is the female who is bound to the home and must live with the other relatives in the household while the husband is away at work. Many divisions of extended families may be initiated by conflicts between females in the household. Although males clearly dominate the overt decision-making in Chinese families, females may influence these decisions in a variety of indirect ways. A more complete study of the Chinese family should also include attitudes of women.

The Ideal Family

The traditional ideal Chinese family has been described as a patrilineal joint family in which all sons continue to live with their parents after marriage.[11] Although this ideal may have been universal, most authors have doubted whether many people ever lived in such families. For instance, C. K. Yang, who studied the village of Nanching in Kwangtung province in 1948–51, writes:

---

* About 6 percent of the men in our sample were Hakka. They were interviewed by Hakka students in their native dialect.

The average family . . . generally consisted of parents, their [unmarried] children, and at times the father's living parent or parents. For the majority, if the parents had two or more married sons, the parents lived with one married son's family but frequently visited the other sons' families. In common with other parts of China, the "large family" where parents and all married sons maintained a common unit of living was in the minority in this village, occurring mainly among the wealthy.[12]

Maurice Freedman attributes the lack of joint families among the poor in part to demographic factors:

A poor family might in the extreme be unable to raise a son to marriageable age and ensure that he stay at home to recreate the domestic unit. The chances were that at most one son would marry and continue the family in the same house. As soon as this son begot a child three generations were present, but the senior generation, represented by the elderly parents, were very unlikely to see a fourth emerge. As soon as these parents died a two-generation family appeared again. The process was repeated: elementary family grew to stem and was reduced once more to elementary. Even though there might be two married brothers at any stage in the evolution of a family, they rarely lived together, with the consequence that no joint family appears in the typical cycle.[13]

Even among wealthy families where there were several married sons, the sons typically remained in an undivided family only as long as the parental generation survived. As soon as both parents died, they divided into separate households. Obviously, in families where there were several sons who survived and married in each generation, division was necessary at some point if the family size was to be kept from growing at a geometric rate.

For purposes of further discussion, we shall define the ideal family as one in which all the sons continue to live in one household with their parents until both parents have died. We can consider this ideal to be supported by two norms (1) that a son continue to live with his parents as long as they live and (2) that brothers continue to live together as long as their parents live. If one has brothers, he cannot accept the first norm without the second. However, the first norm can be modified to require only that at least one son should continue to live with the parents.

It is difficult to measure the extent to which the ideal family is still valued without reverting to behavioral measures. We could not ask the men who were living with their parents whether they liked to live with them because the parents were often around the house during the interview. However, we did ask all the men who were not living with their

312   ALDEN SPEARE, JR.

TABLE 1. ATTITUDES TOWARD THE EXTENDED FAMILY: EXPECTATION OF SPENDING
OLD AGE WITH CHILDREN AND GRANDCHILDREN

Expectation	Migrants	Nonmigrants
Definitely expect to live with children and grandchildren	56.7%	62.0%
Probably will	12.8	13.9
Uncertain	21.2	16.6
Probably will not	6.2	3.8
Definitely will not	3.1	3.8
Total	100.0%	100.0%
N	321	368

SOURCE: The source for this and all other tables in this chapter, unless otherwise noted, is the Taichung Migration Study, carried out by the author in 1967.
NOTE: As stated in the text, the final sample N's were 321 for migrants and 370 for nonmigrants. N's will vary from table to table, however, because of nonresponses for particular questions. Here, for example, two responses coded NA (Not Ascertained) were excluded from the nonmigrant data, leaving an N of 368. Here and elsewhere in the tables, percentages may not total precisely 100.0% because of rounding.

parents whether they desired to live closer to them. Some 96 percent of the nonmigrants and 94 percent of the migrants said yes. Although this question actually tells us nothing about whether the respondents wished to live in the same household with their parents, the high proportions of both groups replying yes tends to support the notion that men in Taiwan still value the extended family highly. Whether their wives, who must bear many of the burdens of maintaining the households, also value the extended family highly remains an empirical question.

Another indication of the extent of belief in the extended family was obtained by asking our respondents whether or not they expected to live with their children and grandchildren in their old age. As shown in Table 1, over two-thirds of the migrants and three-quarters of the nonmigrants said either definitely or probably yes. Most of the others replied that they were undecided. Although fewer migrants than nonmigrants expected to live in extended families, the difference was small, and we can conclude that both groups still valued the extended family. Similar results were obtained from a study of married women in Taiwan conducted at about the same time.*

Maurice Freedman has singled out three "crucial domestic relationships" that vary in relation to one another and that can be used as indicators of adherence to traditional family norms.[14] These relationships

* Unpublished tabulations from the Second Provincewide Fertility Survey conducted by the Taiwan Population Studies Center in 1967 show that 87 percent of the married women in a sample of 4,989 expected to live with their children or grandchildren in their old age.

TABLE 2. STRENGTH OF NORMS RANKING BASIC FAMILY RELATIONSHIPS

Relationship and norm	Migrants	Nonmigrants
Father-son vs. Husband-wife		
Should feel closer to parents	66.2%	76.4%
Should feel equally close to parents and wife[a]	19.7	16.9
Should feel closer to wife	14.0	6.7
Total	100.0%	100.0%
N	314	360
Brother-brother vs. Husband-wife		
Should feel closer to brother	31.0%	41.2%
Should feel equally close to brother and wife[a]	26.5	28.8
Should feel closer to wife	42.5	29.9
Total	100.0%	100.0%
N^b	313	354

[a] This option was not read to the respondents, but was coded when they gave it as a response to the question "To whom should a man feel closer . . . ?"
[b] NA's are excluded from both parts of the question. There were 17 NA's for the first part and 24 for the second part.

are those between father and son, brother and brother, and husband and wife. In the ideal family, the relationship between father and son was the strongest, that between brothers the next strongest, and that between husband and wife the weakest.[15] The relative unimportance of the husband-wife relationship was due in part to the fact that marriages were usually arranged by the parents.

With increased urbanization and industrialization and decreased dependence on the family farm for sustenance, it has been argued, the large extended family loses some of its economic function, and the conjugal family gains the additional function of managing the tensions created by the newer forms of employment.[16] If this is true, then one would expect the relative strength of the husband-wife relationship to increase with urbanization and industrialization.

The traditional norms about the comparative strength of relations with different kin are still widely held. When asked whether a man should feel closer to his parents or his wife, only 14 percent of the migrants and 7 percent of the nonmigrants said he should feel closer to his wife (see Table 2). Most of the rest chose the traditional response—that he should feel closer to his parents. Some compromised and said he should feel equally close to both.

Migrants differed more from nonmigrants in their view of the comparative strength of the relationship between brothers. Although many

TABLE 3. KIND OF MARRIAGE ARRANGEMENT REPORTED BY
MARRIED RESPONDENTS

Choice of bride	Migrants	Nonmigrants
Decided entirely by parents	2.3%	7.8%
Suggested by parents with respondent's consent	55.6	59.7
Decided by respondent with parents' consent	23.0	15.3
Decided entirely by respondent	3.1	1.3
Arranged by other person	16.1	15.9
Total	100.0%	100.0%
N	261	320

NOTE: The total number of married migrants (married at time of interview) was 266, but five cases had to be excluded because the kind of marriage arrangement was not ascertained.

of them still chose the traditional response, many more chose the modern response. Among nonmigrants the reverse was true. A larger number of nonmigrants said a man should feel closer to his brother than said he should feel closer to his wife. A substantial number in both groups refused to choose, saying a man should feel equally close to both brother and wife.

Some of the change in attitudes toward the relative importance of the husband-wife relationship may be the result of changes in marriage customs. The traditional arranged marriage is still the most frequent form among both migrants and nonmigrants, but it was as rare for the son not to be consulted in the selection process as it was for the son to marry without his parents' consent. Thus what usually happened was that the son selected the bride, requested the approval of both sets of parents, and had them make the necessary arrangements for the wedding day, dowry, etc. When both parents on one side were deceased at the time of the marriage, responsibility for arrangements had to be assumed by some other person.

We should emphasize that we have data only on the male side of the marriage arrangement. We would expect to find slightly more females with partly or entirely arranged marriages.

Migrants were somewhat more modern than nonmigrants in this regard. Twenty-six percent of the migrants had selected their bride themselves, whereas only 17 percent of the nonmigrants had done so (see Table 3). Since most of the migrants were married before they moved, one cannot necessarily conclude that the change in marriage customs was directly due to urbanization. An alternative explanation is that men who experience the more modern form of marriage are more likely to respond to the opportunities offered by urban employment. However, it is possible that a more modern outlook obtained either through education or previous urban contact led the migrants to seek both a more modern kind of marriage and a job in the city.

We can conclude that the traditional ideal Chinese family is still highly valued in Taiwan, both among men remaining in rural areas and among men moving from these areas to the city. However, migrants do hold somewhat more modern attitudes toward the family than nonmigrants. In particular, migrants are more likely than nonmigrants to stress the importance of the husband-wife relationship.

Opportunity to Live in an Extended Family

Opportunity to live in an extended family can be defined in various ways. One can consider that a person has this opportunity if he has the appropriate relatives, regardless of where they are living, or one can consider that a person has the opportunity only if these relatives are living in the same town. An even more restrictive definition of the opportunity would take into account whether or not the family farm or business could support an extended family. This last definition seems to be implied by those who state that the opportunity to live in an extended family was limited by economic conditions. Since it seems to us that family members live apart by free choice and that the only real limitation on the opportunity to live in an extended family is the existence somewhere of the appropriate members, we prefer the least restrictive definition in this category. However, since it seems to us that a man becomes a principal member of an extended family only after marriage, for purposes of this discussion, we shall define opportunity to live in an extended family as being married and having the appropriate living relatives.

We shall define "appropriate relatives" as at least one married brother or at least one parent, or both, and shall accordingly be interested in two forms of family extension. The first is vertical extension, whereby a married couple lives with one or both of the husband's parents.* This is normally called a stem family. The second is horizontal extension, whereby two or more married brothers live together. We shall refer to this as a fraternal joint family. Usually, married brothers do not live together unless they also live with their parents. When two or more married brothers live with one or both parents, we shall refer to this as a paternal

* We shall not deal with the matrilocal stem family because matrilocal marriage is no longer prevalent in Taiwan. Only about 3 percent of the men in our sample area lived in such families.

TABLE 4. OPPORTUNITY FOR MARRIED RESPONDENTS TO LIVE IN
EXTENDED FAMILIES, BY AGE

	Married		Appropriate relatives available		
Age	Number	Percent	Living parent	Married brother	Both
		Migrants ($N = 233$)			
23–27	57	53.3%	96.5%	69.6%	66.1%
28–32	82	86.3	91.5	90.1	81.5
33–37	63	95.5	87.3	82.5	74.6
38–42	31	100.0	76.7	93.3	70.0
Average		74.3%	89.8%	82.9%	74.3%
		Nonmigrants ($N = 320$)			
23–27	71	66.4%	98.6%	77.5%	76.1%
28–32	80	88.9	94.9	69.6	64.6
33–37	90	98.9	80.0	78.7	64.0
38–42	79	100.0	67.5	83.8	56.3
Average		87.2%	84.7%	77.4%	64.9%

NOTE: Includes migrants married at time of move and nonmigrants married at time of interview. We have excluded two migrants for whom marital status at the time of move could not be ascertained and three nonmigrants who were widowed or divorced. For some cells the number of cases may be one less than that shown in column one because of missing information.

joint family. This list is not exhaustive. We have not considered such possibilities as a joint family in which a married couple lives with the husband's parents and an uncle or aunt, or extended families involving the wife's relatives.[17]

Most of the men we interviewed had the opportunity to live in an extended family of one sort or another. Altogether, 87 percent of the nonmigrants and 74 percent of the migrants in our sample were married, a smaller difference than would have been expected. The difference would probably have been larger if we could have corrected for the bias in our sample with respect to this item. The proportion of married men varied with age. The largest difference in this proportion between migrants and nonmigrants was in the 23–27 age group (see column 1 of Table 4). This means that among younger men, the single were more likely to migrate than the married. In the two older age groups virtually all those interviewed, both migrants and nonmigrants, were married, and thus no statements can be made about the relationship between marriage and migration in these groups.

Although slightly fewer migrants than nonmigrants were married, those who were married were more likely than the married nonmigrants to possess the necessary relatives for an extended family. Among married migrants, 90 percent had a living parent and 83 percent had a married brother. The corresponding figures for nonmigrants were 85 percent and 77 percent. Altogether, 74 percent of the migrants and 65 percent of the nonmigrants had the opportunity to live with both types of relatives in a paternal joint family.

The percentage of respondents with living parents naturally declined with increasing age. However, even among men aged 38–42, over two-thirds had the opportunity to live with their parents, and over half had the opportunity to live in a paternal joint family.

These results contradict the often-encountered view that mortality and small family size limited the opportunity for most people to live in extended families. However, some of the differences between our findings and those of earlier studies conducted on the mainland of China may reflect Taiwan's considerably lower mortality and possibly higher fertility. Between 1925 and 1944, the period during which the men in our sample were born, the average crude birthrate was about 43 per 1,000, and the average crude death rate about 20 per 1,000.[18] This left a considerable margin for family growth. The mean number of living siblings (including the respondent) was 6.0 for migrants and 5.4 for nonmigrants. Only 5 percent of the migrants and 11 percent of the nonmigrants were only sons. Fifty-one percent of the migrants but only 41 percent of the nonmigrants had three or more brothers.

There is no evidence that migration was precipitated by the death of one's parents or that migrants lacked disproportionately the opportunity to live with married brothers. In fact, as noted above, the reverse appears to be the case. Migrants had more opportunity than nonmigrants to live in extended families (see Table 4). It can be concluded from these data that most men had the opportunity to live in extended families and that the availability of this opportunity had little effect on migration. The additional finding that migrants came from larger families than nonmigrants will be discussed in some detail later.

Extended-Family Experience

The extent to which a group of people is judged to adhere to traditional family norms varies with the way in which adherence to these norms is defined and whether opportunity to adhere to them is controlled for. If adherence is defined as living with one's parents and *all* one's married brothers, then only about one in four of the married nonmigrants would qualify. If it is defined as living with one or more married brothers, then the figure rises to about one in three.*

---

* Exact estimates cannot be made because our data on coresidence extend only to three brothers. Thus for men with four or more brothers we do not know where the fourth and younger brothers were living. We failed to obtain any data on location of brothers for migrants before they moved.

TABLE 5. EXTENDED-FAMILY EXPERIENCE AMONG MARRIED RESPONDENTS
WITH OPPORTUNITY FOR IT BY AGE

Age at reference point[a]	Ever lived with parents	Ever lived with married brother	Lived with parents at move[b]	Living with parents at interview	Living with married brother at interview
			Migrants		
23–27	89.1%	56.4%	58.2%	10.9%	0.0%
28–32	89.3	56.2	65.4	14.7	0.0
33–37	87.3	69.3	56.3	30.9	11.5
38–42	87.0	75.0	34.7	17.4	0.0
Average	88.7%	62.5%	57.7%	18.3%	3.1%
N	208	192	208	208	192
			Nonmigrants		
23–27	89.7%	74.5%	—	78.7%	49.0%
28–32	92.0	83.7	—	74.6	49.0
33–37	91.6	84.3	—	73.6	44.3
38–42	98.1	80.5	—	48.2	28.4
Average	92.5%	81.0%	—	70.0%	42.1%
N	267[c]	247		271	247

NOTE: As detailed in the text above, opportunity for extended-family experience is limited to
married men having a living parent or a married brother. All others are excluded from this table.
[a] Time of move or time of interview as specified in the column heading.
[b] No information was obtained on whether migrants were living with a married brother or
brothers at the time of their move.
[c] Four nonmigrants for whom overall living experience was not ascertained have been excluded
from this column.

On the other hand, if we look at the percentage who have ever lived
in extended families, we find that among the married nonmigrants who
had the opportunity to do so, 93 percent had lived with their parents
and 81 percent had lived with their married brothers for some time
following their marriage.

The typical pattern seems to be one in which men begin married life
by living with their parents and married brothers, if they have any, and
gradually break away as they grow older. This pattern becomes clearer
if we examine the percentages living with parents and married brothers
by age, as shown in Table 5.

The first column of Table 5 shows that the percentages of married
men who have ever lived with their parents differed very little among
the four age groups or between migrants and nonmigrants. The custom
of beginning married life in the home of the husband's parents appears
to have changed little with the urbanization and industrialization of the
last twenty years. However, there seems to have been a slight decline
in the percentage who ever live with married brothers at all. This may
mean that men are breaking away to form separate households earlier

than they used to and are less likely to remain until their next brother is married.

The proportion of married men living with their parents at the time of interview or just prior to moving was, of course, lower than the proportion who had ever lived with them. Whereas the proportion who began married life with their parents varied little among age groups, the proportion who continued to live with them until interviewed or until migration declined with age, the most marked drop occurring in the 38–42 age group (see column 3 of Table 5). Thus by the time men reached the age at which their own sons were old enough to work (many young men begin work as soon as they finish primary school at age 12 or 13), more than half of the nonmigrants who still had a living parent had moved into a separate household, and nearly three-quarters no longer lived with any married brothers. These data clearly document a pattern of family breakup that is independent of mortality. Among married nonmigrants in the sample as a whole, the proportion in this age group who continued to live in a stem or paternal joint family until interview is about one in three, since only two-thirds of the men aged 38–42 had a living parent. However, this is still a sizable proportion when one considers that by the age of 42 many men are nearing the age when they become grandparents and the family cycle begins again.

Few married brothers continued to live together after the death of their parents. Among nonmigrants with married brothers, 46 percent of those with a living parent were living together at the time of interview, whereas only 20 percent of those with no living parent were doing so. In many cases among this 20 percent, the parent or parents had died within the last few years.

More migrants had broken away from their parents prior to migration than had nonmigrants prior to interview (see Table 5). Since migrants had made more previous moves, both to cities and to other places outside the cities, than had nonmigrants, some of these breaks had probably occurred as the result of a previous move.

The move to Taichung city usually resulted in the division of existing extended families. Whereas 58 percent of the married migrants able to do so had lived with their parents before moving, only 18 percent continued to do so in Taichung. Only 3 percent of the migrants were living with their married brothers in the city.

Most married migrants moved with their wives and children. A few moved to the city alone and stayed there a few months before the rest of their conjugal family moved. However, it was much more common for men to commute to the city daily before moving than to move to the city alone. Only 4 percent of the married migrants were living apart from their wives at the time of interview, which was, on the average, one year after the move.

The high incidence of migration of the entire conjugal unit as opposed to the husband only is undoubtedly a function of distance. Other data we have analyzed indicate that a higher proportion of men moving from outside our sample area to Taichung city had moved alone.[19] Also, because men who move alone are less likely to register than those who move with their families, our sample undoubtedly underrepresents the proportion of men moving alone. Gallin reports a much higher frequency of separation of conjugal units in the migration of men from Hsin-hsing village in Chang-hua county to Taipei city.[20]

These findings tend to support the view that rural-to-urban migration is associated with a change from an extended family to a conjugal family. Whereas our data indicate that extended families naturally tend to break up as the principal members grow older, the move to the city resulted in an earlier break for the migrants.

Farm Size and the Extended Family

Much of the discussion of economic constraints on the opportunity to live in an extended family has centered around the limits imposed by farm size. Maurice Freedman has made a clear distinction between wealthy rural families and poor ones, arguing that only the wealthy could support a large number of family members in one household.[21]

The median size of farms in our sample area was slightly less than one hectare. Even with intensive rice cultivation, farms of this size can adequately support only one nuclear family. However, in Taiwan, farm size places no absolute limit on the size of rural families because people can find nonfarm employment in rural areas or commute to the larger towns or cities for work while living in the rural area. Forty-five percent of our nonmigrant households were not engaged in any substantial farm operations.* Although many of these households were located in the towns and the one small city included in our sample area, many were in rural areas.

In Table 6 we have divided our sample into three groups: those who

---

* It is not possible to make a clear distinction between farm and nonfarm households in Taiwan since even in the city many households have vegetable gardens and keep chickens. We considered a respondent to have come from a farm household if he gave an affirmative answer to the question "Does your family own or operate any farm land?" and if his family tilled at least 0.1 hectare themselves.

TABLE 6. EXTENDED-FAMILY OPPORTUNITY AND EXPERIENCE, BY FARM SIZE

Farm-size category	N	Have a living parent	Ever lived with parent(s)	Living with parent(s)	Have a married brother	Ever lived with married brother	Living with married brother(s)
			Migrants ($N = 232$)				
Larger farms	45	95.6%	88.4%	62.8%	77.8%	65.7%	——
Smaller farms	43	93.0	97.5	75.0	88.4	73.7	——
Nonfarm households	144	86.8	85.6	50.4	82.6	58.0	——
Average		89.7%	88.5%	57.7%	82.8%	62.5%	——
			Nonmigrants ($N = 320$)				
Larger farms	68	95.6%	96.7%	87.6%	75.0%	88.2%	62.7%
Smaller farms	107	84.1	93.3	65.5	81.3	86.2	32.2
Nonfarm households	145	80.0	89.6	63.8	75.0	73.4	40.4
Average		84.7%	92.5%	70.0%	77.4%	81.0%	42.1%

NOTE: As noted in the text, larger farms are defined as those capable of producing NT$24,000 a year in income; smaller farms as those producing any lesser income. Percentages of both samples who were living or had ever lived in an extended family are based on the number who had an opportunity to do so. For migrants, "living with" refers to their situation just prior to migration; for nonmigrants, "living with" refers to their situation at the time of interview.

lived on larger farms, those who lived on smaller farms, and those who lived in households not actively engaged in farming. We have defined larger farms as those capable of producing an average income, after taxes, of NT$24,000 or more per year.[22] This figure, being equivalent to US$600 in 1967, would provide an annual per capita income of $100 for six family members, which is about the average size of conjugal units. If this income is accepted as more or less of a minimum, then no farms producing less income should be considered capable of supporting joint or extended families.

Considering first the nonmigrants in our sample, we find that the opportunity to live in an extended family differed somewhat with farm size. Men on smaller farms were less likely to have living parents than those on larger farms. This may have been due either to a relationship between farm size and mortality or to the fact that some of the smaller farms were the result of land divisions following the death of parents. Men in nonfarm households were less likely than those in farm households to have living parents. Although farm size was related to the opportunity to live with parents, it was not related to the opportunity to live with married brothers. In fact a slightly higher proportion of men on smaller farms had married brothers than those on larger farms.

In accord with Maurice Freedman's discussion, we found that extended families were more prevalent on larger than on smaller farms.

Whereas 88 percent of the nonmigrants on larger farms who were able to live with their parents were doing so, only 66 percent of those on smaller farms were doing so. The difference was even greater with respect to joint families. Of those who are able to live with married brothers, 63 percent of the men on larger farms but only 32 percent of those on smaller farms were doing so (see column 7 of Table 6). However, if we look at the proportions who have ever lived with parents or married brothers, we find much less difference between smaller and larger farms. Thus small farm size may not preclude the formation of an extended family, but it may mean that the family will be divided sooner rather than later.

The nonfarm families in our nonmigrant sample were similar to the smaller-farm families with respect to the maintenance of larger units. Many of the nonfarm families had given up farming as recently as the last generation. Thus we are unable to determine whether the extended family persisted among them as a mere carry-over of customs from the recent farm experience, or as a genuinely functional form, providing labor for the family business as it once provided labor for the family farm. The latter explanation seems plausible since many non-farm households operated small businesses that provided employment for family members.

Turning now to the migrants, we find that they show a similar relationship between farm size and opportunity to live in extended families (see Table 6). However, there is a negative relationship between farm size and whether or not the migrants actually lived with their parent or parents before moving. This relationship may be a function of the correlation between farm size and migration to Taichung city.

The relationship between farm size and migration can be determined by comparing the frequencies in column 1 of Table 6 for migrants and nonmigrants. A higher proportion of migrants than nonmigrants came from nonfarm families. But among those who came from farm families, a higher proportion of migrants than nonmigrants came from the larger farms. We have attempted to explain this surprising finding elsewhere by showing that men from larger farms were more likely than those from smaller farms to have obtained secondary school education or special vocational training.[23] Thus the men from the larger farms were in a better position to obtain urban employment than those from the smaller farms.

We must remember that we are considering only one form of migration here, and that the total movement off farms may show a different picture. In Table 7, we look at the data in another way. The picture is

TABLE 7. NUMBER OF SONS WHO ARE FARMERS, BY FARM SIZE

Farm size	N	None	One	Two or more	Total
		Migrants			
Larger farms	60	38.3%	33.3%	28.3%	100.0%
Smaller farms	59	57.6	27.1	15.3	100.0%
Total	119				
Average		47.9%	30.3%	21.8%	100.0%
		Nonmigrants			
Larger farms	76	19.7%	22.4%	57.9%	100.0%
Smaller farms	109	25.7	20.2	54.1	100.0%
Total	185				
Average		23.2%	21.1%	55.7%	100.0%

NOTE: Includes single and married migrants who lived on a farm before moving and nonmigrants who lived on a farm at the time of the interview. For migrants, the number of farmers is simply the number of the three oldest brothers who are farmers. For nonmigrants, the number of farmers is the number of the respondent's three oldest brothers who are farmers plus the respondent if he is a farmer. We have excluded from this table 4 migrants and 19 nonmigrants who had no brothers and a small number of cases where farm size or brother's occupation could not be ascertained.

somewhat incomplete because our information was limited to the primary occupation of the respondent and his three oldest brothers. Although 89 percent of the nonmigrants came from families in which there were two or more sons, only about half of these families had two or more sons who were farmers. In nearly a quarter of the families, no son was a farmer. Furthermore, there was only a small difference between the smaller farms and the larger farms in this regard.

The largest difference in Table 7 is that between migrants and nonmigrants. Less than a quarter of the migrants from farm families had two or more brothers still engaged in farming and about half had none. We do not know how many of the migrants or their brothers planned to return to farming when the father who was currently tilling the land died. It is probable that, instead, many of these farms will be sold or rented at that time.

In the past, the typical relationship between farm size and migration has been described as follows: when land is limited and there are several brothers, only one brother remains to till the land and care for the parents in their old age, while the others move out.[24] Although the other brothers may legally inherit part of the land, they derive little benefit from it because it is sufficient only to maintain the brother who remains on the land. On larger farms, the land is usually divided among two or more of the brothers. Although our data generally conform to this pattern, the relationships are much weaker than might be expected. Clearly, farm size is no longer so important a factor in determining family breakup or migration to the city as it may have once been. As economic development and industrialization proceed, urban opportunities may induce many men to move to the city who could make a living in the rural areas. On the other hand, the improvement of agriculture and the increase in opportunities for nonagricultural employment in or near rural areas may enable some men who might once have been forced to migrate to remain in the rural areas. The result of these changes is that a decision to move to one of the large cities is based more on a comparison of relative opportunities than on necessity. Men who decide to move are more likely to be those who possess the education and skills necessary for urban employment. Since education and vocational training involve costs, the opportunity to obtain education and special skills increases with farm size. Thus it seems logical that men from larger farms will be more likely to migrate than men from smaller farms.

Effect of Number of Siblings and Birth Order on Migration

We have already indicated that most men in our sample had several brothers and sisters. The mean number of siblings (including the respondent) was 6.0 for migrants and 5.4 for nonmigrants. Only 5 percent of the migrants and 11 percent of the nonmigrants were only sons. Fifty-one percent of the migrants and 41 percent of the nonmigrants had three or more brothers. Although the differences between nonmigrants and migrants are not large, it is clear that migrants had more brothers on the average than nonmigrants. Thus to some extent, migration can be interpreted as motivated by a "push factor" consisting of the pressure of family size on family resources.

A large number of siblings can also be seen as a "pull factor" in migration. Information concerning job opportunities tends to flow primarily by word of mouth. Three out of four of the migrants in our sample said they had learned of their first job in the city through friends or relatives. Thus as soon as one member of a family has moved to the city, he becomes a potential source of information on urban job opportunities for other members. Since men in large sibling sets are more likely to have a brother who has previously moved to the city, they are more likely to hear about urban opportunities than men in smaller sibling sets. Furthermore, some migration is motivated by the desire to live closer to family members who have already moved. Elsewhere I have shown that the presence of close relatives in the city, especially parents, is one of the strongest factors determining whether or not a man will move there.[25] Even when a migrant does not desire to live with these relatives, they can provide help in moving and a place to stay until he can establish his own residence in the city.

Although the "pull factors" related to sibling size are important, the "push factors" are probably more important.[26] Marion Levy has argued that the extended family can be a source of stress that motivates migration.[27] In the traditional extended family, the family head, usually the oldest male, makes the major decisions of the family and controls the family budget. All members of the family with outside income give over most of their earnings to the family head each payday, and this pooling of income can cause stress, particularly if different members make different contributions. Although stressful situations arising from this sharing can be resolved by setting up a separate household in the same village, it may often be easier to move to the city where the urban job opportunities can serve as an excuse for the division of the family.

Many migrants achieved greater control over the expenditure of the money they earned by moving. Whereas only 50 percent of the migrants had controlled their family finances before moving, 83 percent controlled them after moving. The fact that only 56 percent of the nonmigrants controlled their family finances suggests that this factor alone is of little importance in discriminating migrants from nonmigrants. However, the desire for financial autonomy may have acted to neutralize some of the benefits usually felt from having relatives at the place of origin.

G. W. Skinner has shown that filial attitudes vary with the number of siblings one has, one's place in the birth order, and the number of older sisters one has.[28] Filial attitudes are strongest among men in small sibling sets, among the earlier-born, and, if number of siblings and birth order are controlled, among those with older sisters. Assuming that migration to the city varies inversely with strength of filial attitudes, one would expect migration rates to increase with number of brothers and with later birth, and to decrease with number of sisters when the first two were held constant. In Table 8 we have calculated the ratio of migrants to nonmigrants by number of brothers and place in the birth order. These ratios, which are proportional to migration rates, have been calculated so that the average ratio is 1.00 for ease of comparison. The results are consistent with our earlier statement that migrants have more brothers on the average than nonmigrants. The migration ratio for only sons is particularly low, less than half the average.

Birth order appears to be important only for first sons, who are less likely to move than later sons. Although the overall relationship between migration and birth order indicates continuing increase in migration with lateness of birth order beyond the first son, this relationship does not hold up when the number of brothers is controlled. In fact, the migration ratio for families with four or more sons is higher for intermediate than for later-born sons. This may reflect the fact that the intermediate

TABLE 8. RATIO OF MIGRANTS TO NONMIGRANTS BY BIRTH ORDER
AND NUMBER OF BROTHERS

Number of sons (including respondent)	N		Birth order among sons			
	Migrants	Nonmigrants	1st	2d–3rd	4th or higher	Average
1	16	40	.46	—	—	.46
2–3	140	179	.85	.95	—	.90
4 or more	165	151	1.10	1.37	1.25	1.26
Total	321	370				
Average			.83	1.13	1.25	1.00

NOTE: Ratios are adjusted so that the ratio for the entire sample is 1.00. Ratios less than 1.00 mean there are fewer migrants than average, whereas those greater than 1.00 mean there are more migrants than average. The table includes both single and married respondents.

sons have more opportunity to acquire education and urban skills than the youngest sons.

We are unable to adequately test Skinner's third proposition, that the number of older sisters affects filial attitudes and hence migration, because we lack data on the age of sisters. However, we have calculated sex ratios of small and large sibling sets separately for migrants and nonmigrants (see Table 9). The sex ratios are inflated because they are based on a sample of men rather than households.* Nevertheless they are valid for relative comparisons of migrants and nonmigrants. Our results seem to support Skinner's proposition, in that migrants have slightly fewer sisters than nonmigrants. Thus sisters appear to play a role in holding families together.

In summary, we have shown that migration is greatest among men with many brothers, men intermediate in birth order, and men with few sisters. Of these relationships, the most important is the increase in migration with the number of brothers. Since economic opportunities both in the rural areas and in the city were essentially the same for men in large and small families, this finding is best interpreted as a response to the stress of large families, rather than as a response to differing economic situations.

Interaction Among Members of Divided Families

Although the move to Taichung city usually separated the migrant and his wife and children from their relatives, it did not necessarily mean an end to all extended-family relations. As Litwak has pointed out, the cohesion of an extended family can be maintained after division through

* Households with four brothers and one sister receive four times as much representation in our sample as households with one brother and four sisters.

TABLE 9. SEX RATIOS OF SIBLING SETS BY SIZE OF SET

Set size	Migrants	Nonmigrants
Small sibling sets (5 or fewer)	2.26	2.08
Large sibling sets (6 or more)	1.43	1.31
Total	1.61	1.54

NOTE: Sex ratio calculated as number of brothers (including the respondent) divided by number of sisters. Because we have a sample of men, we have overrepresented households with many brothers and few sisters and underrepresented those with many sisters and few brothers. This causes the sex ratios to be considerably greater than unity.

frequent visitation and the exchange of aid.[29] Taichung is reasonably accessible to most of the villages in our sample area. All but two of the 46 villages in the nonmigrant sample either had regular bus or train service or were adjacent to villages that had such service. Thus it was reasonably easy for men who moved to Taichung from this area to keep up relations with relatives who had stayed behind.

Migrants who were not living with or adjacent to their parents after moving generally returned to visit them at least once a month. As Table 10 shows, only 20 percent saw their parents less often. In comparison with nonmigrants who were not living with or adjacent to their parents, migrants were almost as likely to see their parents at least once a month. However, migrants were far less likely to see their parents at weekly or more frequent intervals. Thus migration to the cities resulted in a definitely reduced frequency, but did not eliminate interaction with the husband's parents. A similar pattern was found for interaction with brothers. Nonmigrants were able to have much more frequent interaction with their brothers because they generally lived closer to them than the migrants to their brothers.

Since married couples generally visit the wife's parents less often than the husband's parents, migration resulted in less change in the interaction with the wife's parents. Thus the relative frequency of interaction with the wife's parents was much higher for migrants than for nonmigrants. This indicates that migration may lead to an increase in the relative importance of the relationship with the wife's parents. This view is supported by the responses to the question whether or not respondents wished to live closer to the wife's parents. Sixty-one percent of the migrants, but only 40 percent of the nonmigrants, replied yes.

Many migrants continued some exchange of economic assistance with relatives, usually parents, who remained behind. Approximately 30 percent of the migrants sent money back to their relatives and about 10 percent received money, food, or fuel from them.

TABLE 10. FREQUENCY OF INTERACTION WITH RELATIVES IN
SEPARATE HOUSEHOLDS

Frequency of interaction	Husband's parents	Closest brother[a]	Wife's parents[b]
	Migrants		
Several times a week	15.7%	18.9%	13.2%
Once a week	15.2	16.4	8.9
Once or twice a month	48.8	37.4	30.6
Less often	20.4	27.3	47.3
Total	100.0%	100.0%	100.0%
N	211	238	235
	Nonmigrants		
Several times a week	45.7%	37.4%	18.7%
Once a week	10.2	11.2	5.9
Once or twice a month	27.1	23.2	37.8
Less often	17.0	28.1	37.5
Total	100.0%	100.0%	100.0%
N	59	107	256

NOTE: The table includes all married men who have the appropriate relative(s) but are not living with them or in an adjacent household. For migrants the reference point is the time of interview (after the move).

[a] "Closest brother" refers to the brother living physically closest, regardless of whether or not he was married.

[b] Frequency of interaction with wife's parents includes visits made by either the respondent or his wife.

Finally, although migration to the city resulted in a reduced frequency of interaction with the husband's relatives, it did not radically affect attendance at large family gatherings. Attendance at weddings, funerals, New Year's celebration, and religious festivals was almost as frequent among migrants as nonmigrants (see Table 11).

Summary

We have discussed the relationship between the extended family and rural-to-urban migration in a Chinese society undergoing rapid urbanization and industrialization. We have found that the traditional ideal family in which all married brothers continue to live together with their parents in one large household was still widely valued in rural Taiwan. This was true both for men who remained in the rural and semirural areas and those who moved to the city. However, men who moved to the city placed slightly less value on the traditional extended family and were more likely than nonmigrants to view the ideal brother-brother relationship as weaker than the husband-wife relationship.

Although previous writers have emphasized the limitations imposed

TABLE 11. LARGE FAMILY GATHERINGS ATTENDED DURING THE PAST YEAR

Number attended	Migrants	Nonmigrants
None	26.8%	21.6%
1–3	33.8	39.8
4–6	22.6	17.7
7–12	11.3	11.9
13 or more	5.5	9.1
Total	100.0%	100.0%
N	310	362

NOTE: Table excludes a small number of NA's. The number of family gatherings attended includes those attended by either spouse.

by mortality on people's opportunity to live in extended families, most of our sample of men aged 23–42 had the opportunity to live with their parents and married brothers. In particular, there were very few men who did not have at least one brother. It may well be that during the last twenty years in Taiwan the opportunity for men to live in extended families has been greater than ever before. Mortality rates fell without a corresponding drop in fertility rates during the period when these men were born (1925–44).

Most men in the region we studied began their married life in extended families and gradually broke away so that by the time they had reached the age of 40 or so, typically only one brother remained with the parents. Although both migrants and nonmigrants in our sample tended to begin married life in extended families, the migrants tended to break away sooner than the nonmigrants. When the migrants' households prior to moving were compared to the nonmigrants' households at interview, fewer extended families were found among the former.

The move to the city usually resulted in a breakup of the extended family if a previous breakup had not already occurred. Most men moved with their wives and children, but few moved with their parents or other relatives.

For most migrants, the move to the city and the resulting breakup of the extended family was more a response to the greater economic opportunities in the city than the result of absolute economic necessity. Most men were employed before moving and could have found other non-farm employment within a short distance had they desired to stay with their relatives. Migrants came disproportionately from larger farms and from nonfarm households rather than from the smaller farms where necessity was presumably the greatest. This reversal in the expected relation between migration and farm size may be due to the fact that men from larger farms had more education and vocational training than those from smaller farms and were thus better equipped for urban employment.

The probability of moving to the city tended to increase with the number of brothers a man had. This relationship was interpreted as a response to stress in large families and not as a response to differing economic conditions, since there was little relationship between number of brothers and economic factors affecting migration. When family size was controlled, migration was less frequent among first sons than among later-born sons and less frequent when there were many sisters than when there were few sisters.

Finally, although migration to the city generally resulted in the further breakup of extended families, extended-family ties were maintained through frequent visits and often through the exchange of money and other forms of aid. Migrants generally returned for funerals, weddings, New Year's celebration, and other large family gatherings.

The Integration of Village Migrants in Taipei

BERNARD GALLIN & RITA S. GALLIN

Taiwan's population rose from some 3 million in 1920 to over 14 million in 1970. During the same half-century, the land under cultivation has increased by only one-fifth. (The 749,000 *chia** of 1920 had increased to only 896,000 *chia* in 1966.)[1] Food production has kept pace with population growth only through technological advance. In any case, the pressure of these growing numbers of people on the relatively stable land base has become increasingly severe and, despite the Land Reform of 1949–53, rural Taiwan suffers from underemployment, landlessness, and family farms far too small to support all family members.

For many of the people faced with these problems, or for those whose standard of living has not kept pace with their rising expectations, the solution has been to move to the larger cities of the island to seek employment. In the late 1940's, these migrants provided services for the large influx of mainlanders,† and, in the years that followed, they worked in the businesses, factories, and service jobs that burgeoned during the early stages of Taiwan's industrialization. (Between the early 1950's and 1966, industrial productivity more than quadrupled, and between 1960 and 1966, it more than doubled.)[2]

Rural-to-urban migration in Taiwan, however, is hardly a new phenomenon, nor is it a consequence only of rural economic pressures. The proportion of Taiwanese living in cities rose from 10.5 percent in 1920 to

---

* One *chia* equals 2.39 acres.
† These mainlanders included not only military personnel, but also civilians in government, education, and business. Many mainlanders have dispersed to other areas of the island, including small urban centers and the suburbs, to take up government positions or business or other employment; they frequently move around the island, and this movement is reflected in the general internal migration statistics in Taiwan.

15.2 percent in 1950 to 24.4 percent in 1966.[3] Natural increase accounts for part of this growth, but migration has played the major role, for fertility rates are lower in the cities than in the countryside.[4] As a result, fully one-third of the residents of the island's two largest cities as of 1956 were Taiwanese in-migrants; 33.6 and 34.9 percent of the residents of Taipei and Kaohsiung, respectively, had been registered originally in some other locality in Taiwan.[5]

The subject of this chapter is a subset of these rural-to-urban migrants. First we briefly examine the differences between migrants whose destination is a nearby city and those headed for more distant urban centers and distinguish these out-migrants from nonmigrants in their native villages. We deal specifically with natives of four primarily agricultural villages—Hsin-hsing, Ta-yu, Yung-p'ing and P'u-yen*—all situated in P'u-yen *hsiang*, a rural township in Chang-hua county, approximately 130 miles from Taipei in the west-central coastal plain of Taiwan (see Map 1). Data for this discussion have been drawn from the official household record books (*hu-k'ou*) maintained in the P'u-yen township public office.

The body of the paper treats long-distance migrants to Taipei, concentrating on Hsin-hsing villagers with whom we have worked in three field studies, in the village, in the more extended local territorial system to which the village belongs, and in the city.† Our purpose is to show

---

* Data drawn from family records in the public office include the total population of the four settlements, numbers of migrants to each place, and age and educational background at the time of migration. Official family records are known to be inaccurate in certain respects; for instance, a certain portion of migrants register late or not at all. However, since there is no reason to assume a biased distribution of these errors, a comparative analysis on the basis of these statistics is justified.

† Data on Hsin-hsing villagers were collected during three periods of fieldwork in Taiwan. The first, supported by a Ford Foundation Foreign Area Training Fellowship, was an ethnographic study of the village conducted in 1957–58. The second, conducted in 1965–66, consisted of a two-month restudy of the village followed by eight months of research in Taipei on Hsin-hsing migrants. These efforts were supported by a Fulbright-Hays research grant and by a research grant from the Asian Studies Center at Michigan State University. The third, occupying ten months in 1969–70, continued in more intensive fashion the earlier study of Hsin-hsing migrants in Taipei, and was aided by a grant from the Midwest Universities Consortium for International Activities (MUCIA).

We are grateful to Bernard's graduate assistants, Mr. Chen Chung-min, who contributed to the analysis of the raw field data, and Mr. Huang Shu-min, who provided not a little insight along with his expert assistance. We are also indebted to the Institute of Ethnology, Academia Sinica, Taiwan, and especially Professor Li Yih-yuan, for valuable cooperation and assistance and for sponsoring Bernard as a Visiting Fellow during both 1965–66 and 1969–70.

The rural and urban studies concern basically the same population and can therefore be examined comparatively in terms of these populations' structural and behavioral differences as they pertain to the questions of migration and integration into city life.

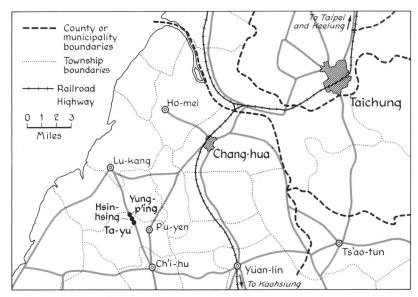

MAP 1. P'U-YEN TOWNSHIP (Chang-hua county) in relation to transport routes and nearby urban centers. The administrative units at the upper right are T'ai-chung county and Taichung city; the unit at the lower right is Nan-t'ou county.

how these migrants relate economically and sociopolitically to the urban situation and how their networks of relationships, especially those based on kinship, village, and occupational ties, affect their integration into Taipei life.

Out-Migration from Hsin-hsing and Three Other Villages

The four villages in question were all originally settled in the late eighteenth century by Hokkien immigrants from the coastal region of southern Fukien. Hsin-hsing, with a resident population in 1970 of 580, is the smallest and also the poorest of the four villages. The registered population of Ta-yu, Yung-p'ing, and P'u-yen, numbering 1,742, 1,325, and 1,378 respectively as of 1970, were on the average somewhat more prosperous and better educated than those of Hsin-hsing. Only P'u-yen has any local industry; as the seat of the township, it also houses the public office, farmers' association, and health station.

Residents have been emigrating from all four villages for more than twenty years, as they have from other villages in the general area. In Hsin-hsing, this emigration has resulted in large part from the growing

TABLE 1. OUT-MIGRATION IN FOUR TAIWANESE VILLAGES, 1945–70

Destination or category of migrants	Village of origin							
	Hsin-hsing		Yung-p'ing		Ta-yu		P'u-yen	
	Number	Percent	Number	Percent	Number	Percent	Number	Percent
Taipei	266	28.1%	252	14.9%	196	8.9%	167	9.0%
Keelung	—	—	—	—	53	2.4	—	—
Kaohsiung (including Tainan)	54	5.7	8	0.5	51	2.3	78	4.2
Total long-distance stream (Taipei, Keelung, Kaohsiung)	320	33.8%	260	15.4%	300	13.6%	245	13.3%
Taichung and Chang-hua	—	—	22	1.3	28	1.3	86	4.6
Nearby market towns	47	5.0	80	4.7	135	6.1	151	8.1
Total short-distance stream (Taichung, Chang-hua, nearby towns)	47	5.0%	102	6.0%	163	7.4%	237	12.7%
Total out-migrants, both streams	367	38.8%	362	21.5%	463	21.0%	482	25.9%
Total registered population, 1970	580	61.2	1,325	78.5	1,742	79.0	1,378	74.1
Total living population originally registered in the village	947	100.0%	1,687	100.0%	2,205	100.0%	1,860	100.0%

SOURCE: Here and for all the tables in this chapter unless otherwise noted, the source is the household record book (*hu-k'ou*), 1970, in the public office of P'u-yen township.

intensity of population pressure on the land. This problem has been less severe in the other three villages, and in consequence emigration began somewhat later there and has progressed at a slower rate than in Hsin-hsing. The proportion of Hsin-hsing villagers who have emigrated since the mid-1940's is 38.8 percent of the combined total of the number of people currently registered as village residents and the number recorded as having moved. The comparable statistic for the other three villages combined is 22.7 percent—still a sizable proportion (see Table 1).

Despite these different migration rates, emigration from all four villages has followed similar patterns; certain types of people have migrated to certain types of localities. It is useful to distinguish two streams of migrants. One consists of villagers who have moved short distances to local towns like Lu-kang, Ch'i-hu, and Yüan-lin, or the nearby cities of Chang-hua and Taichung (see Map 1). The second stream consists of villagers who have traveled to larger, more distant cities, in particular the industrial centers of Taipei (including such de facto suburbs as San-chung municipality and Pan-ch'iao township), Keelung, and Kaohsiung. The second stream is by far the larger of the two. About 87 percent of the migrants from Hsin-hsing, 72 percent of those from Ta-yu, 65 percent of those from Yung-p'ing, and 51 percent of those from P'u-yen traveled to the large, more distant cities (see Table 1 for the absolute figures).

Short-Distance Migration

The two streams differ in several respects. Those who migrate only a short distance tend to come from families of comparatively high socio-economic status. Generally, they have ample landholdings, surplus capital, or both, and family members are not tied to the land. A frequent purpose of local migration is to diversify their economic base.

Males who migrate short distances are usually married at the time of migration (or at least by the time the move is registered at the local public office). On the whole, they are also better educated than migrants who move longer distances. Table 2 shows a distinct preference on the part of villagers with a junior- or senior-high-school education for local as opposed to long-distance migration.

For the most part, short-distance migrants engage in some kind of small business or small-scale manufacturing, work as technicians or craftsmen, or are employed as professionals or civil servants. Very few become laborers or unskilled workers. In large part, then, they are upwardly mobile, and they view the urban places nearby as more advantageous than the distant urban centers. In the nearby places, they have relationships with people who can help them achieve their social and

TABLE 2. EDUCATIONAL LEVEL OF MALE EMIGRANTS AND NONMIGRANTS
AGED 15–59 FOR FOUR TAIWANESE VILLAGES, 1945–70

Village of origin and migratory category	Educational attainment					
	Illiterate	Literate (no formal schooling)	Primary schooling	Junior high	Senior high	Total
Hsin-hsing:						
Long-distance migrants	18.1%	3.2%	64.9%	7.4%	6.4%	100.0%
Short-distance migrants	14.3	—	57.1	14.3	14.3	100.0
Nonmigrants	15.3	8.3	56.3	10.4	9.7	100.0
Yung-p'ing:						
Long-distance migrants	26.1	—	62.5	5.7	5.7	100.0
Short-distance migrants	15.4	7.7	34.6	11.5	30.8	100.0
Nonmigrants	16.1	5.4	59.7	12.4	6.5	100.0
Ta-yu:						
Long-distance migrants	23.4	2.1	66.0	5.3	3.2	100.0
Short-distance migrants	23.1	5.1	56.4	5.1	10.3	100.0
Nonmigrants	17.5	3.0	63.3	9.5	6.7	100.0
P'u-yen:						
Long-distance migrants	19.8	1.2	62.8	8.1	8.1	100.0
Short-distance migrants	8.5	5.1	54.2	13.6	18.6	100.0
Nonmigrants	17.1	3.1	55.8	18.1	5.9	100.0

NOTE: By "short-distance" is meant migration to localities in Chang-hua county, T'ai-chung county, and Taichung municipality. "Long-distance" refers to migration to all other localities in Taiwan. In practice, destinations are limited to Kaohsiung and Tainan municipalities to the south and to greater Taipei, including Keelung and San-chung municipalities to the north. The figures for nonmigrants refer only to people registered *and* resident in the villages during 1970.

economic goals. In addition, those migrants who attempt some new business generally find the competition less intense in local towns and in the slower-growing nearby cities than in Taipei and Kaohsiung and therefore better suited to their sometimes limited business experience. At the same time, since some of these local migrants continue to maintain significant landholdings in their home village, moving to such nearby areas makes returning home relatively easy when they must care for their land or attend to village affairs.*

Long-Distance Migration

That the great majority of migrants from these four villages go to large cities rather than to less urbanized townships is exceptional for Taiwan as a whole. In 1967, proportionately more migrants from rural townships such as P'u-yen moved to urban townships than to large cities

---

* The statistical basis for this statement and several others stemming from the 1969–70 research cannot be offered here because the analysis is not yet complete. These statements, then, are based on information collected from local and migrant informants.

(see Table 3).[6] It seems clear that the largest cities are most attractive to migrants with little capital and few skills, for only there can they find relatively high-paying employment. Thus, among the four villages in question, the big-city long-distance stream predominates most strongly (87 percent) in Hsin-hsing, the poorest, and least strongly (51 percent) in P'u-yen, the richest (see Table 1).

Until very recently, P'u-yen township had no local industries and few job opportunities. Even today, such industries as do exist pay far lower wages than their counterparts in Taipei, Keelung, and Kaohsiung. In general, local towns and cities have had relatively little to offer villagers with limited capital, poor education, undeveloped skills, and networks of relationships with people of similar limited backgrounds. In these circumstances, and given the fine transportation system in Taiwan, it is not surprising that a high proportion of poorer emigrants from the four villages head for the largest cities. The discussion that follows focuses on the 84 Hsin-hsing males who emigrated to Taipei, since for this subset available information is more detailed.

Hsin-hsing migrants started moving to Taipei in 1945, and the flow continues even today. The earliest period, 1945–50, saw the heaviest migration, namely 37 (44 percent) of the 84 males. These earliest migrants were older and more often married at the time they moved than were

TABLE 3. DIRECTION OF MIGRATION IN TAIWAN, 1967

Origin and destination	Estimated gross migration (in thousands)
Large cities to	
Large cities	42.3
Urban townships and small cities	75.5
Rural townships	46.8
Total	164.6
Urban townships and small cities to	
Large cities	107.9
Urban townships	103.7
Rural townships	92.9
Total	304.5
Rural townships to	
Large cities	75.9
Urban townships and small cities	105.4
Rural townships	72.9
Total	254.2
Overall total	723.3

SOURCE: Alden Speare, Jr., "The Determinants of Rural-to-Urban Migration in Taiwan," Unpub. Ph.D. diss. (University of Michigan, 1969), p. 45, Table 3.1.
NOTE: Figures here include both mainlanders and Taiwanese.

TABLE 4. MARITAL STATUS AT THE TIME OF MIGRATION FOR MALE MIGRANTS
FROM HSIN-HSING TO TAIPEI, 1945–70

Marital status	Years of migration			
	1945–50	1951–60	1961–69	Total
Married persons:				
Number	20	7	8	35
Percent	54.1%	26.9%	38.1%	41.7%
Single persons:				
Number	17	19	13	49
Percent	45.9%	73.1%	61.9%	58.3%
Total number	37	26	21	84
Persons under 17 at the time of migration:				
Number	11	15	9	35
Percent	29.7%	57.7%	42.9%	41.7%

SOURCE: As in other tables, plus interviews.

TABLE 5. LANDHOLDING IN HSIN-HSING OF MALE MIGRANTS TO TAIPEI
AT THE TIME OF MIGRATION, 1941–69

Landholdings	Years of migration			
	1945–50	1951–60	1961–69	Total
Total number of migrants	37	26	21	84
Migrants without land:				
Number	10	9	4	23
Percent of all migrants	27.0%	34.6%	19.0%	27.4%
Migrants with land:				
Number	27	17	17	61
Percent of all migrants	73.0%	65.4%	81.0%	72.6%
Landholdings (chia):				
Total owned land	7.27	8.32	5.89	21.48
Average owned land	0.27	0.49	0.35	0.35
Total tenanted land	3.91	2.46	3.22	9.59
Average tenanted land	0.14	0.14	0.19	0.16
Average total holding	0.41	0.63	0.54	0.51

SOURCE: Interviews and land records of the Land Bureau of Chang-hua county.
NOTE: 1 chia = 2.39 acres.

those who followed in later decades. During the 1950's and 1960's, the
flow to Taipei tapered off slightly, and migrants were more often single
and young (see Table 4).

The families of Hsin-hsing migrants own less land on the average than
do villagers in Taiwan as a whole and significantly less than the average
Hsin-hsing resident whose members have not migrated. Table 5 shows
a significant difference between the 1945–50 cohort and the 1951–60
cohort in the average size of landholding. It should be noted, however,

TABLE 6. OCCUPATIONS OF MALE MIGRANTS FROM HSIN-HSING UPON
ARRIVAL IN TAIPEI, 1945–70

Occupations	Related to activities in the Taipei Central Market	Unrelated to the Taipei Central Market	Total
Cart driver (laborer)	30	4	34
Pedicab driver	0	7	7
Manual worker	1	0	1
Shop clerk	13	2	15
Factory worker	0	3	3
Vegetable gardener	2	0	2
Apprentice	0	4	4
Servant	0	2	2
Sanitation worker	0	1	1
Carpenter	0	4	4
Technician	0	1	1
Peddler	3	3	6
Shopkeeper (merchant)	4	0	4
Total	53	31	84
Percent	63.1%	36.9%	100%

SOURCE: Field interviews.
NOTE: The manual worker was an unskilled laborer working for a construction company. The
terms cart driver/laborer are used interchangeably throughout the text.

that many migrants, particularly the young single men who are more
prominent in the second cohort, come from lineal families whose holdings have not yet been divided between the migrant and his brother(s).

Hsin-hsing migrants to Taipei have a generally poor educational background. Their educational level is lower than that of Hsin-hsing villagers
who do not migrate or who migrate to nearby towns and cities (see
Table 2). In keeping with their low level of educational attainment, the
majority worked as laborers on their arrival in Taipei (see Table 6).
Over time, a few became shopkeepers. Others became clerks in the
Central Market, but not a few of these quit to become laborers because
of the higher pay. In any case, the majority of the men from Hsin-hsing,
and from the other three villages as well, became laborers when they
arrived in Taipei, and a majority are laborers even today.

Most long-distance migrants perceive their move as one of economic
necessity, although in a strict sense this was by no means the case. Some
migrants are from families whose landholdings were adequate for their
needs. Others are from large families that wanted to diversify their economic resources or supplement their income. Perhaps, too, a certain
amount of venturesomeness played a part in the decision to move; the
city pulls people to it with its promise of excitement and high-paying
jobs.

Nonmigrants

Villagers who have remained in Hsin-hsing have had to adapt to the land problems that led others to migrate. Some, former landlords or rich peasants who have managed to accumulate capital, have established small local stores in the village and sell pesticides, fertilizer, or groceries. One family has established a rice mill and another a small factory within the village where metal springs are fabricated on a contract basis for a machinery manufacturer. (Both are strictly family enterprises, however, providing no work opportunities for other villagers.) Several of the better-educated pre-reform landlords have taken local civil-service positions. All of these men supplement their income from the land by diversifying their economic interests at home.

Village families without adequate landholdings, the majority in Hsin-hsing, have turned to other sources of income in order to remain in the village. Some have sent members to the city to supplement the living they make from their small landholdings. Members of other families take seasonal jobs as farm laborers, work in local industries, or peddle goods or services in the local area.

Many residents now farm their land more intensively with short-term cash crops. Improvements in transportation over the last ten years have made vegetable cultivation for city markets feasible in the Hsin-hsing area. Labor-intensive truck farming is profitable, however, only when the family's labor pool is large enough to obviate cash payments for field labor. In addition, the growing of vegetables for market is a precarious enterprise; weather, plant disease, crop failure, and market glut all pose threats to the farmer. Thus, some village families have been unwilling to run the risk of converting to vegetable farming. Some who did run the risk succumbed, whereas others lack the labor needed to truck-farm. Land-deficient households in these situations have in many cases emigrated to the cities as a last resort.

Hsin-hsing Village Background

Over the last twenty-five years, Hsin-hsing village[7] has been losing population steadily, but this loss is only partially reflected in the records of the township public office, where registrations show a relatively stable number of people. The registered population of the village was 609 people in 99 households (*hu*) in 1958, and 612 people in 112 households in 1966. In fact, although 612 people were registered in Hsin-hsing, only 506 actually lived there. The rest were living in the localities to which they had migrated (see Table 7).*

---

* In this section and throughout the remainder of the chapter we use figures collected in 1965–66. The more recent figures, introduced in the earlier portions of this

TABLE 7. PLACE OF RESIDENCE AND REGISTRATION OF EMIGRANTS AND
NONMIGRANTS FOR HSIN-HSING VILLAGE, 1956–66

Place of registration	Place of residence			Total registered population
	Hsin-hsing	Taipei	Elsewhere	
Hsin-hsing:				
Male	236	46	25	—
Female	270	23	12	—
Total	506	69	37	612
Taipei:				
Male	—	96	—	—
Female	—	96	—	—
Total	—	192	—	192
Total resident population	506	261	37	—

Within the village, families are grouped in the first instance by patrilineal kinship into lineages (*tsu*) or incipient lineages consisting of a few
recently divided family units. The families within a lineage share a demonstrated common ancestor in the village itself. Virilocal marriage per-
petuates localization by surname. Although twelve surnames are represented in the village, four—Huang, Shih, K'ang, and Shen—account for
some 80 percent of the population. There are more kin groups than surnames, however, since in certain cases resident families of the same surname are descended from two or more unrelated earlier settlers. Regardless of size, these *tsu* groups live in separate compounds or in house
clusters within the village.

The *tsu* functions as a ceremonial group, drawing its members together
for ancestor worship and life-crisis rituals. The *tsu* also has political importance. The more powerful *tsu* within the village form coalitions in an
attempt to coordinate and control village affairs. Influential members
mediate in conflicts within and between the lineages.[8] In addition, *tsu*
coalitions control the internal politics of the village, and elected offices
tend to be held by members of the larger *tsu*. That large *tsu* are considered influential can be seen from the fact that unrelated families who
happen to bear the same surname as an influential *tsu* try to identify
themselves with the group in order to gain some of the sociopolitical
benefits and security that accrue to its members.

Unrelated families and individual families within the *tsu* do not by
themselves wield power within the village. But the family unit still stands

---

paper, have not yet been analyzed sufficiently to yield the kinds of data presented
here. The differences between the 1965–66 and more recent figures, however, are
minor; there are overall increases in the migrant population, but the general proportions of the various categories have changed relatively little.

as a source of security and is important in structuring relationships. Nuclear families predominate, there being 65 of this simple type as against 29 stem and 5 joint families in the village.

A nuclear family is converted to a stem family when a daughter-in-law is brought in for a son, and a stem family becomes joint as other sons marry. But inevitably the family breaks up into conjugal units, each starting anew as a nuclear family. In the wake of family division, however, mutual aid, cooperation in daily tasks, and ritual interaction among the component units persist for at least a generation.

Kinship is by no means the only basis for social relations within Hsin-hsing and the more extensive local system to which it belongs. A variety of voluntary associations draw unrelated families together and provide opportunities to develop friendships and relationships that cross kinship and even class lines.* Moreover, recent developments have steadily diminished the significance of kinship in Hsin-hsing. The land-reform program of 1949–53 expropriated some of the corporate and private land-holdings of the lineages and the few local landlords; as a result, the position of the traditional landlord leaders within kin groups and in village politics was weakened. The recent Land Consolidation Program, which began in the early 1960's, eliminated a former basis for agricultural cooperation among kinsmen. This program redistributed the farmers' fragmented landholdings and provided them with blocks of land, whose new locations draw them into different cooperative relationships that cross kin and village lines. The development of township-wide political factions is diminishing the importance of traditional bonds. And, finally, the more frequent intercession of government agencies and organizations in times of conflict has tended to undermine the importance of the *tsu* group in mediation.[9]

Hsin-hsing Migrants in Taipei

The first migrants from Hsin-hsing found work in Taipei as laborers in the Central Market area of Ch'eng-chung district (see Figure 2). Within a few years of their arrival, several other Hsin-hsing men had joined them, attracted by their offers of help in obtaining jobs and housing. Over the years, the great majority of migrants to Taipei have taken jobs similar to those of the first migrants and settled in living quarters close to each other with the help of fellow villagers and kinsmen already in

* Hsin-hsing villagers participate in the Farmers' Association, public and private irrigation associations, cooperative agricultural labor teams, and such intervillage associations as the committee, drawing on twelve villages, that organizes the annual procession to honor the goddess Ma Tsu.

TABLE 8. MIGRANT UNITS: FAMILIES AND PERSONS RESIDING APART FROM THEIR FAMILIES IN TAIPEI AND HSIN-HSING, 1965–66

Category	Joint	Stem	Nuclear	Individual	Total
Hsin-hsing migrant units in Taipei	2	5	29	41	77
Migrant units that belong to *chia* with members residing in Hsin-hsing	0	0	5	41	—
Persons in the 77 Hsin-hsing migrant units in Taipei:					
Male	8	20	83	31	142
Female	8	15	86	10	119
Hsin-hsing residents in the *chia* to which migrant units belong:					
Male	0	0	13	78	91
Female	0	0	11	83	94
Total membership of *chia* with members residing in Taipei:					
Male	8	20	96	109	233
Female	8	15	97	93	213

SOURCE: Field interviews.

the city. As a result of this chain migration to Taipei, and greater opportunities there, none of the Hsin-hsing migrants for the period 1945–70 went to the closer cities of Taichung and Chang-hua (see Table 1).

By 1965–66, 261 natives of Hsin-hsing resided in Taipei (see Table 7). Of this total 220 fell into 36 family units (2 joint, 5 stem, and 29 nuclear); the remaining 41 Hsin-hsing migrants worked in Taipei while their families lived in Hsin-hsing. Five of these 36 family units considered to be based in Taipei* have an additional 24 members, mostly children or parents, still residing in Hsin-hsing where they maintain the families' landholdings† (see Table 8).

* The term "Taipei-based family unit" refers to a co-resident group of related persons that includes at least one conjugal couple and that resides in Taipei. Even though other members of the *chia* or economic family, such as children or an old parent, may reside in the village, the family is still considered to be based in Taipei. Similarly, a "village-based family unit" refers to a co-resident group in Hsin-hsing that includes at least one conjugal couple, even though certain members of that *chia* are migrant residents of Taipei. Thus, a co-resident group in Taipei of related persons not including a conjugal couple are counted separately as "individual persons."

† In addition, while most members of these 36 family units are officially *registered* in Taipei, 13 of them still have 50 of their members registered in Hsin-hsing. Since the land reform of 1949–53, many village migrants incorrectly believe that they could be considered absentee landlords and so lose their land unless they maintain proof of residence in the village by continuing their registration there. Similarly, many tenant-farmer migrants maintain registration in the village for fear that landlords might reclaim their land. However, even families that have transferred their residence registration to the city continue to maintain their registration in the village

TABLE 9. MIGRANT UNITS IN TAIPEI WITH AND WITHOUT LANDHOLDINGS
IN HSIN-HSING, 1950 AND 1965

Migrant unit	Family type			
	Joint	Stem	Nuclear	Individual
1950				
Without land:				
Percent	0%	50%	21%	14%
Units	0	2	4	2
With land:				
Percent	100%	50%	79%	86%
Units	2	2	15	12
Total	2	4	19	14
1965				
Without land:				
Percent	0%	40%	34%	16%
Units	0	2	10	7
With land:				
Percent	100%	60%	66%	84%
Units	2	3	19	34
Total	2	5	29	41

SOURCE: Interviews and land records of the Land Bureau of Chang-hua county.

Approximately three-quarters of Hsin-hsing migrants to Taipei between 1945 and 1969 operated land in the village at the time of their initial move, and in 1966 the same proportion still owned or rented some land in the village (see Tables 5 and 9). The first migrants, those who moved during 1945–50, operated less village land at the time of their departure than subsequent migrants—an indication, as the migrants themselves suggest, that the economic situation of the earliest migrants was extremely serious (see Table 5). Nevertheless, later migrants still feel that their landholdings were inadequate to meet family needs.

The move to Taipei is usually made piecemeal. In the typical case the male family head or a grown son goes first to Taipei. The men move initially without their wives or families and send part of their earnings back to their families in the village. At the outset, they return often to the village, to plant and harvest crops or to observe festivals or rituals. However, as time goes on, the family normally hires part-time farm labor to care for more and more of the agricultural activities, so that many men gradually make fewer trips to the village and limit their visits to the most important rituals such as deaths and weddings and some of the

family books in the township public office. Family information recorded by the migrant in his family record book in Taipei is forwarded and recorded in the Hsin-hsing family record book kept at the township public office.

major festivals—the village god's birthday, the Ma Tsu procession, and the New Year.

Over 85 percent of the villagers who have migrated to Taipei have remained.* Single men usually return to the village to marry girls selected either by their parents with their agreement or, more rarely, by themselves in Taipei. In the latter "love-matches," the girls almost always have been migrants from the south, and the couple has asked a fellow villager or a matrilateral or affinal relative to serve as marriage broker. In either case, after the marriage, the groom immediately returns to his job and, usually within a few weeks or months, his wife joins him in the city.

After a period of adjustment to some kind of regular work, married migrants usually bring their families to live with them. In the typical case, the wife came to Taipei six or seven years after her husband, accompanied in many cases by other members of the family. Sometimes the wife decides to move to the city after becoming suspicious of her husband's activities there—suspicions touched off by irregular remittances or by tales carried back to the village by other migrants. In such cases, the wife and younger children go to Taipei, to "cut down on family expenses" by cooking and making a home for the man.

The move soon becomes established as relatively permanent for many of the villagers whose families have joined them in the city, particularly for those who have left the village because they were dissatisfied with their economic condition there or with village life and openly preferred to live in the city. Nonetheless, the majority of the migrants retain their land in the village, oftentimes more for security than as an economic investment, since they usually derive little or no income from their land. Nineteen of the 29 Taipei-based nuclear families have arranged for a kinsman (brother or parent) to tend their land in the village. These kinsmen retain most if not all of the proceeds from the land in return for their work.† It is not unlikely that in holding onto their farmland many families wish to be prepared for any contingency, such as the loss of jobs or the coming of another war. None of the heads of these families was prepared to say that farmland had been retained because they themselves intended to return to live and work in the village some day. In fact, three

---

* In all only 45 of the several hundred persons who migrated from Hsin-hsing to Taipei for work have returned permanently to the village. Included among these 45 are many who went to Taipei as seasonal workers and several others who simply did not like life in Taipei and so returned to the village.

† When one of several brothers migrates from the village, family division is often postponed indefinitely. The migrant's potential share is tilled by his brothers, who retain the profits. A migrant in this situation tends to feel that he can do without the meager income from his land so long as he holds his city job.

of these families have sold a portion of their land: one to build a house in Taipei, another to buy a delivery-cart engine, and the third to pay for the marriage of a son.

Whether or not farmland is retained, none of the Taipei-based families have sold their Hsin-hsing living quarters, even when all of their members live in Taipei and seldom return to the village. These rooms are simply sealed, used for storage rooms by the migrants or by relatives in the village, or lent, normally without charge, to village relatives. A house, and land if it is considered ancestral (i.e., has been inherited, rather than purchased on one's own or through the land reform), seems to be retained largely for symbolic reasons: selling it would signify the final breaking of ties. In addition to the symbolic implications for those involved, it could bring some criticism from others.

Eventually, most of the Taipei-based migrant families (including most of those who retain their village land) become rather settled in their work and return to the village only on special occasions such as the New Year or large village festivals. Migrants usually do not return home to observe ancestor worship nor do they worship in Taipei. The frequency of visits to Hsin-hsing seems to be based primarily on the presence or absence of family connections or landholdings in the village. Home visits are necessarily limited by the expense—the costs of the trip itself and the attendant loss of income. In addition, the work of many migrants, unlike their former agricultural occupation, does not permit them to come and go as they please.

For the majority of the migrants who arrived prior to 1960, this work is in the service-type jobs that were readily available in the 1950's (see Tables 6 and 10). Those who came in the 1960's, when village families had grown used to the idea of sending their young, especially girls, to work in Taipei, more commonly hold factory jobs; and this is particularly true of the females. The number of factory jobs increased substantially in the early 1960's and, at the same time, the availability of more lucrative service-type jobs decreased. Younger people, therefore, often could find jobs more easily than their elders, whose family responsibilities necessitated wages higher than those that factories or shops generally pay to unskilled workers.

In 1966, about 65 percent of the male migrants held jobs in the vegetable section of the Taipei Central Market or jobs connected in some way with the vegetable market (see Table 10). Only four of the 38 cart drivers were working in jobs not connected with the vegetable market, and two of these four men worked for a lumber yard directly across the street from it. Thirty-four delivered vegetables (unloaded from large

TABLE 10. OCCUPATIONS OF MIGRANTS FROM HSIN-HSING
IN TAIPEI, BY SEX, 1965–66

Occupation	Related to activities in the Taipei Central Market		Unrelated to the Taipei Central Market		Total	
	Male	Female	Male	Female	Male	Female
Cart driver (laborer)	34	0	4	0	38	0
Pedicab driver	0	0	9	0	9	0
Taxi driver	0	0	1	0	1	0
Shop clerk	4	0	1	0	5	0
Factory worker	0	0	1	8	1	8
Vegetable gardener	1	0	0	0	1	0
Apprentice	1	0	0	0	1	0
Craftsman	0	0	1	0	1	0
Carpenter	0	0	4	0	4	0
Rag collector	0	0	1	0	1	0
Peddler	5	1	2	0	7	1
Shopkeeper (merchant)	5	0	3	0	8	0
Total	50	1	27	8	77	9

SOURCE: Field interviews.

trucks at the market entrance) either to the individual vegetable stalls within the market, from the Wan-hua freight station to the market, or from the market to the customers of the wholesale vegetable merchants.

The heavy concentration of Hsin-hsing villagers in cart driving is attributable to the fact that the postwar expansion and reorganization of the Central Market was just gaining momentum when the first wave of migrants arrived. However the first migrants got started, they helped their fellow villagers and kinsmen find similar jobs. In most instances, later migrants came to Taipei expecting to obtain work in the Central Market, even if only delivering vegetables on a small handcart.*

Five of the eight shopkeepers among Hsin-hsing migrants sell vegetables wholesale inside the Central Market. Two of these men came to Taipei during the late 1940's and became clerks for established merchants at extremely low wages. Gradually they learned the trade and, with accumulated savings, opened their own businesses inside the market when costs were still moderate and space still readily available. A third shopkeeper also began work as a clerk upon arrival in Taipei during the early period, but he became impatient and left this job to become a cart driver at a much higher wage. Unlike other migrants who began their careers in this same way, he managed to open a business in the late

* Such aid to fellow migrants is still forthcoming. Of the seven Hsin-hsing men who were driving pedicabs in 1966, when such cabs were banned from the streets of Taipei, four later found work in the Central Market.

1950's. On the one hand, he "apprenticed" his son to a vegetable merchant to learn the trade and, on the other, he followed an exceptionally frugal regime in order to save money to buy a business for himself and his son. The remaining two Hsin-hsing merchants are younger men in their thirties who recently opened businesses in the market after first working as clerks: the capital for one business came from a wife's dowry and for the other, from both the husband and wife's accumulated savings. Of all the migrants the five merchants are the most financially secure today.

These merchants and the men who work as cart drivers and clerks in and around the Central Market see each other regularly during their working hours. They usually start work shortly after 1:00 A.M., when the vegetables begin to come into the market, and end at about 11:00 A.M., when the business day is over and everything is cleaned up. Most men do not go home immediately after work; some cart drivers remain in the market and do extra work for merchants, while others, the majority, relax by talking, joking, gambling and sometimes drinking together. They finally leave the market for home sometime after noon.

Home for the majority of the migrants is in Wan-hua in the Shuang-yüan district or in the vicinity of the Central Market in Ch'eng-chung district (see Map 2). Both districts are inhabited by large numbers of people from other counties or municipalities in Taiwan and by people who have generally poor educational backgrounds (see Map 3). (On the basis of inferences from the P'u-yen township data, we would assume a great proportion of these people are rural-to-urban migrants.)

Migrants usually attempt to find living quarters near kinsmen or at least other villagers. As a result most Hsin-hsing natives live in residential clusters of fellow villagers and kinsmen, and even the outliers usually live within visiting distance (see Map 2 and Table 11). Migrants who

TABLE 11. DISTRIBUTION OF HSIN-HSING MIGRANT UNITS
BY DISTRICT AND SURNAME, TAIPEI, 1965–66

Surname	Shuang-yüan	Ch'eng-chung	Other five districts	Total
Huang	48	12	19	79
Shen	40	10	2	52
K'ang	29	10	8	47
Shih	6	25	6	37
Li	22	—	—	22
Wang	—	12	1	13
Others	1	—	10	11
Total	146	69	46	261
Total percent	56%	26%	18%	100%

SOURCE: Field interviews.

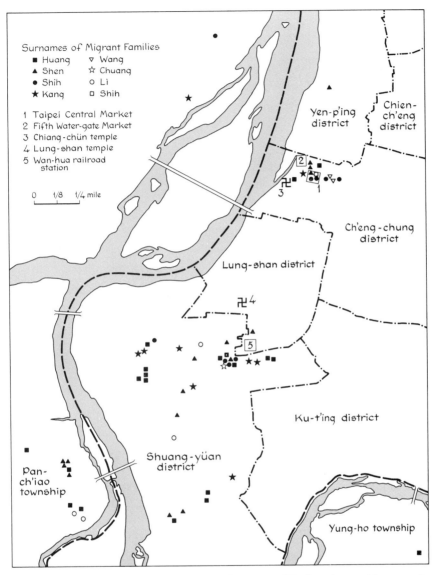

Surnames of Migrant Families
- ■ Huang   ▽ Wang
- ▲ Shen   ☆ Chuang
- ● Shih   ○ Li
- ★ Kang   □ Shih

1 Taipei Central Market
2 Fifth Water-gate Market
3 Chiang-chün temple
4 Lung-shan temple
5 Wan-hua railroad station

0   1/8   1/4 mile

Yen-p'ing district

Chien-ch'eng district

Ch'eng-chung district

Lung-shan district

Ku-t'ing district

Shuang-yüan district

Pan-ch'iao township

Yung-ho township

MAP 2. THE WESTERN DISTRICTS OF TAIPEI, 1966, showing residences of migrant family units from Hsin-hsing village. The residences of six family units are off the frame of the map: one Shen family to the northeast in Chung-shan district, one Shih family and one Chuang family farther east in Ch'eng-chung, one Shih family farther southwest in Yung-ho, one Chuang family farther west in Pan-ch'iao, and one Huang family farther north in San-chung.

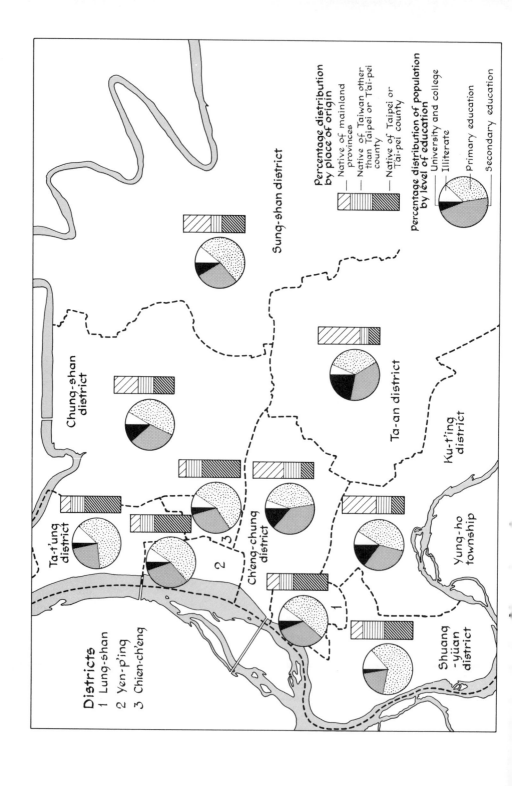

Districts
1 Lung-shan
2 Yen-p'ing
3 Chien-ch'eng

Ta-t'ung district

Chung-shan district

Sung-shan district

Chien-ch'eng district

Ta-an district

Ku-t'ing district

Yung-ho township

Shuang-yüan district

Percentage distribution by place of origin
Native of mainland provinces
Native of Taiwan other than Taipei or T'ai-pei county
Native of Taipei or T'ai-pei county

Percentage distribution of population by level of education
University and college
Illiterate
Primary education
Secondary education

live outside the two central districts tend to be from Hsin-hsing's smallest kin groups or from isolated families. A few of these outliers are young persons working in factories or shops and living in quarters furnished by the employer. However, most of the migrants who do not live in the two central districts either have independent jobs or work in small businesses that are totally unrelated to the Central Market. Not one of them works in the Central Market. Some live and work with affinal relatives and others with natives of P'u-yen township outside Hsin-hsing.

Seven of the Taipei-based families own their own houses, in each case well equipped and boasting several rooms. In several instances, two or more families of cart drivers have jointly rented a large apartment; each family is assigned a bedroom, while the sitting room and other facilities are shared. In at least one such case, the sharing families, all Huangs, are agnates. In virtually all such cases, the Hsin-hsing migrants happily note that living together in this manner is like being in a large family situation once again.

Most families, however, rent tiny places, usually no more than one very small room, and share cooking, washing, and toilet facilities with all the other families in the rented house. Within a particular house, families are seldom kinsmen or even from the same village or area; conveniently located and inexpensive houses are scarce and the migrants must rent what they can find.

Integration into City Life

To what extent have Hsin-hsing migrants continued to rely on kin- and village-based networks to satisfy their needs in the city? We have seen that upon arrival in Taipei, almost all of the migrants depended upon village-derived connections to take care of their immediate needs for employment and housing. As a result, the majority have jobs in the Central Market, which has natural centripetal consequences. The vegetable merchants have daily contacts with their fellow migrants. The cart drivers work and relax together every day; the gossip in which they engage tends to foster a community of interest and makes the Central Market the communication node of the Hsin-hsing community and, to a lesser extent, of the migrant community from Chang-hua county as a whole.

Within the market many of these people have organized themselves into groups somewhat akin to guilds and *pang*, which the government allows to function as "monopolies" in the interest of orderly market operation. The first such group organized was the Vegetable Merchants' Association. In order to maximize their profits, merchants needed two kinds of predictable labor services: delivery of wholesale produce to their stands in the market, and delivery of large loads of produce to major buyers outside the market. The association's first efforts, therefore, were directed toward organizing workers into two stable labor groups to perform these services. Migrants from Chang-hua county and particularly from Hsin-hsing dominate these groups. Over half of the members of one group, which has a contractual arrangement with the Vegetable Merchants' Association, are from Hsin-hsing and most of these men are from one patrilineage. The other group has the tacit recognition of but not a contract with the Association. It was organized by a Hsin-hsing villager and more than half of its members are from the village.

The preponderance of Hsin-hsing migrants in the two labor groups is not surprising; men from Hsin-hsing were among the earliest arrivals in the market, formed the largest village grouping there—compared with any other single identifiable place—and were most familiar with the vegetable merchants. In addition, at the time the two labor groups were formed, many of the migrants' relationships still were based on kinship or village identity or both. It was reasonable, then, that when organization occurred such criteria defined the membership.

One might have expected, however, given these conditions, to find a much higher proportion of Hsin-hsing migrants in these groups. Since their arrival in the city though, all of the migrants have developed new and intense reciprocal relationships with people not from Hsin-hsing—usually also migrants—on the basis of such shared experiences as being employed in the same market or living in the same area. (We will return to this point below.) Over time, many of these bonds have come to be considered more effective bases for developing the trust and cooperation necessary for the effectiveness of the groups than the ones brought from the village. As a result, when positions became available in the groups over the years, they began to be offered to city-based friends rather than to kinsmen or fellow villagers.

Despite the admission of "outsiders" to the groups, however, Hsin-hsing workers continue to exhibit a sense of unity among themselves within the market. Along with non-group villagers—later arrivals who were not able to find places in the more favored groups and who deliver small loads of produce on hand carts—Hsin-hsing laborers form an informal coalition that tries to protect its members against police harassment for alleged violations of regulations, demands for protection money from police and *liu-mang* (hoodlums), and competition from other groups. The coalition's success in this endeavor depends not only on sheer numbers, but also on support from influential merchants who sometimes help when they feel orderly market operation might be affected by problems among the laborers. The coalition's performance has varied over the years, but Hsin-hsing laborers view membership in the coalition as a means of obtaining a degree of security within the market and so it remains an active grouping.

Outside the market however, the Hsin-hsing laborers have failed to organize themselves into a cohesive mutual-aid group. Nor have they joined with other migrants from the Lu-kang or P'u-yen township areas to form a formal regional organization. This is partly because they have only a small population of natives in Taipei and only a few potential members from these places commanding resources, and partly because they do not feel much threatened as a group.

Nevertheless, laborers do report that they are "looked down upon" by Taipei natives because they are "outsiders" (*ch'u-wai jen*)—a term apparently applied to anyone from outside the immediate area of Taipei. And they believe that this attitude, along with their limited personal relationships with influential people, are responsible for their failure to secure government welfare benefits and services such as credit, legal aid, and protection. Thus, despite the limited threats directed against the migrants as people from a particular place, their belief that they are discriminated against and do miss opportunities came to provide a founding principle for a county-based association in Taipei. The group was organized in the early 1960's by several politically ambitious men from Chang-hua county who, in order to develop a clientele and following, used these beliefs and "t'ungism" to recruit members from among the large number of Chang-hua migrants in the city. Suggesting that ties based on a common county of origin were meaningful links that implied acts of reciprocity, these men promised prospective members patronage in exchange for political support.

Almost all the Hsin-hsing migrants responded to these recruitment "pledges" and joined the Chang-hua County (Regional) Association. Few, however, report having derived benefits from their membership. The association leaders' regular promises of aid appear to be met in part only around election time, when the association acts as a viable grouping representing the community of migrants. At all other times it serves primarily as an arena in which its more successful members organize alliances they can translate into social, economic, and political advantages. However, since the Hsin-hsing laborers usually manage to organize relationships through their associational activity only with people whose resources are as limited as their own, their membership fails to provide them with any beneficial ties to patrons or power brokers.

As a result, the only groupings to which the laborers belong that enable them to counter threats directed against them are their occupational groupings. But these groupings are exclusively economic in interest and proletarian in membership and provide them limited opportunities outside the Central Market. Thus the laborers believe that their most promising avenue to success in the city is close and effective relationships with the Hsin-hsing merchants, who they hope will call upon their ties with people of higher standing on the laborers' behalf when necessary.*

The merchants, for their part, are integrating themselves into Taipei by means of their increasing participation in sociopolitical associations. They take care, however, to preserve their village-based relationships. Such relationships enable them to make a contribution to the leaders of their new groupings and help ensure that they will remain welcome among them. Many of these associations serve primarily as a vehicle for the ambitious, and the merchants are recruited into them so that they can exert their influence on the lower-class migrants to promote the leaders' political interests. Thus the continuing ties maintained between the Hsin-hsing laborers and the Hsin-hsing merchants are mutually useful. On the one hand they bolster and secure the merchants' positions among their new associates and on the other hand they provide the laborers with an indirect access to power. The two groups of migrants therefore continue to depend, at least partially, on each other in the city.

In addition, village-based relationships continue to have significance within the two distinct groups of migrants. For example, laborers frequently lend each other small amounts of money without any interest or join each other's moneylending or credit clubs. At the time of a wedding or other festive occasion when many people must be entertained, they will offer their services as hosts. And often they will send *hung-pao* (a gift of money wrapped in red paper) on the occasion of a wedding, even when they are not planning to attend the dinner for which such a gift is obligatory.

The explanation they give for this practice is "that it is done to make *jen-ch'ing*," a term meaning the expression of good will or feeling. The gesture, however, is more than merely expressive, since laborers anticipate that the gift will be reciprocated when they celebrate a similar occasion. A migrant, in fact, when he uses the compound *jen-ch'ing* in speaking of its occurrence in his relationship with another, always uses

* For a more complete discussion of the continuing relationships within and between the two groups of Hsin-hsing migrants, see Rita Gallin, "Migrant Networks: Taipei, Taiwan," unpubl. M.A. thesis (Michigan State University, 1973).

it with the word *ch'ien,* meaning to owe. Thus, the practice is used as a means of creating personal-obligation ties with others.

The main reason laborers seem to take this care in maintaining their relationships with each other is that in the city an uncertainty exists about such relationships. The migrants no longer live in a small community in which residential concentration, socioreligious and political activities, and formal organizations draw them together, foster reciprocal relations, and exert pressure on individuals to conform to expected norms of behavior. (Their joint participation in occupational groupings has tended to reinforce their pre-existing kin and village ties but does not commit them to become involved with one another in other contexts.) As a result, although kinsmen and fellow villagers represent a source of help and security that most likely can be tapped in times of need, these relationships are considered voluntary, not obligatory, and laborers believe they must be nurtured.

In addition, the laborers believe it is necessary to seek out people other than kinsmen and fellow villagers with whom they can ally themselves and on whom they can depend. Most frequently they establish friendships with workmates or neighbors, also usually migrants. At the outset, these relationships are casual and primarily involve occasional get-togethers to eat and drink. Over time, many increase in intensity and evolve into close and cooperative ones involving exchanges of goods and services in both ritual and nonritual contexts. On festive occasions friends are entertained and at the time of a wedding or death, friends help out with gifts of money or with actual physical assistance. In addition, friends frequently visit each other's homes informally and, in time of financial need, furnish short-term loans without interest.

These relationships, however, like village-based ones, involve only voluntary actions of individuals or families. Friends, therefore, in order to be more certain of each other's potentiality as sources of aid, will sometimes organize themselves into a sworn-brotherhood group. Migrants believe that such groupings "unite people" by encouraging subscription to a common set of norms and by introducing a degree of obligation into relationships. Thus, they tend to guarantee that aid will be forthcoming when needed, since the sanctions of the group can be mobilized to oblige individual sworn brothers to fulfill their obligations.

Despite the utilitarian quality of these groups, however, the emotional ties of friendship define and characterize the relations among and between its members. Not all sworn-brotherhood groups, however, are organized as an outgrowth of warm and close friendships. Sometimes such groups are formed solely to maximize the socioeconomic and political opportunities of their participants; friendship may be used as a vehicle to enroll members and solidify their loyalties, but participants are recruited selectively with consideration given to the potential contribution of each individual to the group.

All five of the Hsin-hsing Central Market merchants belong to one such group, which includes among its 28 members a Taipei city councilwoman whose father is a National Assemblyman; the neighborhood chief (*lin-chang*) of Ch'eng-chung district; a member of the board of the Ch'eng-chung Cooperative Bank; the head of the Chang-hua Regional Association; and the vice-chief of the Provincial Water Bureau. During the proceedings that culminated in the formation of the group, the anticipated contributions of the different members were articulated: the merchants were to develop a following for the politically ambitious "brothers" in exchange for economic and sociopolitical favors. Notwithstanding this frank statement of expected advantage, the group does attempt to foster camaraderie by holding dinner parties at members' homes every third month, and members participate in the life-cycle rituals of each other's families in their role as fictive brothers.

Joint participation in the sworn-brotherhood group and overlapping membership in other groupings have reinforced pre-existing ties between the merchants and encouraged closer relations among them. Since they compete for both customers and farmers' agents (from whom they buy their produce), they had previously maintained only rather formal relationships with each other. Their close and intense relationships usually were not with their fellow merchants, but with others whom they had met since their arrival in the city. As they have become more involved in associational activities, however, they have had the opportunity to meet and relate with each other in an arena other than the one in which they normally compete. As a result, they have developed closer and more cooperative relationships with each other, and village and kinship ties continue to have meaning for them.

Summary and Conclusions

Earlier we saw marked differences between the people who move from villages to nearby urban towns and cities and those who move to the larger and more distant cities. Unlike Speare,[10] we found that these migrants to large cities did not have above-average educations and were not better off financially; on the contrary, they had below-average educations and usually were the more economically depressed residents of the areas from which they migrated.

The variance between these two findings may be due in part to differences between large cities such as Taichung (the focus of Speare's work) and urban-industrial centers such as Taipei, the historical fact of the influx of mainlanders into these latter cities, and a host of other factors. Taiwan's fine systems of communication and transportation make the most distant city easily accessible. A chain of relationships with earlier migrants—like the one that drew Chinese from southeast China to southeast Asian countries over the past several hundred years—attracted the Hsin-hsing area migrants to large distant cities. Most of these migrants therefore were not part of the stepwise migration stream in which rural migrants first move to urban towns—perhaps taking the jobs of townspeople who have migrated to cities—and later move to cities.[11] Instead, the great majority of migrants from Hsin-hsing and the three other villages we considered emigrated directly to the distant industrial centers where well-paying employment is available for people with limited resources.

Within the city, the migrants from one village, Hsin-hsing, do not form a cohesive urban community, but they are bound by certain formal and informal ties. Most work in related occupations within the Central Market. When occupational organization occurred there, particularistic criteria determined the core membership of the favored labor groups, and Hsin-hsing villagers dominate the groups. Membership in these groups, however, is not based solely on ascribed bonds of common origin; many men were recruited into the groups in later years on the basis of common experience. Nevertheless, as the largest single village grouping within the market, Hsin-hsing laborers have organized an informal coalition there that actively protects and promotes their economic interests.

Outside the market however, the Hsin-hsing migrants have neither a large enough population nor enough wealthy or influential people to organize an active "t'ungist" group. In fact, the only regional level with a large enough population to support a *t'ung-hsiang* group in Taipei was the county from which the migrants emigrated. The county-based association that was organized, however, is seen as essentially irrelevant by most laborers since it neither helps them to counter the discrimination directed against them, nor helps them to articulate with and operate within the institutions of the city and the wider society. The association is, however, seen as an active and viable grouping by its more successful migrant members, who use it to create advantage for themselves outside the group.

The sociopolitical integration of migrants into city life depends, then, to a large degree upon class. The Hsin-hsing laborers for the most part lack meaningful relationships with people of higher standing within the city, and many of the problems they face are not easily solved. The Hsin-hsing merchants have extended their relationships upward in the city's social and political structure and have increased their ability to maneuver socially, politically, and economically.

The two groups of migrants, however, continue to maintain relationships with each other in order to satisfy their needs and to promote their interests. These relationships, not surprisingly, tend to resemble patron-client models, rather than alliances of equals. The merchants offer to exercise indirect influence on those with power to help the laborers meet certain economic or personal threats. In exchange, the laborers offer a clientele and political following, thus providing the means by which the merchants can secure cooperation from those with power.

Thus, kinship and village-based relationships continue to be significant for most Hsin-hsing migrants, even though institutional supports that help ensure unity and cooperation in the village—such as ritual, politics, kinship organization, and concentrated residential patterns—cannot and do not function in the city. These relationships, however, are less structured in the city and are not oriented around the total group as a group. Instead they operate mainly on the individual family level and on a selective and voluntary basis. Nevertheless, the ties of mutual identification that are reinforced by overlapping social networks and modes of social participation—especially those stemming from related occupational activities—function to hold the majority of this migrant group together as a quasi-community within the city of Taipei.*

* At the same time, the relationships between the members of this quasi-community in the city are reinforced by continuing relations with their home village of Hsin-hsing. These relations are maintained through money remittances, necessary activities connected with village landholdings, occasional visits organized around kinship functions, and a few elaborate Hsin-hsing village festivals that draw both laborers and merchants—along with their money—back to the village for one or two days at a time.

Migrants and Cities in Japan, Taiwan, and Northeast China

IRENE B. TAEUBER

Migration, the growth of cities, and spatial differentiation are aspects of the transformations associated with modernization. The interrelations between these processes and modern social and economic developments have been documented and studied for the European cultural area and for Japan. Demographic transformation has now been shown to characterize the developing areas along the Pacific perimeter from Korea to Singapore. The major questions pertain to the population of China.

This chapter presents some materials from an investigation of China's population in the modern period. It is limited to areas once under Japanese rule and thus subject to the Japanese statistical system. In the first section, some aspects of Japan's great cities are described as models against which other cities may be appraised. The second section considers Taiwan, a milieu that promoted population growth but retarded cityward migration and demographic transition. The Liao-tung peninsula (specifically, the Kwantung Leased Territory and the South Manchurian Railway Zone) is the subject of the third section. Here, commercial and industrial development, accessibility to North China, and an influx of migrants contributed to urban growth and to rural-urban differentiation. The fourth section focuses on three Manchurian cities, approximately one-half to two-thirds of whose inhabitants were migrants, in a region itself populated mainly by migrants.

In the concluding section five hypotheses are advanced as stimulants to further study, including especially an examination of their relevance to the mainland. During China's quarter-century of socialist transformation, controlling migration and population distribution has been as central in demographic policy as controlling the rate of population growth. Early in the period, swift urban growth suggested comparability with

previous experience in the Northeast; but later, guided migration between cities and rural areas became a major factor in development strategy. The drive to equalize opportunity required that urban-rural differentiation be reduced. Allocations of youth and transfers of adults influenced both the scale and the direction of movement. The extension
of city boundaries to include agricultural belts and the growth of industrial activities in the communes limited the usefulness of conventional definitions of "urban" and "rural."

Migrants, Great Cities, and Demographic Transition: Japan

Analyzing the dynamics of the population of China requires reasoned
queries and testable hypotheses, which in turn require data. The like-
liest sources of such data are the records of Japan, where periodic reports
on population have been compiled since the first half of the eighteenth
century.

The Japanese experience confirms the assumption that the initial focus
of research should be change rather than stability, adaptability rather
than resistance to change. The prime areas of study, then, are the great
cities. Within them, the key people are the migrants and their children.
As they increase in numbers, interact with the native-born population,
and are assimilated to urban ways of living and thinking, they link in
their persons the advancing modern of the cities and the changing traditional of the countryside.

The mere presence of migrants in cities does not insure transformation.
If all migrants are local, interchanges between cities and rural areas may
continue an ancient order rather than contribute to a new one. If migrants from a distance remain segregated while in cities and eventually
return to the areas from which they came, migration may have a negligible impact on the society in question.

Insularity and cultural homogeneity combine with limitations of scale
to bar a direct transfer of the pattern of the Japanese past to the Chinese
future. Many aspects of Japanese institutions, political forms, and social
disciplines are distinctively Japanese. Moreover, since Japan modernized
a century before China, there were major differences in medical and industrial technology, developmental status, communications, and social
order. Japan was similar to China, however, in the prevalence of hand
labor in irrigated agriculture, in the pressures of population on land,
and in the economic organization that sustained great cities. In both
countries, the early phase of industrialization was related to the pursuit
of national power and the requirements of military strategy. Japanese
industrialization was more visible to the Chinese than Western indus-

trialization, both because of geographic propinquity and because of Japanese imperial development of certain areas of China.

Death rates declined slowly during Japan's early period of modernization, and natural increase accelerated gradually. At these rates of growth, Japan's rapid economic development meant that her increasing manpower could be absorbed in towns and municipalities rather than in villages, in nonagricultural rather than in agricultural labor. The number of farm households changed little as sons other than the eldest left the villages for the armed forces, the cities, or the imperial areas. Migration was the human aspect of economic and political development, as of demographic transformation.

The population of Japan increased from 56 million in 1920 to 73 million in 1940, an overall increase of 31 percent. During this period, the urban population (all municipalities) increased 173 percent, while the rural population decreased. In 1930, one-third of all interprefectural migrants were enumerated in one or the other of the six largest cities—Tokyo, Yokohama, Nagoya, Osaka, Kobe, and Kyoto. Almost two-thirds were enumerated in the six prefectures that contained these great cities.

More than half the people living in each of the six great cities in 1930 were in-migrants. This fraction quantifies but does not delineate the role of migrants in the cities. The in-migrant streams were dominated by young men. Some two-thirds to three-fourths of the population in these cities between the ages of 25 and 29 were in-migrants. These movements of young adults transferred the locus of family formation and childbearing from rural to urban areas. As early as 1930, more than four-fifths of the children under ten in the great cities were locally born.

The fertility of the urban population was lower than that of the rural population. In each of the six metropolitan prefectures for each of the intercensal periods from 1920 to 1940, the fertility of women was lower in the great cities than in the areas outside them. In each of the six, and outside them, there was a fairly steady decline in fertility over the two decades. The same situation prevailed in all cities of 100,000 and over; fertility was lower in the cities than in the surrounding areas of the prefectures—and it was declining. City growth, declining fertility, and migration were interrelated demographic processes in Japan.

Migration, Rurality, and Stability: Taiwan

The demographic history of Taiwan and its path to modernization are distinctive, whether the comparative perspective is China or the Pacific perimeter. Isolation from the mainland after 1896 cut off the migrations that would have tended to equalize economic pressures with those of the mainland. Taiwan's colonial status, economic dependence, and social subordination created a population dynamic different from that of agrarian China, rural Japan, or the other occupied areas of China. Secure and increasing production, social and political order, and an expanding land frontier were conducive to the persistence of early marriage and high rates of childbearing among the married. Birthrates changed little during the first half of the twentieth century; the age structures recorded in 1930 and 1935 were similar to those recorded in 1905 and 1915.

Regular and sufficient subsistence, barriers to epidemics and external hazards, and improving sanitary and health programs reduced the death rate from about 40 per thousand before 1905 to little more than 30 in 1915 and a little below 20 in 1940. In 1905 the birth and death rates were about equal; by 1935 the birthrate was more than double the death rate —45.7 and 20.9 per thousand, respectively. The population was increasing 2.5 percent a year (see Map 1 and Table 1). The Chinese population of Taiwan increased from three million in 1905 to five million in 1935.

Migration and mobility occurred in Taiwan, but apart from movement to the more sparsely settled southern and eastern areas and to the frontiers, migration was relatively infrequent and mostly short-distance.[1] In 1930 nine-tenths or more of the people enumerated outside the south and east had been born in the districts where they lived. This stability characterized all age groups and both sexes, although lifetime migrant cumulations were somewhat greater in the productive ages from 15 to 50, particularly for men. These and other detailed comparisons between

TABLE 1. POPULATION AND THE COMPONENTS OF CHANGE
FOR ALL TAIWAN AND BY DISTRICT, 1930–35

District (shū)	1930 population (thousands)	Percent change 1930–35			Percent urban, 1930
		Overall	Natural increase	Net migration	
Taiwan	4,314	13.20%	13.4%	−.2%	10.4%
T'ai-pei	787	11.1	10.9	.1	25.2
Hsin-chu	681	7.0	13.3	−6.2	6.0
T'ai-chung	983	14.4	14.7	−.4	4.0
T'ai-nan	1,113	14.9	14.7	.2	11.1
Kao-hsiung	598	15.3	12.9	2.4	7.6
T'ai-tung	54	19.8	8.1	11.8	n.a.
Hua-lien	72	29.9	11.1	18.9	n.a.
P'eng-hu	56	10.1	12.8	−2.7	n.a.

SOURCE: Taiwan [Sōtokufu], Sōtoku kambō, Rinji kokusei chōsabu, *Kokusei chōsa, Shōwa 5 nen: Kekka hyō, zentō hen* (1930 census, final tables, all-Taiwan summary volume; Taipei: Rinji kokusei chōsabu, 1934); Taiwan [Sōtokufu], Sōtoku kambō, Chōsaka, *Taiwan jinkō dōtai tōkei: Gempyō no bu* (Vital statistics, detailed volumes; Taipei: Chōsaka, 1925–30).

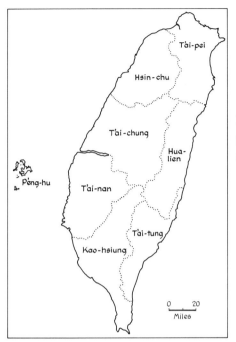

MAP 1. FIRST-ORDER ADMINISTRATIVE UNITS (*shū*) IN TAIWAN, 1926–45

the stable and migrant groups in 1930 suggest traditional life patterns of movement rather than those associated with economic development of an industrial type. The characteristic male-dominated migrations of Chinese populations had occurred in the sparsely settled eastern districts.

The many variations in the migratory patterns of Taiwan during this period cannot be discussed or even summarized here. The major characteristic of the population was stability, especially as compared with other Chinese areas or Japan. In 1930, even in the parts of Taiwan where migration was most frequent, more than three-fifths of all the people had been born in the district where they lived. The native-born numbered more than half even for the age groups whose migration rates were highest.

The extent of this stability and the nature of the movements that did occur are suggested by the relations between districts of residence and of birth.[2] In 1930 only 4.3 percent of the Chinese born in Taiwan lived outside their district of birth. The major losses of the native-born had occurred in Hsin-chu and P'eng-hu. Most of Hsin-chu's migrants were in T'ai-chung or in T'ai-pei; most of P'eng-hu's migrants were in Kao-hsiung. Most movements were over short distances to adjacent districts.[3]

TABLE 2. URBAN-RURAL DIFFERENTIATION IN MARITAL STATUS
FOR SELECTED AGE GROUPS OF THE TAIWANESE
POPULATION, ALL TAIWAN AND BY DISTRICT, 1925 AND 1935
(Percent single)

District (shū) and year	Urban			Rural		
	15–19	20–24	25–29	15–19	20–24	25–29
Women:						
Taiwan						
1925	75.1%	24.5%	9.2%	70.0%	14.4%	3.0%
1935	75.8	24.4	8.8	71.3	15.9	3.3
T'ai-pei						
1925	72.5	28.9	14.4	61.0	14.0	4.6
1935	74.8	28.7	13.6	62.4	15.3	4.7
Hsin-chu						
1925	67.5	17.8	5.8	67.0	16.9	5.1
1935	68.5	18.9	8.3	67.2	18.5	5.3
T'ai-chung						
1925	73.0	20.1	5.7	73.2	14.7	2.1
1935.	74.4	18.8	5.1	74.2	16.6	2.6
T'ai-nan						
1925	83.0	24.3	6.4	70.2	9.6	1.3
1935	79.5	26.2	7.3	71.5	11.0	1.4
Kao-hsiung						
1925	74.4	18.3	3.6	78.8	19.7	3.0
1935	77.2	19.5	4.1	81.0	21.9	3.9
T'ai-tung						
1925	—	—	—	59.4	16.7	7.2
1935	—	—	—	59.4	16.7	7.0
Hua-lien						
1925	—	—	—	60.1	16.2	7.2
1935	—	—	—	56.3	14.9	5.8
Men:						
Taiwan						
1925	95.6	60.3	27.7	94.6	54.6	21.0
1935	96.3	57.9	22.1	94.0	49.0	16.0
T'ai-pei						
1925	94.8	59.6	29.4	94.2	54.4	23.4
1935	96.5	60.5	24.9	94.8	54.7	21.1
Hsin-chu						
1925	92.7	49.6	16.9	91.3	46.6	17.0
1935	93.2	46.5	13.9	91.8	46.8	16.0
T'ai-chung						
1925	95.6	56.4	25.0	95.6	55.9	20.9
1935	95.3	51.0	17.6	94.1	47.5	14.3
T'ai-nan						
1925	97.4	65.8	30.1	95.3	55.4	20.1
1935	97.1	61.6	23.9	93.9	44.5	12.4
Kao-hsiung						
1925	96.3	61.2	26.0	95.5	59.2	23.1
1935	96.9	57.5	20.5	95.4	53.5	17.8
T'ai-tung						
1925	—	—	—	92.9	59.5	22.1
1935	—	—	—	94.5	60.0	23.2
Hua-lien						
1925	—	—	—	94.3	61.1	23.6
1935	—	—	—	92.6	54.9	23.1

SOURCE: For 1925, Taiwan [Sōtokufu], Sōtoku kambō, Rinji kokusei chōsabu, *Kokusei chōsa, Taishō 14 nen: Kekka hyō* (1925 census, final tables); for 1935, *op. cit., Kekka hyō, shūchō hen* (Final tables, districts).
NOTE: Lunar ages were used for 1925; Western ages for 1935.

Concentrations of in-migrants were higher in urban than in rural areas and in newer rather than older cities. These were the expected patterns of an agricultural region where increasing scarcity of land in older centers could be relieved by migration.

Differences between place of residence and place of birth reflect the net movements of lifetimes. In Taiwan, in- and out-migrations were registered along with births and deaths. Occasional tabulations permit the computation of migration rates by age and sex for all Taiwan and for each administrative district within it.[4] In 1930, males were more mobile than females in the frontier areas; elsewhere, differences between the sexes were slight. Young adults (aged 15–24) were more mobile than children, the aging, or the aged, but the differences were slight in contrast to those prevailing in the great cities of Japan or Manchuria. Migration generally flowed from the older and more densely settled districts of the north and west, toward the developing regions of the south and the east.

The patterns of migration reflect adjustments to changes in the availability of resources and employment. Population increase was a major force for change and a stimulant to migration in Taiwan during the 1920's and 1930's. Natural increase amounted to 9.3 percent from 1920 to 1925, 12.5 percent from 1925 to 1930, 13.4 percent from 1930 to 1935, and 13.3 percent from 1935 to 1940. The direction of change was upward in each of the administrative districts.[5] There was a persistent if not entirely regular pattern of net migration: T'ai-pei, the most urban district, showed a relative balance of in- and out-movements, whereas Hsin-chu showed a net loss throughout the period, and T'ai-chung and T'ai-nan were beginning to show net losses by the end of the period. There were major migrant increments only in the south and east. Even here, relative gains were highest between 1925 and 1930. Throughout the period, though, most districts absorbed most of their natural increase within their own boundaries. In no period did any district lose as much as half its natural increase through net out-migration.

The earliest harbingers of declining fertility among peoples of Chinese and related cultures are increasing ages at marriage for women. In Taiwan few women over 24 remained unmarried in 1925, the highest percentage (14.4) being reported from urban T'ai-pei and the lowest (1.3) from rural T'ai-nan. The situation was little changed by 1935 (Table 2) with increases in three districts, decreases in two districts, and a barely perceptible decrease for all Taiwan.

During the decade between 1925 and 1935, there were some slight increases in the proportions of single women between the ages of 15 and

TABLE 3. CHILD-WOMAN RATIOS, ALL TAIWAN
AND BY DISTRICT, 1925 AND 1935

District (*shū*) and year	Children under five per thousand women aged 15–44					
	Total		Urban		Rural	
	All women	Ever-married women	All women	Ever-married women	All women	Ever-married women
Taiwan						
1925	759	1,043	677	1,007	769	1,047
1935	869	1,173	785	1,129	882	1,179
T'ai-pei						
1925	728	995	643	984	759	997
1935	809	1,093	725	1,086	843	1,096
Hsin-chu						
1925	764	1,039	689	964	769	1,043
1935	869	1,166	783	1,088	875	1,171
T'ai-chung						
1925	792	1,089	670	962	799	1,097
1935	893	1,199	809	1,107	902	1,209
T'ai-nan						
1925	753	1,030	680	1,048	761	1,029
1935	907	1,199	805	1,172	921	1,202
Kao-hsiung and P'eng-hu						
1925	765	1,085	779	1,067	763	1,087
1935	854	1,215	874	1,208	851	1,216
T'ai-tung						
1925	687	966	—	—	687	966
1935	755	1,022	—	—	755	1,022
Hua-lien						
1925	649	863	—	—	649	863
1935	824	1,045	—	—	824	1,045

SOURCE: As in Table 2.

TABLE 4. ESTIMATED FERTILITY IN TAIWAN, 1920–35

Measure and time period	Taiwan	Urban	Rural
Gross reproduction rate:			
1920–25	2.94	2.59	2.98
1930–35	3.21	2.84	3.27
Female birthrate:			
1920–25	43.5	39.0	44.1
1930–35	46.1	41.6	46.7

NOTE: Gross reproduction rates and female birthrates were estimated by using the ratio of female children aged 4 or under to women aged 15–44 and the female expectation of life at birth for search and interpolation in systems of model stable populations. West model life tables were used as being most appropriate for the mortality of these age sectors of Chinese populations.

24. This was true in urban and rural areas in Taiwan as a whole and in most of the administrative districts. Marriage occurred later in urban than in rural areas, but differences between the two were remaining stable. Changes in the marriage age for men, larger than those for women but still not dramatic, were generally downward.

The Taiwanese milieu was conducive to the persistence of the early marriage and frequent childbearing that are presumed to be the ideal. The ratios of young children to women shown in Table 3 give a broad view of the pattern for Taiwan as a whole and for its individual districts. Three statements summarize this pattern. First, variations among the districts and between urban and rural areas within them were limited both in 1925 and in 1935. Second, the ratios were lower for urban than for rural areas. Third, the ratios were higher in 1935 than in 1925. This was true for all districts and for both urban and rural areas within them.

Direct analysis of the fertility of the Chinese population in Taiwan during this period (Table 4) confirms the pattern seen in Table 3. Again, fertility was lower in urban than in rural areas for both 1925 and 1935. This was true for each district and for all Taiwan. But fertility was higher for all Taiwan, and in both urban and rural areas, in 1935 than it had been a decade earlier.

In summary, then, during the 1920's and 1930's the population of Taiwan was changing only slowly in the ways usually associated with modernization. There was only a small increase in the relative proportions of the single among young women. Fertility rates not only failed to decline, but actually rose between 1925 and 1935. There were urban-rural differences, but these were not major. The overall demographic picture was more consonant with tradition than with transition.

Migration, Urbanization, and Diversity: The Kwantung Leased Territory and the South Manchurian Railway Zone

Over the centuries, many Chinese have migrated overseas or toward the less developed regions of the country. During the Ch'ing era, the primary destination of non-overseas migrants was southwest China; from the end of the Ch'ing up to and perhaps into the era of the People's Republic, it was northeast China, particularly Manchuria.

The Liao-tung peninsula, with its harbors at Port Arthur (Lü-shun) and Dairen (Ta-lien), affords the major sea entrance to China's northeastern provinces. Japan ruled two highly strategic portions of the peninsula from 1905 to 1945: the Kwantung Leased Territory (KLT) at its southernmost tip (Map 2) and the South Manchurian Railway Zone (SMR Zone), a narrow belt running the length of the Railway. The

Chinese migrants brought agricultural and industrial development, transportation and communication networks, rural expansion and urban concentration, and stimuli for internal migration. Imperial Japan brought not only massive capital investments, but also order and administration, including a population registration system and a series of censuses.

Development in the two Japanese-controlled territories was diversified, but there was a steady movement away from the dominance of agriculture. As the population grew from 375,000 in 1905 to 1.3 million in 1930 and 1.6 million in 1935, it became increasingly migrant, urban, and nonagricultural. In 1907 two-thirds of the gainfully employed Chinese worked in agriculture; in 1935 two-thirds worked outside agriculture.

The demographic relevance of the 1.3 million people living in the KLT and the SMR Zone in 1930 lies in their distribution and characteristics rather than in their numbers (Table 5). Half of the people lived in the SMR Zone and in the cities of Port Arthur and Dairen. One-sixth lived in the rural areas surrounding these two cities in the Kwantung Leased Territory, and the remaining one-third lived in the three predominantly rural northern districts of the KLT: P'i-tzu-wo, P'u-lan-tien, and Chin-chou. The rapid industrialization and urbanization that had occurred

TABLE 5. SELECTED CHARACTERISTICS OF URBAN AND RURAL
POPULATIONS, KWANTUNG LEASED TERRITORY, 1930

Adminis-trative unit	Population (thousands)	Percent Chinese	Chinese		
			Sex ratio (males per thousand females)	Percent occupied in agriculture	Percent born in China
Port Arthur municipality	34	59.4%	2,160	3.1%	57.4%
Lü-shun (rural)	104	99.4	1,043	77.3	8.1
Dairen municipality	293	66.2	2,698	.9	80.1
Ta-lien (rural)	120	97.0	1,435	35.7	38.2
Chin-chou	117	98.4	1,156	64.0	11.4
P'u-lan-tien	151	99.0	1,147	79.0	8.3
P'i-tzu-wo	137	98.9	1,064	62.2	8.6
Total KLT	956	87.3%	1,411	35.4%	30.8%

SOURCE: Kwantung [Kantōchō, 1919–34], Chōkan kambō, Chōsaka, *Kantōchō kokusei chōsa, Shōwa 5 nen: Kekka hyō.* 1, *Shōtai oyobi jūkyo;* 2, *Jinkō, taisei, nenrei, haigū kankei, honseki, minseki, kokusei, fūtsū kyōiku no yūmu, shusseichi, naijū no toshi* (Kwantung census of 1930, final tables: vol. 1, households and residence; vol. 2, population, sex, age, marital status, permanent place of registration, national origin, nationality, elementary education, place of birth, and year of arrival; Dairen, Chōsaka, 1931–34); Kwantung [Kantōchō, 1919–34], Chōkan kambō, Chōsaka, *Kantōchō kokusei chōsa, Shōwa 5 nen: Hirei hen* (Kwantung census of 1930, ratio tables, Dairen: Chōsaka, 1931–34). Vol. 1 for data on population; vol. 2 for place of birth; *Hirei hen* for percentage employed in agriculture.

NOTE: China was defined as including Manchuria but not the South Manchurian Railway Zone.

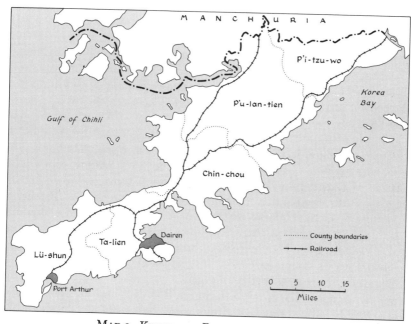

MAP 2. KWANTUNG PENINSULA, 1920–35

during the decades of colonial rule had brought about major differentiations in the economic roles of migrants as opposed to natives, urban as opposed to rural residents, and younger as opposed to older age groups. In 1930, native-born and older people were more rural and agricultural, whereas migrants and younger people were more urban and industrial. The percentage of gainfully occupied Chinese men who worked in agriculture was 37 at ages 10–14, 19 at ages 25–29, and 59 at ages 60–64. Some 55 percent of all Chinese men were employed in manufacturing, commerce, and transportation. The roles of Chinese women remained traditional: most of the few women reported as gainfully occupied were employed in commerce, and married women seldom worked outside the home.

Even such a simple outline of changes documents the significance of this area to the study of Chinese demography and demonstrates the need for analyses of its migratory patterns, urban-rural differentiation, and transformations in marriage and reproduction patterns. Data from the censuses of 1920, 1925, 1930, and 1935 as well as from the registration records permit us to reconstruct the dynamics of earlier decades and to analyze changes occurring between 1920 and 1935. Since the social and economic changes that took place during the period are separately measurable, and since there are reports on in- and out-movements and births and deaths for both areas from an ongoing registration system, the population dynamics can be traced with some precision.

Projecting from this microcosm to all Manchuria or to all China is patently invalid. But the analyzed experience of one area provides a basis for formulating hypotheses and exploring theories about another. Moreover, direct comparisons can be made between the great cities in the KLT and the SMR Zone and those elsewhere in Manchuria in 1940.

The demographic similarities and contrasts between the Chinese in Taiwan and those in the leased territories merit intensive analysis. The existence of two distinct but related subcultures with a comparable statistical record provides an almost perfect experimental design for studies in the comparative demography of Chinese peoples. Briefly, as already noted, the Chinese population of Taiwan exhibited a predominant stability, whereas the Chinese in the KLT and the SMR Zone exhibited continuing mobility. But within the KLT there were rural counties whose people remained in villages and continued to work in agriculture. The prevalence of migrants in any given district was related directly to the degree of urbanization in that district. Rural populations were mainly native-born, but natives were almost strangers in the urban areas.

In 1930, 60 percent of all the Chinese in the KLT, whether native-born or in-migrant, reported their province of belonging* as Liaoning, whereas 30 percent reported Shantung and 10 percent Hopei. Almost all the rural people said they belonged in the adjacent province of Liaoning, whereas most of the Chinese in the cities claimed Shantung. In the SMR Zone, most urban Chinese said they belonged in Hopei. In general, the more urban the area, the more distant the origins of its migrants.

Reported places of belonging suggest historic origins, whereas reported differences between place of residence and place of birth indicate migration within a lifetime. Counts of migrants indicate the size of the currents of movement in and out. In 1930 there were 149 in-migrants and 134 out-migrants per thousand Chinese present in the Kwantung Leased Territory and the South Manchurian Railway Zone. In the KLT the rate of in-migration was 98.7 and the rate of out-migration 79.8. The net gain from a gross movement of 178.5 per thousand population was only 18.9. Within the Territory, rural areas lost and urban areas gained in the migrant interchanges.

---

* The "province of belonging" is the province with which a respondent identifies. It may be his place of birth or the province from which his family migrated a generation or more ago.

TABLE 6. MIGRATION RATES AMONG CHINESE MEN, BY AGE,
KWANTUNG LEASED TERRITORY AND THE SOUTH MANCHURIAN
RAILWAY ZONE, 1930

Age group	Rate per thousand			
	In	Out	Gross	Net
16–20	265	215	480	50
21–25	317	300	617	17
26–30	296	275	571	21
31–35	220	209	429	11
36–40	222	204	426	18
41–45	176	169	345	7

SOURCE: Kwantung [Kantōchō, 1919–34], Chōkan kambō, Bunshoka, Kantōchō jinkō dōtai tōkei (Vital statistics for Kwantung; Dairen, Chō-saka, 1930).

In 1930, as throughout the lifetime of the people in the area in 1930, most in-migrants came from China and most out-migrants went to China. The migrant Chinese were mainly men, and they were mainly young. The age-related rates of migration per thousand population for the KLT and the SMR Zone combined illustrate the place of migration in the life cycles of the men and the limited increments resulting from high gross migration rates (see Table 6).

At each age, from youth to late middle age, those who moved in were more numerous than those who moved out. The rate of gain per thousand men tended to decline with age. At age 51 and thereafter, there were net losses in the interchanges.

Men migrated for economic reasons; those women who moved did so primarily in relation to family and marriage. The age patterns for women were similar to those for men, but the rates of migration were substantially less in each age group. Retention rates were higher, though, and there were net gains at all ages from childhood to advanced old age.

The many changes in the industrializing enclave of Japan's colonial territories on the Liao-tung peninsula were interrelated. There were not enough young people growing up to meet the area's labor needs. People migrated in from China to fill these needs, and more of them stayed than left. The migrants moved into industrial, commercial, and even professional occupations, but generally at low levels and often with temporary tenure. Few of those who were educated had more than the traditional education of the old order nor did they have the primary schooling of the new.

People with roots in the KLT or in the SMR Zone prior to the industrial development made up a small proportion of the areas' youth, but they were a substantial proportion of those in the middle and older age groups. Their educational levels, skills, and capabilities were those of traditional China. The majority of young adults were immigrants from China, with whatever education and training had been available in the areas and the social classes from which they came. The formation of families and the transmission of culture and values were mainly responsibilities of immigrants rather than natives. The heritages being transmitted were those of the villages or towns of adjacent Liaoning, Shantung, and Hopei provinces.

The population structures in the successive periods and the processes that were transforming these structures from period to period were those of early and limited modernization. The population dynamics were those of a peasant people stimulated by a governing group that was itself not far from peasantry. One of the simplest measures of population structure is the proportion of the population under fifteen years of age. Table 7 gives this proportion for various segments of the Chinese population of the KLT at five-year intervals from 1920 to 1935. Among males, the percentages under fifteen were lowered by the high rate of in-migration, particularly the predominance of adult male migrants. The percentages for females were less affected. In the rural districts, more than 40 percent of all females were under fifteen, and there was no discernible trend over time. In the large cities the relative numbers of males under fifteen increased over the fifteen years covered by the table, reflecting the growth of a native population.

What was the internal dynamic of growth in this population with its large migrant component? Was a trend toward higher age at marriage, lower mortality, and declining fertility emerging, or did the dynamic still resemble that of traditional Chinese populations?

As mentioned above, one of the earliest indicators of basic demographic change is an advance in the age at marriage. Although the overall proportion of single people in the Chinese population of the KLT changed little during the years between 1925 and 1935, there were increases in the proportion of single women between the ages of 15 and 19 in both urban and rural areas, ranging from 15.1 percent in Port Arthur to 3.2 percent in P'i-tzu-wo. Among women between the ages of 20 and 24, the rises were smaller, ranging from 5.6 percent in Dairen municipality to 1.5 percent in rural Ta-lien. (In the 25–29 age group, and indeed in all age groups thereafter, the picture was one of near stability.)

The ratios of children to all women and to all women who had married were lowest in Dairen municipality and highest in the most agricultural counties, varying more or less directly with degree of urbanization between these two extremes. Altered marital status was a major

TABLE 7. PROPORTION BELOW AGE 15 IN THE CHINESE POPULATION,
BY SEX, KWANTUNG LEASED TERRITORY, 1920–35

Administrative unit	1920	1925	1930	1935
Both sexes:				
Port Arthur munic.	23.6%	24.4%	26.0%	28.7%
Lü-shun (rural)	42.6	41.5	40.2	40.4
Dairen munic.	11.7	16.9	20.2	20.6
Ta-lien (rural)	30.2	35.9	33.3	33.7
Chin-chou	41.3	40.0	39.2	39.7
P'u-lan-tien	39.7	39.0	39.0	39.0
P'i-tzu-wo	40.5	39.2	39.8	40.1
Total	33.9%	34.7%	33.8%	33.9%
Males:				
Port Arthur munic.	17.8%	18.6%	19.8%	22.7%
Lü-shun (rural)	41.7	41.0	39.4	40.0
Dairen munic.	8.0	11.6	14.6	15.0
Ta-lien (rural)	24.6	32.5	28.9	29.5
Chin-chou	40.8	38.9	37.7	37.7
P'u-lan-tien	38.1	37.2	36.9	36.8
P'i-tzu-wo	39.6	37.8	38.9	39.1
Total	29.0%	30.5%	29.5%	29.4%
Females:				
Port Arthur munic.	38.4%	38.2%	39.2%	40.0%
Lü-shun (rural)	43.4	42.0	41.1	40.8
Dairen munic.	34.5	35.0	35.2	35.8
Ta-lien (rural)	40.1	40.1	39.5	39.7
Chin-chou	41.9	41.2	41.3	42.1
P'u-lan-tien	41.4	41.0	41.5	41.5
P'i-tzu-wo	41.5	40.7	40.8	41.3
Total	41.2%	40.4%	40.0%	40.2%

SOURCE: For 1920, Kwantung [Kantōchō, 1919–34], Rinji kokō chōsabu, *Kantōchō rinji kokō chōsa, Taishō 9 nen: 10 gatsu 1 nichi: Gempyō, dai sankan, Jinkō no bu, sono ni* (Special household and population survey of Oct. 1, 1920, Tabulations, vol. 3, population section, part 2; Dairen: Rinji kokō chōsabu, 1924); for 1925 and 1930, Kwantung [Kantōchō, 1919–34], Chōkan kambō, Bunshoka, *Kantōchō kokusei chōsa, 2, Kekka hyō* (Kwantung census, vol. 2, Final tables; Dairen: Bunshoka, 1927, 193?); for 1935, Kwantung [Kantōkyoku, 1935–45], *Kantōkyoku kokusei chōsa, 2, Kekka hyō* (Kwantung census, vol. 2, Final tables; Dairen: Kantōkyoku, 1939).
NOTE: Lunar ages were used for 1920 and 1925. Urban Lü-shun includes Port Arthur; urban Ta-lien includes Dairen.

factor in changes in fertility in the rural counties. However, the variation in the ratios from the most urban to the most rural areas persisted in all years, even when the ratios were limited to married women.

More precise indicators of changing fertility are presented in Table 8. Gross reproduction rates declined between 1920–25 and 1925–30, but changed little between 1925–30 and 1930–35. In 1925–30 the gross reproduction rate for Chinese women in the SMR Zone was similar to that for Dairen municipality. Female birthrates for the same period ranged from Dairen's 31.8 to P'u-lan-tien's 45.1.

TABLE 8. GROSS REPRODUCTION RATES AND FEMALE BIRTHRATES FOR THE
CHINESE POPULATION, KLT AND THE SMR ZONE, 1920–35

Administrative	Gross reproduction rate			Female birthrate		
unit	1920–25	1925–30	1930–35	1920–25	1925–30	1930–35
Port Arthur						
municipality	2.65	2.57	2.38	40.0	38.6	35.8
Lü-shun (rural)	3.25	2.93	2.99	47.7	43.4	44.1
Dairen						
municipality	2.19	2.09	2.08	33.5	31.8	31.5
Ta-lien (rural)	3.02	2.71	2.68	44.9	40.4	40.0
Chin-chou	3.23	3.00	3.17	47.4	44.3	46.1
P'u-lan-tien	3.24	3.06	2.93	47.5	45.1	43.2
P'i-tzu-wo	3.16	2.97	2.97	46.6	43.9	43.7
Total KLT	3.05	2.78	2.77	45.3	41.4	41.1
South Manchurian						
Railway Zone	2.03	2.06	2.04	31.1	31.3	31.0

SOURCE: As in Table 7.
NOTE: Rates estimated according to the procedure outlined in the note to Table 4 above, with
lunar ages adjusted to Western ages for 1925.

Thus there are some indications of demographic transition of the type
associated with modernization in these areas of the Liao-tung peninsula
during the 1920's and the 1930's. Highly structured differentiations between cities and rural areas existed at the beginning of transition, and
persisted in the early decades. The interrelations among migration, urban
growth, industrialization, and changing marriage and reproduction patterns will be discussed within a broader context that includes the Manchurian cities.

Migrant Cities in a Migrant Region: Manchuria

In 1909–11 there were perhaps 22 million people in the Northeast. By
1940 there were 43.2 million. The area of industrial and urban concentration was a wedge of five provinces extending northward from the
border of the Kwantung Leased Territory to the junction of the South
Manchurian and Chinese Eastern railways at Harbin (Map 3). Located
in these five provinces were twelve of the fifteen largest cities of the
region, including Mukden with a population of 1.4 million, Changchun
(Hsin-ching) with 554,000, and Harbin with 662,000 (1940 figures).
Since these three great cities had been the experimental areas for censuses in the mid-1930's and were then surveyed again in the census of
1940, statistics on migration and other demographic variables are relatively abundant.

Mukden. In 1935 the population of Mukden was almost half a million.
Eighty-four percent were Han Chinese, and these were distributed

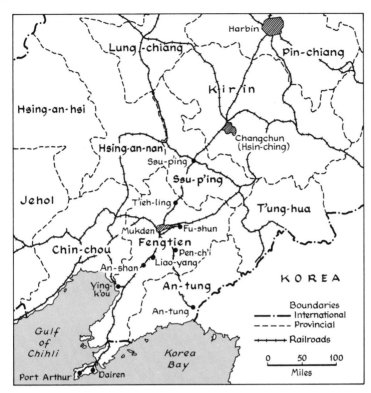

MAP 3. CENTRAL MANCHOUKUO AND KWANTUNG, 1940, SHOWING
PROVINCIAL BOUNDARIES AND MAJOR CITIES

throughout the city. Three-fourths or more of the people in each of the city's six police districts were Han.

Although Mukden was the industrial and transport center of a swiftly advancing migrant region, almost 40 percent of the people living within its limits in 1935 had been born there. Three-fifths of the city's people were Manchuria-born, a little more than half of the men and three-fourths of the women (Table 9). The first generation of migrants and their descendants were producing an indigenous population. Ninety-four percent of Mukden's children under five had been born somewhere in Manchuria; 78.2 percent of them in the city itself. The fathers of Mukden's children were predominantly immigrants, though: more than half the men aged 20–49 had been born in China. The picture differed somewhat for women. The long-distance migrants were largely males; wives and children, if any, were likely to have been left behind in the

TABLE 9. BIRTHPLACE OF MUKDEN RESIDENTS, BY SEX AND AGE, 1935

| | | Manchuria | | | China | | | Japanese Empire | |
Age	Total	Mukden	Else-where in Feng-t'ien county	Else-where in province	Total	Shantung	Hopei	Japan	Korea
Both sexes:									
0– 4	94.0%	78.2%	6.1%	7.4%	4.0%	1.2%	2.7%	1.0%	.9%
5– 9	85.4	64.4	6.8	10.5	11.5	3.9	7.3	1.4	1.6
10–14	76.8	54.1	7.7	11.3	20.5	8.2	11.6	1.0	1.6
15–19	58.2	33.5	7.1	12.0	38.6	11.3	25.5	1.5	1.7
20–24	51.0	28.0	6.2	11.4	43.2	13.5	27.4	3.0	2.6
25–29	50.2	26.4	6.2	11.9	44.7	15.1	27.2	3.1	1.9
30–39	46.0	24.7	5.6	10.7	49.8	17.4	29.6	2.2	1.7
40–49	47.3	27.5	6.7	9.4	49.1	18.3	28.1	1.6	1.6
50–59	57.7	35.1	8.8	10.5	39.4	15.6	22.1	1.3	1.3
60 & over	70.0	44.7	10.8	11.2	27.4	11.0	15.5	.7	1.6
Total	60.9%	39.2%	6.8%	10.6%	35.3%	12.2%	21.4%	1.9%	1.7%
Male:									
0– 4	94.2%	78.2%	6.2%	7.4%	3.9%	1.2%	2.6%	1.0%	.8%
5– 9	85.1	63.9	7.0	10.5	11.8	4.2	7.3	1.2	1.6
10–14	74.3	51.5	7.6	11.5	23.3	9.1	13.3	.9	1.5
15–19	50.6	26.6	6.0	11.7	47.0	13.0	32.0	1.1	1.2
20–24	41.8	21.0	4.9	10.2	53.4	16.4	34.1	2.7	2.0
25–29	41.6	20.2	5.1	10.6	53.6	18.2	32.5	3.0	1.6
30–39	38.0	19.3	4.5	9.2	58.4	20.5	34.7	1.9	1.4
40–49	39.3	22.1	5.3	8.0	57.5	20.9	33.3	1.6	1.2
50–59	49.5	29.6	7.5	9.1	47.7	17.9	27.5	1.5	1.2
60 & over	63.8	40.9	9.7	9.9	33.6	13.1	19.3	.8	1.5
Total	52.6%	32.3%	5.8%	9.8%	44.0%	14.8%	26.9%	1.8%	1.4%
Female:									
0– 4	93.9%	78.3%	6.0%	7.3%	4.0%	1.1%	2.7%	1.0%	1.0%
5– 9	85.8	65.0	6.7	10.4	11.1	3.6	7.3	1.3	1.6
10–14	80.1	57.6	8.0	11.1	16.9	7.1	9.3	1.2	1.8
15–19	75.9	49.9	9.8	12.5	18.9	7.4	10.2	2.2	2.9
20–24	69.7	42.2	8.7	14.0	22.9	7.7	14.0	3.5	3.7
25–29	68.1	39.5	8.6	14.7	25.9	8.8	15.9	3.3	2.5
30–39	63.8	36.8	8.1	13.9	30.7	10.7	18.4	2.7	2.4
40–49	63.6	38.5	9.4	12.2	31.9	12.9	17.5	1.8	2.2
50–59	70.8	43.9	10.9	12.8	26.2	11.8	13.3	1.1	1.7
60 & over	77.0	48.9	12.1	12.6	20.3	8.6	11.2	.7	1.7
Total	75.1%	50.8%	8.5%	12.0%	20.5%	7.6%	11.9%	2.0%	2.2%

SOURCE: Manchoukuo, Kokumuin, Sōmuchō, Tōkeisho, *Dai ichiji rinji jinkō chōsa hōkokusho. Toyū hen, dai sankan, Hōten shi* (First provisional population survey report, cities, vol. 3, Mukden; [n.p.]: Tōkeisho, 1937), Table 7.

villages, towns, and cities of North China. Two-thirds to three-fourths of the mothers of Mukden's children, i.e. females aged 15–49, were Manchurian-born.

This prevalence of indigenous females in cities with large migrant components in their populations is so basic to the formation and acculturation of urban populations that it merits closer inspection. Table 10 gives percentage distributions by area of origin for Mukden's Han population, of whom 242,000 were male and 132,000 female.

The immigrant group in the city was in constant flux. The length-of-residence data presented in Table 11 for Chinese male immigrants aged 29–49 indicate that a majority are recent arrivals. More than 58 percent of these men had been in the city five years or less. The migrants from China tended to concentrate in the lowlier occupations, whatever their length of residence in Mukden.

Crude birth and death rates for the city of Mukden for the 1920's and 1930's, even if they were available, would be so distorted by the migrant structure and the sex imbalances in the city's population as to preclude comparisons with other cities and other periods. Gross reproduction rates differed from one ethnic group to another: 2.31 for the Han, 2.21 for the Manchus, 3.08 for the Muslims, 1.92 for the Japanese, and 2.18 for the Koreans. There was limited variation among the districts of the city.

Changchun (Hsin-ching). In 1935 Changchun was the capital city of the recently established Empire of Manchoukuo. Its total population was

TABLE 10. GEOGRAPHIC ORIGINS OF THE HAN CHINESE POPULATION
OF MUKDEN BY SEX, 1935

Birthplace	Total	Male	Female
Manchuria:			
Mukden	37.6%	30.3%	50.9%
Elsewhere in			
Feng-t'ien county	6.2	5.3	8.0
Fengtien province	10.4	9.5	12.2
Chin-chou	2.8	3.0	2.3
Other	1.7	1.7	1.7
Total	58.7%	49.8%	75.1%
China:			
Shantung	14.3%	17.0%	9.4%
Hopei	24.9	30.6	14.1
Other	2.1	2.6	1.1
Total	41.3%	50.2%	24.9%

SOURCE: See Table 9.

TABLE 11. OCCUPATIONAL DISTRIBUTION IN SELECTED OCCUPATIONS BY
BIRTHPLACE FOR MEN AGED 20–49 IN MUKDEN, 1935

Birthplace and years of residence for China-born	Total	Public service, professions	Manu-facturing	Commerce	Trans-portation
Manchuria	54.2%	64.3%	47.0%	32.8%	24.8%
China:					
5 yrs. or less	58.5%	50.5%	65.4%	55.9%	59.9%
6–10	19.1	22.2	16.0	18.7	22.6
11–15	9.5	11.2	8.3	10.1	9.0
16–20	5.5	6.5	4.8	6.0	4.6
21 or over	7.4	9.6	5.5	9.3	3.9
Total	45.8%	35.7%	53.0%	67.2%	75.2%

SOURCE: See Table 9.

248,000, ethnically distributed as follows: 210,000 Han, 6,000 Manchus, 5,000 Muslims, 22,000 Japanese, and fewer than 4,000 Koreans. These ethnic groups tended to concentrate in certain districts of the city and in certain occupations. Gainfully occupied men among the Han were concentrated in manufacturing and commerce; among the Manchus, in manufacturing, commerce, and government service; among the Muslims, in commerce. The Koreans worked in agriculture and in manufacturing, whereas the Japanese men were mainly official and professional, with a secondary concentration in manufacturing. There were also major ethnic differences in the prevalence of the various occupations among those few women who worked. Han women worked in commerce with a secondary concentration in service, Manchu women worked in service occupations, and Muslim women in commerce.

Like Mukden, Changchun was a city of migrants. Among the Han Chinese that made up the overwhelming majority of its population, only 42.6 percent had been born within the city. Also, again as in Mukden, many of the children had been born in the city, whereas many of the younger adults were in-migrant. It should be noted, however, that many of the migrants came from elsewhere in Manchuria: half of Changchun's male population and almost 70 percent of its female population in 1935 had been born in Manchuria. These proportions are averages for the diverse groups in the city: 90 percent of the Manchus, 75 percent of the Muslims, and 60 percent of the Han Chinese (but only 10 percent of the Koreans and practically none of the Japanese) had been born in Manchuria.

The sex ratios (males per thousand females) among the various ethnic groups reflect the age- and sex-selectivity of the migrant component in

Changchun's population. In the age group 15–29 these ratios were 2,090 for the Han, 1,387 for the Manchus, 1,553 for the Muslims, 1,133 for the Japanese, and 1,916 for the Koreans. Whatever the age group, the relative numbers of males and females varied by place of birth. Sex ratios were almost normal among those born in Changchun. A selective in-migration of families from Hsin-ching county (immediately surrounding Changchun) yielded a high proportion of females. The sex ratio in the total population born in China was almost 3,400. At ages 20–39 the sex ratios were 4,500 for those born in Shantung and almost 4,000 for those born in Hopei.

The migrant cumulations of the Han in Changchun were recent, at least among those born in China. Two-thirds of the China-born Han men enumerated in Changchun in 1935 reported that they had last entered Manchuria sometime within the preceding five years (Table 12).

Most of the in-migrants from China were between the ages of 15 and 39. Whether married or single, most of the men had moved alone. There were 9,155 men for every 1,000 women among migrants aged 15–19 who had been in Manchuria less than a year. These imbalances were smaller in the older age groups, but there were still at least five men for every woman until age 60 and over. The imbalances also declined with increasing length of residence in Manchuria.

The fertility of the population varied among ethnic groups and among the districts of the city. In 1935 the gross reproduction rate was 2.49 for the Han, 2.43 for the Manchus, and 2.91 for the Koreans. The rates for individual districts varied between 2.00 and 3.33. The lowest fertility rates characterized the three districts disproportionately peopled by government officials and professional men. Gainfully occupied women, although still relatively rare, were more prevalent here than in other districts. The highest fertility rates were reported from the two districts where agriculture predominated. Fertility was at rural levels in these two districts, with gross reproduction rates of 3.32 and 3.33. Female birthrates were above 45, and more than 40 percent of all females were under fifteen years of age. In-migrants were less prevalent than in the other districts. Reported sex ratios showing female children outnumbering male children may reflect the underreporting of male children that appears to have been widespread among the Han in Manchuria.

The four districts that were intermediate in occupational structure were also intermediate in demographic characteristics. Recent in-migrants were less prevalent than in the more administrative districts, but more prevalent than in the agricultural districts. Fertility rates were also intermediate between the two extremes.[6]

TABLE 12. LENGTH OF RESIDENCE, AGE COMPOSITION, AND SEX RATIOS
AMONG THE CHINA-BORN HAN POPULATION OF CHANGCHUN, 1935

| Age group | Total | Years since last entrance | | | | |
		Under 1	1–2	3–5	6–11	12–15
Percent by length of residence, males:						
0– 4		38.4%	48.4%	12.8%	—	—
5– 9		18.5	38.1	26.1	16.9%	—
10–14		21.8	26.2	17.3	31.1	3.3%
15–19		26.2	41.8	14.3	12.3	3.9
20–24		24.6	35.5	16.0	16.5	3.3
25–29		21.8	33.2	15.9	17.1	6.6
30–39		17.7	29.8	15.8	17.7	7.8
40–49		13.5	23.9	13.8	19.2	9.0
50–59		10.1	17.6	12.1	16.6	10.2
60 and over		6.8	14.0	8.6	14.2	9.3
Total		19.0%	30.3%	15.1%	17.3%	6.7%
Percent age composition, males:						
0– 4	.8%	1.6%	1.3%	.7%	—	—
5– 9	1.8	1.8	2.3	3.2	1.8%	—
10–14	3.2	3.7	2.8	3.7	5.8	1.6%
15–19	9.8	13.5	13.6	9.3	7.0	5.8
20–24	15.3	19.8	17.9	16.2	14.6	8.3
25–29	16.5	18.9	18.1	17.4	16.4	16.5
30–39	25.7	23.9	25.3	26.8	26.4	30.1
40–49	16.5	11.7	13.1	15.1	18.4	22.3
50–59	7.9	4.2	4.6	6.3	7.6	12.1
60 & over	2.4	.8	1.1	1.3	1.9	3.3
Total	100.0%	100.0%	100.0%	100.0%	100.0%	100.0%
Males per 1,000 females:						
0– 4	1,072	1,021	1,093	1,121	—	—
5– 9	1,064	1,123	1,066	994	1,087	—
10–14	1,590	3,314	1,662	1,246	1,266	1,545
15–19	3,987	9,155	6,290	3,068	1,809	1,277
20–24	4,143	7,336	5,569	3,084	3,216	1,919
25–29	4,099	6,786	5,674	3,246	2,735	3,444
30–39	3,917	7,585	5,934	3,682	2,309	2,790
40–49	3,733	8,051	5,923	3,976	2,597	2,271
50–59	2,893	5,644	3,844	3,000	1,940	2,335
60 & over	1,804	2,512	2,029	1,506	1,108	1,356
Total	3,365	5,909	4,593	2,900	2,229	2,330

SOURCE: Manchoukuo, Kokumuin, Sōmuchō, Tōkeisho, *Dai ichiji rinji jinkō chōsa hōkokusho: Toyū hen, dai ikkan, Shinkyō tokubetsu shi* (First provisional population survey report, cities, vol. 1, Hsin-ching special municipality; Hsin-ching: Tōkeisho, 1937), Table 10.

NOTE: The China-born number 38.8 percent of the population overall and 47.1 percent of males. Since residence durations of more than 15 years are omitted, percentages cited in that portion of the table do not total 100.

Harbin. Harbin was distinctive among Manchurian great cities in the diversity of its people. Some three-fourths of its 500,000 inhabitants were Han. One in each six was Russian, Japanese, Korean, or without nationality.

The Chinese of Harbin, like those of Changchun and Mukden, were a migrant group. Only one-sixth of the males had been born in Harbin, whereas two-thirds had been born in China, and another sixth elsewhere in Manchuria. The sex ratios were 1,041 for those born in Harbin and 3,759 for those born in China. The demographic base for the development of an indigenous Chinese urban population was still small in 1934. There were 118,000 Chinese females in the city, but only 41,000 of them had been born there. In relative terms, 34.7 percent had been born in Harbin, 24.9 percent elsewhere in Manchuria, and 40.1 percent in China.

Occupational differences were associated with the cultural diversity and the demographic instability. Agricultural areas within the city employed one-eighth of all Harbin's gainfully occupied Chinese men. The fraction was above one-fifth in six of the city's thirteen districts, and above one-half in four others. Almost 43 percent of the gainfully occupied men were in commerce or transportation, 26 percent in manufacturing. Almost 8 percent of the women were reported as gainfully occupied, but in work (agriculture, commerce, and household service) that did not conflict with traditional roles.

The extension of education and its associated transformations were slowed by the lack of facilities and the migrant character of the adult population; but they were in process. Data on primary schooling for Harbin's residents contain five categories: completed, not completed, attending school, no education, and not yet started school. Percentages of Chinese children aged 5–9 who were attending school were 14.4 for boys and 6.6 for girls. The comparable percentages at ages 10–14 were 34.3 for boys and 20.0 for girls.

The educational achievement of Chinese men and women in the successive age groups from 15–19 onward suggests a process of social development and modernization. In all age groups, in Harbin as a whole and in each district of the city, far more men than women had completed primary school. Likewise, far more women than men had never attended school. The proportions of men and women with no education were highest in the more agricultural districts, whereas the proportions having completed primary school were highest in the more industrial districts. The percentages of primary school graduates were highest in the youngest age groups and declined with advancing age; percentages without schooling increased with advancing age. These relationships were far

TABLE 13. SELECTED DATA ON MARITAL STATUS AMONG THE HAN CHINESE
OF HARBIN, 1934

Age group	Percent single		Married men per 1,000 married women
	Men	Women	
15–19	85.1%	64.3%	999
20–24	56.2	13.5	1,503
25–29	40.6	3.5	1,757
30–34	28.8	2.0	2,134
35–39	26.8	2.4	2,248
All ages	46.8%	40.2%	2,063

SOURCE: Harbin, Kōsho, *Harubin tokubetsu shi kokō chōsa kekka hyō* (Results of the household survey of Harbin special municipality), 1935, part 5.

stronger for men than for women and for the more industrial districts than for the more agricultural ones.

In Harbin, as in the other large cities, age at marriage was relatively advanced for both men and women. As Table 13 shows, 40.6 percent of Han men were still single at ages 25–29, and 13.5 percent of Han women were still single at ages 20–24. The percentages shown in the table are difficult to interpret, particularly for men, since many of those having moved without wives may have been reported as single. However, it is plausible to argue that the reported numbers and percentages single were maxima for men and minima for women. If so, the ratios of married men to married women in the different age groups are conservative indicators of the abnormalities introduced into the demographic structure and the reproductive potential of the population by the migration of married men without their families.

The Other Cities

The description of migration, migrants in cities, and the structure, characteristics, and differentiation of city populations in Manchuria has thus far been limited to three great cities. Are these three typical or atypical of Manchurian cities in general? Specifically, did their lower fertility as compared with the rural areas surrounding them prevail in this region where rural and urban areas alike were so dominated by migrants? The answer can be given definitively, and it is yes. Table 14 gives the gross reproduction rates for Chinese women in Changchun and in the cities and counties of the five densely settled provinces of Manchuria in 1940.

In Manchuria, as in the other Chinese areas of record and in Japan,

TABLE 14. URBAN-RURAL DIFFERENCES IN GROSS REPRODUCTION RATES
FOR ALL MANCHOUKUO AND SELECTED PROVINCES, 1940

Provinces	Total	Cities	Counties
Manchoukuo	2.99	2.36	3.05
Changchun	—	2.47	—
An-tung	2.72	2.60	2.73
Fengtien	2.73	2.28	2.86
Ssu-p'ing	2.91	2.19	2.93
Kirin	3.21	2.41	3.23
Pin-chiang	3.03	2.39	3.12

SOURCE: Manchoukuo, Kokumuin, Sōmuchō, Rinji kokusei chōsa jimukyoku, *Kōtoku shichinen rinji kokusei chōsa hōkoku: Chihō hen* (Reports of the special census, 1940, provinces), 1941–43.

fertility was lower in the great cities than in the surrounding rural areas. It was lower in industrial than in agricultural regions. It was highest in the regions of recent or ongoing land settlement. Migrants to the industrial cities adapted to the marital patterns and the reproductive levels of the urban populations. Migrants to the rural areas and the agricultural frontiers maintained the high fertility of the traditional rural society or even adapted to the patterns of more abundant childbearing in a rural milieu with lessened pressures of people on land and other resources.

Some Reflections

The structures and dynamics of the Chinese and related populations in great cities during the 1920's and 1930's were determined by the magnitude and selectivity of the migrations and by the natural dynamics within the cities. Analysis of these factors for the cities of Japan, Taiwan, the Kwantung Leased Territory and the South Manchurian Railway Zone of the Liao-tung peninsula, and Manchuria yielded results so similar that summarizing them would be repetitious. These cities were clearly between two East Asian worlds. The decades studied were the terminus of Japanese imperial expansion and transformation, whether inside or outside Japan. They were preludes to the decades during which a unified China and a transforming perimeter would alter the outlook for East Asian populations and hence for all earth's growing populations.

The earliest census and registration data reflect some aspects of the structure and dynamics of traditional cities. The later demographic data, by contrast, may be viewed as bases for postwar orders, whether in Japan, Taiwan, or China. Obviously, then, the dynamics of migration, city growth, and differentiation in the cities of Japan, Taiwan, and northeast China in the interwar years are crucial in interpreting the change from the relative demographic stability of the ancient order to the swift demographic transitions of the modern order. The following tentative generalizations may stimulate further research:

1. Cities were concentrations of migrants. Their population structures reflected migrant habits and age- and sex-selectivity in migration. Most of the migrants came as young men. Many remained in the cities for limited periods only, but enough stayed to yield increasing numbers of the mature and the aging. Most women moved in relation to the movements of men, whether fathers, husbands, or other relatives or family members.

2. Indigenous populations of the urban-born developed swiftly, but urban transformations were retarded by the continuing predominance among the young adult population of migrants from more traditional areas.

3. As the children and later descendants of the migrants matured, the urban populations became more nearly normal in their age and sex distributions. Increasing proportions of those entering the labor force were urban-born; increasing proportions of the young people forming families were remote from the rural heritage.

4. Age- and sex-selectivities in migration, the associated age and sex structures of city populations, and higher ages at marriage and lower fertility for women in cities characterized traditional societies as well as industrializing societies. Both stability and mobility, both homogeneity and differentiation, can be discerned in the dynamics of traditional populations. Adaptability and diversity were the heritage of the developing areas rather than products of development.

5. In areas of comprehensive economic and social change, the rural-urban differentiations in reproductive levels persisted along with downward movements in the fertility of women. In this setting, migration and the changing locus of the population contributed to declining fertility and slowing rates of population growth. Migration, city growth, and differentiation within cities or among areas were neither sufficient stimulants nor necessary harbingers of the declining fertility that signified demographic transition.

Notes

Notes

Introduction

1. *Mémoires concernant les Chinois* "par les missionaires de Pékin" (Paris: Nyon, 1776–1814), vol. 8, pp. 217–19.

2. China, Chu chi ch'u, *Chung-kuo jen k'ou t'ung chi tzu liao* (Statistical materials on the population of China; Taipei: Hsüeh hai ch'u pan she, 1971; reprint of the 1940 original), p. 16. The date to which these figures refer is not stated, but is presumably the 1930's.

3. *Baron Richthofen's Letters, 1870–1872* (Shanghai: *North-China Herald* Office, 1872), p. 117.

4. These are estimates based on (1) Tōkyō chigaku kyōkai, *Chu Shina oyobi Nan Shina* (Central and southern China; Tokyo: Tōkyō chigaku kyōkai, 1917), map facing p. 160, and (2) Minami Manshū tetsudō kabushiki kaisha, *Hoku Shina keizai sōran* (Economic survey of North China; Tokyo: Nihon hyōronsha, 1938), appendix, pp. 2–4.

5. A. Hosie, *Three Years in Western China* (London: G. Philip and Son, 1890), p. 30.

6. J. L. Buck, *Land Utilization in China* (Nanking: University of Nanking, 1937), vol. 3, pp. 420–22.

7. Imahori Seiji, *Chūgoku hōken shakai no kikō* (The structure of Chinese feudal society; Tokyo: Nihon gakujutsu shinkō-kai, 1955), p. 19.

8. D. Gillin, *Warlord: Yen Hsi-shan in Shansi Province 1911–1949* (Princeton, N.J.: Princeton University Press, 1967), pp. 79–102; von Richthofen 1872, pp. 86–87, 95.

9. China, Chu chi ch'u, *Chung-kuo jen k'ou* . . . 1940, p. 102.

10. J. E. Spencer, "Trade and Transshipment in the Yangtze Valley," *Geographical Review*, 28 (1938): 113–14, 117.

11. Imahori 1955, pp. 19, 23.

12. South Manchurian Railway, *Third Report on Progress in Manchuria, 1907–1932* (Dairen, 1932), pp. 17, 40; *ibid., Fifth Report on Progress in Manchuria, to 1936* (Dairen, 1936), pp. 163–64.

13. See Irene B. Taeuber's paper in this volume, pp. 374–77.

14. U.K. Naval Intelligence Division, *China Proper*, 3, appendix iii.

15. C. M. Hou, *Foreign Investment and Economic Development in China 1840–1937* (Cambridge: Harvard University Press, 1965), p. 14; Muramatsu Yūji, *Chūgoku Keizai no shakai taisei* (The social structure of China's economy; Tokyo: Tōyō Keizai shimpōsha, 1949), p. 61.

16. J. K. Chang, *Industrial Development in Pre-Communist China* (Chicago: Aldine, 1969), p. 71.

17. H. B. Morse, *The International Relations of the Chinese Empire* (London: Longmans, 1910–18), vol. 3, p. 337.

18. For an outline of the pattern see the *North-China Herald*, Jan. 16, 1912, p. 2; and Kuo T'ing-i, *Chin tai Chung-kuo shih shih jih chih* (A chronology of modern Chinese history; Taipei: privately, 1963), vol. 2, pp. 1405–38. On the urban character of the revolution see the papers by E. J. M. Rhoads and M. Elvin in this volume, and the important qualification provided by Winston Hsieh's paper. The main authorities for the general position adopted here are M. C. Wright, ed., *China in Revolution, The First Phase, 1900–1913* (New Haven: Yale University Press, 1968); M. Elvin, "The Gentry Democracy in Chinese Shanghai, 1905–1914," in J. Gray, ed., *Modern China's Search for a Political Form* (London: Oxford University Press, 1969); J. H. Fincher, *The Chinese Self-Government Movement, 1900–1912*, Ph.D. diss. (University of Washington, 1970; Ann Arbor, Mich.: University Microfilms, 1971); E. Friedman, "Revolution or Just Another Bloody Cycle? Swatow and the 1911 Revolution," *Journal of Asian Studies*, 29, no. 2 (1970); and M. B. Rankin, *Early Chinese Revolutionaries: Radical Intellectuals in Shanghai and Chekiang, 1902–1911* (Cambridge: Harvard University Press, 1971).

19. Von Richthofen 1872, p. 84.

20. *Population of Great Britain: Abstract of the Answers and Returns* (House of Commons: London, 1822), especially pp. 161 (Liverpool), 521 (Glasgow), 551 (London), 611 (Manchester), 669 (Bradford and Leeds); and *Census of Great Britain, 1851* (Eyre and Spottiswoode: London, 1854), *Population Tables*, Section 2.1, London A1, etc. I am grateful to Dr. T. H. Hollingsworth for having pointed these out to me.

21. M. F. and T. H. Hollingsworth, "Plague Mortality Rates by Age and Sex in the Parish of St. Botolph's without Bishopsgate, London, 1603," *Population Studies* (1971): 145.

22. Yü Hung-chün, ed., *Shang-hai shih nien chien* (Shanghai municipal yearbook; Shanghai: Chung hua shu chü, 1937), section C, pp. 25–26; China, Chu chi ch'u, *Chung-kuo jen k'ou. . .* 1940, p. 42.

23. Preface by Hu Shih to Han Tzu-yün, *Hai shang hua* (Shanghai: Ya tung t'u shu kuan, 1926; *North-China Herald*, Apr. 22, 1911, p. 231; Apr. 29, p. 299.

The Treaty Ports and China's Modernization

1. Joseph Levenson, in particular, has beautifully elaborated the importance of the distinction between "modern" and "Western": see his *Confucian China and Its Modern Fate: The Problem of Intellectual Continuity* (Berkeley: University of California Press, 1958), especially pp. 117ff. Definitions and explorations of "modernization" in a variety of historical and regional contexts are also provided by C. E. Black in *The Dynamics of Modernization: A Study*

in Comparative History (New York: Harper and Row, 1966). Levenson and Black, among others, have examined the dimensions of "modernization" as a helpful concept to the point that it is acceptable to use the term without further discussion of its meaning. For other partly definitional discussions of the political aspects of modernization, and for a point of view, see Barrington Moore, *Social Origins of Dictatorship and Democracy: Lord and Peasant in the Making of the Modern World* (Boston: Beacon Press, 1966), and R. P. Dore, "On the Possibility and Desirability of a Theory of Modernization," in *Report of the International Conference on the Problems of Modernization in Asia* (Seoul, 1968).

2. For a more detailed discussion of this long historical process and some of the factors involved, see my "Traditionalism and Colonialism: Changing Urban Roles in Asia," *Journal of Asian Studies*, 29 (1969): 67–84.

3. R. Redfield and M. Singer characterized these cities as "heterogenetic" as opposed to the "orthogenetic" cities of the Asian tradition in their "The Cultural Role of Cities," *Economic Development and Cultural Change*, 3 (1954): 53–73. B. F. Hoselitz suggests a typology that labels these and other colonial cities as "parasitic" in his "Generative and Parasitic Cities," *ibid.*, pp. 278–94.

4. The Manchurian treaty ports (except for Newchwang) were a separate and later development under what amounted to Japanese colonial control after 1905. Hong Kong is of course similarly a separate and wholly colonial matter.

5. A few representative studies may be cited here: Anil Seal, *The Emergence of Indian Nationalism: Competition and Collaboration in the Later Nineteenth Century* (Cambridge: Cambridge University Press, 1968); N. S. Bose, *The Indian Awakening and Bengal* (Calcutta: K. L. Mukhopadhyay, 1960); David Kopf, "The Urbanized Intelligentsia of Calcutta and Their Asian Counterparts in the Nineteenth Century: Encounter, Modernization, and the Reinterpretation of Traditions," unpubl. manuscript for the Third Conference of Bengali Studies, 1967; Warren Gunderson, "Modernization and Cultural Change: The Self-image and World View of the Bengali Intelligentsia as Found in the Writings of the Mid-Nineteenth Century, 1830–1870," unpubl. paper, mimeo., 1965.

6. See for example the brief run of railway figures published by the Nationalist Government, which show a very low level of operation especially in terms of kilometer/tons hauled: *Statistics of the Chinese National Railway, 1915–1929* (Nanking, 1931). Much of what the railways did carry was troops and military supplies. These figures are further analyzed in R. Murphey, "China's Transport Problem and Communist Planning," *Economic Geography*, 32 (1956): 17–28. The state and development of the economy as a whole after 1911, including the railway system, is clearly summarized and interpreted in A. Feuerwerker, "The Chinese Economy, 1912–1949," *Michigan Papers in Chinese Studies*, 1 (1968).

7. These are multitudinous, not easy to use, and frequently ambiguous. They do suggest at least impressionistically a volume of internal trade and a prominence of merchants that does not agree well with traditional or official stereotypes. A recent effort to analyze the commercial economy of one important area, based in large part on gazetteer materials, is Fu I-ling, *Ming tai Chiang-nan shih min ching chi shih t'an* (A study of the economy of the urban

population of Kiangnan in Ming times; Shanghai: People's Press, 1957). A good deal of material on seventeenth-century trade is provided in Sung Ying-hsing, *T'ien kung k'ai wu*: E-tu Zen Sun and S-c. Sun, eds. and transl., *Chinese Technology in the Seventeenth Century* (University Park: Pennsylvania State University, 1966). The discussion of interprovincial trade and efforts to assess its size in Dwight Perkins, *Agricultural Development in China* (Chicago: Aldine, 1969), pp. 345–65, are useful but highly speculative and are in any case largely limited to the post-1870 period.

    8. The report "Shinkoku menka mempu oyobi menshi yunyū keikyō" (The outlook for imports of raw cotton, cotton cloth, and cotton thread in China), which appears in *Dai Nippon menshi bōseki dōgyō rengōkai hōkoku* (Report of the United Association of Japanese Cotton Spinners; Tokyo, 1898), is cited (pp. 523ff) by Hatano Yoshihiro in *Chūgoku kindai kōgyō-shi no kenkyū* (Studies in China's early industrialization; Kyoto: Tōyōshi kenkyūkai, 1961). I have used Hatano only in a summary English translation generously furnished to me by Mark Elvin, as part of the series prepared and edited by him titled *Michigan Abstracts of Chinese and Japanese Works on Chinese History*, and am of course indebted to him for calling this work to my attention in the first place.

    9. Hatano 1961, pp. 529–30.
    10. Hatano 1961, pp. 533–34, 551–52.
    11. Nakahara Teruo, "Shindai ni okeru sōryō no shōkinka ni tsuite: Sōun kenkyū no hitokoma" (The marketing of tribute grain during the Ch'ing period: One aspect of the study of tribute-rice shipments), *Shigaku kenkyū* (Hiroshima), 70 (1958): 46; and Nakahara Teruo, "Shindai sōsen ni yoru shōhin ryūtsū ni tsuite" (The flow of commodities on grain-transport ships during the Ch'ing period), *Shigaku kenkyū*, 72 (1959): 67. I have consulted only a rough condensed translation of these articles prepared by Mark Elvin, to whom I am deeply grateful.
    12. Hoshi Ayao, *Mindai sōun no kenkyū* (A study of the transport system of the grain tribute during Ming; Tokyo: Nihon gakujutsu shinkō kai, 1963). Again I have been dependent on Mark Elvin's summary English translation, now published as "The Ming Tribute Grain System," *Michigan Abstracts of Chinese and Japanese Works on Chinese History*, no. 1 (Ann Arbor, Mich.: Center for Chinese Studies, 1969), pp. 30ff. The same practices and orders of magnitude continued in the Ch'ing and are further described and estimated in Nakahara 1958, p. 46.
    13. This is of course the main point of Nakahara 1958, for which the article provides ample documentation.
    14. *Ibid.*, p. 46.
    15. *Ibid.*, pp. 46–50.
    16. *Ibid.*, p. 49.
    17. Nakahara 1959, pp. 69–70.
    18. Nakahara 1958, pp. 53–55.
    19. Nakahara 1959, p. 77.
    20. Hoshi/Elvin, pp. 60–61.
    21. *Ibid.*, pp. 86ff.
    22. Saeki Tomi, *Shindai ensei no kenkyū* (A study of the Ch'ing dynasty salt monopoly; Kyoto: Tōyōshi kenkyūkai, 1956).

23. *Ibid.*, and Thomas Metzger, "T'ao Chu's Reform of the Huaipei Salt Monopoly," *Papers on China*, 16 (1962): 1–4. Metzger draws on Saeki's earlier work and on a great variety of other sources.

24. Metzger 1962, p. 4.

25. *Ibid.*

26. *Ibid.*, pp. 30–31.

27. For brief but provocative remarks on this matter, see Thomas Metzger, "Ch'ing Commercial Policy," *Ch'ing-shih wen-t'i*, 1, no. 3 (Feb. 1966): 4–10. Lien-sheng Yang, "Government Control of Urban Merchants in Traditional China," *Tsing Hua Journal of Chinese Studies*, n.s. 8, nos. 1–2 (1970), provides a valuable survey of varied data on the role and status of merchants, especially in late Ming and Ch'ing times. These data demonstrate merchant success in entering the gentry group via examination and purchase, the relatively light level of regulation and taxation or exaction, and the genuine concern of the state not to ruin or even seriously to impede merchant activity. Yang further stresses the nonrebellious character of merchants in general and the infrequency of any merchant-led uprisings or even of protests during the Ch'ing, suggesting that they had their own vested interest in the existing system that protected and rewarded them. P. T. Ho, *The Ladder of Success in Imperial China: Aspects of Social Mobility, 1368–1911* (New York: Columbia University Press, 1962), pp. 53–91 and esp. 83–84, describes the upward mobility of merchants through the examination system, the purchase of degrees, and more general routes in the surprisingly fluid social system of late traditional China. More conventional, or perhaps literal, readings of official policy and actions with respect to merchants may be found in Jean Escarra, *Le droit Chinois* (Paris: Librairie du Receuil, 1936), and T. Jernigan, *China in Law and Commerce* (New York: Macmillan, 1905). F. L. Dawson, "Law and the Merchant in Traditional China," *Papers on China*, 2 (1948): 55–92, takes for the most part a similar view, but does point to the relative operational strength of the guilds as semi-independent merchant groups, and also to the effectiveness of official connections in protecting and nourishing individual merchants and collective commercial enterprises.

28. A. M. Craig, J. K. Fairbank, and E. O. Reischauer, *East Asia: The Modern Transformation* (Boston: Houghton Mifflin, 1964), p. 150.

29. Adam Smith, *The Wealth of Nations*, book 5, chap. 1 (vol. 2 of the Everyman Edition), p. 217.

30. *Ibid.*, book 1, chap. 3 (Everyman, 1: 16–19); book 1, chap. 11 (Everyman, 1: 188); book 4, chap. 9 (Everyman, 2: 174).

31. See, for example, M. D. Morris, "Toward a Reinterpretation of Nineteenth Century Indian Economic History," *Journal of Economic History*, 23 (1963): 606–18.

32. H. D. Fong, *Cotton Industry and Trade in China* (Tientsin, Chihli Press, 1932), vol. 2, p. 230.

33. For more details, see H. D. Fong, "Rural Weaving and the Merchant Employers in a North China District," *Nankai Social and Economic Quarterly*, 8, nos. 1 and 2 (1935).

34. *Ibid.*, no. 1.

35. Hatano 1961, pp. 530, 532–33, 548.

36. Ch'en Shih-chi, "Chia wu chien ch'ien Chung-kuo nung ts'un shou kung

yeh ti pien hua ho tzu pen chu i sheng ch'an ti ch'eng chang" (Rural household hand cloth making and the rise of capitalist production before the Sino-Japanese war), *Li shih yen chiu*, 2 (1959): 17–38.

37. P'eng Chih-i, ed., *Chung-kuo chin tai shou kung yeh shih tzu liao* (Materials on the history of modern China's handicraft industries), 11 (Peking, 1957): 189ff. Too late for me to make extensive use of it in this treatment, Albert Feuerwerker has produced a summary analysis of trends in cotton textile production, trade, and consumption in late imperial China titled "Handicraft and Manufactured Cotton Textiles in China, 1871–1910," *Journal of Economic History*, 30, no. 2 (1970). In brief, it confirms and provides additional detailed evidence for the general propositions advanced here.

38. S. G. Checkland, "An English Merchant House in China After 1842," *Bulletin of the Business Historical Society*, 27 (1953): 162–63, 168, 170, 181.

39. Wang Ching-yü, "Shih chiu shih chi wai kuo ch'in hua chih yeh chung ti hua shang fu ku shou tung" (The rise of Chinese merchants as investors in foreign-controlled enterprises in the late nineteenth century), *Li shih yen chiu*, 4 (1965): 39–74. It is worth noting in this connection, however, that it was common practice for Chinese investors and managers not to disclose more than a fraction of the full amount of their investment or capitalization, in an effort to minimize taxation and other exactions and, in the case of industrial establishments, to avoid restrictions on factory conditions. This was common knowledge, but by its nature hard to document. The same applies to the widespread use by Chinese of foreigners as fronts under whose name ownership of enterprises was listed; this brought a great many advantages and was correspondingly common. It seems probable that the true total of Chinese investment in "modern" as well as traditional enterprises was significantly greater than any surveys or even estimates suggest. I am grateful to my colleague Cheng Chu-yüan for reminding me of these points.

40. See K. C. Liu, *Anglo-Chinese Steamship Rivalry in China, 1862–1874* (Cambridge: Harvard University Press, 1962).

41. Detail on the role of Chinese investors in these activities is provided in Wang Ching-yü, ed., *Chung-kuo chin tai kung yeh shih tzu liao chi yao: ti erh chi* (Materials on the history of modern industry in China, second series), 2 vols., Peking, 1960.

42. *Ibid.*, vol. 1, pp. 68–69.

43. Chung-li Chang, *The Income of the Chinese Gentry* (Seattle: University of Washington Press, 1962), pp. 139ff, argues that by the 1880's the profit returns from trade had become substantially greater than the financial rewards of landholding, especially as land prices rose. See also P'eng Chih-i, "Shih chiu shih chi hou ch'i Chung-kuo ch'eng shih shou kung yeh shang yeh hsing hui ti chung chien ho tso yung" (The importance and function of urban handicraft and trade organizations in the late nineteenth century), *Li shih yen chiu*, 1 (1965): 81–90, on the changing profitability of alternate uses of investment capital.

44. The best treatment of the experience and problems of the government-managed enterprises after 1870 is Feuerwerker 1968. For an analysis of a single undertaking that manifested many of these problems, especially the shortage of both investment and operating capital, see his "China's Nineteenth Century Industrialization: The Case of the Hanyehping Coal and Iron Com-

pany Limited," in C. D. Cowan, ed., *The Economic Development of China and Japan* (London: Allen and Unwin, 1964), pp. 79–110. Feuerwerker has also examined a different case, that of a privately owned Chinese firm (although it profited from official connections) whose striking success was due at least in part to its ability to obtain ample capital, dependent in turn on its success in maintaining a consistent high rate of return to investors: A. Feuerwerker, "Industrial Enterprise in Twentieth Century China: The Chee Hsin Cement Co.," in Feuerwerker, Murphey, and Wright, eds., *Approaches to Modern Chinese History* (Berkeley: University of California Press, 1967), pp. 304–41.

45. See, for example, Gunderson 1965.

46. I am indebted to B. H. Farmer for this expressive phrase, which he uses illuminatingly in his "The Social Basis of Nationalism in Ceylon," *Journal of Asian Studies*, 24 (1965): 431–39.

47. *Awakening Japan*, transl. Erwin Baelz (New York: Viking Press, 1932), p. 17, quoted in W. W. Lockwood, "Japan's Response to the West," *World Politics*, 9 (1956): 37–54.

48. The phrase originated with Bill Bradley, the All-American basketballer; see J. McPhee, *A Sense of Where You Are* (New York: Farrar, Straus, Giroux, 1965).

49. There is much *hubris* in attempting to deal in a short paragraph with that for which Joseph Levenson has given us a magistral guide and interpretation. I can only acknowledge my gratitude, and my indebtedness, to *Confucian China and Its Modern Fate: The Problem of Intellectual Continuity* (Berkeley: University of California Press, 1958), *The Problem of Monarchical Decay* (1964), and *The Problem of Historical Significance* (1965). *Liang Ch'i-ch'ao and the Mind of Modern China* (Cambridge: Harvard University Press, 1953), " 'History' and 'Value': The Tensions of Intellectual Choice in Modern China," in A. Wright, ed., *Studies in Chinese Thought* (Chicago: University of Chicago Press, 1953), "The Province, the Nation, and the World: The Problem of Chinese Identity," in Feuerwerker, Murphey, and Wright, eds., 1967, and *Revolution and Cosmopolitanism: The Western Stage and the Chinese Stages* (Berkeley: University of California Press, 1971) provide further penetrating discussion of identity, "culturalism," nationalism, and provincialism. Levenson's tragic death prevented the completion of a larger manuscript on which he was engaged and which I had the good fortune to see in its early stages and to discuss with him at some length: "Provincialism and Cosmopolitanism: Chinese History and the Meaning of 'Modern Times.' " He also read and commented on an earlier version of the present essay, to my great benefit.

50. "Marketing and Social Structure in Rural China," *Journal of Asian Studies*, 24, no. 1 (Nov. 1964), no. 2 (Feb. 1965), no. 3 (May 1965).

51. For a brief provocative essay suggesting a more appropriate perspective on regionalism and provincialism in this period, see Ernest Young, "Political Provincialism in Early Twentieth Century China," unpublished paper delivered at the 1968 Annual Meeting of the American Historical Association in New York.

52. E. O. Reischauer, ed. and transl., *Ennin's Travels in T'ang China* (New York: Ronald Press, 1955).

53. J. Gernet, *Daily Life in China on the Eve of the Mongol Invasion*, transl. by H. M. Wright (New York: Macmillan, 1962).

54. *China in the Sixteenth Century: The Journals of Matthew Ricci, 1583–1610*, transl. L. J. Gallagher (New York: Random House, 1953).

55. This paragraph is based on a personal communication from Louie Kui-on, a native of the village in question and now a graduate student at the University of Michigan, plus his unpublished summary of his grandfather's recollections as related to him, and his conversations with other former residents of the village now living in or visiting Hong Kong.

56. The most convenient treatment of the matters summarized here is Chi-ming Hou, *Foreign Investment and Economic Development in China, 1840–1937* (Cambridge: Harvard University Press, 1965).

57. *Family Revolution in Modern China* (Cambridge: Harvard University Press, 1949); *The Rise of the Modern Chinese Business Class*, Part I mimeo., (New York: Institute of Pacific Relations, 1949); and "Contrasting Factors in the Modernization of China and Japan," *Economic Development and Cultural Change*, 2 (1953): 161–97. See also, among others, Benjamin Schwartz, "Modernization and the Maoist Vision: Some Reflections on Chinese Communist Goals," *China Quarterly*, no. 21 (1965): 3–19.

58. I list here only a few of the more important examples: the various accounts of the McCartney mission and its inland journey from Peking to Canton; G. T. Staunton's account of the Amherst mission, *Notes of Proceedings and Occurrences During the British Embassy to Peking in 1816* (London: J. Murray, 1824); John Phipps, *A Practical Treatise on China and the Eastern Trade* (London: Charles Knight, 1836); J. F. Davis, *The Chinese: A General Description of China and Its Inhabitants* (London: Charles Knight, 1836); H. H. Lindsay and K. Gützlaff, *Report of Proceedings on a Voyage to the Northern Ports of China* (London: B. Fellowes, 1834); Karl Gützlaff, *China Opened*, 2 vols. (London: B. Fellowes, 1838); David Abeel, *Journal of a Residence in China and Neighboring Countries* (New York: Leavitt, Lord and Co., 1835); W. H. Medhurst, *China* (London: J. Snow, 1838); the several accounts of Robert Fortune, all published in London by J. Murray: *Three Years' Wanderings in the Northern Provinces of China* (1847), *A Journey to the Tea Countries of China and India* (1852), *Two Visits to the Tea Countries of China and the British Plantations in the Himalaya* (1853), *The Tea Districts of China and India*, 2 vols. (1853), *A Residence Among the Chinese* (1857), and *Yedo and Peking* (1863); L. Oliphant, *Narrative of the Earl of Elgin's Mission to China and Japan* (New York: Harper and Bros., 1860; F. W. Williams, ed., "The Diary of S. Wells Williams," *Journal of the North China Branch of the Royal Asiatic Society* (hereafter JNCBRAS), 42 (1911): 1–232; Evariste-Régis Huc, *The Chinese Empire*, 2 vols., transl. from the French (London: Longmans, Brown, Green, and Longmans, 1855); W. Dickinson, "Narrative of an Overland Trip Through Hunan from Canton to Hankow," JNCBRAS, 1 (1864): 159–73; A. S. Bickmore, "Sketch of a Journey from Canton to Hankow," JNCBRAS, 4 (1868): 1–20.

59. Fortune 1847, p. 196. The statement is left unchanged in a later edition described by Fortune in the introduction as "corrected by later experience" (Fortune 1853b, p. 96).

60. Lindsay and Gützlaff, 1834.

61. At Shanghai, there was no reason to assume that it was inflated; tribute

rice shipments would not normally reach their peak until the latter part of the summer.

62. A weekly average of 550 ships averaging 158 tons entered the port of London between 1840 and 1842 (*Tables of the Revenue, Population, Commerce, etc. of the United Kingdom and its Dependencies;* London: 1840, 1841, 1842). Such an assessment is not necessarily inconsistent with categorizations of Shanghai earlier in this paper as a "second-rank regional market." As of the 1840's, its population was apparently much less than that of Nanking, Foochow, Sian, Chengtu, and Chungking, let alone Peking, Soochow, Canton, Wuhan, and Hangchow. Although the volume of trade at Shanghai was clearly large, it was probably smaller than that at Canton and Foochow, Wuhan, and Tientsin, at least. Unfortunately we have no estimates for these cities comparable with Lindsay's for Shanghai. That Shanghai, despite its commercial prominence, was nevertheless a small regional center by comparison with the long list of larger cities tells one a good deal about the bases of urban growth, functions and size in traditional China. By the 1920's the high tide of foreign power and commercial success in China and the pinnacle of economic Shanghai as the lion of the treaty port system (before the blows of world depression, boycotts, and Japanese invasion), Shanghai again ranked among the first three or four ports of the world. How much change did the foreigners, for all their energy, self-confidence, and "progress," succeed in producing?

63. Oliphant 1860, p. 565.

64. Bickmore 1868, pp. 1–20.

65. Davis's work, *The Chinese: A General Description of China and Its Inhabitants*, first appeared in 1836, in two volumes; but after the war it was extensively revised and augmented in successive editions, each of three volumes, which drew on his later experiences. He was the first widely read English interpreter of China, and was able to draw on a twenty-year residence, beginning at age eighteen (in 1813) when he joined the Canton factory staff of the old East India Company. In 1816 he accompanied the ill-fated Amherst Mission to Peking, and hence saw something of the "interior" on the trip back to Canton by inland waterways. In 1834 he was appointed second superintendent of trade at Canton under Lord Napier, and served as superintendent for a year on Napier's death at Macau shortly thereafter. From his first arrival at Canton, Davis had studied Chinese, and had long experience as an interpreter and translator in the dealings of the Company and the Crown with Chinese officialdom. His career in China concluded with a term as Governor of Hong Kong (1844–48), in which office he also had general responsibility for the British position in the five mainland ports.

66. Fortune 1853, vol. 2, p. 12.

67. *Ibid.,* pp. 17ff.

68. *Ibid.,* pp. 19–20.

69. Davis 1836 (4th ed., 3 vols.), vol. 1, pp. 195ff, 200. Davis was doubtless right to attribute a large part of the prosperity to the existence of a peaceful civil order, although this surely worked both ways.

70. *Ibid.,* p. 202.

71. *Ibid.,* vol. 2, p. 67.

72. *Ibid.,* p. 119 (italics in original).

73. *Ibid.*, p. 27.
74. *Ibid.*, pp. 29–30.
75. *Ibid.*, p. 103.
76. *Ibid.*, p. 90.
77. Huc 1855, pp. 332–65.
78. This estimate was mainly responsible for numerous charges that Huc was at best a teller of tall stories, at worst a liar who wove his entire story out of whole cloth and had never even seen Wuhan—see for example the well-known account edited by N. B. Denys, *The Treaty Ports of China and Japan* (London: Trübner, 1867), p. 440. The controversy over the validity and accuracy of Huc's remarks was much later settled definitively by Paul Pelliot in his carefully detailed critical introduction to the Broadway Travellers' edition of Huc and Gabet's *Travels in Tartary, Tibet, and China,* transl. W. Hazlitt, vol. 1 (London: Knopf, 1928), pp. v–xx, which draws on and adds to Pelliot's earlier article, "Le voyage de M. M. Gabet et Huc," *T'oung Pao,* serie II, 24 (1925–26); 133–78. Pelliot concludes that Huc "had a somewhat ardent imagination" but did not intentionally falsify or mislead. He spoke excellent Chinese, although he could read only simple texts. "He invented nothing, but he transposed his material in order to please, and he succeeded" (*Travels,* p. xxxv). As Pelliot suggests, Huc's account should not be depended on in specific details, and certainly not for its estimate of the population of Wuhan in 1850–51, but in general his description may be accepted as valid.
79. Perkins 1969, pp. 297ff.
80. The separateness of the Manchurian economy, an important part of the argument here, seems to me clear and substantial enough to warrant deducting Manchurian trade figures from any attempt to show trade volume, foreign or domestic, as a measure of the treaty port impact on the Chinese economy after 1905. By 1920, total Manchurian foreign trade reached (in round numbers) 270 million Haikuan taels while that of China Proper in 1920 totaled just over one billion. By 1925, these figures were respectively 365 million and 1.3 billion, by 1929 559 million and 1.7 billion. (Figures from the Maritime Customs series, as assembled for comparison in *The Manchukuo Yearbook,* [Tokyo: East Asiatic Economic Investigation Bureau; 1934], Table 4, pp. 579–80.)
81. The likin revenue statistics offer a rough but grossly incomplete indication of internal trade movements. I am inclined to feel that Perkins (1969, pp. 345–57) attempts to extract more meaning and validity from them in this connection than they possess, but his discussion does, among other things, lend support to the point made here about statistical illusions created by the expanding coverage of the Customs figures.
82. These comparisons are based on figures provided in the *Memorandum on International Trade and Balances of Payments, 1912–1926* (Geneva: League of Nations, 1927 and 1928), vols. 1 and 2; and on the *Yearbook of International Trade Statistics* published by the United Nations. Both publications attempt, in spite of the difficulties involved, to make trade data internationally comparable. The U.N. figures, which cover the 1930's, are based on "new" U.S. dollars, i.e. dollars of the gold content fixed in 1934, and on the rates used by each national authority responsible for external trade statistics to convert national currency into foreign currency values.

83. *The Cradle of Colonialism* (New Haven: Yale University Press, 1963), p. 224. The same point is made by J. C. Van Leur in *Indonesian Trade and Society* (The Hague: W. Van Hoeve, 1955), pp. 162ff and 170ff, and by M. A. F. Meilink-Roelofez, *Asian Trade and European Influence in the Indonesian Archipelago* (The Hague: M. Nijhoff, 1962), pp. 134ff and 178ff.

84. Letter dated Jan. 12, 1864, to Bruce's sister, Lady Augusta Stanley, discovered by Jack Gerson in the Elgin/Bruce archive in Broomhall, Scotland, and printed in *Ch'ing-shih wen-t'i*, 1, no. 5 (Apr. 1967): 11–14.

85. Skinner 1965: 211–28.

86. See, for example, P'eng Chih-i 1965: 81–90.

87. Sept. 9, Sept. 23, and Nov. 7, 1879; and Mar. 25 and Apr. 10, 1880.

88. See their application to the China case in Marion Levy, *The Rise of the Modern Chinese Business Class*, 1949.

89. See K. C. Liu, *Anglo-American Steamship Rivalry in China, 1862–1874* (Cambridge: Harvard University Press, 1962) and "Steamship Enterprise in Nineteenth-Century China," *Journal of Asian Studies*, 18 (1959).

90. See Shih Kuo-heng, *The Early Development of the Modern Chinese Business Class*, mimeo., Part II (New York: Institute of Pacific Relations, 1949), p. 38.

91. Yen Chung-p'ing, *Chung-kuo mien fang chih shih kao* (Draft history of the Chinese cotton industry; Peking: K'o hsüeh, 1955), p. 122.

92. *Ibid.*, p. 158.

93. Sources of financing for Chinese mills, and interest rates paid, are given in Yen Chung-p'ing 1955, pp. 182–85 and 233–37.

94. Charles K. Moser, *The Cotton Textile Industry of Far Eastern Countries* (Boston: Pepperell Manufacturing Co., 1930), p. 68.

95. See L. G. Ting, *Recent Developments in China's Cotton Industry* (Shanghai: China Institute of Pacific Relations, 1936); C-M. Hou 1965, pp. 153ff.

96. As recorded in the Maritime Customs, *Annual Returns of Trade*.

97. I have read with much profit and drawn in general terms here on an unpublished manuscript by Ramon Myers tentatively titled "Entrepreneurship and Industrial Development in Modern China."

98. See for example Ou Chi-luan, *Kuang-chou chih yin yeh* (Traditional banking in Canton; Canton, 1932), esp. pp. 209ff; and Wu Ch'eng-hsi, *Chung-kuo ti yin hang* (Chinese banks; Shanghai, 1934). Chu counts 540 "native" banks in Canton in the early 1930's (p. 237).

99. Wu Ch'eng-hsi 1934, pp. 70ff.

100. On the "modern" Chinese banks, see also L. G. Ting, "The Chinese Banks and the Financing of Government and Industry," *Nankai Social and Economic Quarterly*, 8 (1935): 578–616; he counts 146 such banks in China as a whole (excluding Manchuria) in 1932, and "over 300" foreign and Sino-foreign banks, whose total assets were considerably greater. The article also distinguishes three types of "native" banks, but stresses their interlocking connections throughout the China market and their practice of making loans on personal credit. Frank Tamagna, *Banking and Finance in China* (New York: International Secretariat, Institute of Pacific Relations, 1942), includes a brief survey of the development of "native" banks, the decline of the Shansi banks, and the rise of "modern" banking.

101. The pioneer study of the diffusion of innovation is Torsten Hager-strand, *The Propagation of Innovation Waves* (Lund: University of Lund, 1952); his larger study of 1953, translated by A. Pred as *Innovation Diffusion as a Spatial Process*, was published by the University of Chicago Press in 1967. I am, however, indebted to Prof. Hagerstrand for calling this point to my attention in a personal conversation.

102. This also happens to have been the first full decade of the operation of the new treaty system set up in 1858–60 but not fully functioning until the end of the Taiping and Nien Fei Rebellions and the effective opening of the Yangtze.

103. Maritime Customs, *Reports on Trade*, 1879; Report on the Trade of Tientsin, p. 263.

104. *Ibid.*, p. 271.

105. *Ibid.*, 1890 and 1891.

106. *Ibid.*, 1899.

107. *Ibid.*, 1920.

108. *Ibid.*, 1928.

109. *Ibid.*, *Decennial Reports on Trade*, 1922–31, Tientsin, p. 412.

110. *Ibid.*, pp. 337–39.

111. *Ibid.*, p. 413.

112. *Ibid.*

113. *Ibid.*, p. 340.

114. *Ibid.*

115. *Ibid.*, p. 341.

116. *Ibid.*, p. 344. Exports too had flourished right through the 1920's, but began to fall off after 1929.

117. The best population figures are for Shanghai; these are collected and analyzed in R. Murphey, *Shanghai: Key to Modern China* (Cambridge: Harvard University Press, 1953), pp. 10, 19–24, where the connection between city population totals and disorder outside the city is established. Figures of comparable reliability are not available for any of the other treaty ports, but available evidence, principally in the Annual and Decennial Reports of the Maritime Customs, suggests a closely similar pattern. These reports also suggest that, as at Shanghai, many temporary and permanent in-migrants were comparatively well-to-do; after all, it was the well-to-do who would have had most to fear from civil disorder.

118. Ta-chung Liu and K. C. Yeh, *The Economy of the Chinese Mainland: National Income and Economic Development, 1933–1959* (Princeton, N.J.: Princeton University Press, 1965), pp. 66, 69, 89.

119. See *Statistics of Chinese National Railways, 1915–1929* (Nanking, 1931), and note 6 above.

120. See Murphey 1953, pp. 89–90ff.

121. Even the missionaries for the most part had close links with urban bases, without which they could not have functioned; this included period-ically the intervention of the treaty port system in the form of gunboats or po-litical pressures on the center and the provinces, as well as the more regular streams of supply.

122. "Long Live the Victory of Peoples' War," *Peking Review*, no. 36 (Sept. 3, 1965): 9–30.

123. For a discussion of some of these same ideas, including anti-urbanism, but in another context, see my "Man and Nature in China," *Modern Asian Studies*, 1 (1967): 313–33.

The Ningpo Pang *and Financial Power at Shanghai*

1. This paper owes a sizable intellectual debt to modern Japanese scholarship; in particular to the work of Negishi Tadashi, whose fascination with the relationship between political power and private interest groups in China has been the source of many insights. I am also indebted to Professors Mark Elvin and G. William Skinner for penetrating and careful criticisms of my conclusions.

2. See Chie Nakane, *Japanese Society* (Berkeley: University of California Press, 1972), p. 7, where Dr. Nakane takes issue with this view. A theoretical statement supporting such a view may be found in S. N. Eisenstadt, *Modernization: Protest and Change* (Englewood Cliffs, N.J.: Prentice-Hall, 1966), pp. 1–5.

3. For a discussion of this and other theories of nationalism, see Kenneth B. Pyle, "A Symposium on Japanese Nationalism, Introduction: Some Recent Approaches to Japanese Nationalism," *Journal of Asian Studies*, 31, no. 1 (Nov. 1971): 9–10.

4. *Shina kaikojō shi: Chūbu Shina* (hereafter SKS; A documentary study of the treaty ports in China [vol. 1], Central China; Tokyo: Tōa dōbunkai chōsa hensanbu, 1922), p. 993.

5. In 1757 Ningpo, Amoy, and Ting-hai were closed to foreign trade, which was thereafter (until 1842) confined to Canton.

6. Negishi Tadashi, *Shanhai no girudo* (The guilds of Shanghai; Tokyo: Nihon hyōronsha, 1951), pp. 31–32.

7. *Shang-hai ch'ien chuang shih liao* (hereafter SHCCSL; Materials on the history of native banking in Shanghai; Shanghai: Jen min ch'u pan she, 1961, p. 9.

8. Hallett Abend, *Treaty Ports* (Garden City, N.Y.: Doubleday, 1944), p. 64.

9. *Ibid.*, p. 70.

10. SKS, pp. 993–94; H. B. Morse, *The Trade and Administration of China* (London: Oxford University Press, 1921), p. 226.

11. SKS, p. 996.

12. *Ibid.*, pp. 998–99; compare H. B. Morse, *The Chronicles of the East India Company Trading to China, 1635–1834* (London: Oxford University Press, 1929), 5: 57–58.

13. SKKJS, p. 997.

14. Morse 1929, p. 49.

15. Cited in W. C. Milne, "Notes of a Seven Months' Residence in the City of Ningpo, from December 7th, 1842, to July 7th, 1843," *Chinese Repository*, 18 (1844): 348.

16. China, Imperial Maritime Customs, *Decennial Reports* (Shanghai: Statistical Department of the Inspectorate General of Customs, 1922–31), 1: 24.

17. Ōya Kōtarō, "Shanhai ni okeru dōkyō dantai oyobi dōgyō dantai"

(Native-place and occupational organizations at Shanghai), *Shina kenkyū*, 18 (1928): 258.

18. Hamada Jun'ichi, "Sekkōhō oyobi Neihahō" (The Chekiang clique and the Ningpo clique), in *Gendai dai Shina* (Today's China; Tokyo: Gendai dai Shina kankō kai, 1931), p. 948.

19. For a contrasting interpretation, see Morse 1921, p. 272.

20. Fei Yüan-kuei, P'an Feng-chan, and Wang Ping-kang, according to Ōya (1928, pp. 262–63). Negishi (1951, p. 37) lists four founders: Fei, P'an, Ch'ien Sui, and Wang Chung-lieh (possibly another name for Wang Ping-kang.)

21. Negishi 1951, p. 37; Negishi Tadashi, *Chūgoku shakai ni okeru shidōsō* (The leading stratum in Chinese society; Tokyo: Heiwa shobō, 1947), p. 147.

22. Ōya 1928: 275.

23. These suggestions are set forth in my paper "Finance in Ningpo: The *Ch'ien Chuang*, 1750–1880," in W. E. Willmott, ed., *Economic Organization in Chinese Society* (Stanford, Calif.: Stanford University Press, 1972), pp. 47–77.

24. Negishi 1951, pp. 102–3.

25. *Ibid.*; Ōya 1928: 262.

26. In general the term *hui-kuan* is thought to refer to native-place associations and *kung-so* to occupational associations, but the terminology is not consistent. See Wu Hsing and Yao Wen-nan, comps., *Shang-hai hsien hsü chih* (hereafter SHHHC; The continuation of the Shang-hai county gazetteer; Taipei: Ch'eng wen ch'u pan she; reprint of the edition of 1918), ch. 3, p. 1a.

27. A provocative analysis of the interrelationships among the various *pang* in Shanghai is found in Ōya 1928. The division of *pang* into three types is Ōya's distinction.

28. Kagawa Shun'ichirō, *Sensō shihon ron* (Chinese native banking and capital; Tokyo: Jitsugyō no Nipponsha, 1948), p. 17.

29. Ōya Kōtarō, "Shanhai ni okeru dōkyō dantai oyobi dōgyō dantai" (Native-place and occupational organizations in Shanghai), *Shina kenkyū*, 19 (May 1929): 126.

30. Kagawa 1948, p. 18.

31. *Ibid.*, p. 112.

32. See Negishi 1951, pp. 116–17.

33. Nishizato Yoshiyuki, "Shinmatsu no Nimpo shōnin ni tsuite" (On the Ningpo merchants at the end of the Ch'ing dynasty), *Tōyōshi kenkyū*, 26, 2 (Sept. 1967; hereafter Nishizato 1967b): 207. For a brief discussion of the significance of Ningpo ties in comprador circles, see Yen-p'ing Hao, *The Comprador in Nineteenth Century China: Bridge Between East and West* (Cambridge: Harvard University Press, 1971), pp. 174–75.

34. See Chang Kuo-hui, "Shih chiu shih chi hou pan ch'i Chung-kuo ch'ien chuang ti mai pan hua" (The compradorization of Chinese native banks during the latter half of the nineteenth century), *Li shih yen chiu*, 6 (1963): 85–98.

35. Ōya 1929.

36. Negishi 1951, p. 37.

37. *Who's Who in China: Biographies of Chinese* (Shanghai: The China Weekly Review), 1925 ed., pp. 253–54; 1936 ed., p. 72.

38. Nishizato Yoshiyuki, "Shinmatsu no Nimpo shōnin ni tsuite" (On the Ningpo merchants at the end of the Ch'ing dynasty), *Tōyōshi kenkyū*, 16, no. 1 (June 1967; hereafter Nishizato 1967a): 23, n. 67.

39. Negishi 1947, pp. 142–46.

40. I have not been able to ascertain the foreign title of this firm.

41. SHCCSL, pp. 730–34.

42. *Ibid.*, p. 731.

43. Negishi 1947, pp. 142–43.

44. SHCCSL, pp. 734–43.

45. *Ibid.*, pp. 734–37.

46. Some sources say 1867. See Negishi 1947, p. 156; Fang T'eng, "Yü Hsia-ch'ing lun" (On Yü Hsia-ch'ing), *Tsa chih yüeh k'an*, 12, no. 2 (Nov. 1943; hereafter Fang T'eng 1943a): 48.

47. Fang T'eng 1943a: 48.

48. *Who's Who in China*, 1925 ed., pp. 954–55.

49. Negishi 1947, pp. 160–61.

50. The account of the strike that follows is based on that of Fang 1943a: 49–50. Other accounts can be found in Negishi 1951, p. 34; C. F. Remer, *A Study of Chinese Boycotts: With Special Reference to Their Economic Effectiveness* (Baltimore: Johns Hopkins Press, 1933), pp. 13–14; and H. B. Morse, *The Gilds of China* (London: Longmans, Green, 1909), p. 48.

51. Negishi 1951, pp. 34–35.

52. Nishizato 1967b: 210.

53. Negishi 1951, pp. 36–37.

54. Kagawa 1948, p. 124.

55. Fang T'eng, "Yü Hsia-ch'ing lun" (On Yü Hsia-ch'ing), *Tsa chih yüeh k'an*, 12, no. 3 (Dec. 1943; hereafter Fang T'eng 1943b): 62; Frank H. H. King, *A Concise Economic History of Modern China* (Bombay: Vora and Company, 1968), p. 91; Yang Yin-p'u, *Shang-hai chin jung tsu chih kai yao* (Some important aspects of the organization of Shanghai finance; Shanghai: Commercial Press, 1930), p. 116.

56. Yang Yin-p'u 1930, pp. 116–18.

57. Yamagami Kaneo, *Sekkō zaibatsu ron—sono kihonteki kōsatsu* (A study of the Chekiang financial clique: Some fundamental considerations; Tokyo: Nihon hyōronsha, 1938), p. 101.

58. Nishizato 1967a: 20.

59. See Negishi 1951, pp. 112–15; *Who's Who in China*, 1925 ed., pp. 696–97.

60. Fang T'eng 1943b: 62.

61. The other was the Chekiang Industrial Bank (*Che-chiang hsing-yeh yin-hang*), established in 1906.

62. See Fang T'eng 1943b: 62; and Yang Yin-p'u 1930, pp. 116–18.

63. Negishi 1951, pp. 337–82.

64. Ōya 1929: 127.

65. Nishizato 1967b: 211–12. On the continuity of traditional guild organization and the organization of the Chinese chambers of commerce, see Shirley S. Garrett's account in this volume.

66. Nishizato 1967b: 212; Ōya 1929: 143–44.

67. See Marie-Claire Bergère, *La bourgeoisie Chinoise et la révolution de*

1911 (Paris: Mouton, 1968; hereafter Bergère 1968a); Bergère, "The Role of the Bourgeoisie," in Mary C. Wright, ed., *China in Revolution: The First Phase, 1900–1913* (New Haven: Yale University Press, 1968; hereafter Bergère 1968b), pp. 280–88. See also Jean Chesneaux, "The Federalist Movement in China, 1920–23," in Jack Gray, ed., *Modern China's Search for a Political Form* (London: Oxford University Press, 1969), p. 133.

68. These continued at least until the corruption of Ch'en Ch'i-mei's military regime alienated the Shanghai bankers from the revolutionary movement in its turn. See Mark Elvin, "The Gentry Democracy in Chinese Shanghai, 1905–14," in Gray, ed., 1969, pp. 57–58.

69. Fang T'eng, "Yü Hsia-ch'ing lun" (On Yü Hsia-ch'ing), *Tsa chih yüeh k'an*, 12, no. 4 (Jan. 1944): 59–60.

70. Negishi 1951, pp. 64–65.

71. Fang T'eng 1944: 59–60.

72. See Bergère 1968b: 263.

73. Negishi 1951, pp. 66–67.

74. See Andrew James Nathan, *Factionalism in Early Republican China: The Politics of the Peking Government, 1918–1920*, unpubl. Ph.D. diss. (Harvard University, 1970), pp. 106, 109; Negishi Tadashi, *Baiben seido no kenkyū* (A study of the comprador system; Tokyo: Nihon tosho, 1948), p. 310.

75. Ōya 1929: 146.

76. Negishi 1951, p. 377.

77. See Lloyd I. Rudolph and Susanne Hoeber Rudolph, *The Modernity of Tradition: Political Development in India* (Chicago: University of Chicago Press, 1967).

78. I have been inclined to regard the continuity of elite leadership in Ningpo organizations as an example of cooptation that acted to undermine the articulation of lower-class interests. But Mark Elvin has correctly pointed out that this same phenomenon can be used to support the opposite view that there was as yet no serious polarization of class interests within the Ningpo community.

79. See Fang T'eng 1943b, pp. 64–65.

80. SHCCSL, p. 101.

81. See Bergère 1968b: 280–82. Yü Hsia-ch'ing was appointed an assistant director of foreign affairs, and Chu Pao-san became financial administrator in mid-November, replacing Shen Man-yün. For these and other details I am greatly indebted to Mark Elvin's culling of the Shanghai consular archives and the *North-China Herald*.

82. See SHCCSL, pp. 742–43, 730–37, 747–50.

83. *Ibid.*, pp. 730–34; Nishizato 1967b: 206–7; *Who's Who in China*, 1925 ed., pp. 253–54.

84. See Negishi 1951, p. 141; and Mark Elvin's account in this volume and in an earlier study (Elvin 1969).

85. See Shirley S. Garrett's study in this volume, pp. 219–20.

86. Negishi 1951, pp. 147, 149. Traditional guilds (*kung-so*) were reorganized as associations (*kung-hui*) by order of the Ch'ing government in 1903–4 (see Ōya 1929: 127). The Bankers' Association had the distinction of being the only new association in Shanghai that did not grow out of a former guild. No effort has been made here to investigate this difference fur-

ther, although formal as well as functional variations could be expected and should prove interesting.

87. Negishi 1951, p. 143. For a biography of Sung Han-chang, see Howard L. Boorman, ed., *Biographical Dictionary of Republican China* (New York: Columbia University Press, 1970), vol. 3, pp. 195–97. A biography of Chang Kia-ngau appears in *ibid.*, vol. 1, pp. 26–30. At the time Sung was the manager of the Shanghai branch of the Bank of China, and Chang was his assistant.

88. See Ōya 1929: 111; Negishi 1951, pp. 104–5, 109.

89. Negishi 1951, pp. 118–19.

90. Kagawa 1948, pp. 121–22, 155.

91. SHHHC, ch. 21, pp. 14b–15a.

92. Feuerwerker 1958, p. 21. Chou Chin-piao, also known as Chou Chin-chen, was a leading Shanghai banker and a power in the Chamber of Commerce, whose reputation was scarred by the events of the 1910 financial crisis. See Elvin 1969, p. 48 and p. 65, n. 2.

93. Nishizato 1967a: 20.

94. Negishi 1951, p. 340.

95. *Ibid.*, p. 353.

96. See Negishi 1947, p. 202.

97. See Bergère 1968a, pp. 74–93; Bergère 1968b: 284.

98. Ōya 1929: 165–66; Negishi 1951, pp. 368, 377.

99. Negishi 1951, pp. 376–77. The events of the spring of 1927 and the attempted reorganization of the Chambers are discussed in Shirley S. Garrett's study, in this volume, p. 227.

100. See Harold Isaacs, *The Tragedy of the Chinese Revolution* (Stanford, Calif.: Stanford University Press, 1951), pp. 145–85. On the role of the gangs in the crisis see Y. C. Wang, "Tu Yüeh-sheng (1888–1951): A Tentative Political Biography," *Journal of Asian Studies*, 26, no. 3 (May 1967); Kagawa 1948, p. 14.

101. Typical of the references to this period is that of O. Edmund Clubb, *Twentieth-Century China* (New York: Columbia University Press, 1964), p. 144.

102. Fang 1943b, p. 63. For a discussion of the precarious position of the modern Chinese banks in the early Republican period, see Nathan 1970, pp. 148–57.

Merchant Associations in Canton, 1895–1911

1. See Etienne Balazs, *Chinese Civilization and Bureaucracy: Variations on a Theme*, transl. by H. M. Wright (New Haven: Yale University Press, 1964), especially chaps. 2–7.

2. For an overview of the changing role of the merchants at the end of the Ch'ing, see Marie-Claire Bergère, "The Role of the Bourgeoisie," in Mary Clabaugh Wright, ed., *China in Revolution: The First Phase, 1900–1913* (New Haven: Yale University Press, 1968), pp. 229–95.

3. For a brief history of Canton, see Ezra F. Vogel, *Canton Under Communism: Programs and Politics in a Provincial Capital, 1949–1968* (Cambridge: Harvard University Press, 1969), chap. 1; also, "Kuang-chou shih yen ko shih lüeh" (An outline history of Canton city), suppl. to *Kuang-chou shih*

shih cheng pao kao hui k'an (A collection of Canton municipal government reports; Canton, 1924).

4. Vogel 1969, pp. 29, 369.

5. Frederick W. Mote, "Cities in North and South China," in F. S. Drake, ed., *Symposium on Historical, Archaeological and Linguistic Studies on Southern China, South-East Asia, and the Hong Kong Region* (Hong Kong: Hong Kong University Press, 1967), pp. 154–55.

6. John C. Kerr, *A Guide to the City and Suburbs of Canton* (Hong Kong: Kelly & Walsh, Ltd., 1904), p. 4; "Description of the City of Canton" (hereafter "Description" 1833), *Chinese Repository*, 2, no. 4 (Aug. 1833): 155–59; Vogel 1969, pp. 26–27.

7. "Description" 1833: 159.

8. Arnold Wright, ed., *Twentieth Century Impressions of Hong Kong, Shanghai, and Other Treaty Ports of China* (London: Lloyd's Greater Britain Publishing Company, 1908), p. 784. A more elaborate description in the same vein comes from William Archer in the *South China Morning Post* (hereafter SCMP; Hong Kong), Oct. 22, 1912, p. 7: "Here is no rectangular planning and no wide avenues. The city is a bewildering labyrinth of alleys, none of them more than nine or ten feet wide, and most of them so narrow that you have only to spread your arms in order to touch the wall at both sides. Rickshaws are as impossible as motor-cars in Venice. . . . You must either walk or be carried in the slim sedan chairs. . . . Most of the streets are vaulted with bamboo matting so that the whole place is like a gigantic cavern subdivided into a million subsidiary vaults. By day the place is appalling, but by night, when the vaults are dimly lit, and ten thousand naked brown bodies glisten in the Rembrandtesque illuminations, the whole scene, with its hideous vociferations and unspeakable odours, approaches very near to one's most lurid dreams of hell."

9. Kerr 1904, p. 73.

10. B. C. Henry, *Ling-nam, or Interior Views of Southern China* (London: Partridge, 1886), pp. 45–46; N. B. Dennys, *The Treaty Ports of China and Japan* (London: Trübner, 1867), pp. 142–43, 149, 153, 166; Kerr 1904, pp. 20–21; French consular dispatch from Canton to Peking, Sept. 7, 1911, made available to me through the courtesy of Marianne Bastid.

11. Dennys 1867, pp. 153–54.

12. *P'an-yü hsien hsü chih* (hereafter PYHHC; Continuation of the P'an-yü gazetteer), 1931, ch. 12, pp. 31a–31b.

13. John Watt, "Leadership Criteria in Late Imperial China," *Ch'ing-shih wen-t'i*, 2, no. 3 (July 1970): 19–21.

14. T'ung-tsu Ch'ü, *Local Government in China Under the Ch'ing* (Cambridge: Harvard University Press, 1962), chap. 10.

15. Chang Chung-li, *The Chinese Gentry: Studies on Their Role in Nineteenth-Century Chinese Society* (Seattle: University of Washington Press, 1955), pp. 51–52.

16. Feng Tzu-yu, *Ko ming i shih* (Anecdotal history of the revolution; Taipei: Shang wu yin shu kuan, 1953–65), vol. 1, pp. 76–80; Harold Z. Schiffrin, *Sun Yat-sen and the Origins of the Chinese Revolution* (Berkeley: University of California Press, 1968), chap. 7.

17. See Edward John Michael Rhoads, "The New Kwangtung: Reform and Revolution in China, 1895–1911," unpubl. Ph.D. diss. (Harvard University, 1970), chap. 10.

18. Vogel 1969, p. 29; see also the annual *Returns of Trade and Trade Reports* (hereafter TR), compiled and published by the Imperial Maritime Customs (Shanghai), for Canton during these years.

19. *Nan yang hsiung ti yen ts'ao kung ssu shih liao* (Materials on the history of the Nanyang Brothers Tobacco Company; Shanghai: Jen min ch'u pan she, 1958), pp. 1–2; Howard L. Boorman and Richard C. Howard, eds., *Biographical Dictionary of Republican China* (New York: Columbia University Press, 1967–71), vol. 1, p. 364.

20. Vogel 1969, p. 21.

21. Samuel C. Chu, *Reformer in Modern China: Chang Chien, 1853–1926* (New York: Columbia University Press, 1965).

22. Yen-p'ing Hao, *The Comprador in Nineteenth Century China: Bridge Between East and West* (Cambridge: Harvard University Press, 1970), pp. 184–95.

23. Kerr 1904, p. 8.

24. *Ibid.*, pp. 16, 17; John Henry Gray, *Walks in the City of Canton* (Hong Kong: de Souza and Co., 1875), pp. 250–51, 281.

25. Gray 1875, p. 20; cf. Katō Shigeshi, "On the Hang or Associations of Merchants in China," *Memoirs of the Research Department of the Toyo Bunko*, 8 (1936): 45–83.

26. Kerr 1904, p. 12; Gray 1875, pp. 168–69.

27. Kerr 1904, p. 33; Dennys 1867, p. 184.

28. SCMP, June 16, 1906, p. 7. The remark was made in connection with the gentry's alleged attempt to take control of the Kwangtung Railway Company.

29. Hosea Ballou Morse, *The Trade and Administration of the Chinese Empire* (London: Longmans, Green, 1908), p. 69; Jacques Gernet, *Daily Life in China on the Eve of the Mongol Invasion, 1250–1276*, transl. by H. M. Wright (New York: Macmillan, 1962), p. 29.

30. Jung-pang Lo, ed. and transl., *K'ang Yu-wei: A Biography and a Symposium* (Tucson: University of Arizona Press, 1967), p. 71.

31. Hosea Ballou Morse, *The Gilds of China, with an Account of the Gild Merchant or Co-hong of Canton* (London: Longmans, Green, 1909); John Stewart Burgess, *The Guilds of Peking* (New York: Columbia University Press, 1928); Ho Ping-ti, *Chung-kuo hui kuan shih lun* (A historical survey of *Landsmannschaften* in China; Taipei: Hsüeh sheng shu chü, 1966).

32. PYHHC, ch. 12, p. 32a; Tōa dōbun kai, *Shina shōbetsu zenshi* (A complete gazetteer of China's provinces; Tokyo: 1917–20), 1, 973–82.

33. PYHHC, ch. 12, pp. 32a–32b. Unfortunately, the location of specific guilds is not known.

34. Morse 1909, p. 37.

35. Ho Ping-ti 1966, pp. 51–52; see also the data on Canton compiled by the Chinese Imperial Maritime Customs in *Decennial Reports on the Trade, Navigation, Industries, etc., of the Ports Open to Foreign Commerce* (hereafter DR; Shanghai), 1892–1901, p. 198.

36. Kerr 1904, pp. 11, 12, 18, 37–38; Gray 1875, pp. 194–97, 269–70.

37. Ho Ping-ti 1966, p. 46; Morse 1909, pp. 53–57; DR 1882–91, pp. 537–40, 635–36.

38. Burgess 1928, chap. 12; Sybille van der Sprenkel, *Legal Institutions in Manchu China: A Sociological Analysis* (London: Athlone, University of London, 1962), pp. 89–96. I have discovered practically no information concerning the operation of the guilds in Canton itself, apart from the regulations of the Beggars' Guild (*Ch'i-erh-t'ou hui-kuan*), as quoted in Gray 1874, pp. 255–60. I am thus dependent on what Burgess and others have said about the guilds elsewhere in China.

39. Morse 1909, pp. 18–21, 27–28.

40. J. G. Kerr, "The Native Benevolent Institutions of Canton," *China Review*, 2, no. 2 (Sept.–Oct. 1873): 88–95; "Description" 1883: 263–64.

41. *Nan-hai hsien chih* (hereafter NHHC; Nan-hai county gazetteer), 1910, ch. 6, pp. 10b–12a; J. G. Kerr, "Benevolent Institutions of Canton," *China Review*, 3, no. 2 (Sept.–Oct. 1874): 108–14. According to SCMP, Jan. 10, 1912, p. 11, the headquarters of the Charitable Institutions was located on the Bund outside the Ching-hai Gate.

42. G. B. Endacott, *A History of Hong Kong* (London: Oxford University Press, 1964), pp. 155–57, 173–74, 246–48.

43. *Hong Kong Telegraph* (hereafter HKT), mail supplement, Aug. 11, 1902, p. 3.

44. Albert Feuerwerker, *China's Early Industrialization: Sheng Hsuan-huai (1844–1916) and Mandarin Enterprise* (Cambridge: Harvard University Press, 1958), pp. 70–71; Yen-p'ing Hao, "Cheng Kuan-ying: The Comprador as Reformer," *Journal of Asian Studies*, 29, no. 1 (Nov. 1969): 20; Richard C. Howard, "Introduction to 'The Chinese Reform Movement of the 1890's: A Symposium,'" *ibid.*: 7–14; John Schrecker, "The Reform Movement, Nationalism, and China's Foreign Policy," *ibid.*: 43–53.

45. Feuerwerker 1958, pp. 70–71; United Kingdom, Foreign Office archives (hereafter FO; London: Public Record Office), 228/1905, Scott, Canton, to Satow, June 18, 1905; *North-China Herald* (hereafter NCH; Shanghai), Sept. 23, 1904, p. 684; cf. Lo 1967, pp. 107–8.

46. PYHHC, ch. 12, p. 32b; TR 1899, p. 562; TR 1900, p. 550; Feuerwerker 1958, pp. 47–48. It is unclear where the Seventy-two Guilds was located, though presumably it was in the Nan-hai half of the city where nearly all the guilds were.

47. Feuerwerker 1958, p. 71.

48. *Ibid.*, pp. 70–71; H. S. Brunnert and V. V. Hagelstrom, *Present-Day Political Organization of China*, rev. by N. Th. Kolessoff and transl. by A. Beltchenko and E. E. Moran (Shanghai: Kelly & Walsh, 1912), no. 774.

49. *Nung kung shang pu t'ung chi piao* (hereafter NKSPP; Statistical tables of the Ministry of Agriculture, Industry, and Commerce; Peking, 1908–9), 1st ser., ch. 4, pp. 9b–10b; NHHC, ch. 6, p. 8b; *Tung fang tsa chih* (hereafter TFTC; Shanghai), 3, no. 3 (Kuang-hsü [hereafter KH] 32/3/25): Shang wu 39. In the 1920's, the Canton Chamber of Commerce was located in the New City near the T'ai-p'ing Gate.

50. SCMP, Jan. 6, 1913, p. 4.

51. NKSPP, 1st ser., ch. 4, pp. 9b–10b, 32b–33b, 44a–46a; 2d ser., ch. 4, pp. 24a–24b.

52. TFTC, 1, no. 12 (KH 30/12/25): Shang wu 154–57; cf. NCH, Dec. 23, 1904, p. 1404.

53. TFTC, 2, no. 11 (KH 31/11/25): Chiao yü 298; T'an Li-yüan, "Ssu shih ch'i nien lai pao yeh shih kai lüeh" (A sketch history of the press in the last forty-seven years), in *Hua tzu jih pao ch'i shih i chou nien chi nien k'an* (A commemorative volume on the seventy-first anniversary of the *Hua-tzu jih-pao*; Hong Kong, 1934), p. 5.

54. Roswell S. Britton, *The Chinese Periodical Press, 1800–1912* (Shanghai: Kelly & Walsh, 1933), p. 125; T'an Li-yüan 1934, p. 5.

55. NKSPP, 1st ser., ch. 4, pp. 9b–10b; 2d ser., ch. 4, p. 24a.

56. On the nationalist movement in Canton at the end of the Ch'ing, see Edward J. M. Rhoads, "Late Ch'ing Response to Imperialism: The Case of Canton," *Ch'ing-shih wen-t'i*, 2, no. 1 (Oct. 1969): 71–86.

57. On the anti-American boycott, see Chang Ts'un-wu, *Kuang-hsü sa i nien Chung Mei kung yüeh feng ch'ao* (The agitation in 1905 over the Sino-American labor treaty; Taipei: Institute of Modern History, Academia Sinica, 1966); Ting Yu, "1905 nien Kuang-tung fan Mei yün tung" (The 1905 anti-American movement in Kwangtung), *Chin tai shih tzu liao*, 1958, no. 5, pp. 8–52.

58. *Hua tzu jih pao* (hereafter HTJP; The Chinese Mail; Hong Kong; on deposit at the Hong Kong University Library), KH 33/10/16, p. 2; 10/18, p. 2; 10/21, p. 2; SCMP, Nov. 22, 1907, p. 7; HKT, Nov. 21, p. 4; Nov. 23, p. 5; Nov. 26, p. 4.

59. HTJP, KH 33/10/3, p. 3; 10/7, p. 2; 10/14, p. 2; HKT, Nov. 7, 1907, p. 4; Nov. 8, p. 5; TFTC, 5, no. 2 (KH 34/2/25): Nei wu 143.

60. HKT, Nov. 22, 1907, p. 5; HTJP, KH 33/10/17, p. 2; 10/20, p. 2.

61. Meribeth E. Cameron, *The Reform Movement in China, 1898–1912* (Stanford, Calif.: Stanford University Press, 1931), pp. 108–12.

62. *Tung hua lu* (Tung-hua records; Taipei reprint: Ta tung shu chü, 1968), KH 31/11/20, pp. 5787–88.

63. *Chung-hua min kuo k'ai kuo wu shih nien wen hsien* (hereafter KKWH; Documents on the fiftieth anniversary of the founding of the Republic of China; Taipei, 1962–65), 1st ser., vol. 16, pp. 597–98.

64. Wang Yün-sheng, comp., *Liu shih nien lai Chung-kuo yü Jih-pen* (China and Japan during the last sixty years; Tientsin: Ta kung pao she, 1932–33), 5: 193–94.

65. See, for example, China, Wai-wu Pu archives (hereafter WWP) (Nankang, Taiwan: Institute of Modern History, Academia Sinica), file of telegrams received, KH 33/10/15, 10/19, and 10/22.

66. Wang Yün-sheng 1932–33, vol. 5, pp. 193–94.

67. HKT, Nov. 23, 1907, p. 5.

68. Rhoads 1969; for a more detailed treatment, see Rhoads 1970, chap. 7.

69. HKT, Dec. 23, 1909, p. 4.

70. Despite much initial enthusiasm, the company evidently never obtained enough capital to begin operation. KKWH, 1st ser., vol. 16, pp. 597–98; TFTC, 5, no. 2 (KH 34/2/25): Chiao t'ung 76–78; HKT, Jan. 8, 1908, p. 4.

71. NCH, May 16, 1908, p. 402; June 27, p. 805; SCMP, July 4, p. 4; TR 1908, pp. 520–21.

72. HKT, Sept. 10, 1908, p. 4; SCMP, Sept. 11, p. 7.

73. HKT, Jan. 28, 1908, p. 4.

74. SCMP, Mar. 30, 1908, p. 7; Apr. 15, p. 7.

75. HKT, Sept. 17, 1908, p. 5.

76. Cameron 1931, pp. 113–14.

77. WWP, Macau file, clipping from the Canton *Shih-min pao*, Hsüan-t'ung (hereafter HT) 1/3/8 and 3/9; HKT, Apr. 29, 1909, p. 4.

78. HTJP, HT 1/7/25, p. 2; cf. Brunnert and Hagelstrom, no. 527A.

79. For the terms of the franchise, see Cameron 1931, p. 121.

80. The sample consists of the assemblymen from the fifteen counties for which there exists an up-to-date gazetteer, and also those from Ch'ao-chou prefecture, who were analyzed in a dispatch in HTJP, HT 1/7/24, p. 2. See Rhoads 1970, pp. 244–45.

81. The ninety-four assemblymen are listed in TFTC, 6, no. 11 (HT 1/11/25). The three Chamber of Commerce leaders were Ou Tsan-sen, Hsiao Yung-hua, and Liang Kun-hsüan.

82. The topics considered by the Kwangtung Assembly are listed in TFTC, 6, no. 13 (HT 1/12/25): Chi tsai 495–96; United States, General Records of the Department of State (hereafter DS) (Washington, D.C.: National Archives), 893.00/351½ and /501, Bergholz, Canton, to State Dept., Dec. 20, 1909, and Jan. 10, 1911.

83. NCH, Nov. 29, 1907, p. 558; HTJP, KH 33/10/27, p. 2; HKT, Nov. 24, 1909, p. 7; Feb. 18, 1910, p. 5.

84. Brunnert and Hagelstrom 1912, no. 525B; PYHC, ch. 9, pp. 8a–14a; DS, 893.101/3, Williams, Swatow, to State Dept., Sept. 17, 1910.

85. On the Swatow town council, see DS, 893.101/1–3, Williams, Swatow, to State Dept., Sept. 17, 1910, Apr. 11, 1911, and May 2, 1911. On the Shanghai Chinese municipal council, see Mark Elvin, "The Gentry Democracy in Chinese Shanghai, 1905–14," in Jack Gray, ed., *Modern China's Search for a Political Form* (London: Oxford University Press, 1969), pp. 41–65.

86. PYHHC, ch. 9, pp. 10b–11b.

87. SCMP, July 15, 1909, p. 7; PYHHC, ch. 42, p. 19a.

88. "Kuang-tung tu li chi" (A record of the declaration of independence in Kwangtung; hereafter KTTLC), *Chin tai shih tzu liao*, 1960, no. 1: 435–37; SCMP, Oct. 28, 1911, p. 7.

89. KTTLC: 439–40; HKT, Oct. 31, 1911, p. 1.

90. KTTLC: 441–49; HTJP, HT 3/9/13, p. 2; HKT, Nov. 3, 1911, p. 1.

91. KTTLC: 449–50.

92. HTJP, HT 3/9/19, *Ching hua lu* supplement, p. 1.

93. KKWH, 2d ser., vol. 4, p. 443; HKT, Nov. 9, 1911, p. 1; SCMP, Nov. 9, p. 7.

94. Kuo Hsiao-ch'eng, "Kuang-tung kuang fu chi" (A record of the revolution in Kwangtung), in *Hsin hai ko ming* (The Revolution of 1911; Shanghai: Jen min ch'u pan she, 1957), vol. 7, p. 230.

95. *Ibid.*, p. 231; KTTLC: 450–51.

96. Kuo Hsiao-ch'eng 1957, pp. 231–32.

97. HTJP, HT 3/10/21, p. 2.

98. See Edward Friedman, "The Center Cannot Hold: The Failure of Parliamentary Democracy in China from the Chinese Revolution of 1911 to the World War in 1914," unpubl. Ph.D. diss. (Harvard University, 1968).

Peasant Insurrection and the Marketing Hierarchy
in the Canton Delta, 1911

1. Winston Hsieh, *Chinese Historiography on the Revolution of 1911: An Analytic Survey and a Selected Bibliography* (Stanford, Calif.: Hoover Institution Press, 1974).

2. Information on the Shih-ch'i uprising, unless otherwise noted, is based on Cheng Pi-an, "Hsiang-shan ch'i i hui i" (Recollections of the Hsiang-shan uprising), in Chung-kuo jen min cheng chih hsieh shang hui i, Ch'üan kuo wei yüan hui, Wen shih tzu liao yen chiu wei yüan hui, ed., *Hsin hai ko ming hui i lu* (Recollections of the Revolution of 1911; Peking: Chung-hua shu chü, 1962), 2: 338–42. In addition to participating as a T'ung-meng Hui activist in the 1911 uprising, Cheng served in the 1940's as Director of the Hsiang-shan County Historical Commission, which sponsored the compilation of accounts of the uprising. Cheng's material is supplemented by my interviews with Mo Chi-p'eng (1892–1972), another participant in the Revolution of 1911. Copies of the unpublished interview records and the manuscript copies of his memoirs are deposited at the Academia Sinica's Institute for Modern History in Taipei and at Columbia University's East Asian Institute in New York City.

3. The name of the Ch'ing army commander killed at Hsiang-shan is recorded in Shang Ping-ho, *Hsin jen ch'un ch'iu* (Spring and autumn annals for the years 1911–12; Peking [?], 1924), ch. 44, p. 10a.

4. Data on lineages in the Lung-tu area are supplied in the following sources: (a) *Hsiang-shan hsien chih hsü pien* (hereafter HSHCHP; County gazetteer of Hsiang-shan, a supplement), which covers data primarily through 1911, though published in 1924; (b) "Shih tsu chih ch'u kao" (Section on genealogies, a preliminary draft), part 2, in *Chung-shan wen hsien* (Documents on Chung-shan [county]), no. 2 (May 1948), 57–70; (c) *Hsi-chiao yüeh pao* (Monthly magazine of Hsi-chiao *hsiang*), vol. 2 (1948), nos. 4 (Apr.), 6–7 (June–July), 11 (Nov.); and vol. 3 (1949), no. 2 (Feb.); and (d) *Hsiang-kang Chung-shan Lung-chen t'ung hsiang hui fu hui ti ssu chieh chi nien t'e k'an* (Special issue in commemoration of the fourth anniversary of the restoration of the Hong Kong Association for Natives from Lung-tu of Chung-shan [county]), 1964. For an analytical treatment of lineages see Maurice Freedman, *Lineage Organizations in Southeastern China* (London: Athlone, 1958) and *Chinese Lineage and Society: Fukien and Kwangtung* (London: Athlone, 1966).

5. G. William Skinner, "Marketing and Social Structure in Rural China, Part II," *Journal of Asian Studies*, 24, no. 2 (Feb. 1965), p. 221.

6. For the Hsiang-shan people's version of the disputes, see HSHCHP, ch. 16, pp. 5a–6b; for the Shun-te version, see Chou Ch'ao-huai et al., eds., *Shun-te hsien hsü chih* (County gazetteer of Shun-te, a supplement), 1929, ch. 24, p. 14b. For scholarly investigation, see Sasaki Masaya, "Shun-te ken kyōshin to tōkai juroku-sa" (The local gentry of Shun-te county and the Sixteen Delta

Sands of the Eastern Sea), *Kindai Chūgoku Kenkyū* (Studies on modern China), 3: 163–232. For a historical perspective on militia control in this area as well as in the Canton delta in general, see Frederic Wakeman, Jr., *Strangers at the Gate: Social Disorder in South China, 1839–1861* (Berkeley: University of California Press, 1966), esp. chap. 15.

7. For lists of annual import and export figures, presumably of years around 1911, see HSHCHP, ch. 2, pp. 15a–16a.

8. *Ibid.*, ch. 5, pp. 3b–4b.

9. See, for example, *Tung fang tsa chih* (hereafter TFTC), 1910, nos. 3, 4, 5, 7, 8, and 10, including incidents in Kwangtung, Kiangsi, Kiangsu, and Anhwei.

10. This specific incident is reported in TFTC, 1910, no. 6. For information on other "tax rebellions" in the late Ch'ing years, see the TFTC news reports and the documents from the Grand Council archives to be found in the section entitled "Jen min fan Ch'ing tou cheng tzu liao" (Materials on popular struggles against the Ch'ing), in Chung-kuo shih hsüeh hui, ed., *Hsin hai ko ming* (The Revolution of 1911; Shanghai: Sheng chou kuo kuang she, 1957).

11. Information on the Kuan-lan uprising in this section is based on Wang Hsing-chung, "Yüeh sheng ti ssu chün ko ming jih chi" (A day-to-day account of the revolutionary struggle of the Fourth Army in Kwangtung), annotated and edited by Chou Hui-chün, in Kuomintang Archives, comp., *Chung-hua min kuo k'ai kuo wu shih nien wen hsien* (Documents in commemoration of the fiftieth anniversary of the founding of the Republic of China), Part 2, vol. 4, pp. 433–39.

Chungking as a Center of Warlord Power, 1926–1937

1. Archibald Little, *The Far East* (Oxford: Clarendon Press, 1905), p. 75.

2. Cheng Li-chien, *Ssu-ch'uan hsin ti chih* (A new geography of Szechwan; n.p.: Cheng chung shu chü, 1946), pp. 285–89.

3. *Ibid.*, pp. 255–65.

4. *Ibid.*, pp. 266–75.

5. Lu Ssu-hung, *Hsin Ch'ung-ch'ing* (New Chungking; Shanghai: Chung-hua shu chü, 1939), p. 188.

6. *Ibid.*, pp. 192–96. See also Cheng 1946, pp. 243–44.

7. See Chou K'ai-ch'ing, *Ssu-ch'uan yü hsin hai ko ming* (Szechwan and the Revolution of 1911; Taipei: Ssu-ch'uan wen hsien yen chiu she, 1964), and *Pa hsien chih* (hereafter PHC; Gazetteer of Pa *hsien*; Taipei: Hsüeh sheng shu chü, 1967; reprint of 1939 edition), ch. 22. The gentry-dominated government established in Chengtu by leaders of the so-called Railway Protection Movement initially replaced Ch'ing authority at the provincial capital, but collapsed amid military disorders in the city after only a few weeks. Power then passed into the hands of military officers. See Chou K'ai-ch'ing 1964, pp. 304–6, and S. C. Yang, "The Revolution in Szechwan, 1911–1912," *Journal of the West China Border Research Society*, 6 (1933–34): 64–90.

8. Yang Ch'ao-yung, "Hsin hai hou chih Ssu-ch'uan chan chi" (A record of the wars in Szechwan after the Revolution of 1911), in *Chin tai shih tzu liao*, no. 6 (Peking, 1958), pp. 60–65.

9. PHC, ch. 6, pp. 54–59.

10. Brief incursions by extraprovincial forces occurred in 1928 and 1933, but the Szechwan militarists made it clear that the outsiders were neither needed nor welcome, and they quickly withdrew.

11. The weakest of these seven militarists, Lai Hsin-hui, was eliminated by early 1929, leaving six commanders in nominal control of Szechwan.

12. Joseph E. Spencer, "Changing Chungking: The Rebuilding of an Old City," *The Geographical Review*, 29 (1939): 47. I am indebted to Professor Spencer for supplying me with several important maps of Chungking from his personal files. Without these maps I would have been unable to locate many of the structures and features that now appear in Map 3, pp. 154–55. See also H. G. W. Woodhead, *The Yangtze and Its Problems* (Shanghai: Mercury Press, 1931), p. 52. For an anecdotal and highly flavored account of life in the Chungking foreign community, see R. T., "One Night in Chungking," *Blackwood's Magazine*, 235 (1934): 581–602.

13. Spencer 1939, p. 58.

14. *Ibid.*, p. 51.

15. Lu Ssu-hung 1939, pp. 1–2.

16. *Ibid.*, pp. 15–16.

17. Woodhead 1931, p. 48.

18. Lu Ssu-hung 1939, p. 177; Woodhead 1931, p. 48.

19. *Ibid.*

20. Lu Ssu-hung 1939, pp. 22–23, refers to these men as "city gentry" (*shih-shen*). PHC ch. 18, p. 5a, refers to the organization of an "Association for the Proper Treatment of the Cemeteries" (*I-chung hui*) by "people of the country" (*hsien-jen*), who contributed funds for transferral and reburial of the remains.

21. Lockhart (Hankow) to Secretary of State, June 12, 1929, U.S. Department of State (hereafter DS) 893.512/975.

22. Lu Ssu-hung 1939, p. 23.

23. *Ibid.*, p. 25.

24. *Ibid.*, pp. 27–33. See also China, Maritime Customs, *Decennial Reports*, 5 (1933): 489.

25. Spencer 1939, p. 56.

26. Shu Hsieh, "Min sheng kung ssu fa chan shih" (History of the development of the Min-sheng Company), *Ssu-ch'uan wen hsien*, May 1966, pp. 17–20. The most comprehensive source on prewar development of the Min-sheng Company is Min sheng shih yeh kung ssu shih i chou nien k'an pien chi wei yüan hui, comp., *Min sheng shih yeh kung ssu shih i chou nien chi nien k'an* (Commemorative volume on the eleventh anniversary of the Min-sheng Industrial Company; Shanghai: Chung-hua shu chü, 1937).

27. T. H. Sun, "Lu Tso-fu and His Yangtze Fleet," *Asia*, June 1944, p. 248.

28. Shu Hsieh 1966, p. 19. See also Liu Hang-shen, "Jung mu pan sheng" (Half a lifetime in the inner circle), *Hsin-wen t'ien ti* (hereafter HWTT), Nov. 18, 1967, pp. 23–24.

29. Shu Hsieh 1966, pp. 19–20.

30. Hsü Ya-ming, "Ssu-ch'uan hsin chien she chung chih hsiao san hsia" (The Three Little Gorges area in the midst of Szechwan's new reconstruction), *Fu hsing yüeh k'an*, 3, nos. 6/7 (Mar. 1935).

31. *Ibid.*

32. Lu Tso-fu, "Ssu-ch'uan Chia-ling chiang san hsia ti hsiang ts'un yün tung" (The rural village movement in the Three Gorges area of the Chia-ling river in Szechwan), *Chung-hua chiao yü chieh*, 22 (Oct. 1934): 107–12. See also T. H. Sun 1944, pp. 245–50.

33. Shu Hsieh 1966, p. 18.

34. *Ibid.*

35. Liu Hang-shen, HWTT, Sept. 2, 1967, p. 25.

36. Liu Hang-shen, HWTT, Sept. 9, 1967, p. 23. See also Hu Kuang-piao, *Po chu liu shih nien* (Living in a turbulent era, 2d ed.; Hong Kong: Hsin wen t'ien ti she, 1964), p. 296.

37. Hu Kuang-piao 1964, pp. 284, 287.

38. *Ibid.*, p. 303.

39. Liu Hang-shen, HWTT, Sept. 9, 1967, p. 24. Also Lü P'ing-teng, *Ssu-ch'uan nung ts'un ching chi* (Agrarian economy of Szechwan; Shanghai: Shang wu yin shu kuan, 1936), p. 44.

40. Liu Hang-shen, HWTT, Sept. 9, 1967, pp. 23–24.

41. R. T. 1934. See also *Ssu-ch'uan yüeh pao* (hereafter SCYP; Szechwan review), 2, no. 1 (Jan. 1933), for a discussion of the condition of workers in Chungking.

42. Hsüeh Shao-ming, *Ch'ien Tien Ch'uan lü hsing chi* (A Kweichow-Yunnan-Szechwan travelogue; Canton: Chung-hua shu chü, 1937), p. 167.

43. Fan Ch'ung-shih, "1920–1922 nien ti Ssu-ch'uan chün fa k'un chan" (The chaotic warfare of the Szechwanese warlords between 1920 and 1922), in *Chin tai shih tzu liao*, no. 4 (Peking, 1962), pp. 19–23.

44. Cheng Li-chien 1946, p. 352.

45. Li Pai-hung, "Erh shih nien lai chih Ch'uan fa chan cheng" (Szechwanese warlord wars of the last twenty years), in *Chin tai shih tzu liao*, no. 4 (Peking, 1962), p. 75.

46. Lü P'ing-teng 1936, p. 486. Also Li 1962, p. 82.

47. Woodhead 1931, chap. 9.

48. Lü P'ing-teng 1936, pp. 405–7.

49. Lockhart (Hankow) to Secretary of State, May 22, 1929, DS 893.512/966.

50. Hsüeh Shao-ming 1937, p. 171.

51. Adams (Chungking) to Secretary of State, Feb. 9, 1926, DS 893.114/549.

52. For the text of one such demand, see Woodhead 1931, pp. 64–65.

53. *North-China Herald*, Sept. 21, 1929, p. 445; Lockhart (Hankow) to Secretary of State, Sept. 9, 1929, DS 893.00/P. R. Chungking 15.

54. Liu Hang-shen, HWTT, July 29, 1967, p. 25, and Oct. 14, 1967, p. 24.

55. PHC, ch. 18, pp. 1a–2b. Connotations of the rubric *fa-t'uan* may vary somewhat from place to place, but the term invariably denotes the chamber of commerce (*shang-hui*), a labor association (*kung-hui*), agricultural association (*nung-hui*), and education association (*chiao-yü hui*) of a given county. See SCYP, 3, no. 3 (Sept. 1933): 147–49.

56. Lockhart (Hankow) to Secretary of State, Oct. 2, 1930, DS 893.00/P. R. Chungking 28. Also *New York Times*, Apr. 6, 1931, p. 7.

57. Lockhart (Hankow) to Secretary of State, May 22, 1929, DS 893.512/966.

58. Report of Consul Adams (Chungking), June 19, 1925, DS 893.512/335.

59. Toller (Chungking) to Peiping, Oct. 9, 1930, Great Britain, Foreign Office (hereafter FO) 228/4292.

60. Toller (Chungking) to Peiping, Oct. 20, 1931, FO 371/15445.

61. Liu Hang-shen, HWTT, Sept. 23, 1967, p. 23.

62. Hsüeh Shao-ming 1937, p. 167.

63. See *Chung yang yin hang yüeh pao*, 5, no. 2 (Feb. 1936), and Hua Sheng, "Ssu-ch'uan chih yin hang yü ch'ien chuang" (Szechwan's banks and money shops), *Ssu-ch'uan wen hsien*, Sept. 1968, pp. 3–11.

64. Lü P'ing-teng 1936, p. 43.

65. For a discussion of military academy cliques in Szechwan, see Chang Chung-lei, "Ch'ing mo min ch'u Ssu-ch'uan ti chün shih hsüeh t'ang chi Ch'uan chün p'ai hsi" (Szechwanese military schools of the late Ch'ing and early Republic, and Szechwanese army cliques and factions), Chung-kuo jen min cheng chih hsieh shang hui i, Ch'üan kuo wei yüan hui, Wen shih tzu liao yen chiu wei yüan hui (Historical Materials Commission, National Committee of Chinese People's Political Consultative Conference), ed., *Hsin hai ko ming hui i lu* (Reminiscences of the Revolution of 1911; Peking, 1962), vol. 3, pp. 345–64.

66. Lü P'ing-teng 1936, p. 264. Also Chou Li-san et al., comps., *Ssu-ch'uan ching chi ti t'u chi* (Economic atlas of Szechwan; Pei-p'ei: Chung-kuo ti li yen chiu so, 1946), map 24.

67. Hu Hsien-su, "Shu yu tsa kan" (Random thoughts on a visit to Szechwan), *Tu li p'ing lun*, Oct. 1, 1933, pp. 14–20.

68. Adams (Chungking) to unnamed recipient, June 19, 1935, DS 893.512/335.

69. See SCYP, 2, no. 3 (Mar. 1933). Just after Liu Hsiang drove Liu Wen-hui out of most of the latter's garrison area, Liu Hsiang and his division commanders were distributed as follows: T'ang Shih-tsun at Jung-hsien, P'an Wen-hua at I-pin, Wang Tsuan-hsü at Nei-chiang, Wang Ling-chi at Wan-hsien, Fan Shao-tseng at Ho-ch'uan, Ch'en Wan-jen at Feng-tu, and Liu Hsiang at Lu-hsien.

70. Report of Messrs. Stirling and Ingram, Oct. 10, 1929, FO 371/19301. See also Lockhart (Hankow) to Secretary of State, May 22, 1929, DS 893.512/966.

71. Lü P'ing-teng 1936, p. 490.

72. See for example PHC, ch. 17, pp. 2a–2b.

73. See p. 2 of O. Edmund Clubb, "Szechwan Feudalism," encl. in Clubb (Hankow) to Secretary of State, May 20, 1933, DS 893.00/12384. Clubb's use of the term "feudalism" here is primarily pejorative, not descriptive. The structure of subprovincial administration was not completely unaltered during the early years of the Republic. One conspicuous change, not confined to Szechwan, was the abolition of the multi-district administrative units known as "circuits" (*tao*).

74. Lü P'ing-teng 1936, p. 490. The heads of county Revenue Collection Bureaus were natives of the county in which they served far more often than were county magistrates.

75. On corruption and profiteering in county government, see for example *Chung-kuo ching chi nien chien* (Chinese economic yearbook; Nanking: Kuo min cheng fu shih yeh pu Chung-kuo ching chi nien chien pien tsuan wei yüan hui, 1935), pp. F-296, 297.

76. Chang P'ei-chün, "Ssu-ch'uan cheng ch'üan chih hsi t'ung chi hsing cheng hsien chuang" (The present state of Szechwan's system of political power and administration), *Fu hsing yüeh k'an*, 3, nos. 6/7 (Mar. 1935).

77. Lü P'ing-teng 1936, p. 490. Also Hsüeh Shao-ming 1937, p. 187.

78. Chu Hsieh, "Ssu-ch'uan t'ien fu fu chia shui chi nung min ch'i t'a fu tan chih chen hsiang" (Szechwanese land tax and supplemental taxes and other burdens of farmers), *Tung fang tsa chih*, 31, no. 14 (July 16, 1934): 90. Also Lü P'ing-teng 1936, p. 490.

79. PHC, ch. 17, p. 21a. For another reference to *hsiang*-based independent militia organization, see *Lu hsien chih* (Gazetteer of Lu *hsien*; Taipei: Hsüeh sheng shu chü, 1967; reprint of 1938 edition), ch. 2, p. 25b.

80. China, Ch'üan kuo ching chi wei yüan hui (All-China Economic Committee), *Ssu-ch'uan k'ao ch'a pao kao shu* (Report on Szechwan; Shanghai: Ch'üan-kuo ch'ing chi wei yüan hui, 1935), p. 236. This account of Szechwanese militia development is corroborated in many places, including Hsüeh Shao-ming 1937. The estimate of half a million militiamen is repeated in Feng Ho-fa, *Chung-kuo nung ts'un ching chi tzu liao* (Economic materials on Chinese farm villages; Shanghai: Li ming shu chü, 1933), p. 827. Another estimate was ten thousand militiamen per county: SCYP, 4, no. 6 (June 1934): 177.

81. Liu Hsiang, *Liu Fu-ch'eng chün chang chiang yen chi* (Collected speeches of Marshal Liu Hsiang; [Chungking], 1927), third speech, pp. 23–93.

82. *Ssu-ch'uan nung min pu pao kao* (Report of the Szechwan Peasant Bureau; n.p., [1927]).

83. From below, of course, the view was very different. A popular expression said that "the army takes the skin, and the militia takes the bone and sinews." Hsüeh Shao-ming 1937, p. 195.

84. *West China Missionary News*, June 1927, p. 11.

85. China, Shih yeh pu (Ministry of Industry), *Erh shih erh nien lao tung nien chien* (1933 Labor Yearbook; Shanghai, 1933), pp. 69–70. The role of the Ko-lao Hui in Szechwan is of major interest in any investigation of social unrest in the province, but information concerning this secret society is too scanty to permit serious analysis. The Ko-lao Hui played a prominent role in the 1911 uprising against the Ch'ing, operating ubiquitously and openly in Chengtu during the early weeks of provincial independence. Its influence is cited in the case of the Mien-yang anti-tax uprising, the main force of which was provided by local militia. See Chou 1965, pp. 304–5. The extent of its influence among "bad gentry," landlords, and landless unemployed "wanderers" is mentioned by Lü P'ing-teng (1936, p. 149). On the Ko-lao Hui in Szechwan in later years, see Sung Chung-k'an et al., eds., *Ssu-ch'uan ko lao hui kai shan chih shang chüeh* (A viewpoint on the reform of the Ko-lao Hui in Szechwan; Chengtu: Ssu-ch'uan ti fang shih chi wen t'i yen chiu hui, 1940), *passim*; Liao T'ai-ch'u, "The Ko Lao Hui in Szechwan," *Pacific Affairs*, June 1947, pp. 161–73; G. William Skinner, "Aftermath of Communist Liberation in the Chengtu Plain," *Pacific Affairs*, 24 (Mar. 1951): 61–76. See also Charlton

M. Lewis, "Some Notes on the Ko-lao Hui in Late Ch'ing China," Guy Puyrai-mond, "The Ko-lao Hui and the Anti-Foreign Incidents of 1891," and John Lust, "Secret Societies, Popular Movements, and the 1911 Revolution," all in Jean Chesneaux, ed., *Popular Movements and Secret Societies in China, 1840–1950* (Stanford, Calif.: Stanford University Press, 1972), pp. 97–112, 113–24, and 165–200, respectively.

86. *North-China Herald*, Oct. 5, 1929. The leader of the "train bands" was said to have sent a petition to the National Government detailing the abuses of military taxation in his area. This might suggest that the Ch'i-chiang militia leadership was of a different order from the *t'uan fa* who controlled local militia in other areas.

87. *Asiatic dispatch*, Oct. 31, 1934; included in miscellaneous unpublished papers of Norman D. Hanwell, Hoover Library, Stanford, California.

88. Handley-Derry (Chungking) to Peiping, July 29, 1929, FO 371/19301.

89. PHC, ch. 17, p. 22b.

90. *Chung-kuo ching chi nien chien*, p. F-296.

91. The plan is reprinted in SCYP, 2, no. 5 (May 1933).

92. Chang P'ei-chün 1935.

93. Ssu-ch'uan sheng cheng fu mi shu ch'u (Secretariat of Szechwan Provincial Government), *Ssu-ch'uan hsing cheng tu ch'a chuan yüan shih cheng yen chiu hui chi lu* (Proceedings of the Conference of Szechwan Special Administrative Inspectors on Political Implementation; [Chengtu], 1935), p. 110.

94. *Ibid.*, pp. 41–42.

95. Berger (Tientsin) to Secretary of State, Aug. 15, 1935, DS 893.00/P.R. Tientsin 86. See also letter of E. R. Leach to I. Kinloch, Aug. 5, 1935, encl. in Messrs. Butterfield and Swire (London) to Foreign Office (received Sept. 16, 1935), FO 371/19307.

96. Mills (Chungking) to Nanking, June 25, 1937, FO 371/20970. At the time Liu left Chungking, a plan for the nationalization of Szechwanese armies, military finances, and military installations was announced. A conference called to implement the plan opened on July 6, 1937, and adjourned two days later after the Marco Polo Bridge Incident opened full-scale hostilities between China and Japan in North China.

97. John Fincher, "Political Provincialism and the National Revolution," in Mary Clabaugh Wright, ed., *China in Revolution: The First Phase, 1900–1913* (New Haven: Yale University Press, 1968), pp. 212–13. Fincher postulates a qualitative and quantitative change in the gentry prior to 1911, and suggests that a much enlarged modern sector of the population appeared in the years leading to and following the Revolution of 1911. Szechwan in the 1930's seems to show that such a burst of social modernization, if it took place at all, was not sustained in the province. Rather, there was a regression to pre-revolutionary modes of operation, as highly educated young Szechwanese left the province and failed to return, and as militarist regimes retreated to pre-revolutionary methods of administration and control. This regression might have been due in part to the failure in early Republican China to achieve what Fincher calls "the combination of a national issue with strong local economic interests," such as the railway issue had been in 1911. See *ibid.*, pp. 212–16, and Hu Kuang-piao 1964, p. 279.

98. Lü P'ing-teng 1936, pp. 183–85.

99. On the evolution of the militia in nineteenth-century China, see Philip Kuhn, *Rebellion and Its Enemies in Late Imperial China: Militarization and Social Structure, 1796–1864* (Cambridge: Harvard University Press, 1970), pp. 89–90, 161–62, 170, and 212.

100. Short-lived departures from this usual relationship of military ruler to populace might be discerned in the case of the Kuomintang armies early in the Northern Expedition and at certain times and places in the career of Feng Yü-hsiang.

Educational Modernization in Tsinan, 1899–1937

1. "Educational Systems," in *International Encyclopedia of the Social Sciences* (New York: Macmillan, 1968), vol. 4, p. 510.

2. G. William Skinner, "Marketing and Social Structure in Rural China," *Journal of Asian Studies*, 24, no. 1 (Nov. 1964), 24, no. 2 (Feb. 1965), and 24, no. 3 (June 1965); and "Cities and the Regional Hierarchy of Local Systems," in Skinner, ed., *The City in Late Imperial China* (Stanford University Press, forthcoming).

3. "Educational Systems," p. 511.

4. *Tzu-yang hsien chih* (Tzu-yang county gazetteer, 1888), ch. 5, p. 12a.

5. Tilemann Grimm, "Academies and Urban Systems in Kwangtung," in Skinner, ed., *The City in Late Imperial China* (Stanford University Press, forthcoming).

6. M. C. Bergère, "La bourgeoisie Chinoise et les problèmes de développement économique (1917–1923)," *Revue d'histoire moderne et contemporaine*, 16, no. 2 (Apr.-June 1969), pp. 246–67.

7. Yüan Shih-k'ai, *Yang shou yüan tsou i chi yao* (hereafter YSK Memorials; Collection of memorials from the Garden of Cultivating Longevity; Peking, 1937), ch. 10, pp. 4a–7b.

8. YSK Memorials, ch. 10, p. 6a; Chang Chih-tung, *Ch'üan hsüeh p'ien* (Exhortation to Study; Peking, 1928), 2, p. 7a–7b.

9. YSK Memorials, ch. 10, p. 4b.

10. *North-China Herald* (hereafter NCH), Oct. 30, 1901, p. 827; Nov. 20, 1901, p. 964; Nov. 27, 1901, pp. 1018–19.

11. *Shan-tung t'ung chih* (Shantung provincial gazetteer, [1915]; hereafter STTC), ch. 88.

12. NCH, May 7, 1902, p. 887.

13. Yeh Ch'un-ch'ih, ed., *Chi-nan chih nan* (hereafter CNCN; Guide to Tsinan; Tsinan: Ta tung jih pao, 1914), p. 33; P'eng Tse-i, comp., *Chung-kuo chin tai shou kung yeh shih tzu liao, 1840–1919* (Materials on the history of handicraft industry in modern China; Peking: San lien shu tien, 1957), 2: 534.

14. Shu Hsin-ch'eng, *Chin tai Chung-kuo chiao yü shih liao* (Materials on the history of modern Chinese education; Shanghai: Shang wu yin shu kuan, 1928), 1: 59–62.

15. Ch'en Ch'i-t'ien, *Tsui chin san shih nien Chung-kuo chiao yü shih* (A history of Chinese education during the past thirty years; Shanghai: Chung-hua shu tien, 1930), pp. 80–84.

16. CNCN, pp. 26–27; 33–36.

17. "Chiao yü cheng tse tzu i" (My views of educational policy), quoted in Ch'en Ch'i-t'ien 1930, pp. 63–64.

18. *Ibid.*, pp. 64–65; *Chung-kuo chiao yü tz'u tien* (Dictionary of Chinese education; Shanghai: Chung-hua shu chü, 1928), pp. 434–35.

19. Ting Chih-k'uei, *Chung-kuo chin ch'i shih nien lai chiao yü chi shih* (Chronology of Chinese education for the past seventy years; Shanghai: Shang wu yin shu kuan, 1935), pp. 17–21; Ch'en 1930, pp. 71–73.

20. Ting Chih-k'uei 1935, p. 17; Ch'en Ch'i-tien 1930, pp. 66–68.

21. Ch'en Ch'i-tien 1930, p. 68.

22. Shu Hsin-ch'eng 1928, 2: 131–35.

23. *Ibid.*

24. I wish to thank Mark Elvin for bringing this item to my attention in *Shang-hai hsien hsü chih* (A continuation of Shang-hai county gazetteer, 1918), ch. 9, pp. 8b–9a. See also Shu Hsin-ch'eng 1928, 2: 149–56, for a list of recommendations prepared by a conference of educational modernizers to assist the government in acquiring school property. The conference was held in 1906 and attended by men from Kiangsu, Chekiang, and Hunan.

25. Ōgawa Yoshiko, "Shin tai ni okeru gigaku setsuritsu no kiban" (The basis for establishing endowed schools in the Ch'ing period), in Hayashi Tomoharu, ed., *Kindai Chūgoku kyōiku kenkyū* (Studies in modern Chinese education; Tokyo: Kokushisha, 1958), pp. 273–307.

26. Ōmura Kōdō, "Shincho kyōiku shisō shi ni okeru 'Seiyu kōkun' no chii ni tsuite" (The place of proclaiming the Sacred Edicts in the history of Ch'ing educational thought), in Hayashi Tomoharu 1958, pp. 231–37.

27. Shu Hsin-ch'eng 1928, 2: 134.

28. *Wei hsien chih* (Wei hsien gazetteer 1936), ch. 27, pp. 1a–3b.

29. Ōmura Kodo 1958, pp. 267–71; Shu Hsin-ch'eng 1928, 2: 135.

30. Shu Hsin-ch'eng 1928, 2: 131–35; Ronald Yu Soong Cheng, *The Financing of Public Education in China* (Shanghai: Commercial Press, 1935), pp. 124–25.

31. *Wei hsien chih* (1936), ch. 22, p. 7b; ch. 19, p. 14b; ch. 19, pp. 27a–28b; ch. 30, pp. 47a–b.

32. Chiao yü pu (Ministry of Education), *Ti i tzu Chung-kuo chiao yü nien chien* (hereafter CYNC; First yearbook of Chinese education; Nanking: Chiao yü pu, 1934), 7: 325.

33. "The Revolutionary Movement in Chekiang: A Study in the Tenacity of Tradition," in Mary Wright, ed., *China in Revolution: The First Phase, 1900–1913* (New Haven: Yale University Press, 1968), pp. 341–47.

34. Chung-kuo shih hsüeh hui Chi-nan fen hui (Tsinan branch of the China Historical Society), *Shan-tung chin tai shih tzu liao* (hereafter STCTSTL; Materials on Shantung modern history; Tsinan: Shan-tung jen min ch'u pan she, 1958), 2: 221–31.

35. *Ibid.*, pp. 221, 382–84. Based on evidence of such schools at seven of the province's ten prefectural seats.

36. "Huang hsien ko ming shih shih" (Real history of the Revolution in Huang hsien), in STCTSTL, 2: 123–62; "Lü Tzu-jen hsien sheng fang chien chi lu, 1957 nien 9 yüeh" (Transcript of interview with Lü Tzu-jen in September 1957), in *ibid.*, pp. 223–26.

37. CYNC, 3: 350; STCTSTL, 2: 222–23.

38. Tōa dōbunkai, ed., *Shina shōbetsu zenshi [4], Santō shō* (hereafter SSZ; Provincial gazetteer of China, vol. 4, Shantung; Tokyo, 1917), pp. 65–68.

39. Ting Chih-k'uei 1935, p. 40.

40. Cyrus Peake, *Nationalism and Education in China* (New York: Columbia University Press, 1932), pp. 101–2; 160–93.

41. Huang Yen-p'ei, *Huang Yen-p'ei kao ch'a chiao yü jih chi, ti erh chi* (Second collection from Huang Yen-p'ei's diary of educational investigations; Shanghai: Shang wu yin shu kuan, 1915), p. 19; Ting 1935, p. 35.

42. *Wei hsien chih* (1936), ch. 27, p. 24a.

43. Martin Yang, *A Chinese Village: Taitou, Shantung* (New York: Columbia University Press, 1945), p. 182.

44. Huang 1915, pp. 73–75.

45. *Min kuo chih ching hua* (Leaders of the Republic; Tientsin: Peking Leader, 1918?), p. 9.

46. CYNC, 5: 419–20.

47. CNCN, pp. 15–16.

48. SSZ, 4: 64–66.

49. CNCN, pp. 33–40.

50. NCH, 108, July 13, 1913, p. 24.

51. British Foreign Office Archives (hereafter FO) 228/1913 Tsinan Intelligence Report (hereafter TIR) 3d Quarter, 1913, through 4th Quarter, 1914; also Jerome Ch'en, *Yuan Shih-k'ai, 1859–1916* (Stanford, Calif.: Stanford University Press, 1961), pp. 166–96.

52. Howard Boorman, ed., *Biographical Dictionary of Republican China* (hereafter BDRC; New York: Columbia University Press, 1966), 1: 382–84.

53. FO 228/1913, TIR, 3d Quarter, 1914.

54. FO 228/1913, TIR, 3d Quarter, 1914; Huang 1915, pp. 9–10.

55. Prefectures were abolished in 1913. The four circuits were Chiao-tung for everything east of Chang-tien, the town where the branch line to Po-shan joined the Shantung Railroad; Chi-nan for the central Shantung mountains and everything east of the Tientsin-Pukow Railroad; Tung-lin for west of the railroad; Chi-ning for everything south of the city of Chi-ning.

56. CNCN, pp. 25–26.

57. The evidence in CNCN from 1914 conflicts with that in Huang Yen-p'ei's diary of 1915. Apparently Li-ch'eng county did not assume full responsibility until 1923.

58. Shu Hsin-ch'eng 1928, 1: 248–68, contains excerpts from Yüan's *Chiao yü kang yao* (Essentials of education).

59. STCTSTL, 2: 341–42, 400–402.

60. R. W. Luce, "Education in Shantung"; R. C. Forsyth, *Shantung, Sacred Province of China* (Shanghai: Christian Literature Society, 1912), pp. 301–2.

61. Huang 1915, pp. 20–21.

62. Peake 1932, pp. 79–80.

63. Ting Chih-k'uei 1935, p. 17.

64. Monroe was a Columbia professor who served in China as an educational consultant during the 1920's. For his background see J. M. Cattell, *Leaders in Education* (New York: Science Press, 1932), p. 659.

65. Based on the annual summary of business given in Ting Chih-k'uei 1935.

66. Ting Chih-k'uei 1935, p. 86.

67. Yü Tzu-i, "Chi-nan hsüeh wu tiao ch'a" (Investigation of educational work in Tsinan), *Hsin chiao yü* (New education), 6, no. 3 (Mar. 1923): 392–94.

68. Ting Chih-k'uei 1935, pp. 100–101.

69. This magazine was published in Tsinan; the editor was Hsiung Meng-pin.

70. Ting Chih-k'uei 1935, p. 102.

71. CYNC, 2: 39–43.

72. *Ibid.*

73. H. F. Smith, *Elementary Education in Shantung* (New York: Columbia University Press, 1931); Sun Pao-sheng, comp., *Li-ch'eng hsien hsiang t'u tiao ch'a lu* (Record of a survey of Li-ch'eng county; hereafter LCH 1927), pp. 50–59; Ting Chih-k'uei 1935, p. 132. This school did not survive Chang Tsung-ch'ang's governorship.

74. For the history of that institution see Charles H. Corbett, *Shantung Christian University (Cheloo)* (New York: United Board for Christian Colleges in China, 1955).

75. LCH 1927, pp. 50–61.

76. Smith 1931, pp. 127–33.

77. FO 228/3277, TIR, 3d Quarter, 1921.

78. According to some observers the feeling that education is the key to success as an official still continues in contemporary China. R. F. Price, *Education in Communist China* (New York: Praeger, 1970), pp. 106–7.

79. CNCN, pp. 26–28.

80. FO 228/3277, TIR, 3d Quarter, 1922.

81. NCH , Mar. 8, 1919, p. 512.

82. *Shan-tung sheng chih tzu liao* (Materials for a Shantung provincial gazetteer), 1959, part 2 (hereafter STSC 1959.2), pp. 1–19.

83. Chang Kung-chih et al., "Kuan yü Shan-tung hsüeh sheng wu ssu yun tung te hui i" (Recollections of the May Fourth Movement among Shantung students), STSC 1959.2, pp. 22–30.

84. FO 228/3544, letter of July 29, 1919, to British Minister in Peking.

85. Corbett 1955, chap. 15.

86. STSC 1959.2, pp. 79–89.

87. FO 228/3277, TIR, 2d Quarter, 1922.

88. *Ibid.*, 3d Quarter, 1925. See also John Israel, *Student Nationalism in China, 1927–1937* (Stanford, Calif.: Stanford University Press, 1966).

89. Ramon H. Myers, in his study of North China villages, concluded that land distribution had not changed much during the period he studied and that disparities in size of landholdings, already very great, had if anything decreased. The explanation of such stability was the inheritance system of dividing land equally among male heirs. *The Chinese Peasant Economy: Agricultural Development in Hopei and Shantung, 1890–1949* (Cambridge: Harvard University Press, 1970), p. 127.

90. FO 228/3140, Labour and New Chinese Movements, a letter of Oct. 19, 1923, from B. G. Tours to British Minister at Peking.

91. FO 228/3277, TIR, Oct. 1923 to Mar. 1924.

92. Liao T'ai-ch'u "Rural Education in Transition: A Study of Old-fashioned Schools (Szu Shu) in Shantung and Szechuan," *Yenching Journal of Social Studies*, 4, no. 1 (Aug. 1948): 19–67.

93. FO 228/3277, TIR, Mar.–Sept. 1926.

94. *Ibid.*, Mar.–Sept. 1927.

95. The complicated situation has been well summarized by James Sheridan, *A Chinese Warlord, The Career of Feng Yü-hsiang* (Stanford, Calif.: Stanford University Press, 1965), pp. 255–59.

96. Summarized from *Wei hsien chih* (1936), ch. 27.

97. E. G. Woodhead, ed., *China Yearbook* (Tientsin: Tientsin Press, 1934), p. 313; Ting Chih-k'uei 1935, pp. 162–64.

98. Shu Hsin-ch'eng 1928, 4, Appendix, pp. 1–37; Peake 1932, p. 119.

99. C. H. Becker, M. Falski, P. Langevin, R. H. Tawney, *The Reorganization of Education in China* (Paris: League of Nations, 1932), p. 19.

100. *Ibid.*, p. 45.

101. CYNC, 3: 350–58, 411–12.

102. Becker 1932, p. 44.

103. Cheng 1935, pp. 124–25.

104. BDRC, 2: 51–54.

105. Gaimushō jōhōbu (Japanese Foreign Ministry Intelligence Bureau), eds., *Gendai Chūka minkoku Manshu teikoku jemmei kan* (Biographical dictionary of Republican China and Manchoukuo; Tokyo: Gaimushō, 1937).

106. *Shang-tung sheng chiao yü t'ing ti i tz'u kung tso pao kao* (First work report of Shantung Provincial Education Office; T'ai-an: Shan-tung chiao yü t'ing, 1929), pp. 65–66.

107. Lyman Van Slyke, "Liang Sou-ming and the Rural Reconstruction Movement," *Journal of Asian Studies* 18, no. 4 (Aug. 1959), pp. 457–74.

108. Liang Shu-ming, "Tao Wang Hung-i" (Eulogy for Wang Hung-i), *Chung-kuo min tsu tzu ch'iu yün tung chih tsui hou chüeh wu* (The final awakening of the Chinese people's self-salvation movement; Shanghai: Chung-hua shu tien, 1933), pp. 373–80.

109. The work in Ho-tse was delayed, partly because of the problem of banditry in the area.

110. *Shan-tung min chung chiao yü yüeh k'an* (Shantung public education monthly), 4, no. 2 (Mar. 1933), pp. 8off, contains diaries of some of the early lecture-team members.

111. Liang Shu-ming, "Hsiang nung hsüeh hsiao te pan fa chi ch'i i i" (Organization and significance of peasant schools), in *Hsiang ts'un chien she lun wen chi* (Collected essays on rural reconstruction; Tsinan: Shan-tung Tsou-p'ing hsiang ts'un chien she yen chiu hui, 1934).

112. For conditions in the remainder of the old district, see Niida Noboru, ed., *Chūgoku nōson kankō chōsa* (Conditions of Chinese agricultural villages; Tokyo: Iwanami Shoten, 1955), vol. 4.

113. CYNC, 4: 464–66.

114. *Chi-nan shih cheng yüeh k'an* (Tsinan city government monthly), 2, no. 4 (Sept. 1931): 32–34; *Wei-hsien chih*, ch. 22, p. 25a.

115. *Chi-nan shih cheng yüeh k'an*, 2, no. 4 (Sept. 1931), pp. 32–34.

116. Corbett 1955, chaps. 15 and 17.
117. Liao 1948, pp. 19–67.
118. *Ibid.*, pp. 47–48.
119. STTC, ch. 88, p. 23b; Milton Stauffer, *The Christian Occupation of China* (Shanghai: Christian Continuation Committee, 1922), pp. 193–94; *Shan-tung chiao yü yüeh k'an*, 2, no. 12 (Dec. 1923), Annals section, p. 5.
120. Peake 1932, p. 119. "Modern education in China is conceived of as a legitimate and proper tool of the state for indoctrinating the students in the spirit and the principles of modern nationalism."
121. Liao 1948, pp. 49–50.
122. Ichiko Chūzō, "The Role of the Gentry: An Hypothesis," in Wright 1968, pp. 297–318.

The Chambers of Commerce and the YMCA

1. Frank B. Lenz, "Take a Look at China," in *Brooklyn Central* (New York: YMCA, n.d.), p. 14.
2. Shin Tak Hung, in *Women in Industry in the Orient, A Source Book* (New York: The Woman's Press, 1926), pp. 72–73, and H. W. Decker, M.D., *ibid.*, pp. 81–83.
3. S. Wells Williams, *The Middle Kingdom*, rev. and enl. ed. (New York: Scribner, 1883), vol. 2, pp. 87–88.
4. National Archives, Records of the Department of State Relating to Internal Affairs of China, 1910–29, Microfilm Series, General Services Administration, Washington, D.C., 1960 (hereafter NATARC), Microcopy 329, Roll # 116 (hereafter 329–   ), Canton, Oct. 22, 1913, John K. Davis to E. T. Williams.
5. NATARC 329–105, Peking, July 29, 1924.
6. Albert Feuerwerker, *China's Early Industrialization* (Cambridge: Harvard University Press, 1958), pp. 70–71, and Chow Tse-tsung, *The May Fourth Movement* (Cambridge: Harvard University Press, 1960), p. 380.
7. *North-China Herald*, Aug. 15, 1929.
8. Yu-yue Tsu, *The Spirit of Chinese Philanthropy* (New York: Columbia University Press, 1912), pp. 109–10.
9. Mark Elvin, *The Pattern of the Chinese Past* (Stanford, Calif.: Stanford University Press, 1973), pp. 292–93. See also his article elsewhere in this volume, p. 240.
10. Charles Hedtke, "The Genesis of Revolution in Szechwan," a paper read at a conference on the Chinese Revolution of 1911 (Wentworth-by-the-Sea, Portsmouth, N.H.), Aug. 22–27, 1965, pp. 24–25.
11. *Ibid.*
12. NATARC 329–98, Apr. 11, 1911.
13. NATARC 329–98, Sept. 17, 1910.
14. *Ibid.* and NATARC 329–98, Aug. 12, 1910.
15. NATARC 329–98, May 2, 1911.
16. NATARC 329–117, 1283, May 10, 1912.
17. Marie-Claire Bergère, "The Role of the Bourgeoisie," in Mary C. Wright, ed., *China in Revolution: The First Phase, 1900–1913* (New Haven: Yale University Press, 1968), pp. 261–63.

18. Upton Close, "The Chinese Chamber—Power for Progress," *Transpacific*, 3, no. 1 (July 1920): 38.

19. Regulations Governing the Organization of Chambers of Commerce, promulgated Sept. 12, 1914 (hereafter Shang Fa), in Sidney Gamble and John Burgess, *Peking, A Social Survey* (New York: George H. Doran, 1921), pp. 451–71.

20. Li Chien-nung, *The Political History of China, 1840–1928* (Princeton, N.J.: Van Nostrand, 1956), p. 317.

21. Chow Tse-tsung 1960, p. 380.

22. Shang Fa.

23. *Ibid.*

24. Close 1920, p. 39.

25. Gamble and Burgess 1921, p. 200.

26. Close 1920, p. 37.

27. U.S. Bureau of Foreign and Domestic Commerce, Commerce Reports, #1–75, 20th year, Washington, D.C. (hereafter Commerce Reports), Hankow, June 23, 1917, pp. 1112–17.

28. Commerce Reports, Changsha, March 30, 1917.

29. Shang Fa.

30. Gamble and Burgess 1921, p. 195.

31. Close 1920, p. 41.

32. Julean Arnold, in *China, A Commercial and Industrial Handbook* (Washington, D.C.: U.S. Bureau of Foreign and Domestic Commerce, 1920), vol. 2, p. 377.

33. *Millard's Review of the Far East*, Dec. 6 and 13, 1919.

34. Chow Tse-tsung 1960, p. 146.

35. *Millard's*, Jan. 31, 1920, p. 420.

36. Close 1920, p. 41, and Commerce Reports, March 30, 1917, p. 1195.

37. NATARC 329–117, 1283, May 10, 1912.

38. *Ibid.*

39. *Ibid.*

40. Commerce Reports, Hankow, June 23, 1917, pp. 1112–17.

41. Close 1920, p. 37.

42. "Business Practices of Foochow Merchants," *Chinese Economic Journal*, 1, no. 11 (Nov. 1927): 943.

43. NATARC 329–98, 1130, July 25, 1912.

44. Close 1920, p. 37.

45. Commerce Reports, Hankow, June 23, 1917, p. 1115.

46. *Millard's*, Oct. 4, 1919, p. 193.

47. Close 1920, p. 37.

48. Arnold 1920, p. 377.

49. *Ibid.*, p. 250.

50. *Millard's*, Sept. 20, 1919, p. 94.

51. Close 1920, p. 37.

52. *Millard's*, Jan. 4, 1920, p. 371.

53. *North-China Herald*, Oct. 29, 1921.

54. *Millard's*, Dec. 13, 1919, p. 78.

55. NATARC 329–98, 808, Kiaochow, 1923.

56. Commerce Reports, March 30, 1917.

57. Gamble and Burgess 1921, p. 211.
58. Close 1920, p. 40.
59. Jean Chesneaux, *The Chinese Labor Movement, 1919–1927* (Stanford, Calif.: Stanford University Press, 1968), p. 238.
60. Chesneaux 1968, p. 206.
61. Chesneaux 1968, p. 352.
62. NATARC 329–103, 163.
63. Harold Isaacs, *The Tragedy of the Chinese Revolution* (Stanford, Calif.: Stanford University Press, 1951, rev. ed.), p. 145.
64. *North-China Herald,* Aug. 26, 1930.
65. *Ibid.,* July 13, 1929.
66. Kin-wei Shaw and Ziang-ling Chang, "China and the International Chamber of Commerce," *Chinese Economic Journal,* 5, no. 6 (Dec. 1929): 1041.
67. *Ibid.,* 9, no. 2 (Mar. 1933), 286.
68. Frank Tamagna, *Banking and Finance in China* (New York: Institute of Pacific Relations, 1942), p. 68.
69. An extended treatment is available in Shirley S. Garrett, *Social Reformers in Urban China* (Cambridge: Harvard University Press, 1970).
70. Fletcher Brockman, Foreign Secretaries' Reports, 1901, YMCA Historical Library, New York.
71. W. W. Lockwood to "friends," Mar. 10, 1905, Box 65E, YMCA Library.
72. George Lerrigo to Dr. Taylor, March 17, 1930, Box 95F, YMCA Library.
73. Setting-up Conference, Feb. 4, 1930, Box 95G, YMCA Library.
74. *Ibid.*
75. Arthur Rugh to Francis Harmon, Aug. 3, 1936, Box 97C, YMCA Library.
76. D. W. Edwards, Box 99A, p. 22, YMCA Historical Library.
77. Gerald Birks, report, Box 95G, Jan. 28, 1930, YMCA Library.
78. Arthur Rugh, Aug. 3, 1936, Box 97C, YMCA Library.

The Administration of Shanghai, 1905–1914

1. Imabori Seiji, *Chūgoku hōken shakai no kikō—Kuei-sui (Hu-ho-hao-t'e) ni okeru shakai shūdan no jittai chōsa* (The structure of Chinese feudal society: A factual investigation of social groups in Kuei-sui [Huhehot]; Tokyo: Nippon gakujutsu shinkō-kai, 1955), chap. 3; Tou Chi-liang, *T'ung hsiang tsu chih chih yen chiu* (Organizations of fellow-regionals; Chungking: Cheng chung shu chü, 1943), esp. chap. 2 and pp. 70–87; Niida Noboru, "Shindai Konan no 'Girudo Māchanto'" (The guild merchant in Hunan in Ch'ing times), *Tōyōshi kenkyū,* 21, no. 3 (1962): 71–92; Ho Ping-ti, *Chung-kuo hui kuan shih lun* (A historical survey of *Landsmannschaften* in China; Taipei: Hsüeh sheng shu chü, 1966), pp. 112, 131. I am grateful to Professor Ramon Myers for drawing my attention to the Imabori, and to Professor John Fincher for drawing my attention to the Tou Chi-liang.
2. Yü Yueh et al., eds, *T'ung-chih Shang-hai hsien chih* (hereafter TCSH-HC; Gazetteer of Shang-hai county in the T'ung-chih reign; Shanghai, 1871), ch. 2, p. 21a.

3. Yao Wen-nan et al., eds., *Shang-hai hsien hsü chih* (hereafter SHHHC; A continuation of Shang-hai county gazetteer; Shanghai, 1918), ch. 3, p. 1a; Negishi Tadashi, *Shanhai no girudo* (The guilds of Shanghai; Tokyo: Nihon hyōronsha, 1951), p. 9. Negishi says that membership in this guild was restricted to natives of Shanghai, but the SHHHC speaks simply of "*sha*-boat merchants," and such boats were found all along the coasts of Kiangsu and Shantung.

4. SHHHC, ch. 2, p. 22a.

5. TCSHHC, ch. 4, pp. 40b, 43a; SHHHC, ch. 5, pp. 16a, 27a.

6. *Hsin hai ko ming ch'ien shih nien chien shih lun hsüan chi* (A selection of discussions of current affairs in the ten years before the 1911 revolution; Hong Kong: San lien shu tien, 1962), 1: 174.

7. D. Twitchett, "The Fan Clan's Charitable Estate, 1050–1760," in D. Nivison and A. F. Wright, eds., *Confucianism in Action* (Stanford, Calif.: Stanford University Press, 1959).

8. Katō Shigeshi, "Sō no kenkyōku ni tsuite" (On the Chien-chiao treasuries of Sung times), in his *Shina keizai-shi kōshō* (Studies in Chinese economic history; Tokyo: Tōyō bunka, 1953–54), 2: 235–38.

9. TCSHHC, ch. 2, p. 21a.

10. *Ibid.*, pp. 21ab, 22a, 23b–24a, etc.

11. *Shang-hai t'ung jen t'ang cheng hsin lu* (Report of the Shanghai Hall of Universal Altruism; Shanghai, 1846); Yü Chih, ed., *Te i lu* (Te-i records; Shanghai, 1869). The latter work is a survey of the charitable institutions of Kiangsu by a famous philanthropist.

12. TCSHHC, ch. 2, pp. 21a–27a.

13. Yü Chih 1969, 4, no. 4: 2a.

14. Yang I and Ch'ü Ch'ing-p'u, eds., *Shang-hai shih tzu chih chih* (hereafter SHSTCC; Shanghai municipality self-government gazetteer; Shanghai, 1915), Documents section (hereafter Docs) A, p. 27a; Chiang Shen-wu, "Shang-hai shih cheng ti fen chih shih ch'i" (The period of separate municipal administration in Shanghai), in *Shang-hai shih t'ung chih ch'i k'an* (hereafter SHSTCCK; Periodical of the Shanghai Municipal Gazetteer Office; Shanghai), 2, no. 4 (1934): 1222.

15. SHHHC, ch. 2, p. 31a.

16. TCSHHC, ch. 4, p. 35a.

17. SHSTCC, Docs A, pp. 38a–41a; and *ibid.*, Docs A, pp. 29a–37a, and Docs B, pp. 17a–19a.

18. Ho Ping-ti 1966, pp. 38–39, 40–64, 102–12.

19. SHHHC, ch. 3, pp. 1a–16a; Negishi 1951, pp. 7–14.

20. Katō Shigeshi, "On the *Hang* or the Association of Merchants in China, with especial reference to the institution in the T'ang and Sung periods," *Memoirs of the Research Department of the Tōyō Bunko*, 7 (1935): 66–67; D. Twitchett, "The T'ang Market System," *Asia Major* 12 (1966): 205–16; Shiba Yoshinobu, *Sōdai shōgyō-shi kenkyū* (Commerce and society in Sung China; Tokyo: Kazama shobō, 1968), pp. 38–40, 177, 210, 239, 395–96, 410, 487. Almost all the known materials on Southern Sung guilds refer to the capital.

21. Thus we learn from an eighteenth-century gazetteer for Lin-ch'ing in Shantung that in 1466 a guild (*hang*) was formed by three associations (*hui*)

of cotton-cloth merchants from Kiangnan, but nothing is said of its internal character. See Fujii Hiroshi, "Shin-an shōnin no kenkyū" (The merchants of Hsin-an), *Tōyō Gakuhō* 6, no. 1 (1953): 10.

22. Negishi 1951, p. 29. See also pp. 7–8, 15.

23. SHHHC, ch. 3, p. 1a.

24. *Ibid.*, ch. 3, pp. 10a, 13a.

25. *Ibid.*, ch. 3, p. 5a; SHSTCC, Docs A, pp. 138b–139a, 142b, 146b–147a.

26. Negishi Tadashi, *Chūgoku no girudo* (The guilds of China; Tokyo Nihon hyōron shinsha, 1953), p. 151.

27. *Ibid.*

28. Imabori Seiji, *Chūgoku no shakai kōzō—anshan rejiimu ni okeru kyō-dōtai* (The structure of Chinese society: Collective bodies under the ancient regime; Tokyo: Yūhikaku, 1953), p. 262.

29. Imabori 1955, pp. 20–21.

30. Niida 1962, p. 75; Tou Chi-liang 1943, pp. 37–38, 44–46, 65, 83–87.

31. SHHHC, ch. 2, p. 51a; Negishi 1951, pp. 338–42; United Kingdom, Public Record Office, Foreign Office archives (hereafter FO) 227/1561 no. 39, Warren to Satow, June 30, 1904 (enclosure) and 228/1561 Intendant to Senior Consul, June 10, 1907; A. Feuerwerker, *China's Early Industrialization* (Cambridge: Harvard University Press, 1958), p. 372.

32. *North-China Herald* (hereafter NCH), Dec. 29, 1905, p. 707; Feb. 16, 1906, p. 346; Feb. 23, 1906, pp. 396–97, 427; Mar. 2, 1906, p. 468, 495–96; Mar. 9, 1906, pp. 506, 534; Mar. 16, 1906, pp. 603, 625; *Tung fang tsa chih* (hereafter TFTC; Eastern Miscellany), 3, no. 3 (Apr. 18, 1906): *shang wu* 14–16.

33. NCH, Mar. 9, 1906, p. 577; May 18, 1906, p. 401; Sept. 18, 1909, p. 667; FO 228/1603 no. 65, 228/1634 no. 99.

34. The councillors are listed in SHSTCC, Table of Personnel of the Executive Committees, and Table of Personnel of the Consultative Assemblies. Their backgrounds have been traced through the SHSTCC; NCH; Niu Yung-chien, ed., *Min kuo Shang-hai hsien chih* (hereafter MKSHHC; Shang-hai county gazetteer for the republican period; Shanghai, 1936); and Kojima Yoshio, "Shingai kakumei ni okeru Shanhai dokuritsu to shōshinsō" (The great merchants of Shanghai and its independence in the Revolution of 1911), in *Chūgoku kindaika no shakai kōzō* (The social structure of China during modernization), vol. 6 of the *Tōyō shigaku ronshū* (Tokyo: Tōkyō kyōiku daigaku, Ajiashi kenkyūkai, 1960).

35. SHHHC, ch. 2, pp. 22a–31a.

36. Chiang Shen-wu 1934, pp. 1216–22; SHSTCC, Docs A, pp. 1b, 2ab, 53b, 66ab, 67b–68b.

37. SHSTCC, Docs A, p. 173b, appendix.

38. A. M. Kotenev, *Shanghai: Its Mixed Court and Council* (Shanghai: North-China Daily News and Herald, 1925); C. B. Maybon and J. Fredet, *Histoire de la concession française de Changhaï* (Paris: Plon, 1929).

39. *Shen-pao* (hereafter SP), Dec. 18, 1881, p. 1; Jan. 2, 1882, p. 1; May 3, 1882, p. 1; July 28, 1882, p. 1; Jan. 9, 1884, p. 1; May 2, 1887, p. 1.

40. SP, Oct. 27, 1883, p. 1.

41. *Ibid.*, Apr. 13, 1882, p. 1; July 22, 1882, p. 1; May 1, 1887, p. 1. The paper's inspiration presumably came from the early writings of Cheng Kuan-

ying and Wang T'ao. Wang's son-in-law was the *Shen-pao's* editor. See Leong Sow-theng, "Wang T'ao and the Movement for Self-strengthening and Reform in the Late Ch'ing Period," *Papers on China*, 17 (Cambridge: Harvard University, Center for East Asian Studies, 1963): 107, 114–17; S-Y. Teng and J. K. Fairbank, *Research Guide for China's Response to the West* (Cambridge: Harvard University Press, 1959), pp. 14–15; Chien Po-tsan et al., eds., *Wu hsü pien fa* (The reform movement of 1898; Shanghai: Shang-hai jen min ch'u pan she, 1957), pp. 55–57.

42. Li Chung-chüeh, *Hsin-chia-p'o feng t'u chi* (A record of the customs of Singapore; Changsha 1895; photoreprint, Singapore: Nan-yang Book Company, 1947). See also Li Chung-chüeh, *Ch'ieh wan lao jen ch'i shih sui tzu hsü* (Autobiography of old 'Stubborn Yet' at the age of seventy; Shanghai, 1923), pp. 23a–33b.

43. Li Chung-chüeh 1923, *passim*; MKSHHC, ch. 15, pp. 37b–39b; NCH, May 20, 1911, p. 500; Nov. 4, 1911, p. 279; May 10, 1913, p. 348. See also Hu Huai-shen, "Shang-hai hsüeh i kai yao" (Scholarship and the liberal arts in Shanghai), part 2, in SHSTCCK, 1, no. 2 (1934): 502–4.

44. MKSHHC, ch. 15, pp. 25ab.

45. Chin Liang-i, *Chin shih jen wu chih* (Personalities of recent times; Taipei: Kuo min ch'u pan she, 1955), p. 355. See also Li Chung-chüeh 1923, p. 12a; SHSTCC, Docs A, pp. 42a, 98a; B, p. 7a; C, p. 28a.

46. *Min li pao* (hereafter MLP), Nov. 3, 1910, p. 4; Nov. 4, 1910, p. 4; MKSHHC, ch. 15, pp. 22b–23a.

47. MLP, Nov. 3, 1910, p. 4; MKSHHC, ch. 17, p. 9b; NHC, May 6, 1910, p. 336; July 6, 1912, p. 19.

48. MLP, Nov. 3, 1910, p. 4; Apr. 17, 1911, p. 5; Kojima 1960, p. 118; NCH, May 15, 1909, p. 377; May 27, 1910, p. 509; Dec. 9, 1911, p. 656; Mar. 16, 1912, p. 729; Dec. 14, 1912, p. 728; Research Committee on Literary and Historical Materials, Chinese People's Political Consultative Conference, eds., *Hsin hai ko ming hui i lu* (hereafter HHKMHIL; Recollections of the Revolution of 1911; Peking: Chung-hua shu chü, 1961), vol. 4, p. 48.

49. MKSHHC, ch. 15, pp. 11b–12b.

50. NCH, July 26, 1913, p. 263; FO 228/1806, Fraser to Jordan, Nov. 13, 1911; Ch'en T'ing-shan, *Ch'un shen chiu wen* (Old hearsay from Shanghai; Taipei: Chen kuang yüeh k'an she, 1964), Part A, pp. 70, 131; Part B, pp. 114–15.

51. NCH, Aug. 12, 1910, p. 384; FO 228/1634, Warren to Carnegie, June 6, 1906; Yao Kung-ho, *Shang-hai hsien hua* (Shanghai gossip; Shanghai: Commercial Press, 1933), pp. 17–18.

52. SHSTCC, Outline A, p. 1a.

53. *Ibid.*, Docs A, p. 84a; C, p. 50a; and see also C, pp. 34a, 108a; NCH, Aug. 23, 1913, p. 558.

54. SHSTCC, Docs A, pp. 25a, 58b, 64a; NCH, May 12, 1905, p. 319; Aug. 17, 1906, p. 366.

55. Li Chung-chüeh 1923, pp. 172a, 176a; SHSTCC, Docs A, p. 1a; TFTC, 2, no. 9 (Oct. 23, 1905): chronology 65.

56. SHSTCC, Docs A, pp. 1b, 55a, 66a. See also the references given in note 33.

57. SHSTCC, Docs A, p, 159b.

58. TFTC, 3, no. 8 (Sept. 13, 1906): *nei wu* 184, 186; 3, no. 11 (Jan. 9, 1907): *nei wu* 277; 4, no. 5 (July 5, 1907): *nei wu* 233; 4, no. 10 (Nov. 30, 1907): *nei wu* 508–9; etc.

59. Mark Elvin, "The Gentry Democracy in Shanghai, 1905–1914" (Ph.D. Thesis, University of Cambridge, 1967), chap. 4; SHSTCC, Docs C, pp. 106b–107a.

60. Elvin 1967, Table of Personnel of the Executive Committees, Table of Personnel of the Consultative Assemblies. The consulting directors were later replaced by 60 Deputies (*i-yüan*), and the number of managing general directors reduced to four.

61. *Ibid.*, Regulations A, pp. 1ab, 6b.

62. *Ibid.*, Regulations A, pp. 4b, 6b; TFTC, 3, no. 1 (Feb. 18, 1906): *nei wu* 24.

63. *Ibid.*, Regulations A, p. 6b; B, pp. 1ab, 4b; C, pp. 2ab, 6a; Docs A, pp. 7a–8a; *Ta Ch'ing Kuang hsü hsin fa ling* (The new laws of the Kuang-hsü reign of the great Ch'ing dynasty; Peking, 1909), ch. 2, pp. 49b, 51a.

64. On one occasion the general director made the Assembly change its policy by threatening to resign. See SHSTCC, Docs B, pp. 61ab, 95b–96a.

65. Motions from the public were not formally allowed until 1912 (SHSTCC, Regulations C, p. 3a), but were informally permitted at least as early as 1910. See MLP, Dec. 10, 1910, p. 5.

66. SHSTCC, Regulations B, pp. 3ab.

67. For example, MLP, Dec. 7, 9, 10, 13, 14, 15, 16, 19, and 20, 1910, on p. 5 in all cases; Jan. 9, 14, and 18, 1911, on p. 5 in all cases likewise.

68. SHSTCC, Regulations A, pp. 5ab; B, p. 2a; C, p. 3a.

69. *Ibid.*, Regulations A, p. 6a; B, pp. 1ab, 7a; C, 2a, 7b; *Ta Ch'ing Kuang hsü hsin fa ling*, ch. 2, p. 51a.

70. SHSTCC, Regulations A, p. 6b; B, pp. 4b, 5a; C, pp. 6ab.

71. *Ibid.*, Table of the Heads of Departments; Regulations A, p. 1b; B, pp. 5a, 7a–12b; C, pp. 1b, 5ab, 7a–8b, 18ab. The more elaborate schemes set forth in Regulations A, pp. 2b–3a; B, pp. 5ab seem never to have been put into practice.

72. *Ibid.*, Table of Personnel of the Executive Committees, pp. 4a–5a; Table of Police Achievements; Regulations A, pp. 2a, 7b; B, p. 6b; C, p. 8b; Outline A, pp. 1b, 4ab, 6b, 9a, 10b, 11a, etc.; Docs A, pp. 4ab, 55a–56b; B, p. 2a, etc.; TFTC, 3, no. 1 (Feb. 18, 1906): *nei wu* 21–24.

73. SHSTCC, Explanation, p. xiv; Table of Police Achievements, pp. 4b–5a; Regulations A, pp. 7a–10b; B, pp. 8ab, 10ab, 11b–12b; Docs A, p. 2b; TFTC, 3, no. 1 (Feb. 18, 1906): *nei wu* 23.

74. SHSTCC, Regulations A, pp. 9a–10a; B, p. 7a; C, p. 7b; Outline A, p. 4b; B, pp. 5a, 9a; C, p. 10b. A case of a strong departmental link may be found in Outline A, p. 2b. The careers of the twenty-one assistant officers appointed in 1906 may be traced through Outline A, pp. 3a, 4b; Docs A, pp. 4b, 98ab; C, pp. 28b, 70b; Kojima 1960, pp. 117–18, 130; NCH, Aug. 10, 1912, p. 404; Li Chung-chüeh 1923, pp. 198ab.

75. SHSTCC, Regulations B, pp. 8a, 11ab, 14b–16a; C, pp. 19b–21a; Outline C, pp. 12b–13a, 17b; Docs A, pp. 61a, 66a–67b; C, pp. 65b, 67b–68b, 108ab.

76. For example, Hoshi Ayao, *Mindai sōun no kenkyū* (The Ming dynasty

grain transport system; Tokyo: Nihon gakujutsu shinkō kai, 1963), pp. 179–236; Tomi Saeki, *Shindai ensei no kenkyū* (The Ch'ing dynasty salt administration; Kyoto: Tōyōshi kenkyū kai, 1956), pp. 37–56.

77. SHSTCC, Regulations B, pp. 11b–12a.

78. SHSTCC, Outline A, p. 5a; Docs A, pp. 66b–67a, 162a–164a; C, p. 61a.

79. Muramatsu Yūji, *Chūgoku keizai no shakai taisei* (The social structure of the Chinese economy; Tokyo, 1949), pp. 363–72.

80. SHSTCC, Regulations B, pp. 8ab, 10b.

81. *Ibid.*, Docs B, p. 97a.

82. *Ibid.*, Table of Police Achievements, pp. 2a, 3a; Regulations A, pp. 15b–17b; Docs A, pp. 2b–3b, 53a–54a, 15b–17b; B, pp. 28ab, 97a; NCH, Dec. 22, 1905, p. 689; Oct. 12, 1906, p. 72; FO 228/1603 Chinese enclosure no. 52; Yao Kung-ho 1933, p. 25.

83. *Chung-kuo min kuo k'ai kuo wu shih nien wen hsien* (Records presented in celebration of the fiftieth anniversary of the inauguration of the Republic of China), 2d series, *Ko sheng kuang fu* (The Revolution of 1911 in the provinces; Taipei: Cheng chung shu chü, 1963), 1: 386; NCH, Nov. 24, 1905, p. 428; May 18, 1906, p. 401; June 21, 1907, p. 712; June 28, 1907, pp. 749, 768; May 13, 1911, p. 397; Sept. 16, 1911, p. 690; Li Chung-chüeh 1923, p. 186b; Kojima 1960, p. 123; MLP, Jan. 19, Jan. 20, 1911, p. 5; MKSHHC, ch. 15, p. 39a; SHSTCC, Docs A, pp. 128ab.

84. NCH, Mar. 10, 1911, p. 579; Mar. 17, 1911, pp. 624, 637; Apr. 15, 1911, p. 164; May 13, 1911, p. 397; June 10, 1911, p. 663; June 17, 1911, p. 756; July 15, 1911, p. 169; July 22, 1911, p. 228; MLP, Apr. 17, 1911, p. 5; Kojima 1960, 126; HHKMHIL, 4, 11; Li Chung-chüeh 1923, p. 187a; Mark Elvin 1967, pp. 234–36, 241–44.

85. FO 228/1603 Chinese enclosure no. 65; MLP, May 20, 1911, p. 5; May 22, 1911, p. 5; May 24, 1911, p. 5.

86. SHSTCC, Docs C, pp. 67b–68a.

87. *Ibid.*, Docs A, pp. 57a–58a, 86a, 123a, 141a; B, pp. 42a, 43b.

88. Yü Chih 1869, 14, 1: 8a–20b. See also Kung-chuan Hsiao, *Rural China, Imperial Control in the Nineteenth Century* (Seattle: University of Washington, 1960), pp. 202–4.

89. SHSTCC, Docs A, pp. 43b, 92a–94a, 124b–125a; B, pp. 43b, 82a; C, p. 41b; Yü chih 1869, 14, no. 1: 19a.

90. SP, Dec. 14, 1882, p. 1; NCH, Jan. 9, 1909, p. 113; SHTSCC, Docs A, pp. 92a–94b, 124b–125a, 146ab; C, pp. 83a.

91. *Ibid.*, Docs A, pp. 75a, 98ab, 99ab, 109a; B, pp. 15b, 35b, 90b; MKS-HHC, ch. 15, pp. 7b–8a; Chiang Shen-wu, "Shang-hai hsien tsai Ch'ing tai" (Shang-hai county during the Ch'ing dynasty), in SHSTCCK, 2, no. 2 (1934): 518. See P. Kuhn, "The *T'uan-lien* Local Defense System at the Time of the Taiping Rebellion," *Harvard Journal of Asiatic Studies*, 27 (1967), on the general nature of such militia bodies.

92. SHHHC, ch. 2, pp. 44ab; MKSHHC, ch. 15, p. 39a; MLP, Oct. 31, 1910, p. 4; Nov. 3, p. 4; Nov. 5, p. 4.

93. SHSTCC, Regulations C, pp. 11b–13a; Docs C, pp. 28ab, 30a, 32a, 33a, 82b.

94. *Ibid.*, Docs A, p. 160b.

95. *Ibid.*, Regulations A, pp. 11a–12a; B, pp. 17a–19a, 21a–22a; Docs A,

pp. 138b, 142b, 145b–148b, 150a; B, pp. 93a, 97a, 99a; C, pp. 103b, 120a.

96. *Ibid.*, Regulations A, pp. 11a–12a; B, pp. 19ab; Docs A, pp. 141a, 143b, 146a, 150a; C, p. 84b.

97. *Ibid.*, Regulations A, pp. 11a–12a; Docs A, p. 140a, 142a; B, p. 90b; C, pp. 9b, 117b.

98. *Ibid.*, Regulations A, pp. 11a–12a; B, pp. 11b–12b; C, pp. 21ab; Docs A, pp. 138b, 140a–142a, 144a, 151a; B, pp. 77a, 97a–98a; NCH, "Municipal Gazette," Sept. 25, 1913, p. 218.

99. SHSTCC, Explanation, pp. 1b–2a; MLP, Nov. 8, 1910, p. 4.

100. SHSTCC, Outline A, p. 6a; Docs A, pp. 121a–127b; NCH, June 14, 1907, p. 648; June 21, p. 712; June 28, pp. 749, 768; July 5, 17, 27, 28; FO 228/1732, Municipal Council to Consular Body, Jan. 26, 1909, and Intendant to Consular Body, Mar. 23, 1909.

101. SHSTCC, Education Tables, pp. 1a–6b; Public Works Tables, pp. 14ab (see also the detailed calculations in Elvin 1967, pp. 200–202, and Docs C, pp. 24b, 99a); Regulations B, p. 12b; Docs B, pp. 50a, 79a, 87a, 90a; NCH, Apr. 8, 1911, p. 103.

102. SHSTCC, Docs A, pp. 69a–71a; B, p. 94a; Li Chung-chüeh 1923, pp. 177b–180b.

103. SHSTCC, Docs C, p. 32a.

104. *Ibid.*, Docs A, pp. 115a–120a; B, pp. 68ab, 71a–72b. See also NCH, Sept. 9, 1911, p. 659.

105. SHSTCC, Tables of Accounts, 5a–6b. Exchange rate from C. Yang et al., eds., *Statistics of China's Foreign Trade During the Last Sixty-five Years* (Shanghai: Academia Sinica, National Research Institute of Social Sciences, 1931), p. 151.

106. SHSTCC, Docs A, pp. 29a–37a, 61a–63a, 104a–106a; B, pp. 17a–19a; C, pp. 12a–15a, 51a–52a, 100a; Li Chung-chüeh 1923, pp. 173b, 174a, 192b–193b; NCH, July 20, 1912, p. 194.

107. *Ibid.*, Feb. 14, 1914, p. 440.

108. SHSTCC, Regulations C, p. 9a; Docs A, p. 21b; C, pp. 23b–25a.

109. *Ibid.*, Docs A, p. 160a; TFTC, 3, no. 1 (Feb. 18, 1906): *nei wu* 21–24. This was probably inspired by the Mixed Court in the International Settlement. See Mark Elvin, "The Mixed Court of the International Settlement at Shanghai (Until 1911)," *Papers on China*, 17 (1963): 151.

110. NCH, Mar. 30, 1912, p. 8378; Apr. 6, p. 18.

111. Elvin 1967, pp. 241–42, 247–51, 262–63; SHSTCC, Docs C, p. 32b.

112. For example, NCH, Mar. 10, 1911, p. 579; July 5, 1913, p. 24; MLP, Oct. 14, 1910, p. 3 (Wu-hsüeh); Feb. 5, 1911, p. 4 (Ch'ing-ho); Apr. 1, p. 5 (Ts'ai-ho-ching); Apr. 6, p. 5 (Yen-t'ai); Apr. 11, p. 4 (Nan-ch'ang); May 6, p. 4 (Ch'ing-p'u); May 12, p. 4 (Hang-chou); May 22, p. 3 (Sung-chiang); etc.

113. A good illustration of the danger of casually condemning a self-government body on the basis of a few derogatory remarks is Teraki Tokuko's treatment of Ch'uan-sha. See Teraki Tokuko, "Shinmatsu Minkoku-shonen no chihō jichi" (Local self-government at the end of the Ch'ing and during the early years of the Republic), *Ochanomizu shigaku*, 5 (1962). Something was probably amiss in the self-government body at Ch'uan-sha (see SHSTCC, Docs B, p. 61a), but it is as likely to have been excessive reforming zeal as

corruption. Both yamen clerks and rural bullies played a large part in foment-
ing the disorders. See MLP, Mar. 3, 4, 5, 29, and 31, Apr. 10, 16, 19, 23, 24,
25, and 26, May 4, and May 16, 1911, p. 5 in all cases.

City Temples in Taipei Under Three Regimes

1. Fieldwork was made possible by a fellowship from the Carnegie and
Nuffield Foundations through the London-Cornell Project in London. I would
also like to thank Professor G. William Skinner for encouraging me to write on
this topic and, along with Dr. Mark Elvin, for detailed criticism of the conference draft of this report.

2. This paragraph and the following brief historical summary are based
largely on Li T'ien-ch'un, "T'ai-pei ti ch'ü chih k'ai shih yü ssu miao" (Temples
and development of the Taipei area), *T'ai-pei wen hsien*, 1 (1962): 67–77,
and Huang Ch'i-mu, "Fen lei hsieh tou yü Meng-chia" (Communal riots and
Meng-chia), *T'ai-pei wen wu*, 2, no. 1 (1953): 55–59.

3. J. D. Clark, *Formosa* (Shanghai: *Shanghai Mercury* Press, 1896), p. 56.

4. Personal communication.

5. This is noted in *Chu-lo hsien chih* (Gazetteer of Chu-lo hsien), ch. 8
(1716), Bank of Taiwan edition (1962), p. 145. Data on settlement in Taiwan and the effect of official restrictions on migration are to be found in
a paper by Ch'en Shao-hsing entitled "Family, Lineage and Settlement Patterns in Taiwan," given in September 1966 to the Social Science Research
Council (SSRC) conference on family and kinship in China.

6. Lin Heng-tao, "T'ai-pei shih ti ssu miao" (The temples of Taipei), *T'ai-
pei wen hsien*, 2 (1962): 54.

7. *T'ai-wan sheng t'ung chih kao* (Draft gazetteer of Taiwan), ch. 2, ts'e 1
(Taipei: T'ai-wan sheng wen hsien wei yüan hui, 1956), p. 217.

8. *T'ai-pei shih chih kao* (Draft gazetteer of Taipei; Taipei: T'ai-pei shih
wen hsien wei yüan hui, 1965), ch. 4, pp. 32–33; Li Ken-ch'üan, "Meng-chia
ssu miao chi" (A record of Meng-chia's temples), *T'ai-pei wen wu*, 2, no. 1
(1953; hereafter Li Ken-ch'üan 1953a): 40–47; Li T'ien-ch'un 1962; Huang
Ch'i-mu 1953.

9. Lin Heng-tao 1962, pp. 53–81.

10. *T'ai-pei shih chih kao* 1965, pp. 63–73.

11. Lin Heng-tao 1962; Li Ken-ch'üan 1953a, and *id.*, "Ta-tao-ch'eng ssu
miao chi" (A record of Ta-tao-ch'eng's temples), *T'ai-pei wen wu*, 2, no. 3
(1953; hereafter Li Ken-ch'üan 1953b): 78–83. Liu Chi-wan, "Ch'ing tai T'ai-
wan chih ssu miao" (Taiwan temples in the Ch'ing period), *T'ai-pei wen hsien*,
4, 5, and 6 (1963).

12. The evidence for the occurrence of processions in the Ch'ing period is
that they are mentioned as occurring in the Japanese period, in various places
and by various people, and that the current managers and secretaries of the
temples do not remember being told by their fathers that processions had been
initiated in the Japanese period.

13. A good, brief description of the festival in Taiwan is given in Michael
Saso, *Taiwan Feasts and Customs* (Hsin-chu: Chanabel Language Institute,
1966), pp. 66–69. For the seventh-month competitive processions and feasts
see the Japanese compilation by Kataoka Iwao, *Taiwan fūzoku shiso* (A com-

pilation of Taiwanese customs; Taipei: Taiwan nichinichi shinpō sha, 1921), pp. 61–62.

14. The City God was always involved in official prayers for rain. See my "School Temple and City God," in G. William Skinner, ed., *The City in Late Imperial China* (Stanford, Calif.: Stanford University Press, forthcoming).

15. An incense-burner association is a formal bond for many kinds of grouping in Taiwan. I have records of mutual-savings circles, of a renunciation-of-gambling circle, of societies for mutual assistance in funerals, as well as of sworn brotherhoods, groups of compatriots, surname groups, and trade associations that were organized around an incense burner and a patron deity.

16. Quoted in Kung-chuan Hsiao, *Rural China: Imperial Control in the Nineteenth Century* (Seattle: Washington University Press, 1960), p. 472.

17. Kristofer M. Schipper, "Religious Organization in Traditional Tainan," in Skinner, ed., *Late Imperial China.*

18. Rolf A. Stein, "Remarques sur les mouvements du Taoisme politico-religieux au II⁰ siècle ap. J.C.," *T'oung Pao*, 50 (1963). Stein concludes (pp. 77–78): "un système cohérent qui s'est maintenu, avec des variants de forme, depuis les Han jusqu'à nos jours. . . . Chaque fois on trouve un aspect moral et social à côté d'un aspect religieux. Dans les deux cas, le premier aspect s'exprime par une certaine préférence pour une vie communale et l'élection d'un chef sage."

19. As I report in Skinner, ed., *Late Imperial China.* A full description of the establishment of T'ai-pei prefecture is to be found in Harry J. Lamley, "The Formation of Cities in Taiwan," in *ibid.*

20. See my contribution in *ibid.*

21. According to 1933 figures, the association had 22 members in all. Lin Hsi-ch'ing, *Taiwan shaji shūkyō yōran* (Survey of Taiwan religious institutions), "Taihoku shū" volume (Taipei: Taiwan shaji shūkyō kankō kai, 1933), p. 161 and appendix.

22. *Ibid.*

23. *Ibid.*, and interviews with members of the various temples.

24. One of the temple secretaries interviewed compared the lack of personal attendance at local temple ceremonies by local politicians in Taipei, where they are satisfied just to have their names publicized, with the much greater personal attendance of southern Taiwanese local politicians.

25. One example of a man who wielded this kind of power in the Taipei basin during the Japanese period is described by Margery Wolf in *The House of Lim: A Study of a Chinese Farm Family* (New York: Appleton-Century-Crofts, 1968), pp. 47–48.

26. Strictures against both sworn brotherhoods and extravagant feasting in central and northern Taiwan are to be found for instance in *Chu-lo hsien chih*, ch. 8 (1716; 1962 edition), pp. 146–47.

27. Yü Ch'ang-i, ed., *T'ai-pei Lung shan ssu* (Taipei: T'ai-wan chin jih kuan kuang she, 1968), pp. 53 and 68.

28. *Social Base Maps of Taipei City* (Taipei: Department of Sociology, National Taiwan University, 1965), in Chinese and English.

29. *Taiwan shaji shūkyō yōran* 1933, appendix; Yung Feng, "T'ai-pei K'ung tzu miao shih liu" (Sketch of Taipei's K'ung-tzu miao), *T'ai-pei wen wu*, 2, no. 2 (1953): 84–86.

30. Liu Lung-kang, "Ch'eng-chiang jen wu hsiao chih" (Notes on personalities of Ta-tao-ch'eng); and Kuo Hsiao-chou, "Che jen Li Ch'un-sheng weng" (Philosopher Li Ch'un-sheng), both in *T'ai-pei wen wu*, 2, no. 3 (1953): 103–4 and 107–8.

31. I have not made a study of the writings of the movement but base this observation on the frequent statements made to this effect by people in syncretic cults like those of the temples here. One person in a spirit-writing group said that they could call upon Jesus, but they would not be able to understand his response because the writing would be in Hebrew.

32. *T'ai-pei shih chih kao* 1965, ch. 4, pp. 36–37.

33. There is, for instance, the edict prohibiting the San-chiao T'ang (Temples of the Three Religions) in Honan in 1744, mentioned by J. J. M. de Groot in *Sectarianism and Religious Persecution in China* (Leiden: E. J. Brill, 1901; republished, Taipei: Literature House, 1963), pp. 108–9.

34. T'ai-wan sheng wen hsien wei yüan hui (Taiwan Historical Commission), manuscript register of temples in Taiwan.

35. This combination of moral reform and medical cures had a predecessor in Ta-tao-ch'eng in the P'u-yüan She, a foundation established in 1884 as an association for the collective recital of elevating texts and the promotion of proper ceremonial. The founders were two celibate and vegetarian brothers who were also celebrated physicians, one in Han and the other in Western medicine. It no longer emphasizes the recital of ethical texts, just celebrating its deities, which include Fu Yu Ti Chün, Kuan Ti, and Wen Ch'ang. Li Ken-ch'üan 1953b, p. 81; and Liu Lung-kang 1953, p. 104.

36. *T'ai-pei shih chih kao* 1965, ch. 4, pp. 36–37. For the Universal Ethical Society, founded in Tsinan in 1921, see Wing-tsit Chan, *Religious Trends in Modern China* (New York: Columbia University Press, 1953), p. 163.

37. Eberhard has examined oracle slips from other temples in Taipei. Most often they refer to popular plays or to the lives of famous people in Chinese history. W. Eberhard, "Oracle and Theater in China," in his *Studies in Chinese Folklore and Related Essays* (Indiana University Folklore Institute Monograph Series, vol. 23, 1970).

38. Taipei's estimated 1920 population of 153,318 more than doubled in the next twenty years, to 313,152 in 1940. See George W. Barclay, *Colonial Development and Population in Taiwan* (Princeton, N.J.: Princeton University Press, 1954), Table 24, p. 116. Taipei's population had leapt to 923,985 in extended boundaries by 1961. See Taiwan Provincial Civil Affairs Department and Taiwan Population Studies Center (T. C. Hsu and Ronald Freedman, dirs.), *1961 Taiwan Demographic Fact Book* (Taipei, 1963), p. 53.

Migration and Family Change in Central Taiwan

1. William J. Goode, *World Revolution and Family Patterns* (New York: Free Press, 1963), chap. 1.

2. Marion Levy, *The Family Revolution in Modern China* (Cambridge: Harvard University Press, 1949); Maurice Freedman, *Chinese Lineage and Society* (London: Athlone, 1966).

3. Eugene Litwak, "Geographic Mobility and Extended Family Cohesion," *American Sociological Review*, 25 (June 1960): 385–95; Marvin B. Sussman,

"The Help Pattern in the Middle Class Family," *American Sociological Review*, 18 (Feb. 1953): 13–18.

4. Neil Jacoby, *U.S. Aid to Taiwan* (New York: Praeger, 1966), pp. 85–86. Also see the economic indexes presented monthly in *Industry of Free China*.

5. Alden Speare, Jr., "The Determinants of Rural to Urban Migration in Taiwan," unpubl. Ph.D. diss. (University of Michigan, 1969), pp. 108–10.

6. For a summary of urban growth in several Southeast Asian countries, see T. G. McGee, *The Southeast Asian City* (New York: Praeger, 1967).

7. Based on calculations from data in the *Taiwan Demographic Fact Book*, Department of Civil Affairs, Taiwan Provincial Government, 1965.

8. Speare 1969, chaps. 5 and 6.

9. M. F. Nimkoff and R. Middleton, "Types of Family and Types of Economy," *American Journal of Sociology*, 66 (Nov. 1960): 215–25; Morris Zelditch, Jr., "Cross-Cultural Analysis of Family Structure," in H. T. Christensen, ed., *Handbook of Marriage and the Family* (Chicago: Rand McNally, 1964).

10. Alden Speare, Jr., "An Assessment of the Quality of Taiwan Migration Registration Data," *Taiwan Working Paper No. 12* (Ann Arbor: University of Michigan Population Studies Center, 1971).

11. Levy 1949; M. Freedman 1966; Olga Lang, *Chinese Family and Society* (New Haven: Yale University Press, 1946).

12. C. K. Yang, *A Chinese Village in Early Communist Transition* (Cambridge, Mass.: M.I.T. Press, 1959), p. 17.

13. M. Freedman 1966, pp. 44–45.

14. *Ibid.*, p. 47.

15. Levy 1949, chap. 4.

16. Goode 1963, p. 14.

17. For a discussion of the variety in joint families, see Myron L. Cohen, "Developmental Process in the Chinese Domestic Group," in Maurice Freedman, ed., *Family and Kinship in Chinese Society* (Stanford, Calif.: Stanford University Press, 1970), pp. 21–36.

18. Taiwan Population Studies Center, *Taiwan Demographic Reference*, vol. 2, 1965. Ta Chen has estimated that the birth and death rates for Mainland China were 38 and 33 per thousand respectively for this period. Ta Chen, *Population in Modern China* (Chicago: University of Chicago Press, 1945).

19. Speare 1969, pp. 73–76.

20. Bernard Gallin, *Hsin Hsing, Taiwan* (Berkeley: University of California Press, 1966), pp. 122–26. Also see the chapter by Gallin and Gallin in this volume. The Gallins' migrants differ in two important ways from the ones we studied. First, the distance they moved was considerably greater. Second, many of them moved between 1950 and 1955 when economic conditions were less stable than during 1965–67.

21. Maurice Freedman, *Lineage Organization in Southeastern China* (London: Athlone, 1958), pp. 27ff. His argument is supported by data showing the relationship between farm size and family size in John L. Buck, *Land Utilization in China* (Nanking: University of Nanking Press, 1937), pp. 368–71; and Irene B. Taeuber, "The Families of Chinese Farmers," in M. Freedman, ed., 1970, pp. 71–77.

22. This average was imputed from the size and type of landholdings, using data from farm-income surveys: Taiwan Provincial Government, Department

of Agriculture and Fishing, *Report on Farm Record-Keeping Families in Taiwan, 1965*; and Arthur W. Peterson, "An Economic Study of Land Use in Taichung Hsien and City" (Taichung, Taiwan: Research Institute of Agricultural Economics, Chung Hsing University, 1960). The method of calculation is detailed in Speare 1969, Appendix C.

23. Speare 1969, pp. 91–93.

24. Levy 1949, pp. 55–56.

25. Alden Speare, Jr., "A Cost-Benefit Model of Rural to Urban Migration in Taiwan," *Population Studies*, 25 (Mar. 1971): 117–30.

26. In a multivariate analysis introducing expected change in income, cost of moving, possession of job information, and other factors as intervening variables, we found that the largest effect of number of brothers on migration was a direct effect. Speare 1969, pp. 204–5.

27. Levy 1949, pp. 188–90.

28. G. William Skinner, "Filial Sons and Their Sisters: Configuration and Culture in Chinese Families," unpublished, 1966.

29. Litwak 1960.

The Integration of Village Migrants in Taipei

1. Council for International Economic Cooperation and Development, *Taiwan Statistical Data Book* (Taipei, 1968).

2. *Industry of Free China*, 30, no. 1 (July 1968): 54–55.

3. George W. Barclay, *Colonial Development and Population in Taiwan* (Princeton, N.J.: Princeton University Press, 1954), p. 13. Department of Civil Affairs, *Monthly Bulletin of Registration Statistics of Taiwan*, 2, no. 1 (Jan. 1967): 10.

4. Andrew Collver, Alden Speare, Jr., and Paul K. C. Liu, "Local Variations of Fertility in Taiwan," *Population Studies*, 20, no. 3 (March 1967): 329–42.

5. Chu, Hsien-jen, "An Exploratory Study of Internal Migration in Taiwan," Unpubl. Ph.D. diss. (University of Florida, 1966), p. 92.

6. Alden Speare, Jr., "The Determinants of Rural to Urban Migration in Taiwan," unpubl. Ph.D. diss. (University of Michigan, 1969), pp. 29–30; and Paul K. C. Liu, "Population Redistribution and Development in Taiwan," unpublished paper prepared for the Conference on Economic Development of Taiwan, Taipei, June 19–29, 1967, pp. 213–15.

7. For a more complete ethnographic study of this village, see Bernard Gallin, *Hsin Hsing, Taiwan: A Chinese Village in Change* (Berkeley: University of California Press, 1966).

8. For a discussion of the problems of conflict resolution in the Hsin-hsing area, see Bernard Gallin, "Mediation in Changing Chinese Society in Rural Taiwan," *Journal of Asian and African Studies*, 2, no. 2 (Apr. 1967): 77–90.

9. Bernard Gallin, "Political Factionalism and Its Impact on Chinese Village Social Organization in Taiwan," in Marc J. Swartz, ed., *Local-Level Politics* (Chicago: Aldine, 1968), pp. 377–400.

10. Alden Speare, Jr., 1969, pp. 52–61.

11. *Ibid.*, p. 44.

Migrants and Cities in Japan, Taiwan, and Northeast China

1. Taiwan [Sōtokufu], Sōtoku kambō, Rinji kokusei chōsabu, *Kokusei chōsa, Shōwa 5 nen: Kekka hyō, Shūchō hen* (1930 census, final tables, districts; Taipei-Rinji kokusei chōsabu, 1930–34), Table 31.

2. *Ibid.* (1933), Table 30 in each volume.

3. *Ibid.*

4. Taiwan [Sōtokufu], Sōtoku kambō, Chōsaka, *Taiwan jinkō dōtai tōkei ... gempyō no bu* (Vital statistics for Taiwan ... details; Taipei Chōsaka, 1930), Tables 40, 41.

5. Taiwan [Sōtokufu], Sōtoku kambō, Rinji kokusei chōsabu, Dai ikkai Taiwan kokusei chōsa: Dai sanji rinji Taiwan kokō chōsa, Taishō 9 nen (First census of Taiwan, third special household and population survey, 1920; Taipei: Rinji kokusei chōsabu, 1921–24); *Kokusei chōsa, Taishō 14 nen* (1925 census), published 1926–27; *Kokusei chōsa, Shōwa 5 nen* (1930 census), published 1930–34; *Kokusei chōsa, Showa 10 nen* (1935 census), published 1935–37; *Taiwan jinkō dōtai tōkei ... gempyō no bu* (Vital statistics ... detailed volumes published 1920–40); Taiwan, Chu chi ch'u, *T'ai-wan ti ch'i tz'u jen k'ou p'u ch'a chieh kuo* (Results of the seventh population census of Taiwan, 1940; Taipei: Chu chi ch'u, 1953).

6. Manchoukuo, Kokumin, Sōmuchō, Tōkeisho, *Dai ichiji rinji jinkō chōsa hōkokusho. Toyū hen, dai ikkan, Shinkyō tokubetsu shi* (First provisional population survey report, cities, vol. 1, Hsin-ching special municipality; [n.p.]: Tōkeisho, 1937), Tables 10 and 16.

Character List

Character List

Entries are categorized as follows: places (P), temples (T), deities (D), journals and newspapers (J), business firms (B), particular associations and organizations (A), organizational types and categories (O), status terms and official or personal titles (S), and miscellaneous terms (M). Names of provinces, counties, and major cities are excluded; location data are provided for other place names. Particular associations are usually identified by city. No personal names are included.

Ai-yü Shan-t'ang (A) 愛育善堂
   [Canton]
An-k'ang Ch'ien-chuang (B)
   安康錢莊
An-yü Ch'ien-chuang (B)
   安裕錢莊

Cha-pei *ch'ü* (P) 閘北區
   [district of Shanghai]
Chang-tien (P) 張店
   [town in Hsin-ch'ing county,
   Shantung]
ch'ang (M) 塲
Ch'ang-chou (P) 長洲
   [town in Hsiang-shan (Chung-
   shan) county, Kwangtung]
ch'ang-kung (M) 長工
Ch'ang-sheng Hui (A) 長生會
   [Shanghai]
ch'ao (M) 鈔
Ch'ao-chou Pa-i Hui-kuan (A)
   潮州八邑會館   [Canton]
Che-chiang Hsing-yeh Yin-hang (B)
   浙江興業銀行
ch'e-p'iao (M) 拆票
chen (M) 鎮

cheng-shou chü (O) 徵收局
Cheng-yen (J) 正言
Ch'eng Huang Yeh (D) 城隍爺
Ch'eng-chung *ch'ü* (P) 城中區
   [district of Taipei]
ch'eng-pan jen (S) 承辦人
Ch'eng-yü Ch'ien-chuang (B)
   承裕錢莊
Ch'i-erh-t'ou Hui-kuan (A)
   乞兒頭會館
   [Canton]
Ch'i-hu (P) 溪湖
   [town in Chang-hua county,
   Taiwan]
ch'i-lao (S) 耆老
Ch'i-shih-erh Hang (A) 七十二行
   [Canton]
chia (M) 甲
Chiang-su Hai-yün Hu-chü (A)
   江蘇海運滬局
   [Shanghai]
chiao (M) 醮 [communal rite of
   consecration and renewal]
chiao (O) 郊 [guild]
Chiao-tung *tao* (P) 膠東道
   [circuit in republican Shantung]

Chiao-t'ung Yin-hang (B)
交通銀行
Chiao-yang Ch'u (A) 教養處
[Tsinan]
chiao-yü (s) 教諭
chiao-yü chü (O) 教育局
chiao-yü hui (O) 教育會
Chiao-yü tsa-chih (J) 教育雜誌
chien (M) 薦
Chien-ch'eng *ch'ü* (P) 建成區
[district of Taipei]
ch'ien (M) 欠
ch'ien-chuang (O) 錢莊
Ch'ien-shan (P) 前山
[town in Hsiang-shan (Chung-
shan) county, Kwangtung]
Ch'ien-yeh Kung-hui (A)
錢業公會
[Shanghai]
Ch'ien-yeh Kung-so (A) 錢業公所
[Shanghai]
Chih-ch'ün Hsüeh-she (A)
智群學社
[Wei-hsien, Shantung]
Chih-nan kung (T) 指南宮
Chin-chou (P) 金州
[district in the Kwantung Leased
Territory]
Chin-pu (J) 進步
ching-fa li-shih yüan (s)
警法理事員
ching-li (s) 經理
Ching-te-chen (P) 景德鎮
[nonadministrative industrial city
in Fou-ling county, Kiangsi]
ching-wu chang (s) 警務長
Ching-wu Hsüeh-t'ang (A)
警務學堂 [Shanghai]
Ch'ing Shan Wang (D) 青山王

Ch'ing-shan-wang miao (T)
青山王廟
Ch'ing-shui tsu-shih-kung miao (T)
清水祖師公廟
ch'ing-tao fu (s) 清道夫
Chiu Shan-t'ang (A) 九善堂
[Canton]
Chiu-huo Lien-ho Hui (A)
救火聯合會
[Shanghai]
Chou-ts'un (P) 周村
[nonadministrative commercial
city in Ch'ang-shan county,
Shantung]
chu-li yüan (s) 助理員
ch'u-wai jen (M) 出外人
chü wen (M) 具文
Chü-yüeh Hui (A) 拒約會
[Canton]
ch'ü-chang (s) 區長
ch'ü-tung (s) 區董
chüan-wu pan-li yüan (O)
捐務辦理員
Ch'üan Chiao (A) 泉郊
[Meng-chia (Taipei)]
ch'üan-hsüeh so (O) 勸學所
Ch'üan-kuo Chiao-yü Hui Lien-ho
Hui (A) 全國教育會聯合會
Chüeh-hsiu kung (T) 覺修宮
chün kuo-min (M) 軍國民
chün-chang (s) 軍長
Chung-hua Chiao-yü Kai-chin Hui
(A) 中華教育改進會
Chung-kuo K'en-yeh Yin-hang (B)
中國墾業銀行
Chung-kuo T'ung-shang Yin-hang
(B) 中國通商銀行
Chung-shan *ch'ü* (P) 中山區
[district of Taipei]

Ch'ung-ch'ing Shang-pu Tu-pan (A)
重慶商埠督辦
[Chungking]

En Chu Kung (D) 恩主公

Fa Chu Kung (D) 法主公
Fa-cheng Hsüeh-t'ang (A)
法政學堂 [Canton]
Fa-chu-kung kung (T) 法主公宮
fa-t'uan (O) 法團
Fan *chiang-chün* (D) 范將軍
Fang-chen-chi (B)
方振記 (方鎮記)
fang-ch'ü (M) 防區
fen-hsiang (M) 分香
fen-kuei (O) 分匱
fen-ling (M) 分靈
fen-pan ch'u (O) 分辦處
Fu Yu Ti Chün (D) 孚佑帝君
fu-hu (M) 附戶
fu-t'ou (S) 夫頭

Han-t'ing (P) 寒亭
[town in Wei *hsien*, Shantung]
hao-k'o (S) 號客
Hsia Chiao (A) 廈郊 [Taipei]
Hsia-hai Ch'eng Huang Yeh (D)
霞海城隍爺
Hsia-hai ch'eng-huang miao (T)
霞海城隍廟
Hsiang-chün (A) 香軍
[Hsiang-shan county, Kwang-
tung]
hsiang-k'ao (M) 鄉考
hsiang-nung hsüeh-hsiao (O)
鄉農學校
hsiang-yüeh chang (S) 鄉約長
hsiang-yüeh chü (O) 鄉約局

Hsiao-lan (P) 小欖
[town in Hsiang-shan (Chung-
shan) county, Kwangtung]
Hsieh *chiang-chün* (D) 謝將軍
hsien-k'ao (M) 縣考
hsin shih-ch'ang (M) 新市場
Hsin-chuang (P) 新莊
[town in Tan-shui prefecture (to
1875); now in T'ai-pei county,
Taiwan]
Hsin-hsing (P) 新興
[village in P'u-yen *hsiang*, Chang-
hua county, Taiwan]
Hsin-hsing kung (T) 新興宮
Hsin-min ts'ung-pao (J) 新民叢報
hsin-t'u hui (O) 信徒會
Hsin-wen pao (J) 新聞報
Hsing-t'ien kung (T) 行天宮
hsiu-shen (M) 修身
hsüeh-cheng (S) 學政
hsüeh-ch'ü (M) 學區
hsüeh-hui (O) 學會
hsün-fang-ying (O) 巡防營
hu-chi ching-ch'a (S) 戶籍警察
hu-k'ou (M) 戶口
Hu-pu Yin-hang (B) 戶部銀行
Hua-lin ssu (T) 華林寺
Hua-hsi Hsing-yeh Kung-ssu (B)
華西興業公司
Hua-shang T'i-ts'ao Hui (A)
華商體操會 [Shanghai]
Hui-chou Hui-kuan (A) 徽州會館
[Canton]
hui-kuan (O) 會館
Hui-t'ung Kuan-yin Hao (B)
惠通官銀號
Hung-chia-lou (P) 洪家樓
[town in Li-ch'eng county, Shan-
tung]

Hung-chiang (P) 洪江
  [nonadministrative city in Hui-
  t'ung county, Hunan]
Hung-ch'iang Hui (A) 紅槍會
hung-pao (M) 紅包

I-chung Hui (A) 義塚會
  [Pa *hsien*, Szechwan]
i-hsüeh (O) 義學
i-shih hui (O) 議事會
i-tung (S) 議董
i-yüan (S) 議員

jen-ch'ing (M) 人情
ju-tao-chiao (M) 儒道教

kan-she chu-i (M) 干涉主義
Ko-lao Hui (A) 哥老會
k'o (M) 科
k'o-chang (S) 科長
k'o-ch'in pu (M) 課勤簿
k'o-k'ao (M) 科考
Ku-mu Yüan (A) 瞽目院
  [Canton]
Kuan Ti (D) 關帝
Kuan Yin (D) 觀音
Kuan-lan (P) 觀瀾 (官瀾)
  [town in Pao-an (Hsin-an)
  county, Kwangtung]
kuan-tu-shang-pan (M) 官督商辦
Kuang-Chao Kung-so (A)
  廣肇公所
  [Shanghai]
Kuang-chi I-yüan (A) 廣濟醫院
  [Canton]
Kuang-chou Shang-wu Tsung-hui
  (A) 廣州商務總會
  [Canton]

Kuang-jen Shan-t'ang (A)
  廣仁善堂
  [Canton]
kung-chü (M) 公舉
kung-hui (O) 工會 [labor union]
kung-hui (O) 公會 [public associ-
  ation]
kung-i chü (O) 工藝局
kung-li (M) 公立
kung-so (O) 公所
K'ung-tzu miao (T) 孔子廟
kuo-chang (M) 過帳
Kuo-ch'üan Wan-chiu Hui (A)
  國權挽救會
  [Canton]
kuo-min (M) 國民
Kuo-yü T'ang (A) 果育堂
  [Shanghai]

lao-ta (S) 老大
Le-k'ou (P) 濼口
  [town in Li-ch'eng county, Shan-
  tung]
Le-ts'ung (P) 樂從
  [town in Shun-te county, Kwang-
  tung]
Le-yüan Shu-yüan (A) 濼源書院
  [Tsinan]
li (M) 里
li-chang (S) 里長
liang-ting (S) 糧丁
lien-pao fa (M) 聯保法
lin-chang (S) 鄰長
ling (M) 靈
liu-mang (S) 流氓
lu-chu (S) 爐主
Lu-kang (P) 鹿港
  [town in Chang-hua county,
  Taiwan]

Lung-kang (P) 龍岡
[town in Kuei-shan (Hui-yang)
county, Kwangtung]

Lung-men Shu-yüan (A)
龍門書院
[Shanghai]

Lung-shan (P) 龍山
[town in Chen-hai county, Che-
kiang]

Lung-shan ssu (T) 龍山寺

Lung-tu (P) 龍都 (隆都)
[rural area west of Shih-chi in
Hsiang-shan (Chung-shan)
county]

Lü-ho Ch'ien-chuang (B)
履龢錢莊

Ma Tsu (D) 媽祖

Meng-chia (P) 艋舺
[town in Tan-shui subprefecture
(to 1875), Taiwan; now incorporated in Taipei]

meng-yang hsüeh-t'ang (O)
蒙養學堂

mi-hsin (M) 迷信

min-chün (O) 民軍

Min-sheng Shih-yeh Kung-ssu (B)
民生實業公司

min-t'uan (O) 民團

ming-yü tung-shih (S) 名譽董事

Mu-cha (P) 木柵
[suburb of Taipei]

Nan-hsün (P) 南潯
[town in Wu-ch'eng county, Che-
kiang]

Nan-shih Ma-lu Kung-ch'eng Chü
(A) 南市馬路工程局
[Shanghai]

Ning-po Lü-Hu T'ung-hsiang Hui
(A) 寧波旅滬同鄉會
[Shanghai]

nung-hui (O) 農會

Pa-chia-chuang (P) 八甲莊
[settlement in Tan-shui subprefecture (to 1875), Taiwan; now
incorporated in Taipei]

Pan-ch'iao chen (P) 板橋鎮
[township in T'ai-pei county,
Taiwan]

pan-shih tsung-tung (S) 辦事總董

pan-shih yüan (S) 辦事員

pang (O) 幫

pang-hang (O) 幫行

pao (M) 保

Pao-an kung (T) 保安宮

Pao-liang Chü (A) 保良局
[Hong Kong]

Pei Chiao (A) 北郊
[Meng-chia (Taipei)]

P'i-tzu-wo (P) 貔子窩
[district in Kwantung Leased
Territory]

Pin-chiang (P) 濱江
[province in Manchoukuo]

p'ing-chia (M) 平價

p'ing-t'iao (M) 平糶

P'u-chi Yüan (A) 普濟院
[Canton]

P'u-lan-tien (P) 普蘭店
[district in Kwantung Leased
Territory]

P'u-yen hsiang (P) 埔鹽鄉
[township in Chang-hua county,
Taiwan]

P'u-yü T'ang (A) 普育堂
[Shanghai]

P'u-yüan She (A) 普願社
[Ta-tao-ch'eng (Taipei)]

San I (P) 三邑
[the "three counties" of Chin-
chiang, Hui-an, and Nan-an in
Ch'üan-chou prefecture, Fukien]
san lao (S) 三老
san to (M) 三多
San-chiao t'ang (T) 三教堂
San-chung *shih* (P) 三重市
[municipality in T'ai-pei county,
a de facto suburb of Taipei]
shan-t'ang (O) 善堂
Shan-tso Kung-hsüeh (A)
山左公學
[Wei-hsien, Shantung]
shan-tung (S) 扇董
Shan-tung Wu-pei Hsüeh-t'ang (A)
山東武備學堂
[Tsinan]
Shang-ch'uan Hui-kuan (A)
商船會館
[Shanghai]
Shang-hai Shang-wu Tsung-hui (A)
上海商務總會
[Shanghai]
Shang-hai Shang-yeh Hui-i Kung-so
(A) 上海商業會議公所
[Shanghai]
shang-hui (O) 商會
Shang-min Hsieh-hui (A)
商民協會
[Shanghai]
Shang-pao Li-chü (A) 商包釐局
[Canton]
shang-pu (M) 商埠
shang-t'uan (O) 商團
Shang-t'uan Kung-hui (A)

商團公會 [Shanghai]
shang-wu chü (O) 商務局
Shang-yeh Hui-i Kung-ssu (A)
商業會議公司
[Canton]
she-hsüeh (O) 社學
Shen-chen (P) 深圳
[town in Pao-an (Hsin-an)
county, Kwangtung]
shen-i (S) 紳義
Shen-ming Hui (A) 神明會
[Taipei]
Shen-pao (J) 申報
Sheng ch'eng-huang miao (T)
省城隍廟
sheng-li (M) 省立
Shih-cheng Ching-fei Shou-chih So
(A) 市政經費收支所
[Chungking]
Shih-hsing Hsin Hsüeh-chih Yen-
chiu Hui (A)
始行新學制研究會
[Tsinan]
Shih-lung (P) 石龍
[town in Tung-kuan county,
Kwangtung]
Shih-ma (P) 石馬
[town in Tung-kuan county,
Kwangtung]
shih-shen (M) 市紳
Shih-wu Wei-sheng Hua-yen So (A)
食物衛生化驗所
[Shanghai]
shou-chüan jen (S) 收捐人
shu-yüan (O) 書院
Shuang-yüan *ch'ü* (P) 雙園區
[district of Taipei]
Shui-chüan Chü (A) 稅捐局
[Chungking]

Shui-hsün (A) 水巡   [Shanghai]

Ssu Ming Chen Chün (D)
　司命真君

Ssu-ch'uan Min-chün Lin-shih
　Chün-shih Wei-yüan-hui (A)
　四川民軍臨時軍事委員會

ssu-li (M) 私立

Ssu-ming Kung-so (A) 四明公所
　[Shanghai]

Ssu-ming Yin-hang (B) 四明銀行

Ssu-p'ing (P) 四平
　[province in Manchoukuo]

ssu-shu (O) 私塾

sui-k'ao (M) 歲考

Ta Ch'ing Yin-hang (B) 大清銀行

Ta Tao Kung (D) 大道公

Ta-lung-t'ung (P) 大龍峒
　[town in Tan-shui subprefecture
　(to 1875), Taiwan; now incorpo-
　rated in Taipei]

Ta-tao Hui (A) 大刀會

Ta-tao-ch'eng (P) 大稻埕
　[town in Tan-shui subprefecture
　(to 1875), Taiwan; now incorpo-
　rated in Taipei]

ta-t'ung chih shih (M) 大同之世

Ta-yu (P) 大有
　[village in P'u-yen *hsiang*, Chang-
　hua county, Taiwan]

tan (M) 擔

Tan-shui (P) 淡水
　[(1) subprefecture/county and
　river in northern Taiwan;
　(2) town in Kuei-shan (Hui-
　yang) county, Kwangtung]

tang-chih yüan (s) 當值員

T'ang-t'ou-hsia (P)
　塘頭下 (塘頭厦)

[town in Tung-kuan county,
Kwangtung]

teng fu (s) 燈夫

ti-chia (s) 地甲

ti-fang fu-chia (M) 地方附加

ti-pao (s) 地保

t'i-hsüeh shih (s) 提學使

T'ien Fei (D) 天妃

T'ien Hou (D) 天后

T'ien-t'ang-wei (P) 天堂圍
　[town in Tung-kuan county,
　Kwangtung]

Ting Chiao (A) 頂郊
　[Meng-chia (Taipei)]

t'ou-chia (s) 頭家

ts'ai-p'an kuan (s) 裁判官

Ts'ai-p'an So (A) 裁判所
　[Shanghai]

ts'ai-t'uan fa-jen (O) 財團法人

tsan-chu yüan (s) 贊助員

ts'an-shih hui (O) 參事會

Tsu Shih Kung (D) 祖師公

tsung liang-kuei (O) 總糧匱

Tsung shang-hui pao (J)
　總商會報

Tsung-kung Chü (A) 總工局
　[Shanghai]

tsung-tung (s) 總董

T'u Ti Kung (D) 土地公

t'u-tung (s) 圖董

tuan-kung (M) 短工

tuan-tung (s) 段董

t'uan-fa (s) 團閥

T'uan-fang Chü (A) 團防局
　[Shanghai]

Tung-hua I-yüan (A) 東華醫院
　[Hong Kong]

Tung-lin *tao* (P) 東臨道
　[circuit in republican Shantung]

Tung-lu Yin-hang (B) 東陸銀行
tung-shih (S) 董事
tung-shih hui (O) 董事會
T'ung-chiu-yüan (B) 通久源
t'ung-hsiang hui (O) 同鄉會
t'ung-i (M) 統一
T'ung-jen Fu-yüan T'ang (A)
   同仁輔元堂
   [Shanghai]
Tzu-chih Yen-chiu She (A)
   自治研究社
   [Canton]
Tzu-chih Yen-chiu So (A)
   自治研究所
   [Canton]
Tz'u-shan T'uan (A) 慈善團
   [Shanghai]
Tz'u-sheng kung (T) 慈聖宮

Wan-hua (P) 萬華
   [contemporary name for the por-
   tion of Taipei formerly known as
   Meng-chia]
Wan-kuo Tao-te Hui (A)
   萬國道德會
   [Taipei]
Wan-nien-feng (A) 萬年豐
   [Swatow]
wei-yüan (S) 委員
Wen Ch'ang (D) 文昌
Wen miao (T) 文廟

Wen-lan Shu-yüan (A) 文瀾書院
   [Canton]
Wu miao (T) 武廟
wu-lun (M) 五倫

Yang-chi Yüan (A) 養濟院
   [Shanghai]
Yin-hang Kung-hui (A) 銀行公會
   [Shanghai]
Yu-chi Shih-fan Hsüeh-t'ang (A)
   優級師範學堂
   [Canton]
Yü-lan-p'en (M) 盂蘭盆
Yü-ying T'ang (A) 育嬰堂
   [Canton, Shanghai]
yüan-k'ao (M) 院考
Yüan-lin (P) 員林
   [town in Chang-hua county,
   Taiwan]
Yüeh-shang Tzu-chih Hui (A)
   粵商自治會
   [Canton]
Yün-an-ch'ang (P) 雲安場
   [market town in Yün-yang
   county, Szechwan]
Yung-ho *chen* (P) 永和鎮
   [township in Tai-pei county,
   Taiwan; now a suburb of Taipei]
Yung-p'ing (P) 永平
   [village in P'u-yen *hsiang*, Chang-
   hua county, Taiwan]

Index

Index

academies, 102, 173, 182
Adams, Walter, 226
age: and migration, 4f, 337–39, 365, 371, 378–79, 384; and marriage, 15, 316, 365–67, 372, 382
agriculture, 14–15, 177, 207, 249, 303f, 331, 340, 368; Ministry of, 220, 225. *See also* farm size
Amherst Mission, 42, 395n65
Amoy, 23, 224, 265f, 399n5. *See also* Hsia (Amoy) Guild
An-ch'i county, 265f, 270, 273, 275f
An-t'ang, 123f
An-tung, 220, 222f
Anhwei, 7, 40
anti-Christian agitation, 236
anti-tax disorders, 131f, 166–67f, 224, 410n10, 414n85
anti-urbanism, 67–71, 399n123
associations, voluntary, 78–79, 91–117, 172, 215–16, 342, 400n26, 431n15. *See also* occupational associations
athletics, 229f

banditry, 61, 79, 165, 200, 202, 420n109
banking, 20, 30f, 53, 58–59, 73–96, 159, 223, 397n100
Bickmore, A. S., cited, 40
Big Sword Society, 200
birth order, and migration, 14, 324–26, 330
birthrate, 317, 362, 366, 373f, 377, 379, 433n18. *See also* fertility
Board of Education, 173, 178–86, 193
boycotts, 87, 93, 111, 198–99, 218,

221f, 225f, 395n62; anti-American, 108–9, 219
Britain, 27–30f, 75, 111
British East India Company, 75, 395n65
Bruce, Sir Frederick, cited, 50
Buck, J. Lossing, cited, 130n
Buddhism, 259, 263, 273, 276f, 282, 288f, 290–91, 293, 296f
bureaucracy, 25, 36, 97, 102, 131, 156, 177
bureaus for commercial affairs, 105–6

Canton, 12n, 68, 74, 97–117, 213, 215, 222, 399n5; 1911 revolution and, 12, 119, 123, 134–41 *passim*; as treaty port, 20, 62; vs. Shanghai, 40, 58, 240, 245; "city question," 42; and commercial hierarchy, 47, 51f; radical government, 225–26, 228; population, 395n62, 395n65
Canton Chamber of Commerce, 106–8ff, 116, 215, 222–28 *passim*
Canton delta, 119–41
Canton-Kowloon railroad, 130, 132ff, 137
Canton Merchants Self-Government Society, 109–12
Canton system of foreign trade, 12, 42, 74f, 100f
capital, 20n, 21, 30–31, 34, 38, 53–59 *passim*, 79, 392n44; foreign, 9, 22, 58, 79, 84f, 368
capitalism, Chinese, 173, 193–98
censorship, 259
central-place hierarchy, 2, 171, 200, 211f
Cha-pei, 248